A CELEBRATION OF POETS

EAST
GRADES 7-12
SUMMER 2008

creativeCOMMUNICATION
A CELEBRATION OF TODAY'S WRITERS

A CELEBRATION OF POETS
EAST
GRADES 7-12
SUMMER 2008

AN ANTHOLOGY COMPILED BY CREATIVE COMMUNICATION, INC.

Published by:

creativeCOMMUNICATION
A CELEBRATION OF TODAY'S WRITERS

1488 NORTH 200 WEST · LOGAN, UTAH 84341
TEL. 435-713-4411 · WWW.POETICPOWER.COM

ISBN: 978-1-60050-210-1

Foreword

Thank you for joining us in this "Celebration of Writers." We are proud to provide this anthology for you to read. Inside this book you will find the hopes and dreams of a generation of students.

This fall, I received a letter from a young writer. In the letter he thanked Creative Communication for being "A truly courageous group who is willing to invest in the adults of tomorrow." We thank him for these kind words. However, more importantly we are glad that we can contribute to a student's success. Each class that is taken and each project that is completed in school moves a student closer to a successful life. When we invest in our children, we are investing in our future.

I often hear from teachers who tell me about the atmosphere in their classroom when their students are accepted to be published. I am told that it creates an energy and excitement that cannot be created by regular classroom instruction. These feelings can be remembered for a lifetime and can be used as a catalyst to help these students continue to love education. I hope that publishing these writers will make the world a better place.

Thomas Worthen, Ph.D.
Editor
Creative Communication

WRITING CONTESTS!

Enter our next POETRY contest!
Enter our next ESSAY contest!

Why should I enter?

Win prizes and get published! Each year thousands of dollars in prizes are awarded in each region and tens of thousands of dollars in prizes are awarded throughout North America. The top writers in each division receive a monetary award and a free book that includes their published poem or essay. Entries of merit are also selected to be published in our anthology.

Who may enter?

There are four divisions in the poetry contest. The poetry divisions are grades K-3, 4-6, 7-9, and 10-12.
There are four divisions in the essay contest. The essay division are grades K-3, 4-6, 7-9, and 10-12.

What is needed to enter the contest?

To enter the poetry contest send in one original poem, 21 lines or less. To enter the essay contest send in one original essay, 250 words or less, on any topic. Each entry must include the student's name, grade, address, city, state, and zip code, and the student's school name and school address. Students who include their teacher's name may help the teacher qualify for a free copy of the anthology.

How do I enter?

Enter a poem online at:
www.poeticpower.com

or

Mail your poem to:
  Poetry Contest
  1488 North 200 West
  Logan, UT 84341

Enter an essay online at:
www.studentessaycontest.com

or

Mail your essay to:
  Essay Contest
  1488 North 200 West
  Logan, UT 84341

When is the deadline?

Poetry contest deadlines are April 7th, August 18th, and December 3rd. Essay contest deadlines are February 17th, July 15th, and October 15th. You can enter each contest, however, send only one poem or essay for each contest deadline.

Are there benefits for my school?

Yes. We award $15,000 each year in grants to help with Language Arts programs. Schools qualify to apply for a grant by having a large number of entries of which over fifty percent are accepted for publication. This typically tends to be about 15 accepted entries.

Are there benefits for my teacher?

Yes. Teachers with five or more students accepted to be published receive a free anthology that includes their students' writing.

For more information please go to our website at **www.poeticpower.com**, email us at editor@poeticpower.com or call 435-713-4411.

Table of Contents

States included in this edition:

Alabama
Connecticut
Delaware
Florida
Georgia
Kentucky
Maine
Maryland
Massachusetts
Mississippi
New Hampshire
New Jersey
New York
North Carolina
Pennsylvania
Rhode Island
South Carolina
Tennessee
Virginia
Vermont
Washington D.C.
West Virginia

Summer 2008 Poetic Achievement Honor Schools

* Teachers who had fifteen or more poets accepted to be published

The following schools are recognized as receiving a "Poetic Achievement Award." This award is given to schools who have a large number of entries of which over fifty percent are accepted for publication. With hundreds of schools entering our contest, only a small percent of these schools are honored with this award. The purpose of this award is to recognize schools with excellent Language Arts programs. This award qualifies these schools to receive a complimentary copy of this anthology. In addition, these schools are eligible to apply for a Creative Communication Language Arts Grant. Grants of two hundred and fifty dollars each are awarded to further develop writing in our schools.

Anderson County High School
Clinton, TN
Lynn Justice
Ashley Korte
Lori Price

Anthony Wayne Middle School
Wayne, NJ
Lauren Tuosto*

Beacon Middle School
Lewes, DE
Nicole Catanzaro*
Doris Elaine Person

Bishop Denis J O'Connell High School
Arlington, VA
Mary Lou Wentzel*

Bishop Ford Central Catholic High School
Brooklyn, NY
Sr. Mary Towers*

Briarwood Christian Jr/Sr High School
Birmingham, AL
Cindy Janney
Martin Lewis

Bronx High School of Science
Bronx, NY
Kathleen Buchan
Olivia Byun
Dermot Hannon*
Sophia Sapozhnikov

Captain Nathan Hale Middle School
Coventry, CT
Carla Kennedy
Adrienne Manzone
Laura Myslinski*
Jeff Spivey

Carthage Middle School
Carthage, NY
Paula Amato*

Chickahominy Middle School
Mechanicsville, VA
Leah Belcher
Kathleen Martin
Cynthia Sinanian

Colonia High School
Colonia, NJ
Jennifer Murphy*
Danielle Simkovich*

Council Rock High School South
Holland, PA
Rhonda Alves*

Countryside High School
Clearwater, FL
Rosemarie Ceraolo-O'Donnell*

Covenant Life School
Gaithersburg, MD
Denise Griney*

Depew Middle School
Depew, NY
Joseph P. Cena*

E T Richardson Middle School
Springfield, PA
Heather Donnelly*
Trey Reynolds
Kate Walton

Elizabeth Seton Elementary School
Pittsburgh, PA
Bernadine Skraba*

Fort Mill Middle School
Fort Mill, SC
Kimberly Martin*

Grace Lutheran School
Saint Petersburg, FL
Renee McLay
Dan Meissner

Haverhill High School
Haverhill, MA
Katie Eisenhauer*

Heathwood Hall Episcopal School
Columbia, SC
Dr. Sally Plowden*

International School of Boston
Cambridge, MA
Kim Stirling*

Loretto High School
Loretto, TN
Brandon Weaver*

Madisonville Middle School
Madisonville, TN
Laura Mason
Pat Shoopman

Miami Beach Sr High School
Miami Beach, FL
Margarida Pinto*

Most Blessed Sacrament School
Berlin, MD
Cris Kaczmarczyk*

Ocean City Intermediate School
Ocean City, NJ
Martha F. Godown*

Peabody Veterans Memorial High School
Peabody, MA
Kim Catron*

Perquimans County Middle School
Winfall, NC
Tina Mathis*

Pine-Richland Middle School
Gibsonia, PA
Dr. Susan Frantz
Jennifer Latronica*

Ragsdale High School
Jamestown, NC
Susan Miller*

Riverside High School
Greer, SC
Carolyn York Ramey*

Schley County Middle/High School
Ellaville, GA
Patti Wurtz*

Seminole County Middle/High School
Donalsonville, GA
Becky Shamblin*

St Agatha School
Brooklyn, NY
Rosemarie Paredes*

St Anthony School
Winsted, CT
Marilyn Hubert*

Thomson High School
Thomson, GA
Amy E. Proctor*

Thorne Middle School
Port Monmouth, NJ
Joseph Puzzo*

Townsend Harris High School
Flushing, NY
Susan Getting
Charlene Levi*

Trinity Middle School
Washington, PA
Elise Wray*

Unami Middle School
Chalfont, PA
Dianne M. Pizzi*

Westampton Middle School
Westampton, NJ
Nancy Tuliszewski*

Westwood Jr-Sr High School
Township of Washington, NJ
Theodora Pavlou*

William Penn Middle School
Yardley, PA
Vicki Meigs*

Yellow Breeches Middle School
Boiling Springs, PA
Janet Hoffman
Ray Mowery*

Yeshivat Shaare Torah
Brooklyn, NY
Tillie Miller*

Language Arts Grant Recipients 2008-2009

After receiving a "Poetic Achievement Award" schools are encouraged to apply for a Creative Communication Language Arts Grant. The following is a list of schools who received a two hundred and fifty dollar grant for the 2008-2009 school year.

Acushnet Elementary School, Acushnet, MA
Benton Central Jr/Sr High School, Oxford, IN
Bridgeway Christian Academy, Alpharetta, GA
Central Middle School, Grafton, ND
Challenger Middle School, Cape Coral, FL
City Hill Middle School, Naugatuck, CT
Clintonville High School, Clintonville, WI
Coral Springs Middle School, Coral Springs, FL
Covenant Classical School, Concord, NC
Coyote Valley Elementary School, Middletown, CA
Diamond Ranch Academy, Hurricane, UT
E O Young Jr Elementary School, Middleburg, NC
El Monte Elementary School, Concord, CA
Emmanuel-St Michael Lutheran School, Fort Wayne, IN
Ethel M Burke Elementary School, Bellmawr, NJ
Fort Recovery Middle School, Fort Recovery, OH
Gardnertown Fundamental Magnet School, Newburgh, NY
Hancock County High School, Sneedville, TN
Haubstadt Community School, Haubstadt, IN
Headwaters Academy, Bozeman, MT
Holden Elementary School, Chicago, IL
Holliday Middle School, Holliday, TX
Holy Cross High School, Delran, NJ
Homestead Elementary School, Centennial, CO
Joseph M Simas Elementary School, Hanford, CA
Labrae Middle School, Leavittsburg, OH
Lakewood High School, Lakewood, CO
Lee A Tolbert Community Academy, Kansas City, MO
Mary Lynch Elementary School, Kimball, NE
Merritt Secondary School, Merritt, BC
North Star Academy, Redwood City, CA

Language Arts Grant Winners cont.

Old Redford Academy, Detroit, MI
Prairie Lakes School, Willmar, MN
Public School 124Q, South Ozone Park, NY
Rutledge Hall Elementary School, Lincolnwood, IL
Shelley Sr High School, Shelley, ID
Sonoran Science Academy, Tucson, AZ
Spruce Ridge School, Estevan, SK
St Columbkille School, Dubuque, IA
St Francis Middle School, Saint Francis, MN
St Luke the Evangelist School, Glenside, PA
St Matthias/Transfiguration School, Chicago, IL
St Robert Bellarmine School, Chicago, IL
St Sebastian Elementary School, Pittsburgh, PA
The Hillel Academy, Milwaukee, WI
Thomas Edison Charter School - North, North Logan, UT
Trinity Christian Academy, Oxford, AL
United Hebrew Institute, Kingston, PA
Velasquez Elementary School, Richmond, TX
West Frederick Middle School, Frederick, MD

Grades 10-11-12

Note: The Top Ten poems were finalized through an online voting system. Creative Communication's judges first picked out the top poems. These poems were then posted online. The final step involved thousands of students and teachers who registered as online judges and voted for the Top Ten poems. We hope you enjoy these selections.

Top Poem Grades 10-11-12

My Life Is a Highway

The pathways of my life are intertwining
Giving me roads to take
And choices to make.
The roads are always opening up a new journey
And a new destination.

Sometimes the roads I take are rough
Slowing me down, creating obstacles,
But I just have to drive past
And look for the exit…what's important.
But sometimes I'm given smooth roads,
And I glide on them safely to the end.

The roads take me to different places,
Each stop adding character and meaning to my life.
The baggage I carry sometimes weighs down my journey,
But as I continue to drive and take chances
I learn to let go of the unwanted baggage.

I'm always hoping I'm choosing the right road,
And that I will find loving faces at each stop I make.
I know some pit stops will be mistakes,
But one day I will be on the right road
And it will bring me to my home.

Elizabeth Allison, Grade 11
Heathwood Hall Episcopal School, SC

Top Poem Grades 10-11-12

Aquamarine

Aquamarine is the color in my dreams.
It is bright and foreshadowing a new and exciting day that lies ahead.

It is calming and soothing. It paints a picture of a tropical paradise.
The warm, crystal clear water, with its aquamarine hue brushes over the edge of the white sand.

Serenity. Peace. Happiness.

The coolness of the color still gives off a warming sensation.
I can feel the sun that beats on my back, but the heat is cooled off by dipping into the blue water,
as it wraps around me like a silk sheet.

I sink down to the shallows of the water, as the sunlight dances on the surface.
Bright colors of fish and coral pop out at me with the aquamarine shade as its background.

Aquamarine.

A cool, striking, piercing color that ignites excitement and life within me.
A cool blue that relaxes stress and tension.

Aquamarine.
The color of my dreams.

Arayael Brandner, Grade 11
Heathwood Hall Episcopal School, SC

Top Poem Grades 10-11-12

Morning

A light arises in the distance,
marking the start of a new day.
Its glow encompasses the ocean around it,
bringing life into its depths.

The sea becomes awakened,
beginning with its sun kissed waters.
Music fills the air as birds fly past,
singing their soft melodies.

Pastel color illuminates the sky,
filling the heavens with radiance.
The sun shines for all to see,
helping the morning to arrive.

Summer Ceraolo-O'Donnell, Grade 12
Countryside High School, FL

Top Poem Grades 10-11-12

Abandoned Bedroom

She was a messy girl, says her unmade bed
With clothes piled on and an unfolded blanket.
An average-sized girl, shows the
Clothes in her closet and on her bed.
A bookworm she is, announces the
Books on her bookshelf, not so neatly organized.
One who doesn't always finishes what she begins,
Cries her unfinished stories from years ago.

A mysterious person,
Whispers her diaries, hidden in a drawer.
A writer of traditional poetry,
An anthology of poems, including one of hers, proudly proclaims.
And finally, and most importantly,
She is a little kid at heart, reveals her
Chubby stuffed penguin and skinny stuffed octopus on her bed
And the many more stuffed animals in her closet.

Caroline Fu, Grade 10
Farragut High School, TN

Top Poem Grades 10-11-12

What Is a Father?

What is a father? A role model, a guider,
as well as a friend and a provider.
One who's there to finish,
and whose love won't diminish.
It sounds silly to say that it's prevalent today,
the world would be different if things were that way.
Mothers are forced out of their position,
as the so-called man walks out without permission.
They say it takes a man to raise one, I'm one with or without,
but I wonder what I would've been if one was in my house.
Leaders show example, even a father could admit,
if your son's a part of you, then how could you quit?
Experience gives you wisdom, some find out the hard way,
that's not for everyone, doesn't happen always.
So exactly what is a father? Many should stop to see,
because to me it's an example of what not to be.

Clint Gravelle, Grade 10
Jeffersontown High School Magnet Career Academy, KY

Top Poem Grades 10-11-12

On a Summer Evening

On a summer evening
the glinting lantern lights,
glaring out into open sunset.
Flashing fireflies hidden in the dark air.
A cool breeze rustles the black shadows.
I sit there,
amongst nature's stillness,
quietly whispering her silent song,
as the night looks on,
creeping steadily and quietly
on a summer evening.

Abraham Jung, Grade 10
Bronx High School of Science, NY

Top Poem Grades 10-11-12

Social Butterfly

Several around me are hiding their true selves
They flutter around and imitate everybody else
Even though I'm different, my true identity shows
Sometimes I'm glad that I'm not in the know

Some may like my intriguing ways
While others might think I am out of place
Many don't think I make a sound
But they don't know me deep down

My friends and family know me the most
They are the ones who see me flutter and float
Some think I'm beautiful, while others do not
God made everything beautiful, even the rocks

I like attention, this I know
Sometimes that quality doesn't show
Here I am in this thin fragile shell
Waiting to break free and exhale

If they knew me, they might be able to see
My true and breathtaking beauty
Even though I am quiet and shy
Doesn't mean I can't be a social butterfly!

Jasmine Lott, Grade 11
Thomson High School, GA

Top Poem Grades 10-11-12

An Evening by the Sea

Where May burns red into June,
Sand lies beneath my feet.
The waves, they roar and whisper
To a strange rhythmic beat.

I listen to their lullaby,
And I listen to their words
To understand the secrets
Hidden in their verse.

Earth's candle blazes lower,
As Time moves on and on.
Shining brightly one instant,
But in the next is gone.

The Sun's burning red fades away,
Replaced with silver light.
And suddenly we're bathed
In nature's soft half-light.

As the tide rolls in,
I roll away,
Borne off by time's current,
Into another day.

Sean Rayburn, Grade 12
Newnan High School, GA

Top Poem Grades 10-11-12

Katrina's Thunder

Her thunder rolled, her thunder cried
Lightning built up in her eyes
A tantrum like no other
Feel the wrath of Katrina's thunder

Rubble strewn where she'd begun to play
Rooftops sunk in where she'd rested for the day
Flooding rushed into her playground's gates
Playing a different sort of game

Ignoring her doll's cries for mercy, she plays on
Her laughter drowning out their noise
Swinging from the clouds, she goes up and crashes down
Her playroom now a disaster

Winds picked up as she exhaled
Picking things up and discarding them to the ground
A tantrum like no other
We've felt the wrath of Katrina's thunder

Jenna Roland, Grade 10
Lakewood High School, SC

Top Poem Grades 10-11-12

Old House

He became an old house.
The front porch railing with its missing spindles,
That made up his worn smile.
The stiffened joints that echoed the creaking stairs,
As he slowly ambled up to bed.
And the vacant eyes with their shades closed,
Detached from the living world.
The yard and flower beds were left unkempt,
Since he hadn't trimmed his beard in years.
They say his furnace broke the day his wife died.
The cold crept in and filled his bones,
With a terminal ache and longing.
Now all that's left is the leaky roof,
Where the rain soaks in,
And the memories seep out.

Jeffrey Wellman, Grade 12
James Hubert Blake High School, MD

The Silent Rain

On that sweltering day, I wandered out of my ice box.
I breathed in the air and felt the sweet smell of sunflowers fill my lungs.
I listened as the bees buzzed in their usual sprightly choir.
Wandering down the beaten dirt path I admired the jade glow of the light through the leaves.
I walked and walked until the signs of daylight had passed and night had fallen upon me.
Excitement built up in my chest as we made our way to the abandoned field.
I waited, and waited, and waited.
Then it came in a flash.
Red, White, Blue.
Like fireflies in the sky.
Shooting up like flying panthers.
Boom, Crack, Whistle.
And it was done.
An ashen blanket had descended upon the emerald grass.
Glowing coals simmered gently as men scurried to extinguish them.
As we passed, I watched in dismay.

Courtney Carroll, Grade 10
Haverhill High School, MA

The Simple Days

Ahh the simple days
Where the summers seemed endless and the days went by slow,
Where nothing seemed to matter and all you really cared about were the monsters under your bed
Ahh the simple days
When running through the sprinklers was the best thing ever and getting mud all over the place was no big deal
Ahh the simple days
When the neighborhood kids would go out and play Manhunt
Till the streetlights came on and the mosquitoes were biting at your legs
Ahh the simple days
When ice-cream sundaes and snow cones were the greatest things ever and ice cold lemonade made all your problems disappear
Ahh the simple days
Too bad they don't really exist anymore
Now it's all just a memory and something I will pass down to my kids and not let them take it for granted
Because the simple days do come to an end
But I will always remember those days and never forget that I was once a kid
Ahh the simple days
They never end in my heart

Joanna Kamouzis, Grade 10
Peabody Veterans Memorial High School, MA

Change

Change is like the wind,
At times it moves slowly and silently through the calm meadows of your life,
Yet it can rummage through your forest like a wildfire,
Feelings and emotions change creating an everlasting soul.
Change is like the ocean,
At times it swishes and flows with the motion of the earthly life inside it,
Yet it can crash and cut at your weakness,
Memories and stories will grow teaching the everlasting soul.
Change is like the petals on a beautiful flower,
At times it will be beautiful and vibrant,
Yet it can become shriveled and closed,
Only the pure water and intelligence of the surroundings and flower can overcome the closed time,
That gives honor and wisdom to the everlasting soul.

Katie Over, Grade 10
Miami Beach Sr High School, FL

My Pride and Joy

My car is like my pride and joy,
When I drive it I feel more like a man and less like a boy.
I enjoy buying new things to make it cooler,
But when I got mud tires the ride was less smoother.

I take it off-road all of the time,
And the car gets covered with lots of grime.
It has a radio so I can talk to friends
When I drive on the highway its antenna bends.

I like my car because it is mine
And no one's resembles it, so it's one of a kind.

Burk Knowlton, Grade 11
Heathwood Hall Episcopal School, SC

Search for an End

Sand falls through my fingers slowly like a drip
And a pile forms at my feet
But the stare is not broken
Searching for some type of end.
To reach and begin and choose the mistakes to make.
To touch and start and drive the darkness from my heart
To find and commence and wake up with eyes free of gray
To feel and arise and live with a mind unclouded by lies.
But this faulty optimism runs short
For a closing to this
Lies in the beach undiscovered.
And with my eyes clouded white there I will wait
For a cessation to rise.
And bring me to the new world
Bright and gold
But till then I'll linger
For without an end
Nothing bold nor beautiful can be born.

Peter Walsh, Grade 11
East Islip High School, NY

Untitled

As the summer breeze comes and goes
what remains are our worries and woes
along the ridges of and ocean that never sleeps
are the answers that everyone desperately seeks

We try to reach in
longing to grasp onto secrets untold
but fail
as the waves reaching the shores unfold

Then
the waves retreat back
taking all those little things we lack
washing away the memories of what was
and what could've been
without those fateful faults

Elizabeth Jho, Grade 12
Great Neck South High School, NY

To a Friend

What a blessing you are! I love you, dear friend.
Can I even begin to explain the joy knowing you
Has brought me, the truths about love
You've taught me? The purity in the love that you show
Has blessed me more than you'll ever know
And the smiles you bring and the faith of your walking
Sing to me of eternal love
And joy that bubbles up in the soul
Yielding patience and peace as it overflows.
Thank you for walking, for talking when silence
Had to be filled, and for your stillness
Blessing so many tranquil moments.
For your willingness to listen to me,
To befriend me when I so needed a friend,
For your encouragement and laughter and ease,
I thank you. May God bless you, dear friend!

Brittany Darst, Grade 11
Darst Family Home School, NC

Friendship

A firm bond that shall never terminate,
Like the charm of a rose always cherished,
Although gradually it will be perished,
It is worthy enough to ruminate.

It is like the secure gravitational force,
Holding the sun and planets conjointly,
However distant or remote they may be,
Supporting each other during the course.

As cogent and virile as the fine nature,
Impelling its way through troubles,
Step by step in might it redoubles,
Recovering rapidly from disadventure.

The best relation existing on Earth,
Forever bringing a great deal of mirth.

Qurat-ul-ain Gulamhussein, Grade 10
Division Avenue High School, NY

Freedom with the Wind

Freedom, with the wind
On the open road
How *simple* it is
To ride along
Bumpin' and jumpin' along the way
Worrying about *nothing* in the universe.
What a wonderful feeling that is:
To have *freedom* splashed across your face
Like ice water on a hot day
If only things were that way
If only for *once* in our stress-filled lives
We could take a complete break
Where society *dies* for a day
And all we have is the open road and the
Freedom with the wind.

Bobby Schrader, Grade 11
Council Rock High School South, PA

Books

Books are good.
Books can take you places
People cannot.
Books inspire and motivate you
In ways others cannot.
When you are reading a book
You can forget all your troubles.
Books are the key to education,
They help you learn and grow.
Books are the key to a happy life.
Gregory Lambros, Grade 11
Bishop Verot High School, FL

Listen to Beethoven Play

Listen to Beethoven play
Watch the petals flow away
See these fingers press the keys
Sway with the music's breeze

Don't forget to water the flowers
Let the sun shine its power
All to Moonlight Sonata

Your eyes will slowly drift closed
This is the path that you chose
Don't fight it, please, rest with ease
Don't worry, I won't leave

By your side, I will stay
For forever and a day
Playing this, Beethoven's song
To you, my heart will always belong

All to Moonlight Sonata
Alexandria Tondu, Grade 11
Home Instruction Schools, NY

Sunrise

The sun appears
Over tall trees
Bringing warmth
And destroying darkness.
It appears so quickly
That one moment it is dark
Then it becomes light.
The bright new colors shine.
Like the stars once did.
Orange and yellow
Replace black and dark blue.
The cold fades away
And it becomes so warm
That you forget
The cold was even there.
The sunrise is great.
Christopher Law, Grade 10
Schley County Middle/High School, GA

Dying to Live

They say that every day we die a little
Pieces of us gone with every tick of the clock
But if we are slowly dying we gotta still be alive
Every day we live a little too but is it truly living?

Despite this all I can do is keep rolling on
Critics say this is just like a trend
They say it will fade after time has passed away
But by then will too much have passed with it?

Is today the day or will I die a little more
Before I live a little more, before I plunge
Plunge so deep into the murky pool of tomorrow
Blindly like the night I'll swim with only you to guide me

But today is not, cannot, be the day, but why
Why is the question time will never tell
But I'm still standing here knowing what needs to be done but not how
All I do, can, know is that we live and die a little each day
And I only want to live and die with you by my side
Matt Frank, Grade 10
Trinity High School, KY

A Look Through My Eyes

As I gazed upon my stage,
I smelled the desire to overcome and the encumbrance of fear,
the aroma of each slowly penetrating to the tip of my nostrils
forcefully granting permission to enter.
My focused eyes facilitated a mental blueprint,
an iterate slide show that evoked trickles of salty sweat to magically appear.
Each droplet a remorseful admonition of the long blistering hot days,
and hours upon hours of strict preparation.
The essence of the warm muggy air made its presence felt.
As I deciphered the grandeur of this moment.
I glanced ahead and slowly advanced to the front of the band,
the thought of fear growing with each impending step.
It felt as if I was subliming under the elongated arms of the stadium lights.
Although —
The world was blinded of these occurrences
only able to see the poise and composure that comes with being a senior, a leader.
The intensity of the crowd roared.
My time is now
I proudly rose my glowing instrument
Closed my eyes and graced the world with the beauty of music.
Drewe Cosby, Grade 12
Jeffersontown High School Magnet Career Academy, KY

Infatuated

The twist of notes crawling inside my ear,
The thought of never getting a chance to hear what I love to hear
The force of the bass that thumps my heart,
The thought of the vocals that makes my heart start,
The movement of my feet, the motion of my hands shaking,
Never to realize that music made me infatuated.
Imani Pressley, Grade 10
Ragsdale High School, NC

Portraying the Portrait

She trips the light fantastic in a traditional dance,
though its rhythm has changed through the years.
Its steps still remain the same:
she juggles the weight of a thousand china plates
and slaying the boogeyman before bed.

Her tasks are not simple, though others will say she has life
much easier compared to her man.
But has he ever once tried
captaining a ship whilst acting the role of crew
and nursing an invalid colored red?

No, her shift does not cease when the sun rests its eyes to sleep
nor when the light forsakes the dark sky.
She slaves and she slaves all night
and all day, almost always stressed out and in pain
just waiting for him to bring home the bread.

Megan Cornwell, Grade 12
Cullman Sr High School, AL

Nature Is a Part of Me

Nature is a part of me
One with the dirt under me
Spinning around and round
With clouds of dust gathering

Nature is a part of me
Up in a tree
Not making a sound
Waiting for movement on the ground

Nature is a part of me
Seeing a faded reflection of me on the water
Waiting for the bobber to go down
While sitting on this dirt mound

Mat Neal, Grade 11
Thomson High School, GA

Waiting for Spring

Sitting on the back porch swing, swaying,
A warm breeze rustles the hodgepodge of leafy trees,
The backdrop of this late spring day.
A glass of icy cold iced tea in hand,
The droplets of dew cooling my hands.
My sister sits beside me,
Her head lying on my shoulder.
I rock us slowly back and forth.
We laugh sometimes.
Sometimes we just enjoy the silence.
The rays of sun reaching us beneath the awning;
Its warmth penetrates right to the inner core.
There is no better day to remember
When the snow sits heavily on the house,
Threatening to never leave.
But this memory warms and comforts
For the days in which we can sit on the back porch swing,
Iced tea in hand, sun shining…
These days are not too far away.

Michi Aman, Grade 10
Our Lady of Mercy High School, NY

I Scream for Chocolate Chip Cookie Dough Ice Cream

The chocolatey, creamy, cold love of mine,
Is only the BEST and tastes so fine.
Floating in my bowl as if it were in paradise,
Nothing can compare this feeling precise.
This unique, delicious, exquisite pastry,
Has always been extremely tasty.
Each time I take a bite,
I savor this ice cream with all my might.
Chocolate Chip Cookie Dough is a blossomed rose,
Only difference is, it does not give you a stuffy nose.
Here's to Chocolate Chip Cookie Dough,
Awarded with "Best Ice Cream" title and a bow.
My watering mouth during dinner,
Thinking of dessert is such a killer.
Chocolate Chip Cookie Dough ice cream,
Awaiting for me or so it seems.
Lovely dessert, do not worry anymore,
The freezer you're in won't be a bore.
Do not worry about the sun you once felt,
Its rays will not reach I would not let you melt.

Grace Ayudant, Grade 10
Colonia High School, NJ

Step Up

Why must I always be the first one to say "I'm sorry?"
You say you love me, but you can never manage
to utter those simple words.
I know forgiveness can be hard,
but isn't losing a friend much harder?
It seems as if you're so quick
to give our friendship away.
Like an old shirt, I don't seem to fit in your life,
But you seem to fit in mine.
To me, you're the shirt I can never seem to give away.
However, when does love overpower dignity?
Time and time again, I say those words
only to have them never said to me.
I'm simply waiting for you to step up,
But I fear you have already stepped off.

Tamika Normil, Grade 10
Bishop Ford Central Catholic High School, NY

Barack Obama

The new and improved
the icon of hope
here he is at last

The long-awaited Iowa's own
brings up a brighter future

His quick political rise
becomes very respected

Now I know "our time has come"

Courtney Couplin, Grade 11
Carver Vocational Technical High School, MD

Love

When I first met you my heart dropped never knew love could take my heart my mind was wondering but my heart was still placed on your personality I never knew that my dreams could be fulfilled thinking about you late at night wondering how you feel wondering do you love me but I guess that my dreams have already been fulfilled — when you ask me do I love you sometimes I wonder why and sometimes I wonder how but then I start to think it don't take one person to have love it takes two to make one the one love that can pour down a vine that never dies out.

Quaneice Ware, Grade 10
Dave Thomas Education Center West Campus, FL

My Fiber, His Prose

They sought out the rectitude
Callously, sometimes hopelessly
They implored me to engage in a candidness I had never known
To reach inside and wrench out
That deep and heavy melancholy
That once adorned my emerging and faithless soul
My attempt at this elusive candidness arrived
A materialization of those unsettled accretions of grief and tenderness
The thoughts were aligned and scattered:
Perhaps it was his charming flowerbed, that profusion of magnetism and lies
Or maybe the false timidity he revealed
Either way, we collided.
Sprang together concurrently with a forcer greater than anything I could have suffered through on my own
And now, now that the intensity and despair of it all has subsided,
I am left with but a ruthless wonderment
One that strives to know whether this surreal reality was true
Or a mere masquerade that I so happened to catalyze
So draw up and assembly, dearest garrison, the speciousness has come out
Has announced itself with the entire false splendor I always knew it deserved
Grant me equilibrium and cleanliness and reprieve from this imprudence
And for now, I will remain simply and unobtrusively crossed.

Jacqueline Brandon, Grade 11
John Dewey Academy Searles Castle, MA

The Teenagers

The girls gaze into the photo lens waiting for the opportune moment to smile
The girls covered in blue dresses, light from the dance floor shining all the while
Light embraces their faces with a certain glow of superiority
Everyone glances with a tint of curiosity
Flawless attire their hair in curls, as they wait, for the flash
They grasp each other, embraces and hold on for dear life, to hope this moment will last
They want to show their past
They are the beautiful girls
That they, even if for just one moment, are the centers of the world

For this is what friendship is
The connection of being one person not her of his
The bond that we share with each other
As sisters, mothers, and brothers
The unique beauty in us all
Through the rise and the fall
As it runs through the soul, as it travels from one hand to the next hand
If only for that one moment as the flash is approaching, for the stand

Emily McGeney, Grade 10
Peabody Veterans Memorial High School, MA

The Doctor

Ever toiling,
Imprisoned by the walls of the hospital
The pale yellow paints smeared on the walls
Chipping
The color a fruitless attempt at a ray of cheer.
Surrounded by the familiar aroma of soap
And corpses rotting in the morgue
Nursing the minor abrasions of a small, whimpering boy
Tenderly applying a bandage and handing him a lollipop
Then moving on to the amputee in the next room.
A syringe
A steady hand
All it takes to make the pain disappear,
To make it all evaporate into thin air.
The cure washing through the body
Like white water
The ailing all but forgotten
Another rescued patient
Another life saved
All in a day's work.

Prisca Osuji, Grade 11
Columbia Sr High School, NJ

Writing

Meditate.
Close your eyes.
Take a deep breath.
Search your mind, body, and soul.
Travel to the end of nowhere.
Float on cloud nine.
Reach the unreachable.
Exhale.
Release the thoughts into the atmosphere.
Place the ideas upon the paper.

Ashley Mims, Grade 12
Thomson High School, GA

My Struggle

I feel like there's a storm in my head,
That I can't get through.
I try and I try but there's nothing I can do.
I said I pace and I think,
I wish I could wake,
From this horrible dream,
That makes me so mean to the people I love,
Even the Lord up above.
I just wish He would make me a beautiful dove,
So I could fly away to a happy place.
Where I don't have to live in this struggle between love and hate.
It's like a constant battle that I know I'm going to lose.
I continue to fight and receive bruise after bruise.
I don't know what it's for, maybe it's all I know.
Or I'm scared where I'll go.
If I just quit, and don't fight any more.

Cory S., Grade 12
Audubon Youth Development Center, KY

Sadness Is a Computer

Procrastination got the best of me again,
70 degrees outside and I'm stuck in my room,
Only me, the blinding screen, and the click of the keyboard,
It is due by midnight to her email.
The time is 11:45,
A message comes up and says to recharge the computer,
Losing time, I ignore it and kept going,
The screen goes black and my paper is gone.
Sadness is a computer.

Ben Burstein, Grade 12
Tucker High School, VA

Cassius

A man who was looked up to by some,
And looked down upon by many.

His reputation was debased as time went on
Easy to predict a self sacrifice before too long

A man who brought much sorrow
For he did not know how to borrow.

He could only filch and sin,
Romans were grateful that he bears no kin.

A mastermind of trickery and manipulation,
Greeted by Caesar with bitter salutations.

Cassius saw friends and minions one in the same,
There was no love in his relationships. He is to blame.

A great evil was within this man
A tarnished sense of direction, led to his heinous plan.

Chris Perry, Grade 10
Council Rock High School South, PA

Every Little Lie

not a single tear will fall from these eyes for you tonight
and the look on my face shows everything's all right
I turn off the lights and pull back my stage face
where the ugly truths and thoughts have been placed
and as soon as the daylight breaks
I push it all back in with the mask in place
you look at me to make sure everything's fine
your beautiful blue eyes
tell me a million little lies
I smile
and spit each one back at you
and you soak each one up like it's the finest wine
this secret I keep inside, and every day I hide
the sun will reflect it back in your mocking eyes
and as soon as it begins to rain the tears will flow freely
down with the pain,
drained of everything kept inside
freed
of every little lie

Natasha Bailey, Grade 12
Kennett High School, NH

A School Morning

5 a.m.
red-tinted darkness
beating with a pulse
right behind my eyelids
the music plays
my footsteps sway
jam spread on rye toast.

6 a.m.
stiff denim jeans
then a checkered skirt
a black silk screen tee
slightly damp hair
the smell of something burnt.

7 a.m.
red is for lipstick
glitter on my cheek
black dipped ink
the clock ticks promptly
to the breath of my own heart.

Kaitlyn Ernst, Grade 10
Valley Regional High School, CT

Abandoned Love

I stand by the telephone
Waiting for the call
Does it come, No!
Not at all
I make excuses for him,
Like I always do.
He will never realize,
The pain he puts me through.
It comes late one night
I stammer and answer hello
But, does an answer come...No No No
Finally I hear him mutter
Oops wrong number.

Anna Urban, Grade 11
Loretto High School, TN

So Far Away

I walk this street
In line with every beat
Strumming my guitar
And though I've come so far
Further I must go
To be with you I know
I must be the best you've seen
And even though I'm just a teen
I believe this is true love
So I'll call to them up above
To help me see you
Even though I'm so far away

Joe Martin, Grade 10
Monson Jr/Sr High School, MA

Patriotism

The patriotism — of a heroic young man
Who grasps the flag he loves and never letting go
Through the raging bitterness war still he did not let go.
He marches into battle, waving the banner of freedom —
All across the bloodstained land —
Countrymen beside him fall on their knees
Still he stands willing to fulfill freedom's pleas —
He marches on amidst the slaughter of war
He stumbles and he falls amidst the many sounds of war
He stands again still grasping the flag he loves and never letting go
He falls again, blood flowing from his faded navy blue uniform
He lies on the ground clutching the flag he loves
For freedom's cause a patriot is gone.

Marco Garcia, Grade 11
Fort Lauderdale Christian School, FL

This or Nothing

Staring down a narrow, red rubber runway
Heart is beating out of my chest
Palms are sweaty
Trying to remember everything
Strong plant, swing through to vertical, turn
The perfect form is replaying through my head
Close my eyes, I have 90 seconds
Mental preparation, assurance
Open my eyes, I'm ready
Ready to put my last jump on the line
It's this or nothing
I open my eyes, step back with my right foot
Forward, and run slow at first, then progressing
5 lefts, 4, 3, 2, 1, flat, flat, plant!
Pulling, pulling in the air to a vertical position, open my eyes and it's all upside down
"Turn, Turn!" I hear coach yell, and I swing, turning over the crossbar at nine feet
For the first time
The adrenaline rush, the euphoria, I scream in happiness, accomplishment
Coach says, "Are you ready for the school record now?"
Reply: "What's another three inches?"

Becca Kovach, Grade 10
Blue Mountain High School, PA

Cry Now

Whoever said civil rights were civil?
We can fight day and night, in the sweat and the drivel,
Until the bloodstains, soak through the skin,
And reach the souls, that beg for equal sins,
Once upon a millennium, there was a point and place,
Where groups were abominated, by the color of their face,
It was decided that for the dominant race, there wouldn't even be a race,
It was always white power, while blacks get eyes full of mace,
No matter the crime, the punishment's still the same,
If you're black, the nominal memory of you went and came,
We're almost better today but we'll never steer clear,
Of the hatred and racism, that generates blood and tears.

Max Twer, Grade 10
Council Rock High School South, PA

Morning Sun

Your eyes are like the morning sun.
Every time they look down on me, they shine.
They slowly and carefully take every inch of me in.
I look towards the open window and
See the sun rise above the horizon.
You tilt my head back to kiss me,
And I see the morning sun in your eyes before I close mine.

Stephanie Kitchens, Grade 10
Thomson High School, GA

Remembrance

You carry the light that once guided my heart,
Now cascading darkness captures my mind,
Leaving me lost and afraid to go on.
There is no path before me,
No future out laid,
No hopes, no dreams,
All aspirations are slain.

Our memories scream at my conscious,
Haunting my thoughts,
Devouring all happiness,
It claws away at my lingering sanity.
I've often wanted to erase our life,
Moments of laughter and love,
Of bliss and delight,
So I'd have motivation to lay dead,
As cold and ashen as yourself.

Life is the tragedy,
Death is asylum to such pain,
The forever peace for my tortured soul.

Kerrie Carvalho, Grade 12
Rancocas Valley Regional High School, NJ

Burning Enlightenment

The words came as piercing insight,
Splitting to the core.
Burning enlightenment.
The words ceased but the pain continued.
They controlled his state of mind.
Though twisted and skewed,
They were honest.
Brutally honest.
Hurtful truth.
Burning enlightenment.
This honest insight changed his state of mind.
He now understood that he was blind.
Blind of everything good.
Ignorant of truth.
Now that he knew,
What must he do?
He feared his life of ignorant bliss,
But it controlled all of what he could see.
Only those words of piercing insight,
Could truly set his soul free.

Phillip Wennerstrom, Grade 10
Chattanooga Christian Schools, TN

A Shadow in the Night

A shadow moves towards you during the night.
This shadow stumbles and falls to its knees.
The shadow begins to beg and make pleas.
You move in to see this tremendous sight
Just to be confronted with a great plight.
The shadow seems to be a man of needs.
The man is weeping and sweating beads
Of blood. He shouts as if He's in a fight.
This man is calling out to His Father.
For another way for us to be saved.
But the man must die for our behavior.
Prayers get Him to where death doesn't bother
Him. The way for eternity was paved.
This shadow, this man, He's Lord and Savior.

Moriah Chitwood, Grade 10
Cambridge Christian School, FL

Truth

to live is to love,
to love is to feel,
to feel is to hurt,
to hurt is to lose,
to lose is to hate,
to hate is to heal,
to heal is to change,
to change is to risk,
to risk is to love
Love is a risk everyone takes,
some of us win,
some of us lose,
it's a lottery of hearts,
you never know what to expect,
just keep playing the odds and pray for the best.

Tara Hobbs, Grade 11
Loretto High School, TN

Untitled

There in you, lies a heart
that's been broken too early
There, in your hand, is a rose
picked too early

Your heart, inside you, is chipped.
It will heal in time,
but it won't be quite the same.
The rose, in your hand, loses petals.
They will grow back in time,
but they won't look quite the same.

Your precious heart, protected inside you
will eventually stop beating
And a rose, protected by the palm of your hand
will eventually wilt
and die.

Katie Crusenberry, Grade 11
Leesville Road High School, NC

I Am From

I am from honeysuckles, Sunday afternoon barbecues, and chocolate chip cookies. Sunday afternoon walks, good night kisses, cat naps, baby dolls galore, pink bows, dresses, and frilly little socks. Freshly popped popcorn, sleeping bags on the floor, and cases of late-night giggles.

I am from birthday cake, Sprite and Kool-Aid, Grandma's spaghetti, blowing bubbles in chocolate milk, and sparkling sugar cookies. Peanut butter sandwiches, Pop Rocks, Rice Krispies and milk late at night, and sneaking candy from Grandma's kitchen, even though we knew she wouldn't care.

I am from "Are we there yet?" "We're not there yet, are we?" "Get out of my room!" "Bubba did it!" and "Hurry up, we're gonna be late to be early!"

I am from people whose names I don't even know, and ones whose names I will never forget.

I am from a loving brother, wonderful parents, grandparents that spoil me rotten, a beautiful best friend, and great friends that I know always have my back.

Courtney Timmerman, Grade 11
Thomson High School, GA

A Ripe Heart

I gave you my heart on a gold chain.
You took it in your hands and felt its gentle pulse.
Then you weighed it, squeezed it, and pressured it.
I flinched.
Finally, you looked at me and placing my heart back into my trembling hands said, "It's not ripe yet. Give it more time."
Then you turned and walked away.
After you had gone, the heart in my trembling hands shattered.
I felt pain — a pain worse than anything on Earth or in Heaven.
Quickly, the pain left but a hundred scars remained.
Quietly, with shaking hands, I picked up the pieces of my broken heart and tucked them back inside my chest.
A silver key appeared and with it,
I locked my heart away, placing the silver key beside the locked door to my heart.
Years later, you came back, and asked for my heart again.
But I refused.
The more you asked, the weaker I became until I finally unlocked my heart and gave it to you with my head down.
Again you weighed, squeezed, and pressured.
This time I didn't flinch.
And this time you pronounced my heart ripe.
Then, gently, you placed my heart back inside my chest.
You took the silver key that also lay there and we left it behind,
As you took my hand and led me on.

Karis McMahan, Grade 10
Arlington Christian School, GA

Dance Your Heart Out

We turned up the volume, ready to start. The song then began the very first part.
Rhythm and flavor, as we moved to the beat. We were exact and sharp as we moved our feet.
Next, we heard the blast of the speakers. You could feel the vibration in our sneakers.
We spun and turned from left to right, and as a team we looked tight.
The floor under us went bam! We continued flowing with the jam.
We had precision and poise, as we had brought the noise!
The crowd went wild and applauded from their seats.
Louder and louder you heard the bass. We left good impressions on everyone's face.
For the finale we had energy and heart, as we gave our all dancing our hearts out, for the very last part.
Then the lights dimmed on the stage, and the curtains closed with the crowd amazed.

Brianna Luu, Grade 11
Joppatowne High School, MD

Stories

My eyelids tell a story
of long lost hope for the godforsaken world

when love is the answer
and peace is the choice

when diversity is tolerated
not a speaking soul unvoiced

A story
of leaders who have lost control

when love rules the world
and all their hatred lost

when living free is law
and freedom has no cost

A story of love that lives
but
my eyelids lie.

Anna Meany, Grade 10
Greenwood High School, KY

Reflection

At the end of the day,
What do I realize?
Was it how well I played the prelude?
Was it exact or concise?
Was the phrasing just right?
How could I characterize the ebb and flow?
Was it cantabile —
Did it sing?
In all these things,
I concentrate.

Aaron Dixon, Grade 11
Thomson High School, GA

Early Morning Walk

The grass had a scent of morning
As it swayed in the wind
The sun was just rising over the horizon
As it sprinkled light on the budding flowers
Because of our invading of its habitat
A fawn ran into the street
Its hooves clacking on the tar
A man quickly getting into his car
The turning of the engine
Created an echo in the still morning
The fumes coming out of the exhaust
Creating more of a hassle for the Earth to deal with
A bird chirping in the distance
Makes another bird chirp back
And they both fly away
Into the foggy sky
Merrily together

Michael Ferragamo, Grade 10
Haverhill High School, MA

Cheerleading

Bright lights hit that floor, there's no turning back now
My hands start to shake, why is everything loud?

I can't hear myself think as they call out our name
My team runs out beside me they all feel the same

Put on a smile leave your worries at the door
Responsible for each other, united on this floor

In our hearts all as one
Two minutes that make or break us, it's one or it's done.

Sisters at heart throughout the sweat and the tears
Give each other our best as we throw away all fears

It's over now body and souls on the floor…
Completely exhausted, insanely anxious
But always wanting more —

On that competition floor.

Erin Phelps, Grade 10
Ragsdale High School, NC

Slumber, Her Lover

Sleep runs his fingers down the back of her neck as
He coaxes her forehead towards her wooden desk
Sleep is feeding off her thoughts
Voraciously thriving on her stress
Sleep is discrete, caressing her cheek
Dragging her to bed by the lace of her dress
Sleep does not die, he will not be denied
And when her eyes feel weak
She'll be sleeping with sleep

Christopher Lizzio, Grade 11
Harborfields High School, NY

Yom Hashoah

How can people be so cruel?
People lived under one man's thought and rule
Such an awful series of events transpired
None of them expected none of them required
The Holocaust is what I speak of
Where was the aid of the man above?
It was a thing so abominable
Why couldn't we just be amicable?
Concentration camps enslaved my people the Jews
The sick, rich, poor it didn't matter who
History is forever changed Hitler is the man to blame
Death of innocent young and old
Those Nazis obeyed orders and did what they were told
It was a moratorium
Shot guns, gas chambers, crematoriums
Did nobody realize over six million dead?
It all could have been prevented
We cannot forget not now not ever
We must spread the word and remember forever
On this Yom Hashoah I write with regret
As I tell of the awful endeavor

Sydney Spinner, Grade 11
Townsend Harris High School, NY

Sunlight

Where is the sunlight?
As I sit here
Inside my dark room
Lit by only lamps
And my luminescent dreams

Where is the sunlight?
The moon is all I see
A moon that only glows
I don't mind staring down the sun
Even if I my sight slowly wears away

Where is the sunlight?
Is it hiding from me
Or is it I that am hiding?
These dark curtains
Separate me from this bright mystery

Where is the sunlight?
I want to bathe in its heat
I want to spend a moment
Screaming with laughter
With the flower in the sky
Showering me with its radiance
Ashfia Alam, Grade 10
Jericho High School, NY

Red

My favorite color is red,
Red is the color of my bed.
I have always liked this color,
Better than any other.
Some say it is the color of death,
I say it is the color to impress.
My favorite football team is red,
So is the tint on my head.
Red will always be my favorite color,
I doubt I will ever pick any other.
Owen Black, Grade 10
Schley County Middle/High School, GA

Music

The sound is
Moving

Makes the hair on my back
Stand up

Without it we are
Nothing

For
The
Silence is deafening
Daniel Karambelas, Grade 10
Haverhill High School, MA

The Tide

Looking out at the waves crashing in,
A refreshing breeze almost takes my breath away.
And as I'm sitting here,
A feeling of change has come over me.
Staring out at the dark water, not knowing what is at the bottom,
Realizing that's me.
Becoming fully aware that I'm too afraid to reveal myself to the world —
Too discomforted to let people look beneath my surface.
But why am I this way?
That answer is still a mystery.
However, one thing that is known,
I am a dark, crashing wave with a refreshing breeze drifting over me.
That gentle flurry of shyness that floats above my head,
If only it could be replaced with a hurricane of confidence.
Looks as if all we need is a new tide,
Something to randomize all the little things flowing against the current.
Ashley Kirk, Grade 11
Hiram High School, GA

Just to Make Sure

How can I be sure,
That when this is all over, we'll still talk again?
How can I be sure,
That once we part our ways, our lives will still cross again?
How can I be sure,
That once I say goodbye, we'll still say hello again?
How can I be sure,
That when We become only a You and a Me, we'll still come together again?
How can I be sure,
That after a few years, months, days, you'll still remember me again?
But,
When you laugh because of her right in front of me,
When your shoulder brushes mine in the hallways and you take no notice,
When our eyes catch a glimpse of our guilty souls and we look away,
When our footsteps carry us far from our upcoming intersections,
When my heart forces me back from holding on to yours,
That's when you can be sure,
That's when I am sure.
Linda Chu, Grade 10
Bronx High School of Science, NY

My Father

Some people say you are my father, to this I don't agree.
Please don't get angry or mad, just listen and you'll see.
You were there to hold my hand when I was learning how to stand.
You were there to pick me up whenever I fell down.
You were there to dry my tears and chase away all my fears.
You were there to care for me whenever I got sick or hurt.
You were there to hold me tight when I was scared at night.
You were there to listen when I was angry or upset.
You were there to ease my pain when sometimes it was in vain.
You were always there for me with guidance and with love.
Some people say you are my father, to this I don't agree.
Simply put a Daddy is what you'll always be to me.
Jordanna Wagner, Grade 11
Cab Calloway School of the Arts, DE

I Was Twelve

I know you are still here.
I can feel your presence inside me.
I remember it like yesterday; the day you left me.
It was five years ago.
I was too young; I still need you.
I didn't want to see you that day.
I wanted to be with my friends,
I was twelve.
Mommy forced me to go.
It was too hard to see you like that.
I couldn't handle it.
In my eyes, you were always so strong.
I never knew what was going on.
No one would tell me,
I was twelve.
I miss you.
I didn't want to see you that day.
I don't remember the last thing I said to you.
I hope I wasn't angry.
I never liked to see you disappointed.
I couldn't help it though, I was twelve.

Kelsey Fisher, Grade 11
Washington Township High School, NJ

Fairytale Love

Once upon a time, there was a boy,
Who brought a girl so much joy.

They were perfect for each other; two of a kind,
Their love was true and never blind.

They spent most all of their time together,
On cloud nine; they felt light as a feather.

She loved his bright eyes and sense of humor,
Always making jokes about a silly rumor.

He loved her smile and the way she cares,
When she walks in a room he always stares.

They used to wonder, "Is this the real thing?"
But around one another, their hearts would sing.

With their lives always filled with fun and laughter,
It's no wonder they lived happily ever after!

Sarah Shehorn, Grade 11
Countryside High School, FL

My Love

I never knew what love was until I saw you
I never knew what love felt like until I was in love with you.
I never told you what I felt and I never will
For now I will keep dreaming
And maybe someday my dreams will come true.
Now is time to say goodbye
But my love will still be there…in my heart, for you.
Now I can say that I know you
And if I know you, then I know what love is.

Ada Hernandez, Grade 10
Miami Beach Sr High School, FL

Breaking the City's Heart

Laying here under the stars alone
the green grass beside me used to be warm
love so strong it could break a wall of stone
I lost myself and your tears start to form
I said "we're through" I couldn't explain
you swore to me that you could try to change
I never meant to cause you that much pain
maybe I was wrong you could rearrange
I will remember how you said my name
I miss the way you looked at me
I kissed you at the football game
our love was like a wavy blue sea
though we went on our separate ways
I have loved you all these days

Shannon Silvia, Grade 10
Peabody Veterans Memorial High School, MA

I Hope

I hope you can't sleep
because your mind is filled with thoughts of me.
I hope every time you're in your room, bathroom, or car
your brain erupts with memories of us.
I hope when you use our chapstick
you can't help but remember how we tasted together.
I hope every time you open your phone
you see our picture.
I hope you think of what you did
and what could've been.
I hope you felt the same about me
as I did you.
I hope you don't hurt as much as I do.

Samantha Yellen, Grade 12
Anderson County High School, TN

Cupid

Dare to dream of minute puffy clouds
Sitting upon a kingdom of luscious lamentations
Zeus calls upon you for deeds unknown
A journey of love with a tiny arrow and bow

Sniping, shooting, potions of lust
Snaring, daring, tonics of love
With weapon in hand and wings afloat
A small boy makes decisions, remote

With clear eyes and mischievous hearts
Love conquers all with a tiny arrow and bow
A deceitful smile, an imagination of love
Lovers connect inconsequently

A bond of love formed with no sense of hate
A man with a tiny bow and arrow goes crazy not wild
Love formed and then a union of hate
Love conquers all into an emotionless state.

Connor Macdonald, Grade 12
Wamogo Regional High School, CT

Eulogy

His feet were weightless like white feathers on the water
His hands could save and feed thousands of poor sinners
The countenance showed His merciful and generous heart
He was fair to both the fool and smart.

Why did they have to tear him down?
Is it because He loved everyone, willingly remunerated good deeds and forgave the bad
Shared the joy of the happy and the sorrow of the sad
Helped the lads who lacked luck, and never ignored anyone in need for hands
And established a refuge, for the homeless and the sick, on nothing but sand

People full of hatred
Who had a fear for someone sacred
Stabbed Him, slapped Him, and spat on Him
Betrayed and ashamed so many times, He still did not turn His back against them
He was the fire that melted the icy hearts of the narrow-minded
He was the detergent that cleaned the stains people had in their lives

Though He was the light people were seeking
Now where is He? On the bloody, wooden cross of sin
With his hands pierced with the cold, iron nails of hatred
With His body twisted awkwardly, red sweat all over on it
Yet with the smile on His face, as He erased the dirty marks humans had made from the creed

Jeghang Wee, Grade 11
Heathwood Hall Episcopal School, SC

Life's Lessons

Our greatest prejudice is against death.
It spans age, gender and race.
We spend immeasurable amounts of energy fighting,
fighting an event that will eventually triumph.
Though it is noble not to give in easily,
the most alive people I've ever met are those who embrace their death.
They love, laugh and live more fully.

She would say,
"Some men see things as they are and say, 'Why'
I dream things that never were and say, 'Why not?'
To conquer your flaws, you must first accept them.
But above all, you must do the thing you think you cannot do."

He would say,
"Great minds discuss ideas; average minds discuss events; small minds discuss people.
You have to learn to follow before you can lead.
But above all, let us not look back in anger, nor forward in fear, but around in awareness."

It is not life that hands you that bowl of cherries;
It is *they* who make the bowl *and* the cherries.
However, some cherries are rotten, some seedless, some stemless but they are all edible.
They are on their last cherries and no matter how hard you try to fill up the bowl,
You can't. A hero need not speak for when he is gone, the world will speak for him.

Selman Mujovic, Grade 10
Bronx High School of Science, NY

Changes

Changes is why we are born
It's why we are brought to this planet.
Changes are what makes us breathe and
What makes us speak our minds.
We wonder if changes are really on our mind,
If it's by our side.
Without the change there wouldn't be
A single heartbeat dancing, singing and laughing,
Changes are what we will aim for
To make this Earth a better place
For now and forever.
Changes.

Azahira Rosales, Grade 10
Miami Beach Sr High School, FL

essential simplicities

it's the most beautiful thing you can imagine,
like your mind's just flowing free.
it's better than almost anything,
that you could even hope to believe.
the ink across the paper,
my mind discovering me,
words just overflowing,
words i didn't even see.
my body's overtaken,
by a mind i long to know,
and as my heart is breaking,
i surrender; i let go.
i find my freedom on the paper,
release it through the pen.
my head and heart are shaking
but i revive myself once again.
i can feel the life within me,
expressed throughout my words.
i've found what it is that saves me
i've found how to heal the hurt.

Katharine Laundrie, Grade 11
Jamestown High School, VA

Take My Hand*

Some people think life is just a game
　You have to be careful
Or your life will never be the same
　Trust me with this one
I threw my life away
　Because of drugs and selfishness
Hold your parents close
　No matter what they say
Take everything for granted
　Choose your friends by who YOU are
Not who THEY want you to be
　So before you throw your life away
Take my hand and
　Talk to me

Damyon Norway, Grade 11
Eckerd Family Youth Alternative School, VT
Dedicated to Autum

Vulnerability

Snow
　Drifts
　　Down
Your hands: blue.
Your heart: chill.
Our love in an icy cover.
What can I do to revive it?
If only you could tell
If only you could move your iced lips;
They are tinged an azure shade,
A sprinkle of frost,
And petrified eyes.
You are so cold
And I am so helpless.

Kathleen Euler, Grade 12
North Allegheny Sr High School, PA

Addicted

You inject me with sweet affection
You intoxicate me with love
I inhale the *Polo Black* scents of you
Then reality disappears and the sun
And the moon become brighter

I can't get enough of you
I'm high on the blunt of adoration
I'm addicted

I constantly want more and more
Never growing tired of the ecstasy
I'm inebriated with happiness
I'm addicted

The powderiness of love has overcome me
No one can save me
You've pricked me with the spike of passion
I'm addicted to you

Elizabeth Simpson, Grade 10
Lee High School, AL

Haven

Forests dance and sway under breath of breaking day,
　as cloud in heaven unite in canopies of white;
　o'er all the eastern sun will make its fiery run
to touch the western rim as night falls fast and dim.
　Behold the evening star shining clear afar!
　Behold the lunar orb in pearly fashion formed!
　Waters clean and fair do wreathe with misty air,
where ferns and fronds abound and drape in greenest gown
　the fertile loam of earth to greet the sunlight's birth.
　Hail the morning star; light and life unbarred!
　Hail the azure sky where wind and birds do fly!
　Beauty sweet uncovered; love and life discovered
　within this haven fair far past all danger's snare;
　yet I must turn and go to meet with friend and foe,
　to wage both love and war till I return once more.

Renee Fisher, Grade 12
On Eagle's Wings Home School, NC

Waiting Patiently

Waiting patiently
I don't know if tomorrow will come
What will tomorrow bring?
Where will I be?

Waiting patiently
What will I do?
What if something happened to me?
What if?

Waiting patiently
I'm growing tired
I'm getting weak
I'm starting to collapse

Waiting patiently…

Vinshayra Hunter, Grade 10
Seneca High School, SC

Time

The past may be long passed
But do not forget it
for it can make the future
that much more simple
Do not condemn the present
for you will forsake the future
and if you break the future
You will be lost in time
You will be lost in time

Alex Hoyt, Grade 10
Haverhill High School, MA

Space and Silence

It was the bang of a shotgun
Without the blast
The havoc
The fear
The resolution
Face
No time like the present
Time is irrelevant
Your
The space is more important
Than the words ever were
Fear
The words left unspoken
Were the clearest I've ever said
Listen
To the echoes
Bouncing
Like Hell screaming
Or Heaven's
Raptures on high

Casey Mitchell, Grade 12
Beaver Area Sr High School, PA

Remember When

Remember when we were little kids
Remember how we would always talk about running away
Remember how we just wanted to leave this small town,
You said you wanted to become a doctor
Remember when you left me for drugs
I also remember standing beside your casket
Crying for hours because my best friend was dead
Reading in the newspaper sixteen year-old girl killed in a car crash,
I do not remember you as the girl who ended her life.
I remember you as my best friend.
I left this small town and lived out your dream of becoming a doctor.
When I come back I remember all the memories some good some bad.

Correna Reynolds, Grade 10
Wirt County High School, WV

Friends

This is dance class, twenty-four girls to be exact
Dancing in unison in one big room with the bars all around
To ensure that we cannot fall
Even though we often do
While we try to learn from our own mistakes
So we do not hurt ourselves too often
Gray floors, and white walls decorated
All with pictures of beautiful dancers that we strive to be
We must wear the same thing, while we throw our bodies into the air
Knowing no one is there to catch us, but we try to make it seem easy
For a moment, we make that special connection with the music

This is friendship, laughing, crying, and cliques included
Talking about boys and family, and what happened that day
Laughing at the weirdest things, but most of all trusting each other
Creating a relationship, and knowing the other person will always be there
All the fun we have and good times together
Just holding on to one another and knowing that someone cares.

Shauna Gillis, Grade 10
Peabody Veterans Memorial High School, MA

Promise Me, It's Forever

Like words from your heart written on paper,
to no end but from one start it always can be misread.
Like actions from your moods done and redone in person,
out of love? It always can be misunderstood.
The things that you do, I get so intertwined,
I always want you to fully believe, how much you truly mean to me.
From new memories to old times, and heartbreaks to new loves,
this time I hope that you will promise me, it's forever.
So much changing through so much time, I recover and regain
after losing so much and now in pain.
I thought I could never turn around and look back at what changed.
All I need is strength, encouragement, faith and love.
Strength for holding on, encouragement for holding on longer,
faith to stay holding on and hopefully never fall, and love for you to hold on with me
and to promise me, it's forever.

Brenda Browder, Grade 10
Hudson High School, FL

Love

A thought, a whisper.
Does it matter? Does it exist?
An essence, a sort of being,
A lingering hope of something great.
Is this false? Withering away with time.
Just a feeling, a matter of the heart.
Will it fade as tarnish,
Escaping through the cracks of what we don't know?
A kiss, his lips. They are soft, but too sweet?
Is it an illusion, a trick? A mind game at best.
It couldn't be. It has to exist.
It's there, somewhere. It has to be.
I can feel it, I can see it.
I believe I can even touch it.
Its existence grants me life.
A thought, a whisper
Is screaming inside my conscience.
'Hear me, hear my cry.
I am here, do not be deceived.'
'I exist, I matter'
It is real, my love. It is real.

Anna Stuckey, Grade 12
Nansemond River High School, VA

1984

Depressed, distressed, and sad was Winston Smith,
Believing happiness to be a myth.
A member of the Outer Party,
He was watched both day and night through telescreens
And could not speak his mind because of fear
That someone from the government might hear.
One day at work he found forbidden love
This Julia was sent from up above.
She led him to the Golden Country where
The two could be alone without care.
A room above an old shop would be theirs
Until the Thought Police did find them there.
To Minipax Room 101 they went
Both tortured 'til they loved the government
"I love Big Brother" Winston had to say
As he sat in the Chestnut Tree Café.
The doublethink which Winston once despised
Had come to be a way of life most prized.

Lauren Procz, Grade 11
Council Rock High School South, PA

Mirrors Multiplied

I loved him until he loved me,
Then mirrors multiplied, which simplified life
And that cleared up the matter because
Love is a thing that can never go wrong.

But with his name, but clear in time,
Some people mind and I was one.
Right and left have now met success.
Vulnerable, yes, but never pure.

Jessica Brooke Atteberry, Grade 11
Anderson County High School, TN

Misspelled Goodbye

Good morning sunrise,
Shining light upon
The people weaving in
And out of each other's lives.
Good morning thunder's vibration
As the clouds disappear as
The rain pours and the rain
Is lost in evaporation,
Yet remaining invisibly in air,
And I can feel the humidity,
But the ground is left dry
Like the rain never fell there.
The rain is on its way
To becoming clouds that
Filter and fade, dissolve and diminish,
Like you they never stay.
Like you they cast shadows in my sky
As your absence lingers in my mind;
Like you're gone without a trace,
And like you've misspelled goodbye.

Yasmin Bendaas, Grade 12
West Forsyth High School, NC

What Happens Next

What happens next when you walk into the darkness,
You hear nothing, you see black
All you can do is feel

What happens next you feel this thing
That's so soft and warm
Then you get this feeling all through your body

What happens next then you step into the light
But it still looks like it's night
What a way to live
But when it's night I don't feel right

What happens next he's lost in his eyes
I can see so well but I wish he could
He's blind he goes through this every day
At night he's always in the light
But stays in the night.

Ridley Lassiter, Grade 11
Overbrook School for the Blind, PA

Kitchen

This kitchen is a story book.
With each meal adding a new chapter.
It's seen newborns and seniors
It has the vantage of wisdom that often comes with age.
But it also can make you feel youthful again.

It's almost as if
Every copper lined pan
Stays warm for you,
Knowing you'll always come back.

Redding Kingery, Grade 11
Heathwood Hall Episcopal School, SC

Vast

A canvas,
Spread roughly over a table, hands do not bother to smooth the edges,
Or firmly pat the middle to prevent creasing, rough sketches, deep wounds across its face,
Torrents of gold, rush from within its pores, and escape in brazen tufts.

Pockets of green burst from its sides, memoirs of the returning past,
Long steely knives, sharpened through the cold, an iron grasp upon the lands,
A hold into its depths, it grips and blends the soil at its feet,
And before its passing, tunnels deep.

Flattened in the corners, showing signs of weighted wear,
And patches of bald auburn, where the paint must have missed,
Shallow pools of emerald contrast against an aqua backdrop,
And yellow crests rise from within.

A picturesque landscape, here, the art is simple,
It is outlined and blended, pressed and lifted,
The artist raises the brush four times a year,
And the canvas is altered, from green to gold to brown to white,
But the hands that transform it, always turn it back.

Kathryn Lindquist, Grade 11
Middle Creek High School, NC

Struck by Love!!!

You have done the unthinkable —
Matter of fact the known impossible —
And the love I hold deep down inside for you is truly unstoppable —
From the time you came into my life —
Until now 'cause I want to make you my one and only wife —
See it's something about you but I just don't really know —
'Cause you came out of nowhere into my life and have my soft emotions truly ready to show —
From when I touch your body —
To how your smile makes me melt in front of everybody —
And when I gaze into those light brown eyes —
To how I show you where in my heart you reside —
So take these words until we meet again —
And remember I will love you from deep down within —

Brandon Fabian, Grade 12
Frew Mill School, PA

What I Learned on May 19th

Beneath the whelms of pleasure and desire, you will find deep wonder, a certain lost sincerity. What we desire most is soon lost with the knowledge of suffering. I wish not for what I want but for the needs of others. Today, we are so encompassed with our desperate wantings; never once do we stop and ponder the needs of the slightly unfortunate. Women and children dying due to starvation. Men fighting a battle that seems endless. Victims of depression or disease. Infants abandoned, children tormented, teenagers pressured and adults lost. We all are engulfed with our own lives that we simply forget, unintentionally, the sadness of others. It is no crime to do so but it is our better responsibility to remind those who seem to lose their way. When in doubt of yourself, when suffering seems no more, when your heart aches with the pain of a thousand diving knives; catch yourself. Pain is a devastation we share with others; not one to plunge into empty sided. If we all join together; conquering is possible and attainable. We must not surrender to our will, but stand rebellious. Whatever war needing fight, the battles should not be faced by oneself but with an army of troops. And when audacity strikes, you will step upon the line of the battlefield and look beside you, to find your haunting dreams misleading. In your darkest of dreams, you awake drenched in an all consuming fear. You inhale deeply, searching for an all around calm — of the nerves, of the limbs, of the heart. Once reached, your fear is then lifted, you look around to find the safety and security. I pray you find such comforts.

Heather Delaney, Grade 10
Masconomet Regional High School, MA

The Activist Speech
Bright lights of dark nights,
Lead the way through shadowed fights.
Express the tone of which you fear,
And one day God will surely hear.
Fights break out on every street,
Well known actions caused by heat.
To keep it cool through burning times,
Will end the waves of constant crimes.
Britne Brown, Grade 11
Nova High School, FL

Memories
Talk is cheap.
Music is loud.
Sleep is boring.
I am too old,
I am too young,
What happened to all the fun?
Barbie days,
Sun rays,
Pool parties,
Candy Smarties,
Boys were icky,
I was too picky,
Sleepover nights,
Pink ballerina tights,
Bed times,
Nursery Rhymes,
The big kids looked so cool…
What happened to all the fun?
Katie Merrill, Grade 10
Haverhill High School, MA

Within the Wind
I look beyond the open fire
I see the sizzles of burnt desires
Upon my eyes in which I look
I feel despair for those I took
I hear screams within the night
I fear for my life
Run for the woods, and see the light
I run for it faster
With might I take
Within my thoughts I am awake
Waiting to reach my destination
For love awaits
With my desires, piled up high
They can't be fulfilled
In my empty bed
I want, I pray
For one less pillow to be laid
It will never happen for me
I know this, for my compassion
Is caught within the wind.
Stephanie Fabery, Grade 10
Laurel Highlands High School, PA

Pop-Pop
What do you miss most about life?
Is it falling face first on the beach one year
while you were attempting to parasail?
Is it all of our family reunions?
Do you miss telling old family stories?

I miss…
How you were always optimistic and happy,
even as you were laying in the hospital bed with only a few days left.
The way your sky blue eyes would glisten after you were enlightened.
I miss seeing you all the time…

How is Heaven treating you?
Are there big golden gates when you enter?
Is it really true that you can't get hurt?
Are you always as happy as they say in all of those fairy tale books?
Do you receive all of the balloons and best wishes we give you?
Do you realize how much we love and miss you?
Meghan Johnson, Grade 10
Riverside High School, SC

Escape
Forced to conform.
Denied by society.
Denied because of individuality.
Cast aside by those who created me.
Pushed aside by the robots of a failing civilization.
Made an outcast because of my lifestyle.
Seeing authority as my nemesis, my antagonist.
Torn down by the same drones that brought me into this world.
Imprisoned by the same drones that told me to always be myself.
Held captive by the same drones that cast me aside for just that.
Telling me I could be whatever I wanted, but never telling me
They would disown me for not becoming what they wanted.
Going against the will of my creators, as if they deserve that title
Knowing it is my turn…
Tonight it is my turn…
And tonight…
I'm taking freedom back.
Zachary Tate, Grade 10
Bledsoe County High School, TN

Innocence
A beautiful painting hanging on the wall, valiantly for all to see,
Had colors so brilliant, and a gloss so extreme
That all others wished it they could be.
But dust, in its vengeful ways came drifting on the prowl,
And when they saw this masterpiece, attacked it with a howl,
Dust covered the shining glass, missing not a single part,
And some say a wail was heard coming from the tarnished painting's heart.
The painting waited for someone to come and wash it clean,
but realized with a sob that this moment would never be seen.
The other paintings on the wall laughed with mocking disdain
At this once so perfect painting, which was now hanging in shame.
Rebekah Dennis, Grade 11
Fairhope Home School, AL

Underneath the Hill

Underneath the hill
suffocating
no one understands
the pressure
on top of me
I am deep
within the soil
no one can
bury me
my true meaning
lost forever
Underneath
the hill
Samantha Rodriguez, Grade 12
Preston High School, NY

Words Are Sharp

Words are knives
Cutting through a person's spirit
Offering no resistance
Cutting them to pieces
Leaving behind a torn, ragged picture
Cruel reminder of what was lost
Left alone to endure the pain
Wishing someone would come along
To comfort and hold
To heal the hurt
Created by the words that are knives
Sean Rudder, Grade 12
Hanahan High School, SC

Over You

You used me all wrong,
And now I'm gone,
But you don't care
Because you can bear
The weight and the guilt
Up on that empire you built
Of fibs and lies
But my heart it dies
Inside the pain will grow
But I need you to know
That I'm done with you
And that we are through
You mean nothing at all
You're just a fly on the wall
You never loved me
So leave me be
I'm happy the way this turned out
Now I can go out and about
But now that I see clear
Let me tell you my dear
I'm over you!
Amanda Harding, Grade 10
Woodstown High School, NJ

Innocent First Kiss

Pounding hearts,
A Halloween's scary revenge.
Passion intruding like fireworks
Exploding in the crisp air above us.

Knees buckling,
As if a coldness from a summer night's rain has surpassed me.
A child's begging cry,
Wanting the sweet sensations to never end.
The memories engraved into a scrapbook
Where its expressions can never be erased.

Watery eyes,
I will never let go.
Ripping harm from its path.
My first kiss is forever,
Unexpected and never forgetful.

I will cut the tongue, piercing them deep
Of all those who dare to shield me from heaven's sweet kiss.
The world non-existing,
For only we take part in this fantasy!
Our hearts unbreakable, our bodies untouchable, for we are one.
Marleen Dos Santos, Grade 10
Colonia High School, NJ

The Eagle

Here I sit dreading the day you take me away,
Away from all that I know.
You wait for me like an eagle,
Till you can tear me up and eat me.

You're going to put me to work,
And see if I can handle it.
You're moving me to a new city,
And expect me to sleep.

You're taking away the close ties I've built up with friends and family,
But I'll be ok.
I'm outgoing,
And can make more friends.

I have work ethics like no other,
I have a wonderful family,
That will constantly be visiting,
And a personality that gets me through thick and thin.

So go ahead,
Take me away,
Take me away,
And watch me succeed.
Nicole Viereck, Grade 12
Countryside High School, FL

In a Blink of an Eye

Everything was all good it was just today
Then in a blink of an eye life snatched me away
Where it took me seemed like hell
But here I am today saying it's all well
I had taken the wrong route
Thank God it wasn't too late to ask for an out
Life punched me, slapped me, kicked me to the curb
And put the wrong decisions in my mind
Life left me confused, scared and blind
The real me is what I had to find
Life had me in the palm of its hand
It had me buried; stuck in the sand
Here I am out of the sand
Couldn't do it without those who lend me their hand
It was a hard time I went through
But here I am recovered and new
Thank God I'm back to me
The rain is gone and now I can see

Michele Cancel, Grade 11
Edward R Murrow High School, NY

Old Friends*

You stuck with me through thick and thin
You gave me a reason to believe again
You light up my night when it's dark
I can hear your whispers when we're apart
You taught me your language when you weren't in school
You made the heat seem very cool
When I was sick you knew the trick
You always knew which medicine to pick
Now you're gone
I'm sad, I'm mad
I'm blaming myself like I done something bad
I've lost you now and it's been a while
When I think of you I always smile
If I can ever find anyone who can fill your shoes
I know for a fact I have nothing to lose.

Miranda Edwards, Grade 11
Mount View High School, WV
Dedicated to an old friend…I will never forget you…

Love

I knew you were the one since the day we met,
Standing in the hallway with a hand on your hip,
Those big beautiful eyes I'll never forget,
When we were at the movies watching a flick,

Nothing can compare to the feeling of your touch,
Even the softness of your lips on our very first kiss,
I never thought I would love someone this much,
It's the scent of your perfume that I'll always miss,

I may have been gone for a while,
But trust me I haven't forgotten your smile,
Yes I'm young but these words are true,
It's all I have to show my love for you.

Brian H., Grade 11
Belfast, ME

I'm Having a Real Bad Day

I woke up twenty minutes late this morning
There's no empty seats on the bus, where to sit
Just when I thought things couldn't get worse
I realized I couldn't find my English homework
I'm having a real bad day
Second period only got ten times worse
Some girl named Melannie cheated off my test
It's not that, but she was one of my friends
I'm having a real bad day
I was ten minutes late to geometry class
I didn't even understand the lesson
The teacher wouldn't even help me
I'm having a real bad day
Lunch wasn't any better as I hoped
I couldn't find my friend, so I sat alone
Spanish wasn't bad, but could've been better
I missed the school bus to get home
I'm having a real bad day
My mom and father aren't too happy with me
I have a mountain of challenging homework
I'm having a real bad day

Charlene Scism, Grade 11
Deltona High School, FL

Women

There is nothing that a good woman craves more
Than independence, freedom, and youth galore
Equality with men is a bonus too
But in some worlds, this is all taboo

A strong woman is hard to come by
A man makes her personality go awry
Brutality, ignorance, mistreatment he uses
Just to make a woman do as he chooses

Clearly, an independent woman is one to treasure
She does not judge herself based on a man's measure
Courage and bravery and true happiness keep her free
Following her heart, doing whatever that may be

So reject the perfect stereotype men dream of
Go get a good life doing something you love
A woman should not be easily swayed
To be a woman is to be independent and never mislaid

Taryn Noll, Grade 11
Council Rock High School South, PA

Kitty Cats Cannot Fly

The darkness took over as though on assault.
Can't you come when I call?
Must one make life so difficult?
It's as if you're saying, "I don't fall."
You forget that you don't have claws.
Up the tree you went without pause.
You try and try with all of your might.
But kitty cats cannot take flight.

Cruz Nieto, Grade 10
Schley County Middle/High School, GA

I Miss You!

When I think about you I want to cry.
Everything we went through went down the drain with all our dreams.
I wish what had happen between us never happened.
At times I feel like I wasted your time. (Our time)
Remember those long nights on the phone?
Yeah I miss that! I miss you and us.
I loved you. I still do but we will never be.
I hate hearing about you and other girls in the same sentence.
Where did we go wrong what we had was very special.
I just want you. I want us back, us holding hands, the sweet warm kisses.
Baby once we separated I lost a big part of me. I am not the same without you.
I never wanted you to fall in love with me. I never wanted to fall in love with you.
For some reason I fell for you and I am thankful that I did.
You showed me that not all guys are all the same. You showed me that there are some good in some.
I thought you was the one for me. Maybe one day faith will bring you back to me.

Daneishia Williams, Grade 10
Deltona High School, FL

Seventh Commandment

The flowers are arranged with each petal in perfect position, held with hairspray.
The bride is decked out in a sleazy silk snowball.
The food has been colored, spiced, and primped beyond all intentions of making it edible.
The priest — which priest? — checks his watch every few seconds, hoping he won't miss his favorite show.
The band plays a song so complex that all words of passion are lost in a sea of triplets and rests.
The altar rail is so polished I can see my reflection
And me, I sit here laughing inside, enjoying the irony and my new designer dress.

Blakely Mulder, Grade 10
Gill St. Bernard's School, NJ

His "So Called" Lost Identity

It's more than a lost identity he feels within
It's more like all this thoughts are overwhelming him
Bemused maybe that he can't see, the damage he has caused
Because of the promiscuous knowledge, that shows as his flaws
Like he says, it's as if he's wooden on stage, and the crowd is pumped and stopped screaming his name
Hard for him to see, what's ordinary and what's not, because at all times all seems all right
But all good thing slowly come to an end, even the performance he has perfected over and over again
As the sparks start flying and the crowd becomes un-mute
He's no longer on stage but a part of the group
And no one can hear him because he's one of them now
And the only one who cares to hear what he has to say
Is the viewers watching his life go down
Not a lost identity, no broken heart
But the pain and rejection from all the hurt he's caused
And when the performance became predictable
The viewers cut the TV off because they are tired of seeing him with nonchalance
So now he's really grim and sowing what he reaps never seemed so crazy so that the pain he claims
His account of being lazy in love in life and in what he desires
But he never listened to the voice saying, "Effort is required."
Now to escape the embarrassment he attempts to take a break, but he can't pause time and never his mistakes
It's not a lost identity that is misplaced, but his actions finally blew up in his face.

Sydney Sutton, Grade 10
Parkdale High School, MD

Nothing's Nirvana

When it rains, the air turns white.
The walls go white.
All sense of direction and purpose is lost.
The black window frames outline the room.
My feet are the only thing below me.
Running brings an eerie echo.
Which every step, the past becomes saturated with ink.
Nostalgia alone isn't an option,
And treading forward erases the bygone.
Accepting is Faith's only offer.
Declining Faith yields a fatal fate.

Dianna Cohen, Grade 11
St Andrew's School, FL

Ghandi

Ghandi once said,
"You must be the change
You wish to see in the world"
Ghandi was like a calm stream of positivity
Ghandi is positive energy
For an every staggering society
Ghandi's feet were planted by a stream of water
His roots went deep into the ground
Ghandi could not be moved
If I'm aspiring to be like somebody
If I aspire to be somebody
I aspire to be like Ghandi
Because "You must be the change
You wish to see in the world"

Maurice Keys, Grade 12
Cab Calloway School of the Arts, DE

The Sands of Time

I know that out there
Somewhere an hourglass counts down my time
A figure shrouded in black
Is recording my every honor and crime

Like a constant anvil pressing down on me
Like a constant agony as I see all that can be
They tell me in this life there is no guarantee
But every hour of every day I feel this weight
This terrible feeling that I'm trapped in fate
And all I'll ever say or do is written on a slate

I feel the sand eroding our reality away
Who can say tomorrow's not the last day?
The sands of time will swallow us all
No force can halt or delay Death's call

To the omnipotence of time even sanity succumbs
Human minds fearing the sound of eternity's drums
All will be erased every victory and mistake
Every chain will end and every cycle will break
The time will soon come when we too must part
Our era will end and so will begin a fresh start

Mike Saxer, Grade 11
Northeast High School, FL

One Word

All it takes is just one word
One phrase, one meaning, one saying
Said at the right time from the right lips
To change the world and everyone in it.

One moment, one comment, can mean so much,
That saying it has power;
Every statement that comes out of a mouth
Can cause some happiness or sorrow.

Just remember to take responsibility,
For every idea you express,
Because every thought that's brought to life
Can change each word that comes after.

Josh Kazakevich, Grade 11
Plainview Old Bethpage/JFK High School, NY

Life Without Music in Mazes

Wake me up to the morning's music.
To the vibrations so rhythmic.
Beneath the air, I am so still.
Oh, blind to sound if you will.
Find me first fanning the light away from my ears.
Sometimes I am imagined as one of your fears.

Put me asleep to the night's dew.
Act out secrets I once knew.
Of the color life often feels.
And the music my eye half steals.
Catch me coughing away your treacherous gazes,
For my life without music is endless mazes.

Katlyn Hagley, Grade 12
Wamogo Regional High School, CT

Best Friend

The waves of time crash upon our shore
Taking us further and further to what's in store
My mind breaks into reverie
Your laugh warms me mildly
I miss you so…
Sometimes I look at your faded picture and cry,
"Best friend, oh, how you broke my heart!"
A tempest carries my dreams and cares away
But I still go over what happened to this day
I miss you so…
Pictures in time forever stuck in my head
But my brain is too full — it is fed
Friend, time moves fast and time moves slow
Will we meet again?
I don't know
Be sure of this last notation
Remember my quotation
I miss you
I love you

Stephanie Provenzale, Grade 10
Seneca Valley Intermediate High School, PA

Summer

Summer
Hot, humid, sticky
Sunny, bright, warm
Happy, active, playing
Swimming, laughing, giggling
Summer

Gabrielle Jaeger, Grade 12
Pennridge High School, PA

Beach

One by one the lines go by,
The road lasts forever,
Radio blasting,
Father's jamming,
Covering my ears
Preventing a headache,
Mom head back, feet up
Snoozing,
I close my eyes.
My toes are hot
As they drag across the sand.
Farther down the mushier and colder,
I feel the water.
The tide goes in and out
In and out
Rudely awakened,
"Sweet Home Alabama,"
Volume 45,
One by one the lines go by.

Alison Grace Holder, Grade 10
Anderson County High School, TN

The Waiting Room

Blue skies
Bus stops
Sunrise
Corner shops
Train station
Airport
Vacation
In court
Traffic lights
Long lines
Long nights
Hidden signs
Amusement parks
And snack bars
Last remarks
The sports car
First date
Dreams come true
Soul mate
First tattoo
We're all waiting for something.

Amanda Jones, Grade 10
Bishop George Ahr High School, NJ

Faith

Is a smile brought out from a frown
When life takes an unexpected turn
Faith is keeping your head high,
When life tries to bring you down
Faith is having patience,
With the children you brought into this world
Faith is finding the tolerance to endure chaos
and maintaining the composure to comfort others
Faith is devotion to your family, and always being a source of reliance,
Having confidence in knowing that everything happens for a reason
and everyone has their purpose.

Cherylann Tully, Grade 12
Harborfields High School, NY

Silence

Sometimes I like the quiet
I am soothed by its sweet melody
Losing all my senses it feels nice to just sit and listen to the emptiness
When it is quiet
I find myself at peace
Where hate, pain, and fear can't reach me
I can only hear the silence…
Which for a moment overpowers the violence
The violence that surrounds the world
The violence that towers over every soul
For a moment silence takes control
Until my mind begins to think and my thoughts sink in
For I too hold thoughts of hate, pain, and fear
Thoughts I attempt not to acknowledge
But still they seem to keep me hostage
And though I try to pretend they are not there —
Hide them as if I'm not scared
I am aware my soul may never mend
And just when I'm about to let go and give in
Silence takes control once again…

Star Reese, Grade 10
Clarkston High School, GA

Immigrants

Neglected, harassed and unwelcome
In a country of liberty and freedom
Working hours upon hours for less than the minimum
Considered an interloper in a country built on equality
Border-hopper, illegal and other harsh names ring through the air
Why because now they are getting a voice?
Because now it looks like they may be able to overcome the adversity
The people are growing tired of the same old
Those hackneyed excuses for treating immigrants unfairly
Were we all not immigrants at one time or another
Emigrating from Russia, Italy, or as close as Mexico
I intercede that you put down your harsh words
Put down your weapons of inequality
Allow for the real America to survive,
The land of the free and the home of the brave.

Kevin Christian, Grade 10
Council Rock High School South, PA

sunset

as the sun sets on another day,
over an ocean,
as it burns an image into my eyes,
as it is looked on by hundreds,
as it is put into still frame,
as this is seen by my eyes,
my mind wanders to the time that has gone,
the people that have left,
the love I have lost,
and all I'm doing is smiling,
cause with this sun the day is new,
and all I have to say is it's a beautiful sunset
with all the contrast you could ever want,
may you live your life like a sun never setting
always watching burning the sky,
may your image stay in my eyes for all time.

Joe Santo, Grade 11
Reading Memorial High School, MA

Due

Time is wasting
Here I am still procrastinating
Haven't made one move yet
As far as this goes, I'm still not ready, not even on set
To do this thing, I want to in my heart
The problem is that I really don't know where to start
But I am frozen
From my heart to my mind, can't make a move on my toes
Due dates are truly closer than they appear
It's coming to me and I am still sitting here
Like a bomb, it is due to explode
But I will only survive if I detour this lazy road
Time is wasting
Here I am still procrastinating
It's coming to me and I'm not yet ready
After three weeks all I have is my heading,

Time is up
The teacher says "Everyone please pass up your papers."

Monique Bonds, Grade 11
South Mecklenburg High School, NC

To My Mom with Love

This is to my mom, my aunt you are my world
You are everything to me
You are so good to me
I couldn't put it into words
You give me everything even who I am
And for that I Thank You
You're not only my mother you are my very first true best friend
And I hope our journey will never end
I know you will always be that perfect friend and perfect mother

I love you Mom

Shenese Vaughan, Grade 11
Hamilton High School West, NJ

Just We

We walk slowly
Slow paced steps
Nervous, anxious, palms sweat
Pretend to look away, we both know what we're thinking
You take my hand, it's okay
For the moment we held I felt lost
Everything went away but us as we walked
Walking anywhere…
We had no place to be
Just to be together
Nowhere, nothing, just we

Aileen Gabriel, Grade 10
Peabody Veterans Memorial High School, MA

Happy

With a smile on my face
I walk at a fast pace
To the boy of my dreams
Knowing his love isn't a scheme
His smile is like the sunset setting
More beautiful than I've ever seen before
And his eyes are so dreamy you just can't
Ignore the fact that he's perfect
From his cornrows to his lips
To the chain on his neck
To the shoes on his feet
And when I hug him, I never want to let go,
Because I know when it's over he has to go
Then I'm not happy anymore
And my sadness starts to pour
But at the end of the day I see his face,
And my heartbeat races
Because when he smiles, my love for him embraces
Then I rush to his arms, and I feel so safe
Even though the world around me is so crappy
He makes me feel so happy!

Rynishia Gregg, Grade 11
Darlington High School, SC

My Best Friend

His name was Riley
But I called him Bud
He was 5 years older than me
I guess he was my big brother
He had golden wavy locks of hair
And a wet nose that made me squirm
I would always cover for him if the time came
"Mom it was me who ripped the bag of cookies"
"I knocked over the candle, not Riley"
Until one day, Riley got sick
And was eventually put to sleep
His memory will always live on
I loved that dog
And that will never end
I guess they were right
A dog *is* man's best friend.

Connor Leary, Grade 10
Haverhill High School, MA

A Better Day

Out running one day on Sawin Lane, the sky was a dreary gray,
And as we rain, both Rita and I, we dreamt of a better day.

We imagined tornadoes and things of that sort forming from the clouds in the sky,
And as we ran, both Rita and I, we dreamt of a better day.

There was a low roar from the wind in the trees, and the leaves began to fly.
And as we ran, both Rita and I, we dreamt of a better day.

The clouds swirled about and the wind blew hard sending chills up and down our spines.
And as we ran, both Rita and I, we dreamt of a better day.

We watched the leaves dance to the ground from the trees so very high,
And as we ran, both Rita and I, we dreamt of a better day.

We ran and talked and laughed and joked until we noticed how the time had gone by,
And as we turned back, both Rita and I, we dreamt of a better day.

We looked up at the sky, and to our surprise, we saw many patches of blue.
Rita and I smiled at one another because our dream came true.

Jasmine Caulfield, Grade 10
Sanford School, DE

My Beautiful Borinquen

O' beautiful Borinquen, your beauty amazes me
Your never ending oceans of blue truth have inspired me.
Along sandy beaches, where I first held my father's hand,
I found seashells unique like your people.
On your rocks I sat for hours, and shed these tears of nostalgia.
Your oceans have carried my tears away,
Your gentle splashing waves against my feet along the seashore.
Where God's footprints first appeared, I walked upon.
Your enchanting waves have purified my soul, and cleaned out the evil that had been bestowed.
I dream of the day, where I can go back and breathe your sweet, tropical, rejuvenating air.
I dream of returning on a day, when the sun is illuminating on my body like an angel smiling at me.
Granting hope that tomorrow will be a better day.
When the palm trees are smoothly following the breeze of relief.
And the smiles of my fellow neighbors welcome me.
O' beautiful Borinquen, take me once again to that island, that I once called home.
O' beautiful Borinquen, save me form all that pursues me.
I stand here before you, with nothing and no one
And I say,
O' Precioso Bellisimo Borinquen,
When will I see you again?

Facia Class, Grade 12
Bayside High School, NY

I Miss You

When I was young you were there we would always play games together, and you would play along even if you were busy. When you went on vacation you always took me with you, when you went to parties you took me, wherever you went I would follow. Every day I would come upstairs to your house after school and you would help me with my homework. But then the day came and you left me I couldn't come this time because you went into the eternal rest then I went to my bed and cried. When I saw your daughter the resemblance made me cry even more. I just couldn't believe this happened it was so hard to understand. You were there my whole life then you were suddenly gone. You were and always will be my family, my friend you're my Great Aunt.

Manuel Ellis, Grade 10
Edward R Murrow High School, NY

My Everything Comes from You
There were the good times, the bad times
But we held on tight,
As if tomorrow was never gonna come.
My everything comes from you.

You raised me up high,
Giving me all you had.
Love, passion, strength, and patience.
My everything comes from you.

I was an ignorant seed,
But you never gave up,
As you watered me every day.
My everything comes from you.

I answered with rebellious words.
You received them silently,
Returning back with love.
My everything comes from you.

Through thick and thin,
You stood by me.
Thanks because…
My everything comes from you.
Shirley He, Grade 10
Bronx High School of Science, NY

Is She Me
she doesn't feel like I feel
she doesn't see how I see
she isn't touched how I am touched
yet mirrors she me.

I once walked away and left she behind,
but she was constantly there in my being, heart, mind

is she me?

she I failed and
it's the greatest failure

is she me?

no longer
here she stays

is she me?

she is me
and me is she…
rather, she was me
and me was she; it's no more.
Molly Jones, Grade 11
Louisburg High School, NC

What Is a Friend?
A friend is someone, a person, who laughs.
A friend is caring, and gentle, and kind.
A friend is someone, well it's hard to describe.
They make you laugh and smile, not cry.
They bring you flowers in bad times or good.
Friends like you for who you are.
Smiling and loving, they're sent from God.
They support you when you've fallen down.
They take you above and beyond to great heights.
They're the petals to your flower,
The stitches to your tights;
They're everything you need,
To live a happy and free life.
But tell me now, is it possible to describe,
This wonderful beauty in just a few words?
Can you describe with few metaphors?
I'm so very sorry, but I don't think so.
A friend is a friend.
What more can I say?
Roshni Dutta, Grade 11
Northview High School, GA

I Am From
As the sound of my horses greet me on a frosty winter morning,
The smell of leather, the sight of a young colt on the ground.

I am from the pack trips into the woods,
The smell of burnt food when I try to cook bacon and eggs.

I am from long trails and good times.
Matt Stanley, Grade 11
Thomson High School, GA

Alone
Alone I sit, with my back to a tree
Staring unseeing at the world
All colors and shades
Shapes and bright lights
But all of this pales
To seeing your eyes
They gleam when you laugh
At something I said
When I was being me
On the edge of your bed
I give you a look
Mock resentment, I guess
And you laugh still more
And fall back on your bed
I smile at the sight
Of seeing you smile
And lean close to you
So I can cuddle
Alone I sit, with my back to a tree
Wishing that you could be sitting next to me
Desirae Trumble, Grade 12
Pulaski Jr/Sr High School, NY

All Crazy

You drive me crazy
to the point I have to cry
and I just can't say why
you know how to make
me feel so good inside
but I just can't say
why
Baby I want you to be mine!

Rachel O'Flynn, Grade 10
Samuel Fels High School, PA

The Eagle's Prey

The descending eagle
In the skies
Follows its prey
Squints its eyes
Readily tensed
Adrenaline rushing
Hurdling towards
Something or nothing
With a glint in its eye
A smirk of its beak
It curves straight down
Avoiding the peaks
The prey doesn't know
What fate is in store
If it will survive
Or be no more
C'est la vie
As some would say
But what'll they do
When they're the prey?

Megan Gates, Grade 10
Connections Academy, SC

Mum

You love me
Without reason,
You show me
That you care.

You take me through
Each season,
You're always
Kind and fair,
No matter how I treat you.

My life with you
Is never humdrum,
There are no conditions
Of love from you my mum.

Love always…your daughter.

Cassandra Randall, Grade 10
Davenport School, NH

Heart of a Captive

Run! Run! Run! — God blessed run!
Through the woods — across rivers
Hell is the hunter and you the hunted,
Into the horses' stable, careful not to wake the mares;
Into the barn where the farmer's friend is staying;
Do not disrupt the stillness of the night — you're nearly there;
Stop not for a drink or break; stopping is not an option;
So tense you sprint — sprint into everlasting darkness.

Run! Run! Run! — God blessed run!
Over the hilltops of country — over the jags of the mountains;
Are the dogs tired of chasing? Ha! No dog shall get rest;
I feel your pain — I feel your troubles — my feet hurt just as yours;
Will they chase you this far?
Then accelerate now — swifter than the wind blows.

Run! Run! Run! — God blessed run!
This is no time to quit — slay the Devil himself if he stands in your path;
Feel no fear — feel no pity for others — feel not the woes of your brother;
Whose whip wounds burn blistering hot onto his flesh;
Cease thinking of the cries of your daughter and wife;
Freedom is at the very tip of your tongue;
So rapid your heart beats — so courageous and strong.

Anthoney Brown, Grade 11
Thomson High School, GA

The Wonder Years

Childhood is playing hide-and-go-seek-tag in the leprechaun summer,
Eating every ice cream cone at the beach before being chased by a Hummer,
Never, ever wanting to cheat birthdays,
Only counting down to that play day in May,
And the innocent pleasures I wish I had today.

Childhood is a monster, creeping like a bug, out of closets at night,
Giving every child a dire need for light,
Never a frightened Christmas to be foreseen,
Only a few hasty, horrifying Halloweens,
And the irrational fears that are now unseen.

Childhood is playing with an eccentric, enormous bunny whose ears never end,
Creating a lair game with rules I can bend,
Never letting a petty argument pend,
Only being like Mike Tyson and winning every fight,
And the intense competition I lost one night.

Childhood is always fantasizing about being movie stars,
Knowing one day you will land on Mars,
Never doubting your supreme, gleaming dream is near,
Only waiting for the spectacular premier,
And the magnificent hopes that are no longer here.

Caitlin Ball, Grade 10
Haverford High School, PA

The Escape

Amidst a world of indolence
Where instant gratification is key,
There lies an escape of magnificence
That sets a reader free.

In books we soar over the highest mountains;
Swim in the deepest seas.
Nothing limits what can be done
When imagination is free.

Great stories of love and passion
Paint intricate collages of imagery;
Saving us all from our inaction:
I, at last, am free.

Tracey Landgraf, Grade 12
Countryside High School, FL

Pathway to Reality

Above my head I see a cloud full of dreams
Dreams that swell as I turn eighteen
At this age we begin to party
Remember, kids, don't sip that Bacardi
Hoping to attend the college of Bentley
Gave me a scholarship first time they met me
Looking forward to the life in college
Take initiative and attain the knowledge
Master football, receive my M.B.A. in business
I will achieve my goal, you can be my witness
This is a way to become successful
Less reading, more numbers, it's less stressful
From a simple seed to a blossomed flower
I mature and gain experience every second, every hour
Regret the wrong choices and the times I disobeyed
Grown to realize we need to start slow like a stand of lemonade
I take a step forward and reach for my dream
Now living the real world, wow, I'm already eighteen!

Andy Tran, Grade 12
Doherty Memorial High School, MA

Loss

A stately man, old and craven
Whose hair was black as the raven
Safely tucked within his haven
But he could not hide his woe
For within his hidden soul
Which his guilt now controlled
Was the agonizing truth, the pain of long, long ago

And with every passing second
He would always blindly beckon
Despite knowing the truth, and checking
For that girl he lost long ago
The heavy pain he has carried
His darkest days he has since been faring
Despite his face that seemed not caring
His guilt was crushing his mournful soul

Henry Tiller, Grade 11
Heathwood Hall Episcopal School, SC

The One

She gives my life meaning
She gives my soul a dream
Because when we are apart it's as if it would seem
That our hearts are close together
Because when we kiss it's as if we change the weather
Because it comes from the sun to the rain
And no matter what the change our love stays the same
We share the same dreams
Our eyes meet from miles away
And I will continue to tell you the true things that I couldn't say
I'm sorry for the distance
Because I will run a million miles to break it
I realize that you are no longer here
But until our days are done
Our souls shall remain as one

Ashombue Briggs, Grade 10
New Brunswick High School, NJ

Never Came Back

After I was rid of you
I never thought to miss you
That thing you did that caused me pain
Makes me weep for you all the same

To think our relationship was so strong
Until the day you did me wrong
To think of that day I start to quiver
As my heart begins to tremor

That day you ask that makes me weep
Is the day I could not sleep
The day you said I would never leave out
Is that night I had no doubt
On this night there was no arguing no one was attacked
On that night you left and never came back

Keven Maclin, Grade 10
Parkdale High School, MD

The Enemy

Rage flows through the souls of the berserked,
Eating away the flesh like a disease.
Clawing, ripping, scratching, and gouging.
The life of a soldier as he prepares,
Prepares to engage war with the Enemy.
His death, long anticipated.
Pride will not come with death, but only in battle.
With numbers greater than most,
The Enemy controls the fate of many.
Wherever life may exist, the Enemy will erase it from existence.
The Enemy is an unbeatable force.
Until now!
The crazed soldiers fight even with the odds against them.
The sickening screams of battle enrage and excite,
The Enemy has lost footing and far worse, the battle.
A victory for the unexpected,
The Enemy is no longer.

Jonathan Stauffer, Grade 10
Warwick Sr High School, PA

At Ease

Goodnight my child, sweet dreams with sugarplums and flowers
Relax and let everything that was problems go until the morning brings the sun
At once you can close those eyes and see only what makes you smile and happy
Worry less about everything seen when the eyes are open
Forget about it, nothing else is on you nothing else is on you
Create a picture full of the beautiful memories that's held to your heart and mind
Open beyond the sky and galaxy
Fly like an eagle, swim like a dolphin, run like a cheetah, sing like an angel
Dance with the moon and sun, float on the clouds, and be free
Goodnight my child let the mind be at ease
Forget about the craziness, the frustration, the cruelty, the confusion, and the destruction
In this sphere we call Earth
It's not going anywhere, it will always be there with no peace to be offered
Nothing is going to be missed when you close those eyes my child
Let the mind be at ease that when you wake up you can look at everything differently
That you can grasp it and work as an individual to make that dream your reality
Let the mind be at ease my child so that you can see the future beyond billions of eyes
Hope that your mind and heart can guide those billion eyes one day into a peace of mind
So goodnight my child, and have sweet dreams of the world with love and peace
With the mind, heart, and soul being at ease!

Nicole Kristen Jones, Grade 11
Susquehannock High School, PA

Soul

S tars in the night's sky paint pictures of children dreams allowing imaginations to come to life
O verwhelming fears bring your and our worlds together
U nderstanding your reign of power is of the Omega one that created all you see before the eyes of men
L eaving you for our time together has ended, but I will dream and we shall meet once again

Randall T. Bolling Jr., Grade 10
Southside Academy, MD

Dream Guy

He will put his jacket on a puddle and say walk on it now baby.
Know when to tell me I love you and when I'm acting dumb in a cute loving way.
He would say I'm his everything and I'm first in his mind no matter what.
He would love me no matter what no matter my eyes, body, or health.
He would put me first no matter what even when there is a big football game on and just say I'll look it up later.
He would never hurt me and know what does because of my past.
The word lies wouldn't even be in his dictionary because I would be his best friend
And he would tell me everything and have nothing to hide.
He would let me yell at him and not say a word back because that is how much he respects women.
The only time I would cry for him is when he is away from me for more than a day
Because why else would I cry he's my dream guy.
He would pay for everything and show me in little ways that he loves me and can't live without me.
When I cry and he comes he dries all my tears away leaving me wondering why was I even crying?
This dream guy would make me feel so safe, so safe that I would walk into a burning building with him
And not even think twice about it.
He knows that I am meant to be his and would let me know that after every fight.
He knows that the party life I hate and would leave it all as soon as he makes me his girlfriend.
If he made plans with me he wouldn't go and ditch me he would see the date with me as an order he must complete.
But again they call this guy a dream guy and dreams only happen while you're asleep not awake.

Veronica Echevarria, Grade 12
Dauphin County Technical School, PA

Unrequited

I can give you two good reasons,
To show you she loves you more:
She's so proud to love you and
You know she adores you,
So how can I tell her that you've changed your mind?

This engagement you set before her
For her mind to overturn,
It's as if you never knew
Never cared how she felt.

I guess you'll get what you're wanting,
But have you forgot about her?
You think she'll be fine all alone,
But even you're not sure.

She still loves you, you know,
She can't get over you.
Did you know she still screams out your name?
She still needs you!

You know you're breaking her heart.
Some things never change;
You'll always be the same.

Amber Kerley, Grade 10
Rockwood High School, TN

Unthinkable Love

I argue with myself about You,
I just can't make up my mind.
I'm trying to learn more about You,
But I just can't seem to find.

Who are You really?
And do You love me like You say?
Who am I really?
Are You here with me today?

The more I get to know You,
the more I want to stay.
The more I see Your love in me,
the more I'd love to say:

God, You are my father,
The one who holds me tight.
God, You are my savior,
The one who loves me through this fight.

And though I feel this pain a lot,
I know You'll help me through.
Because I've seen how much You've fought for me,
Even when this day seemed blue.

Hannah Foust, Grade 12
Hickory Grove Baptist Christian School, NC

I Am the Turtle

I am the turtle
Calm and slow
I take my time
And breathe in the fresh air
I try not to let life pass me by.
Sturdy is my exterior
A well used shell of different patterns and shapes
But on the inside
Lays a mushy mess.
The confused chaos deep within
Can be very easily damaged
So a hard exterior comes in handy for protection.
It's tempting just to crawl in my shell
And stay there for a while
Just alone
And not let anyone in.
But I know that's not how life is
And sometimes you need to come out.

Jennifer Pierre, Grade 12
Immaculate Heart Academy, NJ

The Love of My Life

I walk outside and I think.
I think about the times we have shared.
The times when we first held hands.
As I thought about it,
I walked back inside.
You should know how much you touch my heart.
I hope we grow old and never part.
I try again and I walk out the door,
I lock it and turn around.
The love of my life,
The one I care about,
Was standing right before me at the door.

DeJuan A., Grade 10
Audubon Youth Development Center, KY

Tales from the Waves

Foamy white caps break upon the shore
Transporting stories to share among the creatures of the deep
Tales of shipwrecks, pirates, the undead, ghosts, and more
Of mermaids, evil sea witches, and talking fish
Wonderful tales unbeknownst to man
Tales of fiend, friend, and foe
Tales, tales, tales galore
Tales of such as that of the mysterious pirate Jack Sparrow
One who raided, sacked, and plundered Caribbean towns
Searching high, searching low for the perfect treasure
Treasures that glimmer and glow with all the colors of the sun
Gold, rubies, diamonds, coins, and gems
All tools to barter for money and necessities
Pirates who have seen it all
Perhaps even the ghosts
Pirates who honor sacred codes
Leaving their vivid tales
In the trusting hands of the waves

Carrielee Crenshaw, Grade 12
Newnan High School, GA

Inning Number Seven

Inning number seven
Back when I was eleven

I just pitched and got two outs
A fan got up, he screams and shouts

I looked up and saw a man
It was my dad, my greatest fan

Nervous now, I let the pitch go
It was fast and kind of low

The batter swung, he missed the ball
We won the game. We won them all

Inning number seven
Back when I was eleven

Kyle Leja, Grade 11
Countryside High School, FL

Samurai

Bound by honor
Trained since birth
Raised to live by bushido
Lived by the sword
Slayer of the wicked
Protector of the weak
Strength for the frail
Dishonor befalls my house
My lord ashamed of me
Calls for an ancient right of purity
Ritual suicide and silk wrapped blade
Release my soul back to the gods
Death reclaims my honor

Nick Perreca, Grade 10
Smithtown High School West, NY

Changes

Old skin hung,
worn from use.
Still tight,
but much too loose.
Faded colors,
overused,
ever bright,
but lost in hue.
Satisfied,
content per se,
yet
unaccepted.
Not bug,
to beauty,
but one butterfly
to another.

Benjamin Sibley, Grade 12
Henderson High School, PA

Fading Summer; Falling Hearts

Our promises faded away with the summer sun,
Those nights that we counted the stars are surely gone,
Those cute fights and walks hand-in-hand
Washed away with our names in the sand.
And you're falling from me like the leaves from the trees
In the same way that our love drifted with the summer breeze.
The months that we spent together have certainly slipped
Along with the love notes and pictures I ripped.
And you can be sure I'll wrap you in lies,
But whenever I see you with her — tears burn in my eyes.
You've broken my heart like those shells that we stepped on,
The morning that we walked down the beach to view the sunrise at dawn.
With you crumbled my dignity — to be honest I'm quite pathetic
Obviously my words won't win you back — clearly I'm not very poetic.
Well, there are no meaningless song lyrics; there's no hidden message here:
I miss you darling, I still love you dear.

Taryn Williams, Grade 11
Dennis Yarmouth Regional High School, MA

Stripes

They live in all sorts of places.
Painted in the sky as a colorful arch-shaped bridge,
Clinging to tigers and zebras for those who adore nature and the wild.
Some wave proudly on flags to represent its people,
While some prefer to isolate themselves
From the world by hiding in our sock drawers and shoes.
They appear on uniforms to symbolize authority
or spiral down candy canes to show they are sweet.
They are branded onto these locations to draw attention,
To represent beauty or warnings,
To show pride or sweetness.

Calhoun Lawrence, Grade 10
County Prep High School, NJ

The Battle

Why should anything matter
When their spirits are crushed? When the hopes shatter,
And even the mere thoughts of the dreams cease to transpire?
When sources of strength are burned in the fire?
Why should it all matter when devastation breaks in from all walls
With the dying sun, the end, too close for comfort, calls?
Why should it matter when the only thing left are the woes,
When even supposed dear friends have become foes?

Though it seems the sense of humanity has been lost
That the conquerors are always the dominant, the privileged, the oppressive
It is at the point of weakness that it all begins to matter
That it becomes crucial to overthrow the forces which are depressive
For the essence of life is not position in comfort, but the stand in times of hardship
And knowing this, these once-crushed spirits must rise from their abyss
Under the waning crescent moon
Impelled by the necessity to persist
Because it would be a sin to simply let go of all that they have started
And all that they ever had on this Earth and in this life

Saima Mir, Grade 10
Bronx High School of Science, NY

A Musty Smell of Memories

A musty smell of memories
Dancing in sunlight streaming
The ghostly waste of past events.
An exhalation stirs the sound
And wakes specters from their sleep.
Livestock bellow to respond to summons
Between the present and the past.
A wild dash for home blazing
Charred leather saddles on the ground.
Intricate bridles to harness the stars
A whisper to relay the message
With closed eyes I relieve the night
Of feral screams and hoof beats.
The tattoo of my heart beating and yours
Fuel for you was for fire too
Catching and taking lustily
A lethal embrace hot with passion
Engulfing hungrily
The roaring mounts; I open my eyes
To the musty smell of memories and sunlight streaming in.

Kathleen Orlando, Grade 11
Holy Name High School, PA

A Place to Ease My Mind

I want to be in that place that is so familiar to my mind
That place that brings peace and joy, as my feet touch the sand
I want the waves to break through my body
That feeling of peace and serenity to ease my mind

I want to go back in time
Laugh and smile, like no one has seen nor heard before
Make memories that I never felt

With the sun so radiant
And the clouds full of color
I know it won't be long until I'm back here once more
With the ocean over head, this place is one I will never forget

I want to be in that place that is so familiar to my mind
That place that always seems to ease my mind

Erica Gottsch, Grade 11
Hanover High School, PA

Life

Is life really happy as it seems?
Lives lost every day,
Along with crushed dreams,
Nothing comes with ease,
With hard work comes reward,
Those who are blessed don't have to do life's chores,
Why must we be divided,
The rich,
The poor,
But if men were created equal,
Everyone would have to do life's chores.

Nick Smith, Grade 10
Ragsdale High School, NC

Dictionary

I am a dictionary.
I sit patiently in my place —
Waiting to be cracked open.
People come to me for answers
And challenge my words.
With a flip and a flap of my pages
Comes answers to those who inquire.
My pages may yellow
And my ink may fade;
My binding may become brittle,
And pages torn from eager page-turning.
But I will always be willing to share what I have to offer,
Patiently resting on my old shelf;
Ever gathering dust.

Rebecca Hanson, Grade 12
Pioneer Central School, NY

Holding Hands

Holding hands in the hall,
Letting everyone know that we are
Fussing over silly things,
Getting over it with a long hug.
Late night phone calls,
Not staying awake in class,
But just enough time to
Write my first name to his last.

Young boy, little girl, to them
Nothing else matters in this world:
It seems always to end in heartbreak,
Misery and tears,
Leaving them paranoid,
Giving their hearts
All their fears.

Courtney Jones, Grade 12
Carver Vocational Technical High School, MD

In Between

Stuck in between experiencing complete joy,
and being utterly depressed.
Tasting the bitterness of failure,
or the sweetness of success.
Stuck in between finding my true self,
verses what people expect from me.
Should I follow the crowd, or find the courage to break free?
The frustration of being stuck is overpowering,
the possible consequences
of the choices I make stand before me towering.
Being stuck, is being unable to move.
But then again without falling back, there is nothing to lose.
So part of me wishes to be stuck forever
never having to think, "all right…it's now or never."
Then I imagine the fog finally lifting,
my point of view finally shifting.
Being stuck will cease to be reality,
just a silly fear that once had its grasp on me.

Maria Lepore, Grade 10
Peabody Veterans Memorial High School, MA

Superglue

My mother uses superglue to fix everything:
Broken bifocals and shades,
Torn books, and seemingly ruined jewelry.
She says it's the best tool for fixing anything that is broken.
It holds together fragments and remnants of things in disrepair.
That is its purpose.
But I wonder if it could bind together a broken heart?
A heart shattered into so many pieces
That it would take centuries to even begin to attempt putting them back together.
Can it fix an organ on which man refused to operate for centuries for fear of irreversible damage?
Can it repair hurt feelings?
Is it adherent enough to mend my relationships?
Can it contain the pain that only antidepressants seem to treat?
Can it conjoin my heart with my mind and body?
Because life would be so much easier if every aspect of me was on one accord…
But I don't think it can.
Because my heart is not metal or paper…but felt.
But I barely feel it beating now, and superglue can't fix it.
Superglue can't fix everything. I guess it's not that super after all.

Siera Toney, Grade 11
Benjamin Banneker Academic High School, DC

Change Good or Bad?

Our world is changing probably a lot more than it should.
Dirt roads are paved, new highways and intersections are constructed, it's all good…right?
Politics and legal matters change all the time.
Things are different, there's wars and weapons, people dying. Why can't we all just live in peace?
Weapons of mass destruction could easily wipe us off the face of the Earth.
Is the change good or bad?
Our world is everything to us; it's all that we have.
Are we getting too smart for our own good?
Technology is changing, from calculators to computers, what's next?
History has an attendance to repeat itself, like the Ice Age and global warming for example, but what is next?
Is there anything we can do to stop it?
How do we know what to expect, if we are not even aware about what is happening around us every single day.
Many people do not watch news or read the newspaper, many of us are uninformed; society is moving away from what it once was.
Our society is being corrupted by materialism and consumerism, the human race is becoming more and more self involved.
So how do we know what is coming next?

Karly Berezowsky, Grade 12
Montgomery Township High School, NJ

Always and Forever

I never thought I loved someone this much.
I'd give up everything I own just to feel your touch.
Whenever I see you, you make my heart race. Whenever I'm with you, I have a smile on my face.
I feel as if you're the only one for me, and I think it's pretty clear for you to see.

But sometimes I think you might be too good to be true. And that I'm a fool for falling in love with you.
Because I've been hurt so many times before; it's hard for me to love or trust anymore.
I'm just trying to let you know how I feel; so you know straight up — what's the deal.
I'm giving you my all, so don't break my heart. I'm asking you please, don't tear it apart.

I want to be with you bad, you don't have a clue because I want you to officially become my boo.
But I've realized that I have to relax and let things be, and wait for the day until you be with me.

India Dennison, Grade 10
Colonia High School, NJ

There's Something I Must Say
I have a confession
A creeping urge
Feelings so strong
Harsh like the pain I know you're going to feel
I need to say it

I have to confess
I feel worse because there is no remorse
I'm scared you'll hate me but I know you will
I have to tell you

I've tried to erase it from my memory
I acted as if I wasn't doing anything wrong
Innocent as a child
Lying to myself is not working anymore
The words must be said

The buildup is killing me
I feel as though I will burst into tears and never stop
I can't comprehend why hurting you was necessary
Maybe I liked the danger of it all
But there is no fun left just guilt
I'm going to say it
I cheated
Gabrielle Levine, Grade 10
Countryside High School, FL

Hurt from the Start
I sit at home in my little red chair,
Holding my soft Valentine's bear,
You left my heart without a trace,
Shattered everything just to run off with her,

Now my tears catch on the bear's fur.
Hiding all pictures of us together,
Thought I'd be with you forever.

Didn't mean to sound rude and hateful,
But what you did was so unfaithful.
Knew I'd be hurt right from the start,
Like another girl on your heartbreak chart.

Still trying to move on, but with what you did,
I'm just glad you're gone.
Wishing what you did was a crime,
So you'd sit alone and do your time.

Hope you regret
Everything that you've done
Because it's over now
And from my love you are shunned.
Sasha Spencer, Grade 12
Rowan County Sr High School, KY

An Ode to Whitman's
"When I Heard the Learn'd Astronomer"
Facts, charts, and diagrams,
He leaves the lecture.
Outside into the night,
The stars.
He doesn't look at them from a scientific standpoint,
But from a poet's point of view.
It's calming and peaceful,
Some things are better to learn about by yourself.
It's how the poet really feels;
The astronomer wouldn't be as serious.
Mark Mieczkowski, Grade 11
Greater Nanticoke Area Sr High School, PA

A Child's Humble Cry
As I lay in my bed and began to cry
A cry so silent and so soft
For only God can hear my humble cry.
A cry of happiness and a cry of sadness,
When thinking about my father and will he ever come home
Thinking about time when I was a little girl
And how I would never want anything but my father
I would remember when at night
My father would put me to bed
Helping me say a prayer
Or sang a song so soft and sweet.
The day my father left
I thought my world would come to an end,
An end that I would never see again
I would cry every night and day
Just to see him again!
As my tears faded away and my memories stay
I know my father is watching over me
Wherever he at. Will I fall from this cry?
Or will I gain strength from this humble cry
And move on in life?
Jasmine Mayfield, Grade 12
Hickory High School, NC

Don't Let It End
God is this too good to be true
Is it real
Is it endless love
Will it stand
Will it end
Will I wake up one day and realize that it was all a dream
A stage
A phase
Or worse a fake
If it's all a dream then God don't let me wake
Let me sleep
Let me rest
Lord let me stay
'Cause to do so is to take my very life away
Javier Sanchez, Grade 10
Miami Beach Sr High School, FL

I Am What I Am
I am a child of the Asias.
I am an immigrant of the Americas.
I am a Pakistani Muslim and an American citizen.

Two different cultural groups
in my life make me feel like a diverse person.

There are 7 different continents of
the world, and I only belong to three of them.

My identity is like my only true identity,
that I am a Pakistani Muslim American citizen.

I am North America and I am South America,
I am 100% Pakistani and I am part of Asia.

I grew in the states, the cities, the towns, the homes, the soil, the trees, the lakes, the rivers,
the clear sky where the stars accompany me at night, and the fresh smell of the flowers
blooming in the beautiful meadows of my native country.

Now I see not the meadows, the lakes and the rivers,
but instead I see buildings, bridges and tunnels,
and it seems as if the stars have solemnly departed and left me alone in solitude.

Marya Altaf, Grade 12
Information Technology High School, NY

I Thought of You
I thought of you today
My eyes filled with tears as I spoke your name.
I hold your memory in my heart, it seems your smile stares back at me from your picture frame.
I reminisced about us yesterday
I laughed about all the fights that now seemed pointless.
It's funny how we could never stay mad for long, no matter how hard we tried.
What's crazy to me is how I sit alone in silence, and the radio coincidentally plays our song.
I know if you were here, you would remember,
The song that we song so soulfully.
You know, the one that when I'm thinking of you, takes a hold of me,
I cried a few months back
I needed you by my side, but I couldn't get to you.
I needed to hear your voice, to hear you say, baby it's ok, you'll get by, and that everything is going to be fine.
I hurt a year ago
I realized that things had truly changed, I think it finally hit me,
You were really gone, and things wouldn't and couldn't be the same.
I'm going to pray tomorrow
That you're watching over me, and that you know that I really loved you with all of my heart
And I want you to know that I know that even though it killed me for us to part,
We didn't say good bye, I don't believe in that word, because if I did, it would be a lie.
You'll meet me at the gates of heaven, and tell me it been way too long, and as we walk off, all the angels in heaven will sing our song.

Melesha Moss, Grade 10
William Penn High School, DE

Waiting*

My dearest love where have you gone
You've disappeared like a morning dove
You are busy in your life
I understand but it's cutting deeply like a razor sharp knife

Please don't let me stay up late in the night in waiting
This shouldn't be how people should be dating
I hope our relationship isn't fading

I am your flower and you are my bee
Please don't take my sweet nectar away from me
If you were to take it away, I would look upon thee
And ask, what did I not give for you to see

I care about you really I do but at this moment, I feel like a complete fool
Please don't let this continue if so, I would have no choice but to leave you

I've done my time waiting for you
What else do you expect me to do?
Wait even more and feel even more blue?
As you walk around still confused?
Let us communicate and not have a debate
Let us start over so we can relate
Let us both stay up late and talk about our next date

Madison Phillips, Grade 12
Jefferson High School, WV
*Dedicated to Stephen

Eight Belles

The gates open,
Shooting out like a bullet,
Such a beautiful masterpiece of God,
But yet such a fragile beast,
Positions change rapidly in split-seconds,
Men rushing their animals to get to the front,
Adrenaline flowing through the veins of gamesters,
Hoping to win a small fortune on their wager,
All are wondering how such an incredible creature,
Gallops on such bantam and brittle limbs,
The last turn approaches,
An elite animal begins his move to immortality,
Wins by nearly five lengths,
Such an amazing feeling that jockey felt,
Immediately overshadowed by disaster,
A horse lies motionless on the track,
Instantly surrounded by trucks lies the second place-finisher Eight Belles,
The diagnosis is two broken front ankles; instant euthanasia is administered,
Cheers from victory turn into tears of sadness,
A brutal reminder to all,
How fragile and sacred life really is.

Travis Allen, Grade 10
Trinity High School, KY

Abuse

I am your everything.
and I am fully aware
of such a thing.
So it is with great selfishness
and blatant disdain
that I attempt your infatuation.
I turn your heaven to hell,
concern for your well being
a fantastically played ruse.
I am unharmed by your hurt
and my deceit only furthers
as you ask for my forgiveness.
It is with such upheld knowledge
that I land another blow
to your already broken being.
I am your life,
a sense of existence
that no other brings you.
You are of no such value,
you are only of the moment.
I don't care at all for you.

Shasta Barton, Grade 11
Everett Area High School, PA

Like the Crow

Death is like a crow
Unexpected but always
There
Unwelcome but here
To stay

Joshua Foster, Grade 11
Anderson County High School, TN

Masquerade Misery

I splash water across my face,
Mascara and eyeliner,
Eye shadow and lip gloss,
They all drip down my chin,
Revealing something else,
Someone else.
Is that me?
I look closer into the mirror, I can see.

I no longer look pretty,
I no longer am one of you,
I've returned to my true nature,
I've found the real me
And I love it,
No fake make-up do I wear,
No dry powder on my face,
Just me.

The messed up yet wonderfully real me.

Kayla Tidwell, Grade 10
Lee High School, AL

Julius Caesar

D ictator
I mpassive
C ontrolling
T riumphant
A meliorator
T ragedy
O riginal
R epresentation

J ulius

C onquering
A varice
E nhance
S uperior
A cquisitive
R uler

Jenna Sechowicz, Grade 10
Council Rock High School South, PA

Blue and Green

Lime green would describe me
Peaceful and strong
Healthy and light
Bright and right
Blue is another color
The color of the sky
The color of ocean describes me calm
The color of ocean represents my might
I feel cool every time I see it
Blue and green are cool like me

Daniel Mrsic, Grade 11
Countryside High School, FL

Betrayed

Perfidy seems so simple
One person is betrayed
The other does the betraying
There are hundreds no, thousands
Of textbook examples
But no mere text can describe
The feeling of being so vulnerable
Around those once trusted
Once loved
Once cherished
Someone held close to the heart
To turn around and slash open
Old wounds, new wounds
Any kind of wounds
There is no restitution
Things can never be as they once were
No longer trusted
No longer loved
No longer cherished

Amanda Gelb, Grade 10
Council Rock High School South, PA

I Am...

I am tenacious and generous.
I wonder why things are the way they are.
I hear the singing of angels.
I see the future as an obstacle to tackle.
I want to visit Hawaii when the ocean is as blue as the sky,
the sand is as white as paper, and the sun is a glowing ball of warmth.
I am tenacious and generous.

I pretend that I am a three year old in the children's toy aisle.
I feel I am a super hero who is undefeatable.
I touch the foul lines in the game of life.
I worry that my best is never good enough.
I cry because I miss the people who have passed away.
I am tenacious and generous.

I understand that the sky is not really blue.
I say that friends are irreplaceable.
I try to live each day of life as if it was my last day.
I hope that one day there will be a cure for cancer.
I am tenacious and generous.

Victoria Frieswick, Grade 10
Haverhill High School, MA

An Unforgettable Night

Thrust upon her suddenly, with no warning at all,
A new responsibility that requires certain gall,
Was presented to this young woman as if it were a doll.
Quickly, within just a few eternally lasting minutes her life was turned around.
By a change so challenging, so darkly profound.
One that is usually characterized ny a temporary mound.
A new chapter of her life has begun.
However now they are two, not just one.
Learning the ways to take care of a child,
Becoming a person more gentle and mild.
Reluctantly accepting, what she had once before denied.
Assuming duties of one who had died.
Becoming a mother, to a small dependent child.
Entering a world, not a little chaotic and wild.

Dilliane Bonnet, Grade 10
Wyomissing Area Jr/Sr High School, PA

They Think Your Life Is Easy

Life isn't easy when you have to wake up every morning and hear the same old drama,
To lay down every night and tell yourself tomorrow's going to be different,
It's a shame and a little insane when you're scared to go to sleep at night,
Because you're afraid something bad just might happen,
Sometimes,
I just want to scream and say,
I've had enough,
I've been talked about, name called, and falsely accused,
Often I have to ask myself, "Am I the only one going through this?"
Afraid to tell my parents,
Afraid what they might say,
Is it worth a try to sigh and decide to cry?

Banisha Clayborn, Grade 10
West Lowndes High School, MS

The Perfect Love

Perhaps the only perfect love,
Is unfulfilled love.
The girl's crush on the football star.
The boy's admiration of an actress.
They are never to be marred by arguments,
Or tough times.
Yet perhaps it is the arguments and tough times
That make fulfilled love the perfect love.
For they allow the love to grow
Into something more beautiful,
Each time an argument is settled,
Or a hard time is passed.
They allow the love to prove itself to the world,
To show that it cannot be beat.
Perhaps it is those hard times and arguments that make
Fulfilled love fulfilled.

Cara Wood, Grade 11
Trinity School at Meadow View, VA

Only for a Moment

If only for a moment,
That time stood still,
I would be so elated,
For the things going well.
There are no doubts that we are friends,
But can that really come to an end?
I know that is unlikely to happen,
With you so thoughtful and sweet,
Though that barely calms me,
Or puts me at ease.
But for you I will try,
Because I know we can forever be friends.

Jennifer Ching, Grade 11
Brooklyn Technical High School, NY

My Apology

Tears fall and I know how you feel
a feeling I didn't think was real
but it has now broken me down
turning every last smile into a frown.
And as the tears fall I begin to drown
I am sorry I ever doubted you
I just some how thought I knew,
that I was right.
And I apologize for every last fight
for all the names we've exchanged,
I take full blame.
Couldn't believe everything you went through,
now looking at myself I don't know what to do.
For I've become weak
lost the voice to speak
and I need you now to make it through
I no longer know what to do.
So please forgive me for all I've done
because the mistakes I've made have just begun.

Nadine Kazzaz, Grade 12
Glasgow High School, DE

Victim of War

My daddy used to always talk about the war
He was a soldier, a hero, a father I adored
He was big, tough, and mentally strong
I never doubted him because he's never wrong
Life was good until this one day
When a man came and said he had to go away

My daddy looked at me
Eyes filled with sorrow
And promised he would be
Back home tomorrow
But the next morning when I waited at the door
My mom sat crying at the phone
And told me I had a daddy no more
My heart filled with hate
Like heads were about to roll
My heart was pumping at a rate
That I could not control

I remember all the times we played together
But because of them we'll never see each other
It's sad because no one talks to me anymore
Because to them I'm just a sad victim of the war

Anthony Brown, Grade 10
North Andover High School, MA

My Best Friend

My ring is my best friend
It is silver as a spoon
And hard as a rock
The diamonds twinkle like the stars
And there are 19 diamonds that will blind the eyes

The ruby colored stone represents my school
I'm in the class of 2009
This is when I'll leave my school
My ring contains memories that I have made
While I attended Raleigh

The deer on the side represent my hobby
I love to go hunting and be in the outdoors
I like it as much as I do my friends
I live my life deer season to deer season
Just so I can go hunting again

My ring is my best friend
It goes everywhere I go
And never complains to me
This is why my ring is my best friend
It stands for the memories that I made
While I attend Raleigh in the class of 2009

Justin Boone, Grade 11
Raleigh High School, MS

A Maturation Process Like No Other

B asking while the bashing's heart flutters **C** aged in the bondage of parental guidance and puberty **D** oomed by statistics and scholastic scrutiny **E** volved by events that splurge the mind, urban youth **F** ind purpose in sports and rhymes **G** rasped by residential wisdom with continuous chimes **H** olding back your berserk demeanor it seems, that **I** as a person am not fully green, you see life is like **J** eans yes jeans I say husky trying to fit in so you lean this way, into an array of unwanted **K** nowledge an adolescent know it all far from polished **L** oving tunneled vision until his ride loses **M** ileage again doomed by thoughts that's **N** onchalant, a life with twists and turns like crooked fonts **O** nce defined by designer clothes and the girls you taunt **P** aranoid as a result of the gun talk that surrounds you as **Q** ueer reality and distance from the truth devours our youth **R** aging thoughts and emotions overwhelm **S** tereotypic ways from those in shiny suits at the helm **T** oned by events that splurge the mind, urban youth find routes with these words of mine in hope that those confined **U** nshackle lungs be resistant to harmful tobacco educating is my **V** erb legislating with **W** ords making my favorite poets seem absurd **X** eno thoughts so distant from the truth tends to devour our **Y** outh

Ivy Mathews, Grade 12
Suitland High School, MD

A Piece of Me

I am a hopeless romantic and sometimes unrealistic
I wonder what the world would be like if everyone was really treated like an equal
I hear the sound that Christmas morning makes when everyone rushes downstairs
I see the reflections of my family in the water droplets of Ocean Spray
I want to be able to spend one more day with Jonathan DeRoche
I am a hopeless romantic and sometimes unrealistic

I pretend that if I make a wish at 11:11 it will actually come true
I feel like my loved ones are with me even when I am alone
I touch the line where the ocean meets the sky
I worry that I will not grow up to be the person I want to be
I cry when I think about all the things Jonathan is missing down here
I am a hopeless romantic and sometimes unrealistic

I understand that everyone has a path in life that they are set to follow, and life can be messy
I say that you have nothing if you don't have the support of your family
I dream about the secrets of life
I try to live my life to its fullest, leaving no room for regrets
I hope that I will continue to lead a happy and healthy life
I am a hopeless romantic and sometimes unrealistic

Amanda Cahill, Grade 10
Haverhill High School, MA

Brutus and Cassius

Brutus is very naïve, noble, and at times a little crass
While Cassius is very manipulative and street smart
Brutus is naïve when he allows Antony to speak at Caesar's funeral
Cassius thinks this was an inauspicious idea when Brutus allows this to happen
Brutus underestimates Antony's speaking abilities and does not realize how persuasive he can be
when he persuades the crowd to be on his side and not the conspirators'
Brutus trusts Antony when he says that he will not speak poorly of the conspirators
Cassius also manipulates Brutus by concocting a plan to persuade Brutus to join the conspirators
with forged letters he wrote pretending to be from the citizens of Rome
Again Brutus naïvely believes that the letters are actually from the citizens
Cassius is a great strategist and tries to persuade Brutus into waiting until Antony's army
comes to them since Antony's army will be tired while their army will be well rested
Cassius acts very cowardly when he asks his servant to stab him to death
While Brutus is brave and noble and stabs himself with his sword while saying when he's dying
that Caesar has been avenged while he dies slowly and painfully

Bridget Lynch, Grade 10
Council Rock High School South, PA

Leaving

I dread the day I go,
Because I am leaving so much behind.
All the treasures that mean the most,
Fall behind me as I rewind.

There are many things that mean so much,
And I know that they will be dearly missed
Some things as simple as a lunch,
But all so memorable as being first kissed.

I wonder what will be of me,
When all these things are gone
And what people will see,
The many rights or the many wrongs?

I often ponder on these feelings,
Of life and of death
But these questions are of God's dealings,
Until the day of my final breath.

Becky Bivens, Grade 11
Loretto High School, TN

Little Things

In this time of 2008, in this world of tragedies and chaos,
The only way to stay sane is to appreciate the little things.
Most people regret, question and criticize our world…
But then there are those few who enjoy it and sing
Songs of their happiness and songs of the praise
That they have for the rest of their days.
They honor the little things,
The things that make the world go 'round.
They honor the bus driver,
Who deals with the cranky old men.
They are grateful for the policemen,
Who make walking down the sidewalk that much safer.
They rejoice at the fact that they get to choose
What they want to do with their lives.
I want to be like those people.
I want to look under the tragedies and chaos.
I want to appreciate the little things.

Javed Chitaman, Grade 10
Townsend Harris High School, NY

Changing Winds

The winds of change blow past
The current sharp and fast
How will I ever last?

The gentle breeze of summer tides
Close behind it winter chills ride
The struggling leaf, like I, abides

Wherefore come such storms?
That send homes crashing for folks to mourn
What sends them on their way?
That they may go and I may stay

Michaela Lacy, Grade 11
Heidelberg American High School

I Took a Chance

I took a chance and told you how I felt,
Knowing you may reject me, as I feel my heart melt.
I knew what would happen if you knew my deepest secret,
I told you praying and trusting that you could keep it.
But I know now that secrets are meant to be kept,
Unknown to the world, not able to be felt!!
It hurts so bad, because I gave you my all,
You were supposed to be there when I was about to fall.
But you turned your back on me,
And now it's so clear for me to see,
You never cared about me or my heart,
I see it was a game for you from the start!
But I can't be mad, I knew what to expect,
We all play the game, and we all place our bets.
I bet everything I had in loving you,
And now that I've lost, everything is thru!!
I knew what I was getting myself into before it all went down,
…I just wish you the best of luck now!!!!!

Dominique Kelly, Grade 12
Gar-Field High School, VA

You're My Everything

You have made my life better,
And I want to be with you forever.
You cheer me up when I'm down,
And wash away my frown.
You will always be in my heart.
With you, I will never part.
You are the love of my life,
And one day I might be your wife.
You make me feel so loved,
And free like a dove.
We have our ups and downs,
But we always work around.
You are a piece of my heart,
And a work of art.
My love for you though,
Is more than you will ever know.
Sometimes we don't agree,
But you still stand with me.
I don't know what I would do without you,
And it is all because I love you.
You're my everything.

Jessica Leanne Moody, Grade 10
Schley County Middle/High School, GA

Trapped

I am in this body and can't get out,
I am in this mind that I can't escape,
I have these feelings that I can't overcome,
I have these dreams that are too much for me,
I have these dreams no one here to help me,
I am stuck,
Can't go,
I am stiff scared to move,
I am trapped without a doubt.

Rasheeda McCrae, Grade 11
Overbrook School for the Blind, PA

Roses

Looking out upon the garden.
The beauty swarms like bees
filling my soul with joy.
Slowly to appear,
the roses bloom with no fear.
They decorate the world with color,
shining unlike no other.
They swiftly sway
throughout the day.
Approaching is a wind,
causing a sad end.

Chase Shane Cromer, Grade 10
Schley County Middle/High School, GA

Black Cat Eyes

Black cat eyes
Peer from that last delusion
He's coated with tragedy
They said, floating among the lies.

Analyze it.
Over and over and over.
Nothing's jumping around anymore.
Where's the outlet?

That train wreck look
And spastic eyes.
They're so sedated.
Concentrated, he's no book.

Now these words he'll mangle
Too numb to fumble out
Splashes of ripe ecstasy.
That tempest, my fallen angel.

Kyle Jhant, Grade 12
McDowell High School, NC

Another Decision

The road continues on ahead
Through its twists and turns
I follow still through it all
Despite its splits and cracks.
Looking back to the road I followed
No different than the others
I see the paths I could have gone
The breaks I could have missed.
So obvious it was now
The roads I should have gone
Yet when I turn my back on them
I know what's made me strong.
I reach a split and search the paths
And find the one for me
Yet I wonder still what those others held
The things they could help me learn.

Keith Johnson, Grade 12
Smithtown High School West, NY

The Sixth of June

And I couldn't have asked for anything more
Than the night when the whole world stopped for us
And the sun beckoned for us to follow
With my wet Levis painting the street
And your words painting my mind
As we made our way down Lazy Brook
Pacing the road with nothing to find
The flowers all bowed their heads out of courtesy for us
And the water slowed its steady current thereafter
The stars rose to see us on our way
And all of the robins stopped their chatty laughter
As I walked down the golden line that divides the north from the south
We continued our epic chapter
You stood behind me and watched me catch the raindrops in my mouth
All of the moments I tried to capture
Every step begins to quicken as we stumble up Spinning Wheel
And every step is cushioned underneath us
With the gentle puddles of teal
Through the puddles we row and I couldn't have asked for anything more
Than the night when the whole world stopped for us
And the sun beckoned for us to follow

Tara Classey, Grade 11
Masuk High School, CT

Earth's Story

"Extra! Extra! Read the story!" shouted the Martian boy.
"I'll take one." "Fifty credits, and Earth's story you'll really enjoy."
The man opened the paper and scanned the page the boy had said was good
After a glance he then moved on, but he had misunderstood.

He read the sports and world events; things that affected him
At the end of the day he threw the paper away leaving Earth's story only skimmed.
What he didn't know was what the story told and how it would change life's course
See, in that story, if one carefully read, unfolded love's powerful force.

It spoke of a man who did wondrous things to save the human race
Their killing sin was conquering them so He gave eternal life through grace.
The ultimate sacrifice He had made to keep them from their doom.
He lived in their world, died on a cross, and spent three days in a tomb.

He rose again at the call of God to speak and breathe once more.
Then ascended up to heaven's gates, the place He lived before.
The Martian did not know that day what he had thrown away,
His simple excuse was that the story was the same as yesterday's.

The gift of life is held before you; do not let it pass.
Reach for things that really matter, treasures that will last.
Here's the story, lightly put, but carefully read it through.
Unlike the sports and other things, it really does affect you.

Elisabeth Niederman, Grade 10
Forest Lake Academy, FL

The Book of Love

My heart is a book that the world can see
One page ends in an awful tragedy
The next is what I wanted it to be
Another is sung like a melody

There is no folded corner or bookmark
Each page is unique in its very own way
Some pages are light and some are quite dark
A lot are filled with things I want to say

It is easier to have your thoughts read
Then to say them truthfully to your love
But mine is a novel that will not end
No line is the same as the one above

A short synopsis can't sum up the book
The words are from the heart so take a look
Jennifer Pashby, Grade 10
Peabody Veterans Memorial High School, MA

Take Me Away

I feel as if I'm going to cry
I really just wish I knew why

For some reason I know this feeling all too well
Here is like the burning pits of hell
The pain hits me like a witch's spell

I want the hurt to go away
Never to return any other day
I want someone to make it okay
Someone to take me away

Cassidy Geborkoff, Grade 11
Lee High School, AL

I Am

I am astute and adept
I wonder what my future will bring
I hear the loud shrieks of my opponent
I see the bright yellow tennis ball approaching
I want to end this match as quickly as possible
I am determined and focused

I pretend that no one can stop me from my goal
I feel my legs tightening and cramping
I touch the sleek titanium racquet head
I worry that I might double fault at the worst moment possible
I cry that my moment to shine is ending
I am in the zone and will not come out of it until I win

I understand that this is my match point and I have to win it
I say "You can do it!" three times before serving for the game
I dream of being as well known as my idols Venus and Serena
I try to concentrate and not let the excitement overcome me
I hope I never stray from my ambitions
I am Maiah Taylor the future's next tennis star
Maiah Taylor, Grade 10
Coral Reef Sr High School, FL

Nightmare

Mama's here.
Watching me.
Watching me like a growing tree.
Brother moved,
He's got a wife,
A baby, and a decent life.
But Daddy why,
Why can't you be here,
To help me through all my fears?
I look around,
To all the kids,
And wonder why, and pray and wish.
I wonder why,
Why you were taken,
From this nightmare, will I ever awaken?
I pray for you,
Pray that you're with Jesus,
And that He's forgiven all your reasons.
I wish so hard,
To see you again and again
Just tell me when, my nightmare will end.
Ashley Marie Smith, Grade 10
Schley County Middle/High School, GA

To the One I Love

To the one I love so sweet and true,
Words can't express the way I feel for you.
You brighten my day just to see your face,
You're too special in my heart so you won't be replaced.
God made you special and just for me,
And now that you're in my life I'm now complete.
To the one I lost you took his spot,
And since you've given me all of you I'll give you all I've got.
Through thick and thin,
Till death do us part.
These are words we said and we meant them from the start.
So since you're the one I love and the one I need,
I pray to God we can always be for eternity.
Michelle Martin, Grade 11
Alternative Learning Center Central High School, FL

Getting Out of Bed

Why won't I get out of bed?
Could be because I still have work to do
Maybe it's from all the work I've already done
Probably because I'm just too lazy

Why won't I get out of bed?
I did have a late night last night
But was it worth all the trouble that's bound to follow?
That thought is keeping me from getting out of bed

Why won't I get out of bed?
I know perfectly well why I won't get out of bed
It's the same reason I should get out of bed
To go and live life, for better or worse.
Brice Spires, Grade 11
Heathwood Hall Episcopal School, SC

If You Were to Die Tomorrow

If you were to die tomorrow what would you do?
Would you spend your life savings for a cool party with all your friends,
Or buy a new Mercedes-Benz,
Would you go on vacation to your dream place,
Or sit at home and pace.
But if you were to die tomorrow;
Would you take the time to skydive,
Or just say "good-bye!"

Jon Sanchez, Grade 10
New Jersey United Christian Academy, NJ

Remembering Memorial Day

We should all stop and take a second to remember all of the armed forces who sacrificed their lives for us to be free.
They gave up living their lives for people they might not have ever known like you and me.
Pause and remember all of their lives that were taken.
Just try to imagine all the nerves that are shaking.
I believe that we all should care about the fallen flowers
Because they are fighting each and every hour
of each day.
And tears wiped away
for each and every one;
can't take back what's done.
So pause and take a moment out of the day to think about each flower having to be laid down.
And remember about that while they are gone and being put in the ground.
Just know they were fighting for you!

Brittany N. Cunningham, Grade 12
Vision Christian Academy, SC

Divine Temple

Every vigorous antemeridian, the resplendent sun rises upon your sky-high towers, the nippy and untarnished zephyr blustering
And thrashing the flag of the temple, birds chirping and singing devotional songs so that the devotee can clean their heart
Temple is like an another abode of God
The flowers in the Temple's backyard and by the roadside give us the aroma of the pure soul
With the Temple's doors, devotees enroll and sit on the bench or bend down their knees in front of God, like the servants pay respect to their master.
I bow down my head for the favor that you are always stature in my heart; your priest is chanting with his prayers and singing
The devotional prayers and the devotional songs travel through the corners of the baronial ceilings
The divine music adds emotion to my human ears and creates a heavenly bond
You surrender yourself, your soul, your body, your brain and everything you have to God, in order to clear the burden of earthly desires
My body feels blessed by the supreme soul; I can never repay the favors that God sacrificed for me
The light that is in the shrine as the supreme light, no human being can ever face with their human eyes
The light leads me from illusory to bona fide, from the obscurity to luminosity
God is my master, my king, my leader, my president, and my majesty; I acquire love and justice through your blessed Temple
When I go to your temple, I receive eternal peace that can never be obtained from anywhere else except your divine,
Peaceful, beautiful, and celestial palace
No one can break the bond that is tied between you and me, not even you, unless I do some kind of big mistake that can never be forgiven
As I leave the temple's gates, and my heart beats and my body feels hydrated
The divine memory of your temple illuminates my soul to step off your Temple's property; my only wish to you before I go is to
Always be blessed and request to you to always be in my heart forever, no matter what,
I will return to your home if the earthly desires will release me off of their clutches.

Krishnam Dixit, Grade 11
Bayside High School, NY

A Prosaic Coin

Upon a wooden table, a prosaic coin spins,
Soon it may stable; to flick it is a sin.

A man skudders by said table, aloof to the world around;
Impatient, persistent, able. The coin makes no sound.

"Farewell" yells his spouse, a door thunders in return,
Left behind; an empty house, the silver coin still turns.

Punctual, he must hurry, competition is toe-to-toe,
Ambition joins with worry, the coin begins to slow.

Immersed in viscous traffic, pugnacious; he proceeds to weave,
Neglecting certain havoc, the coin still loses speed.

The coin begins to falter, slowed; but does not rest.
As its course now alters, in pain, he grabs his chest.

The coin softly glistens, at last, it soon will set.
Despising past decisions, he's engulfed by cold regret.

The coin has lost all power, from afar comes a distant ring.
Piercingly, it grows louder, then at once, a quiet ting.

Bradley J. Hansen, Grade 11
Chazy Central Rural Jr/Sr High School, NY

Escape

Everyone needs an escape at times.
An escape from drama,
An escape from difficulties,
An escape from life itself.
Sometimes, when I feel like I could cry,
I close my eyes,
And take a deep breath.
I imagine being somewhere beautiful.

I close my eyes and imagine,
An enormous waterfall,
Bluer than the sky in the summertime,
The water pounding and splashing,
Exotic flowers,
In every color of the rainbow,
Thousands of giant sized trees,
Taller than an apartment building in the city,
Then I take a deep breath.

Once my eyes have stopped watering,
And I feel strong enough,
I open my eyes,
And I continue with my day.

Rachel Rueff, Grade 10
Jeffersontown High School Magnet Career Academy, KY

My Experience

Riding in the car, I can see many things
When I look out the window I see…
    Grass, horses, cows and many other things.
This is such a beautiful scene
    because the bright sun and glowing sky,
    makes this scene complete.
This amazed me because I have never
    Seen anything like this before —
    Brought tears to my eyes —
I was enjoying this ride,
    I had then realized I was in
    North Carolina — on the countryside!

Amber Few, Grade 10
Parkdale High School, MD

If I Had To

If I had to I would let the waves take me,
drag me to the depths of the blue,
Let the wind carry me up, up
where I would reach the stars and touch the moon.
If I had to I would
climb to the highest branch of a tree,
From sunset to sunrise
wait to turn into a bird
So I could fly far, far.
Far enough to reach you
Far enough to reach the other side.
But for now I settle on the memories
and on the pictures of you and me,
and stare widely at the night sky
and wish you were staring
back at me.

Kathy Ruano, Grade 12
Uniondale High School, NY

I Am Your Candle Light Tonight

I am your candle light tonight.
I ask myself if you're scared I might burn something.
I hear the window being opened.
I see the wind trying to blow me out.
I am your candle light tonight.

I pretend to be more powerful than you.
I feel your heavy breathing trying to blow me out again.
I touch your fingers; I hope I didn't burn your skin.
I worry myself about setting you on fire.
I cry with wax down to your fingers which hold me.
I am your candle light tonight.

I understand I have to be put out in the morning,
But the night is still young.
I say let me stay with you for a little while longer.
I dream for a next time to be lit back on.
I try my best to keep burning my wax.
I desire your company tonight.
I am your candle light tonight.

Maria Scutaru, Grade 12
The Urban Assembly School for Media Studies, NY

Star*

You truly are a star
giving happiness to everyone
not afraid to be yourself
not afraid to say what you feel
your smiles are radiant
your eyes are bright and full of hope
finding your way and helping others
stay with me, teach me to be
selfless and caring.
Show me how to be myself.
And how to be a friend.
You truly are a star.

Brandy Clark, Grade 10
Camden High School, NY
*Dedicated to Ryne Sanborn

You

You were there for me.
You held my hand.
You picked me up.
You were there to understand.

You dried my tears.
You saw my dreams.
You pieced together my heart.
You are a part of me.

You held me close.
You were my seams.
You protected my name.
You gave me everything.

I love you for it.
Yet, you may never understand.
You are my other half.
I love you, my best friend.

Margaret Catherine LoCicero, Grade 12
Countryside High School, FL

What Is and What Should Never Be

What is should be happy,
What is should be bliss,
What is should be the positives in life
That no one has to miss.

But what really is reality,
In its twisted sense of actuality.
We can't quite understand its brutality,
Or its lack of geniality.

Yet every now and then you find
Someone who is oh so kind,
And that person just redefined
What is and what should never be.

Julia Galea, Grade 11
Kellenberg Memorial High School, NY

Our Sacred Place

I begin to climb the worn stairs to the musty floor where walls crumble
This is the place where the two worlds collide and the universes touch
Crack the window, breaking the stitched cobwebs that hold life
A miracle when the weight on our shoulders is too much.

Sitting on the shingled roof and the rain begins to fall
How wonderful would it be to rid my problems and clear my mind?
Now shivering, the cold creeps through my clothes and soaks my skin
Arms stretch to the heavens, hands shake at the sky.

Gather your feelings and push them closer to the ledge
Thunder booms; lightning kisses the ground as if to respond
Grasp the air for the thoughts that have seeped from my head
Place your eyes to the extending above and see the existence beyond.

Jacqueline Torrisi, Grade 10
Watervliet Jr/Sr High School, NY

Someday You'll See the Sun

Arms spread wide open, staring straight ahead.
Take me far, far away from this place where I lay in bed.
In the distance the trees begin to sway.
With every movement they have something to say.
Come towards me and I'll show you the sun.
It's hard to walk forward, let alone run.
Trapped and alone in this world with no where to go.
The wind whispers "Come, and I'll show you things you could never know."
I look up at the sky, with no limits or walls.
Why is it when I'm here no one can hear my calls?
Let me go so I have no more regrets.
Take me away and for once just let me forget.

Gabrielle Indelicato, Grade 12
Southern Regional High School, NJ

Math Quiz

On Wednesday morning, I was busy taking an exam,
In Honors Advanced Math, a class commonly known as HAM.
The exam was ten questions in length,
The subject was trigonometry, which is my strength.
Each question demanded that I share more knowledge,
My grade seemingly determined where I was destined for college.

The answer to question one was abundantly clear,
As one's reflection is in a polished mirror.
I was prudent, however,
Because second chances on an exam are as often as never.
As I neared the end of the test,
I was filled with a feeling of zest.

I placed my paper on the appropriate desk,
And hoped my grade was statuesque.
I watched as my teacher graded my paper,
And my nervousness began to taper.
In the end, I received a one-hundred,
Why I was so worried, I wonder.

Benjamin Altman, Grade 10
Danbury High School, CT

I Am

I am a beacon shining in the darkness,
Dimmed as I relent and the darkness draws near.
I am a ray of hope glistening at dawn,
Tarnished by my self-serving desires.
I am a student of life,
Learning how to live each day.
I am a daughter; disobedient at times,
Trying to follow the lessons I've been taught.
I am a flawed and imperfect mirror,
Reflecting the love that I have been shown.
I am an image; a symbol,
Refracted from those before me.
I am a quiet storm; gentle, stirring, moving,
Subtly dispersing into serenity.
I am a lighthouse; rooted where I stand,
Reaching out to save but can only do so much.
I am a solemn willow,
Weeping silently for those already lost.

Britni Williams, Grade 11
Meadville Area Sr High School, PA

Untitled

When running out far past the shoreline
the smell of salt can fill the mouth
while, lies in your hand,
a sea stone, white and round.
You unfurl your lips and say
"You are my lucky stone."
I clench my jaw
and force a smile,
hating every stir you sound.
Lucky stones have holes in them.
Perhaps you think I am incomplete,
that I still have places to fill.
Or maybe I am old and withered,
becoming decrepit with the tides.
I clench my jaw
and force a smile.
The smell of salt can fill the mouth.
Don't let that smell get to your eyes darling,
it burns.

Stephanie Schloss, Grade 10
Farmington High School, CT

Running from Destiny

If you knew how far I have came
Where I am, where I stand,
You would have thought that I was insane
Wishin' I still was back on my old plan

I learned there's no one to catch you when you fallin'
And there will be no one to hear you when you callin'
So I made sure I ended my cryin'
'Cause I will surely not be dyin'

I am tired of the running from destiny
It's time to face my reality.

Jevone Lawrence, Grade 12
Woodstock High School, GA

Helpless Innocence

The silent cry of the unborn child
Rings through his murderer's ears;
He knows not what first breath is like,
Nor the fingers or toes one wears.

He wondered what pain or blood was;
What pure gaiety could be;
He thought of the smells he missed out on;
And what sights of God's world he'd not see.

He knew not who his mother was,
Or if she regretted her wrong;
Yet it's fine and okay — *they* always say;
So why does this guilt feel so strong?

His mom never told him, "I love you."
His dad braced him not in his arms.
Instead he was given a gift of cold death —
A death of all innocent harms.

When he was suddenly greeted by Jesus,
Sorrow left, while he stared wide-eyed at Him.
As he folded his hands, and knelt by His feet,
He begged God to forgive them their sin.

Tessa High, Grade 12
Highmark's Home School, SC

Nature

A wolf howls mournfully at the moon.
Turning, he glances at his fallen companion,
His brother and friend.
Snow dots the fallen's flank,
And a shining red gash runs down it,
Made by the fans of a wildcat
Driven off by the pack hours before.
Anguish shows plainly in the mourner's eyes
As he paces to and fro, helpless,
Watching his brother's side rise and fall
Rise and fall,
As long ragged breaths sustain him.
Little time passes before these breaths, eve,
Cease to be, and the now solitary wolf
Lets out a long howl,
As if a denial of the tragedy at hand.
But there is little chance for mourning,
For he must move one, and return to the pack,
Leaving his brother to lay in the snow.
A victim of the nature, in all its beauty,
That once kept him alive.

Emily Norwood, Grade 11
Atlee High School, VA

The Sky Is Yellow with Spring Rain

R eality is thicker in these moments
S ticking in small tufts to the
T rees that line Main St., spilling away from the sky's gray
U nderskirts.
V aguely, I observe people moving, like pinballs, between the post office and their cars;
W e wait patiently for this reality to burst, knowing that we'll find bits in the gutter tomorrow.

Daisy Alioto, Grade 12
King Philip Regional High School, MA

Confidence with Knowing Who You Are

A swan, a queen, a gorgeous diamond
None of the above can describe me
I walk with my head high, my back straight and my hips, the curve.
Beauty what a word, but cannot describe me
Talent a characteristic found in some, but cannot describe me
Money, power, respect will never be above me
My name is a name that is not worthy to be with me.
The Twin Towers were strong towers
But yet it was easily knocked down by a lesser power than itself.
Unlike me, I stand tall and refuse to be knocked down.
My eyes, my hair my body and my lips that got you whipped off one kiss.
You wonder how a person could be so delicate and important that words could not describe them.
I'm not conceited I'm just confident 'cause if I don't believe in myself, who will believe in me?
"Silence" when I enter the room, all eyes on me
I'm treated like a superstar although I'm not rich but am wealthy.
Everywhere I go, people wanna know.
Who I am?
I am me *myself.* That's why I stand out. I am me *myself.* That's why I am loved.
I am me *myself!*

Michelle Isioye, Grade 11
Carmel High School, NY

You Are

You are something genuine, rare, and addiction; hard to grasp.
A vivid dream that I do not want to disturb.
A warm, summer day that's not too hot for fun.
A cool, clear night with stars; full of wishes that you will never be erased from my memory, my life.
You are a rainbow with it rains, giving peace and stability.
A cherry slushy with a neon fuschia straw under the shade of an umbrella on the beach at dusk.
An individual, a hero, amazingly human, a force field.
You are wanted by many, something of much discussion.
High news to a drunken, an epidemic, a chilled iced tea.
A love sponge with leaking character and I soak up the vibe.
A race to the finish line with the opponent right on your heels.
A prize; shared by some, envied by others; my boom box.
You are a challenge; humble, funny, charismatic.
A shaken bottle, a basement party, a banana split.
A 95 mph ride on the back of a truck; beyond average.
A brilliant creature, an evolution, muy único.
A strong figure, Superman, my Dr. Pepper.
I pray that every day I live will be attached to you.
You are my friend, a shoulder, a listening ear.
And if you are the epitome of happiness,
I will never need an umbrella again!

Sophia Gravley, Grade 11
Magna Vista High School, VA

Garden of Souls

tHeir eyes are deeper than all roses
full of life and beauty
easy flowing like the calm gentle spring wind

the flowErs wilt
while bees and butterflies suck the sweet nectar
for they only want it for themselves
do they ever come back

crows start to peck the flowers
and the sweet gentle breeze starts to pick up wind
wAter starts to dry up from the fountain of youth
until it's perished

soon the crows kill all beauty
they drink the pRecious water
even if you try to restore its beauty
they'll destroy it

and yet those few flowers who survive 'til night
pray to the sTars
for they are still young inside
and the moon's light will empower them
'til next time

Jon Dollar, Grade 11
Dekalb School of the Arts, GA

If Water Had a Voice

In a city that never sleeps,
I flow beyond these dark and dirty streets.
I am hot, but sometimes cold.
I live forever, yet never get old.
I flow through your fingers, but you can't hold me.
I am the waves at the beach.
I carry your boats on my back no matter the size.
I give your children a place to play.
I fall from the sky with grace or rage.
I help make life — and take life.
I am a home; I am shelter.
I am your rivers; I am your harbors.
But you have poisoned me!
I have become your ashtray;
Your garbage can; your toilet.
You need me more than anything.
I put out your fires. I clean you.
I quench your thirst. I helped make you.
And now you are helping destroy me.
If only you could hear me!
If only I had a voice.

Christian B. Casanova, Grade 12
The Smith School, NY

The Catcher in the Rye

His brother's death was just the inception,
Of Holden's deep, deep depression.
Being a young adolescent child,
His hatred grew wild.
His mother and father avoiding what they can,
Sending him to boarding school again and again.
Although Holden was indeed censurable,
His problems seemed undetectable.
Attending Pency and meeting old Spencer,
Holden was granted with a wonderful connoisseur.
Cawffle seemed to be a great escape,
Until it turned out there was no such date.
His anger grows and grows inside,
Until one day, when Holden will do more than just cry.

Erin Kerwick, Grade 12
Council Rock High School South, PA

Live. Laugh. Love.

Free from all worries
Hanging out with friends
That's the best part in life
So cherish it while you can

That's how it is
When I am with my friends
We fool around like
Monkeys on vines

We tease each other
And share our pain as well
When tears run down our cheeks
We give a shoulder to cry

Friendship is like a delicate piece of crystal
I take care of it like people do of diamonds
I've learned from experience
True friends always got your back

Don't let other people ruin your friendship
Trust your friend
Otherwise your friendship is worthless

Anila Abbasi, Grade 10
Colonia High School, NJ

Devastation

Waking up in the morning
Losing a loved one
Hearing the word, "No"
Stressing over rejection
Seeking forgiveness in a situation with no hope
Fighting a pointless cause
Arguing with those that make no sense
Embarrassing myself in public
Worrying about what others may think
Answering obvious questions
Repeating bad habits
Recognizing some mistakes are irreversible

Jessica Johnson, Grade 10
Bledsoe County High School, TN

What to Do?

Good morning mind
Are you awake today?
    PLEASE give me a poem…
I have nothing to say
    It kind of feels like
Watching the cursor on
    The computer blink.
Just wish the poem
    Could write itself
It takes you though
    To make it so…
It takes you to make it move
    It takes you
To make the letters
    Of mystery appear across the page
But what to type…
    What to write…
A blank mind is all
    I got, right?
                    Emily Gordy, Grade 10
Schley County Middle/High School, GA

Love Came Rolling In

Love came rolling in
Upon my humble heart
Fearing being torn
Maybe luck could change
This time around.

Crushed and stomped upon
Until it bled velvet
Maybe my heart can get sewn together
Because I am ready for love
And love isn't going to wait on me.
                    Erica Bettross, Grade 11
                    Thomson High School, GA

What I've Left Behind

I wake up in the morning
And you're the first one on my mind
I fall asleep thinking
About what I've left behind

Your smile kept me happy
Your laugh was like a dream
Your touch was unforgettable
And your absence was obscene

When your astonishing eyes shine
They put every star to shame
Then we wished to stay together
And distant we became
                    Patricia Cotton, Grade 10
                    Riverbend High School, VA

Juxtaposition

Love is but a twisted collection of letters,
A word dancing nakedly across life's palm.
Like all others, it is devoid of true meaning.
Real words are those left unspoken,
Those that are sung from the heart.
Perhaps I shall never know of such words,
As I live to question the unquestionable.

Society has long-since deemed me unworthy;
I am the ugly duckling floating in the tranquil river of Father Time,
Left untouched by Mother Nature's caress.
Surely the swan will not have me.
I am not dainty as I should be,
And the dirty blotches of social disorder remain caked on my wings.
But perhaps it is the swan that is unworthy of me.

I rise above my imperfections,
Examining the reflection of what I have become.
I am beautiful in my turmoil,
And I spread my wings to fly.
I will not live by Mother Nature's oppression any longer;
I will follow the songs of my heart,
Finding beauty in every faltering note.

                    Shannon Meany, Grade 12
                    Massapequa High School, NY

Cry, the Beloved Country — Gertrude's Letter

My dearest brother to whom I write,
Please, you tell me not of your disappointment, brother.
For I know, I well know.
Brother, I am sick and the sickness of mine is not evanescent.
Oh, how much regret do I feel of my actions.
But brother, of my decision, I promise it was politic.
That loving home of yours cannot house the shame and sorrow I would have brought.
Brother, if that of my own blood hung his head low,
Then how brother, how will those strange to me learn to accept and forgive?

Here in Johannesburg I have long since had a duty.
And brother, after seven nights pass I am promised to have money,
For I now cook and clean for the white man.
Endless is my work since he enjoined I have the night shift.
Oh, I do apologize for a letter so short,
But the dust and the dishes await and impatient they grow.
Give the little blood of mine a loving and content life,
And pass Gertrude's wish to "go well" to all of Indotsheni.
They need not say "stay well,"
For breath must not be wasted on things so foolish.

— Gertrude

                    Janet Gugel, Grade 10
                    Council Rock High School South, PA

The Tragedy of Julius Caesar

Of those who know of that great play
With a famous line known as "Et tu, Brutus"
Written by a paragon known as William Shakespeare
The play was titled the *Tragedy of Julius Caesar*
The conspirators gathered their plans
While Caesar was oblivious that he was their man
As winsome as Brutus did seem
He was all part of the conspirators' scheme
When the Ides of March finally came
Caesar was no more a part of Rome's fame
That day turned into complete bedlam
The crowd was swaying to both sides
As Antony and Cassius would battle off for a victory
And the end finally came
With Antony's army capitalizing over Cassius and Brutus

Adam Salkovitz, Grade 10
Council Rock High School South, PA

Mother and Child

O Mother, show me the love you feel
To a small child
Who barely seems real
And who you touch with hands gentle and mild

Child, Child you grow and grow
Your heart beats and plays
As you begin to in turn love the people you know
Growing stronger throughout the days

Mother, Mother you gave life
The painful joy of giving birth
It can be filled with agony and strife
But in the end, it's what life is worth

O Child, you were given a gift
Your authorities gave you your mind and soul
And throughout your days they will gently lift
That mind and soul to its desired goal

Susan Weidman, Grade 10
Wyomissing Area Jr/Sr High School, PA

Morning Dawning

Morning knocks on my oak door
Sunlight enters with a commanding roar
Mockingbirds signal me to arise
A new day to bring many a surprise!
As I stir from my adrenaline-crazed sleep
I look outside and hear not a peep
Dew lingers like fur on my favorite sweater
Like it doesn't care about the weather
Like it has nothing left to weather
The clouds are mauve
And reflect the lilacs on my front grove
While rays of light wash my face
And annoying squirrels try to race
I take it slow at my own pace
While the morning shrouds my residential place!

Snehann Kapnadak, Grade 10
Colonia High School, NJ

The Work Force*

I see the ship builders,
And hear the song of the shipyard,
The zap of the welders,
And the zit-zat of the air-powered ratchets,
The song of the compressors,
Humming along, straining to do their jobs
I see the slow ascension of the wooden structure,
And the thump, thump, thump of the hammer,
Hitting the nail into the board,
I hear the whirr of the electric drill,
And smell the sweet, fresh-cut wood,
I see the flashing lights,
And the yellow and black paint,
And hear the beep, beep, beep,
Of the huge hunks of metal
And smell their exhaust fumes
And the fresh, hot, wet tar,
At the end of the day,
I hear the sound of many voices,
Men relaxing, looking back at the day's work,
Preparing for tomorrow.

Nick H., Grade 11
Palmyra, ME
*Dedicated to Walt Whitman

Life

Struggling to stand in the boxing ring
Still feeling the sting from the last swing.
Clinging to the cold tile floor trying to spring up and fight.
Despite the strength of the enemy taking all my energy.
As my lungs begin to collapse and there isn't any air.
Pulling through all the punches and strikes
Like a child trying to ride a bike.

The pain runs deep and it continues to tug at me.
Sinking in the depth of agony disguised by a smile.
Nobody has a clue of what I go through.

Beginning to understand their technique.
In trying to make you weak, but now it's time to speak.
Dodging all the punches and all the obstacles.
Till you're the only one standing and it's the last round.

Heart starts to pound loud and you can hear every sound.
Lungs are no longer filled with debris.
And your heart that was in a prison has been set free.

No one can bring me down
Because it's spring and I've sprung.

Nicole Saxton, Grade 10
Wharton High School, FL

Winter Love
Who said spring was the season of love?
Winter is more or less the season of love.
Imagine cuddling in front of the fireplace
As the flames dance exotically.
And enjoying a coffee cup full of hot cocoa,
And eventually falling asleep in each other's arms.

Lennie Anderson, Grade 11
Theodore High School, AL

The Dreadful Photograph
The dreadful photograph
Dressed in all white with the tips of my hair in a perfect line, itchy, and uncomfortable
Waiting, waiting, waiting…children screaming and crying "Oh that dreadful place"
Finally it's my turn after aging 30 years
I walk in…and I am told to take a seat
All of a sudden a collage of events happen
Move to the right, now to the left, stand up straight!!!
I ponder…what must have I done to deserve this punishment?
They tell me to smile
I try to pull off a fake smile that hides the hate I am expressing towards this person
But it's never good enough for them
They wave a colorful imitation of a teddy bear in my face
All I can think…what am I 3?
Just as I see the light to freedom and victory
I fall back down to the dark black hole when I hear the words…
"Ok let's take another one"
Finally they are done and as I walk out all I can see is the devil in his eyes
I get in the car and think "When am I going to dress into comfort?"
And that was a…
Dreadful photograph

Aaron Pinet, Grade 10
Haverhill High School, MA

Book
Have we become so arrogant as to forget the basic construct of our language?
Entertainment has driven us to a childlike capacity.
For fear of being deemed hypocrite, I do lavish the labyrinth of the web.
But have we no bounds?
Where do we draw a line between fantasy and reality?
Is it too late?
Have we become so intertwined within ourselves we perceive all things
To our own standards?
Has it always been like this?
Is humanity doomed to a pattern of self indulgence?
For aren't all things pleasure also pain?
I fear humanity is drawing to a close.
All things done are done for self and for higher standing.
Creation has been reduced to media and entertainment.
Beauty is a paradigm phantom that continues to reappear
And destroy everything in its path.
Twin to wealth, both a disease of the mind.
Alas, the question remains, is it ourselves to blame?
For we alone create progress and progress destroys good intent
So then, I ask, is the book soiled too?

Cat Mueller, Grade 11
Haverford High School, PA

I Am a Big Girl Now

OMG! I'm turning seventeen
I can't believe it
I smell independence
But a strange feeling at the same time.

I can't believe I'm going to college very soon
I remember as if it was yesterday
The butterflies in my system,
And the fear of the first day of school,
Starting my own way to success

Yes! I'm seventeen now
I'm very proud of it
Now the fear is gone
High school is almost over
And I just enjoy going to class
Without that fear
Yes! I'm seventeen now

It's an awesome feeling
The smell of freedom
Yes! I'm seventeen now.

Dennise Carranza, Grade 12
North High School, MA

Leap of Faith

In this torn world of scorn and fear;
never relinquish your heart's desire,
but to the law of truth you must adhere,
'cause integrity is a grand gift to acquire.
Life's golden rule: never stoop down the level
where you have to compromise your conviction,
'cause selling your soul to the devil
will bring only a doom jurisdiction.

Let not a sour tongue spark you with doubt
nor let yesterday's mistake erase your esteem,
rather let your fruits of labor sprout,
as you climb high to live out your dream.
Staying gold means standing on your own,
so bite the bullet and conquer your goal.
As you enter and exit this world alone,
depend on no one except your own soul.

Life is an abstract art
any wish you can paint
and the most beautiful part
is that there's no constraint,
so don't ever hesitate to take a leap of faith!

Rosella Simogan, Grade 12
Mary Help of Christians Academy, NJ

Nature's Composition

The soft, tranquil sound of a rolling brook,
Mixes with the crunch of autumn leaves.
A cricket chirping to his mate,
Intertwines with the hymn of the birds' songs.
The hushed blowing of the wind,
Amalgamates with the luminous, warm sunlight.
Weak thunder expires in the distance,
Finally passing away after its exhausting fight.
Gentle rain pitter-patters off roof shingles,
Creating a gentle lullaby to soothe the night air.
So calm and pacifying are the sounds of nature in tune.
Harmony.

Ally Chase, Grade 11
Framingham High School, MA

Love and Pain

Each morning the girl awakes in her room
Thoughts of her Prince Charming louder than rain
His unawareness adds to silent gloom
That she feels through all of the unheard pain

A walk on the beach is not a sure fix
To rid her of the heartache and sadness
She knew before that love and pain don't mix
But now this logic adds to her madness

In so many words she can't ever speak
She wants him to know she can always cry
And that he has made her lonely heart weak
Only then she'll feel it was her best try

Soft and sweet, all that is left unspoken
Will forever remain as a token

Krystin Pashby, Grade 10
Peabody Veterans Memorial High School, MA

Release

I am warming to the thought of
Release, three hours of utter
Exhilaration, of heated glances and quick
Hope, a fusion of self-conscious
Movement, harmonic instinct, and heavenly
Ignorance.

I am beginning to
Flow, allowing the hard beat and harsh words to
Run me, to permeate every cell like a
Drug, to seal my eyes and let it carry me
Far, beyond rationality and into true
Freedom.

I am releasing everything except the
Music, intoxicating and alive, right
Now the source of my joy, my misery, my
Being for one night, one rare and delicious night of letting
Go, of honestly forgetting, disregarding everything else but the
Release.

Katherine Kilkenny, Grade 11
Choate Rosemary Hall School, CT

Nature Is a Beautiful Thing

Nature is a beautiful thing;
It's full of wonder and splendor.
It is cautious, never careless;
It is flawless, never defective.

It has life and gives life,
It shares life and takes it away.
It gives those who choose a place to live;
Nature is a beautiful thing.

Blake Allen, Grade 11
Thomson High School, GA

I Am Free!*

Today, I see everything clearly
the big choice,
everything that I left when I flew.
How could I?
How did I have strength?
My huge wings
I still can't control.
I miss you, I miss my nest,
your protection always there.
Today, I see everything clearly
the scar that you left on me
that I will keep forever.
I am free! Thank you!
With my huge wings
I am capable to cross cliffs.
I feel like flying, risking, and then:
to glide over the sea
with more calm than my chest can hold.
Today, I see, I am an eagle!
And solitude is my fear.

Danyla Bezerra, Grade 11
Miami Beach Sr High School, FL
*Dedicated to my mother.

Like a Book

Open my pages and then you'll see
All the different sides of me
Open my pages and then you'll know
All the feelings that I can't show
Open my pages and then you'll find
All the memories I left behind

Go ahead and take me
Off this dusty shelf
Look at my worn cover
And you'll see my broken self

Open my pages
And read my dreams
Don't judge me by my cover
I'm not what I seem.

Sarah Braithwaite, Grade 10
Bronx High School of Science, NY

Backyard

In the morning, I see sun-kissed Apollo flying his golden chariot high in the sky.
He shines light on the morning dew that covers your leaves that stretch out like arms.
Chirping birds bring music to your gigantic ears.
As I pick luscious grapes from your entangled hair of vines,
Bugs crawl around hoping that you will feed them.
Then dawn turns to dusk while fireflies awake from their slumber.
I watch your sleepy eyes light up with the twinkling fireflies and shooting stars.
The luminous moon shines upon your glowing face as the night drones on.
Slowly and softly, your sweet music puts every living creature to sleep.
Petals of flowers close their eyes; small animals snuggle up to their mothers,
I crawl under my covers and think of the treasured memories the next day will bring
as I drift off into my, thoughtful dreams.

Maadhuri Shankar, Grade 12
Bayside High School, NY

The Interminable March

We were marching across a field one morn'
Men, boys, wounded, and sick
Not a word was spoken; not a hymn was sung
The only sound was the constant booming of the distant cannons
Chancellorsville, Gettysburg, Antietam — we've seen them all
This one would be no different.

But that evening the silence was broken
By a young boy weak from walking.
He asked the captain why we continued marching.

We all march for one reason only
To see this country united once more
Until Virginia flies only one flag within its borders
And we shall not stop marching until our goal is reached.

Kennedy Thrift, Grade 11
Thomson High School, GA

Girls

Girls will lie, girls will cheat
Girls are the most horrible people you're ever likely to meet
We fuss, we complain, we stab in the back
Don't make us mad, because we're ready for an attack

We talk about everyone, but we're nice to their face
Forget the golden rule, for us that's not the case
Don't be fooled by our angelic disguise
It's no wonder we always befuddle the guys

Passive aggressive is our middle name
That secret cattiness is our claim to fame
We'll smile and we'll flirt, we'll laugh and we'll giggle
But not at your joke, it's really your jiggle

We hardly ever mean what we say
That's why we switch best friends every other day
So now you've been warned, get the picture — be aware
Don't assume we're telling the truth, because that occasion is rare

Katherine Grant, Grade 10
Peabody Veterans Memorial High School, MA

Mon Ancien Frere (My Former Brother)

"I'm a mess these days" you say during our first conversation in months
and lately it's all I can think about.
You're a mess these days and I don't know why that one sentence
makes me wanna curl up and cry.

I fight every urge to run up to your apartment,
bypass the 50 year old elevator and knock on your door.
I fight against every part of me that wants to save you
for you were never mine to save.

The way I know you're falling apart makes me want to hold you
tighter and fiercer than I've ever held anyone,
and whisper things that would somehow make things right.

Maybe somehow I could piece you together
somehow I could help you smile again
be the boy you once were, be the brother I once had.

But then I remember how I've been burned before
putting myself on the line for you
and I drop you as quick as I held you, like fire in my hands
I walk away from you
as you smolder, and eventually
die out.

Irene Yenko, Grade 10
Townsend Harris High School, NY

Feelings Change

Feelings change no matter what
Even if you don't want them to change
If it's a boyfriend, friend, or sibling
Your feelings will always come out.
Even if you try to fight it or try not to think about it
It will all be worthless because feelings always win the fight.
But sometimes the feelings are true,
And changes can be a good thing,
Like if someone is hurting you or doing you wrong
Feelings could make you strong.
Feelings can make you or break you
Feelings can make you sick
Some people don't even know their true feelings
And try to make them up
And they don't even notice their true feelings just showed up.
Until finally change shows up
That's why people always say "you don't know what you got until it's gone."
But the most important lesson life will teach you
Is not to mess with someone's feelings,
Because karma will always comes back to haunt you
And make you cry and whine too.

Constanza Soncini, Grade 10
Miami Beach Sr High School, FL

Trapped

I don't want to be here
I just want to go somewhere
To a place where I'm free
and it's okay to be me
the whole world I want to see
I don't want to wait
I want to hurry before it's too late
I don't want to be here
and no one seems to care
maybe I should run away
If only I could find a way
but something's telling me to stay
maybe just one more day
but I can't wait
I want to hurry before it's too late
I don't want to be here
Is there anyone out there
maybe I'll be saved
what if I'm enslaved
I can't stay, I can't wait
but I think it's too late…I'M TRAPPED!

T'Sharaye Preston, Grade 11
Frederick Douglass Academy, NY

The Stream

Burbling softly,
Gushing over smooth pebbles
Onward towards its end.

Thea Anderson, Grade 10
Lee High School, AL

Here Is to You

I'm kind of lost without you here
Remembering you still makes me tear
For the good and the bad,
When I am happy or sad

The roses I left on your grave
Your sweet soul, I wish I could save
The pain stings like the freezing cold
The pictures are starting to get old

Peaceful and happy you may be
But oh, I wish you were here with me
To guide me through my teenage years
You would save me a lot of tears

I still have not said goodbye
Driving by your house still makes me cry
The family is not the same
Because without you we remain.

Jodi Bartorillo, Grade 11
Dallas High School, PA

Keep on Going

Every Friday night before I step out onto the football field the same thing runs through my head every week. I will play until I cannot go any more. I will give 110% until the whistle blows. I will keep pushing and driving until the referee blows his whistle no matter what is going on. I will drive my opponent straight into the dirt every time he comes to face me. I will break them down until they cannot move. The pride and strength of our team we will not be defeated we will never give up. The tiger's pride will never be torn apart.

Tyler Wager, Grade 10
Wirt County High School, WV

Mistaken Ambiguity

Hard it must be for a woman to love, but refuse to be loved
Can be trusted and can't build up the ability to trust
Questioning the very veracity of human beings, deciphering what was or could've been love as lust

You are determined to look into her eyes and do so for about a second before she averts them to avoid her gaze from penetrating your skin, and hoping you would be lost in the vast abysses of her eyes instead of intolerable pain

You see right through her and know that she's been hurt but she's oblivious to your discovery whilst her mind travels thirstily seeking trust, listening to everyone carp about moving on, but believing that "happiness is admire without desire"

Impervious to pain because she has built a barrier around her only to peer out precariously through her Venetian blinds, while you see only a shy girl with her hands clasped together or her arms folded

Wondering whether her journey for trust is eternal and whether or not she will remain unlovable

Unable to shake her internal pain that becomes a twinge when it just suddenly comes to her mind, forgetting that the past catches up with you

Trying unsuccessfully to move forward,
feeling like…her turn is skipped every time

Indigo Green, Grade 11
Wilson High School, SC

A Kite's Courage

Lying against the window, watching the minutes go by
Minutes and days that pass in idleness
My tissue paper worn and wrinkled, wooden dowels with dust sprinkled
I have but a feeble and frail frame with no power to change this standstill and languish life
Yet I often find myself facing the sky, a sky so boundless and free
Where dreams can grow and soar through the skies
Like a bird with newly grown wings ready to fly
And if there was only a day when the wind could blow just right
A day with clear sunny weather, no rain in sight
I would stand against that blue sky with the thick and dark ground below me
Feeling the force of the wind brush against my wooden skeleton
That pushes, pressures, and encourages me to fly forward
Then, I steadily drift toward the vast sky
I slightly tilt my tail and look down — the world below me feels smaller and smaller
And I see millions of envious eyes gazing at me in wonder
The sun slightly stings my tissue paper skin — I could care less
And despite the breeze tickling my tail, my paper-thin heart has not felt such optimism, greatness
The day when my walls could break down
The day when I no longer need to wait
The day when I have the courage to fly toward the sun, courage to make life worthwhile
So I lie against the window, dreaming of that day

Jennifer Li, Grade 10
William G Enloe High School, NC

Broken

It's here she lies for countless hours,
In a field of dying flowers.
Broken promises, broken heart,
Now she starts to break apart.
Tears form in her empty eyes,
Wondering how she believed the lies.
Broken sobs, from her broken form,
Cold numbness entering a body once warm.

Now she lies under a bed of flowers,
Proof that her soul was devoured
By the sorrow of love, it tore her apart:
His broken promises broke her heart.

Mikayla Bennett, Grade 11
Hilton High School, NY

Chi-Town's Greatest

I've been told I'm a failure
But I couldn't let it get to me
The crash bent me up
Is there anything left to be?
Jaw wired shut, couldn't even speak
I wrote a whole song, it got me closer to the peak
My career skyrocketed, the story about a kid
Who didn't finish college, I must be a nobody
Drama surrounds me about the songs I write
Like the one about Jesus, I had to fight
For it to be played
I've had good times and bad
George Bush drives me crazy, almost mad
But I'm happy I'm living and I know I'm the best
I've got that Roc-a-fella chain hanging over my chest
Now everybody knows my story, I'm Kanye West.

Grant Mummert, Grade 11
Hanover High School, PA

Selfish Case

I must justify this case,
my brain works at a rapid pace,
results of a pretty face,
is there love or just like,
I cannot find a trace,
while I stare into space.
My thoughts bring pain,
my friends say maintain your self-restraint,
I feel, I feel faint,
just tell them, I know she is not a saint.
They're starting to judge me by what she said,
my blood runs cold from hatred,
it feels like a bullet full of lead,
slamming, slamming, into my head,
my spirit is covered in dread.
Do they really know what came to be,
no, they're too blind to see,
it is not her whose heart is broken,
it is me.

Donal Buie, Grade 11
Overbrook School for the Blind, PA

Dear Beautiful

Dear Beautiful,

And until this day I dare not speak
Of the secret we swore to keep
Deep inside my young heart
Where all my truths were torn apart
And looking into your dark eyes
Like searching for stars in midnight skies
I find the truth to all my fears
The root behind all of my tears
I learned that forgiveness is for the strong
It helps you get up and move along
And now when I wake up every day
I forget the mean things we used to say
When I look at you, I see love
And that's how I knew you came from above
To warm my heart and make me smile
Make each moment seem worth while
And now I know wherever your heart goes
My heart beats faster and constantly grows

Love,
Your Precious

Jenna Mingledorff, Grade 12
Cambridge Christian School, FL

The Great Gatsby

The nights are splendid occasions
Full of wine, champagne, joy
Guests in the pool, more in the study
My brothers and sister all, they know me, they care
Every night they come, we party, we drink to happiness
This is the meaning of life

Let me show you my horses, my house, my car
Look at my money, my wife, my mistress
Am I not great, do you not envy
This is the meaning of life

What should I buy, how should I live
What do I want, what should I do
What do I lack, where is the joy
Where is the meaning in life

The money left, the friends soon followed
My wife departed, my mistress moved on
Who cares for me now, I'm still the same
Why do you flee
What is the meaning of life

Dan Colón, Grade 11
Council Rock High School South, PA

Me and You?

It's kind of scary you see,
To think about you and me.
I don't know what to do
Whenever I'm around you,
My brain just stops
And my heart it drops.
My knees they shake
Almost like an earthquake.
I want to be your lady
And to maybe call you my baby,
The way you make me smile
It always lasts for a long while.
When my hand is in yours
My heart just soars
I know you feel it too
Whenever I'm with you,
I see it in your eyes
You look so hypnotized.
I really do like you
But I don't know what to do.

Angelina Bradley-Russo, Grade 11
Bishop Kearney High School, NY

Promise

Time passes in a blink of an eye
what seemed yesterday is now today
two souls intertwined by destiny
part their ways
with only hope and memories
embedded in their heart
that someday
once more
they will become
one…

Kelvin Garcia, Grade 12
South High Community School, MA

Nature

The clouds all run
  So the sky can shine its best;
The trees part their branches
  To make you a path.
The grass grows
  So you have a carpet on which to lie.

Birds sing and fly and play and dance
  So your ear alone can hear,
And flowers bloom
  For your eyes to see.
Ink pens try to express feelings for you
  But fall short.

Nature operates under your control
  Because it alone can reflect you.

Gabriel Triggs, Grade 12
Newnan High School, GA

Time To

Way back when, when Jesus roamed in sin.
I remember way back when, when Jesus hung on the cross for me.
To think I am truly blessed,
I am blessed when I put clothes on my back; He hung on the cross for me.
I am blessed when I walk into my home; He sacrificed His life for me.
I am blessed when I step into my vehicle; He rose for me.
I am blessed when I nourish my body; He sprang his wings for me.
I am blessed to have the chance to live; He died for me.
When it is time for me to go, Jesus will hold out His hand and call my name.
He will say it is time; it is time to leave all of the destruction, sin, and horror behind.
It's time. It's time to die for Him to live in the golden gates in the sky,
Where all our troubles just fly and say goodbye
Yes it is time. Time to live an eternal life, and leave a wonderful world behind.

Damitri Robinson, Grade 11
Lancaster High School, VA

Let's Break Up

Don't you care about anything else
Than what I wear or about my physical features
Don't you care if I'm a good friend
The world is so twisted up with your lies
You said you loved me for who I am,
and that turned out to be a lie
You said I can be whatever I wanted to be
And that turned out to be a lie
You betrayed with your heart and said that I was your all
and that turned out to be a lie. I need something better
Someone that will send me a romantic letter
Is that you? No!
I need someone who loves me for who I am
Is that you? No!
Your love was as false as a fictional story
I realized you're not the one for me
too many secrets and too many lies
Your insincere apology just added more fuel to the fire
I don't need you I don't want someone that isn't true
I want someone that can be there for me
So, I'm moving on and you can too. Sorry, but I'm done with you!

Kiyana Hunt, Grade 10
Colonia High School, NJ

Don't Go

Please don't go I want you here I don't want you to leave me
I can't image life without you I don't know what life would be
You're hanging on by a thread living day by day
Not knowing what tomorrow brings I can't figure out what to say
You'll be gone too soon it seems I think of you all day long
Why must it be this way this is all so wrong
But there's nothing I can say or do I know it shouldn't be this way
And I feel I'm left with nothing I wish I knew what to say
My heart is thumping faster now and my mind just keeps racing
My legs feel as if they're frozen this, I don't feel like facing
So please don't go I need you here please don't leave me
I can't imagine life without you I don't know what it would be

Danielle Szoss, Grade 10
Deer Lakes Jr-Sr High School, PA

The Seasons

Sweet is the season of spring,
When flowers come in bloom.
The world begins to awaken.
Colors begin to show themselves.
The snow is banished.
New life is born.

Summer is of the sun.
The air is warm and skies are clear.
Fireflies brighten the night.
More birds take flight.

Fall is the season of leaves.
For it is the leaves that carpet the ground.
Colors paint the hillside,
As the leaves begin to change.
Birds begin to leave for their winter homes.

Winter,
The season of sleep.
White is its color.
All things prepare for next year,
As the plants and animals become dormant;
Waiting for another spring.

Callie Hitchcock, Grade 10
Randolph Central Jr/Sr High School, NY

Why?

What am I?
Why can't I do the things they want?
Why do I tell lies?
And make them think what they thought?
Why don't they see it as the truth?
When it really is?
Why can't I get anywhere?
Because of this?
Why can't I change the way I am?
Why can't they understand?
Why can't I make them?
Believing only what they see.
Why do I lead the path I lead?
Why do I see generous?
When they see greed?
Why do you change what I couldn't?
Why do they stop you?
When they really shouldn't?
They dream me a fantasy, and ask me to follow
I turned my once ambition filled heart to one now hollow
Help me change because life without you is so strange.

Sasha Stephens, Grade 11
Pittsfield Middle-High School, NH

Panic

It starts out as a nagging of yours
Keeps getting bigger and bigger
You think it's nothing
You go on with your day
You wonder why you're feeling this way
You go on with your day
You turn around and there it is
Right in your face
It takes you down with it
You can't get away
The only way to stop it
Is not to pretend it's not there
But to face it when you first come in contact
With that nagging feeling of yours
Panic

Conor Halbleib, Grade 10
Trinity High School, KY

Chrome

Hurt and hated
Until you came along
Played and betrayed
Until you came along
With your love

I was alone
Feeling as cold as chrome
Left out in the cold
Covered in mold

I was used
And abused
Ablated from happiness

Without you
I am nothing
Without you
There is no happiness
I love you

Komal Tejwani, Grade 12
Wesley Chapel High School, FL

The Sad Tale

It burns through the neck, and weighs down the mind
It turns them away, and cuts your soul blind
A pendant that mocks, a chain that tempts ends
The soul can't be healed, the wound never mends

A heart has been broken, another begun
A third into chaos, the rest, they shall shun
It does not help any, the time they have lost
Their comrades are asking, "But why at that cost?"

But at the conclusion, she takes off the chain
And hands it to him, whom feels nothing but pain
For the loss of a loved one is nothing to bear
And in this sad tale, all hearts shall not share

Daniel Albro, Grade 10
Fairfield Warde High School, CT

Her Dance

Dance is like a blooming flower.
Her dance is a man's lust.
Why is she dancing?
The girl is filled with happiness.
The touch of the nice cool fog mist.
The sight of seeing her on the moon
With the smell of relief.

Dancing is like approaching heaven.
It is love for someone filling the air.
Her emotions pouring out.
With every step taken.
With the feeling of music playing.
Dance filled with romance.
But who is she dancing for?
Her love for dance is a painter's masterpiece.

Ekta Kothari, Grade 12
Colonia High School, NJ

Lonely Path

Walking down a lonely path,
Hearing the breeze dancing along the trees,
Seeing flowers sleeping in the sun.
Peaceful and quiet, soft buzzing bees.

Yet there is a rose with death lingering near.
Without a friend, on the lonely path.
Fallen petals scattered along the wind,
Exposed to the sun's full wrath.

What did the rose do to deserve this?
The most beautiful flower among them all,
Only one suffering this particular fate,
Yet closer to death the rose falls.

No one is there to know about the rose's fate,
The flower no longer appears,
For death has taken it within its hand,
Only to see a fallen tear.

Shelby Page, Grade 11
Thomson High School, GA

The Value of Life

People are asked what they value the most
Answers vary depending on the various;
Family, money, friends, jobs are tangibles
Love in families;
Happiness in money;
Trust in friends;
Security in jobs
Can't be touched, but seem to always be there,
Making us take tangibles for granted
What should be valued the most
Is life, which shouldn't be taken for granted
Because without it
Tangibles are a lifetime away.

Kim Goidell, Grade 11
Harborfields High School, NY

You

Your evening breeze caresses my face
Your calming waters soothe my soul
Your exciting nights enchant me
When we meet I long that summer never ends
Your thunderous silence engulfs me in my solitude
I yearn for you during the seemingly endless year

Brittanie Papaconstantinou, Grade 11
Bayside High School, NY

The Womb

Artificial insemination in the hills of Boone,
　　the merciless seed of progress forced deep inside
　　　　a land that died alongside another race.
The tops of green breasted mounts crumble,
　　too dry to provide for the ever rooting mouth of civilized society which,
　　　　in its advancement, caps the breasts with steel towers
　　　　as if there was anything left to contain.

There are no cries or pleas
for mercy because the trees
have no mouths in which
to produce a cry or a plea.

And this is how the womb is built
　　　　not by God or the
　　divine　　mechanisms of the body
　　　　　but with dynamite and profit motives,
plastics and machinery producing the Child and a new
world of vacation homes sprouting upon
the green hills of Appalachia.

William Kilgore, Grade 12
Tarpon Springs High School, FL

I Built a Bridge

I built a bridge

To get over the easy and the hard times
To cross and look over when I'm down

To make my tears float away
Underneath there is a sea

Words can't describe what this bridge does for me
It could teach me the right and the wrong

It taught me to grow up so I could be tall enough to see over
The bridge is like a guard it protects me from bad and opens for happiness

I learned from it I made a path
A path towards the right direction instead of falling down

I want to get to the point where I cross the bridge
Go to the other side look back and say I MADE IT!

Chelsey Gerlat, Grade 11
Devereux School, MA

Delicate Daisy in Memory of Shawntae

The beautiful, yellow, delicate daisy
    sitting in a field where it is meant to show happiness
    shows such sadness in my eyes.
This daisy is supposed to show joy
like the fist roller coaster we rode together.
        She screams on the ride
    like she probably screamed the last seconds of her life.
This daisy stands alone in a field of memories
that will never be forgotten or lost.
    This daisy represents all that I have left of her
        all the happiness of my very best friend.

Jennifer Cooper, Grade 12
Cullman Sr High School, AL

On the Road

Joints, bars, clubs, cities, states
Were all places Sal Paradise wanted to see
Life was to have no gates
Life meant just to be
So he set out on the road
With his friend Dean Moriarty
Who spoke in a secret code
A code that was an indecipherable priority
At first, many friends surrounded him
Among them Sal, who was inspired
Their adventurous whim started to dim
Drugs and jazz and sex had expired
They had traveled many places together
As their thoughts drifted apart
Sal could not live like this forever
Dean lost the holy heart

Nadiya Freylikh, Grade 11
Council Rock High School South, PA

The King of All

The heavens marvel and the seas glisten,
The mountains are resilient,
The forests towering.
The eagles soar while the deer roam.
It is only by your hand that all was created.
El Shaddai: God Almighty
I look at how you've blessed me and am speechless.
You've given me a home, a family, and a church.
You have supplied all my requests.
What else could I ask for?
Jehovah-Jireh: The Lord Provides
I used to be scared of many things.
Death, injuries, being alone.
You've changed all that.
There is fear no more in this once timid girl.
Jehovah-Shalom: The Lord is Peace.
On the cross you hung for all to see.
Not for yourself, but for me.
You paid my debt when I could not.
You made a bridge and God now I can see.
Elohim: God, Majestic and Strong.

Amanda Pickle, Grade 11
Samuel W. Wolfson High School, FL

The 'B' and the 'F'

I sit, I think
What does it mean?
Frozen in time
Not a second goes by.

Everyone stares and thinks OMG!
What do I do?
This has never happened to me!

I open my eyes
And to my surprise
A smile starts to grow.

My used-to-be BFF
Says "Well? Hello?"
With his curly hair and his deep blue eyes,
My BFF sighs.

Just drop a 'F' and find a new BFF
Because I just got a new BF
Including my first kiss!

Tiffany Alvarado, Grade 11
Loretto High School, TN

Is It Fair?

Is it fair to say the world is safe,
When man is killing man?
Is it fair to say "I cannot do it,"
When the soldier says "I can?"

Is it fair to fight a war,
For a cause that is unknown?
Is it fair to give up life;
Eye for eye and bone for bone?

Is it fair to say that we are better,
When in fact we hide our fears?
Is it fair to say that we are stronger,
When in fact we pour our tears?

Is it fair to live in fear of death,
And spend your life secluded?
Is it fair to just give up,
And say that life's concluded?

The truth is it's not fair,
To think that we have won.
The truth is he will always fight,
Before his efforts come undone.

Klevis Xharda, Grade 10
Peabody Veterans Memorial High School, MA

True Love

Looking in his eyes
Saying "I do"
Telling him that I love him
And that he loves me too
Together forever
For always now
As we speak
That wonderful vowel
With the ring
You slip on my finger
Tears fall down
As we start to kiss
This is the moment
I never want to miss
Being with you
For the rest of my life
Is going to be
The best years of my life
Paula Shepherd, Grade 11
Anderson County High School, TN

Moving Still

She sees him standing there
She wants to move closer
But she can't move
For something is holding her there
She is bound by something so she
Cannot leave
He sees her standing there
He moves closer to her
Just close enough to place
His hand on her face with the
Most gentle of touch
Emily Nelson, Grade 10
Hudson High School, FL

Evenfall

It is not light,
nor is it dark.
This is a haze
which rests amid
two enemies.
We are awake,
but sleep is near.
Now is time
to return home
as the fading sun
stains the sky
opalescent.
And we chase the rays,
before blackness rises.
Katy Sternberger, Grade 12
Portsmouth Christian Academy, NH

The Dilemma

Had I only thought twice,
As I was walking home late at night,
My heart started pounding with great fear and fright,
I heard, the sounds of
Two coldhearted men beating on an innocent child with great anger and rage,
The cries of a young boy pleading for mercy,
Many pedestrians passed there, but no one seemed to care

So there I stood with a fork in the road,
Bearing this heavy load,
If I act I might get caught in the riot,
Or should I just remain quiet,
Having endured experiences in both joy and tears,
I was sure that my decision was well made for my years,
Deciding to just walk away, I knew that the guilt would always stay

The next day, as I routinely opened the morning newspaper,
The front cover glared at me with much shame and disgrace,
The headline read "Young Lad Brutally Murdered,"
My hands began shaking as I felt my body trembling,
Next to the title was a picture, a picture of my dear nephew,
If I only knew it was you, I would have tried to save you,
Had I only thought twice.

Ilana Shimunov, Grade 12
Shulamith School for Girls, NY

My Voice

Indecision is synonymous with my state of being
The future is only one continuous line of choices
Of questions and answers
Of decisions
Of selections
That will forever alter one's life
How is one sure when the answer is right?
When the choice is correct?
When the selection is beneficial?
Even as my brain makes the conscious decision to record these thoughts
My mind questions their significance and hesitates with each staining of the paper
With these words that may or may not be effective
That may or may not be significant
That may or may not be profound

The words of others continue to invade and perplex my psyche
Until they all become like the maddening static seethe of a radio
And the only intelligible station
The only voice that one can make sense of
Is the voice articulating these words
Articulating these words
Articulating these words

Alexis Jackson, Grade 12
The Christian Academy, PA

Am I Worth It All?

You took me by surprise
You were so different from any other guy
You showed me that they're not all the same
and you made me realize I was not to blame
You make me happy
Even when I'm so down
You've helped pick me back up
and turned my life back around
You can make me laugh
Even when I want to cry
and you think I look beautiful
Even at the worst of times
I don't know how to explain you
You're the absolute best
I'm so glad you stuck with me
and ignored all the rest
You know you didn't have to
put up with all this mess
but for some reason you thought I was worth it
I have no clue why you did
Because I know I don't deserve it!

Kelsey Bare, Grade 11
Sullivan East High School, TN

Rush

The cheers get louder
You know it's almost time
The crowd starts chanting
It's your chance to shine.

The lights shine brightly
You take a deep breath
The practice you've had took hours on hours
You have nothing to fret.

The crowd gets silent
You know everyone is watching
Most are just watching you
There is a few who keep talking

The music starts
It's like your heart pumps more blood through your veins
It happens so fast
After it's over you know you'll never be the same.

Fame is such a beautiful word
Something we all wish we could conquer
The line between normal and fantasy
Is it a lot to ask for.

Holly Parris, Grade 11
Loretto High School, TN

Blank Heart

An unwritten book
Seeking an author's hand
Ink and thoughts,
Pen and mind,
These are the tools that are used
To write upon my
Blank heart
Fill my pages
Rival the sages
Give in to the fever of my blood
Please, steady hand,
Create a loving destiny
For my
Blank heart

Christopher Michael Chaloux, Grade 10
Eckerd Family Youth Alternative School, VT

Musing

Shall I begin to study Love again?
Shadowed by past greatness, I falter, shake,
Forced to match talent and wit if I can.
Yet my Muse whispers, ceaseless, "You must make."

Troubled, I arrange these words side by side,
Knowing my meaning is bound to some flaw,
In describing her grace, its endless tide,
But forward I strive, emotion still raw.

Burden! A burden of pleasure and pain!
The flow of ink marks my only release.
To labor in silence for her is gain,
That I might perfect Love, defect decrease.

Love is her name, to love Love is my goal,
To grasp her image is to grasp her soul.

Jonathan Lin, Grade 12
Whippany Park High School, NJ

I Must Go and Visit the Jungle Again

I must go and visit the jungle again,
With the vines from the trees
And the sweet sound of the chirping toucan.
Oh! How I love the jungle in the midst of its many wonders,
Nature's beautiful harmony serenely whistles in the wind.
The trees prostrate to the friendly creatures beneath,
Shielding nature's sublime beauty.
The rain stops abruptly,
And I feel the intimacy of nature.
How I love the harmonious tranquility
Of the chirping toucan
And the sweet echo of the ribitting frogs.
Nature's song is an ineffable spectacle,
Affectionate and waiting to be
Heard like a maternal bond to a child.
As the night closes its door on the day,
It is time for me to leave.
For I will be back tomorrow…

Jim Schwoebel, Grade 12
Newnan High School, GA

Ze Green Spaceship!

Matt's car is what I call the green spaceship.
Its color is a mix between the Caribbean Sea and an oak tree swaying gently in the breeze,
Creating a color that makes the spaceship itself.
It has a mind of its own and you never know when it will beep for your safety.
If you close your eyes, you will be at a loud concert.
The kind of music that will leave your ears sore and throbbing.
The spaceship is as spacious as the sky,
Its windows are covered in clouds of fingerprints.
Every print with its own individual story to follow.

I will help keep it clean from anything that comes its way.
With my money, I will buy it air fresheners,
It will always smell like it rolled out of the car wash; dirty or clean.
I will protect the spaceship and keep it forever with me.

Jenna Mitch, Grade 10
Colonia High School, NJ

Julius Caesar

Julius Caesar thought he had the prerogative to be the king, little did he know his death would it bring.
Brutus ascribed Caesar to be the fall of Rome, there was only one choice so he and the conspirators met at his home.
Cassius thought of Caesar to be an abomination, for it was he who wanted to be the one to rule the nation.
Cassius wheeled Brutus into joining his side, then Brutus became the leader now the rules Cassius must abide.
Together they contrived a plan that would be talked about forever, some people though don't consider it to be too clever.
Many omens came the night before his death, "Et tu Brutus?" he said with his last gasping breath.
On the Ides of March Caesar met his doom and was killed, while Brutus felt sorrow, Cassius was thrilled.
Antony was angry but he played it cool, he made Cassius and Brutus both look like a fool.
The conspirators weren't a motley crew all being senators and such,
After Antony spoke the crowd decided they didn't like them too much.
Cassius and Brutus ran with the Romans in tow, Brutus was angry with himself for stooping so low.
Killing Caesar turned Brutus into a corrupt person, his actions didn't help Rome, the consequences only made it worsen.
Octavius was Caesar's great nephew who he named heir to the crown,
He and Antony created an army and many soldiers willing to fight they found.
Shakespeare uses his vitriolic nature throughout the course of the play, that makes readers want to stay.

Ali Zinman, Grade 10
Council Rock High School South, PA

Fate

Fate hath grasped the reins of time, in an attempt to warp our minds,
To batter us with horrid thoughts, and strike us down when we think not.
It lurks around each turn we make, and follows us within the dark,
Waiting for the perfect day to strike us all, and pierce our hearts.

The pressure that boils from beneath our flesh, rises to the surface with a hindering rush,
And blurs our minds with a lightning flash, causing all we've known to end,
With a gruesome crash.

Though, fate, it seems to have no flaws, it cannot hold its grasp on all,
For some it makes but empty threats, while others seem to conquer it.

From these words it should be clear, that fate itself is watching you,
And if you fail to realize this, then fate is sure to follow you,
It will engulf your heart and mind, and swallow, every piece of flesh, and while the others pay their dues,
You must pay the greatest one, for though your life had just begun,
All you've known has been undone.

Brett Harvey, Grade 10
Jackson City School, KY

Make Your Move

A chess game before you and me.
We both stare but neither speak.
A pawn or two and a rook you've taken.
I've found myself a knight, but am I mistaken?
Those dark eyes watch mine.
Come on, stop wasting time.
A hand on the chess piece; make your move.
In anticipation, all I can do is wait for you.
I contemplate your stares and glances my way.
What's to come in this silent game we play?
The chess board is still and so are you.
I'm waiting. Come on, make your move.

Jaylee Strawman, Grade 11
Northwood Academy, SC

For My Grandfather

I called on angels to lift your pain away,
Machines will never know you like I do
Suff'ring stops in the shadow of the day.
I know right now what it is time to say,
Though I've never missed someone more than you
I called on angels to lift your pain away.
Soon my eyes swell up and tears fall astray,
I can't help to think you're part of my loved few
Suff'ring stops in the shadow of the day.
As I walk to where you silently lay,
I've felt your love for me; so pure and true
I called on angels to lift your pain away.
And to this very moment I sit and pray,
That I'll see you again in that sky of blue
Suff'ring stops in the shadow of the day.
On this ever-so gloomy month of May,
I'll remember your wink; the 'I love you' clue
I called on angels to lift your pain away,
Suff'ring stops in the shadow of the day.

Gabby Grano, Grade 10
Plainview Old Bethpage/JFK High School, NY

Invisible Girl

Invisible Girl
Hiding in the shadows
Underneath that dark cloud of sorrow
Out of sight to anyone who may love
That transparent face of yours
Invisible Girl
You are no stranger to pain
Your scars wrap around your broken and frail body
And the numbness has kicked in long ago
In your world of agony and defeat
Invisible Girl
Who has done this to you?
The tears on your face
And the hurt in your heart
Will surely fade away
If you step into the light
And let your soul be free.

Danielle Palmieri, Grade 10
New Haven Academy, CT

A Sea of Kindness

What can be said about your kindness
All that you have done for me
Was for the sake of love

For years you have given to me a precious thing
A thing so worthwhile all else seems to be nothing

From you to me bestowed a great knowledge
A knowledge of care, of generosity and happiness

With a smirk you turn a tear of misery to a tear of joy
Your hug gives to me a state of bliss
I think of all that is good when you give me a kiss

This day that honors you
I would like to give you a gift
Take at mind where it came from
And the creation that would grow to love you so much

A sea of kindness you gave to me
Here is one drop back

Daniel Cabrera, Grade 12
Rutherford High School, NJ

Persephone

Her voice is the howl of the cold winter wind
The ice of her skin makes any man cringe
The dark of her hair blots out the sun
Persephone has come; winter has begun.

Down from above, to sit by her King
To her gown the shadows cling
Daughter of life, to death made wife
Leave behind the stillness of a dark winter night.

When she walks the Earth, the green things grow,
Men rejoice, the river Styx runs slow,
And who would think that her evil groom
Would, in his heart, for her make room?

Who could know the loneliness he feels?
Who knows that at her sight, he instantly heals?
Is it possible for death to feel love?
To mourn for his wife, so happy above?

In her heart does she dread the return to his side?
For she was unwillingly made his bride
Now his wait is all but done,
Winter has begun; Persephone has come.

Kelsey Pratto, Grade 11
Peabody Veterans Memorial High School, MA

Love Watchers

She watches the swan,
Glide in the water
Just like the eyes
Of someone you love.
Looking down on you,
You watch the sunset,
Emerge on the faces of the good
Also on the faces of evil
It's just like the fear
Of being near you again.

She watches the moon
And in the moon's face
There is a picture of you,
Smiling, smiling and warming the soul,
To create peace with you.
Love watchers
That's what they do.

Sara Winslow Foley, Grade 12
Devereux School, MA

The Warrior

I am a mighty warrior
Dressed for battle
My weapons are the words
Of truth!!
I am a mighty warrior
Dressed for battle
Bowing before the Lord
My God!!
Seeking wisdom…
Asking for the words
Of truth
Expecting miracles
For this nation's youth!
Mother, warrior, and
Servant of God!!

Gregory Perkins, Grade 10
Heritage Private School System, FL

A Masterpiece

Lines are endless.
They create shapes of all kinds
They create words for expressing
And above all,
They create the opportunity of art.
One line, is just a line
But two is an artwork,
And three is a masterpiece.
Landscapes, portraits, and abstracts
Started from one single line
Followed by two and three
And finally,
A masterpiece.

Colette Weaver, Grade 11
Hanover High School, PA

Your Music

Music seems to fill the air like the oxygen we breathe,
The words escape our lips without any thought.
Words that protrude happily in harmony,
The music in your soul is nothing to be fought.

That song you're hearing is from deep within
Coming from struggles you went through but never stopped.
Just open your mouth and let the feelings flow; that is how to begin.
The freedom that song gives cannot be topped.

It is happening to people everywhere;
Their unique songs of triumph are coming out.
So go ahead and sing your song loud, without care,
You have been through too much junk not to shout.

That music is yours, brought through adversity.
Now all you have to do is open your mouth and sing.

Brianna Danae Harris, Grade 11
Elmira Christian Academy, NY

Ubi Sunt…?

Where now are the kings of old? Out of ken
They have passed, their pyres forgotten.
Where is the bright sword shining, and the high helm gleaming?
Where glints the ring-mail? Where reigns the ring-giver?
Out of mind they have fled, and out of memory wandered.
Where now are the wise? Their wisdom,
Long in the gathering, is swift in the losing;
The lore of long ages is lost to us.
Where is the harp-string sighing, and the minstrel sadly chanting?
Where is the golden feasting hall, and the honey-mead flowing?
Beyond the grasp of song they have gone.
So must all things pass until the world is changed.

Joel Sams, Grade 10
Sams Home School, KY

Looking Glass

If the world looked in a looking glass, what would it see?
It would see war, death, and destruction.
It would see homeless mothers and children dying by the millions.
It would see orphaned animals giving birth to more whose lives would be forfeit.

If the world looked in a looking glass, what else would it see?
It would see charity, forgiveness, and goodwill.
It would see parents adopting orphans.
It would see families graciously giving animals homes.

If the world looked in a looking glass, what else would it see?
It would see both good and evil.
It would see both war and peace.
It would see children both abandoned and adopted.

If the world looked in a looking glass, it would see many things.
It would see which practices we should keep, and which we should abandon.

John Diana, Grade 11
Manus Academy, NC

The Mother We Disappoint the Most

Stop to stare,
Wait to glance,
Look deeply everywhere,
Slow it down every time you get a chance.

What are we doing?
Some people don't get it,
No further we are moving,
Disaster is what we commit.

Once beautiful nature,
Gorgeous open land for miles,
Now nothing more than an old picture,
Not even to get the slightest smiles.

Dirty streams,
Nasty air,
Disintegrating atmosphere,
More and more houses everywhere.

List of many problems,
Where does it stop?
When does it end?
Something positive needs to develop.

Clinton Bullock, Grade 10
Gloucester County Institute of Technology, NJ

Wish

Holding hope and holding dreams
Restitching lives along the seams
Told to stars, to friends you make
Or told to candles on a cake
Written down on New Year's Eve
Made for returns when loved ones leave
Millions falling at your feet
Someone lost you'd love to greet
A peaceful day without a war
And some for those who just want more
I float through windows and walk through doors
I fly sky high and crawl 'cross floors
You jump for joy and cry wistful tears
When I come to end your fears
I solve all problems and ease all days
I help you through in gracious ways
I can break through walls and bring you home
From whatever place you roam
I'll save your life when you don't know
I'll take you where you need to go
I'll give you anything that's true, if I only come to you.

Mollie Hutchings, Grade 10
Argyle Central School, NY

My Funny Valentine

Oh my funny Valentine
Where has gone the time
I hope you know that I am yours
'Cause surely you are mine

Oh my funny Valentine
Let's take a walk down lover's lane
By nightfall you will be glad
That my young sister hadn't came

Oh my funny Valentine
Sit and stare at the moon
The sweet words that come from your mouth
Make me feel as if I might swoon

Oh my funny Valentine
Where has gone the time
I hope you know that I am yours
'Cause surely you are mine

Kaitlin Bresnahan, Grade 10
Haverhill High School, MA

Worries

Every day is filled with worry.
Every night is filled with pain and sorrow.
No matter what I attempt to do.
Worries keep coming through.
The best thing for me to do,
Is continue to be positive,
And refrain from being down and blue.
Every morning I wake,
I pray and ask,
"Lord give me another take."
(on life)

James G., Grade 10
Audubon Youth Development Center, KY

In This Mirror Is What I See

With uncontrollable curls that mock me every morning
and these so called amazing blue eyes
people take me for a dumb blonde
but my hopes and dreams will never die

I am just a girl with way too many burdens
no one knows how hard it really is to be me
because I choose to be safe
I only trust few to really see

my life may look all grand and happy
but you have yet to see
I guess I'm just that good of an actress
to make people really believe

two girls and seven boys: but I am the older of three
there was always football; no Barbies for me
but when tackled I don't pity myself
I don't mind growing up like this,
because now I am a girl who can take care of herself.

Gracie Compton, Grade 11
Cullman Sr High School, AL

What Spring Means to Me?

Spring means flowers blooming
Spring means trees have leaves
Spring means warm weather
Spring means cool breezes
Spring means life
Spring means animals come out to play
Spring means wearing a cute sunny dress
Spring means open toed shoes
Spring means bright colors
Spring means happy not too hot sunshine
Spring means school's almost up
Spring means honeysuckle
Spring means allergies
Spring means a lot to me
It's my favorite time of the year
It's not too hot or cold
And the plants and animals just start coming out.

Rosa Moore, Grade 10
Seneca High School, SC

The Savages

We're in the 15th century
And we're here to take control.
We're here to tame the savages,
Their ignorance pains my soul.
Those Africans, they're savages,
They need our help and we'll provide,
With European dress and style
They'll surely be on our side.
We only want to help them out,
But we may benefit as well.
But that's what imperializing is,
Those savages think that it's hell.
We're proud to be European,
Nationalism, is what it's called,
We love our culture and background,
We'll do anything for it — don't be appalled.
We'll kill and insult the foreigners,
To get the resources that we need,
You think it's cruel but it is not,
Industrialization, we will heed.

Esther Whang, Grade 10
Townsend Harris High School, NY

Her Smile

When her lips depart,
and her dimples set in
this girl with a smile is beauty with no end.
When the door is closed,
and her smile is gone
it will stay hidden away until she sees your eyes,
and how they start to respond.
She hides behind her smile,
so that no one can see
the ache in her heart; the forbidden plea.

Brandii Bonham, Grade 10
Swansboro High School, NC

Unity

Loyalty in our families to true friendships
Unity shapes our society
Unity keeps our nation strong and prosperous
Unity is blacks working with whites
Unity is peace among our fellow European countries
Unity is our bond with the rest of the world
Without unity, our success will turn to failure
And all that we strive for will turn to dust

Ronney Gant, Grade 11
Thomson High School, GA

Regret

Maybe one day when I look in the mirror
Regret won't be staring at me through the glass,
Her cold, lackluster eyes searing my soul.
She takes no prisoners — Regret
One rendezvous with her and she's a scar,
Her infected tissue spreading, spreading,
Until your entire entity is brimming with ancient, withered wounds.
She's ever-present,
Those patronizing pupils never wasting an opportunity
To slow your steps,
Wear your bones
Until you feel aged centuries beyond your existence,
Like a heap of soil beside a grave being excavated,
She continues to grow.
And you can't help but shovel alongside her,
Contributing, defenseless
To your own misery.

Sarah Horton, Grade 11
Heathwood Hall Episcopal School, SC

Causes of World War I

When you think about World War I,
Do you know what caused it?
Was it one factor?
No! There were many that started it.
Alliances were a huge reason why
Tensions grew among nations,
The Triple Alliance and the Triple Entente,
Proved to be harsh creations.
Nationalism, Militarism, Imperialism,
All were causes as well,
Their effects on countries
Pushed people to fight and hope to live to be able to tell.
Is this all?
Of course not —
Don't forget the unification of Germany and social unrest,
After all, each cause led to the killings of a lot.
But the biggest spark of all
Came with the Archduke's death.
After he was assassinated by a Serbian nationalist,
Austria-Hungary declared war after the duke's last breath.
If it weren't for all these causes, World War I may have never started.

Ivana Ilic, Grade 10
Townsend Harris High School, NY

Recital

As I wait offstage in black silence
For the music to start and the curtain to open
Reviewing everything I can in my head, shaking with nerves
I see the light on the stage through the opening curtain
The music begins and I await my counts
To appear on stage, with all eyes on me
I run out to the center, and nail my leap
Run to my position, pirouette, piqué, fouetté
My smile so wide to express my excitement
As I see the connection I made with the audience
This song is quickly coming to an end
The best part is near, the final bow
At the tip of the stage I stand
Looking far out into the crowd
Knowing my parents are out there watching
And supporting me the whole way
I know I have made them proud
And pleased everyone else that watched
As I run off stage to be again with the black silence
But a different feeling comes over me
I am now accomplished

Ashley Gaston, Grade 10
North Tonawanda High School, NY

All I Ever Wanted

All I ever wanted
was to find someone like you
to see down deep inside me
below the surface of my skin.
Someone who won't admire what meets the eye
but respect what's in my heart.
All I ever wanted was to find someone like you
to stand beside me through it all
no matter thick or thin.
Someone to love me
even after beauty fades in age.
All I ever wanted
was to find someone like you.

Kesha Leshay Jerrell, Grade 10
Thomas Walker High School, VA

Ill-appreciated Pain

A bent page, a snapped twig
A soiled broken thingamajig
The torn cloth, the burnt note
The dirty old seldom-patched coat

The death of an ill-appreciated thing
Its beauty lost like a broken wing
It's never wanted yet always there
The wall flower smile, the last time-cracked stair

It waits it hopes for just one chance
But dies of want before its dance
Its last move, one of patient love
It dies, the crow before the dove

Eileen Streeter, Grade 10
Mount Ararat High School, ME

You Were My Rock

If I leave here, will you remember the years?
The days of adventure that made us smile,
Crazy nights and hay ride fears.
You were my best friend, my solid rock,
I stood up for you when others would mock.
I didn't care, I thought you'd be,
Right there standing up for me.
I found out how fleeting friendship can be,
How easy it seemed you took from me,
The closeness I thought would always last,
Now just part of a painful past.
No longer your life am I now a part,
There's no room for me in your heart.
I've taken chances since you shut me out,
Through life, I'll take another route.
I can't say that it doesn't cut,
I tore my heart open and you sewed it shut.
But they say you must live and use what you learn,
So next time the pain will not so burn.
But I promise I thought you would always be,
An important part of my family.

Marissa Miller, Grade 11
Chapman Christian Academy, AL

The Virtue in My Mind

Love is patient, love is kind,
This old virtue spins in my mind.
Everyone says that this is hard to find,
But I think I was just left behind.

Another one is, you see,
That beauty is in the eyes to be.
The one you see under the sky,
Is the one who will fly.

Also, all the stars in the sky,
Each can tell a story, even some wishes to fly.
You can wish your wishes every night,
Especially if you want your wishes to take flight.

I don't know how long this will be,
But we shall clearly see.
I can only ponder on my thoughts of love,
Until I find that one dove.

So, love is patient, love is kind,
This virtue is still in my mind.
I'm now having trouble to find,
But at least I'm not that behind.

Robert Reyes, Grade 12
Raritan High School, NJ

Old and New

Our visions clouded
by the once forgotten diaries;
depicting our pasts.

Smiling eyes while
we read each word carefully,
lost in time.

Sitting out by
the old tire swing, we propel
our dusty imaginations.

New words mean
that our future will be
brighter than before.

Sunlight heating up
the morning, we draw cursive
lines and giggle.

Drowning in the
pages of our books, we
hug and forgive.

Annie Walters, Grade 11
Chatham High School, NJ

The Great Gatsby

The Great Gatsby is more than meets the eye
Jay Gatsby was not just a wealthy man
Jay Gatsby was not just a lavish host
Jay Gatsby was not just an ambitious lover
He was a lot more than that
He was a friend

From the moment I heard of him, he was a mystery
It seemed no one at his parties knew who he was either
He was like a target in hide-and-go-seek that could never be found
He was just a pile of rumors

Without a doubt, my opinion changed when I met him
Behind his visage of mysteriousness and wealth and luxury, there was unhappiness
Gatsby was deeply in love with a woman who was already married
He was determined to win her back

He eventually got what he wanted
So it seems his story ended happily ever after
But although his life was a party filled with guests
His death was a ghost town filled with nothing
To those who did not know him, he remains an enigma
To those who did know him, like me, Nick Carraway, he remains a friend
A special, special friend.

Elisa Swank, Grade 11
Council Rock High School South, PA

For He Is a Flower

With a smile so bright
He lights this world like
A daisy or a sunflower

Although flowers grow in the ground,
He also grows on me

His stem stands tall and proud
Just as he
Nothing thrives off him
Because he is so pure and honest

His beauty is that of a flower's
Different colors
And an everlasting aroma

Through a drought
When thirsting for water
He may appear weak
But only gains strength

For he is my flower
And one day I will pick him
To hold forever

Megan Connor, Grade 11
Thomson High School, GA

Friend

It's May 29th
2nd period Spanish class
I don't understand why I even took this class
The teacher goes on and on and on and on, she doesn't even know my name
So bored
Finally my best friend walks through the door, no one can see him but me
I wave to him and he waves back, I usually see him in every class
But couldn't in 1st period because I had a test
He comes to me and says, "what's up"
He is such a happy-go-lucky guy, never caring about anything
I said, "what's up Sleep, where you been"
"Oh someone in Dr. Castleman's class called me, I'm here now"
Sleep sat on the empty desk next to me
We got into a heated discussion on who would win the NBA finals
We both had Lakers and Celtics in the finals
He thought Boston would win, I thought Lakers would win
Sleep always won in arguments
He said Paul Pierce, Kevin Garnet, and Ray Allen would lead the Celtics to victory
I was just about to say that Kobe and the Lakers would never lose
When I heard my name, the teacher and the class were looking at me
Sleep ran away as usual, I got stuck with detention for sleeping during the entire class

Jacob Sebastian, Grade 12
Central High School, PA

Music

The sound to your ears.
The hideout from your fears.
An escape from reality.
Joy for both she and he.
The beat of your heart.
A true form of art.
A nutrient to the ear.
Evolves each year.
More significant than just a sound,
when creativity and imagination are found.
Comes from the soul and mind.
Lyrics and sounds entwined.
Triggers memories from long ago.
Varies from up tempo to slow.
Can be heard almost anywhere.
From the chirping of birds, to a drum's snare.
Has the ability to move a crowd.
Played in your head or out loud.
It even travels from place to place.
It also can vary from race to race.
Music.

Shayla Lawz, Grade 10
McNair Academic High School, NJ

Journey

The pallid lady stood above,
The caps and shawls and beating hearts.
Stately and commanding,
She promised to shelter them.

On Ellis Island it was another story.
Roughly inspected, amid noise and confusion,
The thumping hearts were forced
To give up the first of many things.

The many things that would change for them,
That had been a part of them.
In this great big stew,
Boiling in the melting pot of New York.

And so they changed their names,
And their surroundings,
And their neighbors.
But did they exchange their culture, too?
Or let one become part of the other,
Being of neither one or the other,
Yet both at the same time.
These immigrants — dreamers, seekers and adventurers
All gazing up at Lady Liberty.

Isabella Oledzka, Grade 10
Townsend Harris High School, NY

A Son's Love*

Dad, without you in my life,
It is always a struggle and fight.
No matter what I do,
I will always love you.
I know things between us were not always right.
Nevertheless, you did not have to take your life.
Sometimes I ask, God, "Why?"
However, I cannot help but break down and cry.
If you were hurting that bad,
I would have helped you because you are my Dad.
When I cry I know it will not be my last,
But I can't sit here and dwell on my past.
I could have helped you through it,
But you went ahead and blew it.
When I had to lay you in your grave,
I felt like I became the devil's slave.
Even though you are gone,
I am going to remain strong,
Because we still have that father and son bond.

Johnny A., Grade 10
Audubon Youth Development Center, KY
*Dedicated to my father.

Summer

The smell of the ocean beneath my nose,
The sand all stuck between my toes,
The cool water touching my feet,
Places to go and new people to meet.

School's finally out, we're without a care,
The warm summer breeze blows through my hair,
It's time for vacation and loads of fun,
How sad I'll be when the summer's done.

We'll have our license to do what we want,
New sunglasses to wear and cars to flaunt,
Staying out late and sleeping in,
I don't want the school year to begin.

Haley Thomeczek, Grade 10
Peabody Veterans Memorial High School, MA

A Teenage Girl's First Crush

A teenage girl's first crush is…well, crushing.
Her body isn't hers nor is her mind.
She finds herself shivering, shaking, and blushing.
Weak, tormented, sick and going blind.
And why? Because some guy might look her way.
Then cast his eyes as quickly to the ground;
Some special one, for reasons she can't say,
Whose voice makes her feel faint when he's around.
But now my crush on you has been returned.
And so the two of us stand on some brink:
It can't be love so young, and yet we've learned
Love does its thing, no matter what we think.
Slowly, slowly now — we mustn't rush:
Let's enjoy this first sweet teenage crush.

Mariam Savage, Grade 10
Parkdale High School, MD

Animals We've Become

Caged; locked up behind bars in factory farms living in conditions far from sanitary or natural.

These animals are the ones who have to suffer and pay.

Beaten and killed unjustly every day.

Enduring the pain, no one seems to care for these social, intelligent,

maternal creatures with strong, magnificent, beautiful features.

For what purpose are they killed? For gluttonous pigs of the 21st century?

In a time when we are so anxious to attain peace, we are the living graves of these "murdered beasts."

So I ask, how?   How can we sit here satisfying our appetites with slaughtered flesh?

When these wondrous creatures God created deserve the right to life

just as much as any human being is granted the right to life and the right to live.

Cold-hearted and cruel, people may never see the light, for they are more stubborn than any mule.

So now who is the stupid species?

When we, humans, are the real dummies.

Twisted and morbid, people disgust me with their torturous ways.

For those who rape poor animals of life for the purposes of food are pathetic.

For these marvelous creatures are no different than you and I.

They have their own language, they reason, and they are loyal.

So I ask why? Why do we kill?

When God's marvelous creatures deserve the right to live and the right to life.

Cristina Corsetti, Grade 10
Durant High School, FL

Hell in the Hardwick Hills

Gray rays emerging from the moon's lustrous craters created an austere August scene

The moist dew drops of day dampened the tarp-like covering of the cabin,

In which a sense of languid torpor lingered with the fumes of parasitic mildew

The dire odor of Dial soap blended blandly with the fungi, and emerging from the mixture was the stench of cheese blintzes

A variety of different-sized horseflies hovered about the cabin's conflagration of forgotten holiday lights

A sudden swish of swift feet in deep sleep broke the mundane beat of heavy breathing

Tremulous scuttles rattled against the warranted weather protected door

A burly, black-bodied beast buried itself in a burlap bag to escape nature's moist tyranny

Its oversized hide belied the rising sun's exothermic warmth

Day is welcomed by the "thud" of music vibrating against the fiberglass of windowpanes

Dawn has broken nighttime's grim encounters

Marisa Sanders, Grade 12
Hackettstown High School, NJ

My Love

Who I love is special, how I love is unique, makes the warriors weak and mutes speak, turns tangible into supernatural, imaginary into real, transforms geniuses into fools, teaches cold souls to feel, gives the dead heartbeats, makes poets' pens dance across sheets

I love hard, pouring out pieces of me, ignoring the ignorant who don't know how I feel inside, giving me just a textbook definition of what love should be, using words as chains, barricades rusted by contempt, forged of steel to hold down young hearts guilty only of reckless love, crazy love, I pray to God above love doesn't taste like this, like the fruit of oblivion, I hope true love doesn't feel like this, every time I get it, it makes me wanna ball my fingers into fists

Love is for fools and I'm too smart, I don't want to have spectators as my heart gets torn apart, I don't want to be clay in my lover's hands, shaped and bent to fit a standard for society's sake, I'd rather have no love if it means I don't have to be fake, forced to fit into the model image of what people want to see, if I have to be chained by love, I'd rather be free

Who I love is special, how I love is unique, it made a warrior weak and a genius a fool, taught me from experience, more than I could learn from school

My love is strong, destined to last to world's end, makes me feel like "wow," it makes me feel guilty as sin, I find myself fighting new emotions that are surfacing within

Love is hard to get and keep every day makes you want to sit and weep, it makes atheists kneel down to God above, it's a deceptive concept, but my young heart does love.

Terez Heckstall, Grade 11
Bertie High School, NC

Nature's Crimson Wonders

Old, tainted Japanese maple,
Small and withering beside the gate,
Branches reaching up to heaven,
Crimson leaves waiting for autumn's fate.

Stepping silently across the branches,
Smooth and broken, twisted and old,
Fragile framing supporting my creeping,
Across the bark covered in mossy mold.

Tar patched bandages heal its wounds,
Of age and generations before me,
Keeping the tree alive through this day,
Beneath each patch another story.

Pushing out through the branches up above,
I gaze into the skies of blue,
Watching as the cotton clouds get brushed by the crimson wonders,
Hoping one day, its life and strength will remain for you.

Erin Sinnott, Grade 11
Saugerties Jr/Sr High School, NY

Writing Poetry

In class today I was told to write a poem.
I never know what to write about, I can't do it alone.
When I go home I sit down to think,
nothing ever comes to mind, maybe colors — blue or pink.
I could write about unicorns or the sky above,
I could write about ooey-gooey things like butterflies and doves.
I'm not very sentimental because I'm only sixteen,
so I could write about my future as a potential beauty queen.
I could write a haiku but it seems a tad too short.
Oh, I just don't know what to do, I'm all out of sort.
Once I have a topic set there is still much more to do,
there are many steps to write a poem but here are just a few:
the rhyming part is hard sometimes because it sounds lame.
Hopefully this poem wins a contest to bring me riches and even fame.
You have to be original or else that isn't good,
the more and more I thought about it the less I understood.
As you can see poetry does not come easily to me,
but if you say this poem is great, I can't help but agree.

Kelsey Incrovato, Grade 10
Peabody Veterans Memorial High School, MA

My Room

Light green, yellow and pastel pink
Sometimes messy but always safe and comforting
Whiffs of memories, experiences and learned lessons
Pictures jump out from every wall, every dresser, and every shelf
They capture smiling faces and hugs wrapped in love from different occasions
Dead roses sit on my dresser, wilted but still beautiful
Every time my room is entered
It is a reminder of where I have been
And where I am going

Margaret Taylor Cain, Grade 11
Heathwood Hall Episcopal School, SC

I Dreamt

I dreamt
you were around me
holding me together
as my ribs burst
and flowers grew from my chest
and your arms intertwined
and became safe vines
and your slow breathing
echoed like the wind
as my eyes pooled to seas
leaving streams from mountaintops
I dreamt.

Kat Daly, Grade 12
Robert W Traip Academy, ME

The Controller

I have love in my soul
And I don't wanna let go
Freedom's in the air
It flows through my hair
War and peace run through my veins
How do I remain sane?
I'm in control
While the world's a black hole
My eyes a brown calm
No sweat on my palms
The might of my brain
Can bring an end to this game

Jacob Kramer, Grade 11
Harborfields High School, NY

Love

Love is like the endless sky.
It just keeps reaching out,
Even though you may
Think there is no more.

Love is like the ocean.
It is so deep and full
Of wonderful things.

Love is like the Earth.
Sometimes its course can be smooth,
While other times,
Its course can be rough like a mountain.

Love is like a rosebush.
It is so beautiful,
But at the same time,
It can hurt you.

Love can be compared to many things,
But nothing is the same,
Because love is unique.

Alicia Escoto, Grade 10
Albert Einstein High School, MD

She's Never Been in Love

She's never been in love,
this bored and jaded girl,
never been held to touch,
no one cares for her brunette curls.
Stubbornly she's refused to dress,
in slim and skanky fashion,
and no one is impressed,
with her brilliance and her passion.
So she's never been in love,
and so beautiful she'd be,
for someone inclined to look,
love would be so easy,
but she's never been in love,
a statue in Eden,
unseen, untouched,
her dreams and desires,
out her beatless heart are bleeding.

Jennifer Michaud, Grade 11
Mercy High School, CT

My Favorite Place

A house hidden in the woods
Screen doors slamming
Wooden floors creaking
A picnic table anticipating company

Worn trail to the water
A long metal railing
Water lapping against the dock
Friends splashing in the water

The tangible form of summer
The promise of fun
The lakehouse
My favorite place

Emily Traylor, Grade 12
Newnan High School, GA

Collateral Damage

Ready, set, hike
The ball goes in motion
Everyone moves, everyone reacts
I am gonna kill the running back

Right, right, right
He takes off running
I follow quickly
We collide, he falls to the ground

He is out
My head is hurting

Devin Brunsvold, Grade 11
Middle Tennessee Christian School, TN

Fireworks and Fish Tanks

I looked on softly, patiently, waiting for a storybook's epilogue.
Fairy tale lies came back to haunt me, welcomed yet spited, they fused with my body.

I would watch crystal fish dance
in the pools of moonbeams in your eyes,
the black silk of someone else's hair,
the bubbling in my face.

Quilts of minor chords wrapped me snugly in a whole note
whole rest, where I dwelt for days like ages.

But I was in love with a jigsaw puzzle
that was missing the one piece I needed the most.

And I was always there,
looking on from the sidelines and ignoring all stop signs.
Seeing you see me, among other things like tombstones and cobwebs.

And I was there, too,
   to see the sun leave your eyes,
      to see you crumble before me
         like a forgotten statue.

Christopher Janigian, Grade 12
The Providence Country Day School, RI

My Last Goodbye

Ever since I was young
I've wanted to work with Special Ed children
At Barry Tech Boces I volunteered
At HiHello Daycare Center in Freeport

As I arrive at the center, I see my four year olds wave down to me from their window
I wave back with a smile on my face

My last day rolled by and had to say my last goodbye to the children
Raven, Amanda, Alejandra
Told me they wanted me to stay forever
Pablo, Gabriel, Sebastean
Said I was their best friend
Aceli and Jasmine told me they love me

I've celebrated a variety of holidays with them
Celebrating with them is the best gift a person can receive

Working with them has been an experience I can *never* forget
Saying my last goodbye was really hard to do
I became so close to them

Now I work at Marcus LEEDS Daycare Center with my 3 year old Special Ed kiddies

Samantha Gastman, Grade 11
Massapequa High School, NY

The Incalculable Soul

What is our role in the universe?
What are we in the grand cosmic scheme?
We define ourselves as "humans,"
But what are the traits behind man?
We chart our world each day with rulers and graphs,
but what device can decipher our souls?
The essence of man's existence,
our reasons for love and despair,
all endlessly debated,
but never resolved.
What is this answer we're all looking for?
Is it some immaculate graph,
a concrete linear path,
something that says here you are and there you'll go.
That's a device we never shall have.
Nor should we aspire to gain.
So what is all this you may ask?
The truth is,
it's for us to decide.

Danny Nemati, Grade 10
Ragsdale High School, NC

I Am Woman, Hear Me Roar!

It shall not be long, until it is known
Until you realize that your phone,
My clothes and the money from the car loan
Are all gone, to the great world of unknown

Is it not sweet
To sit in your seat
And regret the times we did not meet,
Contemplate,
Separate your thoughts
Trying to figure, out what went wrong.

An epiphany,
Come to realize, that I am gone
Stop, and listen, you hear it ?
A loud penetrating silent…sound
For I am woman, hear me ROAR.

Ferneldra Carty, Grade 11
Leonardtown High School, MD

The Final Seconds

The time is quickly passing,
Warriors staring into the eyes of the beast,
20, 19, 18, the beast charges,
The ball is thrown through the air 17, 16, 15,
Hearts beating out of their chest,
Screaming coming from the stands,
Everything comes down to this moment in time 10, 9, 8, 7
Hoping for success, we all hold our breath 6, 5, 4,
The clock is ticking,
3, 2, 1, the buzzer sounds as the warrior hits the ground,
21 to 19,
The Warriors have claimed their victory.

Ashley Freeland, Grade 11
Wirt County High School, WV

A Dose of Reality

Imagine not having the splendors of today's world
and instead, being technology and fortune deprived.
Imagine that your only luxury
was your strong willpower to survive.

Imagine working through the stifling heat,
the searing sun merciless towards your struggles.
Imagine not having a drop of clean water
to quench your thirst or troubles.

Imagine knowing that the rich feast daily,
yet for you, there's not a crumb in sight.
Imagine malnourishment, of feeling feeble and weary,
afraid you'll disappear into the night.

Imagine losing parents to malaria and AIDS,
each day feeling pangs of sorrow.
Imagine fighting a constant battle, you against the world,
never knowing if you'll make it 'til tomorrow.

This is the life faced by many children in Africa
who've lived through hardships our minds couldn't envision.
To send them food and water and vaccinations to live —
in other words, to help them is our mission!

Janelle Viera, Grade 10
Townsend Harris High School, NY

Depths of Reflection

That which must make one
So incandescently happy, I do not know
Perhaps I shall only recollect
The pointless encounters, though
Those times were few and insignificant,
For the joyous moments of mine,
Although force me to put a smile on this face,
Only add to the false pretense that I'm fine.
The cause of this downfall, I dare say
Is yet to be determined, for
The results are quite inconclusive
Only to sacrifice is to find out more.
It is not when or why
This cynical thought was for me to find,
It is a matter of how and who
Has sincerely inflicted upon this state of mind.
This manner of perverse thought
Is acquainted with very few —
Only those who knew me were able
To attempt to understand what I knew.
But perhaps…I just do not know.

Elaina Mercatoris, Grade 12
Brookville Jr/Sr High School, PA

Endless Summer

Oh, how I wish it were summer again.
Oh, how I miss my toes in the sand.
Oh, how I wish I could hear the wind crying.
Oh, how I miss all the seagulls flying.
Oh, how I wish I could hear the roar of the ocean.
Oh, how I miss the smell of suntan lotion.
Oh, how I wish summer was here to stay.
The endless sunshine would chase my worries away.

Hannah Wigal, Grade 10
Wirt County High School, WV

Creeping In…

Confusion, paranoia, destruction constantly creeping in…
Amongst this atmosphere of failure there seems no chance to win.

Lost in the suffocating toxic of hatred and abuse,
Strays a once radiant love whose presence is no longer in use.

Forgotten in the cryptic mystery of corruption and fear,
Lies affection and compassion, which once were so dear.

Drifting within a whirlpool full of rejection and betrayal,
Wanders honesty and faithfulness, now hidden behind a veil.

Smothered under the stifling stench of rebellion and spite,
Is the sweet perfume of peace, now dwindling in its might.

Masked behind a benighted barrier of pride, doubt, and despair,
Sits a mass of eroding hope, seemingly crushed beyond repair.

Arrogance, lust, depression constantly creeping in…
Despite this atmosphere of failure, there's still a chance to win.

Alethia Johnson, Grade 10
LAMP High School, AL

Amelia White

"Dance Amelia Dance," that's all they ever say
for dancing is life, right?
They want me to be tippy tip toeing
shoulders pop popping
fingers rapidly moving
choreography abiding
body always gliding with the beats
their pride dancer, Amelia.
"What a future in dance Amelia has."
Yet how foolish they are, for Amelia's heart is not dancing with the beats.
I want to paint. Painting is my life.
Beats never looked more beautiful then with color.
And the colors blend together on the canvas. No, not blend, dance.
The colors dance together on the canvas.
They dance in one swift motion then collide into each other with my command
Because I am their choreographer.
My little colored dancers. My, what a secret talent I have!
Amelia White, the dancer of colors!

Kaitlin Torres, Grade 11
Paramus Catholic High School, NJ

The Right Choice

I drive away,
But I seem to go nowhere.
The long and dusty road
Keeps growing in the vast distance.
I find myself stuck-in-a-rut
In my confused conscience.
Do I turn back to my everyday life,
Or do I keep going in seek of a new hope.
I finally let go of this feeling in my heart.
Taking months and months to burn out this kindling flame,
I am finally relieved that I can now move on.
But now that it has returned,
I don't know what to do.
Should I trust my heart and try again,
Or will I just be tricked and left hopeless in the dark,
Knowing I wasted my time for nothing.
But you don't seem to realize what I went through
To try and get you out of my life.
But now that you're back,
Give me one more chance and hopefully,
You'll feel like I do.

Frank Cannella, Grade 11
Harborfields High School, NY

The Road to Hope

Dark plants a seed of the light to the east
The sea of gold springs from
A small crack in its hard shell
Hailing over the frozen world
With an Overture of Fanfare
Awake from the darkness
And see the world
Full of gold

What truth lies beyond the road to the light
No one knows its destination
Only the fear grabs the feet
Before thinking of failure
Take an adventure
Towards the glimpse of light
And see the truth yourself

The land where you arrive
May devour your hope with ease
Yet what if it does
A price follows every grant

Go forward on the road to hope
And see the truth yourself

Sunjae Park, Grade 11
Roslyn High School, NY

My Love for You

After this year we have spent together,
I know that our love is forever.
Not knowing your love before,
Now I couldn't love anyone more.
You are the one that I cherish,
With my love that will never perish.
Enjoying the company of a friend,
With that love that never ends.
Through these moments that we shared,
I can tell how much you've cared.
We spent these moments full of fun and laughter,
Knowing something is waiting, it's our happy ever after.

Jennifer Robinson, Grade 11
Jackson City School, KY

Future

The hot, moist heat brushed on my skin,
the calmness of summer was starting to set in.

As I sat looking at the ocean my thoughts began to race,
thinking of how I am going to eventually leave this place.

I will be in a new setting with no one I know,
new people I will meet, new places I will go.

It is scary to think that I will be going far away,
will anyone remember me, the person I am today?

I wonder if I have done everything I could while I was here,
not reaching my potential in this place is something I fear.

The future is blurry but it sure does look bright,
the sun sets on the horizon and I know all will be all right.

Elizabeth Leone, Grade 12
Massapequa High School, NY

Mom

Hello Mom,
That's the only name
I have ever really called you.
So insignificant,
So boring,
So ordinary —
You would think that the name I know you by,
The name that I have chosen to call you,
Would better reflect
Who you actually are.
For you are not any of these things.
Important,
Interesting,
Special.
These words are more suitable
For you.
They are far superior to others,
And you are far superior to most others.
You deserve better.

Andrea Alfano, Grade 10
Bronx High School of Science, NY

Brother Sitting
My brother screams,
I pull my hair,
My daddy acts like he don't care.
A sippy cup,
To ease his nerves,
Baby sitting's for the birds.
But it's not long,
Till it goes dry,
And now is when I start to cry.
Our mom comes home,
And daddy sighs,
Another weekend's passed me by.
Mary Beth Allen, Grade 11
Loretto High School, TN

My One and Only
I never thought I would find you.
The perfect guy just wasn't there.
I looked all my life.
There just weren't any anywhere.
You walked in and out of my life.
I never thought you'd stay.
I wanted you more than anything.
Every night I'd pray.
Then my prayers were answered.
And now you're all mine.
Having you is like a dream come true.
You make my whole world shine.
I thank God every day,
That I can call myself yours.
You're everything I ever wanted.
I love you right to the core.
I never want to lose you.
You'll be mine forever.
You are my one and only.
You'll never be an endeavor.
Tiffany James, Grade 10
Schley County Middle/High School, GA

Pressure in the Pocket
The pocket is collapsing
But no need to rush,
The fans are going crazy
And I wish they would hush.

The first option is to scramble
The second is to throw.
I think I'm going to run it,
Never mind, I'm too slow.

There is no one in the flats
And the tight end is gone,
But thank God there's a receiver
Wide open in the end zone.
Brandon Turman, Grade 11
Thomson High School, GA

512 Sichuan Earthquake
The blue skies suddenly turned dark and gloomy,
The grounds of Sichuan started to quaver, and a second later…
It is scattered into pieces filled with the deceased.
As family members cry and plead longing for their beloved,
Pure hearts discretely tear.

Anguished cries penetrate through minds of many.
The silence and tranquility in which heaven performs upon cannot be foretold.
Children are lining up for heaven, for massive sufferings bring faint hope.
Sorrow overwhelms the world where tears of many…
Becomes ice and slowly melts away by the light of candles.

Ripping apart and quivering every soul, is this horrifying earthquake.
The once enduring home of many lively souls…
Is now corrupted by numerous desperate cries.
With optimistic faith, in an anxious call of searching…
Stay strong and preserve for a better tomorrow.
Kristie Tse, Grade 10
Environmental Studies High School, NY

Where Would I Be Without You?
Where would I be without you?
Somewhere dark and cold.
Like a lonely snowy night.
Me not looking for a new best friend,
you came into my life so unexpected.
Being so quiet and shy and me so loud and obnoxious,
and when I least expected it you were there for me when no one else was.
I know I could never replace you with anyone.
Because you have been there for me through thick and thin.
Jen you're my best friend and I would be lost without you
so promise me you will never leave!
Shelby Kozlowski, Grade 11
Home School, NY

Skynyrd's Innards
The crew finally loaded up the gear, as we wiped away our family's tears.
Goodbye is the last thing we say, before we get on our way.
Sitting in the plane, we're all looking around.
Pilot comes over the speaker, this thing's going down.
We all have one last drink and think of a better place.
We fear the thought of looking the good Lord in the face.
I tried to live my life right, staying out of trouble and fights.
I tried to live by my mama's plan, and be a simple kind of man.
The ground's getting closer, the trees are getting bigger,
somebody call the grave digger.
I think I see Jesus; He's waiting on me.
Guess I'm like a bird; I'm finally free.
Turns out I shouldn't have been so scared; the Lord's a pretty cool guy.
Told me and my friends we could live in His mansion in the sky.
Well don't ask me no more questions, I won't tell you no more lies.
Guess it's time for me to tell my fans goodbye.
Even though I'm gone, I'll always be around.
'Cause I'll live on through my songs.
Josh Quinnelly, Grade 11
East Central High School, MS

My Love

My love for You is one of a lover;
Your reflection is the spark in my eye.
I know I am safe when in Your cover,
I love when I am Your uttermost cry.

My love for You is a most grateful one;
Your gifts to me are Your own hand's design.
I can't give back for the things You have done,
So I know Your love for me is divine.

My love for You is as close as can be,
I love midnight talks underneath the stars;
And when You dry my tears so I can see.
My love for You, and you…me, is just ours.

I have many loves, to You I do bring,
But my respect for You is of a King.

Noelle Chamberlain, Grade 12
Elmira Christian Academy, NY

Never Let Go

I never knew I could hurt like this
And every day life goes on
"I wish I could talk to you for awhile"
"I wish I could find a way to try not to cry"
Then time goes by

Although you'll reach a better place,
Still I'd give the whole world to see your face
And I'm right here with you
It feels like you were gone too soon

I'll be lovin' you always.
Lift your head to the sky cause we will never say good-bye.

Victoria Caso, Grade 11
Mount Olive High School, NJ

Searching

For one to look for something
It first has to be gone astray
Misplaced inside of a space
Where it possibly can't be displayed
Digging deep and hard
And the outcome seems to vary
I get so tired of looking for that one thing
That it drains me out and I get weary
It's all cluttered under a mess
That just won't come clean
But when I discover what it is
I will know exactly what it means
Looking for what you really need
Seems to be sufficient
But you just might lose yourself
Looking for something different
So when it comes to what's right for me
I won't need anything else
By just searching inside of me
I can find what I stand for in myself

Trey Foy, Grade 12
Wando High School, SC

This Land Was Made for You and Me

They say this is the place to be,
To live, to laugh, to love.
So we, ten million strong, came
Life may not be easy;
We eat differently,
We speak differently,
But we found friend and family

The other day, I met a new friend.
His parents were doctors.
I knew what's next.
I did not know how to reply.
Sir Nimbus high above us, darkened and cried.

Then another day we saw a lady
Who spoke of a program for us
So we can light up our caves a bit.
We continued sewing and mowing,
Cleaning and selling, and in a blue moon,
We find ourselves buying.
But we found a spark, and with another one
It might just turn into a warm fire.

Meng Meng Zhu, Grade 10
Townsend Harris High School, NY

The Best of Me

Chaos and clutter,
That's how I see my life.
But I don't know what I would see
If I could see me through Your eyes.

Would I see a child that brings glory to Your life,
That speaks Your name without the cares of this world's strife?
Or would I stare into the eyes of someone lost and afraid,
Searching for the hope of yesterday
And wishing that tomorrow would just go away?

Lord, I stand before You now,
As a child who has lost her way,
To examine myself and with all my heart to say,

I know I have not done my best for You.
I have let the devil get the best of me
But Lord I'm willing to let all of me go
And come to You and be made whole.
I know I'm not perfect,
And never will I be.
But I pray You hear my cry,
And make the best of me.

Molly Littrell, Grade 11
Loretto High School, TN

Dusk

They are coming they are coming are coming to here
To hear the glorious rattle of our life-throat as it dies, falling away along with the petals as our roses gracefully descend
into the evening light
So that their morning vines may shoot above at the crack of next dawn, using our decay, our fragile disintegration as sustenance,
Ashes for nourishment, for those who are coming

And as they approach, as we see their dust cloud augmented against the horizon,
We know that our time has come to succumb
And politely bow in thanks to life,
Before throwing our souls into the sky, thrusting them in fistfuls beneath the topsoil, casting bits off in paper sailboats to float
down the familiar river
The river that will not cast them asunder, knowing its responsibility as bearer.

We finally bring forth that long-hidden ruby-red smile. The one of intimate acceptance, that bares the inner conscience naked,
proud. We finally find the treasure in the last waning moments, after so long.
And so comes the tears, the pearls reserved for this time,
Entrusted to those whom we love, so they may keepsake our jewels within them in this way
We are sharing ourselves and each other, scattering the soul to where it would be most useful, most appreciated, most
treasured, permanent. Safe. They mean us no harm —
It is just our time to fall, with lightness
together embracing, together letting go.

Jacqueline Voluz, Grade 11
Staten Island Technical High School, NY

stuck

i'm stuck in between the world with so many people, so many places, so many contradictions, and so many personalities, so
much potential but it's not being shown, so much hate and not enough love, so much fear and not enough hope, so much lying
and not enough honesty, so many gangs and youth dying but not enough comfort for who's crying, so many hungry and not
enough nourishment. at the end we're all looking for *love*!!!!!!

DeSean Irby, Grade 11
Bonnie Brae School, NJ

Love Twisted

Pay attention, learn some lessons,
Stay focused; keep your mental thoughts motivated,
Flowing through your mind like a person in a maze trying to find a exit,
Lasting so long you get distracted,
Not being able to bring up the last thoughts you had made of, take a deep breath,
Think for a second, ease your mind to a tranquil state,
So peaceful and calm, all thoughts coming back so clearly,
As if never forgotten, strangely felt as if had have been lost at one point,
So many mental states in your mind at once, coming and going, never staying too long,
With every thought different emotions occur.
Anger, depression, sad, confused, oppression,
Yet many more, but lost once again in a maze, a maze of love, twisted in every bit of way,
Can't ever find the way alone, bright light shines someone waits at the end,
Who knows how long they waited, maybe this could be it,
This could, no this is, where your true love waits for you to be by their side,
Under their love and care,
The compassion of the two so vastly open as if handpicked by love itself,
Just for the two to be. Guidance, protection, love and care,
Ever so close, bonds so tight,
Unbreakable as the chains that open the gates of the heavenly above…

Alvin Colon, Grade 11
Eastridge Sr High School, NY

September 11 Memorial Tree

There is no communal grave here
No one's buried here at all
And it wasn't here that whirlwind
Took my loved one in its fall

Everyone used to live their own life
Better worse but living though
Death's a terrifying fairy
Took them all in one great blow

And in one scary, hot embrace
Their souls turned to the sky to flee
And in this quiet park they come
Back to us and our shar-ed tree

In this branch is someone's son
And in that one, reappears the dad
Mommy, brother; and on that leaf
Is a baby never had

There is room enough for all here
To you, we give our earthly bow
There is no communal grave here
No one's buried here at all

Aleksandra Sher, Grade 11
Staten Island Technical High School, NY

The New Past

Time has come, many years have passed
People have changed no one to recognize
A new past growing up moving place to place
No more home to call my own
Starting a new day with a lot to say
No one around to hear me express myself in many ways
Confused and upset
Yet no home to stay in again
Alone in the dark is where I guess I must take my stay in
No one around no one to love or be found
Or felt just a tiny bit is all I ask for a little family
Perhaps here could be the beginning of the starting
Past is that too much to ask?
All I want is to make it right again
Where I would have somewhere to stay
And feel welcomed again
With no type of uncomfort or threats in my way
Here I go again starting a new past just taking the ride of stress
Free happiness no fights drama or anyone telling me what to say
Do or act so here we go again
Starting the new past again.

Mariluz Lopez, Grade 10
Miami Beach Sr High School, FL

Upside Down

Thrashing wildly, unsure which way is right,
I stumble blindly through the grating night.
Am I moving forward, or is a trap awaiting?
The only voice I hear is utterly degrading.
Listening past unearthly screams,
Running from the tormenting dreams,
Blocking out the deceitful charm,
I still can't tell if I'm headed for help or harm.
A voice calls me, instructing where to go.
But how can I be certain, how can I know
That I'll be embraced in a protective hedge,
That He won't lead me too close to the edge?
Yet I am blind, but He can see.
Must simply trust that He'll guide me.
Without Him, I'm sure to drown,
Because right side up seems upside down.

Cynthia Pullin, Grade 10
Grace Christian High School, VA

Our World

I step outside and I am in amaze.
I cannot believe the beauty in which I gaze.
I run my fingers through my hairs.
As I feel the breeze of the unfortunate polluted air.
I lie down and nap in the grass.
But I am disappointed when I am surrounded by trash.
I want to do something about the garbage.
So I can better appreciate the foliage.
I sit up against a tree.
And I wonder is this really me?
I look up at the sky.
And I wonder why o why?
Why do I cry?
I touch the tear from my eye.
And as I remove my hand from my face.
In my heart I know this damage is damage I cannot erase.

Daniel Packard, Grade 10
Haverhill High School, MA

Hold Me Close

Every moment I love you more
You turn from me with rage
I'm sorry, will you love me
Just say yes that's all you have to do
Tell me you love me and I will hold you forever
I am free when I am with you
I once was told that maybe I'm afraid
It was the truth but now I am ready
I am ready to love you
Hold my hand and I will show you
Trust me again, I want to know you
Smile at me the way you do I want to love you
Hold me close and I'll show you
Hold me forever and never let go
I love you

Meredith Kinley, Grade 11
Lee High School, AL

Sunrise

The beauty of a sunrise all agleaming
As it casts its beautiful morning light.
Starting a new day as you are dreaming;
It is a truly amazing delight.

When you wake up and see its bright new wonder
You are happy to see a new day.
It breaks through the dark with great asunder,
A wonderful beginning to a day.

As you wake for a day of glorious school,
You see the sunrise and you then go on
Knowing you have not yet broken a rule,
A smile on your face as you go beyond.

It is a promise of a brand new day
And you want to go on without delay.

Carrie Marshall, Grade 11
Elmira Christian Academy, NY

Snapple

Snapple is the most amazing drink,
It makes me energetic and think.
Snapple lemonade comes in yellow,
Snapple makes me feel very mellow.
I drink Snapple every day,
It's never ever hard to pay.
I collect a lot of Snapple caps,
Diet Snapple won't make you fat!

Snapple is like a waterfall drop,
Once it starts to pour it doesn't stop.
I would die for Snapple,
My favorite flavor is apple.
Snapple is like my own little addiction,
It's out of this world like science fiction.
Snapple is made from the best stuff on earth,
I must have drank it at birth.

Louis Garbarini, Grade 10
Colonia High School, NJ

Winter vs Summer Nights

A winter's night is nothing like the sun
It drains your energy leaving you weak
During these nights you don't have any fun
All I long for is to hear someone speak
Sitting here alone I get lost in the dark
Waiting for the warmth of the sun to come
I wish I could watch the sunrise in the park
When it's warm outside I am never home
Now I feel the sun beat down on my face
I run and play at the beach with my friend
When I go hang out I have my own space
This is how I wish all summers could end
Now you see why winters are not for me
All summer long the beach is where I'll be

Carley Irvin, Grade 11
Harborfields High School, NY

My Father's Kitchen

The business coat resting on the stairs,
The smell of juicy steaks drifting inside,
The sizzle of the browning okra, crisping in the pan,
The sweet smell of apple pie coming from the oven,
The sliding of paws against the tile floor,
The echo of Seinfeld coming from the next room,
The clatter of dishes being pulled from the cupboard,
The smile of a man I'm proud to call my father.

Katie Barton, Grade 11
Heathwood Hall Episcopal School, SC

I Am From

I am from
A beautiful town,
Where people stay strong,
So if you feel that, sing along.
Because they know how to work together.
I am from
A place doesn't cry,
A place doesn't suicide,
A place which is extremely alive.
Because they know how much their life worth.
I am from
A place filled with dreams,
Achieve goal by working with teams,
Mark their plan on the sheet.
Because they know what they want.
I am from
A place filled with happiness,
Has no sadness,
People's hearts have all kindness.
Because they know how to forgive.
I am from a place which is imaginary, which always exist in our hearts.

Mengdi Wu, Grade 10
LaGuardia Arts School, NY

The Blank Page

My anger grows as this page remains wordless
Kills me inside as I can't release burdens
I long to fill this page with meaning and purpose
So lost in my thoughts to find what the first word is
My heart grows heavy, weighed down by rage
I can't stand the thought; I'm a slave to a blank page
So much pain and hate and sorrow that I'd love to give away
These emotions are my focus, how do I not know what to say?
This page laughs in my face with a tone of irony
As it fills me with the frustration that first inspired me
I start to stress over my life and the hell I hold inside of me
As the thought of the blank page all but fades entirely
The thoughts of life fill me with hate and starts to burn in me like fuel
I'm sick of being abused for simply following life's rules
And with thoughts set on pain and how this life is so cruel
I take a step back and realize my page is full

Joshua Thomas, Grade 12
Woodstown High School, NJ

Softball

Up to bat.
Take a swing.
You can do anything.
Just remember, don't swing at balls.

Here comes the pitch, take a deep breath,
It's not like I'm facing death.
It's just a game; it's just a game,
Here comes the pitch; Swing!

There it goes, there it goes,
It's heading for the wall!
Uh oh! It's gonna be a foul ball!
Oh no! It's fair! Was that a catch?!

"She dropped it! Keep going!" I hear the fans scream.
I run, I run at my top speed.
I head for third; oh yeah! I'm there!
Do I keep going? Do I dare?!
Alexis Ambeliotis, Grade 10
Peabody Veterans Memorial High School, MA

Peruvian Sunrise

The bright sun peeks over the rise
As it illuminates, brightens, enlightens the skies.

Islands of peaks creep out of the shade
Revealing the marvelous carvings our God has made.

Crevices of shadows wrinkle the land
Each intricately carved by one mighty hand

Cotton candy clouds blanket valleys below
As more and more landscape begins to show

Like a curtain drawn back to let us see through,
A beautiful sunrise reveals my first glimpse of Peru.
Brittany Carmack, Grade 12
Peachtree Ridge High School, GA

Childhood

There is a boy who's growing up, it's the last thing on his mind.
He is stuck within his childhood
    when everything was fine.
He misses the innocence and dwells on the past,
    the times he really wishes would last.
In a bizarre way he fights to hold on
    to what he has, before it's all gone.
His feelings are kept covert
    and he is misunderstood.
He acts quite debonair,
    the way he thinks a seventeen year old should.
The responsibilities of growing up
    are tearing him apart.
He wants to stay young forever,
    the dream he holds in his heart.
Ashley Wright, Grade 10
Council Rock High School South, PA

What I'd Rather Not Admit to My Mother

Flowing with youth,
Despite her age,
She's one sly sleuth,
One clever sage.

No thought crosses my mind,
Which she fails to decode.
Her soul can't be confined
To such a dull abode.

She aspires to explore
To study and to learn
This zest I just adore!
For this passion I yearn!

She's admirable for sure.
But then, why wouldn't she be?
So wild and yet mature.
Just a replica of me.

We're so alike, both so iconic.
I can't deny the similarity.
I sound conceited, but it's ironic.
How she's better than me at poetry.
Hera Bokhari, Grade 10
Bronx High School of Science, NY

Last Chance

I remember when you walked on me then.
I was broken hearted,
Disillusioned with memories,
I couldn't find you anywhere.
I guess that means it's over now,
And I don't know what to do.
Because now I'm lost.
I lost my personality,
My smile walked away,
And never showed its face again.
I don't know my own name,
But I know it's far from what it used to be.
I was happy as a kid, and now I can't smile.
I felt that I was lost for good, but something changed.
Now someone is walking back to me,
She had my smile in her purse, and my name in her wallet.
She gave them back to me.
I know my own name again,
And erased bad memories, that took me away before.
Now that I'm not alone, I've never been so alive.
I'm alive now, but I'm still working overtime.
Paul Buono, Grade 11
Washington Township High School, NJ

Beauty of Nature

Green trees down a wooded forest
Purple lilacs blowing in the wind
Leaves crackling beneath my feet
The creek flowing rapidly
Beautiful butterflies fluttering around
Blue jays chirping in the wind
Nothing relaxes me more than nature

Samantha Key, Grade 11
Thomson High School, GA

Stay

As much as I want for it to come true,
I know I can't force you to love me
the way I want you to.
Will you make me feel better
or run away forever?
The trust I had for you was undeniable
and the love for you
will forever be uncontrollable.
I'm standing here waiting
for you to come,
but my heart is telling me
it's over and done.
Will you run away,
or will you stay?

Tina Nieves, Grade 12
Patchogue-Medford High School, NY

Helpless

you stare at me,
constantly trying to
figure me out
you NEVER will
this amuses me
I laugh silently to myself
my heart and soul
both dead inside,
what happened to me?
I HATE myself,
caring less and less
with each passing day
cradled like a baby,
my body is numb
I feel nothing
in the mirror I stare blankly
my eyes dead as buttons
listen, can you hear me now?
nothing,
silence,
I am free!

Alisha Kauffman, Grade 11
Hanover High School, PA

Refraction

I see the fragments of what could have been
Inside a part of the dreaded mirror, broken,
And it troubles me not — though my deepening slumber can
Waken, hearken back to talk of thoughtless times

Simpler, I think, it might be surer — back when no sort of life was art or creed
And I could give a glance through child wide eyes, let it go and forget the deed

Broken mirrors are cruel in what they reflect — and the image — shatter'd remains
But it is truer — and I will see it never fades —
I never wish to be again a silhouette

One day I learned the puzzle pieces fell,
Picked them up, rewarmed them from the ice
Not the least bit frightened but aware — Inside I was reflected twice.

[I see a girl with a dimpled face and a pampered, careful air
Then there is one — just lacking grace…That is not — truly — there]

I fall between projected thought
And nearly to the light
Just to the bend past what I ought
And one nearer than I might.

Laura Lowe, Grade 10
Western PA Cyber Charter School, PA

The Thoughts of Life

Day by day we contemplate, day by day we wonder;
As the sun shines among us for a time, slowly but surely floating down for its slumber.
Why do we exist today? In such a modern time.

As the days flow by, we ponder evermore;
Though none show truth of the thought;
Why do we live today? If there no longer grows contradiction.

We live for the glory, for the vengeance, for the pride;
We live to conquer, to govern, to form
Though none can see through a conscious mind,
Evil and Good must preserve the pendulum;
If not, what then would be man's desire?

Though hope still shines from a distance;
For in man hibernates one gleaming Light,
Until man stumbles, until man discerns,
The glory known only to those who seek the greater divine.

The bond of Light within each one creates a vital Entity;
That develops the face of joyfulness, the face of peacefulness, and the face of love;
That so many seek but few ever find.

Ethan Holliman, Grade 11
Thomson High School, GA

Welcome to Florida

Welcome to Florida is what we say.
Where the tourists come to stay.
We are known for the beaches and sun.
If you come you could have a lot of fun.

We have a big city called Tampa Bay.
This is where the Bucs play.
Where the Devil Rays hit the ball.
But, lately haven't hit any at all.

Orlando is full of parties and games.
Don't go if you are lame.
You can bring your kids to Disney World.
And UCF is a good college so I've heard.

We have to pass a test called the FCAT.
But, some seniors don't seem to get that.
We rather go to Clearwater Beach on a hot day.
And watch the palm trees sway.

It has made a home for many.
Just don't visit Ybor City.
So come awhile and stay.
'Cus welcome to Florida is what we say.

Annette Koulouvaris, Grade 12
Countryside High School, FL

We Just Didn't Belong

I've had enough of all the "I love yous"
I'm tired of putting up with you!
And all that you have put me through!!
I've had enough of all the sappy love letters too.
We just don't belong!
    Why did you want to do this to me?!
You cheated! That's it! I'm done with you!!
Why didn't you just tell me and set me free?
We just didn't belong!
    You never meant a word you said.
You faked it all along!
I hate you! I hate you! Get that through your head!
Why didn't you tell me and just set me free?
We just didn't belong!
    I can't believe what you done!
Why didn't you just tell me and set me free?
You deceived me and made me think it was real.
    What went wrong?!
Why didn't you just tell me and set me free?
I guess it's over now.
We just didn't belong!!

Linda Pritchard, Grade 10
Schley County Middle/High School, GA

The Tall and the Proud

The clang, the sound of everlasting strife
Bring a rush of blood to my ears, pounding.
The sword, the dagger, the blade, and the knife;
    All mighty men in a chorus do sing.

When cowards fear, the real men rush forward;
When silence stands, the sword clash will fell it.
This is no place for silence nor coward,
For they are the weak, which shan't endure it.

Here they come! They are the tall and the proud,
    Who have left the enemy in the grave.
And now say what? Hark! The war cry is loud!
Shall our mighty men now once again rave?

Now hear, if you are to sing, sing it loud!
For indeed, they are the tall and the proud.

Seth Douglass, Grade 10
Elmira Christian Academy, NY

Mom and I

I argue with my mom,
So she will let me be.
If I leave,
it would just make trouble for me.
She tries to fight,
so she can make my life right.
I don't listen,
and it just takes me places,
I don't want to go.
All I have to do is listen,
and follow my mom's soul.
Be the best I can be,
so I can end up in the right life.
Mom I love you,
and you love me,
so let's make this plea,
and follow the best lead.

Richard B., Grade 11
Audubon Youth Development Center, KY

Face Up

Damp wood chips and soil slip through my fingers
And sharp strips of bark dig into my back.
A string of smoke from the blazing fire stings my eyes
As I challenge the moon to a staring contest.

This game has been played before
And the moon has never lost.
Lunar forces pull me through the atmosphere
And into an infinity of dust and ash.

I blink.
The stars applaud my effort,
And then I return again
To the soil and the campfire.

Laura Karson, Grade 11
Bronx High School of Science, NY

The Timid Rose

A dragon swoops beneath the clouds in a bright blue sky.
A rose looks up in admiration.

The dragon alights softly on the grass, scales reflecting thousands of tiny suns.

A distance away, the rose watches, shading her eyes with dark green leaves.

Her heart quickens as the dragon pads toward her without disturbing a single blade of grass.

Suddenly afraid, she bows her petaled head, cursing the feeling that crushes her to the ground.

The dragon stoops near her hiding place
To gently move a ladybug from the shadow of his taloned feet.

The rose longs to ride on the dragon's strong, glittering shoulders,
But there is a wall that holds her back.

As the dragon straightens up, the rose throws herself desperately
Against the ivy-covered wall encircling her heart.

The moss at her roots is rained upon by sweet-smelling tears
As she beats against the unforgiving stone in this secret place in her heart.

She nearly collapses into a sobbing, anguished pile of leaves.
But this time, on she struggles, the moss growing ever wetter as the dragon turns to walk away.

At last, with a terrible grinding, a stone falls,
Leaving a jagged hole in the wall that once choked her heart.

The rose wiggles through,
Steps with forced certainty over the fallen stone,
And stands tall at last.

Michelle Bobrow, Grade 12
Great Neck South High School, NY

Autumn Cycle: Falling Leaves, Barren Trees

At the onset of autumn, what comes to mind?
An image of crimson, orange, and gold leaves:
Vibrant colors twirling delicately in the warm fall breeze,
And rustling softly through barren trees,
Auburn branches swaying to and fro with innate ease.

However, as autumn's breeze becomes colder,
Its evenings become longer,
Shortening the length of its day.

The sky darkens at an earlier hour,
A natural phenomenon which even the brightest of stars in the night sky cannot overpower,
Rendering the tree branches to appear as tall, ominous shadows on the leaf-blanketed earth below.

As the night gradually comes to a close,
The clear autumn sun once again shines to expose:
An image of crimson, orange, and gold leaves…

Deborah Borlam, Grade 11
Shulamith School for Girls, NY

Touch

And your heart is where I lay my head to rest,
my face against your chest.
Your eyes are where I look for truth,
without you I am blind,
deaf without the soft beating of your heart in my ear,
you're no longer there to breathe life into me,
I'm dead alive in this place I used to call home,
a walking corpse in this small world.

Keri Kennedy, Grade 11
Fort Myers High School, FL

Step Back and Smell the Roses

The leaves were green
Mountains envelope the scene
Bumblebees sipping honey
The eastern horizon — bright and sunny

Rapid water rushing through
Swishing, sloshing, a vibrant blue
The scent of flowers, sweet and bright
High in the sky — the morning light

Now the clouds have all turned gray
Smog seems to blanket every day
The warning is out but some pollute more
Countless trees fall to the forest floor

The smell of gasoline lingers in the air
The poor Earth keeps turning, how much can it bear?
Weather is changing — drastic hot to cold
Has our world's integrity been sectioned and sold?

Sarah Cottrell, Grade 10
Haverhill High School, MA

A Love That's More

More than a four letter word, love is
a sacrificing feeling of joy, hope, and
peace that can be experienced for as
little as a moment or a lifetime.

More than a four letter word love is the
glimmer in the eye of a mother with child
as she prepares a room for her newborn.

More than a four letter word, love is
a friend who will stick closer than any
brother.

More than a four letter word, love is
a Savior who defied the grave, and is
mighty to save.

More than L-O-V-E. Love will stand
the test of time.

Phârez Roberson, Grade 12
Newnan High School, GA

Pain

You left without a care,
You left me in despair,
I cry not knowing what to do,
I'm still in love with you.

I'm trying to move on,
But I can't accept you're gone,
Please listen and just come back,
Without you my world is empty and black.

I can't get you out of my head,
You're all I think about crying in bed,
I'm so in love with you can't you see,
Nobody could ever love you more than me.

I can't believe you caused all this pain,
Nothing will ever be the same,
You never even had a clue,
And yet I'm still in love with you.

I'm standing back up on my own,
My love for someone else has grown,
I'm now proud to say,
That he's the one I think about every day.

Jerilyn Bradley, Grade 10
Heide Trask High School, NC

My Life

I was the youngest and only daughter.
Before I was one, I could walk and by two, I swam.
I played many sports: soccer, basketball, dance,
Swim team, tennis, and gymnastics at different times.
I've seen the Grand Canyon,
And walked across the Golden Gate Bridge.
On both snow and water, I can ski
And on ice and wood I can skate.
To see every state was our parents' goal.
Where exactly we've been, I'm not sure.
We've seen 27 of 50 states.
I've been baptized with a broken arm that couldn't get wet.
Traveled to Yellowstone once, I saw a buffalo stand still
With birds sitting on his back.
Sitting on a horse, I saw a wild coyote eat his lunch.
My grandparents taught me to fish the weeks
I've stayed with them in the summer.
I've chased billy-goats.
I learned that laughing makes you skinnier.
Smiling makes you younger.
Life is best when it's random.

Becca Leland, Grade 10
Riverside High School, SC

Starvation

What lay in front of me
Provoke what I wanted to see.
It was an endless mistake
In which I could not fake.
Preventing it to stay in
Will cause me to make my own sin.

What lay in front of me
Did not lie there now.
Inside a cylinder trash it will now be
Forgotten, taking its last bow.
It will decay like all the others,
Down in a suffocated multicolored trash.

What lay in front of me
Was nothing eatable
But a hungry beggar child
In the streets of India.
Tenzin Lhadon, Grade 11
Everett High School, MA

The Good Girl

She never sets a toe out of line
She will always just be fine
She will never yell or get mad
She will always go along with the fad
Even when she's down and blue
She will always have a smile for you
She is the good girl all parents want
Because she is always nonchalant
Mary Claire Lordi, Grade 10
Colonia High School, NJ

Free Highway

I'm screaming inside
The truth isn't out
Let me be your guide
Of this usual route.
My life
I'm actually lost
On this free highway
My highway
Maybe I made a wrong turn
Went off the other exit
Now I need to learn
Without a fit.
Emulate others' moves
Get back
Back on that right path
My life.
Because I'm actually lost
On this free highway
My highway.
My life.
Meira Gunzburg, Grade 10
Bais Yaakov High School, MD

The Right One

In doubt; my mind utters
In love; my heart bursts
Which one should I follow?
To take the path unknown, the path of love
Where it's anonymous to me
Feeling like a preemie brought to light
Not knowing what to do, not knowing how to act
Opening my eyes to the real meaning of love
The path of love and affection that leads to pain and deception
Whether I let it take over my life or reject it knowing that I'll regret it
Undecided by the whispers in my head
"Don't fall for it"
"Don't let it take you away"
As my heart exclaims louder than my mind
"She won't let you down"
"She is the right one"
My mind sounds deeper than my heart but I feel it more down in my heart
Terrified of falling in love;
Due to the fact that I've been sentimentally deceived and sentimentally aggrieved
I will take the path unknown and experience the true meaning of love
Jankel Aleman, Grade 10
Miami Beach Sr High School, FL

My Life Questions

They say destiny is made by our choices, but is it really?
Where will I find answers to all my questions, and will I accomplish my destiny?

Is my life nothing but desert?
What else could I insert?

Will I ever experience happiness?
Is my hope hopeless?

Will I ever conquer my fears?
Or will I always cry in tears?

Will my questions ever be answered?
Will my answers survive the blizzard?
Shridhar Patel, Grade 10
Colonia High School, NJ

Amorous Wisdom

Behind these Blue Eyes, a new world unfolds.
There, emerges a secret, that was never told.
The cuts and bruises of internal frustration,
swallow the emptiness of a wasted creation.
Lies and unsureness, beautifully broken in cuffs.
Desperation and unawareness, beauty's not enough.
Wisdom is deep as the depths of the ocean.
But the vision to see beyond thwart rare and gives me a notion.
Seeing is believing but sight is on a limit.
Though my heart is true save vision for those timid.
While I believe lies of truth it was my heart they took.
The world never changed, my eyes were closed when I looked…
Jessica DiDuro, Grade 12
Geneva High School, NY

Growing Up

Drawing pictures in the sand,
Fingerprints and colorful hands.
Practicing cursive and writing on a line.
Playing with Hot Wheels and yelling mine!
It's all so much fun, but time flies by.
One minute you're a kid.
The next you're one of the boyz.
From Head Start to high school.
The unattractive girls to a heartbroken fool.
The obstacles will come.
Some big some small.
You're too short, they'll say.
Some will say, you're too tall.
Your teeth are busted and your clothes are whack.
Taping "kick me" signs when, they pat you on the back.
Someday you'll laugh, others you'll cry.
Be honest with yourself.
Never quit, always try.

Eyron S., Grade 11
Audubon Youth Development Center, KY

A Moonlight Traveler

The moon's satin flows in beams to the Earth,
Glittering on the ice-capped branches.
The snow covered night sings hymns of its birth,
The forest night the moonlight enhances.

A traveler alone, afoot and blushing,
The cold of the night makes white cheeks go pink.
A river she follows so deep and gushing,
A village she finds unmasked from black ink.

The fires from here melt all the heart's plight,
Yet the soft sound of hooves beats in the air.
A figure descends to counter the night.
For love's warm embrace can win anywhere.

A world yet untouched, a world yet unseen,
For powers of darkness fade in light's beam.

Christianna Chamberlain, Grade 10
Elmira Christian Academy, NY

Morning Canoe

I awake to the shrieking buzz of my alarm clock,
Which sends a shiver down my spine at every sound.
I look at the time, five-thirty as I stumble out of bed.
The bed looks so tempting as I get further away.
I dress in warm clothes, for Autumn mornings are frigid.
No light penetrates my window, for the sun has not arrived.
I walk outside, and I am met with a cold rush
    which pours over my warm skin.
I push the canoe onto the water and proceed to paddle.
Nothing can bother me now, for I am alone with my thoughts.
As I watch the world awaken from its slumber,
I see only the good in life,
And in this moment, I am happy.

Sam Taylor, Grade 12
Newnan High School, GA

Young Provider

Life is harder than it may seem,
Especially, when you're a growing, learning teen.
You realize how some things aren't meant to be,
When you finally fall out of love and really see.

I have so many things I'm going through,
If I could go back, there would be some things I wouldn't do.
When I thought I had made it to the end,
I told myself I wouldn't do it again.

I'm so sad and confused,
Wondering why I just didn't refuse.
I can say that I made a mistake,
But there is no way now that I could escape.

It feels so right even though I know it's wrong,
But it's just been going on too long.
I just wish that I could express the way I feel,
I know it won't go away, it is real.

Ebony Barber, Grade 11
Seminole County Middle/High School, GA

Puzzle

The pieces of who I am, have never fit together,
Mismatched from different puzzles, with others lost to nether.

I am many different things, some are real and some invented.
But I cannot discern the pieces, that is something I've lamented.

I'm acrid, I am fragile, I am prideful, I am meek,
I am lovely, I am ugly, I act strong though I am weak.

The fake ones are thorns to me. To have them hurts my heart.
But if I pick the fake ones out, I know I'll fall apart.

And so I'll be this person, I'll stand up brave and tall!
Because if I bear this long enough, this won't hurt me at all.

I can no longer change, this person that you see,
This person is the adult, that I've grown up to be.

Anastasia Stolz, Grade 11
Vincentian Academy/Duquesne University, PA

Beautiful

She tilts her head
Steps out of bed
And idolizes them
They make it seem like rich and proud
Is better without a doubt
They dye their hair, they look like dolls
No one can compare to how they make themselves
She wants to be like them
To have her hair glisten in the sun
To know that she's what everyone wants to be
To feel beautiful she'd pay at any cost
The knife lifted her face, surgery no longer waits
That day her life was lost in vain

Monet Walters, Grade 10
Paramus Catholic High School, NJ

Appreciation
As I start to think,
A tear forms in my eye.
Our time is up,
It's time to say goodbye.
You were always straight up,
And never played around,
Kept me on the right path,
Even though I wanted to clown.
Deep brown eyes,
Big bright smile,
Cannot go unnoticed,
Because it's so worthwhile.
Even though I did a lot of things,
And caused a lot of pain,
All my thoughts changed.
When I began to understand how you feel,
How you cared for other people,
Let me know you were real.
My pen and paper is my communication
All of the above was my motivation.

Matt B., Grade 10
Audubon Youth Development Center, KY

Libby's Closet
Bags are shoved at the top with no order.
Shoes are thrown everywhere.
So many you can't even count.
Emerald ones are her favorite pair.
Her clothes are all lined up,
They're hanging on a rack.
She tries to keep them organized,
But that never works.
She gets them looking one way,
And the next day they're right back where they were.
A spider lies on its back in the corner,
Its legs curled up in the air.
I don't think she even notices,
And I know she doesn't care.
One day she is going to wake up,
And clean her closet,
And it will stay that way —
Forever.

Molly Love, Grade 11
Heathwood Hall Episcopal School, SC

Georgia Autumn
Early in the afternoon,
The sun blazes in the clear blue sky.
The sun is yellow and vibrant orange,
And the weather is slightly hot.

In the woods,
The pine trees offer shade.
The dark brown branches crackle and pop.
The branches fall crisscrossed into a pile.

Grace Milford, Grade 12
Thomson High School, GA

For Angels and Cupid
Holding the Earth's light,
inspiring traditional bedtime lullabies,
suspended in midair
like another level of the world.

There is something celestial
about this field where angels play.
Little puffs of cotton where Cupid is known to roam
form an infinite apparitional realm.

Kayla DiCicca, Grade 12
Northside Christian School, FL

Good Morning Bravery
I wish you felt the movement of the ground beneath my feet
I've ascended into the empyrean
Not blinded by the light, but taken by sight
My palm is faced up, fingers are numb
And the moon grasps hold:
"Don't chase away the stars, tonight we'll make this sky ours"
How sweet the sound of our melody;
The words fall into place
Oh my, my I'm enraptured
As these crows approach my sky they falter by the stars laughter
It has come to this
Your hands are full of me
My hands are too small to bear it all but you hold me
Oh my, my behold this strength
The stars dance across my feet
Rat-tat-tat-tat
For the crows have subsided
And for some reason I can't explain
The sky will never be the same
You cradle me in your smile
Now I can close my eyes.

Samantha Hinkson, Grade 11
Brooklyn Preparatory High School - Harry Van Arsdale Campus, NY

1984
Paranoia running through every inch of your mind,
Big Brother is watching, can he see what you've done?
Every action you make is being closely watched,
Is there a way to escape, can this battle be won?
You aren't safe when you're awake,
For his eye can see all.
Yet peaceful slumber is no better,
For treacherous dreams render imminent downfall.
Your mind is a safe filled with secrets unknown,
As it is being pried at, will it crumble and crack?
Or will your thoughts be kept safe,
Is it possible to hack?
When faced with fears you will discover what you love best,
Your whole life's desires will be put to the test.
Will your thoughts remain unchanged, or will they be laid to rest?
You are being watched.

Luke Kockott, Grade 11
Council Rock High School South, PA

21st Century Strife

The 21st century is filled with children who don't belong.
It seems like someone is always crying because something is wrong.

Where your parents do everything for you but it's never good enough,
they smack you on the wrist and you yell, "that's too rough."

As I look around the room I see black lined eyes and dyed air.
I can't seem to break the urge to stop and stare.
What I'm seeing is such strive to be different,
and such strive makes you and more the same.
Every kid has an excuse and someone else to blame.
So go be emo if you want, go whine along with all your friends;
But I can tell you, you're not being different at all,
you're just following all the trends.

So kid what I'm about to tell you will probably ruin your day,
In order to have originality, you have to have your own personality
and quit living by other people's ways.

So you see, everyone is dying to be so different.
Sitting alone in a dark room and whining along.
Don't you realize that everyone is singing the same song?

Megan Ellison, Grade 10
Wirt County High School, WV

Bruiser of My Soul

Inadequate is the bruiser of my soul
An unbearable look I get when my child looks at me,
To provide sustenance for his empty belly…and I can't.

Depression is the bruiser of my soul
Anguished by the feeling that no one cares but one measly person…
    On the other side of the world…
That couldn't help
Even if they wanted to,
Which brings me back to square one

Ignorance is the bruiser of my soul.
Suffering day to day,
Until I die, is all I can do,
Hoping there were another way to die
Often I've been told that suffering is good for the soul,
But
    What good is suffering if you don't bear a soul?
Misery is the bruiser of my soul.
Morally, there is no happy ending for me,
Unless that one Immortal soul,
Mends my bruised soul
Then felicity would be the mender of my soul.

Gabriella Logan, Grade 11
Chamblee Charter High School, GA

Silence

Sometimes the best sound is
Not a sound
But the lack of sound.
Where nothing is heard
But all can be seen.
A tranquil place
Where one can rest.
A peaceful time
When one can think.
Silence is golden
But gold can break
With the slightest sound.

David Nicol, Grade 11
Hanover High School, PA

Summer's End

XOXO and sealed with a kiss
I've never felt love for a boy like this
Letters wrote and pictures sent
I'll see you at the summer's end
The words on your paper aren't as real
As the love for you I can feel
Miles apart, I still feel your heart
Nothing can break us apart
When I return and we're together again,
Soon enough, summer will end.

Kayla Reese, Grade 10
Ferndale Area Jr/Sr High School, PA

Day

Hey there I can't believe it's you
Please come in stay a while
Leave your shoes there,
Lay your coat there,
Hope you don't mind the mess

So take a seat, relax
I know you've had a rough day
We can listen to some music,
Just sit and talk a bit

I really could spend forever right here
I don't mind as long as you don't
Whether rain or shine
I will be happy

Now I can say
My day is complete
As time I think went by,
It stood still in your eyes, in mine.

Sarah Doucette, Grade 10
North Tonawanda High School, NY

All

Just hold my hand, that's all it takes,
for you to make me smile.
And wrap your arms around my waist,
if only for a while.
Clearly you are all I need,
to make it through the day.
I use the light that's in your eyes,
to help me find my way.

Kati Wilburn, Grade 11
Loretto High School, TN

Life

It's love,
Of the things
You hold near,
And you want to.

It's love,
Of the things
You let go,
'Cause you ought to.

It's love,
Of the world,
All its beauty,
All its art.

It's love,
Of yourself
And your soul,
And your heart.

Hanna Busse, Grade 10
Chantilly High School, VA

Another Florida Day

The tide swells and grows
Then crashes upon the shore
It recedes quickly
Then slams once more
The squawking of the seagulls
Who try to steal our food
Will put the sunniest disposition
In a cranky mood
Lifeguards sit on their post
With raft in hand
Ready to rescue those
Who are far from land
Skim boarders
Are no longer riding on the tide
As the sun sets
The tide continues to swell and grow
And crash upon the shore
Tonight the crowd is gone
But tomorrow there will be more

Jake Severn, Grade 10
Countryside High School, FL

My Definition of America

America is all passion the strongest for its attacks
America is love a love that makes people dream.
America is a friend among strangers.
America is a freedom land to newcomer.
America is a cure to our future.
America is like a dream waiting to come true.
America is like a song in the breeze when you feel at ease.
America is a promise to give you a brighter future today, tomorrow and always.

America lets people live
America lets people pray
America lets people write
But America lets people cry, hate, forget, judge, discriminate.

Anne Pierre, Grade 12
Edgewater High School, FL

My Pigmentation

My pigmentation is not an invitation for discrimination.
This is God's creation that has formed one nation.
It identifies who I am, and where I stand.
It is the color of caramel and carries a sweet smell.
Its texture is smooth, despite a few flaws and a mysterious bruise.
It has been through things in the past years like,
beatings, scars, fights, and a few tears.
My pigmentation is not an invitation for discrimination.
This is God's creation that has formed one nation.
Yes I've been at war and my enemies have knocked on my door
to the point I couldn't take it anymore,
but now I'm okay,
because God has shown me that tomorrow will be a brighter day.
I've been frustrated and aggravated, but I made it.
My pigmentation is the color of my skin,
as you go deeper the spirit of the Lord dwells within.
My pigmentation is not an invitation for discrimination.
This is God's creation that has formed one nation with appreciation.

Ricsheeda Caldwell, Grade 11
Middle Creek High School, NC

Julius Caesar

Once you think somebody is your friend
You want that friendship to never end
Julius Caesar would praise him but they all put on a frown
Brutus does not believe that one man should be dictator
So he started to have a lot of odium on Caesar and became a conspirator
Devious Brutus wheeled Caesar to go to the Senate and made up an interpretation
Caesar believed him and went to get his crown, only for that reason
Brutus was exhorted to become a conspirator by Cassius
When Caesar was dying, his last words were "Et tu, Brutus"
Caesar was surprised that his friend would take part in that attack
However, there was no way Caesar could get him back
Brutus was friends with Caesar though soon became his enemy
He watched Caesar die with equanimity
This shows that not every friend is true
And you never know when they can backstab you

Anetta Dubinchik, Grade 10
Council Rock High School South, PA

A Lover's Torment

He lied in her arms and whispered her name.
His voice called out to the depths of her heart.
His voice was the essence that kept her sane
in the hours before his dreaded depart.
She fought the force that gently closed her eyes,
the force of sleep, common in the dim hour.
These moments with him were too rare to pass by
but she surrendered to slumber's dark powers.
She awoke at dawn and reached to her side
only to feel the emptiness of silk sheets.
"Romeo," she called, and tears fell as she cried,
knowing he had left in the midst of her sleep.
And the nightingale sang a song of lament
of forbidden love and a lover's torment.

Catherine Zhang, Grade 12
Newton South High School, MA

Doubt

And I breathe so soft and slowly
then I close my eyes,
only to see you in my mind.
Such delicate features,
reflected by your kind face.
This place is so familiar
this heart that beats at a steady pace.
Hold on to this disaster.
Humor found in the midst of it all.
We manage to break a smile.
These facades crash and fall.
I felt the sincerity from words that left your lips.
How to feel both nervous and sick.
Stop these shaking fingertips.
Revealed are high hopes that will never come true.
If only then we knew,
everything would soon fade to shades of blue.
These days and hours are breaking through.
It could have been anyone,
but it had to be you.

Heather Intelicato, Grade 10
Holy Cross High School, NJ

Abime (Abyss)

Fading quietly into the dark background
Sweetly humming my prayers
It seems that I have failed to live
And am now no longer among those of this world
I have not died for I have yet to take breath
As if I have fallen into some unseen abyss
I speak soundless words, that form no sentences
No rhyme
I am the rotting remains of something that never was
Meandering around without a purpose
No reason to go on, a true rebel without a cause.
But I lack the cowardice to take my own...
So I fall and continue falling.

Richard Pogue, Grade 12
West Philadelphia Catholic High School, PA

The Sweet Smell of Sky

The sweet smell of sky
How brilliant, how beautiful
That beckons the winged of soul
And biddeth the restless of spirit ascend
To rest in the sun's soothing glow
And when blessed sun dims into sacred moon
And stars form a flock in the night
Still nothing compares —
Nay, no scent of all airs —
To the sweet-smelling fragrance of sky
The odor of time
How musty, how mournful
How nauseating, and unkind
I'd rather avoid it —
Its thick, haunting stench —
And inhale the aroma of sky

Samantha Hawkins, Grade 11
Hawkins Home School, GA

I Won't Get Out of Bed

I won't be getting out of bed this morning
Call my boss and let him know
No, there was no forewarning
Just tell him I'll be a no-show.

I was up all night when I should have been sleeping
I stayed awake like there was no tomorrow
My thoughts were endlessly leaping
As time was stolen not borrowed.

I'm glad you weren't there to witness
You drove me crazy with your silence
You're my own personal sickness
How can someone's mind be so dense?

So if you're looking you can find me
Below covers of confusion and thoughts
On a pillow of no guarantee
In a room of misunderstandings and knots.

Emily Carson, Grade 11
Heathwood Hall Episcopal School, SC

It's Raining Outside

I look outside and I see the rain,
The rain has moistened the two-way lane.
Not only that but I am home alone,
And the true colors of boredom are now being shown.
I am so bored that I'm writing a poem,
So that when my parents come home, I can show 'um.
Because of the rain, there is silence on the street,
I can't even hear a sound nor a beat.
I am looking outside through my window,
I am so bored that I wish I had a Nintendo.
I begin to wonder if we'll ever have a drought,
And suddenly I notice the sun coming out.

Zagham Chaudry, Grade 10
Union High School, NJ

Cupid's Arrow

When I first saw you, I didn't know what to do. Should I have said hi, or asked how are you? Your beautiful eyes put me in a trance, and Cupid's arrow struck my heart. I felt there and then that I was in heaven. Your beautiful eyes and smile, I didn't want it to last for a while. I wanted it to last forever. Forever is a very long time, but when I'm with you I don't care about time. I don't care if time stops. I don't care if the world ends. I will always know that we will be protected. Our love will remain strong and our hearts will be connected. You will always be my light in a realm of darkness. You will be my dark clouds' silver lining. Always remember one thing you are my everything.

Andrew Schneider, Grade 10
Tottenville High School, NY

Yea Though I Walk

Yea though I walk through the valley of the shadow of death I shall fear no evil nor shall I fear no woman or man
Did anyone ever tell you love was a sin?
You shall not repent for the crimes that you have committed
There is no justice or peace for your reckless decisions
The peace you seek is when your body lies still
As your soul wanders into a place unknown
No man lives for his own we all feed into each other like an endless cycle of deceit
I shall no longer be defeated by the emotions rising inside
Later on to find out everything my so called lover said was a lie
It is a shame to have fallen in love when the truth is there is no love everlasting
Only thing everlasting is the promise of death the eternal rest
A wise man once told me "it is frightening to know who my murderers are
When it is written that a murderer strikes its victims in the shadows in the dark of night"
But my murderer struck me in daylight and buttered me up at night
To think it doesn't hurt you to be the reason I die inside
There shall be no more tears from my eyes because my words cry for me
My eyes now like daggers piercing into your soul I can see right through you
You have no feeling inside
This is why I quote
Yea though I walk through the valley of the shadow of death I shall fear no evil nor shall I fear no woman or man
This is my prayer to my Lord. Amen.

Brittany Diggs, Grade 10
Middletown High School, NY

Home Is Where the Heart Is(n't)

The nicotine's got her down, but the coffee's got her flying as high as the plane last week that had her heart beating too fast. The sound of heels against pavement is putting her to sleep, but she's got places to go and people to disappoint.

The beggar on the street asks her for her story, and she gives him a one liner with three and a half meanings and an allegorical question mark. Half-curiosity, she says; half-guilt. Half-me. May have left the rest here; heard this is where the heart is (supposed to be.)

Familiar stepping stones lead up the familiar walk that she'd spent so many years scurrying down, to get away from the house that she was now barging into with zero warning of entrance. The oven was full but the scent could not compare to the sounds that overwhelmed her mind. She stared at rectangles filled with familiar faces, wrinkled at the corners by age. Glancing over the wallpaper that she had always hated, she realized that there was nothing to find but bitter and broken and why she ever left in the first place. It all smelt like holidays that meant nothing and screaming that never ceased and the kind of rubber that burns when you're getting away from a not so home. Here I am, she thought; but here my heart is not.

The nicotine's got her down, but the plane's got her flying. She's heading a thousand miles away from the place that she kind of came from. The place that she never knew and she'd never let know her. Breathing easy for the very first time, she lost herself in the vice of a pilot's voice who knew nothing about her but that she was going to wake up a thousand miles away from where she'd been. Home.

Emily Brown, Grade 10
Ragsdale High School, NC

Upset

I just want to break down and cry but I don't know why
Wait, I do it's because of you
I can't believe it how she makes me want to vomit
Why does he like her more c'mon what for?
I am just as good I wish you understood
Jeez why do I feel this way? I really don't know what to say
You're just a guy that makes me want to cry
But you make my heart race
Why can't I be in first place?
Is it because I'm not pretty enough?
Or don't wear juicy, coach and all that stuff?
Not just you, but everyone
Always picks the other one
I am dead last on your list
And I'm waiting for that one special first kiss
Always and forever I want to be
And I really honestly wish you can see

Andrea Sabo, Grade 10
Colonia High School, NJ

Discrimination

I commiserate for the African Americans back in the day
They lived such hard lives that they dealt, come what may
Almost two-hundred years have passed
But some people can't forget that fast

The noncommittal South had too much to say
Not many stopped them because of the fear to not stay
They either worked or ran
Some even had to fan

In many countries African Americans were not taken seriously
They were to nominal to be free
Africa, Australia, and America had slaves
The Emancipation Proclamation was passed to save

Though it's a law for no segregation
Many still live as though there is a plantation
No one should be treated like dirt and all slavery should cease
I am glad to hear now that there is some peace

Bryanna McQueeney, Grade 10
Council Rock High School South, PA

Memories

Memories come, memories go
But one I won't forget is not letting you go
The pain you put me through…
Still runs through my mind
The embarrassment I felt
Still runs through my heart
The sight of you manipulating my thoughts was there
But it went nowhere
I stayed watched and listened
And at the end all I got is my heart that now listens
Listens to the signs of what he really wants
And knows that being with him would cost me

Taima Gomez, Grade 10
Parkdale High School, MD

FDR: The Man Who Saved a Nation

The flame of hope was burning
Rekindled in this nation
Nothing now could stop us
Short of great inflation
Sadly we did meet this fate
And had a Great Depression
So Franklin was elected
To lead us through this age
No shortcuts would be taken
While he led our nation
We'd earn our title as the best of all
Through fair play and hard labor
As a lion in the jungle
We'd retake our place
Like a quiet bubble on a sea of noise
Franklin kept us behind the scenes till we would know
How to fight economically around the globe
He cleared out isolation
He saved European nations
He led us through a dark war
Our powerful president: FDR

Christopher Hrvoj, Grade 11
Mcintosh High School, GA

Winston's World*

A world without freedom a world without smiles
A world where gray is the color in style
Everyone is on the watch everyone is suspicious
With an eye out for something seditious
Winston's world is like a jail
The misery and hardship make it a terrible tale
The brick buildings of the city only add to Winston's fear
No luck at all can be found here
The world is lonely the world is dark
Nowhere is safe from the bar to the park
Police and mind control and friend versus friend
Winston hopes this world will come to an end

Julie McNamee, Grade 11
Council Rock High School South, PA
*Inspired by "1984."

Glory

Which experience truly teaches the soul,
When the glass feels half empty or when it seems full?
Does a man learn of glory in his moments of pride,
Or when he's struggling against the forces that push us aside?
The deepest well we can fall down is stone cold,
And contains no footholds,
But if we learn to fall and land with grace,
There is no moment where we cannot show our face,

The taste of Glory is only sweet,
After we have picked ourselves up from defeat,

Those who know of no smile when pushed to the ground,
Will never hear the gift of Glory's sweet resounding sound.

Sammi Massey, Grade 11
Georgetown Visitation School, DC

When I Wake

The sun shines through a
dark green curtain and
reflects off my daisy
colored walls,

A soft voice is heard
on the other side
of my door as my
mother gives her wake-up call.

The warm water hits my
face and rolls down my
body and stands in
tub for the drain is clogged,

Clothes go on, then my teeth
are brushed I run out the door
to crank my car and wait 'til the
windshield is unfogged

Traffic is light, my chill
bumps remain 'til I
spring into the classroom
before the bell rings

Kayla Noblit, Grade 11
Loretto High School, TN

My Turn

I used to be weak,
But now I am strong.
Here is my chance
To prove you all wrong.
My life has changed
And now you will see,
Nothing will hold me back
From being all I can be.
I have been through a lot
And from it I have learned.
I was unhappy for so long
But now it is my turn;
My turn to shine.
It is no longer raining
And I can now see the sun.
I have a whole new perspective,
Never again will I be on the run.
You see, I am who I am
And that's good enough for me.
The nightmare is over;
I am finally free.

Kristin Yerkes, Grade 11
Lifeworks Alternative School, PA

Stars

Laying on the edge just letting my feet sway in the wind.
My thoughts wandering into the corners of my mind…
Creating a silence that even I can't control
A silence that scares most people;

Yet here I am just sitting and thinking…letting my thoughts take over my whole body
My whole being;
Letting myself sink down into the earth,
I can't tell the difference between the sun and ground…
It's swallowing me in to the depths of its center…
And I'm just sitting there…letting it take me away from reality.
Taking me to a place that holds secrets
Secrets that would shock most and put others in denial.

I can see the stars just a twinkle of light,
Shining across the black velvet that is the night sky.
Thinking to myself I wonder
Why…
When…
How…
Did my heart get broken?

Margaret Abrams, Grade 10
Paul VI High School, NJ

The Horrors of Algebra

Sorry to be so negative now,
But to be positive, I don't know how.
I'm sure you can see the source of my wrath,
But please tell me how you add letters to math!

And those signs, I never know what goes where,
And let me ask you a question. How can a Y be squared?
And what about that invisible one that always goes with a letter,
A regular one would work so much better!

What about those different kinds of numbers irrational and rational,
I'll start a campaign and it will go national.
We'll protest against algebra trauma
Of broken lives and cries for their mama.

I'm so frustrated I could pull out my hair
I could tear up my math book and not even care!
I can burn it or shred it, oh yes I could,
Or, I could use the garbage disposal, ooo that sounds good!

But, it's the end of the semester, and I'm almost done.
I fought against algebra, and I won!
"But Honey," Mom said "don't you remember,
You have to take Algebra 2 in September."

Gwendolyn Pollock, Grade 10
Home School, FL

No Longer, by You

The vast Brooklyn Bridge gleaming beneath broad daylight,
the armada of tires passing through,
the jubilant smile upon my tiresome face,
no longer misshapen by you.

Now miles away, and heavens apart,
I feel fully alive it's true,
a bittersweet symphony ringing onward for miles,
no longer conducted by you.

An effortless laugh, racing through my lungs,
sends my newly formed path askew,
yet the direction I'm headed on this turbulent road
no longer detoured by you;

and with each revolution on this asphalt expanse
I can feel freedom, liberation passing through,
and this perpetual feeling, this glorious moment,
no longer misshapen by you.

Eddie Gonzalez, Grade 12
North Forsyth High School, GA

Life's Path

As I stare into her eyes I wonder
Of how I wasn't torn asunder
Then I come to the conclusion
That I lived my life in great confusion

In the past I always thought
That all my efforts led to naught
Until one day I learned
That all successes must be earned

So then I began
On my quest to become a young man
Though my decisions sometimes led me astray
My life guided me to become who I am today

Michael Lasko, Grade 12
Perth Amboy High School, NJ

Opposites

Gone, missing, away
By my side, never to stray,
Lone voice on a phone,
A hug or a kiss, a laugh and a smile,
A lame attempt at closeness,
A bond, tight as a knot,
Two forgotten birthdays,
A party to my surprise,
Brags to others of my successes, unknown to him,
Support of my failures, pushing me to never give in,
Tears, rage, and longing
Love, comfort, and a sense of belonging,
I know he loves, a love I sometimes can't see,
A love I always know, feel, and yearn to be
He is my father, trying, but always coming up short
She is my mother, perfect and every part of me.

Taylor Murtaugh, Grade 10
Bronx High School of Science, NY

Friendship Is Danger*

To value friendship is to be ignorant to danger
Especially when great Caesar had such power
The conspirators feared he'd be the decadence of Rome
With Caesar's increasing powers, he just had to go
Even poor Brutus felt his dear friend must die
So the conspirators planned to kill Caesar for the good of Rome
To the Senate Caesar would go with plans of celebration
By all his dear friends the crime would be committed
But Calpurnia expostulated Caesar with her premonitions
Only to be laughed at and be called a silly woman
To the Senate Caesar went in a most vulnerable state
The conspirators circled him, bowing strategically close
Their daggers hidden beneath their togas for a sneak attack
Then Caesar goes down with a mighty fall, killed by betrayal
Even great Caesar should have been cautious
For the friendships he had weren't what they appeared to be

Lauren Myers, Grade 10
Council Rock High School South, PA
Inspired by "Julius Caesar."

This Is Not America Anymore

What has become of the Land of the Free?
All the problems, we try not to see.
Land of the Beautiful, Home of the Brave,
America has turned into a Land of Debris.

People in the cities are homeless.
Many people are becoming jobless.
Mom, dads, and children have extreme hunger.
This is not America any longer.

The media twists things to go their way,
And the truth is not at all what they say.
We turn to people to make us happy,
When we should just turn to God and obey.

A flag with stripes and a field of stars
Is now a symbol of crime and bars.
We all strive for the American Dream.
Everything is perfect as it seems.

Hilary Lassetter, Grade 12
Newnan High School, GA

The Words to Say

I'm just trying to find the words to say
Yet my mind is still thinking in the gray
Maybe I'll reach deep down inside my brain
But still I abstain from thought
This emptiness is something I may have to fight
Though it may appear to be somewhat of a fright
Will it be something that I just need to bear?
Maybe I'll just end up pulling out all my hair
Then an idea comes to me
Will it be something that will set me free?
Or will it just fall back into the dark
Of the stark blackness of the night?

Ian Leidner, Grade 10
Bronx High School of Science, NY

Summer Night

The sunbeams glow between the leaves.
Such a happy day it seems!
The dark night clouds begin to cover.
And to a slightly cooler wind I shudder.
I look up at the sky while the clouds move away:
I see the smiling moon.

Carly Hasting, Grade 10
Athens Bible School, AL

All the World Is a Low Budget Stage

cat walk strut
down a dirty
main street
dance to a beat
drum the sidewalk
restless feet

tap out a song
that only you can hear
sing a song
sing this song
sing to anyone
who's near

it's four
in the morning
dancing in the moon
singing some insanity
feel your heart
it may explode soon

Rose Walpole, Grade 10
Hutchinson Central Technical High School, NY

Marionettes

We are all marionettes
In the hands of society.
We dress and we live
Under its control.
It controls our every thought,
Our every action,
Our every movement,
We've become dependent
Upon not our own
Instincts or feelings
But upon what society thinks and feels.
We are constantly seeking our master's approval,
No longer self-content with who we really are.
We acquiesce to *Seventeen* and MTV,
Afraid to disagree,
Afraid to stand out,
Afraid of our own emotions.
We are society's Barbie Dolls.
We are being molded into
The media's idea of perfect each and every day.

Stacey Norred, Grade 12
Newnan High School, GA

A Day in the Trench

Thunder rolls, over our heads,
The rattling of weaponry, ringing in our ears.
Reluctant heads, peer over the top,
Unsure of their return, to the hellish hole we call home.
Our provisions ran dry, for what seems like ages ago,
As the rats obtained a new meal by the minute.
My friends, lay fallen on the dirt,
Faces drenched with the sorrow, and the pain.
The sun has set on our youth.

Saeed Bhuiyan, Grade 10
Townsend Harris High School, NY

Nightfall

I am the mellow evening light, gently pushing back the sun
I am the stars coming back to life, twinkling one by one
I am the silent moon, unthinking, as I rise without a care
I am the bitter evening frost drinking up the summer air
I am the children's wishful thinking of dreams just out of reach
I am the days slowly shrinking, because for winter, I beseech
I am the smooth black inking that cools the twilight sky
I am the constellations linking to form pictures way up high
I am the chill unyielding to the warmth yet to come
I am the blackness always wielding the sleep that leaves you numb.
I am the one who swallows your world in an angry cloud
And whether daylight follows is what nature has endowed.
I am the fear that lives hidden in the bottom of your hearts
I am what disappears at dawn when I fall again to parts
I am the one who veers away from day at any cost
And if day doesn't follow me, then everything is lost.
I am nightfall.

Hunter Holbrook, Grade 10
The Derryfield School, NH

The Monster in My World

On Monday, the mountain begins as a small pile.
It stretches itself into a corner of my world.
On Tuesday, the mountain has flourished with a fervent pace,
Holding the dirt and sorrow of Monday.
On Wednesday, the once amiable mountain, has now become a monster.
The shadows crawl onto my bed as night falls.
On Thursday, my world is being taken over by the shadow of the monster.
I feed it and hope to make it my friend.
But it only growls at me from the depths of its core.
On Friday, I can't even enter my room
Without the fear of being swallowed alive.
On Saturday, my mom declares war.
She hands me gloves, a shovel, and a gas mask.
I tip-toe towards the door. I hear the monster's thunderous growl.
I gulp hard and loud.
With adrenaline pumping, I charge the monster and attempt to tackle it.
After an hour of fighting, I call for back-up. My mother rushes to my side.
With her bare hands she rips the monster to small chunks.
My world is safe once again.
But on Sunday, a little lump begins to grow.

Lana Bridgham, Grade 12
Prince Avenue Christian School, GA

A Silent Voice

I guess I'ma just have to get used to it.
I need to pick myself up
and learn to stand with my own two feet.
If he doesn't want to love me anymore, I can't chase it,
cause you can't force anyone to do anythin' they don't want to.
But regardless if I'm loved, I'll always be alone.
So life, teach me,
give me the cold shoulder of being neglected or isolated,
but give me the warm feelin' of love and happiness.
Then at once, take it all away and have me feel nothin',
as if I was of little importance.
Don't baby me, be as hard as you could be on a person
so I know not to expect anythin' less and
when I do get the worst things in life it won't be as bad anymore
and I'll finally be able to be happy and set free
because with every bad comes good, so accept the good;
life is life, nothin' comes close to ever being quite like it.
It will make you suffer and succeed at the very same time,
don't take it for granted, you only have one time to live!

Anastasia Del Valle, Grade 11
Mount Olive High School, NJ

Forever

Walking down the sandy beach, hand in hand,
Skipping giant rocks into the water.
Running everywhere all through the hot sand,
A mother sat scared for her young daughter.

Her daughter was in love and happier.
She was scared that she would be very hurt.
The man assured he would never leave her,
And that his true love would not turn to dirt.

The man and woman grew up together,
Got married and had about six children.
They had dreams of happiness forever,
Wanted to be married longer than then.

The woman and man shared lots of laughter,
And they lived happily ever after.

Lauren Cohen, Grade 10
Peabody Veterans Memorial High School, MA

Summertime

The wonders of summer bring much joy
Now you can play every day
And enjoy all of your toys
Look at all the boys and girls play!
But do not forget that summer has an end
And then we go back to school
To make new friends
And learn new things that are oh so cool
But do not forget that school has an end
We will go back to the pool
And pretend once again, that summer never ends

Lexy Khella, Grade 10
St Stephen's Episcopal School, FL

Last Concert at an Opera House

They come with their own arrogant predispositions,
Unkempt fingers clasp to instruments.
These final fateful desperate musicians,
They are in truth merely implements,
To make profit with deplorable renditions,
Alas this din brings far less than a beggar's tin.
Its sound chastises the ear.
It causes the soul to burn in agony from within.
It causes the mind to sear.
It drives many a man to their hell with sin
They scream with bestial whines.
They shall never ever win.
It is the music of their crimes.
No one now sits in the seats.
Pity and sorrow the scene silently entreats.
For there was time when the place was quite grand,
But thanks to the swift greedy hand,
The sweet buttermilk has gone sour,
In this an opera's final hour.

Frank Loeb, Grade 11
Overbrook School for the Blind, PA

Great Depression

Days of work so long and dreary
Suddenly fade to night quite weary.
The moon and stars glow beautifully in the sky
But no one seems to notice, why?
A nation so troubled,
So down and depressed
They cannot even feel the love of a family
Due to times of trouble and great stress.
Many people doubt life and their existence
However, if but one has hope, has faith and persistence
We will come to the dawn of a day
When to great hardships we can say, nay!
No longer can you stay
You may darken our doorstep no longer,
For by the passing of the day we grow ever stronger!

Jarrod Howell, Grade 11
East Central High School, MS

Trapped (Locked-In Syndrome)

holding you hostage in depths of our own body,
I give you a life of anger and frustration,
sparing you no sympathy,
I speak no words
I work in silence
taking control of you and making
you my prisoner,
as long as you are in the grasp
of my deadly hands,
all you possess are wishes and dreams,
I won't allow you to live your life
like an animal in captivity,
you remain trapped behind steel bars,
until I decide to set you free.

Maizie Yates, Grade 11
Harrison County High School, KY

Ties to Time

Time.
Seconds.
Minutes.
Hours.
Are they our enemies?
Or friends?
Like sand through my fingers.
It goes away.
Yet it never does.
Almost mocking,
Restricting, constraining us
To get things done.
Lose it.
Spend it.
Have it.
But the fear is
Will we ever have enough?

Jessica Chu-A-Kong, Grade 10
Townsend Harris High School, NY

The Four Seasons

Warm spring day
Galloping through the water
Swishing through the grass

Ocean tides
Big mighty hands
Pull in the sand

Crackling leaves
Shades of light
Vivid colors

Hot chocolate
Lingering in the kitchen
Turns ice cold

Jennifer Davies, Grade 10
Warwick Sr High School, PA

I Think I Love You

When you walked into my life,
My life changed,
I liked you ever since I laid eyes on you,
You were my first crush,
It was 2nd grade,
Then here we are again together,
I hope it stays this way,
I think I love you,
You make me laugh all the time,
You make me smile,
You make me very happy,
There is something about you,
That makes me love you more every day,
I think I love you.

Jessica Cassant, Grade 10
South Glens Falls Sr High School, NY

Glory's Consequence

Bullets rain upon the soldier in the line.
They drop down, lifeless bodies piling high.
No guilt, yet no glory; for the war is far from over.
Its seems like the opponents back away; yet they get closer.
Stalemate. No victory made.
Just soldiers ducked down in the safety of the shade;
In the trenches. With blood smeared and corpses decayed.
Shell shock strikes upon the men; with dear hopes that these memories shall fade.
"A Great Adventure" it was called; a fight for your nation, bold and brave;
But who knew that such zeal and honor would lead young men straight to their grave.

Katherine Panayotov, Grade 10
Townsend Harris High School, NY

Color

In the framed snapshot of exuberant green, brown, rustic paradise
Peering — gazing — glowing through this singular window, I can see:
For what is a window but an instant portrait of a moment in time?
No expensive camera needed and my morning eyes crave
Unity with these colors.
If perhaps I ventured to sacred territory —
The forgotten hunting ground of yesterday — would I find?
Consider ephemeral Eve's playground:
Her apple was surely the color of my blood.
Just life and all the separate elements, streams of flowing conscience —
No blood shed with that apple.
So indeed, I am never independent.
Subconscious habit picks me up from my sanctuary:
Four poster bed: unceremoniously dragging me to
The altar of my holy mug of coffee.
With all the steam in the world enveloping my sleep-teased features
And tangled hair, I am invisible, so black-and-white sketched.
If only I too was painted in sunlit Technicolor out my bedroom window —

Caroline Paulus, Grade 10
Marist High School, GA

Disconnected Views

Modern lyrical rhymes produce lethal crimes,
Unintended through the youth due to stupid acts and throwing gang signs,
The atrocities I describe, I don't need to front about,
Selling rocks, killing cops, or hustling up on the block,
I am what I am; you see what I see,
We're together, interconnected in this world I believe,
My rhymes are lyrical, my mind is cynical,
I'm no criminal,
Just put on this Earth to spread my thoughts and riddles,
I play games with your mind,
For what reasons were we designed?
Got u vexed, twisted, it's so obscured up in your brain,
You hear, but you think I'm insane,
Take one look at yourself; look deep into that mirror,
So maybe you can see and hear my thought clearer,
One thing I ask, that's all I need,
Believe in peace and harmony,
Truly believe.

Alex Winrich, Grade 10
Trinity High School, KY

NASCAR
N avigate smoothly
A ggression
S tock cars
C ircular track
A drenaline rush
R acing vehicles

Justin L., Grade 10
Audubon Youth Development Center, KY

Axiomatic
oh!
ideas,
are the only thing i've ever loved.

do i
understand the universe?
or do i
think?
therefore i

(believe.)

i look. i hear. i touch.
evenly spaced lines beneath my fingertips,
how far will they travel before the
oh!
adumbrative ideas,
abstruse comprehension
is a system that runs
at equilibrium with futility.

Ashley Ball, Grade 12
Lawrence High School, ME

Tell Me a Story
Tell me a story, be it long or short.
Make it resonate in my mind,
For years to come.
Let it wield its wisdom
With fury and patience.
Hold it for tender pauses, anticipating the next breath.
Let it cross categories and cultures
And be what it needs to be.
For now conceal it from the innocent eyes.
May its experience overpower the naivety of its audience.
Tell it slowly, quickly, mysteriously, overpoweringly,
At the right steps and movements.
Let it weave its way into our hearts
And entangle itself in our amazement.
Let us devour it as if it was the last of its kind.
Let it echo thunder and shadow lightning.
Leave it unfinished and tarnished for time to fill and lessen.
Denounce it, for imaginations to take and mold.
Release it into the wilds of the unknown,
For it never belonged to just one.

Mileini Campez, Grade 12
Coral Gables Sr High School, FL

Wildwood Days and Nights
My summer of 07 was the best ever
Sunny skies and beautiful weather
People and children everywhere
I could even smell the salt water air
Sitting on the beach and splashing in the waves
The ocean was as cool as a glass of lemonade
Airplanes with messages passing above
Teenagers on a blanket falling in love
Nighttime brought loud music and rides
Fireworks bursting in the dark skies
Boom, crash, bang as they lit up the night
I was in awe, of such a spectacular sight
As we walked we got closer and closer
To the fastest and biggest roller coaster
Strapped in tight and my feet dangling down
Screaming as the track swung me around
The night was coming to an end
My pockets were empty, no more money to spend
I put on my pj's and went to bed
And dreamt of tomorrow, where I'll do it all again

Nicole Scanlon, Grade 10
Colonia High School, NJ

The Summer Night
The warm breezes blew through her long brown hair;
The moonlight shimmered from his hazel eyes;
They danced the whole night long without a care;
She saw a shooting star go 'cross the skies.

She made a special wish as it went by;
She wished this summer night would never end;
He held her close and felt like he could fly;
And she would always be his closest friend.

The moon hung like a spotlight in the night;
She loved him more than she had e'er before;
Their love had been brought out into the light;
She was the one he always would adore.

She'd never been this happy in her life;
Now nothing more would ever bring her strife.

Serena Marshall, Grade 12
Elmira Christian Academy, NY

The Fear That Is Held Within Me
The fear that is held within me is that you won't want me
that's the fear in me
the fear that you won't love me
the fear that I'll just be a shadow bright moonlight
the fear that your love for me will fade away
the fear that the love that is needed will vanish
the fear that I'll vanish
the fear that is held in me is that you won't want me
the fear that I'll be alone
the fear that I'll lose my mind
that's the fear in me
the fear that you won't want me

Devitta Jones, Grade 10
Great Bridge High School, VA

The Religion of Friendship

I am a Jew, you are a Jew we share uncommon interests but what makes me so different from you
My beliefs are different does that make me incompetent?
Non relation to you because you think that you are the ultimate Jew we are all of God's children
A Jew is of the chosen land whether our skin is as black or white as any shoe
I'm sorry that I use my intellect far past the ability of what you "Jews" may expect
My path to become Rabbi contradicts everything that I stand for in me there is a faithful Jew and so much more
The commandments are my life but people never look upon the outside world given so much grief and strife.
Hurting inside no more words are ever shared for this I was never prepared
The days grow longer, colder, and harder so hard to bear oh how I wish you were there
I say the Torah was writing by God you say the Toura was written by man inspired by God who knows which is really true?
If I believe something different again does that make me so much more different from you?
We play the same game inspired by different rules and God is our coach
Wait should I take a different approach people come into your life for only three elements reason, season, or a lifetime
Sometimes a lifetime friend is heaven sent you came to teach a lesson I was sent to be your lesson
My gain isn't your loss without you in my life I feel miserable rainy days filled with frost
Will we ever speak again? Will our moment of silence officially be the end?
All the words in the world mean nothing of what I want to say
For this religion of friendship I can never repay I give more because you give less
To God is where we leave the rest I respect you for who you are
I'm proud of you for who you've become and I love you for what you will be
No matter what Jew you see on the outside looking in why? "That's the religion of friendship."

Kanesha Brown, Grade 11
Cab Calloway School of the Arts, DE

Aristocracy

Isn't it ironic how someone can have so much grace and taste, yet have so little heart?
To consider themselves proper and decorous yet treat people so vulgarly and condescendingly?
The old and the new know no difference — the real quarrel is with the common man.
However, competition will arise between two powerful groups.

Gatsby.
Part of the old aristocracy.
Yet, the one who waited outside his love's window to make sure she was safe.
The one whose heart was loyal and only full of love.
The one who isn't what most people perceive of him.
The one who doesn't belong.
The one whose life ends for being a decent human being.

Perhaps, the world is corrupt,
And some of the aristocracy doesn't deserve to be there.
Who can put them in their place, or leave them ruling for centuries to come?
What defines aristocracy anyway?

Erica Keselman, Grade 11
Council Rock High School South, PA

Darker Side

Does everyone have a darker side?
Something we have to keep hidden from the world, maybe something about our history we are ashamed of.
A dark secret that can destroy us from the inside-out should it be unleashed.
Can we protect those we love by keeping our darker side subdued.
Will our secrets get the best of us or will we control it?
Or will this dark side vanquish the light?
Whatever the secret, if forces itself to the light it may destroy us.

Veronica O'Brien, Grade 10
Canajoharie High School, NY

Betrayal

Friends are often hard to come by
The ones you love can make you cry
The caveat given about ones you now hate
Can blazon upon your heart, the thorns to extricate
Greed, hate, envy, but fate will choose
Play the game, don't let the game play you
See all, know all, think high and choose wise
Hardest thing to see is the open-faced lies
Seething, eating, breathing your life
Taking your feelings, fighting your fight
Take the good, burn the bad, and bury the dead
Scorch hatred upon ones who feel sad
They don't want to treat you
They just want to beat you
The heartfelt, the demon, the little children screaming
Who's the one you called Mr. Comrade?
The one who stabbed your back
Now your life is off track

Zach Silverstein, Grade 10
Council Rock High School South, PA

Hypnophobia

Rested, wrapped up in your sheets like a mummy.
You press yourself against the wall,
nearly out cold from the dullness of the cocoon.
The grating of machines gnaws on you.
Your nerves fray, a rope about to snap.
These shivers intensify. It is nearly dawn.
Wide-awake, your eyes are the only giveaway
that you are alive. Indeed.
The pupils dart from side to side.
You, in the safety of your blankets,
wonder if the wall will hold you up.
This pulsing headache has been here for days
and you cannot shake it.
Fervently you pray
for some type of contact with the world.
You are unconnected, disabled like the cable of a phone
yanked out of its socket:
a dead giveaway.
You feel sick.
And the phone rattles on its cradle,
meets silence.

Kelsey Swensen, Grade 12
Annapolis Sr High School, MD

My Tears

I cried inside
Told people you died
My tears were as big as a pond
I talked to myself hoping you would respond
You weren't there when it happened to me
That big tragedy
When my mom rushed me to the hospital,
No you weren't there
When all the people stared!

Tanya Jones, Grade 12
Longwood High School, NY

In Just a Matter of Time

When life doesn't seem to be going right (ooh)
There is only so much you can do
You can run but you can't hide from the voice inside you
You try to make it better
But sometimes it just seems like they will be hopeless forever
For even though dreams aren't always what they seem
You can always dream of what life can be
And will be in just a matter of time
In just a little while hope will return to you
You will be amazed at what you can do
You just have to take what comes your way
And listen to your thoughts and heart every day
In just a matter of time you could be mine
We will never be the same but in dreams we imagine
Any time and any day
I could see the way
As life changes, relationships tear apart
And occurrences may create a bleeding crisis of the heart
What could happen in a matter of time?
Well it's simply divine that every whim
Can come true up a steep climb, once in a lifetime

Delisa Youngblood, Grade 10
Rutherford High School, FL

My Best Friend

I love the times we laugh.
I hate the times we fight.
    It's funny when we talk about nothing,
Til twelve o'clock at night.
    You're my best friend,
And I hope you're with me to the end.

Amber Vansandt, Grade 11
Loretto High School, TN

Eagle of My Soul

Eagle of my soul,
I released you today.
I stood on that road,
Looked to the sky, and said,
"Eagle of my soul,
Fly far away from me.
Soar to the heavens and disappear,
I never want to see you again."
And I watched you fly away, higher and higher.
Until you were no more.
I lay on that road,
Until the sky turned black.
Eagle of my soul,
I can still remember.
Everything I went through,
And everything I shouldn't have seen, but did,
Was because of you.
So, I set you free;
It was time to let you go.
Time to move on from my beloved,
My eagle of my soul.

Parker Phillips, Grade 10
Schley County Middle/High School, GA

The Door

I am the door
That's always in use.
I am the one
They always abuse.

I am the door
That's easiest to open.
I am the one
That cannot be broken.

I am the door
But I am never admired.
I try to fulfill everyone's desire.

I am the door
That's trapped here forever.
Now everyone's left, everyone's gone;
Yet I am still here.
Why don't I move on?

I cannot go with them;
It is not my place,
For I am the door.
And this is my space.

Justin Chin, Grade 11
Heathwood Hall Episcopal School, SC

Rain

Glistening drops fall,
Like small teardrops on your cheeks.
Diamonds from the skies.

Kira Dancewicz, Grade 10
Peabody Veterans Memorial High School, MA

The Breezy Sea

Life is like an ocean
With waves and heavy hidden rocks
It's a journey never to be considered easy
But to be treacherous
Traveling through this sea
Can give a feeling of serene joy
Serene joy is felt for so long though
And can easily be taken away by a wave
There are many waves in life that conflict with my journey
I sometimes get hit so hard that I don't know which wave I should ride
But I remember that the sea calms down and becomes peaceful again
The crisp sound of the sea rocking back and forth
It covers my future beneath its serene color blue
It can scare sometimes but I have to continue the journey
I must submerse myself in it in order to see what else life brings to me
I alone know what I must do to complete it
For I am the only one that is traveling my own journey
The calm serene blue ocean
The word "Peaceful" doesn't give it enough justice
Nothing can or will stop me from completing my life
Because the waves will take me away forever

Kevin Moreau, Grade 11
St Thomas Aquinas High School, FL

Losing a Friendship

If anyone knows how it feels
to lose a friend it's me.
There are many times I wish
I could go back and change
some of the things I did.
Sometimes we can't let
little things get in the way.
There is a saying that goes
sometimes you only get one chance
so make the best of it!
Unfortunately I didn't.
I'm not here to tell you
how to handle your friendship,
but to tell you don't let little things
ruin your chance.
I missed my chance
to be a good friend.
Arguments and other drama
aren't worth losing
a person you care about.
Don't ruin your chance!

Brianna Bell, Grade 10
Schley County Middle/High School, GA

Apocalypse

Once the vagueness of the universe is revealed,
While time and sign beckon the hour,
While gold becomes rust, and hearts ache pain, they lay there, souls slain.
Time ticks away the days we now know as seconds,
For little do they know hell's reverse.
As the shadow of cold death approaches,
As the hands of instance turn their tables.
While humankind wishes its past present, their breaths become shorter.
Eyes turn black, and friends and family forgotten,
Graves grow fresh and trees and cities rotten.
All consciousness of dear world is lost, and once blooming flowers turn to frost.
The sky will lose its lumen, and man will turn upon man,
As lives become destroyed and darkness consumes our core,
The world continues on slow spin, only to reveal the many receding shores.
When doom's hour is finally present,
After the dead have risen from their graves,
They are all questioned.
Once the truth has been spoken,
Whether the voices of the tortured wrongdoers can be heard,
If any sinner can bear the flames of hell, as though an eclipse has occurred,
The tortured will live in infinite darkness, never to see the light of day.

Yasmeen Farraj, Grade 10
Al-Noor School, NY

Music of Soul

This is the night where all work comes in play
All work goes into this day
I step out onto this stage of a one time chance
This is my time, my dance

The strap around me helps me keep my balance
The guitar will show off my talents
The words come out of my mouth
Into the mic my nerves go south

I have my confidence as fans yell my name
Vocal chords are winning in this game
Emotions come as I coordinate arms and rhythm
I love these notes and all that is in them

I love the sound
As I vent to the crowd

Jessica Caruana, Grade 10
North Tonawanda High School, NY

Like the Leaves Before Winter
or the Sun Before the Night

Not against azure skies only in blackest heavens do stars shine
Dreams pervade not by sun nor light yet in sleep's dark shrine
And as I lay still on the cold ground, for you I bleed brine

Death to all things that once brought gladness
Death to all those things that had seemed kind
The truth has shown me that it was madness
That the world I viewed is only for the blind
That the world I lived in was temporally mine

Like the leaves before winter
I bequeath to you, the eyes at me you used to gaze

The new grass growing in the ruins of this scorched field
The Dead beneath us feeding the roses to you I yield

Nate Atwell, Grade 12
Leonardtown High School, MD

A Lover's Prayer

Oh Lord, You who forgive us
and taught us to act identically, in order to live
This girl who I obsess about
hurts me as the stars number
please give me strength to love her more
for, although we're sinners, you are still our Prior
you never want to kick us out.
I do not know why I still love her
Sometimes I want to cheat and be even
but her attractive face magnetizes me
a hundred reasons are already given
for us to be together as we were meant to be.
Please God almighty mollify her spoiled mind
and make her a hard dove to find
as you make me hard to be obtained by bad things.

Siannciado Oleus, Grade 12
Deerfield Beach High School, FL

The Spider's Web

Life is like a spider's web;
today it is here, tomorrow it is history.
Minutes pass, experiences happen, moments fly by.
But then, the tiniest thing happens;
a drop of rain hits our web —
a collision with the smallest bug.
A hole is formed,
but life goes on.
We spin it up, we patch the hole,
we move on.
It is these experiences that shape us
and mold us into things of beauty,
like the spider's web.
Then dawn breaks, and it is gone.
Only a few silken strands remain —
memories from ones we hold dear —
forever stored in their hearts.
A quiet beginning, a quiet end,
unnoticed by some, treasured by others,
the spider's web —
we call life.

Marissa Candiloro, Grade 10
Mother Seton Regional High School, NJ

Reunion

We all have come together to celebrate each other
To rekindle the memories made years before.
All not knowing what to expect
Because of the time lapse since we last met.

Laughing and splashing with the cool ocean breeze
All the bumps in the road sink down with ease.
All that remains is the smiles on our faces,
Warming the atmosphere to 100 degrees.

The early morn' fishing crew arrives empty-handed,
But love still embraces their sun-kissed faces.
Although the fresh fish still swam in the sea,
Our conversation had sizzling flavor.

Gathered around the "camp fire" of life,
We capture the moments that we often take for granted,
Knowing that this could be the last day that fun was forever,
And that playtime was all that was required.

Blaire Teeters, Grade 11
Stoneman Douglas High School, FL

Life's Journey

On that road to that journey
There are excitements, disappointment
Some days, clouds are dark and it's raining
Some days are bright, lit up with light shining
Times filled with sorrow or joy
Don't play with your life toy
Living life there are many lessons to be learned.
You learned from environment
Families and friends.

Karlmicheal Bailey, Grade 10
Parkdale High School, MD

Painting Our Love

We are no ordinary artists;
We're galaxies ahead of our time,
Our love is painted with the colors of
Emotion and passion, art no man defines.

We create the art they laugh at,
The funky red and blue stars,
The epitome of uniqueness to
Us, the work of the truly divine.

Our love is like graffiti;
Misunderstood by most,
Labeled by society by what they see,
Not by what they don't.

Mahalia Floyd, Grade 10
Lee High School, AL

By Any Other Name

If a rose by any other name
Would smell as sweet,
Then why are religions
Persecuted on each other's streets?

If war isn't so savage,
Why is it that
We can't appreciate peace
Until we are all at combat?

If in life, we get
Only what we deserve
Why do innocents
Have others to serve?

If the world was blind,
How handicapped would we truly be?
For when looks are forgotten,
Is reality what we see?

Marisa Ashour, Grade 10
Staten Island Technical High School, NY

Your Kiss

I love you more than you love me,
Your kiss is sweet and deep like the sea.
Your eyes are like the sky,
So beautiful and full of wonder.

I love you more than you love me,
Your beautiful ways are what comfort me.
You are my love, the sweet and brightest dove,
You changed my life with a simple hug.

Your love is kind and romantic,
It is like being enchanted.

I love you more than you love me,
Your kiss brightens me like a Christmas tree.

Anthony Y., Grade 10
Audubon Youth Development Center, KY

Goal Scored

Feet thumping as I run,
Grass crunching under my cleats,
Calling for the ball to be passed,
The thunk as he passes the ball,
Plop! As the ball lands in front of me,
Whack! The shot is taken by me,
Arrrrgh! The goalie dives and crashes to the ground,
Swish the ball in the back of the net,
The screams of my team and the parents spilling onto the field!

Evan Welsh, Grade 10
Schenectady Christian School, NY

Change

Life is all about change.
Everyone goes through change.
This year I went through a lot of change.
Change in my surroundings.
In schools,
With friends,
And even family.
People around me have changed as well.
Some people change for the better,
Some change for the worst
Some don't even change at all.
It was very difficult for me to handle everything.
But life is all about taking chances.
I took a big chance and I made a huge change in my life.
I didn't like it.
However I believe that things happen for a reason.
Everything that happened to me was for a reason.
I knew something good was going to come out of all the change I went through.
It hasn't happened yet.
But I know it will happen soon.

Princess Rosario, Grade 10
Miami Beach Sr High School, FL

Let's Go Back in Time

Let's go back in time,
back to when you could still give me a piggyback ride
and when we could share a single ice cream cone.
I want to relive those moments. The best memories of my childhood.
They go by too fast before you can truly treasure them.

Let's rewind the hands of the clock
to the time when you were my best friend.
We frolicked under the steamy summer sun
until we collapsed by the shade of the leafy oak.
But I never had to worry because you could always carry me home.

Time never stops for us but it keeps moving along.
The wrinkles have aged your face and time has weakened your limbs.
I've grown too heavy to be carried.
No longer best friends but father and daughter, still.
Time can never change some things.

Kar Yi Lim, Grade 10
Bronx High School of Science, NY

Dark and Early Morning

It is torture to remember now,
That dark and early morning,
How the oceans had turned crimson
And all around us lay sanguine pools,
Where the gun shells deafened my ears.
It haunts me now,
That dark and early morning,
Where my comrades around me
Cried for their mothers while they died,
As I watched with shameful eyes.
It shocks me now,
That dark and early morning,
How we had lost so many
But held strong our fortitude
As we pushed forward to break their defenses.
It vexes me now,
That dark and early morning,
The time which was known as our 'Finest Hour,'
The day which began when our boat released its door
On June 6th, 1944.

Christopher Zhang, Grade 10
Townsend Harris High School, NY

Foundations

I wake up
It's morning; it's too early
The lights are alive
Embracing my eyes. It's horrible
My retinas burn, I close my lids
My door is open, I walk out
"I want Cap'n Crunch"
I leave it to soak, I won't eat it
Back to my cave
My clothes, we play a game;
Hide and go seek. "Where are you?!"
Scattered on the floor, nine hundred black shirts
Minimalism
To the mirror, we can be friends or opposite
My hair is wild, I like it
Today we're friends
Brushing my teeth toothbrush frayed
It's too early to care
I miss the bus I planned this
10 more minutes to watch Fox 5 News
In the car, off to school

Nick Szczesny, Grade 10
Colonia High School, NJ

I Will Always Love You

I will always love you
no matter how much pain you put me through.
We have been through so much together,
I will love you forever.
Together again we are meant to be; can't you see?
Sadly it didn't work out that way
but hopefully someday.

Toni Bradberry, Grade 11
Southwestern Central High School, NY

Do You Believe in Magic?

Magic is all around
As far as you and I can see
There is magic even in a bee
Do you hear that magical sound?
Fairies and witches have I found
The very copper key
Having a conversation with a warlock with special tea
The place where they all hide is a mound
Fairy dust and powder
Magical rocks in different colors
Wishing upon a star and it coming true
Magical beings getting louder and louder
Believing in the all powerful nature of mothers
With this magic you're never blue

Claire Vakalis, Grade 10
Colonia High School, NJ

Why

I wonder why we feel pain,
the throat tightening pain of mistakes gone by,
one that makes breath elusive.
The butterfly pain of guilt,
a fluttering nausea trickling from the soul.
The overwhelming pain of loss and loneliness,
a hollow heart, numb and teary.

I wonder why we love,
exposing ourselves only to be hurt,
searching for love, an obsession every day,
finding it and the vulnerability to more pain and loss.

I wonder why we die,
leaving our loved ones.
Death itself, causing so much pain.
Why,
for it tears apart the blocks of security
everyone works so hard
to build.

Kendall Nicosia-Rusin, Grade 11
Hollis Brookline High School, NH

To Whom It Concerns*

To whom it concerns I'm only sixteen
But I really am much sadder than I seem.
To whom it concerns my heart is in two
But they all argue there was nothing I could do.
To whom it concerns when he spilt his blood red
He didn't consider who else would wind up dead.
To whom it concerns I'm starting to heal
But I'm starting to imagine the pain he used to feel.
To whom it concerns I know that he loved me
But I also could see he wasn't the man he used to be.
To whom it concerns I'm accepting his death
But please understand I will never forget.

Alyssa Ames, Grade 12
Brunswick High School, ME
*In loving memory of Willie the greatest step dad
a little girl could ask for.

Drumbeat

A rum pum pum
the beating drum
the beating heart
collide

A rum pum pum
they're burning down
the little town
tonight

A rum pum pum
and here, they come
and still they're
synchronized

A rum pum pum
the heart and drum
the beats they then
divide

Cassandra E. Gorcsos, Grade 11
South Brunswick High School, NJ

Diamonds Are Forever

They shine like a star
It sparkles like a polished stone
It is good for jewelry
It is the hardest gem in the world
There are fake ones and real ones
DIAMONDS ARE FOREVER

Jon Schilmeister, Grade 10
The Baird Center, MA

This Dream

Every day I pray,
I hope, I dream
That he'll return to me.
A dream that I have prayed
For ever since he left me.
I looked up to him as my hero,
I looked up to him as a friend,
I looked up to him as my father
But yet he still not there.
I used to wake up in the morning
Running to his arms.
I used to wake up in the night
Running to his room.
I used to wake up every day
Knowing that he was mine.
But I never thought that day would come
That he was never there.
That day that I woke up and
Didn't see him there.
He's gone
Now he's gone for good.

Janna Prieto, Grade 10
Miami Beach Sr High School, FL

Loneliness Is a Table

The young man is sitting, reading a book in the middle of the restaurant.
I see him touch something in his pocket, but I think nothing of it.
He is alone.
There is no one across from him to talk to,
No one to notice how he is dressed or his sadness.
He finishes his meal.
Pulling his cell out of his pocket, he checks the time,
Sighs, leaves a tip and walks out into the night.
Left on the table is a note: *If my wife comes, tell her I left.*

David Mistler, Grade 11
Tucker High School, VA

Cry, the Beloved Country

Cry, the beloved country for those that cannot see
The brutality of Johannesburg, the dreams that cannot be
Hopes have been torn from the lonely traveler's hand
And thrown to the ground like the driftwood deserted in the sand.

Young men and women from all different sects
They walk to their future to see what's next
Inadvertent to their surroundings they are lost in the crowd
Impassive and stoical, lost in the clouds.

The nature is dead, there is no life
There is no happiness when looking at the horizon just strife
The once prolific valley has turned to dust
The buildings are decaying from rust

Kumalo leaves the city with less dignity than he came with
Because of the infraction by his son
He is left with a new daughter and a child so young.

Karis Quanstrom, Grade 10
Council Rock High School South, PA

Peace

Waterfall.
Rocks sparkle under the soft light.
Serene.
Aquamarine bubbles twirl.
Graceful.
Green blanket, stained red by the falling sun,
dying between the blades of grass.
Luna appears, glistening.
Stars surround her, their leader, the moon, goddess of the night.
The black backdrop displays her, center stage.
Watercolor flowers dance, led by the light breeze.
Words follow, the song of nature, whispered throughout.
The breath of life.
Bells chime, signaling the start of a new day.
Butterflies twitter, welcoming the last ones who continue to dwell on sweet dreams,
to awaken and greet the sun.
Dawn approaches. Shyly at first, yet always determined to let light seep to all.
Owls back away, preparing to sleep.
Peace at last.

Amanda Bragg, Grade 10
Nature Coast Technical High School, FL

Mother

M is for mistakes I made and they were dumb.
O is for overconfidence that I had, but I was wrong.
T is for treatment that I went through.
H is for healthy corrections that I made too.
E is for everything I put her through.
R is for respect I give her as a growing young man, too.

Avren S., Grade 10
Audubon Youth Development Center, KY

The Railroad

O' Railroad — my friend can you hear me?
I ventured your incalculable links that wound me to see sights
of horror and serenity,
the sights you had to offer a simple human being
just as me…
There on the hill I watched your smile stretch upon concave and linear course —
through your window I came to see and ask…
My life —
where are you taking me?
Take me to where the infinite waves progress,
colliding with the jagged cliff's edge,
Take me to the path along where the apple trees
grow —
the only place I know.
And with you, all the visible silhouettes blur as they perch themselves upon you —
reminding me of your sole purpose.
So take me farthest from home,
let the tracks bring me across the cities, around the globe
where the angels will sing chorus for us —
the traveler says while returning —
Take me to the vineyard so the fresh dews may remind me of you.

Megan Rossomangno, Grade 10
LaGuardia Arts School, NY

Overused

We can start with once upon a time, but there's no happily ever after.
Why don't you tell them all about our closing chapter?
You mixed things up like words in a blender.
Do you remember everything you ever sent her?
You know, concrete cracks under pressure, and I knew I could do better
But your overused phrases always kept me bent over backwards
Or maybe head over heels.
And you made it feel like gym class
Where I'm gonna be picked last.
Once again.
My heart stopped cold, my throat swelled shut, my tears started route
After major system failure the rest followed suit.
Soon you became a still frame, a snapshot in my head.
So why was I still hanging on every word you said?
But now I'm starting to forget, though I know you're never gone.
But it's nice to hear my heart beginning a new song.
I got your picture in my pocket.
I'll save it for a rainy day
Or better yet, I'm gonna let it fade away.
It sounds cliché, I'm sure it's true.
But so was everything ever said by you.

Terra Fasold, Grade 10
Shikellamy High School, PA

James

It's the way how every day
Feels so sunny
Makes my hands tingle
And stomach feel funny
With smiles so bright
Never-ending nights
Without your arms around me
Holding so tight
The moon keeps me sane
When I want to run
'Cause it's out of my control
While I'm still young
I see my future
In your big, brown eyes
Every single time
Our lips collide
Like the beach
Against its morning tide
My love is true
I promise you this
I'll hold on forever
And swear with a kiss

Jenny Barch, Grade 11
Walsingham Academy Upper School, VA

The Unforgotten Sting

I know the feeling
Where the trust is lost
I feel unappreciated
Used, filthy, ugly,
The pain — too much to take
The memories — never forgotten
The joy — gone
My face — just blank.

I can't look at myself
I lost my dignity, pride, self-respect
The passion in my eyes is lost
The beauty of life is gone
The freedom of choice is taken
What's left is this body of ruin
That refuses to let me be.

In the inside, I'm just screaming;
Where is that girl I used to know
My life is just taken from me
I — have no power.

I just wanna say, "feel MY PAIN."

Joselie Marie Louis, Grade 11
Everett High School, MA

Understanding My Life

Growing up has its dilemmas. Afraid to grow up your way, and say,
what it is that you did and what it means. My heart runs rampant, full of emotion.
Whether to scream, laugh, cry, or love. What a hole I put myself in, I choose life.
To live is to reject and to be rejected. To accept and be accepted.
On a journey to satisfy the flesh, but in the meantime, creating inevitable mess.
Learning to deal with others, and battling your own demons.
Choosing what comes first and what comes last. I lost my friend the other day, and I learned to stand on my own.
I felt the warmth of body heat and I let my mind wonder.
I have new connections, some for fun and some for lessons.
Trying to figure the whole me and what I am seen to be.
The abstract of my soul is out on a poster for the world to see.
Trying to make definitions for the words that are happening, is different for you and me.
My comfort door behind me, I try to hide behind, but the angel that lives there closes it.
I have been put out into this cold, wet world and left to dry. Building my own shelter, so I can go inside.
I wonder what the future holds, and what will be come of me.
I do certain things in order to control my destination, but it's too far to reach out into a foggy distance.
My mind is not contained within the walls of my oppression.
I search for the goodness in life to fly through certain recessions.
My thoughts are up on a cloud, and I try to fly them higher. Music is my plane, but also an inhibitor.
I often hide behind isolation, to relieve myself of exposure.
I write my heart onto this paper, and I believe I am getting closer.

Amber Bowie, Grade 12
Kinston High School, NC

The One

there are times when you think, are they the one. there are times when you wonder if things are gonna last, every time i see his face and think…he is the perfect guy. i look in his eyes and i know that he cares. being around him everything is good, all problems begin to fade. when his arms are around me i feel safe. every time we kiss everything around us disappears. you can always tell if he is the one by the way you feel around him, and every time you're apart you know he is thinking about you like you are thinking about him. you know you are in love when you are the happiest you have ever been no matter what happens.

Sammy Garvey, Grade 12
Marshfield High School, MA

I Am From

I am from an old country road, with deer running along each side, riding 4-wheelers where we made our own paths
I am from spending time with my dogs, and hiding from them just to see if they could find us
I am from fishing trips in my pond, thinking Jaws lived there, learning to shoot a gun, and the wonderful feeling of shooting my first deer
I am from horseback riding bareback, having the time of my life, and giving my friends rides on my pony, laughing hysterically as he threw every one of them off
I am from hot summer days working in the yard, rides on top of the tractor with Dad, and spending days at the lake with the family, while trying to learn to ski but never being good at it
I am from early morning breakfasts cooked by Chef Dad, being chased by mean roosters, and the duck that thought he was a dog
I am from parties at my house with all of the family, spending summers running barefoot around the yard playing in the sprinklers, and spending my allowance on bread for the animals
I am from inventions, such as a slip and slide out of shampoo and shower curtains, sleeping in tents in the yard with friends and being scared to come out for fear of the bats flying overhead, having sleepovers and midnight concerts in the yard on the picnic tables where our only audience was the chickens
I am from the best mom a girl could ever have, who I have always considered to be my mother and one of my best friends, she can make me laugh till tears run down my face with her awesome sense of humor and energy like no one I have ever known
I am from good and bad memories, but knowing that I have the best life I could ever want, where being at my house is better than being anywhere else in the world, and I am proud to say that I am from my very own heaven on Earth.

Melissa Landrum, Grade 11
Thomson High School, GA

My American Dream

I have a dream that one day soon
I'll affect our nation that's seen nothing but gloom;
To set them up in God's big hand
And without fear or shame they'll stand.

To help them remember how this all began,
When God made man with nothing but sand;
To look back and see what our nation once stood for,
When we cared for the sick, the outcast, and poor.

If only our country could wake up and see
All the things we've messed up, and what we should be.

Daniel Lutcher, Grade 10
Elmira Christian Academy, NY

A Vow of Silence

Is it a vow of silence
Or an outspoken voice
That will eventually give us the choice?
To choose how we live
To choose who we love
To interpret the truth of the heavens above?
A simple silence
Is just a second without words
Without these words can we truly be heard?
But too much spoken
Can belittle the speaker
Then have we accomplished what we're after?

A moment of silence
Can accomplish little
But any word spoken can change perspective.
It can change our attitude.
It can change our lives.
Speak out; don't leave your voice unheard.

Gabrielle Atkinson, Grade 12
North Bullitt High School, KY

I Am From

I am from
Blooming flowers, birds chirping,
green shrubbery, and the smell of fresh air.

I am from
Jambalaya; bacon, grits, eggs, and croissants;
fresh shrimp, salmon, crawfish, and crab.

I am from
"Ashley, Brandon, and Terrence time to get up,"
and "Don't make me fire your little butts up,"
and "Good morning Beautiful."

I am from
Glenn Turman, Aretha Franklin,
Rev. Dorothy Hart, Yetonia and Terry Turman,
but most of all I AM FROM GOD!

Ashley Turman, Grade 11
Thomson High School, GA

Erie

E
R
I
E
The lure of the lake;
Pulsating, gyrating, flowing
It draws me near, it reels me in
I become liquid under its persuasive spell
I sling a rod, I gather some bait, I snarl some tackle
Morning, noon, and night are all equally opportune
Weather often hinders but I never relinquish
Waves crash, clothes dampen, sun bakes
I tentatively cast, the lure plops
Slowly I crank, crank, crank
The line retrieves — the wait
Unbearable, Strike! Jerk!
Faster and faster
Jump, splash
Out of water
The verve of a fisherman

John Imbery, Grade 11
Grafton High School, VA

Craven

Rustic, ancient, barely standing
Red lights glaring
Devils? Seraphim?
This place called Craven…
Upon, once did I enter
Lune, they fancied me. Lune, I say.
Quickly halted, was their judgments.
Say to me perhaps?
Fancy you, also, me to be mad?
The devilish deed complete: murderer,
They say, murderer? Humble me?
Why "never" did I answer.
Again though they believed me not.
"Mad, mad?" I said.
"Devoured." "Engulfed," they respond.
But why you ask? By what, not? Do I?
Gluttony, pride, envy, sloth, greed, lust, wrath
Yes, seven fine lovers: yet still they fancy me mad.
Fancy, I, mad and a murderer?
No, never, never, mad I say!

Mike Slaughter, Grade 12
Mount View High School, WV

Was It the Kiss?

The sky shone star-kindled gold today
With clouds bursting vivid hues of sheer joy
A kaleidoscope of vibrant pigments
Reflecting my jubilance
Why does the world mirror my gaiety?
I must know!
Is it because you kissed me last night?

Tory Christian Rogers, Grade 11
Theodore High School, AL

Guardian Angel

Angelic smile and dainty wings,
Greets me as trumpets sing.
My Guardian has come to lift me up,
High above enchanted sky.

Guide me O blessed angel,
Fill me with your wisdom.
Teach me to live with moral ways,
And protect me from darkened days.

Give me strength to hold my own,
When threatening times are near.
Defend me and keep me safe,
If ever harm should appear.

And as I face these evil times,
My fear I shall not abide.
For I know that deep within,
My Guardian Angel is by my side.

Kristen Bentley, Grade 11
Theodore High School, AL

Untitled

You
Saunter around,
Gloating in your perfection
This picture-perfect image
That I have come to loathe
I
Shatter the image
Scattering seemingly bulletproof shards
Amongst the pining.
You
Shall not have power
Over my personality
I
Kick away the weak followers of
Normality
They
Know nothing
Of
Me.

Emily R.A. Bilodeau, Grade 11
Cheltenham High School, PA

Temptation

Alluring
Enthralling
Passionate
Desire.
Temptation sets
The world
On
Fire.

Haley Wilson, Grade 11
Liberty High School, SC

Heaven

Let us proceed then, you and I to that grand palace in the sky
Like a child wandering aimlessly from land to sea, to feel so free
By the light of that inner flame so bright, warm and untamed
We shall find the gates of Heaven we shall ascend up to Heaven
See the angels come and go passing into the holy glow
Take my hand and we shall go wearing robes as white as snow
To the world up in the clouds many miles above the ground
We shall escape the drooling jaws of death and refill our lungs with that holy breath
Standing in front of the pearly gates knowing that God holds our fate
In we go, both you and I into that grand palace in the sky
'Tis not a dream, 'tis not a dream even though that's what it may seem
We have eluded the devil's power to make it to this glorious hour
Let us relax, you and me and live here for eternity

Miles Bumgardner, Grade 12
Winston Salem Street School, NC

A Loss for Words

This feeling indescribable these thoughts random but very true
The way she looks at me I would never undo
Her, beauty, sweetness, and wit draws me so nervously close
Anxious, scared, excited it's crazy because I love this the most
Slightly fallen or completely shattered to pieces this guard I put up so well
Everything I thought I knew about these things have gone to hell
In my head again and again she's so tempting like a little sin
She's very on my mind
I swear I hear her voice drifting in the wind
At a loss for words to say the least
Will we write this story with a happy end?
Close your eyes fall back I'll catch you and take me by the hand

Chris Hickman, Grade 12
North Henderson High School, NC

Eying Something Fishy

Charting the sea and watching out for the big fish above,
You must keep your eyes peeled
For other's scrutiny and vision may perceive more than you can.
Above and below the undulating water lies a perilous world full of criticism,
Which is spewed out by the sharpest sharks.

Unaware of your potential to get fried,
Laziness overcomes you
You are halted by drooping, complacent fins,
Not able to see and not wanting to see.

Why would you be so lethargic when there's so much to see
Look around — AYE —
Because when danger comes and baits you
You will need to be wide open.

Now your pair of dark circles darts around feverishly,
Stimulated and held open by beating long fins
Curled in the most beauteous fashion.
Having understood the importance of "eye and I,"
You are now ready when the shark gives you the fisheye.

Sasha Weiss, Grade 11
Jericho High School, NY

Why Am I So Confused About Life??

What is life to you and me??
Life is so confusing
sometimes it feels like it's worth it
what does life do for us?
Oh my God!!!
So many questions about life
that it is impossible to get any answers
sometimes it feels like if I should give up everything
life can create lot of problems
life can make you feel happy, sad, angry, and so on
life is timeless, can change you every minute of your life.
To me life is like a roller coaster
it goes up slowly, a minute later
it just drops you down like a big shock
that it takes a while to catch your breath
life can do lot of things to you
that you are not aware of
why is life so confusing
when I get the answer
I promise to tell you what it really means…

Syeda Ali, Grade 11
William C Bryant High School, NY

Bugaloo

Known to be ignored
and sometimes left with mom
Yet in my teenage life
My brother is the bomb
Together we play with whatever's around
Socks or sabers or swords
As long as I'm there to play at the moment
Our time together is our reward.
A dynamic duo, always near to each other
Our separation is seldom seen
We work together in all we do
Forgetting he's six and I'm fifteen.
His nickname is one given by dad
Not Bud or Kid or Scooby-Doo
In the classroom he's known as Aaron R
But at home he's "the Bugaloo"
Aaron and I, two brothers bonded
Our relationship is as strong as steel
When people see us side-by-side
They see a love that's real.

Adam Ridenour, Grade 10
Calvary Christian Academy, FL

My Momma

Ever since day one, she was there for me.
Without you around, I don't know what to do.
She showed me in life that nothing is free.
She took care of me ever since 92.
Lord knows she tries real hard.
And she gives all her thanks to God.
All my life my momma stayed true.
And all I have to say is I love you!!!

Trevon Woods, Grade 10
Miami Beach Sr High School, FL

Greatest Goddess of All Time

The queen of my eyes, the sea and sunshine,
We've been to hell together as Satan tried to harm,
Threatened my eyes, cursed me to be blind,
Yet, not even his soul could resist your charm.

Our kingdom will rise to the highest of heights,
And your name will be forever screamed
Into the late hours of all nights
Until your image creeps into people's dreams.

Poseidon sinks my boat, no matter if Zeus shocks me,
Even when Aphrodite lusts me against you.
I'll spoil their plans; next to this god you're destined to be
With all my abilities, you'd not add something new.

To allow you to pass without me is a crime,
As Odysseus I'll make you the greatest goddess of all time.

Shane Young, Grade 12
Carver Vocational Technical High School, MD

The Beauty of Spring and the Dullness of Winter

Just like a child,
We saw through eyes of joy.
Our hearts and souls,
just as warm as the sun.
Our spirits flowing,
just like the wind.
Our beauty and radiance,
like a flower blossoming in spring.
Our joy and innocence,
just as beautiful as the season.
Eventually, spring turns over,
then winter takes over.
The world becomes a cold place.
Our souls are buried under the snow,
our beauty and heart, as cold as ice.
Our innocence has vanished like the sun.
And just before our eyes,
we've turned into people,
we no longer know.

Brittney Gunter, Grade 11
Bristol Plymouth Vocational Technical School, MA

My Brother's Keeper

The bachelor brothers
Bread-and-butter
Monthly milk from their cows
Dungarees stained with patches of manure
Boom, Boom, Boom
Dead in bed
Like a doornail
National news
A confession?
Or just a mistake gone awry
'I was nervous and shook up'
The bachelor brothers

Joe Hofmann, Grade 10
Colonia High School, NJ

Fighter

You're a fighter,
Waiting for anything to come your way,
Ignorant people, obstacles, and hazards come every day.
Everyone else would run away if they had your life.
But you take it like a soldier even when you cry.
You try not to show your emotion,
Even though you cannot take it some days,
A friend might try to understand what you're going through,
But in reality they will never know until they are you.
You are strong, independent, and intelligent.
Always there for somebody as you watch from the side,
Seeing everything as the day goes by,
Ready to pick up the pieces for everyone you love,
You are the care taker, soldier, and fighter that will always show up as the days go on!

Kimberly Fine, Grade 11
Miami Killian Sr High School, FL

Dirt Road

It feels like the weight of the world is tumbling on my shoulders
My legs start to quiver and these minutes seem longer
I have no clue what to do, God please make me stronger
The world's getting darker and my body's getting colder
Can anyone help me, it seems like no one wants to
I'm stuck in a pool of pain and I don't know what I'm going to do
You don't know what I'm going through
Take your pain, times it by ten, and it doesn't even add up to what I'm going through
I feel like I'm walking a dirt road with no end
All these curves and bends, I'm all alone and with no friends
I pretend that there's someone beside me that can lend
A hand to help me out but then I notice the dirt road again
Maybe this feeling is just a phase and it'll be gone in a couple of days
But it's got me in a rage and plus my job doesn't do well in pay
I just want to be listened to but my story…no one's heard it
The long dirt road, I stare it down with great courage

Kyle McCarty, Grade 10
Ragsdale High School, NC

Wonder and Beauty

As I look at this world's wonder and beauty a few thoughts begin to come to me.
When I see the beauty of dove I think of one's ability to care and to love.
When I see the river flowing I think of human persistence to never want to stop going.

As I look at this world's wonder and beauty a few thoughts begin to come to me.
I begin to think of the love of family, telling you never to stop believing.
I think of your friends that are by your side when you need somewhere to hide.

As I look at this world's wonder and beauty a few thoughts begin to come to me.
I think of the wisdom of the old with all their memories as precious as gold.
I think of the young whose book of life has barely begun.

As I look at this world's wonder and beauty a few thoughts begin to come to me.
I think of freedom and liberty and all of the things that has been given to me.
It is funny what one begins to ponder when one gives a good look at nature.

Matthew Ditsworth, Grade 11
East Central High School, MS

Mystery

Who knows, did you see them?
what, where? and now enticing superstitions
drip from my skin.
life is built from the ground, built from the dirt of adventure
to the roof of what the future holds
no one knows
who knows…

Anthony Valenti, Grade 12
Cab Calloway School of the Arts, DE

Calypso's Sorrow

Why do those undying gods
Always take what is not theirs?
They do what they will
Unmindful of the wants, the needs,
Of their very own sister.
They brought that wandering man,
That man of suffering,
Nothing but grief and pain.
Then they brought him to me,
Floating in the salty sea.
I nurtured him, made him whole once more,
I fed him, housed him, and loved him.
I gave him all the time in the world, and for what?
So that they can come and take him away
Because it is what they desire.
He is alive due to me,
With no help from those gods, arrogant Zeus, brutish Poseidon.
What right do they have to take him?
To tell me to let him go,
Even though I fed him, housed him and loved him for these long years
What gives them the right?

Adam Sands, Grade 11
Riverdale Country School, NY

One Child at a Time

Every day you seem to complain
about everything you don't have
you seem to love receiving than giving
you don't care about what's happening to others
as long as it's not to you

but while you are being too selfish to think about others
there are children dying of AIDS, starvation, and loneliness
if only you can take a moment and put yourselves in their position
feel their pain, hurt, and cry every tear they cry

you feel that you can't change the world
you feel like you are invisible
you feel no one will notice

you can be the difference
these children crave for
you can mend a broken heart
you can save a generation
one child at time

Damilola Adedeji, Grade 11
Union High School, NJ

Choose Your Own Way

Do what you want
Choose your own way
Don't just follow the crowd
Cause they say "Go this way!"

It ain't right to follow your friends
And it ain't right to be the passenger.
Be a leader for once
And choose your own way.

You want to follow them
But you know it ain't right
Cause it ain't what you want
So choose your own way.

Take a swing at the curve ball
That life throws at you.
Follow the path
That you know is right for you.

You'll sigh in the end
If you follow a friend
So choose your own way,
Don't make your own pain.

Jessica Groom, Grade 11
Swampscott High School, MA

Ending Heartache

Regret
Wishing I could turn back time
Despair
I can't believe I let it die
All the signs were there
But I just let it pass on by

Joy once surrounded me
Now all I feel is pain
It seems I have everything
But what I want
I cannot gain

Wishing I could turn back time
To fix my one mistake
To let you know the truth
Before it is too late
To enjoy the way it was before
And never let it die
To change my heartache into joy
And end my soul's demise.

Erin Hartsfield, Grade 11
Loretto High School, TN

Pop Cried

How many people ever really see their dad cry? Well, I saw my dad cry for the first and only time. Dad, you are the strongest man I know. Today I saw you cry. I know it had something to do with me and I know what it was. You see, I've been trained. I've been trained for all kinds of things. I'm trained to turn and stare death in its face when it's chasing after me. I'm trained to take a bullet and keep moving. Even the sight of broken bodies can't make me stumble. The chill of fear that runs down my neck when my buddy next to me is shot in the head isn't enough to stop me. The loud ear bursting and earth shaking sound of a bomb going off can't make me shutter. I have seen it all, but no matter how I've been trained, nothing could prepare me for the tears rolling down your cheeks. You cry for me. You are proud of what I've done, but sad for what I've been through. Today in church, we all cried. Nothing in this world is as strong as love. The love for his son is the only thing that ever made my pop cry.

Jordan Ball, Grade 10
Schley County Middle/High School, GA

En. Light. Ened.

"Yeah, I'll try to make it this Friday to your, thing, maybe." Bah.
Bulging bags carried through my elongated eyes, arched down in a horizon. Support-less lanky limbs, toil-less,
Pushing up against a salmon painted sky. Toes tow across the coarse pavement trekking hills. Switch off.

"So, yeah, I think I like him a little, but seriously, I can't believe that she'd,"
Candy grins and rolling shrills echo between warm syllabic exchanges. Facing front, she bobs, reverberating, back and forth.
She walks willingly and my hollow harmonies no longer swish swiftly past. Her serious stare promises me. Flick on.

"Sorry! It's my dad's birthday and we're going out to celebrate for dinner.
Um, next time?"
Swordplay slash at cheeks, cheered. Sinking in billowy pillows, droggy and drained without a drive.
Night. Blind. Graspless wonders. A breathless wail.

Closed off.

Rosalie Chung, Grade 12
Jericho High School, NY

Wilting Lilies

Your eyes look in fury to the skies for answers you cannot see because your eyes are closed
your heart search to touch the fire but you can't feel it because your heart is frozen cold
You've deserted yourself on an island where you feel more alone
I try to send you a lily of hope across the water but you refuse it
thinking you can spring to life on your own

You try to kiss the stars so that in fame your name people will remember
but I, I try to kiss the autumn leaves trying to inhale the glory of November

When we both fall into eternal sleep you'll have the weep of people
that in tens of years will just forget your face
But in the autumn leaves, the winter snow in my lily smell
I hope to leave a trace

And that's what I think you want to do really
aside from fame and stars and all
In your eyes all you wish to see is a blossoming lily
and hold it,
deserted island of our famous souls
Protecting it
just like a paper wall.

Anya Artsibacheva, Grade 12
Randolph-Macon Academy, VA

Writer's Block

It was as if the flowers had stopped growing,
As if the soil was now a barren land,
Like if all rivers now had stopped flowing,
And all you saw was dried out golden sand.

It was like climbing up a mountain,
Without the correct, effective gear,
Like trying to reach the mirage of a fountain,
When dehydration was your biggest fear.

It was frustration to its biggest peak,
Like running into a solid brick wall,
Or hear the incessant ticks of a clock,

As if the object of desire which we seek,
Was really next to us all along,
This is what it feels like to have writer's block.

Jennifer De Jesus, Grade 10
Bronx High School of Science, NY

Drop the Puck

The bus was loaded and ready to go
Our record stood an even oh and oh
A bus full of kids ready to play
We had all been awaiting opening day
With a team full of seniors expectations were high
Unfortunately all the hype went awry
As we went for the first time through that gate
We had dreams of being the best in the state
Soon we would realize how lofty the goal
We could not even manage to beat division three Lowell
As the season wore on the true team began to show
The season had reached an all time low
We finished the year a dismal five eleven and three
A far cry from a "post season guarantee"
So for those of us looking for a direction to steer
We can at least remember there is always next year

Matt Fairburn, Grade 10
Haverhill High School, MA

Who Really Cares

When you
Walk by a widow
Or a run down
Beat up shack
Do you ever stop and wonder
Just how much they lack
They may have lost everything
Or maybe passed away
But no matter what
Has caused it all
No one is dismayed
The world has lost the people
Who always seemed to care
And replaced them with
The people that
Are always in despair

Jeffrey Thomas Davis, Grade 12
Jeffersontown High School Magnet Career Academy, KY

The Love That I Have

The love in my heart,
The love in my soul,
I keep it all inside,
Too afraid to let it go.

Afraid to be used,
And dropped to the side.
But that won't happen,
With friends and family on my side.

The love in my heart,
The love in my soul.
Time to spread it around the world,
To the people who need it the most.

This is the love…
The love that I have!

Sasha Augustin, Grade 10
Bishop Ford Central Catholic High School, NY

From Where I Want to Be

Here is where there is a firm ground
a place where floorboards don't move underneath me
and make it hard for me to stand.
Here is where I don't have to worry whether
you are going to be okay and decide
to come out of your shadow of depression.
Here I can breathe. I can feel the rush
of the perfect storm and the relief of the hush
the Man standing, past deep, commanded.
I felt that calm once. Heard my eyelashes touch
in that calm. I remember it.
I remember it like I remember
how fearless we were when we dove
under porches and in almost the same quiet
we discovered skeletons we couldn't touch for sadness.
Here I feel these things.
I can stand on the floorboards. Here, I don't worry
about your shadow, and even in the storm
I can be fearless enough to stand and wait
for its perfect, quiet calm.

Danielle Jodoin, Grade 12
Oak Ridge High School, TN

Will Power Will Succeed

I'm surrounded by my own walls of darkness,
I'm a failure, I have no sources to harness.
I've been told that dreams are not for people like me,
beyond my looks I wish someone could see.
I try too hard but that's not good enough,
all I want is for me to be tough.
I have to be strong in a world so cold,
if only I had the power to be so bold.
I know what I am and I know what I'm not,
in spite all my failures I'm thankful for what I've got.
At least I got a chance, so what if I didn't succeed,
my life, my strong will power will lead.

Revati Lalwani, Grade 11
Englewood High School, FL

If Only

If only we could be free,
Free from discrimination and hate.
Free like the great rivers,
Running toward the seas.

If only we could be free,
Free from the bloodshed of our people.
If only we all could runaway,
Far away from the clashing whips that cut our backs.

If only we could be free,
Free from the guns that pierce our chests.
Free from the cruel names we've taken,
If only we could stop the unwanted deaths.

If only we could be free,
Free like the wild winds of the Earth,
Go where we please without being punished.
O, if only, if only, if only we could be free.

Alicia Wright, Grade 10
Schenectady Christian School, NY

Storyteller

Ignore the wind howling my child,
and focus on the flame.
Draw thyself close about the fire
and listen to my tale.
A haunting story of witches' nine,
who lived in the woods in velvet fine,
of princesses and knights so bold.
Of chants and prayers of druids old.
Of spirits ghostly rides at night,
dancing with the devil in the pale moonlight.
So with shut eyes and open ears
thou shall now come to face thy fears.
Ignore the wind howling my child,
and focus on the flame.

Caitlin Crosby, Grade 12
Leonardtown High School, MD

Julius Caesar

He wanted to gain autonomy
But instead was murdered by friends
He ignored all the caveats
Which in the end, enabled him to realize
That his best friend Marcus
Was not a friend indeed
He was very disconcerted
And didn't know what had happened
He fell to the ground
And with one last breath, said "Et tu Bruté"
And down came the dictator
From oh so high up
He couldn't bear to think
That his best friend Brutus
Would ever do such a thing

Julia Park, Grade 10
Council Rock High School South, PA

When I'm in the Shower

It's dark and my head is down.
The water falls, hits my scalp.
Drips down my wrinkled strands of hair, like grease off bacon.

The steam squeezes and screams through my pores.
Releasing me of stress and aches.

I stand perfectly still clearing my brain.
My eyes are closed.
I focus hard on relaxation to calm my mind.

The water is hot it pierces my skin.
But I love the way I feel when I take a shower.

Symone Neal, Grade 10
Countryside High School, FL

Never Fear

I will never fear the darkness
For I need only to call your name and you will give me light
I will never fear the monsters
For you will whisper in my ear and assure me they are not real
I will never fear the pain
For your hand will grasp my hand and make it disappear
I will never fear the dreams
For they have been shaped by your hands
I will never fear the future
For nothing is unknown with you

You will never fear the end
For I will always be your beginning

Samantha Faso, Grade 12
Nashua High School South, NH

Sweet Summertime

Warm weather, and beach trips.
Cookouts with hot dogs and chips.
Swimming in pools on a hot day.
Oh, how I wish sweet summertime would forever stay.

No waking up early to spend the day at school.
Eating all day 'til you're just too full.
Spending hours with friends, and waking up just to do it all again.
Oh, sweet summertime, please don't end.

Staying out late and watching the stars.
Warm summer nights are the best by far.
Catching glowing lightning bugs in the palm of your hand.
Oh, sweet summertime I'm your biggest fan.

But it's sad to say that too soon it will come.
It reaches late August, and school has begun.
But summer memories never fade.
And until sweet summertime, we'll just have to wait.

Courtney Butler, Grade 10
Wirt County High School, WV

Life

The days pass, the time passes and the Earth seems to stop itself
Life can be so strange "a never-ending pastime"
Made of dreams, nightmares, sadness, happiness, loves, solitudes, desires
Made of people so small — insignificant, tiny parasites
Above all, it's made of the days and nights that cover our dark grim faces,
But behind all this hides the existence of the Omnipotent, the Creator,
The one who has marked the destiny of each one of us…
Life goes on day after day, hour after hour, minute after minute
And we must conquer it so that it does not go wasted,
Because one day watching our script we will notice to have mistaken,
But when this occurs it will be too late
Let's not throw to the wind something so precious bestowed upon us.

Debora Radano, Grade 11
NY

I Am…

I am intelligent and creative.
I wonder what life is like for teens my age in other countries.
I hear the voices of the past.
I see a time when pigs fly.
I want to be remembered.
I am intelligent and creative.

I pretend that sometimes I live in the past.
I feel the presence of ghostly memories.
I touch the lives of those who lived before me.
I worry about what life will be like in ten years.
I cry for the homeless and the pets that love them.
I am intelligent and creative.

I understand that people are different and that will never change.
I say that love is the most powerful force in this world.
I dream of making history come back to life.
I try my best to do what is right.
I hope to be happy when I die.
I am intelligent and creative.

Samantha Krenzer, Grade 10
Haverhill High School, MA

The Porcelain Doll

Have you ever seen a porcelain doll, her skin so fragile and sweet?
Have you ever seen a porcelain doll with hair a golden blonde?
Have you ever seen a porcelain doll sit and wait upon the stand?
Have you ever wondered if she's waiting for someone to take her by the hand?
Have you ever wondered if she's waiting for someone gentle and so kind?
Have you ever seen a porcelain doll wait her entire life?
Have you ever seen a porcelain doll get so dusty on that stand?
Have you ever seen her find someone kind enough to take her by the hand?
Have you ever seen a porcelain doll finally find her one true love?
She thinks that he was sent to her from heaven above,
She looks at him with trusting eyes, then he drops her on the floor,
Her fragile pieces everywhere
She's a porcelain doll no more.

Amy Marsh, Grade 12
South Side High School, PA

Reality

I follow a listless dream
A nightmare in this reality
There's a path laid before me
But out of the corner of my eye
I see what could be
The monster that lurks in my way
Refuses to let me stray
As I yearn for what could be
I follow a listless dream
A nightmare I made my reality

Anna Sprout, Grade 12
Leonardtown High School, MD

Wish

Wish upon a star
For a calm, quiet sleep.
Wish upon a star
For those promises to keep.
Wish upon a star
For a bright and sunny day.
Wish upon a star
For love to come your way.
Wish upon a star
For the wars to start stopping.
Wish upon a star
For the tears to stop dropping.
Wish upon a star
For the peace to fill the air.
Wish upon a star
For an end to all the despair.
Wish upon a star
For these wishes and so much more.
Wish upon a star
For that's what stars are for.

Jessica Fong, Grade 10
East Brunswick High School, NJ

Heaven

Is your house up there
On a Street of Gold
This should be your prayer
For Jesus your hand to hold
As you enter the pearly gate
And behold your Savior's face
I hope you have made this date
And have the Savior on your case
Oh to know no sorrow or pain
To see Him with open arms
And know that he didn't die in vain
Or that you can come to any harm
To meet with all our loved ones passed
And feel nothing but love
Won't that be a blast
To be with Jesus above.

Samantha Barrett, Grade 11
Middle Tennessee Christian School, TN

The Way Things Are

I can't escape my hollowed existence
My lost and merciful soul
The pain I can't help but feel
Wherever and whenever I go
The heart that does not beat
And the tears I keep bottled up
The love I have not found
Cruel fate has left me standing
Alone in my bitter world
Too sad to cry, too angry to scream
You wonder how much you can take
Before you break right down the middle
Your whole world jagged, torn and shredded
My life shattered, ripped and battered
Needing release from the world that keeps
Smacking me down on the hard ground
The icy words that people say
I close my eyes hoping for a break
But instead I get tomorrow.

Amber Moore, Grade 10
Hart County High School, KY

Drifting

Drifting out of space,
Isolated far away from Earth,
Without any directions.
No course to run on,
No path to follow.
So much pain and headache,
Filled with sorrow.
Life is too short,
There might not be a tomorrow.

Driton B., Grade 11
Audubon Youth Development Center, KY

Oblivion

They live their lives as thoughtless mirrors,
Thinking they're better because their skin is clearer.
Like stunning wallflowers without a stem,
Oblivious to the world around them.

They worry about getting dates to prom,
While lives are lost to a suicide bomb.
Strutting through life causing others pain,
Not knowing how fast the sun can turn to rain.

Undergoing surgeries to become more beautiful.
Mistreating the servants who are so dutiful.
Shedding galling of fake and dry tears,
Never showing a glimpse of desires or fears.
They are trophy wives and nothing more,
Without anything true or real to live for.

From young to old they never see,
How beautiful their lives could truly be.
Never admitting their wish, the deadly sin,
To live their lives in more than oblivion.

Alicia Birge, Grade 12
Wamogo Regional High School, CT

The Dream Fixer

She may be opportunity
Or even your best friend.
She takes all the broken dreams
And brings them home to mend.

Dream Fixer, many love you
For mending all the dreams
Gluing back the pieces,
And sewing up the seams.

I've seen my hopes shattered
My dreams torn apart,
My ambitions battered,
And that's only the start.

The world has been so cruel to me,
Time after time after time.
Dream Fixer, you've fixed so many dreams,
Why haven't you fixed mine?

Emma Peterson, Grade 10
New Providence High School, NJ

You Are

When I first saw your face,
You took my breath away
Seeing if you would date me,
Is a step I has to take
you are my strength
When I'm not strong
You are my right,
When I'm wrong
There is not a day that goes by
Without me hearing your voice,
It is like a big rejoice
Your beautiful green eyes dazzle in the light
When I'm in your arms,
Everything feels so right
You are my light to my day,
And my water in my bay
You are the one I want and the one I need
Just as long as you're here with me,
It's only you that I'll please.

Shirletha Wells, Grade 10
East Central High School, MS

A Longing Afternoon

The moist scent of the jasmine blossoms of your perfume;
The fairy-tale melody of your sacred promises;
The disheveled golden locks that hug your cheekbones;
The curl of the tips of your chapstick-covered lips,
I'm running back and forth in your ebony eyes.
"You're my longing afternoon. A best friend,"
You whisper through the shadowed air.
We spend the rest of the day in hollow laughter,
Drowning in ostensible mirth,
Ameliorating, and
Gripping onto the ethereal touches of the longing afternoon.

Cecelia In Lee, Grade 10
Westborough High School, MA

Through My Eyes

If you look through my eyes you'll see what I've been through
And why it is that I don't believe every I love you
If you look through my eyes you'll see how hard I try
Try to put on a fake smile so I don't break down and cry
If you look through my eyes you'll see the past 15 years of my life
The pain I've endured and all of the strife
If you look through my eyes you'll see why it's hard for me to believe everything that people say
And why it is why I am who I am today
If you look through my eyes you'll see all the backstabbing and lies
You'll hear all my silent and mournful cries
If you look through my eyes you'll see how hard it is to move on
And why I'd rather be weak than to be strong
So before you say she always runs away and hides
See what I've been through take a look through my eyes

Daizetta Ellerby, Grade 11
The Middle College at Bennett, NC

Letting Go

Forgive me for all those times I secretly wished you were gone
Forgive me for all those times I blamed you for everything that went wrong.
No matter how much I hated you once before
I never knew how much the future would have in store.
After all this time of suffering, I know I should have seen it coming.
But my mind just wouldn't let me accept it, the thought was overwhelming.
To think that I never got the chance to say good-bye
Brings a tear to my eye, and makes my heart want to cry.
I'm still not able to let you go, although it's selfish, I know.
But before I can truly move on and really let you go.
I need a chance to say good-bye, a chance at your forgiveness.
I remember you once said that words can lead to a great big mess,
But that you'll always find a way to listen, no matter where you are or what I have to say.
And so with this I get my real last good-bye, and you can finally go up, up, and away.
My heart will be able to let you go, and let you enjoy your life in peace.
My mind will never forget you. I'll still be your little niece.

Maria Myrtil, Grade 11
New York City Museum School, NY

A Nothing

The anxiousness — acidic in my lower stomach; the most vulnerable place — waves over me as the pounding of a heartbeat steadily invades my senses. I can feel it, like a drumbeat; playing the cadence to Hell. I can hear it, whispering my name, caressing me with words; arousing goose bumps from my skin. I can taste it, a sourly sweet treat; teasing my palate with restricted delicacies. I can see it — the vibrations it releases; rippling simultaneously.

Time freezes and becomes as dense as the weight of water around me. I'm suffocating. The heartbeat lurches toward me in aggressive yet restrained pulses. Its face — translucent and temporary — flashes while riding each wave. Then it crouches beside me; its eyes scrutinizing my position; its stillness evident from anticipation.

Everything is black and nothing is visible.
An explosion of light — I barely see it gulping the space in front of me like a gluttonous sinner; ravenous for more.

I run, through fate's pause. I end up nowhere.
And the heartbeat grows louder.

Samantha Watson, Grade 11
Ola High School, GA

This Miracle

This miracle is an angel,
an angel sent from the stars.
She is the center of my affection,
my love for her, infinite near and far.

I look at her with guilty eyes,
unable to hide these feelings inside.
I see her through loving vision,
her heart being stolen, my mission.

I'm not with her for now,
though she's always in my heart.
No matter how far I get,
she has been there from the start.

Love is a priceless value,
unable to be bought or sold.
My hopes go no higher,
for together, me and her grow old.

Love is ever living,
to never be deceased.
Love is the grand bounty,
the everlasting feast.

Luke Lovell, Grade 12
Florida Youth Challenge Academy, FL

Earth

I am Earth.
I am in limbo
between the dying
and the dead.

On my surface
walks a creature
that thinks itself above
me
one another
and their morals.

Their disagreements,
diseases,
and destruction
are, bit by bit, destroying me.

When I am fully dead, though,
where will all the creatures go?
If
there are any left.

Elissa Reiskind, Grade 10
St Petersburg High School, FL

Papyrus

When a tree is just growing,
It starts out very small.
It will get leaves and branches as time passes by.
Branches are my ideas and leaves are my details.
Sometimes, I fail, like trees do in the winter
But keep going like they do in the spring.

Nicole Rego, Grade 10
Colonia High School, NJ

Jealousy

It begins during a leisurely stroll through the park,
The air cool, the leaves rustling around you.
You appear normal, a teenager with
Dreams and desires, goals and ambitions.
And yet the darkness is still extant, lurking inside of you,
Only to be seen in the shadows of your eyes,
Restrained from the real world by pure thought,
Strongly desiring to be released toward the sky.
And then the wind begins to harshly blow,
The dogs begin to howl, the cats running for shelter,
And you open your mouth to scream,
To release the feelings of envy from deep within.
For a few of your dreams have come wrapped up in presents,
Only to be opened by others around you.
But nothing comes out, your mouth agape,
And the air is still cold.
Your body begins to tremble,
And without a moment's thought,
You begin running.
But as the wind calms and the sun rises, shedding warmth on all,
Only a distant, running figure can be seen.

Arpan Prabhu, Grade 10
Morgantown High School, WV

Anger

Trying to keep my cool as my blood begins to bubble,
knowing if I make any rash decisions I could get in a lot of trouble.
I try to get away from the problem, the reason why,
but rage has furiously taken over my insides.
I still try to walk away but I fear it's too late,
I won't be able to control my anger if it continues to increase at this rate!
I know how people told me to walk away from fights,
but this person has been bothering me, and holding off has taken all my might!
My blood begins to boil and I decide I'm not taking no more,
but the decision I have just made was very poor!
Fists begin flying as teachers start to surround,
trying to stop the fight as the principle and cop comes around.
They finally break the fight up and the cop takes out two sets of cuffs,
we were then escorted to the office, while a teacher sent up our stuff.
After we both talked to the principle they put us in cop cars,
we knew where we were going and it wasn't that far!
When we got there we were put in cells and later told a date,
Now it's all or nothing, because this decides my fate.
I'm now going to Juvie because of a fight,
I wish I would have controlled my anger, and took everything said light!

Danielle Johnson, Grade 10
East Montgomery High School, NC

The Beauty of Life

Why does life have the capability of changing so fast?
And sometimes take the turn for the better but make us question our past?
Our morals, ethics, and everything alike,
Wants to make us do nothing more than take a hike,
To think things out and wonder if what we're doing is right.
Are we following the straight path or walking blindly through the night?
How is it that years of dogma can be forgotten in one instant?
Beliefs we were so strong in, things we followed on instinct,
Vanish, disappear, without further ado
Endlessly looking for a destination out in the blue,
Sky that holds so many questions and answers both
And yet mysteriously hides them behind the shadow of clouds as if under an oath.
Is it truly our duty to be searching for these answers throughout our life?
If it is, why is there so much strife,
Over what our reason for existence may be?
Why can't we all unite under a common goal peacefully?
Whatever the answers to these questions may be,
One thing will remain forever certainly.
Life, is beautiful.

Shehrezad Haroon, Grade 11
Trumbull High School, CT

Sam

Sitting in a room with a million other people; he walks in as everyone stares
His confidence is high, standing like a steeple; he still doesn't notice everyone's glares.
He tries to say "hi" and make a new friend; but all that comes out is a groan
His greeting attempt has come to an end; as he is left there embarrassed, alone.
What he doesn't realize is that he is weird; people look at him with a feeling of shame
He didn't notice that everyone sneered; and thought to themselves "he is lame."
This is the sad story of simple Sam; but the glum does end here.
For this story was a mere sham; and nothing is as it may appear.
Yes when simple Sam enters a room; eyes do begin to gaze,
But it's his smile like a flower in bloom that sets your heart ablaze.
He is witty and constructive and is always optimistic.
Against all odds he'll be productive; proving judgments wrong about autistic.

Carolyn Ross, Grade 11
Bishop Denis J. O'Connell High School, VA

Julius Caesar

Julius Caesar was a man of courage and honor
And was also very passionate
He knew mostly of war and valor
And preferred to be around men who were corpulent
He was known and loved throughout the city of Rome
For when he passed by people bowed to their knees
The great city of Rome was his only home
And he could always do as he please
But the astute senators did not like and wanted him dead
They were so angry that when they stabbed Caesar they nearly cut off his head
Cassius wheedled his way into getting Brutus's trust
But now whenever they see each other they always start a fuss
Et Tu Brute was what Caesar said as he died
I guess he should've listened to the soothsayer and watched out for the March of Ides

Josh Johnson, Grade 10
Council Rock High School South, PA

The Hunt

It was so very cold,
My heart so very bold,
I was hoping to see a deer,
Hoping not to freeze up in fear,
I sat in a big oak tree,
With my gun on my knee,
A big buck came running out,
It took all I had not to shout,
This was it I was ready,
Held my gun very steady,
As I pulled the trigger,
I knew we had dinner.

Michael Staggs, Grade 11
Loretto High School, TN

More Than a Hippie Sign

Some people say
It's overrated
Impossible
Unrealistic.
Whatever happened to
Love thy neighbor
The golden rule
Everyone is equal?
Peace is more than a hippie sign
It's a concept
A state of mind
A way of life.
Why can't we embrace it?

Cami Fanning, Grade 12
Newnan High School, GA

Imprisoned

I wanna break free
I wanna soar
High above the mountains
Clear across the seas
Floating among the clouds
Drifting in the breeze
But all I see is darkness
Cold steel bars
No space to breathe
Scraps to eat
Nobody cares for me
Lost among the deafening silence
No one can hear my screams
No one can hear my cries
I am abandoned
And I am alone.

Emily Ibanez, Grade 11
Miami Killian Sr High School, FL

A Tale from One Who Has Loved and Lost

Out of the brooding, dark gray mask the sky
wore to convey the heavy, silent day,
there came at once a lilting voice, a sigh
so soft over commanding tone: a ray
of light, of daring hope shines through. What is
this strange response from my embattled heart?

The brazen wind added its call to his.

If all this fog today were to depart,
the wistful sighs of yesterday would be
bleak portrayals, all of what's come and flown
away; the fog which hides the face of he
shines sadly with forsaken tears. My own
are hushed, wasted — a traipsing, hapless stream.

One with the sun, I rise, I run from dreams.

Jen Westphal, Grade 10
Suffern High School, NY

My Mom

My mom is the reason why I am alive
My mom always encourages me
My mom is true
My mom is love
My mom is loyal
My mom is kind
My mom shows how to love and how it feels to be loved
My mom is tough, but sometimes tough love is needed.
I would define my mom as:

M iraculous
O ver comer
T rusting
H onorable
E ver loving
R ich with love

I love you mom

Brandon Dhatt, Grade 10
Miami Beach Sr High School, FL

Anger

Getting angry makes the situation worse,
Control your anger, don't burst
Don't blame your actions on another
You control your anger, not your sister, mother, or brother.

Think before you react,
Be peaceful, don't attack
When you're frustrated just walk away,
Don't make a bad decision and throw your life away.

Vent your anger don't hold it all in,
Scream into a pillow, or talk to a close friend,
Take a deep breath, clear your mind,
Don't make an impulse decision, and always take your time.

Michael Long, Grade 10
Gulf Coast Marine Institute, FL

Metropolitan

A chronic catalyst,
Able to manipulate my masochism
A luxury, I lavish your loose-fitting laceration
I'm always comforted by your gray blanket of methanol

Glamour girl, you gorge my grief
With your perverse panache
When night sheds, beneath jet black,
I'm inebriated under incandescent incantation.

Around you I'm a shark,
Without movement
Morality approaches when this masquerade
Is remit and relinquished

A shame how we are aloof,
'Cause you're my absolute appetite
If not you, I chew and spit
Or swallow, then vomit

The commotion below the concrete scene,
The new sounds via underground,
I long for the day I'm able to capture
Such a recherché realization

Michael Foz, Grade 10
Colonia High School, NJ

Among the Thoughts in the Nighttime

My mind in the nighttime
lays soft, hazy musings in my thoughts,
That which I suppress, too forcefully, during the day
slips in at night,
when I am too tired to remember what is practical.
After midnight, when I am awake
and when
the waves of consciousness lap lightly and patternless,
there are thoughts that ebb the ins and outs
of love, morality, truth and shame
and everything I vowed I would no longer dwell on.
It is this time when I realize
how little is ever truly forgotten or overcome;
the mind, like most things, is not meant to be tamed.
I know you know what I mean
I know you don't always stay up for lack of tiredness
and that,
sometimes,
you wander to keep from the reach of the threatening thoughts.
You and I both, we have not learned
to let them come.

Anna Hadfield, Grade 12
Montgomery Blair High School, MD

Grades 7-8-9

Top Poem Grades 7-8-9

South Carolina Shore

I see now what I have never seen before
The magnificence of nature, captured on an ocean's shore
The undulating rhythm of waves hitting the beach
Leave me coming back each time for more.

Searching through the shells to find the best
I look down and realize how hard this task is to complete
Every one has its own beauty and every one so unique
Finding the best would be an incredible feat.

Lazy days on the beaches looking through the shells
Soft nights at the beaches gazing at the endless sea
It seems so serene, like nothing could go wrong
Its mere existence seems impossible to me.

Perfect at some times yet disastrous at others
How could something so right end up all wrong?
During the times where things seem so hopeless
You have to remember the wave's wonderful song.

And when the storm is over and everything is calm
Every disaster makes you appreciate it all much more
The endless beauty, the endless perfection
That is captured within the ocean's shore.

Jillian Barbaro, Grade 8
Pelham Memorial School, NH

Top Poem Grades 7-8-9

On a Summer's Eve...

The fireflies come out to play;
They dance and jump and twirl and glow.
The twinkle of their dainty parade
Sheds light upon your aching woe.

The crickets chirp a symphony;
It softens the silence of night.
This blissful train of melody
Liberates you of your fright.

A weeping willow's graceful sway
Whispers kindness to your soul.
Charmed by her uplifting ballet,
You're freed from life's fatiguing pull.

The moon's angelic luminescence
Veils the sky in a silver glaze.
As you bask in her moonlit presence,
You're lulled to slumber by her rays.

The cosmic sky is endless blue;
Starred swirls create a fantasy.
They dot the sky like sparkling dew,
Encrypting your dream's legacy.

Amber Barbera-Hale, Grade 9
East Ridge High School, FL

Top Poem Grades 7-8-9

Persevere

My grandfather scales his John Deere,
relaxes in the leather seat,
and cranks the great green giant.
He traverses the rolling pastures
and furnishes the grass with fulfilling fertilizer.
He works into the long hours of the day
with the sizzling sun smirking
at his golden straw hat.
Brackish sweat flows like the Nile
down the arms of my grandfather,
reddened from the August heat.
He perseveres with the will of Superman.
Meanwhile, time, his only nemesis,
tries desperately to thwart his efforts.
The pink sky of dusk is his deadline.
Come morning, the grass will be as green
as his innocent granddaughter.
As he rounds the last foothill,
he wipes his wrinkled brow, quiets the giant,
and walks into the cool air of his house,
the taste of victory still fresh in his mouth.

Tyler Blackmon, Grade 8
Baylor School, TN

Top Poem Grades 7-8-9

The Hammock

Lying suspended between two trees
Has always been the place for me.
Swaying gently in the wind,
No place on Earth, I'd have rather been.

Tall strong trees wave their branches of green,
Sleepily relaxing with me.
Birds chirp softly in the air,
Dandelions everywhere.

Rabbits scurry underneath,
Squirrels hurry up the trees,
Soft wind gently lifts my hair,
Tickles my toes, tan and bare.

Warmth of sun on my legs,
Long, bright, golden rays
Filtering through thick green leaves
Making its way down to me.

Robin Crowley, Grade 7
Trinity Middle School, PA

Top Poem Grades 7-8-9

Soldiers of the Departed

My fingers clasp your hand, although you do not respond.
Your glazed eyes glance up to places I cannot reach.
And in this dry barren desert,
Where the snake dances in the sand,
And the night prowls with the fangs of men,
I hum to you the mournful psalm of the departed.
The shiny metal of your toxin sparks anger in my deepest soul.
Under your helmet I place it,
In remembrance of my service, comrade.
Is this the cause for which I fight?
To be injected with the poison
Of the men who angered quickly,
Of the men who wanted more?
Another day of hearing
The mournful cries of these broken women
Will surely split me open like an egg.
Are we all not victimized soldiers of the same war?
And tonight, while man-made shooting stars
Light up this midnight sky,
My tears will puddle in the sand
As they hum to me the somber stories of the departed.

Megan Munkacsy, Grade 9
Steinert High School, NJ

Top Poem Grades 7-8-9

Each Grain of Sand

I've heard life compared to an hourglass,
where the sands of time just slip away.
Special moments and precious words pass,
lost in flurries of hectic disarray.

Prolong the beauty, always hold fast
to the memories that give you strength and will.
The rushing of wind through the lush green grass,
or the humble sound of a songbird's trill.

Don't wait until your time is spent
and only remember joy, love, grief, and pain.
Don't wait until your body is rent
to wish that your life had helped others to gain.

Devote your life to the greater good.
Enjoy Earth's glorious, majestic grace.
Live life to the fullest, as you should.
Cherish every grain of sand, then you will have earned your place.

Claire Nelson, Grade 7
Chickahominy Middle School, VA

Top Poem Grades 7-8-9

One Window Is All I Need

One window is all I need
To spread my wings and take off
"take a chance, make a wish,
take a risk, and make a change"
Reach out of the darkness
and step into the sun
I won't be trapped like a bird in a cage
I'll just stare out the window,
watch the rain fall and dream until I'm ready.
Taking small steps, I'll learn bit by bit
and one day I'll fly off and soar to live my life…
All I need is one window.

Gina Park, Grade 7
Anthony Wayne Middle School, NJ

Top Poem Grades 7-8-9

Introduction to Poetry

I ask them to take a poem
and yell out the words ecstatically,
like if they just won the lottery
or found out that homework and tests no longer existed.

I say throw the poem high into the blue sky
and wait for a bird to swoop it away,

or run across the poem's lines
and beat the letters to the author's name.

I want them to scuba-dive
in the poem's deep oceans and
blow the words to the surface of the paper.

But they eccentrically look
for treasure, not knowing
the experience is the prize.

They violently begin digging at its ground,
to find out what it really means.

Natalie Petrossian, Grade 8
International School of Boston, MA

Top Poem Grades 7-8-9

My Grandpa Len

Seldom did he visit me,
A stranger in my home,
And blurry though his image is
His voice I still recall.
We'd talk at length of many things,
But my riding caught his interest most,
For in his younger days he rode horses in the cavalry.
His voice would quiver with excitement when that topic did arise,
And gladly did I provide answers to his seemingly endless questions.
How tall a horse and what's his name?
Does he float above the ground like a mysterious fog
Or proudly bounce in step?
What color, pray please tell, is he
— Silvery white, midnight black, or something in between?
I heard less from him as he grew sick, dwindling in strength.
Now he lies peacefully and eternally beneath the golden sun,
Dreaming, I'm sure, of racing through the nights upon a ghostly steed.
In vain Death tries to separate my grandfather and me,
But through the horses I still hear his voice and feel his presence everywhere.
I know for as long as I ride,
His memory will not be forgotten.

Morgan Zaidel, Grade 8
Gill St Bernard's School, NJ

Top Poem Grades 7-8-9

Environment

The sparkling crystal clarity You gave each fish-filled brook
Was changed by man until they had a muddy, oily look.
The gentle rivers we have filled with garbage and debris
Because we thought we owned them and forgot that they're of Thee.
The velvet of the violets we've plowed into the ground.
With heartless selfishness we've slashed the trees where birds abound.
We've leveled off the mountains and with carelessness we've burned
The forests where the animals the ways of nature learned.
We've massacred the buffalo, the salmon and the seal.
The burrows where the rabbits live we've trod beneath our heel.
We cover picnic spots with trash. This ugliness destroys
Each place of beauty once admired by little girls and boys.
Let us respect the natural things we find upon the Earth
And give to each the value and the credit that it's worth.
We need to resurrect the loveliness that once was clear
And give our children reason to enjoy the nature here.

George Zucker, Grade 8
Hommocks Middle School, NY

Love

Holding hands
Walking side by side
Always knowing I'm here for you
Even when you need a ride.
Love is patient,
Love is kind
You'll always be on my mind
Even in the night
When I'm blue
And don't even have a clue.
Can't take my eyes off you,
I know you feel the same way too

Sheridan Davis, Grade 7
Kittatinny Regional High School, NJ

My Decision Unmade

I stand at an intersection
Unsure where to turn
Afraid to take the steps
My silenced heart yearns.
My decision unmade
But the die has been cast
My road has been paved
There's no looking back.
My path has been changed
But I still have a choice
If only I was not afraid
To raise my voice.

Katie Beitzel, Grade 8
Beacon Middle School, DE

The Tree

Sitting silently
A parasol for the grass
Shelter from the sun

Zach DeGiovanni, Grade 7
Public School 334 Anderson, NY

Winter of Wonders

The cold, crisp air hits your face
pinching every nerve
The snow falls slowly in your place
making your path curve

The trees sway back and forth
throwing snow everywhere
More flakes come from the north
falling with gentle care

You can notice the change of mood
turning to quiet and calm
No person acts mean or rude
like the snow set off a huge bomb
of relief

Blair Smith, Grade 8
Milford Middle East School, MA

All at Once

Here I go again with this juggling act
It's in my ear, Chris do this, Chris do that.
I have an assessment meeting at seven, a basketball game at eight,
Thousands of things to do, but no time to concentrate
My homework isn't done; the dog needs to go out
Sometimes I feel like I just have to shout
Give me a break, I'm tired of all this
I can't be myself
No room for laziness.

I wake up too early; go to bed too late
Sleeping is one thing, I need, I can't debate
I get home and the best things I see
Are my bed and my pillow
As my trophy.

Chris Alexander, Grade 9
Unami Middle School, PA

Crimson Red

Angry,
Rage rushes through me like a raging bull.
The smoldering fire is tanning my flesh.
A smoldering vat of fire breathing chili nips at my nose,
Crackling and sizzling,
My furious face illuminates the midnight sky.
The spicy taste of the salsa is tingling the taste buds on my tongue.
While a candle dances with the wind.

Jake Ramsey, Grade 7
William Penn Middle School, PA

Could It Be Love?

I see your face and I can't help but smile
I pick up the phone but hesitate to dial
I hold on to every little word you say
Just to replay it back in my head later that day

I'm thinking about you nonstop
Wishing you were here with me
It's absolutely amazing
You've given me so many sweet little memories

All the little things you do to brighten up my life
It means so very much to me, I can get away from the drama, tragedy, and strife
(that engulfs today's world)

Some friends say that I'm falling for you all over again
And I can't help but to agree
What's in the past stays there
There's somethin special 'bout you and me

My prayers have been answered,
Like always God came through,
I'm so thankful because
I see how truly blessed I am when I'm smiling up at you

Amelia Ford, Grade 8
Dundee Ridge Middle School, FL

Ode to My Grandma

My Grandmother is kind and loving so
she understands me as I grow,
from day to day the years go by,
I will love her til the day I die.
we share lots of secrets, and have many laughs,
we've made lots of good memories don't think of the bad.

Emily Hallman, Grade 7
Saluda Middle School, SC

Let the Music Play

Let the music play
Hold and squeeze me slightly
Hug me tightly
Tell me that you love me
Let there be no delay
Let the music play

When you let the music play
It shows me day to day
Just the way
You love me for who I am
And that lets you hear my heart go bam bam
Let the music play

Let the music play
I'm sure you can be a knight ready to slay
Anything that comes your way
I could be a princess standing in the path during the day
You would come and meet me half way
Let the music play

Karlee Harris, Grade 7
Narragansett Middle School, MA

Serenity

Where the lily pad grows,
Where the wanderer goes,
Where the full moon shines bright
Upon the lake in the night.
Where deep blue resides in the depths,
Where the grass is caressed by the wind's gentle breaths,
Where dreams shine in the stars up above,
And love flies through the sky like a dove.
Where soft sand sleeps upon the shore,
Where the cricket cries just once more.
Where the only sound is the beat in your chest,
As together we lay down to rest.
Where safety and warmth shall last forever,
Where the touch of your hand is soft as a feather.
Where understanding always lies,
As well as deep passion that never dies.
This is where I long to be,
This is what I often see.
Within is the solution and compromise,
It is the light I see in your eyes.

Gabriella Oddo, Grade 7
Bethel Middle School, CT

I Feel

I feel lost
I feel scared when no one's around
I feel anxious as to being tested
I feel abandoned like a baby when its mother leaves
I feel sad when I don't have classes with my friends
I feel lost
I feel as though I have no one to turn to
I feel troubled as the world sits on my shoulders
I feel like a Martian; I don't belong
I feel as irritated as a bee
I feel lost

Cie'dah Graves, Grade 9
Lee High School, AL

I Am…

I am a WWE fan
I am someone who listens to heavy metal music
I am a Guitar Hero playing fanatic
I am me

I will be the next WWE diva
I will be a high school grad
I will be skinny
I will be me

I can do anything
I can be what I want
I cannot dye my hair
I can be me

Jennifer Eisan, Grade 8
Rising Tide School, MA

Love

There's an amazing thing,
That words can't describe.
Is it just a feeling, or is it more?
Why does it make me feel,
Hurt and wonderful all at the same time?
Why do I get it for certain people,
And not for others?
Why is it that it makes me feel
Like you're a million miles away?
When really, you are so close.
Why does it make me cry?
Why does it make me depressed
For no reason at all? Except I'm not with you.
Why does it make me get butterflies
Just because I hear your voice?
Why do I like it?
Why do I hate it?
I don't care. I only care about you.
All I know is that I do,
More than anything.

Hannah Thompson, Grade 8
Plantation Christian Academy, GA

Your Turn

Believe me; I've tried
To fix it —
More times than I can count.
But "nothing's wrong."

I'm not an idiot, love.
I know it's a lie:
Your denial betrays you.

We don't talk to each other —
can't even look at each other.
Don't pretend everything's okay.
It makes it worse.

Because when I ask, you get agitated.
And when I don't,
it gets worse.
Just stop it already.

Can't you look me in the eye?
Shut up with your silence,
And say something for once.

Jennine Nash, Grade 9
Unami Middle School, PA

Tornado

Like a tiger on the prowl
Terrorizing anything around it
Just waiting to strike
Completely hidden until it pounces
And then it's gone like the wind…

Brendan Cosgrove, Grade 7
Anthony Wayne Middle School, NJ

Time for Bed

"It's time for bed!"
My mother had said.
So I brushed my teeth,
And washed my head.

I ran to the window,
And looked very far,
And then I saw something,
The very first star!

I first made a wish,
Then hoped it'd come true.
For if it didn't,
I'd really be blue.

I fell asleep quickly,
When my mom had kissed me.
Then smiled real wide,
And turned on my side.

Andrew Xavier Jr., Grade 7
Orlando Junior Academy, FL

Animal Farm

At Manor Farm, the animals abhorred Farmer Jones
Mr. Jones treated them like dirt and starved them to their bones
The animals could not put up with the harassment much longer
Having a rebellion could only make them stronger
Chaos occurred on the farm
Mr. Jones dealt with much harm
The animals drove Mr. Jones away from the place
They should have seen the look on his face
With Mr. Jones away for life
The animals thought there would be no more strife
When Snowball became the leader, everything was fine
Then when Napoleon took over, a downward plunge was a sure sign
The insidious Napoleon acted like a martinet
The animals worked very hard and used up a lot of sweat
They didn't know which they liked more
Mr. Jones or working for Napoleon until they were sore

Bryan Goldman, Grade 9
Council Rock High School South, PA

Red Wings

Red Wings in the cup, going for the glory,
Looking for themselves, to be in the story.
Of all the hockey players, that played in this game,
To play for the Stanley Cup and give themselves fame.

Lidstrom shooting against the boards, to give to Datsyk to shoot,
And when he scores he usually does, give the scoreboard a salute.
When Zetterburg wins the face-off, to give the Wings the puck,
Draper shoots at the goalie's head, and always makes him duck.

Huddler with a hat trick then the crowd makes a loud sound,
Then look up and you will see, the octopus then comes down.
And then of course we can't forget, Osgood in the net,
He will always make a save, you can always make a bet.

As you see the Wings will win.

Christian Hehr, Grade 7
Depew Middle School, NY

A Ray of Yellow

Yellow is the sparkling summertime sun,
warming my pale soft skin in the glistening daylight.
Blooming buttercups out of the dried summer meadows.
Dotting cheerful baby chicks over the frantic farm
harmoniously herding toasty sunshine into noon.
Yellow trickles on my pink tongue
with pineapple squirting chilled tangy juices,
filling my mouth with vibrant tropical tastes.
Yellow is the sweet smell of honeysuckle
that has been prospering in bushes all spring
relaxing in the wisps and quivers of the refreshing cool breezes.
Yellow is the perky smile on a joyful face every day
that brightens everyone's life and fills it with a brilliant happiness.

Meghan Scarpiello, Grade 7
William Penn Middle School, PA

College

She stood there, by her car, bag in hand
Merely 5, I could not comprehend
The loneliness I would soon encounter
She was my only friend,
See ya kid
I felt hot tears run down the trenches of my cheeks.
The burning sun baked my head
I ran, through the front yard's bushes
As they caressed my gentle skin.
Kneeling down, she let the bag hit the shining grass.
Into her warming arms,
I held her tight, she couldn't leave.

Robert Scordia, Grade 8
William Penn Middle School, PA

Gone But Not Forgotten

With love in our hearts
We watched as we helplessly drifted apart
You went to a sea of light
You saw such a wonderful sight
An unknown world opens its door
As a true new life relives
We held on to the day
As in our hearts, memories of you stay
But still we could not wait for the night
Which would hold you up as a beautiful sight
Because you are a new star in our world tonight

Alexis Cook, Grade 8
Transit Middle School, NY

The Bubbling Brook

Water bubbles down the rocky path of the brook
Sweeping the dirt and pebbles into its rage,
Like a tornado consuming the land like a monster,
Sight
A majestic deer sits at the edge of the brook,
He drinks the water, letting the water slide off his tongue
The cool, fresh taste empowers him, as he drinks his fill,
Taste
The smell of fresh water fills my nose,
It overcomes the smell of fresh flowers entering my nose,
The overwhelming scent causes me to inhale deeply,
Smell
The sound of bubbling water fills the clearing,
Loud enough for any creature to hear
The relaxing sound calms my nerves,
Sound
I kneel on the sandy bank, my fingertip's brushing the water,
The cool feel sends a surge through my body,
I dip my hands in the water, letting the feeling consume me,
Touch

The bubbling brook.

Ben Hsu, Grade 7
Carson Middle School, VA

I'm Me

I'm me when the lights turn on
I'm me when they go out
I'm me all the way an original no doubt,
I'm me which is all I can be,
A role model in which young people look up to me,
Who expect me to be all I can be
I'm me a person who has been set free
Where not even the sky is considered a limit to me
I'm me a person who isn't afraid of success
Even if I fail I still do my best
Always reaching for the top settling for nothing less
I'm me someone God has blessed tremendously
With tremendous heart, tremendous soul, smart mind,
A person who always reaches for their goals
I'm me when the lights turn on
I'm me when they go out
I'm me all the way an original no doubt!!!!

Marquel Reid, Grade 8
N B Clements Middle School, VA

The Green-One-Friend

Green-One-Blanky,
So soft with comfort in my times of need.
With a tomato stain from picnics,
and torn edges from the scary monster nights,
just like a shield to my fears.
From the rich mint-chocolate-chip color,
to the holes that still remain,
the same friend,
the same imaginary protector,
the only difference,
is the sewn holes,
and repaired memories.

Kelsey Lang, Grade 7
Trinity Middle School, PA

Winter Desire

I woke up one morning to find a snowflake
Outside of the window of the bed that I make.

Downstairs by the fire I see a lit candle.
The warmth reminds me of the beach and a sandal.

I stayed inside for hours because it was warm,
Wanting to stay out of the cold winter storm.

I now hear playing an old Christmas song,
One that I've heard for so very long.

I joyfully go outside to build a snowman.
(It's the only thing to do since I cannot get a tan.)

At night I join my family side by side near the fire,
Realizing our day had met our desire.

Lauren Desmond, Grade 7
Westwood Jr-Sr High School, NJ

Incoming

Unbearable stress
Delivers loneliness
Straight to the source
Of where anxiety is buried

It's hard to cope
Sometimes when hope
Is the only thing you need
But the only thing you lack
Lost in an ever-flowing sea
Letting the current drag

When will you stop worrying?
When will you stop thinking?
When will you start dreaming?
When will you start doing?

Kevin Qian, Grade 9
Westford Academy, MA

The Bullied Kid

I once knew a kid who was teased
He never seem to be pleased
No matter what he did,
Everyone laughed at that kid
He cried every time
Which made him commit a crime
Bullied kids grow up mad,
Which makes them very bad
Today he is dead
This makes me hit my head
And say what have I done!!

Ellen Dyche, Grade 8
Yellow Breeches Middle School, PA

Dreams

In our hard lives,
Sometimes we lose steam.
To build it back up,
All we do is dream.

Whenever it seems hard,
Or impossible to do.
We just have ourselves a dream,
And we have strength brand new.

No matter what the challenge.
No matter how much per hour.
No matter what feat it is,
A simple dream will give us the power.

So stop saying "I give up,"
And sinking in your little pit.
Follow your dreams,
And its guaranteed you'll do it.

Anthony Kallhoff, Grade 8
Yellow Breeches Middle School, PA

One with the Sunset

I just lay there,
With an oak to my right,
A blossoming cherry straight ahead.
The spring birds slowly come back north.
A small stream slowly trickles down the road from a hose.
The sunset of pink and gold sinks into purple cotton candy clouds.
An orange sun casts long, growing shadows.
The stream shimmers like broken glass.
Wind whistles melodies in my ears.
Why do I come here?
Why do I feel calm, peaceful?
Why do ideas float in the wind waiting for me to grab them?
Is it different in winter?
Peaceful.
Relaxed.
Wanted.
Alone.
Alive.
Beautifully peaceful.
Beautifully peaceful.
Beautifully peaceful.

Rachael Metz, Grade 7
William Penn Middle School, PA

Zimbabwe Child

I am a Zimbabwe child running in the wild.
No mother no father and nothing to eat,
Stomach aching and blisters on my feet.
10,000 deaths almost every day,
Why can't I have it my way?
No gunshots, no wars
I never felt this way before.
If there was an election for peace on this planet I would be a good candidate.
It's quiet and silent no one can hear my cries,
There are bugs and ants and biting flies.
Why can't I be like the other kids with toys and games?
Being isolated just drives me insane.
I have nothing to eat not even a book to read.
I lay in my bed just looking at night,
Wondering if in the next day there will be a violent fight.
I am a Zimbabwe child running in the wild.

Chelsea Shields, Grade 7
Sewickley Academy, PA

Judged

Running free, she does a turn and a twirl.
Just being a carefree little girl.
Not thinking about drama or global warming;
only about how her mother loved her drawing.
Stopping to wave, as she sees a friend;
they scream and hug, as if the world was about to end.
Anything, pretty much anything I would give, to be that little girl again;
the one without a care, who could dress, speak, and act however;
without being judged.

Jessica Brown, Grade 7
Westwood Jr-Sr High School, NJ

Candy River

The reflection of the lights shine on it,
Like glass reflecting your face.

The imprints shatter it into a thousand pieces,
Like a broken mirror on the wall.

Crackle, crackle, the wrapping comes off,
Unfolding the sea of glass,

Every grain of sugar slowly breaks apart,
Like every part of a dandelion floating in the air.

The melting sugar runs like a river,
Making a waterfall,

And finally the river runs dry,
For the red candy glass is gone.

Marisa Weaver, Grade 7
Yellow Breeches Middle School, PA

The Chipmunk

As I was staring out the window one fine day,
There sat a chipmunk on a bale of hay.
Looking so innocent like a little child,
Though this little animal had come from the wild.
He looked up at me as if he needed help;
Was it food, shelter, or his health?
I wish there was something I could do,
This animal was the size of my shoe!
Before I knew it he was running away,
He must only be wondering about the rest of the day.

Rachael Brush, Grade 9
Schenectady Christian School, NY

The Autumn I Was Eleven

My brothers started to get on my nerves
Permanent fights, screams, awful crisis,
Made the whole family go crazy
It was time for this stupid game to stop

What could have possibly helped that?
A little sister, I thought
Then, one day, this little jewel came
Called Suzanne, she pretended to be my sister

But I knew it was just my imagination,
Suzanne could not possibly exist, I thought,
A dream come true, I could not believe it
But she was there, everywhere

I could touch her gorgeous face,
Smell her little baby head,
Hear her laugh, but also yell
And, all of the sudden, I realized, I had a little sister.

Mathilde Bernaert, Grade 8
International School of Boston, MA

The Ocean

The ocean is filled with the wildest things.
From turtles, to sea cows, to diamond rings.
A lot of this we cannot see, but that will not stop you and me.
We'll dive deep down under the water.
Much like the North American otter.
We'll search the floor for things unknown,
And maybe we'll find some dinosaur bones
Underneath the ocean water.

Hayley Morgans, Grade 7
Bloomsburg Area Middle School, PA

Relaxed

Sea Isle City on the balcony
Kids running on the beautiful beach
Sky, light blue
Fluffy white clouds, dancing
Sun rests on my shoulder
Telephone wires cast long delightful shadows
Pleasantly swaying with the gentle breeze
Ocean leaps and sparkles
Glistening in my face
Sun's rays beam upon the restless water
My heart shaped dune still remains in the sand
The gentle breeze kisses my face
Excited voices from children below me
Everything else, silent
I wonder if snow ever falls onto the beach
Cozy fun loving
Memories, a lot of memories
Never wanting to return home
Relaxed

Joy Hopkins, Grade 7
William Penn Middle School, PA

The Saved, the Abused, the Lost

Nineteen thirty all was well
until Hitler stepped up and took the throne.
He made an organization named the Nazis.
He concocted a scheme
He told himself that he would be the ruler of them all
but first he had to work small.
He never really liked children or Jews
and he thought that they should be abused.
All around Europe thousands of Jews died each day
A very sorry sight.
The children got the worst
no one to save them, always in fear.
They got operated on and badly abused,
many were killed.
Some lucky children lived safely with their parents
while the others were not so lucky.
We grieve the lost and abused,
and hope it never happens again.

Victor Sarmiento, Grade 8
St Stephen's School, NY

The Seasons

There's summer, spring, winter, and fall, so many seasons to have a ball.
Hot, cold, chilly, and even warm, too many temperatures, it's such a storm!

Summer is my favorite season of all. There's no time to go shopping at the mall,
'cause everyone is at the beach or even the pool, trying to stay away from the dreadful school.

Spring is the prettiest season by far, seeing beautiful flowers blooming while driving in your car.
But of course there are some rainy days too. It usually makes many people very blue.

Winter is o' so fun. Playing in the snow until your parents say, "You're done!"
And sometimes you get unusual snow days, where you get to miss school and play all day.

Fall is the windiest season of them all. Leaves all blowing 'round having such a ball.
The leaves all change pretty colors as well, red, orange, yellow, and green, all looking so swell.

So many seasons, all so great, they are too good enough to even rate.
Each season is so special in its own way, how I just love each season each and every day.

Debra DeJoie, Grade 7
Westwood Jr-Sr High School, NJ

What's Going On

Some people see you walking down the street, but they don't know about yo struggle and what you been through
They just see another African American out the hood and look at you like you like you see through
It's so hard livin' in the world today because it's like every youngster has a gun and is making a son
You can't blame a youngin' to be living in straight fear this is one reason all mothers are in tears
I'm speaking about life, history, anything that matters after you read this you'll just leave it alone
Because you don't know that all the problems in the world will soon be gone man what's going on?
What happened to all the stuff that mattered to us our music, money, and children are all fading away like dust
We need all peace through nations and all war to be gone and there's only one question man, what's going on?
It used to be about peace, loving, and living but now it's about killing, money, and who gets the most women
They say stop all the gun crime but saying stop ain't gonna help you save lives
As we speak people living on one life line boy I wish we could sit down and press rewind
So we could start all over again for what used to be for peace loving and families
What's going on?

Jalen Brown, Grade 9
Rockledge Sr High School, FL

Spring

Plop-Plop; new fallen snow begins long awaited liquefaction,
The sun hugs the earth with its bright rays of sunshine
The earth basks in its resplendent brightness
The sun as wonderful as a bright summer's day
Spring calls to the trees and whispers to the animals
Spring is the treaty bringing alleviation to its people
Relief after the brutal war that is winter
During the war animals die, starved trees are stripped of their leaves
Spring comes with alleviation
Spring is luscious fields of green, the golden proud sun and flowers with their sweet aroma
Spring is the best season of all
Whoosh-Whoosh, plip-plop April showers dance bringing water to the ground
Bringing new life to the world
Pitter-patter, streak, dash, check around
Slowly animals come one by one looking for spring's fruits
Spring is by nature's selection the best season of all

Rosh Varghese, Grade 7
Westwood Jr-Sr High School, NJ

Blazing Love

My heart is like an inferno
Burning solely for you
The flames lie eternal in my soul
My love is boiling over scorching me inside
I can take it no longer, I refuse to hide my love
The truth will now show, a feverish wanting to be with you
A fiery need that will be unleashed
And you will love me, and calm the raging heat
But, do not put out the flames

Katherine Gregory, Grade 8
East Rochester Jr/Sr High School, NY

No More Fun and Games

I used to think that life was fun and games,
But one day my life changed.
At the age of thirteen, my Mom got killed.
When I heard it, I didn't believe it, thought I was dreaming,
But when I saw it, I knew it was real,
And wanted to know the reason.
I then had to move with my Dad,
Knew nobody and had nobody with me,
Times alone were sad and I was very mad,
About the situation I had.
After a while I went back to my original "hood,"
Started doing bad things, doing no good.
I was on my own, no place to go;
Wish I had my Mom,
God rest her soul!

Eric A., Grade 9
Audubon Youth Development Center, KY

It Was Just a Dream…I Think

It is so clear in the sky
No clouds are above
The birds are flying high as I can see
There are lots of people there
Having fun in the sun
Not worrying if the skies are going to turn gray
It's going well so far
As I noticed the wind
It was blowing hard
I didn't know why
I looked into the sky
It was getting dark
I have no clue why
It was only 3:00
Then I noticed it started to rain
I kept thinking but I just couldn't think
Of what the problem was
It was really scary the kids started to cry
I heard some noise, it sounded like
A banging sound to me
Then I realized that it was just a dream

Kelsey Bermudez, Grade 8
Seminole County Middle/High School, GA

It Ain't Gonna Be Easy

It's a time of poverty
I tell ya,
Them boys just come and go.
Barley sticking around unattended.
Animals left unfed,
They can get their arm or leg
Broken here and there.

I got no time to kid around,
None of us owners do.
We can't have them come and go like they do.
We lose work, lose money,
Things we can't be losing now,
Not during a time like this.

More of them leave than come here to work!
Give 'em a month or two and they're gone…
The same dreams in their minds:
Land, money, maybe even a family.
A time like this?
It ain't gonna be so easy,
With the New Deal or not…
I'm telling ya…it ain't gonna be easy.

Amy Xu, Grade 9
Bronx High School of Science, NY

Fate

I choose my fate by the things I do
if I am good my fate will be too
I would never buy into what others want me to do
fate's a gift for you to send
fate's a gift for God to end

Alicia Gagnon, Grade 8
Inter-Lakes Jr High School, NH

My Mountain

Gliding down,
Breathing the fresh pine air
Swiftly turning
The mountain moves with me
Blowing by tourists
Laughing at their neon colored one piece suits
Wind whips by me
Like a hurricane in my ears
The sun smiles
A bright shine into my goggles
Sometimes I wonder what the mountain
Would look like without snow
I feel so calm but I'm shivering
On a warmer day it's so exciting
Growing up here
Kept me so close to the mountain
My birthplace
My mountain

Aeddan Flaherty, Grade 7
William Penn Middle School, PA

Snow

The snow stream
is so peaceful that it could
put a baby to sleep —
no loud commotion,
just the snow stream.
What makes it so wonderful?
Is it the sound?
Or, is it the look of it?
Maybe both.

The snow
lies on the top
of the water,
a scattered cloud
in the gray sky.
The muffled white
falling snowflakes
create the constant,
peaceful snow stream.

Scott Kirkpatrick, Grade 7
Ocean City Intermediate School, NJ

Sun

With effort to please us
Every hour every day
It succeeds with its bright
Gold light to bring a smile
To faces and to heat
Each diverse person's heart.

Then, the moon takes over
Gives the sun a night-long break
Though no one's light compares
To its strength, to its heat,
Its smiley power to
Fix someone's cloudy day.

Nicole Levine, Grade 7
Fairfield Woods Middle School, CT

Fireplace

I'll warm you,
keep you kindled,
until the storms have dwindled —
on a beautiful cold winter evening.

Jon Cardenas, Grade 7
St Agatha School, NY

My Dog

my puppy is loud like a horn
wild like a lion
black like night
his mustache is fuzzy grass
his tail is like a sausage
his ears are cat-like

Katelyn Paseler, Grade 7
Thorne Middle School, NJ

Jelly Isn't So Sweet Anymore

Crash! Bluish, murky water washed up and down the shore.
The waves, like a free fall, went up and d
o
w
n.

The cool breeze and the ocean scent,
A candle that's never blown out of the mind, like that moment, a memory.

On the sand I poked the clear, round jelly creature,
the jelly creatures that blanketed the beach.
Carefully, I stepped over them like hopscotch,
trying to avoid being stung a painful death sting.

Adventuring further and further into the ocean,
what felt like a string brushed against my right leg.
At first a soft tingle on my skinny, tanned limb,
then a gust of pain swept through my leg.
My leg gasped for a soothing feeling, but got none.

I marched out of the painful pit of harm, the ocean.
Once I was out I felt refreshed the next second a sharp pain.
The moment wasn't pleasant. The sting made it feel like I plunged into hell.
My leg itched like a wool sweater.
I was stung by a jellyfish, and it all happened at Virginia Beach.

Alexis Appelbaum, Grade 8
William Penn Middle School, PA

Mom and Me

I may not remember the first day we met,
but with each passing day I grew to know
the sound of your voice, and your gentle loving touch.

You looked upon me with watchful eyes,
your heart filled with endless hopes, bountiful wishes,
and sometimes silly surprises.

The gift of sweet innocence here for a moment,
then missed for a lifetime.
"Remember the days, when life was carefree, sweet child of mine."

As I play, the world is my theater.
The grass as my stage, the sun as my spotlight,
the birds as my orchestra, and my stuffed toys as my audience.
I perform the dance of a lifetime.

Your watchful eye always there, never missing a beat of my special talents.
The gift of sweet innocence here for a moment, then missed for a lifetime.
"Remember the days, when life was carefree, sweet child of mine."

As I become older, my princess little girl ways
are being replaced with gossip, boys, and shopping.
Your parenting guidance changes as I look upon you as a friend.
I can share these new adventures life brings to you and me!

Chanel Thibeault, Grade 8
St John's Catholic School, ME

Piano

When I play the piano
I'm in a different land.
Different notes and keys,
and songs I play with please.
Do you know the notes?
How to read music like me?
There's sharps and flats and ABCs,
so it's easy you see,
just follow me.

Kayleigh Gaborek, Grade 7
Cathedral Catholic Academy, PA

A Lack of Focus

The problem is the focus I lack
I find myself living in my own world
I try to listen, but it all goes black.
All of the thoughts in my head become swirled.

While reading, something grabs my attention
I don't know what it is but it just does.
This is what causes me apprehension.
It is more exciting and always was.

How do you fix a problem like this one?
It is difficult with a mind like mine.
I look around and know that I am done.
But I know that it will all be just fine.

If I work real hard, I will win the fight
And I know my future now looks real bright.

Lauren Kleinschmidt, Grade 9
Unami Middle School, PA

Breaking Free

Darkness is all around me.
My chest is pounding.
I'm gasping for air.
But I keep on running.

When I run it's like nothing can touch me.
I can't take it anymore,
My knees drop to the ground.
The dew is cold against my skin.

I roll over gazing up at the stars.
Each one twinkles and shines in their own way.
They all mesmerize me as they create a unique design.

One star catches my eye.
It's not the biggest or the brightest,
But for some reason I love it.

It's time to leave that peaceful place in the grass.
I get up and start running again.

Abbi Fuhrken, Grade 7
Carthage Middle School, NY

Screaming, Silence

I scream,
But I'm silent.
I'm felt,
But not seen.
I'm loud,
And I'm angry.
I'm soft,
And serene.
I am the wind.
Howling above all,
Or quietly whispering,
A song that enthralls.

Jess Genovesi, Grade 8
Southern Columbia Area Middle School, PA

I Don't Want It to End

The first time I saw you
I knew it must be true
You are the one
You shine just like the sun
You make me wonder every night
Why I see you in my sight
I can't believe you're gone
It's been way too long
I wish you would stay
But things can't go my way
I will never know what it would be like
You and me
But now I can see
I hope you understand what I mean
You have no idea what I have seen
I wish you weren't going out with that girl
When I found out it made me twirl
I can't stand it you holding her hand
I just want to bury my head in the sand
I hope we could be together
Forever I just don't want it to end

Allison Kelly, Grade 8
Vernon Center Middle School, CT

Sinking In

Open the page and free my mind,
let loose with the phrases
and let the words I read disappear after,
experience their feelings and senses
and imagine their faces and surroundings,
my imagination bleeds color and creativity,
while I sink into another's place for a time,
until I must return to reality
and face my own adventures and challenges,
with real people and my own thoughts.
May seem lazy, but that's just me,
I've finally closed my mind's eye, but can't not peek once more.

Victoria Langan, Grade 9
Unami Middle School, PA

I Am One

As the furious storm
knocks down
leaf on leaf
dozens at a time,
from the proud tree
upon the hill above,
I am but one leaf
joining and forming
a river of brown
blanketing the earth.

Geoffrey Duffy, Grade 7
Ocean City Intermediate School, NJ

Shipwreck

"The ship was a beauty,"
says the maiden on the bow.
"It's been here a while,"
says the resident sea cow.
"A treasure it was carrying,"
say the sparkling doubloons.
"The captain was a smart man,"
says the charts of the moons.
"It was a war they were prepared for,"
say the stacks of cannonballs.
"We went down fighting,"
say the holes in the walls.
"Revenge is what we're after,"
say the spirits of the crew.
"Peace is what you need to find,"
says the sea, deep and blue.

Mary Catherine Pflug, Grade 9
Spartanburg Jr Writing Project, SC

The Face

I lay curled in my room
Looking at the clock
Faucet dripping water
Tick-tock, tick-tock
I feel my eyes fluttering
My head nodding off
I'm surrendering to sleep
With a sneeze and a cough
The silence was deafening
Not a soul in sight
Nothing but darkness
And then, a light
"You've arrived" said an ominous voice
My heart in my throat
A ghostly face before me
As white as my faux polar bear coat
"Who's there?" my voice cracking
Silence and then I can't see
I awoke in a sweat
To find the face smiling back at me

Christina Agbonghae, Grade 7
Sandy Springs Middle School, GA

Tomorrow's Supper

Ma wakes up early in the morning,
Around five, before the sun rises.
She is hard at work in the kitchen, even before I even open my eyes.
Pa gets up early too, starts work the moment he's washed up.
He works hard on the ranch to support us, his family.
Ma, my lil' sister Millie, and I all give him hope.
He doesn't bring home a lot, just a few scraps here and there,
barely enough to feed lil' Millie alone
But Ma makes the best of what we have; she cuts down her own portions
until we have enough to eat.
Once, Pa came home empty-handed.
He did not have the small bags he usually brought food in.
He walked into the kitchen with a long face, and turned to MaMa.
"There's a lotta men workin' for 'em now. A lot more men then there are barely,
so he decided to let me go. He gave me a few shillings."
He opens his hand 'n dumps it on the table, coins race out.
Ma takes the change and places it beside her.
She whispers, "What will we do for supper tomorrow?"
Pa shakes his head slowly, and walks away.

Shahana Ganesharajah, Grade 9
Bronx High School of Science, NY

When We Were Younger

Do you recognize me, in the shadows of the dark?
Do you remember when we were younger?
You would hold my hands, and tell me that you love me.
Do you remember all the good times we had? Do you even remember me?
Tell me you do. Tell me you love me. Tell me that I'm not invisible.
Tell me a story from when we were younger.
Tell me how much I mean to you.
Tell me something, show me a sign.
Please I'm begging you. I want you to remember.
I want you to remember all the good times, even the bad ones.
I want to be in your mind, to let you know how much you mean to me.
How much we mean to the world.
Please remember.
Please.
Please remember what we had.

Chelsea Spring, Grade 7
Depew Middle School, NY

The Beach

The beach is a wonderful place to see.
And a wonderful place to be.
The beach sand is soft as a pillow and gives you space.
The smell of the fresh water makes the beach a nice place.
The nice blue sky; and crashing of the beautiful waves.
It is such a free and beautiful phase.
The waves crashing were so loud that it seems as though there was a car crash.
The waves move back and forth making loudest bash.
The beach makes me feel so joyful.
The view is so alive and wonderful.
Sometimes you just watch the setting of the beach on your chair.
Sometimes you just want to enjoy the coolness of the beach and this you can't bear.

Uzoamaka Ibeh, Grade 9
Colonia High School, NJ

Making Memories at the Beach

My favorite time of the year
Twenty seven days, it's drawing near.
No clocks, schedules, or ringing bells
My toes in the sand I'm picking up shells.
Waves crashing beneath my feet
Behind me my footprints are stamped on the beach.
Sugar white shores this time so sweet
Later in the evening I'll be bound to be beat
In the hardest arcade games or on the go-cart track
There is nothing at all that summertime lacks.
As the first bell rings beginning the new school year
I'll hold myself back from shedding a tear.
I'll look back and remember the summer
Being in school will seem like a bummer.
I have not a single doubt in my mind
There is no time better than summertime.

Jordan Carroll, Grade 8
Briarwood Christian Jr/Sr High School, AL

Venus

As the arrow pivots and hits my chest,
I never knew Cupid
could catch me like this.
All I want is the gentle warmth
of her forever-lasting kiss
Knowing I can't feel her soft lips,
Knowing I can't compare the texture of her skin
To the summer breeze.
Venus must be incarnate
Because beauty like this is surprising.
If I were an artist, I would capture her image
As if she were a goddess
The drifter says this magic moment
takes me by surprise
How I felt when I met her
I guess Venus isn't the only goddess after all!

Jean-Garmel Marcelin, Grade 9
Bishop Ford Central Catholic High School, NY

Love's First Kiss

Love's first kiss is a joy to be remembered.
For its kiss is as a flash of lightning.
Lighting up your insides,
and makes your heart rumble as thunder.
The rain that accompanies it, makes love grow,
and the rainbow, the path that love follows.
The sun produces the rays of hope,
to keep love burning bright.
Although, love may hit many bumpy roads,
there will never be forks in the road to separate our love.
For love's first kiss, is the best kiss,
enjoyed by two sharing the thunderstorms of life.
Their hearts beating at a tempo together.

Amber Reuthe, Grade 9
Carbondale Area Jr/Sr High School, PA

The Smile

A cool, gentle breeze on a hot summer day,
A warm, friendly smile to brighten your way.
A kiss from your mom,
A hug from your friend,
That let's you know that they're there 'till the end.
A joke heard in the hall,
A card in the mail,
A surprise from your dad,
The happy wag of your pet's tail.
Homework done early,
Better yet, none at all!
A warm cup of cocoa,
A trip to the mall.
A level up on a video game,
A song heard on the radio,
Watching a movie,
Or someone saying they love you so.
A penny on the sidewalk,
The sun on a cloudy day,
Are all reasons to smile today or any day!

Madeleine Morin, Grade 7
Tequesta Trace Middle School, FL

In the Dark

In the dark
surrounded by nothingness
robbed of my light
cause you left me for her,
taking with you the last fragment of my soul
even though you promise to love me till death do us part.

Dumbari Kara, Grade 9
South Gwinnett High School, GA

Exposed

Blood is quickly rushing to my head like fast lava.
My bloodshot eyes are starting to water.
I try to yell, but nothing comes out.

My head feels as if it is a volcano about to explode.
I can almost see my thumping heart pounding out of my chest.
My knees are buckling as I collapse.

I lean on my feeble knees as I cry.
Everything had gone wrong.
This was not meant to happen.

I feel embarrassed, revealed, and uncovered.
My blushing cheeks turn crimson red.
Sweat slowly drips down my forehead.

I am feeling torn apart, devastated and destroyed.
All my precious memories are rapidly bursting into flames.
My secrets are in the open air.
Exposed.

Benjamin Baxter, Grade 7
William Penn Middle School, PA

So Called Friends

So called friends
say they would be your friend to the end.

So called friends
will never end.

So called friends
always do bad.

So called friends
will make you mad.

When they are done with you,
you won't feel sad.

No part of you is left
so remember to think about yourself.
Christina Gaddis, Grade 9
Kate Griffin Jr High School, MS

Tall Creature

Walking skyscrapers
Found only in Africa
Orange Dalmatians
Tongue as blue as blueberries
Reaching for green leaves
Jennie Upton, Grade 9
Unami Middle School, PA

Silence

Silence,
the language of patience,
the feelings of depression,
the calm before the storm.

Silence can help or destroy,
kill or heal,
be depressing or happy,
or just confusing.

Silence,
a universal medicine,
a slow-killing poison,
a neutral area.

Silence,
the emotion of the gods,
the life of death, the death of noise,
the rebirth of emotion.

Silence,
my personal haven,
my feelings of depression,
my little package of emptiness…
Daniel Smith, Grade 8
Takoma Park Middle School, MD

Daddy

Daddy you put my perspective of the world in a whole different view.
From all the hard times I have been put through.
The hurt and pain I will overcome.
But my heart still aches sore and numb.
Daddy you're like no other you're there for me every day.
Even when I don't feel like talking you're there anyway.
Even though I can't see you nor touch you, I know you are there.
The only time we communicate is through a prayer.
I remember that day just like no other.
I was at my neighbor's house when I got that call from my mother.
She told me to come home we needed to talk. So I left regretting that walk.
When I got home she sat me down, looked at me with a sad face, that made me frown.
She broke the news that you had died. My heart broke and I cried.
Fifteen-hundred miles away. I couldn't do anything but sit and pray.
I was only twelve when you died of cancer. But right now I really need an answer.
Why you, what did you do? I know it was cigarettes, yes it's true.
Now I know the answer for your tragic death.
But I would have done anything to have seen you take that last breath.
Candace Ballance, Grade 9
Great Bridge High School, VA

Grass Green

Hearing the roar of the lawn mowers,
Inhaling freshly cut grass.
Rolling down steep hills and getting mouthfuls of green fringy leaves.
Bugs buzzing, flowers sprouting, birds chirping,
The beauty of nature.
Stepping in patches of crab grass,
Striking like the quills on a porcupine.
Waking up to a fresh morning dew smell,
And just enjoying the wonderful grass green color.

Kelsy Gumbert, Grade 7
William Penn Middle School, PA

Lord I Am Yours

You gave Your life for a child who was torn.
Through the sorrows and pains You wore those thorns.
Not caring for Your life, but for those whom You wanted.
Lord I am Yours from the moment I first heard
Of Your love and grace I read in Your Word.
My Father, my Father, I give You my life. Oh Lord
Lead me through the plan that You have in store.

Lord I am Yours through the moment I die.
Seeing life on this Earth, always through Your eye.
Although there are sorrows and tears to cry,
You, Lord, will wipe away every tear until dry.

Lord I am Yours from the moment I first praised.
My Father, my Father, I worship You with praise.
The wonders of Your love are seen in Your gaze,
When You looked at me from the grave on the day You were raised.
Lord I am Yours.
Caroline Driggers, Grade 8
Briarwood Christian Jr/Sr High School, AL

Average

How troublesome it is
To be an average person
Truly never seen
Never greater
Never smarter
Just there in existence
Waiting for someday
When you're more than in between

Alejandra Buitrago, Grade 9
Bishop Denis J O'Connell High School, VA

My Father's Heart

My father's heart
Is just the start,
Of a great piece of art.
I know he likes it when I sing,
Cuz the expression on his face, it's the most beautifulest thing.
Although his voice sounds like a chicken wing,
I guess I admit I like to hear him sing.
My father's smile,
Is so worthwhile,
My dad is more than a friend,
If you don't like him just pretend.
But please don't break his fragile heart,
Cuz that would not be very smart.
Overall, my dad's the best,
I'm obsessed and you're impressed.
So please remember that his heart,
Is just the start of a great piece of art.

Michelle Contreras, Grade 7
Westwood Jr-Sr High School, NJ

Don't Judge a Book

it seems like people are always in a hurry
always so quick to judge
but why the rush?
take the time to say hi
take the time to get to know someone
what do you have to lose?
people will judge you at a glance
see what you are doing
see what you're wearing
see who you're with
"she's reading — she's a nerd"
"he's wearing this brand — he's spoiled"
"she's hanging out with her — she's weird"
no matter who you are
someone is willing to look at you
and find something they don't like
no one is exempt
so you don't have to read the book cover to cover
but skim the pages a little
you won't lose anything
but there's something you may gain — a FRIEND

Erika Polner, Grade 8
Beacon Middle School, DE

Him

I wonder if he noticed me
There in the hall
I wonder if he noticed me
Noticed me at all
I'm not supposed to like him
That's what Jordin said
But when I ponder it
Roaming round in my head
Cause when I see him in the gym
My heart stops just thinking
What to stop and say
But really when I think about it
I can't like him no not at all no way
To him I'll never be but a smudge on the wall
So when I think I love him
I must think twice
Cause he will never notice me
But all right anyway ok!!!

Cassandra Rhodes, Grade 7
Rohanen Jr High School, NC

How Do You See Orange?

Palm trees brushing in the crisp cool air,
that's now being warmed by the sun,
as if it were breathing.
The scattered waves pierce along the shore,
creating their own melody.
The hot sand buries your feet,
making you feel like you're being swallowed alive.
Sticky sweet salt water taffy rests in your mouth,
calming your spirits.
The quiet wind carries the ocean's scent,
as you escape off into the beautiful sunset.

Missy Cassady, Grade 7
William Penn Middle School, PA

No Excuse

You hear me crying throughout the night
The more you hit me the more I'm in fright
You hit me so hard I have bruises everywhere
That goes to show how much you really care
You say you love me but I don't believe
Why in the world would you conceive
You can see the tears rolling down my face
Why oh why did you bring me into this horrible place
My greatest fear is that someday I'll be
Just like the person who has done this to me
The pain you inflict gets worse and worse
Pretty soon you'll be watching me get put into a hearse
Sooner or later I'll be dead
I wonder if it's tears that you will shed
Please stop the child abuse
There is absolutely no excuse

Rocco Faccone, Grade 9
Colonia High School, NJ

Life
Pain.
It's this pain that keeps me comfortably numb. This pain that makes life worth living. Pain that makes the deepest hurt, but feel so good. It's this pain that I long for at the longest hours of my darkest days.

Hate.
Hate boils inside of me, waiting to explode. Hate for all that has gone wrong. Hate for all that I have done wrong. Hate for all who did me wrong. Hate for anything and everything.

Hope.
There's hope for a new day. A day where life isn't so hard, a day where life doesn't seem like I'm stuck inside a jail cell. Hope for a time where I don't want to say goodbye and disappear with no one knowing. Hope that is always worth waiting for.

Heather Creamer, Grade 7
Ocean City Intermediate School, NJ

I Am from My Own Little World
I am from,
A vending machine with an unlimited supply of candy, chewy chocolate chip cookies,
cookies and cream ice-cream, popcorn, and orange soda.
Boxes stacked high with pizza, Boston cream doughnuts, and marble cake.

A library of fantasy books full of magic and adventure waiting for me to join in.

A scrapbook and album full of pictures and memories of the year before.
Friends, classmates, and teachers worth remembering.
Field trip to Pt. Pleasant, the Brownstone, Trenton, and many more.

A vacation traveling to a place with houses all the same and ancient castles made of stone.
Also, being of Southeast-Asian decent with village scenes of boats sailing
and people fishing in rivers with cool, fresh air blowing around.
Cities overpopulated with people and transportation.
Rice with chicken, fish, shrimp, beef, or anything else being the main dish eaten.

A family with a father, mother, older sister, and younger brother.
Naughty little cousins in Bangladesh with innocent faces,
the cutest of eyes and chubby face, but always looking to play.

I am from my own little world!

Sabrina Fatima, Grade 9
John F Kennedy High School, NJ

Rumor
That rumor she created was like a chain reaction like waves in a puddle.
You knew that it was far from the truth
But that didn't stop you.
You told everyone.
People then thought different from her then what they truly knew from years of talking to her.
The stares she got the next day felt like 1,000 words of rejection stabbing right into her.
But then she confronted her, she only said,
"Thank you for showing me who I really am.
Thanks to the rumor I know what I really am and what I'm really not."
And with a smile on her face she walked away,
The kids at the school forgot about it like it never happened.
She realized that words were just words;
Sometimes powerful, but also meaningless.

Lindsay Chmieleski, Grade 7
Depew Middle School, NY

My Love, Volleyball

I get myself in position, as I'm on the court.
Sweat is trickling down my face, boy I love this sport.

Waiting for the serve, for I want to dig it high.
I'll make it easy for the setter and not make it go by.

So the serve comes over. The ball is now in play.
I dig it how it should be, with no one in my way.

The setter sets the ball, and it goes to middle front.
She jumps as high as she can and doesn't hit it blunt.

The other team panicked and didn't know what to do.
They let the ball hit the floor because, wow! It flew!

We got the point and won the game volleyball is for me
Because I can play it with no shame, and it fills me up with glee!

Kripa Venkatakrishnan, Grade 7
Pine-Richland Middle School, PA

Walls

Surrounded by silence, and locking in sound
By these four walls we are bound
By the limits that they push down
While they protect us, as they surround
They see our movements through our youth
To our secrets, they hold the truth
If these walls could make a sound,
And by silence, they weren't bound,
Would they talk or would they cry?
If you asked them, would they lie?
Would they weep or would they scream?
Would they share what they have seen?

Phoebe Bowe, Grade 9
Nottingham High School, NJ

My Heaven

A tall building towers over me.
I remember my first time there
I was afraid as the giant loomed over me.

Now I walk right in.
My favorite section is towards the back.
I skip in, not a fear left.

An hour later I emerge into a sunlit parking lot
a basket trailing at my side laden with a hundred heavy books
each one as special as the next.

I am content
for my friends are beside me
in a little straw basket
each one waiting to be read.

Katja Shimkin, Grade 7
Merritt Academy, VA

Ode to Glitter

You sparkle you're never dull,
Isn't that remarkable?
Just a small dab is all you need
Purple, pink, white, blue so many colors to make you fab
Which one is right for you? I like them all.

You shine, you're pretty,
And I like to throw you all the time.
Whoever made you sure was witty;
Because glitter you're perfect!
You're right for every occasion,
You're there by my side…
Until I spill you on the floor,
Then it's your time to go away,
Under the carpet and out of my way!

You flutter to the floor,
Onto the couch, and out the door.
You smile on someone's eye's bring out their best,
You're a lifesaver in disguise.
You make things fun,
You make things thrive,
I'd wear you all the time because you make my eyelids shine!

Liz Tsolakis, Grade 8
Beacon Middle School, DE

My Twins

Of course they are tall,
strong,
individual, and totally independent.
One was taller though.
Never once,
did anyone think
they could fall so easily.
No Band-Aid was able to bandage their wounds.
So they were broken,
And they fell,
taking everything in them,
forever.

Holly Turcich, Grade 7
Tomlin Middle School, FL

Dawn of the Day

As the sun sets over the mountain,
The creatures come alive.
Chirping and croaking,
As the night flies by.
Lives are changed,
As they see this sight.
Pity none because it takes no plight.
Beauty resides in the trees and flowers.
Life flows through the wind and showers.
Daily life on the edge,
Has triggered something that will never end.

Emily Hoats, Grade 7
Salisbury Middle School, PA

A Flower's Song

As I listen
to spring's sweet
loving symphony,
I hear the melodies
of pink blossoms
dancing in the gentle breeze.
As the flowers seek
the sun's nurturing warmth,
I too am a flower seeking
the spring's loving symphony,
to fill my heart
with renewed beauty
and inspire me
to perform my song,
expressing my true colors.

Kirsten Kershbaumer, Grade 7
Ocean City Intermediate School, NJ

Butterfly Fly Free

Once I saw a butterfly,
Fluttering freely in the sky.
Flying until it dies,
Never coming back to my surprise.
Leaving behind winter's chill,
While still keeping its free will.
All winter I cannot see it,
Returning in spring will be its spirit.

Robert Ward, Grade 7
Glades Middle School, FL

Climb Higher

The higher I climb
the harder I fall.
If at the top,
I lose grip and drop
I know people will
catch me below.

If I climb all the way up,
I may or may not drop,
but it's a chance
I'm willing to take.
I'll climb and climb,
until I
conquer the foe.

On my way down
I can't help but think,
"Will they catch me if I fall?"
And best of all,
I know that below
they will all catch me,
once I fall.

Jack Handshaw, Grade 7
Ocean City Intermediate School, NJ

Colors of Nature

The gentle breeze of a cool summer day
criss-crosses in and out of nature
across a field of orange and yellow.
Cattails warily sway
in the breeze
as a glorious flaming sunset
marks the start of twilight.
A low valley is
streaked with vibrant colors
on an artist's canvas.
The gentle, wafting breeze
sways blades of emerald grass
spear by spear
until the entire meadow dances.
Nature's endless colors
unrivaled in beauty
are so fragile, yet so magnificent.

Stephen Basile, Grade 7
Ocean City Intermediate School, NJ

Frogs

I (A frog)
Jumped
And landed
On a lily pad
And continued
Jumping from
Lily pad to lily pad
Throughout the
Large, beautiful pond.

Sara Bryson, Grade 7
Oakvale Elementary School, WV

Our One Moment

I fell for you,
When our eyes met,
That seems impossible,
But you did it,
And I just think,
That to feel this way,
You'd have to be the one,
There's no doubt,
That we were meant to be,
Because to be charmed,
As quick as I was,
I must have known,
This was it,
Because since you've come,
You showed me the signs,
As if you knew it too,
And for that,
You're all I've asked for,
Only more than I expected.

Emma Whisted, Grade 7
Bates Middle School, MD

Sunshine

Sunshine swoops down
Gives the world a warm embrace
Delicately dangles in the sky
Shelters us under its wing
Until night falls

Sydney Shaw, Grade 7
Anthony Wayne Middle School, NJ

Together, But Apart*

When I fell down,
you two helped me up.
You two worked together,
but apart.
You took one hand,
she took the other,
together you both showed me the way.
She helped me create,
my "white room."
You taught me,
what true writing was.
Both of you helped me,
to stop looking back.
Together you helped me see,
who the real, true me is.
Two people, I do thank,
for helping me become,
who I was supposed to be.

Kelsey Wilcox, Grade 9
Aucilla Christian Academy, FL
*Dedicated to Mr. Matthew Campbell
and Jessica Hunt

EBay

You don't understand
The pain you put me through
And I just have to say
Please don't bother me
I was highest bidder
With one hundred ten dollars
And then you came along
You were the sniper
That shot me down
With two seconds left to go
I had it in my grasp
It was all mine
And then you paid the fine
I do not know you
But I can already tell
That I do not like you that well
You took it away from me
And I do not see
How I could ever forgive
Someone that mean

Kyle Sosnowski, Grade 7
Depew Middle School, NY

Pride

My sittu lives far away
on the countryside of the mountains.
She raised my mother to become a
strong woman and treats her
like the sun and loves me like the air.
I am proud of the woman whose hair is as
silver as the winter clouds
and who whispers like a church mouse
sings praise songs in her house
cooks for the family
and only needs
a cappuccino and a hug
to be happy.

Nicole LeCates, Grade 8
Beacon Middle School, DE

Just Because...

Just because I get good grades
It doesn't mean I'm not good at sports
It doesn't mean I'm a nerd
    Just because I get good grades
It doesn't mean I like to read
It doesn't mean I always do my homework
It doesn't mean I don't act up sometimes
    Just because I get good grades
It doesn't mean I'm in all gifted and talented classes
It doesn't mean I don't have a social life
You should still include me
Just because I get good grades...please just give me a chance

Hunter Beck, Grade 7
Anthony Wayne Middle School, NJ

Misery

Alone. I walk to the plate
The center of attention.
Parents and children all around me
Yelling. Screaming.
I'm the center of attention and scared to strike out.
It's up to me to win the huge game.
I step in the rectangular box
And pull the heavy bat up over my shoulders.
I squat on my trembling knees
Waiting for the pitch.
BOOM!
The ball had zoomed past me
Into the catcher's mitt.
Ball one.
The next pitch came faster.
I swing the heavy bat and miss the ball.
Strike one.
The next pitch was horrible.
It whacked right into my thumb.
I dropped the bat. My thumb grew bigger.
I was in horrible pain. It was definitely broken.

Brandon Stern, Grade 8
William Penn Middle School, PA

Fulfilled Beach

Pounding waves,
Colorful sail ships,
Smooth, hot sand.
The light blue sky is like a clear, blue stream.
The sun's rays wrapping you up in a blanket of warmth,
Cotton ball clouds.
Glinting sea,
Swooping seagulls,
Young kids screeching,
Soft winds rustling the vibrant umbrellas,
Loud voices,
Quiet radios.
When will I come back?
Does it snow here?
Do fish sleep?
Fulfilled,
Relaxed,
Exciting.
Pounding waves,
Pounding waves,
Pounding waves.

Quinn Hlatky, Grade 7
William Penn Middle School, PA

Lonely

I am pure loneliness
Empty air, a passing cloud
I am, I was, I am always going to be
An empty space
A lifeless vessel
No spirit, no soul
I am a vase
That is drowning
I am a shallow ocean
A half eaten orange, never looked at twice
An unwanted being
I am everything that never was
I am nothing new, nothing old
Never happened, never wanted
No beginning, no end
I am an empty vessel
I am, I was, I am always going to be
I am lonely

Beena Biju, Grade 9
Sewanhaka High School, NY

Life

Life is everything.
It consists of many things,
Love being the most powerful.
And until you have figured out,
Which one you are going through,
Your life is not what you believe it to be.

Ashleigh Latham, Grade 7
School of International Studies at Meadowbrook, VA

Clay

I touch the clay
So smooth and cool
Like waves dancing
On the shore
I throw it and mold it
Into the desired shape
When all is smooth
And all is perfect
I cut it away
From the wheel
The oven of fire is
Hungry for clay
The white clay
So smooth so soft
Has been made
For a good use after all
The vessel can last two weeks
A hundred years or more
It will bring memories
Of the sweet days
Of long ago
Joanna Bak, Grade 9
Unami Middle School, PA

Crossover

the sun dips its fingers into the sky
trying to fathom the temperature
and if it dares tread on
he skinny-dips
swirling ripples with his feet
suddenly
an electric wave of ice
jolts through his body
wincing he flees
tricking the moon in
without hesitation she dives face-first
into the pool of sky
embracing the sudden rush of coolness
the sun blushes out of embarrassment
and flushes
and the sky is a cushioned red blanket
padded with furry cotton clouds
settling on the Earth
slowly fading to a navy amethyst
as a symbol
of moon's invitation
Kevin Xiong, Grade 7
Peabody Elementary School, MA

Books

I'll spark you,
help you sleep.
Bring dreams you'll forever keep —
on a dappled autumn afternoon.
Nicholas Andrade, Grade 7
St Agatha School, NY

The Untruthful Truth

I thought you were my true best friend
But no, I was wrong
You act like it when it's just me and you
But when someone more *important* is in the picture, you twist my words
and make me feel like the last pick for your team of the little game you're playing
So now I see the mask you wear to cover your lies is becoming a part of you
Do you deserve my friendship?
Or are you just telling me another canard?
I wonder how you would be without me
No one to talk to
No one to manipulate
No one to fall back on
Secret betrayal
Courtney Thornton, Grade 8
Depew Middle School, NY

Home Sweet Home

The sun rose bright above the tall green trees,
No cloud in sight,
A slight breeze picked the leaves off the field,
A buck stepped out of the tree line,
The animal spied around the plain looking for any predators,
He sniffed at the pink ribbons that lined up in front of him,
One step more, then another until he was dead center,
The birds chirped all around him as he looked for food,
In a flash his ears popped up,
In the distance almost a microscopic sound of crumbling,
Just over the ridge a giant backhoe plowed through the trees,
It ripped the roots out like they were in butter,
The buck scampered back into the trees,
The shadow engulfed him,
Hiding himself from the menacing machine,
The animal watched in fear as the man at the controls tore through the earth,
With every dig, it beat down on the heart of the native,
He came back the next day to find a crater size hole in the ground,
From that day the buck and his herd would leave their old environment forever.
Greg Kosiras, Grade 8
William Penn Middle School, PA

Just Because I Seem Kind Hearted

"Just because I seem kind hearted,"
Don't take advantage of me,
Don't use me for your own gain.
"Just because I seem kind hearted,"
Doesn't mean I don't have emotions,
Or get angry and have commotions.
"Just because I seem kind hearted,"
I am not close to perfect since the roller coaster is always a ride.
I may not pick your side, but at the end that causes me to want to hide.
So never get let down or act like an annoying clown.
"Just because I seem kind hearted,"
Is a way for you to know to come to me.
"Just because I seem kind hearted,"
Don't be like me; be who you are, but find that special key.
Neetu Nirappil, Grade 7
Anthony Wayne Middle School, NJ

Grandpa

My grandpa passed away on January thirty-first
The pain is still here and my heart still hurts.
Although he was stubborn I loved him so,
Why did he have to leave me, why did he have to go?
Yes I do cry, I cry for he is dead,
I wish he was still here and maybe I wouldn't be sad.
I try to think about the good times we had long ago,
And remember he loved me, he loved me I know.

Monica Zeisz, Grade 7
Depew Middle School, NY

I Love You

My life changed
The day you said you loved me.
When I heard those three words
You touched my soul.
The world that seemed so unbearable to me
Changed in just a second
To give so many possibilities for a better life.
You gave me something to believe in.
Something that was worth waking up to.
I carried your love around
Like a badge on my heart.
At the end of the day
I had someone to rest my head on.
Your love was what kept me going.

Desiree Colon, Grade 9
Bishop Ford Central Catholic High School, NY

Said I Love You

It was on the beach in early June
We were watching the crescent moon
Listening to the song of the setting sun
The evening that had just begun
I could hear your heart in beat with mine
Keeping exact and perfect rhyme
I looked up and said I love you for the first time.

As days progressed our love did too
Never stopped only grew
When you said it I knew it was true
The look in your eyes
Proved the words held no lies
Even when you said I love you
For the thousandth time.

I was sitting to your right in the passenger seat
You were laughing at my singing, said I couldn't hold a beat
I remember headlights, a swerve, and a crash
They say that drunk man was driving too fast
Hanging in the air the feeling of death
You knew it, I knew it, so you used your last breath
To say I love you for the last time.

Emily Muro, Grade 9
Unami Middle School, PA

Life Changes

Change, it's a word that can't be described
Yet you can notice it.
It's all around you
It'll always be surrounding you.
Wherever you might be, from the day you were born
Till now
You'll always see it.
Change happens
You can't stop it
It happens day by day
You can't realize it
If you look back and see things closer
You'll observe it.
You can't explain it nor can you feel it.
At times you ask yourself "What happened?"
You recognize that CHANGES happened.
You can't prevent it; you have to go along with it.
Changes are just another part of life.
Life is life.
You'll always have to live up with it
Keep up with it.

Daniella Soares, Grade 9
Miami Beach Sr High School, FL

High Heels

I walk through mud, I walk through rain
And even there I don't complain
I am a little taller than all my friends
Until I am worn down and my life ends
I clang on hard wood floor
While I dance next door
I go to fancy places
And see many new faces
But when I come home I am thrown aside
Until on someone's foot I take a ride

Dominique Seamon, Grade 8
Covenant Life School, MD

What's Love???

What is love?
Somebody please explain
I think I love this girl,
Although I don't think she knows my name.
Does love mean a pretty girl?
Somebody please tell me what it is!
Should I?
Or should I not know because I'm just a kid.
What is love?
Is it real?
How does love feel?
Does love exist?
Does love mean a hug or kiss?
Or just someone you know.
Somebody please explain love because I need to know!

Devonte Bailey, Grade 9
Seminole County Middle/High School, GA

Rain

It falls from the sky,
but not a soul knows why.
It brings the end to a sunny day.
No longer can children go out and play.
Listen to the heartbeat,
see the flash of light.
Watch as this rain
becomes a wondrous sight.

Down, down, down it goes.
Seeping through your shoes
and in between your toes.
The umbrella is leaking,
you feel it on your skin.
And then you start to wonder,
will it ever end?

Bethany Buckner, Grade 8
Madison Middle School, WV

I Was Killed

A week ago today,
Or maybe it was yesterday,
I was killed.
I was being drilled.
People above me
They said that they loved me
But come to find out,
They were sucking the life out of me
Like water in a drought.
I couldn't take it any longer
I wasn't getting any stronger
I started to cry
Then I said goodbye.

Brittanie Covington, Grade 7
St Andrews Middle School, SC

A Key

I think I have found something
To open up my door
To the world around me
I will see so much more
That something is a key
A key that I find great
To make the key
You fold your hands and
Simply begin to talk
That wondrous key
Will hear you
Don't you ever doubt
For that key is something special
Something beautiful
Something great
This key is all around us
Just reach out and pray

Matthew McIntosh, Grade 9
White Station High School, TN

Ode to My Elephant Blanket

You may never know how much I like you.
Peanuts scatter the front of you
while brown drenches the back.
You're beautiful when you are fresh and clean,
making the pink that lies with the peanuts shine radiantly.

The elephants triumph the blanket.
Their bodies make me feel safe even when it's the darkest of nights.
Your fragile ties keep you woven together.
I never want the sea of warmth you provide to go away.
Lovely blanket, how I like you so.

Sarah Beattie, Grade 7
Christ the Teacher Catholic School, DE

My Godbrother

With eyes that shine across the room and cheeks that are so rosy.
He is cuddled up in my safe arms, and I know he feels cozy.
With ears that are so very small and lips that are so thin.
He is so cute you tend to get goose bumps on your skin.
With arms that look so big and fat he looks as if he is strong.
When doctors test him with other kids they feel like something is wrong.
With a tummy that is so very fat and filled with yummy food.
To take away his bottle will quickly change his mood.
With legs that are so filled with energy all he does is move.
And when he hears music on he dances to the groove.
With nails that are so nice and long and feet that are so wide.
He knows that he has special feet, and moves them with pride.
His laugh is big and extremely cute, so he is never sad.
His face looks so very innocent, so he is the opposite of bad.
He dwells in the Big Apple among many Yankee lovers'.
But it gets so cold in New York City, he is always wrapped in covers.
You can't imagine the amount of love I have for this little boy.
And when he comes to visit me I will spoil him, toy after toy.
This adorable child is blessed with a tremendous father and mother.
And I am so proud to have Matthew Luis Bumbalo as my godbrother.

Francis Curiel, Grade 8
Archimedean Academy, FL

School Again

School comes again, what a shame.
It seems like just yesterday that summer was beginning to blossom.
Children whine and complain.
No more late nights playing Internet games.
There's homework on the first day of school?
Come on teachers, at least try to be cool.
Buying uniforms and getting up early,
You're taking away our happiness.
Doing essays after essays,
Not a single break.
Giving out assignments like there's no tomorrow.
Giving us homework like we don't have a life.
I would never let my kids suffer like this.
My mom should've thought about having me twice.

Alicia Payne, Grade 9
White Station High School, TN

Should I Write of How I Dislike Poetry So?

Should I write of how I dislike poetry so?
I must say it confuses me to no end.
When I think I get it, I really don't know.
I think I see the pattern, understand the trend.
I believe I can grasp the very concept,
Appreciate the meaning of what's said.
I then find myself seeing how adept
And skillful can be a poet's head.
I believe I am none of the sort.
I have my mind so closed and so stressed.
It's sealed from poetical purpose, like a fort.
And with it so, writing is not my best.
Then when I relax, it is easy to see,
Now just how easy poetry can be.

Sean Killian, Grade 9
Unami Middle School, PA

Last Day of School

It's the last day of school —
Everyone's excited!
It's my last day to be cool —
The teachers feel delighted!
No more classes
No more studying
No more demerits
Till next year.
But for now I'm good
I'm in a good mood
I'm wearing clothes under my uniform
So when the bell rings
I'm taking off the uniform
So people can see me rock my name brand clothes.
I wish I didn't have to go to summer school
Because that's not cool!

Kalil Brown, Grade 9
Bishop Ford Central Catholic High School, NY

What Would Happen?

What would happen if I died today?
Would I merely be a memory that got lost and thrown away?
What if I left, without saying goodbye?
Would you cry?
Or simply wipe the tears away in haste?
What would happen if I said I loved you?
Would you whisper it back surely?
Or walk away as if nothing had occurred?
Because if you died
I would cherish those memories.
If you left
I would be left with questions why.
So Lord, what if we let our faith die?
What if we all deserted You?
What if we all stopped loving each other?
What would happen?

Leigh Rohrbach, Grade 9
Forest Park High School, VA

Frog

I flow down rivers
Like a relaxed hunter
In the wide open air.
My lunch finally arrives
With my color blending with surroundings
I snap a bug.

Victoria King, Grade 7
St Anthony School, CT

Maybe…

Maybe —
she *does* have a voice,
she *does* have something to say,
she *does* have inspiring words of wisdom to share.
But, will anyone listen?

No, they just see some quiet and shy classmate —
just a classmate to ignore and pass by in the hallway.

OR MAYBE —
if someone listened,
she would be HEARD and known that
she is just like them in many ways,
she is a nice, friendly, goofy girl just like everyone else.
Maybe —

Kyle Sherman, Grade 7
Ocean City Intermediate School, NJ

Poetree

Itching to get outdoors
But chilly winds of March prevent
Want to watch plants sprout
Getting ready makes one content

Get a jump on the season
Start indoors
Don't bother waiting
Get down on all fours

Make a small hole
Plant the seed in the dirt
Water it gently
Not too much — just a squirt

The sun stays up longer
Seeds start to sprout
They grow into seedlings
No longer cold out

Let the sun fall upon the greens
They need a transplant — they've grown so well
Now's the time to go outside
What fruit will they yield? Only time will tell.

Richard Benner, Grade 9
Unami Middle School, PA

'Twas the Night Before Thanksgiving

'Twas the night before Thanksgiving and all through the house, everyone was hungry, even my mouse.
We all stared at Mom, running and busy, it made me sick, and even dizzy.
I tried to help by cooking the turkey, only to find that it tasted like beef jerky.
The chocolate milk was thick, brown and gooey, I don't know what came up the straw that tasted so chewy.

I ran outside as quick as I could, got out a bag and puked out what I should.
My mom is no cook, but a lot of fun we all played football when dinner was done.
My cousins all tried to tackle my friend, he couldn't outrun them, so he fell in the end.
But he turned and tickled them and they laughed so hard, they couldn't even run just one more yard.

I stole the ball and went off running, no one could catch me, my legs were humming.
My team won the game and we had so much fun, that I didn't want Thanksgiving Day to be done.
Later that night when I got home, I heard a loud noise, and started to think about Christmas toys.
I wanted a tree and wanted it now, I screamed at my mom and she had a cow!

She sent me to bed to unwind a bit, only to find me throwing a fit.
I wanted out of my room and I wanted a tree, why was that so hard for her — to see!
Christmas is so close to Thanksgiving Day, I can't wait for it to be out of my way.
Around the corner, just waiting for me, is that soft and decorated Christmas tree.

I fell asleep on that Thanksgiving night, with no pretty tree, not one in sight.
But when I woke up early the next day, all I could see was a tree — oh yeah.
We took out the decorations one at a time, my favorite one is colored lemony lime.
The last thing we did was put on the star light, it made the room nice and so bright.

Kristin Allocco, Grade 8
William R Satz Middle School, NJ

Paradise

The sun is just one giant lightbulb that sets off our ideas.
The Earth is just a giant tetherball used in the gym class of space.
Each and every day is just another time to say "Thank God I'm Livin'."
Every minute is just more time to enjoy.
Not all of the world thinks this way and is so grateful of life.
Our world is a paradise with other mini paradises inside of it.
We need to keep our world a remarkable place.
One day, one day, this will all become reality when humankind decides to take care of our
World and show R

E
S
P
E
C
T

Jimmy Naplacic, Grade 7
Ocean City Intermediate School, NJ

You Said

When I met you, you said you would never do anything to upset me. I can't believe I fell for that bunch of lies. Did you not think I would not notice you talking garbage behind my back? You said you loved me, but the next day I see you with another girl. You came back and said give me a second chance, I can do better. I can't believe I took that lie. You said I was the only girl for you, but yet you continued to look for other girls, but I ignored it and thought you were just being friendly. I am beginning to hate you and your guts, but at times you can be the sweetest guy around. So I decided to keep you around but then you said I don't understand why you are mad at me. You were too uptight with yourself and other girls to realize what you were doing to me. So now I am glad we are through.

Kaylin Carter, Grade 7
Depew Middle School, NY

The Beach's Life

The glimmering sun,
Peachy soft sand,
Warm inviting waves,
Sandy boardwalks,
And fun filled amusement parks.
Some small puffy clouds, suspended in midair,
Layers of sun, settle on my skin,
And the clear blue waters wash away newly pressed footprints.
Crashing waves indulge the sand with life,
Calling seagulls swoop down for food,
The gentle breeze whooshes around chattering people.
Does the sand ever go cold?
Is the life of the beach ever killed?
Will we be able to be here in 20 years?
Happiness emanates from every soul.
Anxious children run to the water.
Relaxed adults lounge under the beaming sun.
I've never felt more wonderful.
Wonderful.
Wonderful.
Wonderful.

Chris Lagunilla, Grade 7
William Penn Middle School, PA

Step Closer

In for the excitement, in for the thrill?
Ready for revenge, or ready for the kill?
Aching for peace, deep inside your soul,
yet you won't admit, all that you have stole.
You're ready for the quiet, yet you love all the action,
so why doesn't it come, up to your satisfaction?
Something's still missing, but what could it be?
There's a hole in your plan, and I hold the key,
all you've known is hate, so what are you lacking?
You're splitting your soul, and your heart is cracking.
Never heard a cry, never strived to aid,
never saw a smile, darkness was your shade.
Happy memories you never knew, never caring what you had,
so will you tell me then, is it worth being sad?
You brought pain upon yourself, choosing darkness over light,
and that my friend would be like, choosing blindness over sight.
Diminish your fears, and don't be afraid,
'cause you can come back, even when you have strayed.
So step in the light, even though you can't see,
for I am right here, so step closer to me.

Courtney Dibble, Grade 8
Warren L Miller Elementary School, PA

Empty

The person that you love the most just left you
The thought that nobody is with you
The thought that there is no reason to be alive
The feeling like you have no soul

Alberta Reyes, Grade 9
Highland Park Middle/High School, NJ

Rolling Freedom

Kick. Push.
No limits of where to go
Riding down the streets
Pavement under your feet
While life is holding you down
You go and break free
And now you see
This is the way to be
You are rolling free
No restrictions
No destination in sight
Just you and this endless route
The one that you have sought after
Making curves down the street like a master crafter
Not even thinking about life's problems
Not thinking of how to solve them
All you're trying to do is
Roll free!

Nick Sufleta, Grade 9
Unami Middle School, PA

Ode to Power Tech

Oh power, how I enjoy you.
So powerfully full of power and technology.
Laughing in the face of those who slack.
Waiting to instinct the worthy,
the dream, those who long for.
Your steel and other various metals
you impart the knowledge of worth
of strength to build
Love…it is Power Tech Shop

William Bungert Jr., Grade 9
Mid Valley Area Jr/Sr High School, PA

Summer

Summer is a time for fun
Summer is a time for sun
In summer we go to the beach
Or enjoy a fresh peach.
We stay home in the A/C getting cool
While we're out of school, children play
On a hot sunny day.
The summer craze
Continues in the scorching blaze.
The bugs fly
In the warm sunny sky.
We swim in the ocean, pool, or lake
So in the summer sun, we don't bake.
The rays of the sun upon us beat
As we try to avoid the hot summer heat
So we say good-bye to summer's call
We cannot wait for the season Fall.
I never thought the start of school
Would ever seem so cool!

Steven Hickey, Grade 9
Bishop Ford Central Catholic High School, NY

Jake's Routine

In his soft, flawless skin
he sleeps so peacefully,
but then he wakes up
and we sit and play.
He is hungry.
We have lunch.
Mushed bananas for him
macaroni and cheese for me.
We play.
His toys laugh and make music.
He jumps and giggles.
Crawls from here to there.
He is finally tired
and lies down
for another nap
with Doby, his teddy bear.

Ariel Gordon, Grade 8
Beacon Middle School, DE

My Sister

Jamie is my best friend
I will love her until the end.
She's the girl I talk to,
When I'm mad at my friends.
We laugh and we cry
She reminds me of the sky.
We argue and we fight
When it's bright or when it's night.
My sister is the best
I think she is better than the rest.
Jamie is my best friend.
I'll love her 'til the end.

Jessica Bates, Grade 7
Chichester Middle School, PA

The Catch of Life

Father to son
Man to boy
Chest to eye
Glove on left hand, ball in right
A white sphere is smacked off the tee
Ball sails through the air
Falls, one bounce, two, three into glove
Ball goes back and forth
Flying through the air, like an airplane
Looking to land
Only to land feet in front of the hangar
Ball takes off again reaching the glove
Ball in air, wizzz
Ball in mitt, smack
All grown up
Eye to eye
Man to man
Father to son

Sam Waldorf, Grade 8
William Penn Middle School, PA

My Favorite Outdoor Place…The Soccer Field

Fields are as soft as white, puffy clouds,
Soccer balls aim toward soccer goals.
Proudly, the pavilion stands tall,
People run by on long zigzag walking paths,

Glistening, glowing, glittering river,
Gently, a light breeze pushes my hair,
Beyond the pavilion, coaches and teammates happily laugh and scream,
Behind me, dogs and puppies bark loudly,

What does it look like with new fallen snow?
Do animals sleep there quietly at night?
Happy,
Relaxed and fun,

Glistening river,
Glistening river,
Glistening river.

Caitlin Coia, Grade 7
William Penn Middle School, PA

Blue

Once upon a time there were blue skies, but today it is red for a Holocaust.
Red for the color of war where they abolish and demolish.
But never for the color of their hope.

Once upon a time there were parents who wore blue, but today they wear gray.
Gray for the color of uniforms worn while they are beaten and broken.
But never for the color of their faith.

Once upon a time there were children who wore blue, and today it is still blue.
Blue for hope. Blue for faith. Blue for a brighter tomorrow.
But always for the color of you and the color of me.

Linnet Leon, Grade 7
Glades Middle School, FL

Just Because

Just because I'm a girl,
Doesn't mean I hate sports,
Doesn't mean I don't like video games.

Just because I'm a girl,
Doesn't mean I love to start drama,
Doesn't mean I'm scared as a mouse whenever I see the smallest bug.

Just because I'm a girl,
Doesn't mean all I care about is looks,
Doesn't mean I'm obsessed with boys.

Just because I'm a girl,
Don't treat me different than everyone,
Don't exclude me from certain things.

Just because I'm a girl — just let me be me.

Alexa Beck, Grade 7
Anthony Wayne Middle School, NJ

Waves

Spring speeds past me
    pulling me into summer
        in all different directions.
the R
    O
       A
          R of the waves smashing the beach
          yell "Summer is upon us!"
Hearing the shrieks of the children tell me the time —
    Summertime!

Zach Greaser, Grade 7
Ocean City Intermediate School, NJ

Beauty and the Beast

Sitting alone in the shade of a tree;
I look upon the beauty of life,
great and small, that surrounds me.
All is quiet; but everything is making noise.

Then comes a roaring beast,
destroying in a single instant
all that was green.
No respect was shown
for things that should not be disturbed.

I remember that even in this isolated part of nature,
I cannot hide from Mankind's destructive touch.

I talk to the Beast
who shows no evil or hate —
only confusion.
Is he completely unaware of nature's beauty?
Can he be taught to respect the wild?

This gives hope that
all is not lost.
Nature will grow again,
if only it is respected.

DJ Gilhooley, Grade 7
Ocean City Intermediate School, NJ

Pain in Darkness

Darkness —
a void of nothing.
I am a part of darkness;
therefore I am nothing
I notice people who want to be darkness at times
and see the darkness in the eyes.
People who are treated wrong,
or always alone at different events;
this is the darkness.
People who are the darkness
and nothing more
have the worst pain of all.

Kevin Hemple, Grade 7
Ocean City Intermediate School, NJ

Where I Belong

The scent of the salty water warms me.
The grasp of the sand between my fingers,
Like silk, falls to my feet.
Shells a swirling white and pink,
Snuggle beneath the golden blanket.
The sun is on fire against the horizon.
Sparkling blue gems gleam in the evening set.
I wonder about the world.
Is this where I belong?
I glimpse at the sea again and find my answer.
I belong to the sea, long and broad.
I will be there always,
As here is my home, beautiful and clear.
Colossal waves lap against the smoothened boulders;
Moving further and further downstream,
Closer and closer to their destination.
I stand and watch until dark when I must return home.
Capturing the last of the moment,
I walk away.
But I will be back again tomorrow.

Ashley Gilmore, Grade 7
Chazy Central Rural School, NY

She's Only Seven

Seven years old pretty and smart.
How could you leave her
With such a heavy heart?
She's broken inside
Nowhere to go nowhere to hide.
What kind of father is that?
You've destroyed her dreams and crushed her spirits
When she tries to talk
You refuse to hear it.
You made her cry so many tears.
When she closes her eyes
It's your voice she hears…
She was only seven but now she's thirteen
And now when she sees you
She expects you to scream.
She never forgave you, she might not ever
But living without you
Has made things better.
Seven years old pretty and smart
How could you leave her?
You must have no heart.

Erica Woodward, Grade 7
Carthage Middle School, NY

Mothers

A mother is an important thing,
For without a mom everything will go "bing."
Every mother will share but one thing,
And that is a child for loving.

Christopher McDaris, Grade 7
REACH Home School, VA

My First Time at the Beach
The sand feels warm,
Wedged between my toes,
The sun shining,
High, up in the sky

I hear the seagulls,
Chattering with each other,
And smell the salt water,
Lingering in the air

The waves crash,
Against my bare feet,
It makes me want to jump,
Into the body of water

I find a shell,
Pick it up,
And clasp it in my hands

It's smooth, round, perfect
I want to bring it home,
But for now I set it down,
And let the waves take it away.
Marissa Chisholm, Grade 7
Carthage Middle School, NY

Together
A rose is a symbol of love.
A dove is a bird from above.
A woman is for a lovely evening.
A man is there for a woman to love.
A ring is for a woman.
Together they are one.
Their love is beyond compare.
They may go to great places together.
Express their likenesses together.
They will not leave each other, because
they
are
in
love
together.
Jodie White, Grade 7
St Stephen's School, NY

Trees
The trees sing when their leaves rustle
The trees talk when the wind goes by
When you try to talk to them, they reply
When you touch them, they move
The rain falls on the trees
and it drips down as if it was crying
The trees sit alone in the empty forest
Waiting for a friend to arrive
Kathryn Muehlberger, Grade 8
Milford Middle East School, MA

My Best Friend
The one that I will always love
Even if he is always annoying.
We can fight all night and fight all day,
Never for hurt, always for play.
No matter how many times our mom tells us
To settle down we never listen.
Our bond, an Everlasting Gobstopper,
That will last forever.
He is quiet like a mouse
And shy as a cat.
Even if he doesn't speak a word, I always know how he is feeling.
There can be a smile stretching from ear to ear or
A tear r-o-l-l-i-n-g
D
O
W
N
His gentle face.
He is my best friend and will always be there.
Who is he?
My brother.
Amanda Pace, Grade 8
William Penn Middle School, PA

Love
Just because two people dated
Didn't mean they loved each other
It was not love it was infatuation
They hid their pain under fake happy smiles
She was strong headed and didn't let anyone stop her
He was possessive and moved her away from her friends and family
They never trusted each other
The lack of trust was the reason their relationship ended
Without trust your relationship will crumble like a house without a foundation.
Nicole Bain, Grade 9
North Tonawanda High School, NY

The Story of Jane Eyre
Jane Eyre was a lonely girl;
Mistreated and beset by her "family"
She longed for something to love and to hold
She feared she would never get it,
Not even when she was old
Bessie was the only one who treated Jane with some respect
She had great compassion for the young girl
Jane was ecstatic when she had the opportunity to leave Gateshead
She felt like a wastrel to her aunt and cousins
Lowood wasn't much better than her old home
Except Jane made a friend she truly loved;
But Helen soon passed on and Jane felt alone again
Finally, Jane left Lowood and went to a place called Thornfield
She met Mrs. Fairfax, Adele, and Mr. Rochester
Things weren't perfect at first, but they soon settled and Jane was happy.
Finna Wang, Grade 9
Council Rock High School South, PA

The Gingerbread Man
Freshly baked,
Right out of the oven

Little boys and girls,
Laid flat on the rack

Warm, spicy, delicious, and sweet,
All to create this tasty treat

As the cookies lay flat to cool,
We can't wait for the various decorating tools

Icing, candy, and sprinkles, too
It is just enough to make your tummy tickle true.

Sarah Prins, Grade 7
Pine-Richland Middle School, PA

Reflection
You sit by a lake.
You dream by a river.
Dare to look down into the cool, murky water.
And your reflection greets you in any way it can —
A smile, a frown, maybe even a funny-face, upside down.
You giggle, you laugh.
The reflection copies you.
You sing, you dance.
The water copies you again, swaying to and fro.
Doing its undefined dance of a reflection.

Alysia Nichols, Grade 7
Spartanburg Jr Writing Project, SC

A Rainbow Without Color
Crisp air on a warm summer day,
    As hot as a fire,
As fresh as newly fallen snow,
    As bright as the sun,
This sounds like waves crashing against the shore
    As the sand awaits, to be dampened
As a frown grows into a smile
    This is the color of happiness
The color of excitement, the color of enjoyment,
    The color of fun, the color of laughs,
The color of playfulness, the color of summer,
    And most of all, the color of a smile
Yellow is the color of…Life…
    A world without the color yellow is like
A song without lyrics, a day without minutes,
    A birthday without age,
A fairy tale without a happy ending,
    And a rainbow without colors
Without the color yellow
    We would be living in black and white.
Yellow makes the darkness fade away.

Devin Sophy, Grade 7
William Penn Middle School, PA

Pretend
Alone…unfeeling
I sit here…my expressionless face unrevealing
I'm surrounded by those who mean the most to me
But I don't feel a thing
I'm not even happy
At home…in my bed
I cry endlessly
No reason evident to the eye
Maybe it's something deep inside
Maybe it's the feelings that I hide
Even from myself
Now they're shouting out a cry
Here I am! Stop shutting me out!
For now I'll ignore them
Pretend they're not there
I'll fall asleep crying
And pretend I don't care
I'll wake in the morning
And get dressed for school
Then I'll meet with my friends
And pretend it's all cool

Deven Goss, Grade 8
Noble Middle School, ME

Midnight Garden
I was sitting in a garden full of flowers,
watching the moon glimmer over the pond.
No one coming to look for me,
I sat there hearing the crickets chirp.
Receiving company from the many stars in the sky,
I sat there falling asleep at midnight in a garden.

Pranati Puri, Grade 9
Brandon High School, MS

UH…Sisters!!
It is so annoying having a little sister
But, I'm glad because she isn't a mister
You can't really talk to a brother
She's sort of like a really hurtful blister

I feel really bad for my mother
Also, her significant other
But of course, she is a little angel around them
She even annoys our grandmother

In the morning, she is as irritating as phlegm
It is like you pricked your finger on a rose's stem
Even though she is sometimes annoying, I still love her
Her soul shines in my heart like the most valuable gem

When she is around me, the most wonderful things occur
Even though she can sometimes make me go grrrrrrr
She is pretty irritating to me at times
But, even when she annoys me, she is precious, my sister.

Madison Sandlin, Grade 8
LaVilla School of the Arts, FL

Shot

My heart started to beat
as fast as running feet.
My thoughts started to be fear
but I knew my mom was near.
I started to shake
as fast as a kid eats his cake.
I closed my eyes
and to my surprise
the shot was over and done
and now I can leave and have fun!

Jessica Pellegrino, Grade 7
Westwood Jr-Sr High School, NJ

A Walk

A walk through the woods
can often find

A place to sit
and clear your mind.

To stop and stare
and think.

To love and
be loved.

Adore the nature,
adore the life and the wind,
and the silence!

Not much of a peep or a sound;
just sit and ponder all day long.

So come along, and you will find,
a place to sit and clear your mind.

Katelyn Comer, Grade 7
Oakvale Elementary School, WV

The Santana Taco

I never noticed
The cheesy, saucy sour cream
Covered taco on the road

Once I was driving
In the hot Mexican desert
And the taco was just lying there
Oozing on the hot pavement

I wonder
if Carlos Santana
dropped that scrumptious taco
on the road
And if it was my job
to return it to him

Jess Wise, Grade 7
Trinity Middle School, PA

Things I Thought I'd Never Say

I never thought I'd say it.
But my number just got called.
I never thought I'd say it.
But my life just hit a wall.

I never thought I'd say it.
But I'm a soldier now.
I never thought I'd say it.
But I'm here, how?

I never thought I'd say it.
But my best friend and I are in the war.
I never thought I'd say it
But we're fighting in Vietnam now, and we're fighting in the core

I never thought I'd say it
But I almost got shot in the head
I never thought I'd ever say it
But my friend saved my life by leaping in the way, but now my friend is dead.

Devon Seymour, Grade 8
James Weldon Johnson Middle School, FL

My Hero

You are my guardian angel, my love, my friend
I don't know how I will ever make it till the end.
You helped me through the tears and the bad days
and you always knew exactly what to say
I remember all the days we spent together
and all the dreams we made last forever.
Every night I miss you, and every night I know you miss me too.
I know the stars in the sky are holding you up so high.
I never thought that day would come
when you were never going to return home.
We had the best of times and always had the best goodbyes.
I know you watch over me and the things I do
But sometimes it's just not enough I really need you.
You were my best friend and like I said I need you till the end.
You are my hero, my everything I don't know why this happened the way it did
But I know I'll always love you, and I hope you'll never forget me too.

Brittany Snedeker, Grade 9
Carbondale Area Jr/Sr High School, PA

Rain

Rain is like the heavens above crying down to Earth.
Rain is when a little girls cries because she had a bad dream.
Rain is like when you cry and cry because everything is going wrong.
Rain is when you shed a single tear and it falls down your pretty face.
Rain is like when your heart breaks and no one can replace the pieces.
Rain is when you try your best but your best isn't good enough.
Rain is like your thoughts and feelings kept all hidden away inside.
Rain is when you finally give up and stop trying.
Rain is like you're trying to be something you will never be.
Rain is when you make other people happy, but not yourself.
Rain is like the ocean's storm, destroying everything in sight.

Charity Dickerson, Grade 7
Oakvale Elementary School, WV

Ice Cream

I am cold and icy.
When you touch me you feel a chill!
I'm almost like Antarctica.
I come in many flavors —
cherry, vanilla, chocolate, and many more.
Your tongue might even give your brain a freeze!

Joana Muñoz, Grade 7
St Agatha School, NY

My Dog Caine

As I yelled to my dog Caine, let's go play.
I heard him bark as if the bark meant yay!
I opened the door and let him outside
Then turned and ran to go hide.
As I ran to hide behind the couch.
My mom walked in, ouch.
She didn't seem too mad.
She actually looked glad.
We played outside for an hour
But Caine got dirty so he had to take a shower.

Amber Frick, Grade 7
Thorne Middle School, NJ

Summer

What's my favorite season of the year?
It's summer that I hold near and dear
It's the best time to swim and play of course
But it's also the best time to ride my horse
Galloping down a dusty trail
The wind blowing my horse's mane and tail

Summer is the time when farmers make hay
To line the stalls where my horses lay
I love to ride in the bright sunshine
Leaving all of my worries behind

Summer and horses go well together
And I get to ride in the glorious weather
I can hardly wait until winter is done
So I can ride my horse in the warm summer sun
Summer is the season for fun
I wish it were the only one.

Patience Hartzell, Grade 7
Trinity Middle School, PA

Where I'm From

I'm from two sons, the older but not the wiser;
From Polo shirts and khaki pants on Sundays.
I'm from a busy road with many wrecks and traffic —
(bumper-to-bumper sometimes) in the morning and evening.
I'm from football and baseball games in the front yard and
swimming in our pool to beat the heat.
I'm from Boiling Springs, SC,
and there's no place I'd rather be.

Dylan Swofford, Grade 8
Spartanburg Jr Writing Project, SC

Beginning Poetry

I recommend that they stamp the poem
To the interior of their scalps
And watch as the meaning changes
Or tread in the poem's pool
Being careful not to disturb the serene flow of language
I ask that they pay attention
To the way the dirt has worn through the poem fabric
Or to skip through the poem's labyrinth
Gathering fruits from the idea tree as they go
I want them to sip the glass of poetry gingerly
But instead they gulp it down in one sip

Esmé Valette, Grade 8
International School of Boston, MA

Silent Companion

Hazel eyes,
gray, brown and black coat,
flaccid but gentle perked up ears —
this is how I describe my puppy Nami.
She's a good companion,
always keen to see my family and me.

She's very wary of strangers,
but as the saying goes "Her bark's worse than her bite!"
After a long day of school she greets me with a long howl
and sometimes jumps on the couch to sit right next to me.

Nami —
a good friend to have,
always silent,
always caring,
always a true friend,
always a true companion.

Connor Cowell, Grade 7
Ocean City Intermediate School, NJ

What "Perfect" Appears to Be

I have the body of a model
And that laser whitened smile
But as you walk past me
What you can't see is that inside I'm hollow
I have the grace of a bird in flight
And the face of an "angel"
But in a couple years that face will be ruined by drugs
I know this may scare and confuse you
But I'm not as perfect as I look
Not everything is wonderful in my life
My parents always pressure me to do better than my best
And my friends threaten to leave me
If I don't buy them cigarettes
So you see my life isn't perfect no matter what you think
Don't succumb to drugs and drinking
Even if your life has a kink

Amanda Wachowski, Grade 8
Beaty-Warren Middle School, PA

Animal Inside Me

There is a kitten inside me. With soft fur like a baby's blanket, and it comes out when it is provoked. It lives in my soul and makes me feel protected. It speaks like a five year old begging for a piece of chocolate. It scatters like impulsive raindrops falling from the sky. It makes me want to come out of my shell and confront everything that comes my way. I wish for just one day I could meet her and give thanks for all she has accomplished.

Tanya Cruz, Grade 9
Highland Park Middle/High School, NJ

Butterflies

B eneath the dark shadows
U nder the moon's brightness
T rapped in a lie that never ends
T rying to escape this reality
E ach passing day getting worse
R ecreate yourself for your own good
F ree you wish to be
L eaving a nightmare that won't go away
I s it just fantasy, or recreation for your own good?
E ternity makes you wait for that only chance you have
S it calmly and wait for the right time

You will see what may happen,
Stars shining on the dark pitch sky, she watches from her window
Two lovely butterflies full of life enter her room through the window
Remembering her old self; the butterflies cure her pain flying in circles around her to purify her soul.
Feeling guilt no longer she faints, picturing in her head meeting the love of her life dancing.
Under the moon in the mist of twilight her soul will rest in peace,
No longer tormented but for longed with joyous wonder.

Ana Benencio, Grade 9
Miami Beach Sr High School, FL

Lost

Slipping slowly through the crowds, longing to see the familiar face,
Searching, seeking as I go by, scanning, squinting as I pass,
But everywhere I turn and look, sheens of scarlet are all I see.

Now scampering swiftly through the crowds, longing to see that familiar face,
Hoping so strongly that wishes come true, determinedly daring to find what I know,
But everywhere I glimpse out of my eye, shimmers of scarlet are all I see.

Oh, sprinting shakily through the crowds, longing to see that familiar face,
Fervently praying the familiar prayer, slipping a sweaty hand over my scared heart,
But, somehow, everywhere I slow enough to see, waves of scarlet and silver splash over me.

Now stumbling through the crowds, now sobbing silently, now eyes streaming with silver tears,
Longing to see that familiar face.

But I never would have noticed, if my heart had never soared,
That flying flags of scarlet were before my weary eyes.

As I stumbled and helplessly fell, there was that sweet face in front of me,
And a stronger hand soon reached for my own, and lifted me to my unsteady feet,
But I contentedly let myself fall back to the ground, for that familiar face not I had found.

Yes, on my knees I surely saw what had been here all along.

Sarah Jane Thielman, Grade 8
Briarwood Christian Jr/Sr High School, AL

The Black Death

It was evil like the villains.
People crying among bodies,
Scattered across the floor.
The death is coming near,
Too cold to be strong,
It's like I'm melting away,
Into a puddle of water.
Look at me if you dare!
If you do,
You die!
The skies turn gray,
And spun with fear.
Babies left to die on the streets.
What a torture it can be.

Nimmy James, Grade 9
New Hyde Park Memorial Jr/Sr High School, NY

Memories

Step by Step
Breath by Breath
You walk down the road of your memories
Flashbacks
pictures
sadness and agony
pain and regret
joy and happiness
love and amicable moments
no longer a blur
like you have always dreamed of
No longer just a picture
No longer just a story
Memories making your heart jump with excitement
or ripping tearing spitting and piercing it
despite the pain,
you never want to leave the past.

Dana Aigotti, Grade 7
Westwood Jr-Sr High School, NJ

The Disney World Adventure

Oh that magical time at Disney World.
The sound of kids wailing
like a goose with laryngitis
and the sound of music blaring
into my ears like a fire siren.
The sight of many smiling faces
with smiles that went as high as the heavens.
I saw many costumed characters
with big, blue-starred hats.
The sun's heat beat down on me
like a hammer pounding
every last drop of energy out of my body.
Sweat rolled down onto my rosy cheeks.
Luscious smell of cotton candy filled the air.

Camille Villena, Grade 7
Trinity Middle School, PA

No One Knows How Hard It Is

No one knows how hard it is to live without you.
No one understands how I feel.
They say don't look back,
keep moving forward,
and I pray to God I can without you here.
It's hard to go on without you
Sometimes I feel like I can't move on
Go with me everywhere,
share your wisdom and your love.
No I can't move on alone.
Shine down from heaven above.
Hold my hand,
Walk with me,
carry me when I can't.
They say it's ok,
but the truth is it will never be that way.
Your chair will be empty,
just like the whole in my heart.

Felicia Weisberg, Grade 9
Hudson High School, FL

Friends

A friend is someone
who would be there for you
in your ups and downs.
A friend is a person
who would be by your side
in your good times, and your bad times.
This friend would always still be with you
even if you moved away from the town you were in.
They would call you on the phone,
and they would talk for hours with you.
Friends

Kaitlin Whalin, Grade 7
Hebron Middle School, KY

What It Takes

Will I have all the nerve that it will take?
Will my mind have the strength to survive?
Can my will, alone, be enough to make
A calm life in a city so alive?

New York. Such a city of excitement.
The town that has left so many alone
Will you throw me to the streets broke and bent?
Will you rip apart the life I have sewn?

The opportunities that await there
Can only be reached with a strong belief
By believing in dreams, and with strong dare
Any person can obtain their relief

Any person's dream can end with a touch
In this wicked city I love so much.

Amy Gimpel, Grade 9
Unami Middle School, PA

Naive

You,
With your jet black hair,
I couldn't help but stare.
With your eyes so beautiful,
you seemed so intangeable.
You were perfect.

Me,
with my skinny jeans,
constantly in a day dream.
With my confidence so low,
little did I ever know
you thought I was perfect, too.

Us,
with our music playing so loud,
always making a scene in the crowd.
Though we had best intentions,
I failed to mention
we'd never be perfect
for each other.

Tia Carter, Grade 9
Riverside High School, SC

Crushed Then Relieved

Losing what you love
Is when you fall from the sky above
Whenever you think about her
Time is running near
But it's not too late
Run faster than you can
Before they close the gate
The faster you run
Your heart beats drums
Wait, she's there
Catch her now
The gate's swallowing
But how
Then you storm through the gates
She's in your arms with you
You both shed tears of joy
Because the beginning is new

Tyler Dos Santos, Grade 9
South Lakes High School, VA

Love

Love is like a digital camera
Instead of taking pictures
It takes in someone's heart

Love is like a digital camera
It can be taken wherever
It flashes with happiness
And gets shared with family and friends

Brittany Miles, Grade 9
Thomson High School, GA

Windy Shores

Obviously, incredible, windy
Air blowing at the speed of a race car
Expectantly beautiful slated rocks
Water crashing against the eroding shore
Windy, peaceful
Sunset off the great mountains in the distance
Slate slabs acting as a wall on the shore
Sun bouncing off the water
Noises whisper across the air right across the water
In the foothills of the Maine woods pine trees whirling in the great gust
Kindling crackling in the bonfire water crashing upon the beach
Feeling warm inside knowing that I can relax
Beautiful wanting to stay
Knowing that the next morning that you need to canoe it
What will it be like in the winter?
Snowing, frozen
A ghost town
Animals not coming out because too cold too bland
Crested in the wild
Crested in the wild
Crested in the wild

Bill Schaub, Grade 7
William Penn Middle School, PA

My Family Is a Car

My dad is the steering wheel; he knows the direction we need to go.
My mom is the accelerator;
she is the one who gets us moving when we need to be somewhere.
My brother is the tires; he is always on the move.
I am the headlights; I always like to be able to see where I am going.
My family is a car.

Jenna Marcantonio, Grade 9
North Tonawanda High School, NY

Sweet Summer Days

My toes sank into the soft, hot sand I laid my towel out and planned
To sit in the sun for hours upon hours to make my skin tanner

The kids threw a colorful beach ball 'round the kids clumsily fell to the ground
They leaped into the big waves like a kitten pouncing towards a fly

It was time to visit the boardwalk the air was a sweet carnival
It smelled of cotton candy and ice cream I was falling into a wonderful dream

The rides were full of screaming children cute little faces filled up in my head
The bumper cars crashed into each other the children smiled and yelled

The ocean settled and looked very calm walking on the beach at night is very soothing
The sand in between my toes felt good life is great when you're at the beach

It was time to settle down and go to bed listening to the waves rolling onto shore
Made me go to bed very quickly I couldn't wait to wake up in the morning
And do it all over again it is summer!

Tara Maybury, Grade 8
Westampton Middle School, NJ

Waste Not; Want Not

With the greenhouse gasses
And the melting ice masses
And the drowning polar bears
And the endangered plants everywhere,
Strong natural disasters
And diseases spreading faster
Many more floods, no doubt
And a vast severe drought
With devastating forest fires
And temperatures getting higher and higher
Something has to be done
Or else we won't have any more fun
How about recycling
Or, instead of driving, biking
Or eating and using things that are organic
And planning a landscape that is botanic
Or changing the bulbs in our lights
And unplugging the cell phone charger tonight
We all have to remember what our lives are worth
And do our job to help out Mother Earth

Eva Tuszka, Grade 9
Bishop Denis J O'Connell High School, VA

He

He is noble, he is brave and strong.
He is caring and he sings a song
About his life and that is not a lie
You can see his story through his eyes.
He is caring and he is loving,
He is humorous and cunning.
He has seen many things and been through so much more
He is more than he seems if you look to the core.
He is joyful and happy and loves his life every day,
The future, the present and past pictures of white and gray.

Courtney Camden, Grade 8
Cape Henry Collegiate School, VA

Ghost Opera

A phantom, standing waiting for a call,
the call of his fans screaming his name.
Violin in hand he clambers onto the stage, fans silent in awe
his instrument is risen up to his chin
"Ladies and Gentleman the show is about to begin!"
The enigma draws his bow, his arm flies to and fro,
smoke dancing from his fingertips
flowing along with his melodies,
voices sang out like angels singing from heaven.

The phantom's violin begins to shriek in a demonic cry,
sparks from the bow begin to fly
the music accelerates and the singing ends
Ghosts ascend down into the audiences hands
The onlookers possessed, the paragon's army raised
Surely this beat will bring about the end of days!

Michael DeFreitas, Grade 8
Murray Middle School, FL

Full Life

I never noticed the huge pine tree down the hill,
always filled with birds nesting and resting.

Once I saw a cardinal with a black left wing
swoop in, to feed the babies
who had just hatched only to find one had gone on.

I wonder where the baby went,
did he fly?

Maybe he went to find his mom,
maybe he went to find food,
maybe he is moving on, am I?

Connor Durko, Grade 7
Trinity Middle School, PA

Identify Me

Who was I, am I, will I be?
Why can't you tell me?
Why can't you see?
All my friends know, as they say,
What they'll be someday.
"I'll be a doctor," says one, "An astrophysicist," says another.
So then why can't I know?
"It's normal," says my mother.
"You're smart. You'll figure it out," says my brother.
Everyone but me seems to think that.
I just don't agree.
Don't seem to get what I did to deserve this tit-for-tat.
Why betide me such woe?
Why is this so? Why can't you see?
I haven't a clue, just what'll I do?
I always wanted to be somebody and to go somewhere,
but who, and where, I still don't know.
Please, my faith is running low,
A clue towards my right path is all I ask.
I just need a little help to identify me,
To remove my covering mask.

Peter Jafferakos, Grade 9
Bishop Ford Central Catholic High School, NY

Skating

This is my safe place
where I spend most of my time,
where I can be calm with myself.
The place where nothing else matters,
but the sound of wheels coasting.

I learn new things,
I fall, but get back up.
Life lessons are learned, and goals are damaged.
I skate for life, not to be sponsored.
I skate for myself, and only myself.

Ryan Bakely, Grade 7
Ocean City Intermediate School, NJ

0.05

If I had a nickel,
For every time I've heard
"Bless your heart,"
I'd be driving in my Mustang,
From my Victorian mansion,
As I ran my campaign
Giving a smile for the camera's flash,
And shake your hand,
As you speak in your dumb little drawl.
Bless your heart.

If I had a nickel,
For every time I've heard
"No offense,"
I'd be living in a plantation house,
Next to my prized stable,
In an antique rocking chair,
And in a polite Southern accent,
State that your Yankee politics,
Are superficial and idiotic.
No offense.

Sarah Phillips, Grade 9
Arab High School, AL

Lucky Charm

There once was a kid who was lucky
Who loved the word Kentucky
He was a charming boy
Who one day got a toy
It looked like a little rubber ducky

Luc Nguyen, Grade 7
Texas Avenue Elementary School, NJ

My Cup of Restraint

My cup of restraint,
Forcefully built,
Is pouring in
And filled with guilt.

I had so much to say,
Trust me, it was a lot!
I should have been me,
Or so I was taught.

My cup of restraint,
Built with guilt,
Is just a small cup though
So wait 'til it tilts.

It'll crash in pieces,
Oh surely it'll break!
But I should just move on with life,
For my good's sake.

Vagdevi Kondeti, Grade 7
Anthony Wayne Middle School, NJ

Trapped

I'm trapped inside of something,
That isn't even me.
Doing what I'm told to,
Not what I believe.
Forcing a smile,
To set upon my face,
But with each passing moment,
I feel I'm out of place.
I need to break away,
And be free to come undone,
But I'm forced to stay,
My battle is not yet won.
One day I'll get away,
And be able to be free,
But until then,
I'm trapped inside
Of something that isn't me.

Chelsea Allen, Grade 9
Hudson High School, FL

Olympics

Spring, summer, winter, fall,
Athletes train through them all.
Swimming, diving, running, more,
They want to get the highest score.
Even though gold is the goal,
It is only for one soul.
Hopefully our team will win.
If they don't, we'll try again.

Christina Nagy, Grade 9
White Station High School, TN

Practice

Beats and rhythms flowing round
Flailing sticks all around
Telling stories to me
Of the happenings that day.
These stories,
Never the same,
Sometimes of shame.
The deeds told of
By these extensions of me
Can never be retold.
So bold
These stories
Not restricted by moral views,
Drums are heartbeats
Stale and cold.
These stories,
Some long
Others short
Told by memories,
From I, the storyteller.

Keven Anderson Beach, Grade 9
Riverside High School, SC

The Wintertime of Year

The icicles glistened
Among winter air
Gleaming with sparkles
Shimmering to glare

The snow crunches
As white as sheets
It lays motionless
Where it and objects meet

The dripping branches
Lay solid with bliss
Covered with white
As sweet as a kiss

The whole street is quiet
As moonlight appears
Don't you just love
The wintertime of year

Stephanie Levin, Grade 7
Carson Middle School, VA

Nature

Its beauty alone can be seen for miles,
It blows in the wind,
Our nature smiles,
Nature shows its love to the Earth.

Keeping us from falling apart,
Its moods are restless,
Our nature's controlling gesture,
Nature lives for us.

The whistling sound of what we hear,
It has a peaceful battle with us,
Our nature alone has the power to win,
Nature is Earth's loving sin.

Megan Reid, Grade 7
Inter-Lakes Jr High School, NH

Book

Crackle go the pages,
pop go its words.
Little does it seem,
to get into a book.
Its words are so big,
they might even give you a hug.
But when it meets a friend,
they never separate.
It also thinks about you,
just like you do too.
But when you fall asleep,
it's still there right beside you.

Sabrina Samolyuk, Grade 7
St Agatha School, NY

Waiting

I've been waiting for something.
I don't know what
I don't know where.
I just know that something is there.

Watching the waves roll through the sea
Hearing them as they crash and flee
Looking at the sunset as the sun says goodbye
I stare and lie down as I watch it go by.

Darkness has come to end the day
As the moon smiles at me
I go to bed safe and sound
Just waiting, waiting to be found.

Paolo Ramirez, Grade 9
Unami Middle School, PA

Golden Memories

Every four years looking for gold medals
Like rare gems in the ground hard to win gold
Countries all round competing for the gems
Running and pushing all to grab ahold.

Event after event countries come bound
Fingernail chewing suspense in between
One goal set to be better than the rest.
Winning is like a treat on Halloween.

The world watches in anticipation
As their country fights for the first place treats
Several going to watch in person
Arenas with people so no one cheats.

When over everyone goes back home
To rejoice about the huge victories.
The contestants celebrate at home,
Always remembering the memories.

Austen Poynter, Grade 9
White Station High School, TN

I Found Grace

I closed the door
On everything You gave to me. I yearned for more
And because of that I am empty. My heart is torn,
Because You know what's best for me, and I ignored
Your plan for my life, and what it should be. I start the day
Casting off all my insecurities. I go my own way,
Blind to my eternity. And the only one
Who can change this hardened heart of mine is Your Son…
He's the only one. So where is Grace?
Where is hope? Where is love? I will embrace
Your love for me, and up above You see my face.
I will replace my old ways, 'cause in You I found grace.

Ben Parks, Grade 9
Briarwood Christian High School, AL

The Beach

Sea salt floating in the gust of light air,
The crowing of the selfish seagulls,
Rainbow colored beach umbrellas waving,
Endless amounts of lobster colored visitors grazing under them,
I taste the disgusting sea water I had swallowed in my swim,
Toddlers splish-splashing around in the foamy water,
Ghostly crabs running in and out of their tunnels at sunset,
Old treasures found as sandcastles grow,
Depleted people say their final goodbyes to the cooling sand,
Stargazers park their blankets in the dunes,
Life really is good.

Ryan Karch, Grade 7
William Penn Middle School, PA

The Rain

The sky transforms from a crisp blue, to a frightening black,
The sun slithers behind the dense black blanket,
Slowly, drops of pure water trickle from the sky,
Then, faster and faster, until it batters the roof,
Boom! The thunder is as deafening as a bomb,
The lightning strikes, illuminating the dark sky,
The rain slows down until finally it stops,
The dark clouds push their way out of the sky,
The sun peeks out of the new billowing clouds,
Then, across the pale blue sky, a rainbow appears,
With shades of red, orange, yellow, green, blue and purple,
But, slowly, it fades until it's seen no more,
Birds began to chirp and everything seems to come alive again,
There is nothing better, than watching the rain.

Rebecca Grube, Grade 8
Cocalico Middle School, PA

Who Am I?

Who am I?
I am like a bird trying to fly
But I can't because I am chained to the ground
By the cold iron of poverty.
Who am I?
I am like the mighty lions that wish to roam free
But can't for I am imprisoned inside a small cage.
Who am I?
I am like the sheep that graze in the fields
But have to keep a watchful eye
Of the wolves of the rich.
Who am I?
I am like the roses
That bloom beautifully in the summer
But are shriveled up by the cold winds of sadness.
Who am I?
I wake up and know that I have to work
Four jobs every day for the rest of my life
Just to pay off my mortgage.
Who am I?
I am the lower class.

Antonio Miranda, Grade 8
The Knox School, NY

David

The way he looks at me,
his eyes so soft and green.

The way he holds my hand,
his arms so tough and lean.

The way he says "I love you,"
sends chills down my spine.

And I'm so glad to know,
that he's forever mine.

Karla Ginn, Grade 7
Perquimans County Middle School, NC

Thunder

On our planet
Not in the ocean
In Europe, not in a huge country
But in a beautiful city
Named Paris
Among French kissers
And bread eaters
No fast food
But delicious pastries
In "ma petit maison"
Not too small
In a cozy kitchen
Not old fashioned
But not high-tech
Sitting under the table
Escaping the
Crack of the thunder
And the pounding of the rain
Not too scared, just petrified
There we were
Me, myself, and I.

Audrey Owens, Grade 8
Hommocks Middle School, NY

Nature's Soul —

The sun
shines upon my soul
lifting my mood
while the wind
blows me into
a spiritual state.
The sky glows
a beautiful, baby blue
welcoming birds
soaring upon their wings.
Nature whispers —
awakens my heart
to embrace the creation
of this magnificent Earth.

Katie Johnson, Grade 7
Ocean City Intermediate School, NJ

Six Room

The sun smiles down on me warming my skin
Clear blue skies surround me like a warm coat on a cold winter's day
I can barely hear over the roar of the roller coasters
The soft breeze gently flows through the small plant surroundings
This place is so amazing and wonderful
Like I'm in a whole new world outside of reality
I wonder when I will be back again

Taylor Zaccaro, Grade 7
William Penn Middle School, PA

Who Am I

Who am I
I am me
a young black child stuck in a corrupt life style
hurt pride bring anger all a part of being black is what I'm told
So I ask myself who am I really

Who am I
people tell me since I'm black I'm nothing
I think otherwise and don't pay it no mind
I'm determined to establish something positive with my life
Self really who am I

Who am I
since I'm black I should have a lethargic life
people think blacks should be overlooked because of prior history
growing up as a black child is the hardest part of life
Growing up being black I ask myself who am I

So my question is self who am I
Really who am I

Eldrige Beauford Jr., Grade 8
Southside Middle School, FL

Nobody But Me!!

The scent of perfumes and colognes overpower me,
As I linger behind the very curtains that extinguishes my shadows
My courage to go out and perform in front of an enormous crowd, awaits me
Waiting for the curtains to open
Nobody but me!!
I hear the audience clap
As I dance my final silhouette
I feel free as an eagle flying across the night sky
I spread my wings and try to find some closure
Nobody but me!!
Watching these unfamiliar faces look at me while I take my final bow,
Applauding for a standing ovation,
Still hearing the smooth music to my ears
Nobody but me!!
Then why is it that I feel nothing?
Isn't this what I want to do!
I guess fame isn't worth a dime
If you don't have anybody to share it with
Nobody but me!!

Rasheedah Russell, Grade 9
Colonia High School, NJ

Moonlight Stroll, Midnight Love

Under the glistening crescent moon,
Two lovers walk along the river's groove.
They walk together hand in hand, side by side
Completing each other perfectly, one soul, one body, one mind.
As the purity of the crescent is transitioning crimson red,
The lover's passionate flame turns ice cold.
They quarrel alongside the riverbed,
Trying not to shed the tears they hold.
The crossroads of their destinies lie before them.
Each lover takes a different path,
Never to see the other again.
As the moon evolves to a sparkling sapphire blue,
Their footprints remain together as one.
The closer the footprints get to the zero hour,
The further they drift off into the night,
To be washed away forever into the dark abyss of the water...

Kinsey Sheppard, Grade 8
Baldwin Middle School, NY

Summer's Day

She's smiling,
She's so surprised today.
The super summer sun crawled in
Ready to glare on the tanners that lay.

The sun's yellow and shining bright,
She never thought it would happen,
The sand is soft like cotton.

The perfect day to be at the beach,
The perfect day for the ocean,
She got there in one quick motion.

Sipping soda,
Riding waves,
Running along the beach.

Thank you sun for coming out,
She said,
Thank you for letting me enjoy my summer's day.

Kim Oppenheim, Grade 7
Westwood Jr-Sr High School, NJ

Kennecia

Kennecia
Cool, fun, athletic, goofy
Daughter of Anita Dunn and Michael Hamilton
Lover of basketball, having fun, and music
Who feels confident, independent, and silly sometimes
Who needs a cellphone, money, and a laptop
Who fears small places, heights, and wasps
Who would like to see New York, ATL, and LA
Who lives in Clarksville, Tennessee
Hamilton

Kennecia Hamilton, Grade 8
Montgomery Central Middle School, TN

Trees

Trees are tall that grow towards the sun,
Trees hang swings that can be great fun,
Trees make the world go 'round,
Trees make the leaves that fall down.

Trees make music for everyone to hear,
Trees are not to be feared,
Trees make homes so birds can nest,
Trees provide shady spots for the weary to rest.

Trees make great stands for birds to sing,
Trees are what make the wood ring,
Trees provide the wood for our homes.
Trees made the paper for this poem.

Trees are the green that is seen from above.
Trees are beauty you can't help but love.
Trees are a miracle sprung from the sod.
Trees truly are the handiwork of God.

Taylor Smith, Grade 9
Corinth High School, MS

A Best Friend

She shines like the sun
When the sun is no where to be seen;
She makes things more alive.

She's like the older sister I never had
We take care of each other
In good times and the bad,
She is always there.

She cares for everyone,
And loves unconditionally
Even to those who treat her poorly,
And do wrong by her.

Bubbly and fun
I'll love her forever,
She's my best friend and "my sister."

Morgan Crissy, Grade 9
Bishop Denis J O'Connell High School, VA

This Game

This is, what we call, the game of life.
People win, people lose.
Players cheat, lie, steal, bluff, and quit.
There is no such thing as fairness,
If you can't keep up, then you're done for
Like a tempted fish lured in by the fisherman's bait and caught.
In the moment of struggle for freedom
You break free, or get chained down.
This is, the game of life.

Shirley Yu, Grade 9
Bronx High School of Science, NY

The Boogeyman

His breathing sped up; her heart rate increased.
What would you expect when they were about to be deceased?
Not a sound could be heard in the lonely room.
There was certainly a feeling of deep gloom.
Anyone could see the fear in their eyes.
They were standing up to the media's lies.
So what made them do this, what was the force?
Why, it was the Boogeyman of course.

The Boogeyman is the destroyer of thought; if you congregate you will surely be caught.
The Boogeyman is the destroyer of free will; follow his orders, for he does not hesitate to kill.
The Boogeyman is the destroyer of information; he most certainly will deny you this sensation.
The Boogeyman is the destroyer of rights; do not resist him, for he wins all of his fights.

These criminals would surely pay.
Their thoughts were meant to be kept at bay.
All 15 people hid under the table,
Which was telling them their situation would not stay stable.
The books around the room were evidence of their crime.
How could they get rid of them in time?
Suddenly, a large, beeping object hit a woman's thumb.
It was then that they knew the Boogeyman had come.

Zach Lustbader, Grade 9
Livingston Sr High School, NJ

It's All You!

We have grown so close this past year.
However, becoming so close introduced all *your* drama.
Every day it takes a toll on me.
I try not to let it bother me but then I think it's all you.
I wasn't the one lying.
I wasn't the one betraying my parents and
I wasn't the one involved it was all you!
Just thinking that thought makes me angry.
I want to be friends with you, I really do.
But it has to go away!
I can't take much more of this.
Soon this situation will get to the point where I won't know what else to do but not be friends with you.

Nicole Champagne, Grade 7
Depew Middle School, NY

From the Strong to the Weak

Lock me up, take away my electronics; but life will go on. Beat me, yell at me, tell me I'm worthless; for no one can tell me how small I am, I decide how big I will be. Tell me I'm stupid, paper has more patience than people. Hate me with every atom in your body; God will still love me. Strip me of my possessions and smile because you think you have defeated me; I will do the time, I will not allow the time to do me. I will make the prison my home. Keep me in and I will refuse to go out. Intimidate me and realize that I am the intimidator; for as Martin Luther King Junior once said, "we must build dikes of courage to hold back the floods of fear." You must never let fear hold you back, or let doubters hold you back. Look for the most important strength of all — the one that comes from inside of you. Take risks; for what doesn't kill you will only make you stronger. Accept the truth even when it is not to your liking. The world is full of pain and misery. There will be times when you will feel as if you are wandering in darkness and you see a light, and you chase it…only to realize that it's not there, over and over again. But we must pull ourselves together, there is no time for self pity, we must endure, for more pain and suffering awaits up ahead in our pursuit of happiness. So I say this to you, keep your head up, don't let anyone put you down, and hold on to your dreams…for your dreams will take you to wonderful places.

Natanaelle Germain, Grade 8
Chestnut Ridge Middle School, NY

Summer in Disguise

The white and crispy cotton crunches beneath my toes.
It falls so swiftly and gently and lands upon my nose.
How the sugar nuzzles me as it's falling from the sky.
I shudder from the coldness as the flakes go passing by.
I flail my arms and twirl around and then I close my eyes.
I open them to a whole new world, a dream and a surprise.
Although I am shivering, I stay to watch the show.
A winter goddess, blanket of cloud, a thing that we call snow.
I bid farewell and give a salute and say all my goodbyes.
It's a winter wonderland, summer in disguise!

Courtney Gilmore, Grade 7
Chazy Central Rural School, NY

Tony

Tony was a wonderful father and friend
You could always trust him until the very end
I still can't believe it happened
It is something I will always dread
The remembrance of him is still implanted in my head
Along with all of the terrific things he said
Sort of like a hero; Tony
Because he was always truthful and never a phony
Me, Avie, Adam and all others who loved him
Will try to stay strong and never cave in
Although he was not my blood relative
He could have been
Because of all the great things he did for me and Avie
Which make me very grateful as you can see
If only you knew him you could feel
All of these feelings that seem so surreal
So for now, Tony, it is farewell and goodbye
Until the day that I see you up in the sky

Heather Deaver, Grade 7
Garnet Valley Middle School, PA

Message to God

God what is wrong with me?
What am I doing wrong?
Every day and night
I make bad decisions.
I wish I could stop, but
I feel like a bird trying to fly, but can't
because the wind is too strong!!
If You were me, what would You do?
I need the answers now!!
I want to be a good person.
I am not an adult,
but yet You leave me with all these decisions!!
GOOOOSH!!
I hate these decisions!!
God I am asking You,
please help, I need it the most
NOW!!!!!

Matthew Dernoga, Grade 8
Beacon Middle School, DE

Wondering

If you could be a bird in the sky
    Would you wonder "if" or "why"
Or maybe would you understand
    The kindness sadness of this man
Would the love of these two
    Amaze or wonder, confuse you

If you would be the moon, up high
    Would you know "if" or "why"
Or maybe you would just know the way
    You'll understand what she wants to say
And what about the way he feels
    Could you show him what is real

If you were me wondering with a sigh
    Would you understand the "if" and the "why"

Time goes by the world goes 'round
    And all these people are earth bound
But their meanings pure and true
    Are remembered and told to you
And as you wonder "if" or "why"
    The stories are told and the world gets by

Emily Mitchell, Grade 9
Holy Cross Academy, VA

Friends

I have a lot of friends
Friends that are girls
Friends that are boys
I have one true friend, Carly
If a friend is mad at me, Carly is there for me
We both think the same and say the same things
We are the best of friends
Friends may come and go
Carly will always be my best friend

Annie Zayatz, Grade 7
Brielle Elementary School, NJ

The Art of Laughing

What joy there is to having a good laugh!
A simple chuckle to a loud guffaw.
We giggle 'till our bodies bend in half.
There is a mile of space between our jaws.
Is it possible to die from laughing?
I've spent many hours to find it out.
Is there really any point in asking?
As long as you have things to laugh about.
There once was a poor boy who couldn't laugh.
It's sad what happened to him in the end.
The kids all thought he was a hermit crab.
Because of this he could not find a friend.
So what is there to do when life's a bore?
My doctor's prescription: go laugh some more!

Lisa Zhou, Grade 9
White Station High School, TN

The Church Bell

Ding dong! Ding dong!
The church bell is ringing!
Can't you hear its joyous song?
Ding dong! Ding dong!
Look high up into the steeple.
There it is! Gently rocking,
Singing its song to the people!
Ding dong! Ding dong!
Listen to its mellow notes.
They drift far, ever so far,
Farther than Sir Lancy's boats!
Ding dong! Ding dong!
It rings from dawn 'til dusk.
Never resting, never sleeping,
Always letting angels fly!
Ding dong! Ding dong!
Astride the breeze the notes go leaping,
Waving the sleepy town good-bye!
Slowly away the note rolls,
As the bell tolls:
Ding dong! Ding dong!

Ashley Kaysen, Grade 7
The Holy Name of Jesus Academy, NY

The Pond

A calm placid pond
Everything in sight at rest
A calm breeze blows by
A quiet and still night
Disturbed by a fallen leaf

Natalie Lindo, Grade 7
Pine Crest School, FL

My Passion

My passion for it
How much I give to it
How much it gives back
It's just like a perfect person

It makes me happy
It makes me cry
It keeps my head straight

It makes me want to do well in school
It makes me want to be a leader
It makes me a man

It changes me when I'm on its field
The smell of the grass is wonderful
The feelings it gives me — sad or bad

My will to win is high
It sucks to lose
But I will always love the game

Devante Green, Grade 7
Oakvale Elementary School, WV

Seagulls Chirping

Seagulls chirping at one another as they swiftly swoop from the sky
The waves crashing effortlessly along the shoreline
Sand seeps soothingly out from between my toes
Early birds have gotten there early to claim their accustomed spot
In the early morning, the beach is being groomed
The sun is still a dark orange peeping above the trees
My shadow is long and skinny stretching across the groomed sand
The water is glimmering like glitter spilled all over the sea
A nearby flag is dancing in the breeze
The chains clattering from the lifeguards detaching their gear
The sound of wind whistling as it blows by a flagpole pulley
And the sound of sand skipping across other particles of sand
I wonder if people come to the beach in the winter
I wonder if the huge ocean ever freezes
I wonder if the crabs still come up onto the fine sand
I wonder if the waves get bigger, or smaller
When I am there I feel like a new person, I feel like I can do anything
I feel that I always have a friend there, that I am never alone
Seagulls chirping, seagulls chirping, seagulls chirping

Matthew Kraus, Grade 7
William Penn Middle School, PA

What Happens to a Girl When She's in Love?

Can you see the way he makes her smile?
Her smile is as bright as the sun,
When he is near.
When he touches her hand, she feels no pain, no fear.
He makes her day brighter.
Her love for perfume is sensational with the smell of roses and twinkling tulips.
She loves it when he tells her "Your perfume smells good."
Does her voice change when she is around that special someone?
Yes!
These are the signs of a girl in love.
Will you be the next girl in love that everyone envies?

Kayla Hernandez, Grade 8
Public School 31 William Lloyd Garrison, NY

Cheerleading

At a cheerleading competition
First up on floor
Ready to compete
Getting ready to accomplish more
My nerves are a bunch of tangled wires ready to explode
I feel like I'm going to be sick
I get on the floor and feel like a load
I do my tremendous backhand spring and then get up to do a jump
I fall to the ground, and you hear a rapid snap
I start crying and screaming
I get carried away on a mat
I'm going to the hospital
Only dreaming of what will happen to me
I broke my ankle and hurt my knee
Now all that's left is a cast put on

Brianne Janosko, Grade 7
Pine-Richland Middle School, PA

Happiness

I sit in this world *always* thinking
of the best and *never* the worst.
God painted this Earth with all sorts of color
to symbolize the joy I celebrate.
I live like the sun,
shining, glowing, and making life.
It's definitely the best medicine —
easy to cure, easy to find.

Samantha Sullivan, Grade 7
Ocean City Intermediate School, NJ

Sunshine on My Soul

The sun shines from a distance
warming my heart, spirit, and soul.
I long to see the beautiful painted colors
of the dawn awake from the dark night.
The rays penetrate my mood when I am irritable;
a torch that lights my soul from miles away,
giving fire to my life.
Feeling the warmth mask my face
is a wondrous feeling.
The sun is the heat of my body.
I cannot thrive without the light
given off my the enormous orb of fire every day.
It turns the seasons, turns the day,
and turns my life.

Jackie Jernee, Grade 7
Ocean City Intermediate School, NJ

Summer I Was 10

The summer I was ten,
Was a life changing time.
2 digits already. Wow.
Spring I was 9, summer I was 10.

School was at last finally out.
Yet I could not have found enough joy.
My school only went until 4th grade.
Leaving my friends, headed to new doors.

Leaving a place you knew almost all of your life so far
Isn't as easy as it might look.
Entering a new place full of new people
Made me as nervous as I could be.

What if the people didn't like me?
What if I didn't like them?
What if I was totally different to them?
Yet all these what ifs would not have helped me.

I have not totally left my old school.
I have not left the place I live.
Nothing much can really change.
It can only get better from here.

Yannick Boeck-Chenevier, Grade 8
International School of Boston, MA

Race Day

It was Sunday in mid February and the biggest race of the year
fans filled the seats waiting to cheer.

Moments before the event began
we stood at our seats and honored the flag.

With forty-three cars all lined in a row
waiting for someone to tell them to go.

The sun in our eyes, barely able to see
I couldn't' help but wonder who the winner might be.

As the two hundred laps finally came to an end.
They handed the black and white cloth to my friend.

Chadd Nowak, Grade 7
Depew Middle School, NY

The Gift of Nature

One Saturday while walking in the park,
I noticed the gift of nature
I hear the squirrels playing with each other
running through the crunchy leaves and going up the trees.

As I sat down on a park bench,
I noticed the gift of nature
I listen to the baby birds in the nest chirping
waiting for their mother to bring them worms.

When I left the county park,
I noticed the gift of nature
the clouds in the sky darkened
and the rain started to fall.

James Dogali, Grade 7
Westwood Jr-Sr High School, NJ

Overcoming the Cold

The weather is colder than ever today!
There is no trace of life in sight.
It may be too cold to go out and play;
Be careful to not get frostbite.

Where are you going my friend the sun?
Are you sleeping during this storm?
Your presence has been missed a ton,
Without your company, it is not very warm.

Your enemy, the cold, has taken control.
The clouds have invaded the sky.
But don't give up, you should be able
To scatter the clouds if you are sly.

Bright ally, destroy your mortal foe
Then all Earth's happiness will show.

Josiah Baldwin, Grade 9
Elmira Christian Academy, NY

4th of July

During
4th of July,
Eric
And I
Will set
Off fireworks
While our
Parents gaze
At the show
And clap
Louder
And louder
For the
Flying flames,
Sizzling sparks,
And bursting boxes
As we
Turn night
Into
Day.

Matthew Rohr, Grade 7
Chickahominy Middle School, VA

Freedom

Japanese rice balls
My mom's kind voice
Mamaw's pumpkin pie
My friend, Rachel
A first kiss

Hannah Beasley, Grade 7
Madisonville Middle School, TN

He Is Here with Me Today

Every day I wake up feeling
The same sad and depressed way.
But I must always try to remember
That He is here with me today.
Some people will just shut Him out
And go along on their way.
But without Him I must declare,
There is no point in being here today.
So whenever I need guidance,
I will just sit down and pray.
And I will always try to remember
That He is here with me today.

Katherine Barker, Grade 8
Excel Christian Academy, GA

Jellyfish

Jellyfish
Wet, jellyfish
Swimming, stinging
Shocking isn't it?
Lightening.

Joshua Hubert, Grade 7
St Anthony School, CT

Maui Memories

Maui memories made
Bubbles explode, a quintillion perfect spheres
Sunbeams dart like mallet fish, kissing the reef with soft rays
A pair of smiling eyes slip down from an algae slide
Past my mom and I it swims
The baby sea turtle paddles leisurely back home
Past school of babbling angel fish, past mammoth undersea bats
We snorkel through this majestic shelled soul's backyard
the coral extends a hand, indigo fingers to shake
A lionfish and nurse shark dine together at the sandy seahorse restaurant
A delicious spaghetti ala seaweed feast
An eel rests its scaly head on a broken bed of hardened lava
Bubbles drift through broken fangs, sinew flexes with vicious strength
A crab sketches an engraving in sand, legs and claws swirling
Di Vinci's undersea brush, a Mona Lisa on the ocean floor
A reverberating whistle, Maui memories made
Sand and water, salt and volcanic rock
Turtles and rays, sunshine and happiness
Maui memories made

Michael A. Biksey, Grade 7
Trinity Middle School, PA

Love

Love is born from respect and kindness.
Love looks like flowers blooming on a sunny spring morning.
Love sounds like ocean waves rolling up on the shore.
Love feels like the longest roller coaster ride ever.
I would give love to the entire world because everyone deserves some
Love.

Carolina Hildago-Daza, Grade 7
Glades Middle School, FL

Friends

It's been days since we last talked
But the days just keep adding up
Yet we always seem to miss them as they fly past our face
Saying we'll be friends forever but forever's a lie
Nothing lasts forever not even love but the point here is not love
But friendship a treasure that we shall all cherish
Enjoying every living
Waking breathing day we spend together
Whether fun or fights
We still stand strong for we are the past, now and future of our decaying world
Running blind
Falling down
Helping our fallen companions up
Wiping the blood from our eyes
Shedding pain
Losing friends
Along the way
We are a family
An army
A whole
A force that can't be devoured

Michael Pereyra, Grade 9
Miami Beach Sr High School, FL

Ode to My Cell Phone

Oh cell phone, oh cell phone, how I love you so
I use you every day so please don't go

When you call to me Brrrrrrrringgg Brrrrrrrring
You beckon me with your little white key

And when you want to send a message you just press send
And when you want to close a call you just press end

You are so small, mighty and a fierce hue of red
But yet I kiss you g'd night and put you to bed

Oh how I love you so I really really do
I wish I could have the power you do

Every day I give you to my teacher
And when someone calls I put them on speaker

And when I lose you, every day I look for you I really really do
And finally when I find you I'm not blue

Oh cell phone, oh cell phone, how much I love you so
I use you every day so please don't go

Colleen Bassett, Grade 7
Most Blessed Sacrament School, MD

The False Hopes of Love

My love for you is a giant sea,
One look at you and I am filled with glee.
But, you glare right through me,
No one wants to be with me.

Am I that unsightly?
Am I that bad of a person,
That you cannot so much even lend a hello?

You messed with my heart before,
Had me intertwined in your fingers.
I WAS deeply attracted to you.
Until, you were unfaithful.

Now you're with what's his face,
Doing God knows what.
I wish you stuck with me,
Oh, if only you stuck with me.

Joel Antipuna, Grade 9
Gloucester County Institute of Technology, NJ

In the Band

In the band, four people stand
All with instruments in their hand.
The crowd's attention they demand.
They hope they're good, so they don't get canned.

Christopher Stevens, Grade 9
Redeemer Lutheran School, PA

Briana

B old is the word that defines me the best
R emember the good days in my life
I n the end I will achieve at anything
A chieving everything I want and desire
N ever put myself down in life
A ccepting everything I get in life

Briana Quanataya Mike, Grade 9
Seminole County Middle/High School, GA

Felt

The waves crash against the ocean's shore,
The lightning flashes more and more.
The thunder roars in empty skies,
All your words, all your lies.
The darkest blue, the deeper sea,
I thought that all you needed was me!
Now my world crackles and shakes,
I've figured out, you're just a fake.
All the stars come tumbling down,
And all you have is just a frown.
You shouldn't waste your words on me,
There's nothing left for you to see.
The sun that burns against your skin,
The same that heats the roofs of tin.
Will melt you down from tip to end!
The words you speak are all the same,
I know I'm not the one to blame!
I hope this leaves you empty inside,
For you are the thing that I *Despise*.

Haley Vick, Grade 9
Lee High School, AL

Forbidden Mirrors Truth

Tears leak
Bleeding with immense pain
Uncovering all your truths
Unraveling pure rage
What is truth friend?
A perspective on things that you hid behind?
Things that you run away from?
That you make so difficult to find
Strips of fiery drip, and gush from beneath walls of secrecy
Surfacing a forbidden truth
Searching for the enemy
What becomes of the lies that we tell?
The secrets we keep? What becomes of it all?
What about the tears that leak?
From forbidden truths
This is what you discover
You must never judge a book
By the essence of its cover
You must understand what those riddles are
Because a sheet of water shows you your true colors
Through eyes you have never seen, that's what mirrors are

Shaunice Green, Grade 9
Warren East High School, KY

Growing Apart

We met when we were little,
We always got along,
But as we got older,
Something went wrong.
We started off as best friends,
We were sisters at heart.
Now I can see
How we are growing apart.
It seems like only yesterday
You promised you'd be there
Now you're throwing me aside
And you don't even care.
You made a lot of new friends
You slowly walked away
And when I try to talk to you
You had nothing to say
What happened to the girl
That I used to know back then
I have one thing left to say
Don't talk to me again

Brittany Vatter, Grade 7
Depew Middle School, NY

War

The howl of the wolf
Signals the fight
Telling the vultures
Of a feast tonight

Calling the beasts
To unwillingly brawl
For the kingdoms clash
And in the end will fall

The bloody battle
Declines to cease
While the loved wait
And pray for peace

Bargaining for land
With the lives of men
Neither caring nor paying
For their horrid sin

Jenny DelVecchio, Grade 7
Jamestown Middle School, NC

What If

What if I become a MLB player
I might play for the New York Yankees,
What if I became a legend?
I could break records,
What if I make it big like the Babe?
I would be a role model for kids,
Do dreams really come true?

Cole Bray, Grade 7
Perquimans County Middle School, NC

Rolling Down a Hill

I
stood
there, sleigh
ready in my hands,
speechless, staring at the
spectacular hill before me. Its
lush green grass awaited for rails to
slide down to its bottoms. Anxiously, I
ran up to the top, dragging the resistant sleigh
tied to my tiny wrist. I reached the top. I stopped,
looked down, and blinked. It was no dream. The small
hill stretched down before me seemed to go on for miles. A
tiny smiling ant at the bottom of the hill yelled at me, "You can
do it!" My mom's motherly sweet voice made its way to the very top,
encouraging me, giving me bravery. With a deep breath and a forceful sigh,
I sat on my small sleigh and with a push, I started happily rolling down the hill.

Maria A. Mendoza, Grade 8
William Penn Middle School, PA

The Silenced

We were friends, we talked all the time
But now for some reason you're just quiet
I try to find out what's wrong but you don't respond
But then I remember what I did
I try to apologize it was just a joke
I didn't mean to make you sad when I called you those names
I didn't know it would make such an impact
I understand how bad you feel, so I will give you your space
But for now we will just have to ignore each other and just stay in silence

Shawn Kemp, Grade 7
Depew Middle School, NY

I Am

I am nice and happy when family comes over
I am nice and happy when I hit the ball deep
I am nice and happy

I am nice and happy when I am with my friends
I am nice and happy when people enjoy me for who I am
I am nice and happy

I am nice and happy when I get good grades
I am nice and happy when I make people laugh until their tummy aches
I am nice and happy

I am nice and happy when I bond with my sister and we become two peas in a pod
I am nice and happy when I am watching movies with my family
I am nice and happy

I am nice and happy when I am able to relax and unwind on my feelings
I am nice and happy

Are you nice and happy?

Joseph Hummel, Grade 8
Westampton Middle School, NJ

Two Lonely Rings

As they sit on the bench, her eyes gaze upon him.
His luscious locks the color of sand,
his arm wrapped around her holding her hand.
She looks into his eyes, so deep and hollow knowing
that nothing will ever be the same.
Everything has been different since the day that man came.
Trust was no more as shame came to play.
The only thing that was left, were two meaningless rings.

Haley Acuna, Grade 7
L E Gable Middle School, SC

Daddy's Little Girl

I miss you
Nobody can replace you
But is it okay to let people in
Sadly I must think you'd say no
Then I think and cry
When I cry and think
How could a girl my age feel like a 21 year old
I miss you so
My heart breaks inside as I think of you
I can't believe you're gone
You never seem to call back
It's almost as if you're just a ghost
How I wish for you and mom
But I guess it never could be
I'll always be a daddy's girl
Even though you're never around
It makes me think
Am I really daddy's little girl?

Kailee O'Donnell, Grade 7
Schenevus Central School, NY

What Is Love?

Love…what is love as we know it?
Is it a word like any other, just said to be said
A four letter word that means so much
And so little, in seconds.

Love…what is love to you and me?
After a "hello" and before a "good-bye"
I love you; I love you.
Yes, I already know
Do you know what it means
or are you running a show?

Love…what is love to you and me?
Will it ever be more than "hello" or "good-bye?"
Take your time before you speak
Because words may never show
All this talk about love may never ever grow.
They say love will grow as time goes by
But my love is real
It "ain't" takin' no time.

Jessica Phillips, Grade 9
Bishop Ford Central Catholic High School, NY

Life Isn't Fair

In a city I've never heard of,
In an alley far away,
A beggar girl sat quietly
Through the freezing night till day.
She knew she did nothing wrong,
To be getting what she got,
But Fate never stood on her side
And got nothing that she sought.
She never wanted anything more,
Than life just by itself,
And to be able to pay for things she wanted,
And to not resort to stealth.
She wanted people just to know,
That she was good inside,
But as time passed on and nothing changed,
The faith inside her died.
I want someone who will love me,
I want someone who will care,
Though I know I did nothing wrong,
Life just isn't fair.

Kimberly Huang, Grade 7
E W Thurston Middle School, MA

Sports

Sports are great.
I've played them since I was eight.
Almost anyone can play a sport.
But sometimes people tell you, you are too fat or too short.
They try to tell you what to say and do.
But I think the choice should be up to you.
When people are good many start to brag.
They make you want to hit them and watch them gag.
Although I make sports sound pretty bad.
There are things about them that are pretty rad.
Things like having fun.
And being in the sun.
You can play if you're not wealthy.
Sports will always keep you healthy.
I think everyone should play.
That's why I wrote this poem today.

Brian Rybak, Grade 7
Depew Middle School, NY

It's a New Day

Clouds hover as…
     a family moves…
thunder strikes when someone is lost…
     rain depresses flowers as pollen washes away…
          fog distorts images behind its MASK until…
               The
               SUN
GOD appears — beginning a NEW DAY,
     The reason TO LIVE LIFE!

Dane Brasslett, Grade 7
Ocean City Intermediate School, NJ

Life Is Hard

Life is hard when you don't have a mother or father there for you.
Life is hard when everything doesn't seem to go your way.
Life is hard when you have a young child and when you can barely take care of yourself.
Life is hard when you need someone to talk to and there's no one to turn to.
Life is hard when your life feels like a tire running out of air.
Life is hard when you lie down and all you could think about the what ifs and the what nots.
But when you look at it, life is hard but it takes you to hold your head up make it easy.

Shenika E. Taylor, Grade 8
Broward Detention Center, FL

The New Kid

Bones the bully was big as ever strong, tough and sometimes clever
he took everyone down and with you your lunch opened the bag and crunched, crunched
you can try to fight back but that will only get you a trip to the nurse
you can try to be brave and get revenge but you'll be bruised first
there was no kid on school campus who could ever take him down
so everybody just looked at him with frowns

One day there was a new kid who talked to no one just sat quietly
Bones gave him a tap on the shoulder very angrily and violently
the new kid turned around knowing the reputation of the mean guy
then shook his head carelessly and stood up in a silent reply
Bones shoved him trying to snatch the boy's lunch like his usual attacks
and swung a fist but missed as the boy ducked and knocked him straight on his back
the whole playground stopped jaws dropped but not as low as mine did
screamed in glee at the top of our lungs and praised the new kid

Caroline Koko, Grade 8
Stone Mountain Middle School, GA

Ax Handle Saturday

It was so vivid as I would ever remember, something too strong to bear
I didn't think I could hold up my own on Laura Street way over there
We were going to "work" like we did every Saturday morning
I had just wished that God or someone would have given me the slightest warning

We had just walked through the threshold of white vs black we were just too startled to turn around and go back
They hit us with bats, ax handles and all they seemed to colossal, and I felt so small

It got harder and harder, the pain kept getting worse
I wasn't giving up 'til the blacks came out in first
People were watching, and acting like it was okay
This tragedy happened three months after May

They had finally broken us up, and took away the pain
I was hoping and praying to God above, that it wouldn't happen again
We had cuts, bruises, bloody noses, and broken hearts
The time was now, for a brand new fresh start

We were all desperate, and thriving for change the whites all acted, like *we* were the ones acting strange
They all acted like Martin Luther's evil conniving enemy the whites were the lock and we *needed* the key

It was so vivid as I would ever remember, something too strong to bear
I didn't think I could up my own on Laura Street way over there
But we all pulled through, and came out tall years passed by, and we came together as all.

Kaitlyn Birch, Grade 8
James Weldon Johnson Middle School, FL

The World of Sweets

In the world of sweets,
There are chocolate covered mountains,
And lollipop flowers, each with its own taste and color,
Then the sun would be made of honey.

There would also be bushes that grow jaw breakers,
And others that grow gumdrops and gummy bears.
Candy canes would grow like vines on red twizzler trees.
The mud would be chunky peanut butter.

The rainbow would be made of skittles,
And the clouds would be soft cotton candy.
The volcanoes would spit out fudge,
And it would rain lemonade.

The rivers and waterfalls would be smoothies and slurpees.
The grass would be pixie stixs of different colors.
And the mints would form the rocks along the hershey path.
The icebreakers would be the snow on the mountains tops.

In the world of sweets,
Where everyone's dream of candy and chocolate come true,
No one can become overweight or be told not to eat,
And no one can get cavities and everyone is jolly.

Nicole Castaneda, Grade 9
Bishop Denis J O'Connell High School, VA

Discipline Beats Talent*

I was the hardest working man
I always strove for the best
As a kid I biked and I ran
I was never able to give it a rest

Influence came from my dad
He was the captain of his high school team
He trained me patiently and never got mad
Easy he did make it seem

I trained for hours and hours
That is what made me so clutch
I was decent but did not have superpowers
I did want to be talented like such

High school is where it all started
I was the quickest man on the team
The territories I passed were uncharted
Easy I did make it seem

That is how I become famous and proud
Hard work is needed for everything in life
That was my story I just told out loud
It is not as easy as having a wife

Roy Lederman, Grade 7
Pine Crest School, FL
*Based on "If I Was Famous."

A Global Warning?

What has come of this world?
A place we have come to know and love
Have these problems just appeared
Who are we to judge?

I mean, the ice caps are just melting
So what if there are holes in the sky
These HUGE problems need taken care of
And here are the reasons why:

Our kids will never see a polar bear
The gasoline shall pollute the air
Thus causing harmful oxygen
For which us humans are unaware

So what will happen?
Please don't cry!
There are possibilities
Please be sure you try!

So have a go at it!
Do be brisk!
For if you don't,
Our future will be at risk!

Madeline Waugh, Grade 7
Massabesic Jr High School, ME

School

I like school because I can learn
Like these subjects math and social studies
Social studies and math are my favorite
I learn something new every day
Social studies helps me think about our environment
I like our physical features
They are mountains, rivers, oceans, and lakes
And math is my favorite subject
You can learn expressions and equations
I learned that today and I got it through my head.

Javis Tucker, Grade 8
Seminole County Middle/High School, GA

Water

Flowing from the beginning to the end of the Earth,
I have sat still and roared in places,
Amazing people with my greatness.

Rejoicing and happiness I have accomplished
But this is just one side of me
As well I have destroyed
And set many people in a great crisis.

There is no place where you cannot find me,
Even in the most scorching desert
I leave many traces.

Francisco Loayza, Grade 8
Covenant Life School, MD

Snowflake

A small snowflake
Twirling and dancing
The vast sky
Setting sun
Freezing wind

Jessica Valenta, Grade 8
St Anthony School, CT

4 Seasons

4 seasons, each unique and different
In their own way
Each bringing new things
All of them beautiful

Spring brings flowers
And little creatures
Awakening from a long nap
Summer brings sun
A light that illuminates
Our nights, and lengthens our days
Fall brings changing colors
Of different hues and shades.
And the preparation of the rest to come.
Winter brings crystal snowflakes
Along with a chilling breeze
Replacing the once luscious grass
With a thick sheet of white slush

4 seasons, each brings something new
But takes away the affinity of the old
Though each season,
Brings a new beauty all year round.

Milik Coffer, Grade 7
Carthage Middle School, NY

Peace in My Eyes

Most people tease
But, will we ever truly have peace?
Do you think this is a game?
I and others feel the same.
We do not want to play,
We are here to say,
Stop the fighting, put down the guns.
They are not very much fun.

We want no more reruns of,
People dying,
Then families crying.
A father should be able to see
His baby instead, he is fighting overseas.
Do you see what fighting does to us?
War makes too large of a fuss.
Follow me if you must,
Because in peace, we must trust!

Kelsey Morrison, Grade 8
Yellow Breeches Middle School, PA

America on Pause*

America is on pause, is stopped on a dime
America is greedy, wishing all the time
I see America walking, onward to its goals,
Others are just wandering, going on a stroll.
I hear America crying because it sees the dead,
A high schooler has to repeat because he's a little short on creds.
I smell America cooking, most of it is fried,
With healthier eating, some might not have died.
I feel America's heart beating, if it only were one,
We would not be at war, and life could be more fun.
I notice America is ignoring, ignoring the gift of life
This saddens God and stabs at His heart like a knife
I hear America complaining about a job it was told to do
Why work somewhere, when all you do is rue?
America is not perfect as you would expect,
But can't we come together, and treat everyone with respect?
I hear America cheering for their favorite sports team,
While soldiers are fighting to hold onto the American dream.

Darren Lesher, Grade 8
Beacon Middle School, DE
*Inspired by Walt Whitman's "I Hear America Singing"

Remember

Remember all the times we shared when you were here with me?
I remember being with you
It's just too much to believe
But there's nothing else I can change, and nothing I can do.

Remember when we laughed and cried
it all went so fast
I thought you'd always be by my side
But that's all a memory of the past.

Remember you said we'd always be together
It was all too good to be true
But now it's just me
And there's no you.

Amanda Gruenbaum, Grade 9
Unami Middle School, PA

Me, Myself, and I

What's it like to be "me?"
Why don't you ask "myself?" He knows!
"I" am the distinctive, four-leaf clover,
in a field of other, *ordinary* clovers.

"Me" couldn't be any happier,
being different the way "myself" is.
While looking at "I" in the mirror,
it's evident I have the extra — the rare —
leaf of *originality.*

Intelligence, Focus, Clarity, Originality —
Me, Myself, and I

Dale Roeck, Grade 7
Ocean City Intermediate School, NJ

The Goldfish Pond

The little goldfish swim around a lake,
With beauty and mystery through their fins,
The fish have a freedom that no one can take,
The fish won't be caught and put into bins.

Their scales are glistening in the warm sun,
As they slowly swim through the deep green reeds,
They play around and have tons of great fun,
The goldfish have no cares and no real needs.

The fish are gold in the blue water hole,
As darkness surrounds them, they seem so bright,
Their color is neon, unlike black coal,
The fish move around the pond with delight.

These beautiful goldfish are full of joy,
This is a part of nature, not a toy.

Lennon Cooper, Grade 8
William R Satz Middle School, NJ

Living Through Life

Have you ever felt like everyone hates you,
or just one friend is mad,
or when you do something not perfectly,
your whole day goes bad.
Have you ever tried looking,
through someone else's eyes,
or tried to be something,
which you despise.
Or ever tried to prove something,
to make someone proud,
but later snapped out of it,
and found out your head was in the clouds.
When you see someone who seems mad,
do you take the time to smile,
and in a race do you always
run the extra mile.
When you're down and gloomy,
there will always be a light,
just reach out and touch it,
and all will be right.

Mary Moore, Grade 7
Chickahominy Middle School, VA

When I Cry

When I cry I feel like I have died.
When the tears hit my face it feels like
a soft drip of water running down.
When I cry it feels like I've been stabbed.
When I cry it's the worst feeling.
When I cry it feels like I lost hope for everything.
When I cry I just sit there and feel bad.
When I cry it feels like I'm all alone.
That's how I feel when I cry.

Zach Livada-Raso, Grade 7
Oblock Jr High School, PA

Light and Dark

The light and the dark
Each other deplore.
These two great forces
Are in constant war.

Light banishes dark
With each coming day,
While dark quells the light
Each eve in this way.

But without the one
The other is naught.
These two need each other
Though oft' they have fought

Though both these powers
Draw each other's ire,
The light and the dark
Each other require.

Nicholas Hentschel, Grade 9
Bishop Denis J O'Connell High School, VA

Beyond the Stars

Beyond the stars
I will be better than you
You all will see
I know you don't believe in me
But when on that field
The world will see me
I will be playing in the game
I will set a record
And be in the Hall of Fame
Beyond the stars
I will be.

Rashawn Miller, Grade 8
Seminole County Middle/High School, GA

The Sun and Moon

The sun and moon
Light and night
Cold and heat.
They both go around the Earth;
Smile at the world.
The summer belongs to the sun
Where it embraces the Earth with its rays.
On the other hand the moon
Sometimes confused
For a gigantic ball of cheese in the universe.
When the sun sets
The moon appears.
Then when the moon disappears
The sun comes out;
Morning is born.

Jorge Jimenez, Grade 9
Miami Beach Sr High School, FL

Mom, I Love You

I love you, Mom
We fight a lot
I hate when you yell
You hate when I yell
We fight a lot
Now I'm with Dad
You hate when I yell
What happened?
Now I'm with Dad
I'll never forget you, Mom
What happened?
Why did you say that?
I'll never forget you, Mom
You hurt me inside
Why did you say that?
I know you still love me
You hurt me inside
I hate when you yell
I know you still love me
I love you, Mom.
Megan Buttiglieri, Grade 8
Noble Middle School, ME

One Window Is All I Need

One window is all I need
to see the future
to look to the past
and take in the present.

One window is all I need
to see myself for who I am
to correct my mistakes
and move on.

One window is all I need
to prepare for the challenges ahead
to figure out my life
and live it to the fullest.

One window is all I need
to go to new places
to look where I have been
and go.
Sarah Brown, Grade 7
Merritt Academy, VA

7th Grade

7th grade
Work, work
Wake up early
Tired, work, fun, awake
Sleep, play, TV
Video games
Summer
Matthew Waters, Grade 7
Perquimans County Middle School, NC

The Fire

They tell you over and over again,
Taunting you like what you're doing is sin
They say you can't do it, just give up
Your futile actions are like drinks from an empty cup.

They don't understand your life's true desires
And the frail but hard-to-kill spark of eternal fire
Burning bright inside you, seeking the best of best
And making you know you're different from the ignorant, cold-hearted rest.

They MUST have let their fires go out
Failures smoldering them until there's no other route
Why else would they stop you, even mock you?
If they had that glowing ember, they would have faith too!

Kindle that fire, shelter it from wind and storm
And one day your dreams will come in any shape or form
Hope is the kindling, wishing is the match
Together they can burn open that rusty, dream-deferring latch

And if that fire goes out at last with a sigh,
Your dreams, like smoke, will drift away and fly
Fading away until nothing is left but scattered ashes:
A reminder of what could have happened, but got whipped away by cold lashes.
Grace Liu, Grade 9
Dacula High School, GA

At Half-Past Three

"CRASH" went the snowmobile,
And down he went, so sincere,
His pain, he tried to conceal,
But his heart, we could all hear.

With a smile he said as he went,
"I love you all, and don't you forget!"
With a kiss, his mother bent,
To tell her she loved him and her pain etched on her face, so wet.

He smiled some more,
and said, "God planned this for me,
I'll arrive at his door,
At half-past three."

His eyes began to close,
As his body began to shake,
He had a faint twitch on his nose,
And he started to make…

His road quite clear,
His path shining as bright as could be,
The end has come near,
As he knocks on God's door, at half-past three.
Kelsey Worden, Grade 8
Princeton Elementary School, ME

Filling Ears with Melody, Hearts with Harmony

She strokes the ivory keys.
Music pours
From her fingertips.
She sways
With the piece,
Lost
In the depth of the ballad.
Filling ears with melody,
Filling hearts with harmony,
She strokes the ivory keys.

Stephanie Kim, Grade 7
Carson Middle School, VA

Where Did All the Flowers Go?

Where did all the flowers go,
Their glowing hues so lush?
For now I only see barren earth,
In a field painted with war's brush.

Where was the mockingbird's melody,
Where were the flocks of doves?
For no swish of wings nor olive branch
Flutters in the sky above.

Where was the children's laughter,
Beside the river of flowing tears?
For no ray of smiling innocence
Pierced the dark shadows of fear.

Where were the congressmen's calls,
As blood tainted our angels' wings?
For when America's bombs tore through the air
Our flag waved on silent strings.

Where did all the flowers go,
To where did their petals fly?
When will color again flood this land,
As a new sun rises in the sky?

Winnie Shao, Grade 8
James Weldon Johnson Middle School, FL

Reliable

I hold you in my rough working arms.
I protect you against the odds.
I bring you down when you need a rest.
But I am as gentle as a fragrant spring breeze.
I bring you up when the world has brought you down.
I am a reliable type of person,
Who will clean up after your mistakes.
I will set you out into the world,
When your time is right.
I will cry but never hold you back.
I am the Father you wished you had.

Eleanor Park, Grade 7
Pemetic Elementary School, ME

School

School…
I know I have to go there
I know it must be done
Although it isn't cheerful
Although it isn't fun
I know I'll get through it
I know I'll be all right
It's something I must do
I won't put up a fight

If I complain, it will get worse
Nothing will get better
That is not a good source
I will just let it settle

All I can do is learn
It can't be that bad
But what I know for sure
I'll have more than I had

Nile Otu, Grade 9
Bishop Denis J O'Connell High School, VA

Darkness

D arkness envelops the world
A t night when everyone's in bed
R insing away the greed and leaving
K indness in its stead
N ever will we see the world in this true
E nchanting virtue
S unlight's absence makes us blind
S ightlessness prevents a permanent change of mind

Tamara Thomson, Grade 8
Princeton Elementary School, ME

Nothing More to Say

Mom, there is nothing more than love —
between us is nothing that we cannot change.

Mom, as I grow and the seasons unfold,
your love is the sun —
her gentle arms reach down through the dark forest,
in your brilliant beam I am found.

Mom, you're the one whose love is true.
I remember swinging with you,
how my world soared —
I became your fairy princess,
you were my daylight abroad.

Mom, without you
the sunflower of your love would never know
the robin's morning song or the kiss of summer rain.

Mom, is there anything more to say?

Robin Reynier, Grade 8
Briarwood Christian Jr/Sr High School, AL

Rain
I fall from the sky.
Every second my little drops come down,
like opals hitting the ground.
You get wet.
Drip! Drop! Drip! Drop!
Michelle Maldonado, Grade 7
St Agatha School, NY

Never Give Up, Never Surrender
I reach for my dreams,
and set my own goals.
And yet I remain
a broken soul.
But I never give up,
I never surrender,
to evil thoughts
and all my nevers.
Now I fly to my dreams,
even if I fall.
And memorize my goals,
even if I forget them all.
So I'll always try,
even when I fail.
And isn't that what makes life
more than just heads or tail?
Rebecca Henenlotter, Grade 9
Oakton High School, VA

Why Hate
Hate is a strong word
That is used very often
What people don't realize
Is it can hurt others

Why hate
When there are other words
Why hate
When you can love

Some words are stronger
Others are personal
You should know what to say
Before you speak

Next time you're talking
With friends or family
Think before you speak
And remember:

Why hate
When there are other words
Why hate
When you can love
Jessica Prible, Grade 7
Depew Middle School, NY

Color
Clean is not important
Amount is what you need
Tidy rooms get messy
Trained kids then clean
Bright sounds like fun
Dirty sounds like not
Another word for bright is fun
But another word for dirty is work
T.J. Shedd, Grade 8
Fort Mill Middle School, SC

Forever Friend
I'll hold your hand and help you up
When someone lets you down
I'll dry your tears from your eyes
And hurt the one who told you lies
I'll listen to what you have to say
When others talk all day
I'll be there for you
Just give me a cue
I'll be your best friend
Until the end
I'll make you smile
Even when it's been a while
Through good and bad
I'll always be the friend you've had.
Emily Hershey, Grade 8
Yellow Breeches Middle School, PA

Seasons
Chirping
Kids are playing
The pools are opening
The weather is getting warmer
It's spring

Hotter
Tons are outside
People are having fun
Ice cream melts in your hand outside
Summer

Cooling
Squirrels gather nuts
Leaves begin to fall down
Kids gather at parks and have fun
Autumn

Freezing
Hibernation
Kids sled and ski
People build snowmen and ice skate
Winter
Tayler Howie, Grade 7
Yellow Breeches Middle School, PA

Freedom
pizza
drive on the road
sweet roses
brand new car
swimming in a pool
Mateo Mauricio, Grade 7
Madisonville Middle School, TN

Forever Waiting
I stood there
In pouring rain,
Waiting for him.

Time flew by
Still waiting
For the one I still loved

Not wanting to remember
That he and I
Were no more.

A single tear
Rolled down my cheek.
I was forever,
Waiting.
Amanda Leyva, Grade 8
Carthage Middle School, NY

A Single Flaw
Wake me up late.
Don't call me for school.
I've gone to dig bait.
Summertime rules!

After I fish,
I'll dive in the pool.
I'll do what I wish.
Summertime rules!

Lying around
On this beautiful day,
Soft summer sounds —
No homework today!

Every good thing,
A sick prankish scheme,
Hot dogs and swimming,
A teenager's dream!

One thing missing
At this time of year
Summertime's perfect
But football's not here!
Greg Jones, Grade 9
Unami Middle School, PA

Emotional

When I'm emotional I play.
What about you, do you play?
I play my guitar when I'm sad,
plucking the strings and feeling the vibration.
But when I'm mad I play my drums,
beating and letting it flow.
When I'm happy I play my keyboard
fingering a light touch on my soul.
In the end, I am spent
and I am free.

Dallas La Marche, Grade 7
Ocean City Intermediate School, NJ

God's Eyes Through Lies

Lies and betrayal are being told
By people who make life more cold
But God will help me through the road
I don't know who to believe
But God taught me how to see
To see the lies that I receive
But I'm still smiling because I deserve to
And one day I'm going to know the truth
And then I'm going to know what to do
But right now it's too hard to hold the pain
The pain of playing someone else's game
Which is lame 'cause the pain is the same
Which no one wants to play
But I'm going to win someday
And everything will be ok
All because God showed me the way

Adena Rankin, Grade 7
Kernan Middle School, FL

Dawn's Roses

The fall roses have all withered and died,
Their petals are soaked with the tears I cried.
They have been drowned in a lake of sorrow,
Crushed they will not rise again tomorrow.
Unable to feel the cold harsh winter,
Which would pain them like a thousand splinters.
They would be crushed without mercy or care,
More painful then pulling out your own hair.
But all this will not be the end,
For spring will come and they will rise again.
Spring showers will wash away the pain,
Replacing it with the cool drops of rain.
The water will wash away all my fears,
So I can hear the sound of rainfall in my ears.
And so the roses will bloom once more,
No longer will they lie broken on the floor.
Not covered with the darkness of night,
Their petals will shine as bright as the light.
As they stand tall I shall walk on,
Towards the warmth and brightness of dawn.

Michelle Joyce Yabes, Grade 9
Bishop Denis J O'Connell High School, VA

Summer: My Summer Friend

Remembering —
the times we spent together
drawing pictures on the preschool floor
and dressing dolls out in the field behind the school.
We were companions — never to be torn apart
like summer days at the beach;
the sea and shore just fitting together
with the cool water washing over our feet.
As we made sand castles under the July sun,
nothing could ruin our friendship except the winter.
Those cold winter days when school would start,
Summer and I would end
and our companionship would be lost.
Remembering —
the times we spent together
as I walk by the deserted preschool.

Juliann Baker, Grade 7
Ocean City Intermediate School, NJ

A Friend Is a Friend,
But a Best Friend Is a Mentor, a Guide, and a Gift

A friendship, strongly sewn,
is a gift from the unknown.
Through thick and thin,
whether you lose or win,
a friend is always there.
And it's not just for themselves they have learned to care.
Through the hardships of life, and all the wear,
they help you to choose the right way to go,
helping you take the high road, not the low.
A best friend can always make your spirits lift;
a best friend is a mentor, a guide, and a gift.

Maia Edwards-Borowicz, Grade 8
Villa Maria Elementary School, PA

Miracle

Your hair pulled back in a knot,
Your cherry blushed cheeks tear stained
And your constant movement from pain
In a beat-up creaky hospital bed,
You fake a smile anyway
Just to comfort me.
You tell me that you will be fine,
But someone else will not be
As you brushed back my hair
Your fingers like a comb.
I knew the severity of it
So I kept hope when there was all doubt.
You left and worried —
Then you came back and you were crying,
Not from the deep denial and despair of the loss
But tears of joy for the new hopeful beginning.
Miracle.

Jordyn Distler, Grade 8
William Penn Middle School, PA

The Break Up

Pretty please don't hurt me, I gave my heart to you,
I sincerely said I'm sorry, but you said it was totally not true,
My heart hurries to someone else now, someone who won't make me blue,
You're soaring to super heights, while I'm living the low life,
I wasn't ready for you to consider claiming the title of my future wife.
Heaven help your soul, I thought you'd just cry,
I didn't know breaking up our beautiful relationship would make you fall down and die.

Nicari Legette, Grade 7
Johnakin Middle School, SC

Too Afraid*

I heard them tell us "no," and quickly walked away,
My friends, they sat and protested, but I was too afraid to stay.
"Summer of the Freedom Riders," in 1961,
My brothers proudly rode those buses, but I watched 'til they were done.
The times, I hear, are "a-changin." They all sing of hope,
But I sing of sadness, in November, '63, we all must cope.
"Let's stand up and march!" My sisters said today,
I watched from a distance, as Dr. King led the way.
Musicians bind together, tell us to do the same,
My parents applaud, but I sink my head in shame.
MLK delivers one last speech, "I've been to the Mountaintop!" he said,
The next day he ascends as far as he'll go, staining the ground with red.
Robert Kennedy pleads for peace, after the crowd gasps and cries,
"Don't get mad, stay together," "To the mountaintop we still can rise!"
Months later he's shot down too, "It seems the good, they die young,"
A decade of standing up is almost over, and I haven't even sung.
"We've got what we wanted!" The nation all cries,
White and black, hand in hand, tears falling from our eyes.
I tried to stand up, finally, it was my time! But being too afraid, I was too late for the climb.

Lauren Harris, Grade 8
James Weldon Johnson Middle School, FL
*The ballad of an African American during the 1960's

Teammates

Fourteen sweaty teammates all around me learning and having fun playing basketball
Dribbling and passing the rust colored ball.
The familiar feel of the leather in your hands. Shooting lay-ups, three-pointers, and free throws.
The blinding glare off the shimmering backboard. Getting pumped from the roar of the crowd.

Goofing around in the locker room unaware of the smelly socks permeating the air
Reminiscing about all the other years running endless laps around the gym
While listening to music blasting out of the speakers.

Clowning around, laughing, and joking
Cheering one another on but knowing when to be serious.
Even Coach Mitchell being like a teammate to us with his braided locks.
Our mentor.

Just playing our hearts out winning games by double digits
Sitting on the wooden bench waiting to go in.
Cheering, clapping, and supporting one another.
Having this time to remember forever. It will be ingrained in our memories
When we are old and gray with knobby arthritic knees.

Chase West, Grade 9
Riverside High School, SC

Fun in the Field

I never noticed
The kids playing baseball
Up in the field on my hill.
There could have been more than 20,
And all participating,
Sweaty and smelly
Just like the Majors.

Once I saw the littlest of them
Hit one right over the fence
While I sat and watched them.

I wonder why
They're always on my hill
And don't play regular baseball
On a team.

Maybe it's because
They'd rather play for fun
With friends
Or maybe they do

Marquel Matusic, Grade 7
Trinity Middle School, PA

The River

The river down by your house
Is the most important thing to me
That's where we met,
Had our first kiss,
And now we're here,
Together,
Married, with a house
On that same river.

Carly Wyche, Grade 7
Brielle Elementary School, NJ

Much More

You really don't know,
I can tell you can't see.
The wonderful feelings,
that you're causing me.
I think I might tell you
you probably should know
there are many feelings,
that I can't possibly show.
I walk around
thinking of what I could say.
Deep down inside
I know you'll realize some day,
that although I didn't let you know
and you needed help to see
I'm just a friend to you,
but you're so much more to me.

Laura Perry, Grade 8
Carthage Middle School, NY

In Need

As I am floating in my bed,
I cry so softly in my head.
For what do I see,
It shouldn't be?
Thousands of animals
Abused and in need.
We are so greedy, this mankind.
For one is sold, five may die.

Nicole Haulman, Grade 8
Yellow Breeches Middle School, PA

Too Tall

Five ft. ten,
Still growing.
Is it never going to stop?
Until too tall.

Will it end when I'm 20?
Or maybe 13.
Maybe this year,
Maybe the next.

"How's the weather up there"
One kid asks.
It's not so great being,
Too tall I reply.

Five ft. ten,
Still growing.
Is it never going to stop?
Until too tall.

Andrew Benson, Grade 7
Carthage Middle School, NY

Unanswered

was my story never found?
did I walk this world without a sound?
am I desperately losing this fight?
or am I trying, with all of my might?
will you be there in the end?
or will you walk away, and just pretend?
do you see me when I scream?
or do you think I'm just a dream?
will you catch me when I fall?
or will you lay there, on the wall?
are you my greatest mistake?
or a regret I refuse to take?
am I just taking up space?
or am I the start of a new race?
is the rain falling for the sky to cry?
or just to keep me inside?
am I writing this for myself?
or am I writing this, for someone else?

Gracie Conrady, Grade 7
Trinity Middle School, PA

Spring

Flowers bloom in the spring
and birds chirp and sing.
People are outside walking
and others are in the yard talking.
It is a great time of year that kids like
and they get to play outside and bike.
We hope for good weather
and start to plan a family get together.

Colleen Hiles, Grade 7
Pine-Richland Middle School, PA

Just Because…

Just because I'm quiet
I'm not perfect
I'm not mean
I'm not a nerd
I'm not a freak
Just because I'm quiet
I have friends
I like to sing and dance
I like to have fun
I like to go shopping
I can be funny
Just because I'm quiet
I don't think I'm better
I have feelings
I have opinions
I have flaws
Just because I'm quiet —
If you talk to me, I'll talk back.

Amanda Cunha, Grade 9
Unami Middle School, PA

Freedom

hot, juicy ham at Christmas
Jesus' voice saying, I love you
hot chocolate
good times
wonderful

Meagan Atkins, Grade 7
Madisonville Middle School, TN

I Like a Boy!

I like a boy.
I did not know his name.
He was older than me.
Like anyone would know.
I really didn't want his name
all I want to do is know him even more.
Every time I see him,
my eyes are as bright as the stars
my smile is ear-ear.
But all I can think about is the boy I like!

Kimberly Hatcher, Grade 7
Rohanen Jr High School, NC

End of the World

The sun dimming
People screaming
Screech, go the cars
Birds dying
Animals going crazy
People saying their "goodbyes"
The sky getting darker and darker
No moon, twelve o'clock
Buildings falling; people falling
The sun burns out
It's cold
There is no sound of anything
The world has ended

Emily Simpson, Grade 8
Garnet Valley Middle School, PA

Dreams

Dreams are hopes floating by,
Things wanted but not there yet.
Dreams are wishes shooting high,
Reaching out and soon to get.

Dreams are goals set to achieve,
Waiting there to accomplish.
Dreams are air, always needed,
Staying strong and fair from vanquish.

Dreams are songs not discarded,
In a cavern called our hearts.
Dreams are crowds so bombarded.
Dreams are with us until part.

Kendall Peel, Grade 7
Mahanoy Area Middle School, PA

Cloudy Skies

Lost in a sea of clouds,
Hidden and out of sight,
Trying to steer the plane,
Wishing with all her might,

The plane shook perpetually,
A tunnel of clouds did form,
All those tiny white specks,
Around her they did swarm,

The plane began to fall,
She yelled at the control,
Her life flashed before her,
Once she thought life was dull,

Her life was no longer dull,
With her spirits the plane rose,
She landed her plane safely,
But she tripped and broke her nose.

Rory Greever, Grade 8
Fred S Engle Middle School, PA

Sticky Soda Spill

Boy, don't you just hate it when,
You become as uncomfortable as you've ever been.
Nobody likes to have a big spill,
Be real careful and I don't think you will.
Here's how it goes, when that yummy, sweet soda cup,
Falls all over and it's so hard to clean up.
Make sure that your glass is always stable,
And not too far towards the edge of the table.
The feeling of the soda is sticky, wet, and just not right.
It goes through your clothes and ruins your night.
The penguin waddle is how you'll be walking,
While everyone else is comfortably talking.
Especially if you are wearing white,
You should not drink Coke so try some Sprite.
The liquid immediately goes straight through your jeans,
There are many ways you can and should prevent this by all means.
What your mom always told you is oh so true
To push the glass back, or it will fall on you!
Just hear what I say and you won't end up
Like the poor, poor people who have spilled their soda cup.

Jennifer Graw, Grade 8
William R Satz Middle School, NJ

You

Every day I see you pass me by without a glance
My heart is screaming out but blinded by your appearance
You made me wonder if I had a reason to live
But then I realized you're the reason to live
I want you to notice who I am
I'm not just the short girl over there
I'm a personality too
Well here I go screaming my heart out wishing you would hear me
Too bad there's only silence

Angela Troidl, Grade 7
Depew Middle School, NY

Everyone Has Problems

Everyone's different
Different lives, different homes, different feelings
bad feelings, good feelings, okay feelings
hidden secrets
bad childhood, good childhood
It doesn't matter
Some people will judge you
Don't worry about them
They have problems too
Maybe harder or not as hard
But they are still problems
People want you to feel sorry for them
But why should you?
If you think your situation is worse
You think it should be the other way around
but always remember
There will always be someone in life with a bigger problem than you.

Kelly Smith, Grade 8
Beacon Middle School, DE

Inside This Fish
Inside this fish
Is an infinite world of mystery and adventure
This world has not been explored much by non-natives
But is known almost entirely
By the collection of inhabitants that roam here
Along with all the dreams, discoveries
And reality of this realm
There is much more than can be imagined in a lifetime
And infinite potential to those who are here
While that being unknown
It's inside this fish
Barry Anderson, Grade 7
Christ the Teacher Catholic School, DE

Holding My Guitar
Standing up in my room.
I listen to the mellow sounds.
My favorite songs fill my head
As I strum on my guitar

I close my eyes and begin to see
The lights all shining down.
The stage is lit and the fans are shouting
As I walk the frets of my guitar

As I finish the song I open my eyes.
I have returned to my bedroom.
The fans have stopped their shouting
And there I stand alone holding my guitar.
Jon Thomas Williams, Grade 9
White Station High School, TN

Crashing Waves
Salty air, crashing waves.
Sand as hot as burning coals beneath my bare feet.
The powerful sun shining, no clouds.
People talking, shaded under their colorful umbrellas.
Sharp seashells surrounded my striped towel.
Boats lined the horizon in the distance.
The sun beats down on the clear blue sky.
My shadow, stretching long behind me.
The water glittering like gems in the sun.
The seagulls scream as they fly above my head.
A light breeze blows softly against the grass filled dunes.
Under me, the sand crunches lightly.
Does it snow?
Will I come back?
When?
I'm relaxed, warm and happy.
Excited and worry free as I listen to the
Crashing waves,
Crashing waves,
Crashing waves.
Bridget Congdon, Grade 7
William Penn Middle School, PA

Aruba
Aruba is hot Aruba is fun
Sitting on the beach in the sun
Watching waves so high
Jet skis on the ocean fly
Their riders thinking do or die
Watching all these great sights
Amazing things amazing flights
Aruba Aruba a great place to be
Aruba memories come back to me
Jordan LeVea-Rokicki, Grade 7
St Francis of Assisi Elementary School, NY

Non-Conformity
Don't make me be what I'm not
It'll break my spirit and crush my will
This lack of individuality will make me rot
I'm done with it, I've had my fill.

I just want to be me
I don't want to be you
I want to set my spirit free
I'll not do something that I'll rue.

I do things my own special way
My peace of mind
Is not a worthy price to pay
For you to be kind.

I'll keep to myself
And hang with my friends
But as for this poem
Well, this is the end.
Chris Bober, Grade 9
Unami Middle School, PA

Summertime
While walking along the shore
Waves violently crash
And sand squishes in between my toes
Crabs skitter across the cool, foamy water
As the gentle breeze dances in the warm air
Dolphins leap in the distance
And a large boat far out in the shimmering water
Footprints are deeply printed in the soft sand
The sun dips down in the darkening pink sky
With a few scattered fluffy purple clouds nearby
The glistening ocean turns pink
And several seagulls simultaneously squawk overhead
I wonder where the gulls go at night
And hope I don't ever have to leave this beautiful place
Which makes me feel relaxed and calm
The treasured memories are brought back
And make me want to linger there forever
Summertime, summertime, summertime.
Brooke Peterson, Grade 7
William Penn Middle School, PA

Never See the Same

To depict every —
    moment sound heartbeat;
oh, how I wish I could.
    To look in their eyes
    and see the rest of the world;
to count every iris
    see every cone
pick all the colors
as though they were a rainbow.
    Take your rainbow splashed eyes
    look up look up look up
to the ocean embedded sky.
Tell me what you see —
    but no matter
    you'll never see the same sky
as me.

Samantha Ruszkowski, Grade 7
Ocean City Intermediate School, NJ

Rowing

Oarlocks snap
"Catch!"
"Catch!"
Slicing through choppy water
Like butter, swift and smooth.
Lurching forward,
Approaching our prey.
Orders belted out
Crawling up the slide
Banging with our legs
Crews on either side
Approaching the line
Grunts of exhaustion
Sweat hangs off our skin
Crossing the finish.

Tina Murphy, Grade 8
Galloway Township Middle School, NJ

One

One discourse
being made, going into
a mishmash of sound.
The cacophony is loud —
different sounds of drums,
cymbals, and guitars
not being in one
single harmony.
Then the discourse
becomes one —
a piece of music that
can be heard
around the world,
in one loud
breathtaking sound.

Dante Stone, Grade 7
Ocean City Intermediate School, NJ

Mysterious Man

I never noticed the guy washing and drying his clothes at the river
While he stays outside until he shivers.

Once I saw this man while I was on a field trip on a ship.
He was washing his clothes.
I asked everyone who he is, but nobody knows.
He then began to dry his clothes on the rocks.
He washed everything from shirts to socks.

I wonder why he is washing his clothes there.
Does he just not care?
Why can't he go to a laundromat?
It's a shame he can't do that.

Maybe he can't afford to wash his clothes at a laundromat.
Maybe he doesn't care what people think about that.
He might want to try something new,
So he washed his clothes in the river's blues.

Dustin Galentine, Grade 7
Trinity Middle School, PA

Break Up

A sad girl crying her eyes out on her bedroom floor.
Big puddles of tears crawling down her face.
Hearing the last goodbye going down the hallway from a loved one.
The room went dark and dull.
Tears were filling up her eyes.
Thinking over and over that there will be no more hugs, dates, or kisses.

Messes in the living room.
Full of ice cream and empty cartons.
Watching TV all night.
Her friends try to make her remembrance forgotten.
It didn't work.
She is not like a sunny day filling up the rooms with light anymore.
She is now like a stormy day filling the rooms with darkness.

She finally remembered your friends.
Will be there for you when in need, right when she remembered.
She had forgotten anything had happened.

Jackalyn Schwartz, Grade 7
St Andrew's Episcopal School North Campus, MS

Painting

She paints on a smile for the world to see,
But really all the while she's holding secrets from you and from me.
The brush moves with such grace and paints moods of many,
But sometimes when she's painting, she wonders if there is really any.
When she gets tired of painting that same fake face,
Her true colors will, for the first time, show.
And until she meets her time, her place,
No one will ever know…

Sarah Trainor, Grade 8
Unami Middle School, PA

You Will Go Far

It seems like my tears seem to never go away,
As I watch people's lives slowly fade away.
Cocaine, Methadone, Alcohol, or Ecstasy,
These can all kill you but sadly you'll never see.
You think your life is a joke and a game,
But think about the others you're driving insane.
People who care for you that you don't even know,
They pray every night hoping you don't go.
Even your children are affected by these drugs,
Growing up knowing they'll soon pull the plug.
Begging and begging that you'll turn your life around,
You tell them you will but keep falling to the ground.
Hopefully one day you'll see how many you're hurting,
Mostly yourself with these poisons you're inserting.
Soon you'll realize what a beautiful person you are,
Kick the drugs behind, and I promise you,
You will go far!

Brittany Turner, Grade 9
Westerly High School, RI

Wintertime

In winter of youth it was my best friend
Fingers crossed, waiting for the fall to end
The hours went on, the inches increasing
School closing was the wish I was seeking

Innocence of childhood play was all well and good
But the magic of it all no on well understood
Sweet day, so calm, so crisp, so bright
The morning was welcomed by a blanket of white

The sun rises; bringing an avalanche of warmth
The melting beings; nature's hard work, dissolving away
Without even having a say
On if it wanted to stay

The drops dropping; the world awakening
It was time for the day to begin
Shovels shoveling, snow blowers blowing, sleds all stirring
School was closed, winter was here to stay
After all, the snow finally got its say

Jessica Ferreira, Grade 8
Milford Middle East School, MA

The Candy Store

Candy is tasty, candy is great,
You better go get some before it's too late.
For all the little children will be going to buy,
The scrumptious candy, there are plenty to try.
Gumdrops, lollipops, chocolate and many more,
I dearly advise you to go to the store,
And buy those sugary treats that many adore.
So anytime you feel like you're in a bore,
Just take a magical trip to the candy store.

Alex Gulati, Grade 7
Westwood Jr-Sr High School, NJ

The Faithful Drummer Boy

The drummer boy of the Civil War
Could not stand to endure
The suffering of his Confederate countrymen
Would their suffering never end?

To God he prayed, every day
For the war to go away
Every day they would fight
The end of the war wasn't in sight

All others lost faith long ago
That dreaded war would never go
Only the drummer boy kept on praying
With God, the drummer boy was staying

After many great battles, they admitted defeat
The enemy they fought, swept them off their feet
However, the Union let the drummer boy go
Prison was a place no little boy should know

The drummer boy didn't just have this luck
God saved him, while his men were stuck
The faith that the drummer boy kept
Saved him, while his countrymen wept

Kevin Lauerman, Grade 9
Bishop Denis J O'Connell High School, VA

Home Alone

Home alone, the first of many.
Knowing I'm safe, but feeling I'm not.
A proud moment of growth, I'm old enough now,
but a moment of shame for this secret I keep.
I fear the dark corners and the fright that overcomes me.
Is that a sound I hear?
Or does my mind play tricks on me?
I hear the phone, it breaks the silence.
A voice on the other end.
The realization that I am alone, I feel the fear wash away.
As I wonder what will be on TV!

Ashley Varela, Grade 7
Westwood Jr-Sr High School, NJ

The Beginning of March Madness

Squeaking shoes across the court
The swishing of nets
Bending rims from the pulling of arms
The blow of a whistle
Two people jumping for a ball
The never-ending sprinting of legs
Strategizing coaches pacing across their line
Constant battle of agility
Bodies soaring towards the basket
The ring of a buzzer brings an end to the battle

Nate Roberts, Grade 7
Pine-Richland Middle School, PA

Beauty in Society

Beauty in society,
Like a game of baseball.
Swing the bat hard
With perfect form —
You're safe.
Swing it timid
And miss the ball —
You're out.
The giant wave of trends
Crashes down to the ground.
The flow of water carries us,
Rushing us by robots.
Fake hair, fake tan, fake nose,
Thin, slim, and slender,
White blonde hair like straw.
Plaster a smile across your face,
Even in the saddest of times
And you're free to go home.
Round third, the coast is clear.
Because in society
Fake is a beautiful, powerful home run.
Sarah Mills, Grade 7
Westwood Jr-Sr High School, NJ

Sky

Sky's the battlefield
The sun is the red warrior
Moon is the loser
Jackson Douglas, Grade 9
Thomson High School, GA

Dog/Cat

Dog
Cute, happy
Running, playing, smiling
Eat, sleep, claw, whiskers
Pouncing, rubbing, yawning
Funny, purring
Cat
Cheyenne Langhirt, Grade 7
St Agatha School, NY

Autumn

Autumn is when the wind blows high
Grey and blue is the sky
Leaves turn brown and yellow
People walk by and say hello
Storms come and go
Sometimes fast and sometimes slow
Trees blow left to right
All through the cool dark night
Leaves fly everywhere
But they go nowhere
Autumn is when the wind blows high
Raja Cole, Grade 7
Piccowaxen Middle School, MD

Love

You said she loved you and you loved her.
You premeditated to spend the rest of your life with her,
But as fast as you could say the world "Love"
She was gone and she had passed away.
The days soon turned into months,
And within this time you said you were hurting ever so much.
They sat there and told you they knew how you felt,
But truly they had no idea.
Your world began to feel deficient.
It felt as though everything you put faith into was completely mislaid,
So you withdrew from your life that day.
Things just weren't worth your stay.
This girl was your world.
She was your everything.
She showed you how to laugh when you had tears in your eyes,
And now she is no longer here.
You cry tonight wishing she was with you.
With all your heart you pray.
You thought there was nothing left of you though there must have been something left.
If you found the faith to pray you got all you need right there,
Because you found faith through one of the hardest times of all.
Samantha Phillips, Grade 9
Countryside High School, FL

I Miss Them All

I miss them all.
I miss them a lot.
I miss my mother, I miss my Nanna Murphy.
I miss my Uncle John.
But even though they are not with me they keep me going on.
If they were here they would be very proud of me.

I also miss my dogs Peaches and Bailey.
They were the greatest dogs in the world.
These are the ones who I miss the most.
I miss them all.
I miss them a lot.
But now just my father is all I got.

Matthew Hook, Grade 7
Depew Middle School, NY

The Meaning of Love

Love is tender, love is kind,
Love is a song, one I hope to find,
Loves has many funny faces,
Of time and pretty places,
Love is like a baseball game, some you lose and some you win,
You must give it one try or it would be a sin,
There is the love of a puppy, the love of a brother,
But the greatest love of all, is the love of a mother,
Mothers are loyal and give good advice,
Mothers are songs we want to hear twice,
Though you may not like what she has to say,
She will hold you and embrace you, and her love will never stray
Zach Panza, Grade 7
Pine-Richland Middle School, PA

Through the Forest Run

The soft, rustling pine smell,
relaxed me on my calm expressionless face.
The cool gentle breeze,
brushed along me,
as I slowly swayed
through the rough minty forest floor.
The light,
beating on top of the sour, bird chirping filled trees relaxed me
and gave me a beat.
As I quickly rushed through the bird singing forest,
twigs snapped in thunder as I ricochet from tree to tree
like a speeding bullet.

Peace Peace Peace

Maks Kuts, Grade 7
William Penn Middle School, PA

Trapped

Thinking, thinking not sure what to do,
Simple decisions have to carry me through.
Working nonstop for a distant goal,
Trying too hard I might run into a pole.
Hard times may come and good will go,
Leaving me trapped, all alone.

Dreaming, dreaming of a hope ahead,
Looking into my future before lying down in bed.
Finding some way to get through the day,
Reaching for something so far away.
Hard times may come and good will go,
Leaving me trapped, all alone.

Doing your best and not carrying through,
So many people counting on you.
Feeling off in a distant land,
Wondering if anyone can give me a hand.
Hard times may come and good will go,
Leaving me trapped, all alone.

Down in a dungeon locked up so tight,
Trapped in myself struggling to put up a fight.

Jill Hall, Grade 9
Unami Middle School, PA

Track

My track shoes turn me into a cheetah
My spikes are claws
They strike sparks from stones
They dig into the earth and secure me to the spinning planet
They make me faster than anyone
The wind of my own running puts tears into my eyes
I am a cheetah
Made of wind and fire

Natasha Lear, Grade 9
Unami Middle School, PA

Damaged But Fixed

When something was wrong,
You knew I would be there.
Just to comfort you.
I told you I'd be on your side,
And you told me you'd be on mine.
But that was yesterday.
I can't believe I trusted you.
You lied,
Then put me behind.
You're like a tornado that swept through me.
You can't stop the tears of a damaged heart girl,
Wanting to find true love.
I'm gonna forget you,
Because I think I found somebody else.
Someone I can count on.
I should have went on this path earlier.
Because I finally feel safe.

Hannah Gullo, Grade 7
Depew Middle School, NY

Just Life

I didn't understand.
I once thought that hatred and death was all there was.
I didn't understand.
Now I found something new.
This would be called love.
Still
I don't understand.

I don't understand
Why have I never felt this way before?
I don't understand
Why is life the way it is?
Just life
I don't understand.

Brandon Johnson, Grade 7
Palmyra-Macedon Middle School, NY

I Miss You

I wish that I could show you
How much I truly care
All our little jokes and the memories that we share
Our arguments are stupid
Our fights are pretty lame
I guess I never thought
That it would never be the same
I miss your gentle smile
I miss your warm embrace
You've always been the one
To shelter me from a world with so much hate
You held me when I need you close
Dried my tears when I would cry
And when I stop to think
This is just about some stupid guy

Kristina Peck, Grade 8
Carthage Middle School, NY

Inside

Inside a heart is a constant beat,
It beats and beats and beats,
It is as dark as a midnight sky, all alone just waiting in the dark,
Inside is a bunch of holes taken by things that have gone and it can no longer love like it used to,
Inside it screams for help because it is drowning in a sadness that can never be fixed,
It is like a lump of clay all dried up and useless,
No one is there to love and cherish it,
It is no longer beautiful, it is no longer caring,
It is just a lifeless thing,
Inside a heart is a constant beat,
It beats and beats and beats.

Katy Carter, Grade 7
Grace Lutheran School, FL

Petals

My heart has wilted like a flower. My feelings for you once have now become dry, the thirst has been unbearable. The sun has scorched my petals. One by one they drifted off. My leaves have become brown and crisp. The weeds wrapped around my roots when I saw "her," the brand new bouquet planted beside me. Fresh and watered. I, stand twisted and bent, with the force of gravity overruling my head. My colors have fallen taking the ground for a bed. I pray for the rain to begin again. I wish for you only to be my friend. I hold on dearly to my last petal. But, it seems the tighter I hold on, the more loose it becomes. I'm sure my condition is fatal. I feel the breeze and the time is growing nearer. And then one day it happened. So gracefully in the snow. My petal had fallen, I've become so old. My petals will return next spring I'm told. I will stand so tall with all my petals, proud and bold.

Isabelle Coyne, Grade 9
Westhill High School, NY

A Tribute to Teachers

Teachers are…
Like the sun,
Emitting incandescent light rays of knowledge onto us budding flowers
Like compasses,
that activate and attract our magnets of curiosity and help guide us in the right direction
Like potters,
Who help make and mold us into intricate clay masterpieces,
Their dexterous hands performing every wisdom-filled molding with care
Like chefs,
Who add the ingredients of learning into our brewing brains
Like sculptors,
That make their own markings on each student's stone,
Where it will perpetually stay,
So precious it cannot be washed away like sand by the water,
Or forgotten by the sculptor artist and by the work of art itself
Like water,
Nourishing and filling us sponges with knowledge until we are teeming with valuable information
Like cheerleaders,
Perky, energetic, and filled with spirit, cheering us all the way and boosting our morale in all of our endeavors.

Elvina Yau, Grade 8
Jericho Middle School, NY

Why

Why would you want to break my heart and take our love and break it apart? And now I'll cry myself to sleep just to think about why you would scar me. Now my heart is filled with this empty space that I can't fill. And it will go to waste I guess I didn't know how much I had you until you were gone. Now I'm all alone, wiping tears from my eyes, not even trying and some days I feel like dying. I know you love someone but that someone isn't me. I just don't understand why you don't love me.

Cortnee Taylor, Grade 7
Depew Middle School, NY

Sunday Dinner

A dinner on first Sunday,
I can hear the yelling voices,
The dog barking outrageously,
And the kids running,
The pleasant aroma of chicken on the grill,
And baked beans cooking on the stove,
From everywhere the family comes,
Thousands and thousands of miles.

Uniquequa Wilcher, Grade 9
Thomson High School, GA

Torn

I am only a fragment high above ground —
head in the clouds, eyes scorched
by the glaring rays of the luminous sun,
torn from all directions by the howling wind,
battered and beaten by the stinging rain.
Gravity has yet to drag me down to Earth.
But gravity wants to wrench me down,
and if I surrender; it will!

So, I must find a way to stay aloft because
by myself, without direction — I cannot survive alone.

High above ground, head in the clouds
eyes scorched by the glaring rays
of the luminous sun I am only a fragment —
this much I know is true; but I know I am not alone.

Peter J. Markel, Grade 7
Ocean City Intermediate School, NJ

Depress

Lying there, me looking at his face
Like the softness of the wind blowing against me
Like the lifelessness of a cut down hollow tree

The emotions flowing through my veins
The thoughts going through my head
And the tears rolling down my face

The sound of thunder, I do not move
Rain pours down, I stand and stare
My clothes are drenched from the cold freezing rain
Still no movement occurs

Eye to eye, I look at the body to see
He is truly gone, but he is apart of me
My heart, for a beat is missed
His heart stopped, for he is breathless

The emotions flowing through my veins
The thoughts going through my head
And the tears rolling down my cheek
Lying there, me looking at his face.

Danielle Farmer, Grade 9
Burlington County Institute of Technology, NJ

Freedom

Sweet watermelon on the Fourth of July.
A Memorial Day parade marching through the streets.
Cookouts all summer long.
Our bright, colorful flag blowing softly in the wind.
A caged bird released to fly.

Savannah Dalton, Grade 7
Madisonville Middle School, TN

Boo*

I did something bad long long ago
I got in with a bad crowd that I did not know
We harassed a lady as we cussed and we drank
I was locked up in jail with my friends to thank
My father wouldn't have it, he wanted me home
He put me in the basement with nowhere to roam
I skulked underground for countless years
Soon the outside world was one of my fears
I began hiding things inside of a tree
I left it right where the little girl and boy could see
The children had fortitude, they wanted to visit
But my brother was averse, he didn't like it one bit
He closed up the hole in the tree, my portal to the real world
I couldn't bear it, my head swirled
I had to follow the girl home from the play
There was a man behind her, he seemed to sway
He had a knife and I pushed him down
We fought for a while, but I wore the crown
Bob Ewell died when he fell on the sharpest of knives
But I had my two new friends, thankful that I saved their lives

Alexi Blessing, Grade 9
Council Rock High School South, PA
*Inspired by "To Kill a Mockingbird."

I Am

I am wild natured and adventurous.
I wonder what will happen when I travel.
I hear snakes hissing as I succeed.
I see joyful spirits in my parent's room.
I want to become an appreciated doctor.
I am wild natured and adventurous.

I pretend to know a lot about people.
I feel death breathing down my back as I explore.
I touch angels' wings as I fly in my dreams.
I worry what will happen when my next mishap comes.
I cry when I see people who have nothing.
I am wild natured and adventurous.

I understand how I will need to succeed.
I dream I will get to have complete joy.
I try to do my best.
I hope someday I will achieve my dreams.
I am wild natured and adventurous.

Marsell Holley, Grade 8
Germantown Middle School, TN

Trout

Trout
Smart, stealthy
Swimming, eating, hiding
Hardest fish to catch
Biting, fighting, losing
Swimming, landing
Caught

Michael Longacre, Grade 9
Unami Middle School, PA

The Morning Glory

A soul with a warm glow,
Sits in the eternal peace,
A precious gift to the world,
For those who are blind can see,
That its beauty is eternal,
More eternal than the foggy morn',
As it unfolds into a burning presence,
Comfort surrounding what was,
But a cold and uncertain night,
The morning drags on,
A slight breeze,
A breeze that carries the day,
The spirit leaves with the comfort,
The wind takes the spirit,
The brightness of it taken by day,
The loving energy shriveled,
The restless heart of the world,
Gone in an instant,
Only to be back tomorrow,
The beauty of the Morning Glory.

Richard Donaty, Grade 7
Ni River Middle School, VA

On a Quilt

The golden sand, the emerald earth
The scarlet fire sweeps the feathers
Off its feet.

The cross seams the symmetrical design,
Opening the angle, from right to left,
Searching every passageway out.

The birds have been noticed,
The snakes have been scared,
Are the animals yet to arrive?

You begin to see Jesus, the Christ of God,
You begin to realize Religion.

On a quilt, you see animals come along
To come join together
To make a rainbow
With texture and pattern.

Shameen Akhtar, Grade 7
Peabody Elementary School, MA

The Intellectual

I live,
Trapped in a world that can't,
Comprehend my existence.

I strain,
Living under the scope,
Whose master waits within a protective bubble of glass,
Begging for it to be shattered, yet in fear of the very thing he seeks.

I thrive,
Making sense of the world,
Understanding that which would as soon be destroyed,
That which I protect.

I suffer,
Feeling the joys and pains of myself,
Of the world, as no one else can.

I cry,
Knowing that they,
The ones who fear and reject me,
Are the ones who most wish to join me.

I smile,
Knowing, embracing myself,
Helping others to embrace their world.

Daniel Sonnenberg, Grade 9
Gill St Bernard's School, NJ

My First Day in the Jungle

"Beep Beep Beep Beep Beep"
The sound of the new school and
A new school year.
I walk down the crowded stairs
Trying to find my new homeroom
With my heart beating as fast as a cheetah.

I walk into the room, seeing my new teacher.
I see some old friends and walk over to them.
The teacher calls my name and I say "Here"
The morning announcements come over the loudspeaker and
Dismisses us to our first class.
I walk down the huge hallway hoping not
To walk into the wrong classroom.

After a long first day I get on the new bus and sit down near friends.
I turn on my iPod and we start talking to each other.
When I get home I say hi to my mom
And then she asks
"So, how was your first day of school?"
I stare her right in the face and said
"Fine, just fine."

Tom Kenny, Grade 8
William Penn Middle School, PA

A Seasonal Cycle

Call out to the hummingbirds
as they fly with their fragile wings;
"April's showers bring May's flowers;"
with a breeze, the wind chime dings.

As they fly with their fragile wings,
the sun comes out of hiding.
With a breeze, the wind chime dings,
tough schedules no longer colliding.

The sun comes out of hiding,
but it soon will not be found.
Tough schedules no longer colliding,
for now, like the leaves on the ground.

But it soon will not be found.
[What is "it?" Would it be snow?]
For now, like the leaves on the ground are
my sighs as I stare down below.

What is "it?" Would it be snow?
No, but it may be my soul.
My sighs as I stare down below
will come from a heart of the winter's cold.

Tiffany Lo, Grade 9
Churchill Jr High School, NJ

Hope Is a Flower

There is no sun in this camp to shine,
Only the wounded and sick who moan and whine.
There are no flowers growing tall and true.
There are no families, no "I love you."

There are no tears, no it is just water,
A father crying out for his daughter.
Through all of his suffering and all of his pain,
All he hopes is for the sky to rain.

The rain washes away the sorrow.
Rain brings hope for life tomorrow.
And as the father lies awake at night,
He hopes that his precious daughter sleeps tight.

For when she awakes to a gloomy dawn maybe she too
Can have a flower growing in her heart, tall and true.
But there is no sun and there aren't any flowers,
Yet there is hope at heart, hope that brings many powers.

There is love present; there is peace too.
Along with the flower growing tall and true.
With the girl's heart beating with such great power,
She lets the sun shine down on the flower.

Ally Briegel, Grade 7
Holicong Middle School, PA

Springtime

Finally it is that time of year.
The sound of birds chirping is all I hear.
Animals come out of hibernation,
and feel the warmth heating up the nation.
Flowers begin to bud like new romances.
The cool breeze makes the trees do dances.
The wind flies through my hair,
sending the scent of fresh air everywhere.
But dark clouds start to fill the sky,
covering the sun up so high.
Then it begins to pour,
making the rest of my day a bore.

Madeline Stenken, Grade 9
Unami Middle School, PA

Tangled Branches

Its tangled branches form a net,
my shield against the outside world.
The hundreds of tiny leaves,
tiny magic carpets ready to take me away.
I sit against the weather beaten trunk
on a warm sunny day
and allow a book
to take control of my mind.
Or, on a crisp, starry night,
lie beneath on the rusted hammock,
peering through its woven pattern
as confusing as my own thoughts.
Wisps of dreams fly too quickly
through my mind for me to grasp.
The stars help guide me back
to more certain thoughts,
but time's cut short
when another loose dream flies through,
bringing me back to my labyrinth
of never-ending thoughts,
underneath the tangled branches.

Ciara Boyle, Grade 7
Ocean City Intermediate School, NJ

Good Grades

The way a good grade
Fills you with satisfaction,
Relieves you of frustration;
Makes you want to get even better.
Encourages your knowledge,
Fills you with hope honor to yourself.

But the hindrance of life will always
Be there to haunt you.
To worry you and convince you to go another path,
Convince yourself what the right thing to do is.
Get an education; it's worth the wait.
The future will bring you a life of luxury.

Jasmine Whitaker, Grade 7
Ambridge Area Jr High School, PA

Night Shades

As night falls across the sky.
Shades of baby blue give way to
Darker shades then to gray.

Reflections of fireflies, and the
Mystic moon are caught in pools
Of the waterfall spoon.

A magic melody floats away, as the
Sound of water and insects sway.
The smell of jasmine lingers in
The light cool mist.

And the cheek of a maiden will
Soon be kissed.
A lightning bolt and sound of thunder,
Soon disturb her listless slumber.

As the sun rays fall across the sky, the
Maiden must bid the night goodbye.
Though with her, her dreams will stay.
As again she awaits the end of day.

Jennifer Wolford, Grade 7
Oakvale Elementary School, WV

The Feeling of Being Alive

You'll just smile
And walk on by.
Ignore them with ease
And not even try.

Show them your strength
And not care what they say,
You'll laugh and you'll sing,
And do as you may.

It's the feeling of triumph,
And what you strive
Is the simple feeling
Of being alive.

Emma Fisher, Grade 9
Mahanoy Area High School, PA

Crimson Butterflies

Everyone is like a beautiful butterfly.
Their wings are different,
And it makes them unique.
Some are small and others big.
They live their lives,
And so do we.
But some things cannot live forever.
But when we die,
We are flown to heaven,
On the wings of a butterfly.

Crystal Bieber, Grade 8
Paxon Hollow Middle School, PA

Biking in the Sun

The path of small stones crunches softly under my rubber tires,
As my bike makes the path seem to grow smaller by each rotation my feet make.
Sand rises like hot air.
The curious fish peek outside their wet world,
As the frogs hop up to say hello,
Hello world,
Hello you,
Hello summer.
The bright sun massages my back, fierce, but gentle.
The muddy canal water shimmers, sparkling
In the sun's mystical beauty.
Frogs croaking cheerfully,
Birds squeaking hurriedly,
All together in the gloriously sung chorus of nature.
Sometimes I wonder
If I can ice skate on this canal during the winter.
This place makes me feel excited, relaxed, and joyful.
Like summer is actually going to begin.
Finally.
Finally.
Finally going to begin.

Laura Giancarli, Grade 7
William Penn Middle School, PA

A Beautiful Day

Blue as a blue bird is the sky
On such a beautiful day the birds fly so high
Into the blue sky the birds go to fly
Sudden and shimmering is the grass wet with dew as if about to cry
The wind blows so light and then it dies
Plains plateaus pastures all start to sigh
As the bright old sun starts to die
The moon flies over the sleeping creatures from up in the sky
Then it starts again
For blue as a blue bird is the sky
On such a beautiful day the birds fly so high

Matt Mandeville, Grade 7
Westwood Jr-Sr High School, NJ

Dang!

I couldn't believe it happened
  It was a warm and sunny weekend
    The anticipation was building in me like a rocket getting ready for takeoff
      I grabbed my board and took off for an afternoon of twists and turns
      As I approached the quarter pipes they looked like enormous wooden death traps
    I had no fear facing what was ahead
Up and down and all around where would it take me
  Dang! It was all slow motion and suddenly it happened
    A day of fun had turned the next few weeks of my life totally around
      My ankle pulsed with pain as I limbered home
    In an instant my fun had turned to pain
  My pain had turned to imprisonment

Dang!

Jordan Maund, Grade 7
Depew Middle School, NY

Masked
The mask disguises her true self.
She puts up an act for all to see.
But if you tore down the mask,
You'd see who she really was.
Look deep into her bright blue eyes.
Who is she really?
Is she who she portrayed herself to be?
No.
She is much different than that.
She is a whole other person.
A person needing to break out of her shell.
Wanting to show herself to all.
Not that you would ever know.
She is calling out for you to help,
But will you help her?
No.
You never even knew
That she needed you
To be her savior.

Nicole Rothner, Grade 8
Beacon Middle School, DE

I Am
I am lovable and caring
I wonder what I will do in the future or be in the future
I hear woods of the fire crackling
I see colors at the corner of my eye
I want to be rich and have a nice future
I am lovable and caring

I pretend I am someone I'm not
I feel proud of my life
I worry about what could happen in the future
I touch a whole new world
I cry when I hear fights between family
I am lovable and caring

I understand my mom and dad won't get back together
I say I can go through all of my troubles in life
I dream I will have a good future and nothing bad happen
I try my best in school between all of the stress
I am lovable and caring

Chelsea Young, Grade 7
Oblock Jr High School, PA

No Matter Where
No matter where my life takes me
he will always be in my heart even if I don't want him there

I keep telling myself that I can do better than that
but when I find a guy that's better than him I leave

I thought our love would have never died
but within a few months we broke up and I still love him

Kimberly Airey, Grade 8
Sangaree Middle School, SC

Stand Strong
I have been hurt and cheated,
I have tried and failed,
But someone once told me,
That life is hard,
There is no way to get through it without pain,
But if you hold out and never give up,
You will make it,
So I am here to say,
That I am coming ever stronger,
And I will hold on that much longer,
There is no stopping me.

Stephanie McCormick, Grade 9
Heritage Jr High School, NY

My Emmiebelle
Emmiebelle runs and jumps and plays;
Catching bugs to earn Mommy's praise.
Annoying her brother is her favorite sport.
"Emmie" she is called for short.

Emmie needs braces, and that's no lie.
She sticks out her teeth as if asking, "Why?"
Emmie shows love with sloppy kisses;
And sleeps in my arms whenever she wishes.

Emmiebelle thinks she's tough and mean;
Plays in the dirt and won't stay clean.
Emmiebelle shows a stubborn streak;
She knows the rules, but she won't be meek!

Emmie knows acting cute is fun;
In contests for beauty, she has often won!
Like a model in her stylish clothes,
Emmie looks adorable wherever she goes.

Can you guess who Emmiebelle could be?
She's my puppy, I tell you with glee!

Sarah Crouch, Grade 8
Briarwood Christian Jr/Sr High School, AL

Midnight Sky
It looks like a midnight sky.
The city looks sluggish and slow,
A robbery could happen and nobody would know.
He is sly and as cool as the sky.
Everything is calm, cool, and collective.
It looks like a mysterious valley,
Just like an alley.
The sky is midnight blue
Which is true.
The plants are all different
It looks like a midnight sky.

Rebecca Crosson, Grade 7
Gowanda Middle School, NY

Jimmy

There once was a boy named Jimmy
Who had a friend named Timmy
Jimmy never let him out of his sight
Timmy watched him day and night
So they got a new buddy, named Kimmy

Rabiul Sany, Grade 7
Texas Avenue Elementary School, NJ

How Is Life Like

Life is like a burning candle.
It continues burning,
If you hold tight onto it,
But it goes off without knowing.

Life is like a running race,
Where there are audiences,
Competitors and many obstacles.
But, never give up,
Even if it feels like touching a fire.

Life is like an ice cream,
And is so sweet.
It lasts for a short period.
So taste the taste of it,
Before it melts away.

Life is like a garden,
With many flowers, many dreams.
Each flower pays out.
When the flowers dry,
The dreams are broken,
But, when the flowers bloom,
The super souls are awoken.

Tenging Lama, Grade 9
Newcomers High School, NY

The Memory

Twisted, tangled
Beaten, mangled,
So different than
It started out.
Cut to pieces
Taped back together
Remade, reshaped
And changed
Forever.
Like a canvas,
Never blank again
Once color is painted on.
When our minds
Mold a memory
To our liking,
In an instant,
The truth is gone.

Jacqueline Litwin, Grade 8
Community Middle School, NJ

Untitled

With your mind set on warfare and your heart full of pride,
you stood tall to protect your own [country] and for our liberty, you died.
If there was a way to thank you, before you left this Earth,
I would show you all my gratitude, for all your hard work.
Hopefully you've crossed over to a place where you can be,
free from enemies, bullets, bombs, or any type of artillery.
Where food is abundant and clear water runs for all eternity,
where you are able to walk and talk, side by side, with your enemy.
Where fighting is forbidden, and death is prohibited,
only kindness, love, and respect exhibited.
Though the war is not over, it is believed to be won,
and though you are gone, your heart beats on.

Candace Williams, Grade 8
White Station Middle School, TN

Nostalgia the Irritable

Memories are simplistic things,
Like bottle caps or plastic rings.
The things they evoke, however, are complicated,
The emotions that come are never satiated.
Nostalgia tends to never be a reasonable animal,
When coaxed, the chagrin of many, it may become an angry preacher.
Spewing nosy words in your head,
Haunting you when you got to bed.
Sometimes if you're lucky you'll catch it in a good mood,
It won't be nosy, irritable or even rude.
As I diligently search through the almost endless pile,
Tossing to the side the bad pictures every once in a while,
I begin to wonder if nostalgia is trying to get me.
I come across the children, a small black dog plus those three
They all sit upon the snow strewn steps with bright, grinning faces,
Like victorious greyhounds after winning three races.
I feel my own lips begin to curve into a crescent shape,
And there they stay, refusing to move as if pinned by masking tape.

Alexandra Doyle, Grade 8
Masconomet Middle School, MA

Trash

Just because there's trash everywhere,
Don't add to the mess,
Don't just ignore it,
Try and clean it up.
Just because there's trash everywhere,
Doesn't mean no one cares about our planet,
Doesn't mean you can just do nothing,
Doesn't stop people from trying to make the world,
A better place.
Just because there's trash everywhere,
Still try and help clean it up,
Can't wait 'till it's all cleaned up,
Just because there's trash everywhere — you don't have to add too.

Samantha McGowan, Grade 8
Garnet Valley Middle School, PA

Where He Belongs

The day we got him was the best of them all
An energetic body
He was oh so small
Defenseless and weak
He was the cutest little pip-squeak
And after he had grown
He became my very own
Where he made my heart into his home
With all the memories
And exciting stories
Then one day
He passed away
And I felt as though he would forever be gone
But then I remembered
Something about him that I would always look back upon
That he had made that special little place
In my heart
Where he would always belong

Casey Johnson, Grade 8
Whitinsville Christian School, MA

Orange Breeze

The hot sun attacking my skin with warmth,
The soft sand,
Tickling my feet beneath me,
Feeling relaxed on this beautiful,
And peaceful day,
The waves crashing behind me,
I can hear the music flowing in the air,
And I can taste the orange,
Tangy, slushy swim in my mouth,
I can hear the little kids yelling,
Having so much fun,
I can imagine them catching sand crabs,
And making castles,
If only I could see,
Boy what a dream that would be.

Jack Ziemer, Grade 7
William Penn Middle School, PA

My Friend, My Guardian, My Teacher

He's there to greet me every morning with a smile on his face,
the one that cheers me up whenever I've got a problem to face.
Throughout the day he's the one who wants to play,
our time to shine, our time to play.
So P.E. is his time of day,
as the sun closes in on the school day.
The final bell rings it's time for us to go,
away from the school, where else would we go?
As I leave I say goodbye to that one true friend I've had in mind,
when night time comes I may rest my mind.
Until tomorrow comes when I shall see him again.

Lexie Center, Grade 9
East Pasco Adventist Academy, FL

Why Now?

Life is like a pencil that keeps on getting
shorter and shorter until one day it runs
out — that one day should be peaceful,
that one day should be elegant, that one
day should be an excellent day.

"Live life to the fullest!" That's how she was,
always holding on, with a grip so tight
not even God could break it.

All of those memories — good ones, bad ones,
funny ones, serious ones — have stopped
because the pencil has run out of lead!

We have sorrow, a big emptiness —
like part of our hearts was erased.
Why did she leave us? "It was her time,"
is what I am told, and I know
that nobody can hold on forever,
but — why now, why now?

Mark Pfander, Grade 7
Ocean City Intermediate School, NJ

Was the House a Home?

I never noticed the old creaky house
I drive by on my way to school.

Once I ventured up the creaky old steps
and looked inside the dirt-smeared windows.
The high ceilings looked laced with cobwebs
and dust lay thick on the furniture,
but I could tell that this was once a beautiful mansion.

I wonder if the dirty windows once sparkled with light
from the crystal chandelier that hung in the hall?
I wonder if laughter and love rang out with these walls?
I wonder if children once ran through the long halls?

Maybe, one day, this house will have a family again.

Alyssa Guerrieri, Grade 7
Trinity Middle School, PA

Every Day

Every day I see him along the halls or in the gym.
Every day I'm in a daze and in the back I hear them say
why do you like him.
That's all I hear them say!

Every day I do not care, it's the only thing I can say.
But I really don't care!

Every day my thoughts never change.
Cause when I'm in a daze
he's all I ever know!

Myranda-Lynn Johnson, Grade 7
Rohanen Jr High School, NC

Waterfalls in the Fall

Milky white ribbons
On a mountain of colors
Cascading ever further down
This one stands out from many others

Wider and thicker at the base
Though slender at its highest point
Into a pool of frothy foam
In the middle is its joint

In the winter, it will be frozen
Down it will come, chunks of ice
And then onto spring and summer
When the weather will again be nice

Laura Herrle, Grade 8
Pine-Richland Middle School, PA

My Sister

"Do this,
Do that,
Pick up this,
Pick up that." —
That sounds like my sister.
Always giving commands
And complaining.

But, when I need her,
She's there,
When I have a problem, she listens.

When I'm upset,
She helps.
She does everything
She can
To see me happy.

She's my best friend,
My idol,
My sister.

Irfa Sheikh, Grade 7
Carthage Middle School, NY

Dreams

Dreams come to us when we are asleep
Dreams come to us when we are awake
Dreams are not always good
Dreams are not always bad
Dreams make us feel happy
Dreams make us feel sad
Dreams come in all languages
Dreams come in all colors
Dreams enter each and every mind
Dreams are truly colorblind

Juan Rodriguez, Grade 7
Glades Middle School, FL

The Great Hit

With the crack of my bat,
The fans started to cheer,
It soared over the wall,
The Mets began to jeer.

As I rounded third base,
I took my last stride,
I crossed home plate
Full of Yankee pride.

I checked the scoreboard,
It said two to one,
In the bottom of the ninth,
I'd hit a walk-off home run.

As we gave our high-fives,
The press gathered around,
The stadium still awake,
Booming with sound.

When the night was done,
I was batting .348,
I was so proud of myself,
I felt like a baseball great.

Max Teng, Grade 7
Westwood Jr-Sr High School, NJ

Riders of the Past*

Dragons roamed the land
From the ocean to desert sand
Free hunters in the skies
The wild, brave, and the wise

There lived elves and humans
The magical kingdom weakens
Riders rise and dragons fly
When villagers scream an outcry

Evil strikes in the darkness
Crumbles all the Riders' boldness
Swords and claws slash and clash
Fire burns the land to ash

Elves disappear in the forest
The humans, by far, were weakest
Dwarves, in their mountains, hid
Urgals, from all, were forbid

Enemies' blood stains the blade
The Foresworn were the nights' shade
From their dragons, the Riders sprawl
This is the story of their downfall

Monica Pradel, Grade 7
Pine Crest School, FL
*Inspired by the book "Eragon."

Buddy

The day I've been waiting for has come
This day is the day I get a dog
The waiting is over
I will always have a buddy
Always someone to talk to
When times get rough he will be there
To comfort me and protect me
He is my best friend
The waiting is over

Chris Mazgaj, Grade 7
Depew Middle School, NY

A Friend

A friend, lost
moved away
gone forever
not here to stay

Far away doesn't work,
you can't see each other,
far away doesn't work
it's really a bummer

You forget to e-mail,
you forget to write,
you're too busy,
with your new life

A friend lost
so far away
loses her old friends,
not here to stay.

Brittany Sangastiano, Grade 8
Westwood Jr-Sr High School, NJ

First Step Experience

Beautiful sunsets
Like a rainbow covering the entire sky
Warm, calming water
Waves rushing over my wrinkled feet
Bringing a few shells to the shore
Moist sea breeze filling the air
Carrying a pleasant scent of salt water
Sand between my toes
Sometimes burning like the sun
Sometimes cool like the summer nights
Palm trees swaying
With the rhythm of the wind
I seem to fly with the seagulls
Soaring over the busy water
Taking this experience
With the first step
Onto the sandy beach

Hadley Farabee, Grade 7
Trinity Middle School, PA

A Football Legend
The one who they call sweetness is not a myth
But actually a legend
He runs and runs
Battling his way through defenders
With his elusive power and balance and speed
He also ran over thirteen thousand yards
And he won a Super Bowl in his career
This legend may be the best of all time
And this legend's name is Walter Payton.
Juq'Wuan Murphy, Grade 8
Seminole County Middle/High School, GA

Forgetting
My papa often forgets,
sometimes he throws a fit
then he hesitates to sit.
He forgets every second or two
but he doesn't know what to do.
He never wants to be left alone
or even leave his home.
He loses track of time and
never wants to spend a dime.
His forgetting makes me sad
and sometimes even mad.
But he's not the only one for
this poem is not even done…

My grandma has this problem too
but what am I supposed to do?
She's always misplacing things
and the pain of this really stings.
I miss the old times before I was ten.
It was not the same as it has been.
And even though it is very sad…
I will NEVER forget the good times we've had.
Rocco Fumerelle, Grade 7
Depew Middle School, NY

Goodbye
You call me
and all you say is "Hi."
In my heart,
I know what you mean
and that is goodbye
"Why do you lie?" I ask.
There's no answer from you.
Then, you tell me that you love me,
I don't believe you though.
Then, the next day
You tell me that you'll always remember me,
You also tell me that you promise.
However, I know
that some things
will just never happen.
Katherine Tarre, Grade 7
Varsity Lakes Middle School, FL

The Baseball Life
I love the smell of fresh cut grass,
and playing kids from last year's class.
Stepping up to the plate,
the pitcher's eyes are full of hate.
As the pitcher beams,
I see the rotation of the seams.
As the ball comes in,
the world begins to spin.
I start to swing,
and the bat says, "ping."
The crowd bursts
as I run to first.
I try to run like a deer with grace,
as I tap on the second base.
Then I fly like a zooming bird,
down the line, and on past third.
The away team is screaming words of hate
as I happily sprint across home plate.
James Delgato, Grade 9
Unami Middle School, PA

I Will Have to Stop Becoming Stressed Out
I will have to stop becoming stressed out
Now I can find it a difficult juggle.
I need to be all smiles, and stop the pout,
If you ask me, school is such a struggle.

I have so much going on, I'm aware.
The charity work is fun and rewarding.
I will be happy, I promise, I swear.
I have to play sports, they are awarding.

I know I'm guilty, I have some issues
I am going to spin out of control.
My new outlook is here, pass the tissues
I must stop, 'cause this is bad for my soul.

I do not always have to be correct
If I do not breathe, I will become wrecked.
Ashley Kershaw, Grade 9
Unami Middle School, PA

One Window
One window is all I need
To feel free and be me
I can dance and sing without being made fun of
I can dress how I want and express myself in every way
When being in my ideal world you won't see my cry
I can use my imagination and make my dull world colorful
This time I won't be just another face in the crowd
For once it's not about them it's about me
When the time is right I'll take a step back into reality
Bari Nedick, Grade 7
Anthony Wayne Middle School, NJ

Danger

Danger feels like your heart's pounding so hard from terror your chest could rip open
Danger sounds like people screaming insanely, glass shattering piercingly, and alarms ringing hysterically
Danger smells like stinky smoke filling your living lungs with the aroma of tears running down your cheeks
Danger looks like ferocious flames racing high like the sky, people with terror-stricken faces, and your vision slowly darkening
Danger tastes like anomalous amounts of scorching sauce in your mouth smoldering you to the millionth degree

Elizabeth Sayan, Grade 7
Most Blessed Sacrament School, MD

The Bird That Could Not Fly

The bird chirped and the bird sang. The bird tried to fly but fell with a bang.
The bird kept trying but it could not soar. The other birds teased him more and more,
But whatever the bird did he could not soar.

Month after month the days flew by. The little bird could not leave its nest.
Each day the bird tried but couldn't get it right, except for one dark intensifying night,
The bird jumped from the nest and began to take flight.

The bird began to soar. The higher he went the happiness grew more.
The next day the birds took flight. The young little bird soared with them as they roamed.
The bird had so much fun the bird did not want to go home.

The bird made many friends, and didn't want it to end the bird could always lend a wing to a bird in need,
Because the other birds showed him the best places to feed. A bird in need reminded him when he could not fly.
He loved the feeling of his wings in the sky.

The bird could not lie. The bird was in love.
The bird was in love with a beautiful dove.
The bird lived happily ever after.

Myles Fabritz, Grade 8
Westampton Middle School, NJ

Tangled

Ivy clings to a garden wall.
A tangle of leaves and dry stems twisting chains around the helpless brick;
it crawls, circles around the lonely stone.
Rough granite wears at my bare back, as I fall into peace with a solid thought,
staring helplessly at the storm-ridden clouds and listening to chirping, angst-filled robins.

Alone,
but surrounded by a thousand insects,
stinging, biting, creeping to blackmail
my fragile self and my esteem shatters,
each bite produces a single bitter behest —
Perfection.

A war rages between my twiddling thumbs
as I balance myself between the crumbling blocks,
aching from holding the world for so long.
The wind's single sigh tumbles the wall stone by stone.

Without a place to root its feet
the ivy brittles and coils with time,
while the absence of the garden wall rejoices —
Freedom.

Bailey Blumenstock, Grade 7
Ocean City Intermediate School, NJ

Flowers

Bright and shiny petals
Like little diamonds
Super strong standing straight stems
That are strong as metal

When you run walk or play
You usually see a flower every day
You look at them they smile back
They are God's craft made out of velvet
And believe me they will always grow back

Molly Hourigan, Grade 7
Westwood Jr-Sr High School, NJ

This Boy

This Boy…
was suffering on the inside
but was terrified to show it
because he wanted to be strong.
He had a faith I'd never seen
but tried to hide it
because he thought he was weak.
He would try so hard to be himself,
but eventually would hide beneath a mask
because he didn't want to show his pain.
He would teach me about life
but still wouldn't understand his own
because he was scared to think about his own.
This Boy…is my hero.

Christianna Burns, Grade 7
Ocean City Intermediate School, NJ

Ode to Music

I grew up fighting the fight
Then music came into me and saved my life
I used to be a thug
Then I realized I was as slow as a slug
I said to myself: What am I doing?
And I thought it was my life that I was ruining.
I was so caught up in doing drugs and getting into trouble
That I didn't realize I was trapped in a bubble.
I didn't used to care and went to many courts
Then I turned my life around and started playing sports.
In school I used to get bad grades,
Then someone really close to me got murdered with a blade.
After that night I was filled with shock
I felt my time to go getting closer on the clock
So I started writing poems to show my expressions:
It's your life you shouldn't be stressing.
I love making beats
To go with the rhythm, the words that I speak
I am so happy that music came into me
Music saved me from the penalty.

Joe Ruggiero, Grade 8
Milford Middle East School, MA

One Window

One window is all I need,
To see the world around me,
To feel the breeze inside me,
To hear the sound all around,
To find myself deep inside,
To make my heart pound with fury,
To hear myself speak and feel the wind on my skin.

Sara Puleo, Grade 7
Anthony Wayne Middle School, NJ

Mary Don't You Weep

Mary don't you weep
Rest your head and sleep
For this is God who speaks
For your Son is now with me
So Mary don't you weep
So close your eyes in peace
For I have set Him free
So Mary while you cry
I will let Him dry your weeping eyes
For He has not died He is yet alive
So Mary don't you weep
Just leave your pain with Me
So Mary you will be ok
I know you will find your way
So Mary don't you weep
Because you will be here some day
And you will be here to stay
So Mary don't you weep
For this is God who speaks
For your Son is now with me
So Mary don't you weep

Diamond Williams, Grade 9
Seminole County Middle/High School, GA

Soldier

Soldier, soldier you defend me as a friend,
you will be there for me until the end,
defending America is your plight,
and you won't give up without a fight,
you held the light of liberty,
to set this country free,
you defend us to this day,
and put all threats at bay,
every day you risk your life,
but you end all strife,
I know it must be hard,
with something so big to guard,
when you hear someone cry,
you are quick to reply,
you are the elite,
and you never accept defeat,
you abolish danger to zero,
you are my hero.

Brian Maher, Grade 8
Florida State University/Florida High School, FL

Holding Hearts

Crimson kisses
Your hand in mine
Romeo and Juliet
We'll recite our lines
We'll jump from this balcony
Flee to the sea
Run from the tragedy
Just you and me.

Danielle Johnson, Grade 9
Thomson High School, GA

A Forbidden Surface

When the leaves turn a perfect gold
And a delicate red, the
Trees relinquish ownership
Sending leaves fluttering down.

The air becomes colder still,
The wind shivers violently.
The shifting season brings change,
Full clouds invade darkened skies.

Snowflakes fall from up above,
Agilely reaching ground.
The mangled surface rigid,
The pond now frozen in time.

Twigs and ruts scar the surface,
Buggy parts remain behind.
An angel's upturned face just
Sympathetically staring.

Gliding across is forbidden,
Which makes it intoxicating.
The luminescent moon will still
Forgive you and spotlight your zeal.

Jenna D'Angelo, Grade 9
Unami Middle School, PA

My Open Palm

My open palm,
Come grab a hold of me,
I'll be your Indian guide,
Follow me and you'll see.

I will show you,
I'll lead you to the light,
Come grab a hold of me.

I'll make your life bright.
Don't be scared,
Dare to dare.
I can share my world,
With someone special like you.

Natasha Trout, Grade 8
Ephrata Middle School, PA

Trapped Inside

trapped.
in the dark forest of my mistakes.
I try to break out but the wall is too tough,
the love is nowhere near,
and I see the people I hurt the most floating inside my head.
I wish I could go back to a time where things were happy.
I'm trying to find my way through the forest, but I think I am going in circles.
it all looks the same, dreary and gray.
I see the sun shining through the swinging tree branches,
and I think to myself,
whenever will I be free?

Amy DeVoe, Grade 7
Anthony Wayne Middle School, NJ

Spring

I know it's time when nature calls,
in with spring and out winter crawls.
The leaves come out fresh and green,
and branches that are crisp grow in between.

The sounds birds make are as mellow as a flower,
and there is no surprise why people can't only listen for an hour.
Baby chicks are born,
ready to yell like a horn.

Flowers bloom,
smelling like a beautiful perfume.
Adding the colors of the rainbow to any field,
and now you know why all pedestrians must yield.

Up in the sky you see clouds blow away,
letting you know it is a wonderful spring day.
Spring, spring, the best time of year,
spring is here so let out a cheer!

Amanda Pirola, Grade 7
Westwood Jr-Sr High School, NJ

Believe in Your Dreams

When you have a dream, do you believe?
Do you believe that it is true or may become true?
Do you tell people your dreams, or keep them to yourself?
Or do you just think that dreams are nothing,
When you wake up do you just put them to the back of your mind,
As if when you sleep, you sleep in a black hole,
And nothing is happening?
If or when you tell people your dreams,
Do you feel better if it was a scary dream or a threatening dream?
Or do you feel embarrassed because it was a dumb dream,
And now have people laughing at you or bring it up in an awkward place.
It does not matter as long as *you* believe in them.
Your dreams, your decisions.
To believe or not to believe,
Make that decision for yourself;
So hopefully you believe.

Emily Tredo-Klosko, Grade 7
Depew Middle School, NY

I Wonder

I wonder when I'm in the hall
Does he even notice me at all?

I wonder when I walk by
Does he ever smell the perfume of cinnamon spice?

I wish I could express how I really feel
If I was brave I know I will

I wonder when I grow up
If we'll be toasting two glass cups

I wonder if he'll ever know
How dearly I love him so

I wonder how we'll meet
Or will I always walk past with my head down looking at my feet

My mind will wonder forever and ever
Until the day we may come together

Sekiyah Jones, Grade 8
Seminole County Middle/High School, GA

iPod

I am sleek and small.
I store many songs, videos, shows, and pictures.
I shine on brightly.
I am light to carry,
and easily go in your pocket.
I love music and listen to it all day.
I never sleep,
but play 24/7.
The latest technology never leaves me,
as I am an iPod who's a nano and blue.

Trisha Paz, Grade 7
St Agatha School, NY

Art Class

I enter the art room
And ask the children to let their imagination fly
To only think about silly creatures and bright colors

Close your eyes and relax your mind

I wanted them to think about paradise
Somewhere, where there is no pain or misery
A place where there's no turning back

Where you can only smell pure air
And see nature all around

Though apparently, this was not so easy
When they took the paint brush in their hands,
They automatically froze.

Farrah Ridoré, Grade 8
International School of Boston, MA

The Color Changing Mountains

It was like nothing I ever saw before
It was really really great
But no one would believe me because I was only three
They kept thinking that it wasn't real
That I was just a kid
Some thought I was crazy
Some thought I was foolish
Even my parents didn't believe me
They thought my imagination
Was acting up again
But you will believe
That I'm not crazy
Those color changing mountains
Are as real as you and me.

Brandon Hodges, Grade 7
Newtown Friends School, PA

Fierce and Frightening

Flashing, flashing all around
Bolts of lightning hit the ground
Angels bowl and make you jump
Clouds burst like water pumps

Shut the windows, lock the doors
Watch outside as the rain pours
Wondering when the fierce winds will halt
Waiting on the next lightning bolt

Staring, staring into the sky
Wondering when the frightening will pass by
Hail stones crash hard into the earth
Crushing flowers, just given birth

Hoping for just one ray of sun
Oh when will this storm finally be done?
Waiting for the rainbow to appear
To dry the tears of the angels and make the little one cheer

Brandi Clark, Grade 8
DuBois Area Middle School, PA

Time

Time is like a door.
You never know what's going to be on the other side.
Every day is like a new world.

It goes by too fast.
When you are doing something it seems to go by fast.
But when you are just sitting there it seems like forever.

Time is like gambling.
You never know what is going to happen.
But someday time will stop for you.

Chase Cantrell, Grade 7
Charles D Owen Middle School, NC

Men's Ways

How fine men can be.
When trying to impress girls.
And then the truth shows.

Amber Winslow, Grade 7
Perquimans County Middle School, NC

Screaming My Name

Howling my name to the sky
It doesn't give a reply
Begging for me to come out of hiding
Searching everywhere but beside you
I'm here, already beside you

Days become useless hours to you
Everything flows together
You've stopped searching for me
But I'm right here
Don't you see me?

I look in the mirror
I'm transparent
When did I learn to walk through walls?
Like I did just now
"I'm right here" I whisper to myself
I wish my lies could come true
But I realize where I really am
Six feet under
And never found

Tiffany Farr, Grade 8
Irmo Middle School, SC

Yellow

Hanging in the air
is the sharp smell of tropical fruit.
The wind secretly
creeps up behind me like footsteps.

My smile broadens
at the sweet taste of happiness.
The sun warms me
as I sit idly on a sandy beach.

Into my curly hair
the ocean softly sprays a mist.
The sun's hot rays
leaves on my face a golden color.

Smiling sunflowers
stare back at their creator with pride.
Lilies standing tall
release their sweet scent into the air.

Finally, as I reflect
yellow simply comes to mind.

Chris Ghildyal, Grade 7
William Penn Middle School, PA

A Wish

A wish to be free, to ride with glee.
A wish to be who you are, without looking very far.
A wish to soar, more and more.
A wish to dance happily with the leaves, among the trees.
To whisper a secret that won't be told,
With the passage of time no one will know.
A wish for nothing bad, nor anything sad.
For all people to accept one another, as their sisters and brothers.
A wish for serenity all around, for peaceful, quiet sound.
A wish for no fights,
Although people think it is right.
That all animals be treated fair,
Small ones too, like the hare.
Our world would forget their hungry greed,
And do for a stranger a very good deed.
To help people of all ages,
No matter their size or wages.

A wish. A single wish.
That is burred deep down in people's hearts.
So hard to reach,

But keep trying…

Kelly Brzyski, Grade 7
Depew Middle School, NY

Are You Afraid of Fast?

I try to alleviate myself from the pain, from the speed,
Making sure nothing comes upon me, like my brother.
Thou canst stop me from the horrors I pain, bullets came by,
I ran away it should never come back, I will make sure never
To see the speed of anything, I will never want to see anything boisterous.

So tell me, will I hide in a cache and never come out,
Or should I capitulate and overcome this nightmare,
But this fear is too colossal, so tell me, how I desist
Something like this, can you help me?

Stop talking so fast, stop driving the car at fast speeds,
Don't run I beg of you. Help me, I'm lost in speed,
I have gone crazy believing myself I can become a great man.
I will run like the wind, and listen to Mother Nature
Screaming away while her velocity starts to rip apart
Can I overcome this fear? I don't know?

I will not leave myself alone, I will stay inside
And lock myself up, so nothing will hurt
Help me, this fear is too colossal, so tell me,
How I desist something like this, can you help me,
Or can you help me?

Abdul Khail, Grade 7
Plainview-Old Bethpage Middle School, NY

Fishing
I like fishing, fishing is like hunting except you are casting.
I like it because it's exciting to catch a fish.
Some can be big, some can be small.
But they are not easy to catch at all.

Eric Parham, Grade 7
Charles D Owen Middle School, NC

Ode to Birds
Oh majestic creatures!
Bird are
Soaring in the air
Without a care.
Where they are going?
How free you are in the sky
Than being in a classroom as I sigh.
The sky's the limit for you,
And the ground is the limit for me.
How free you are soaring up and down.
Flying south for the winter
And north for the summer,
While I shiver in the cold,
Or sweat under the powerful sun.
You are as free as a cloud in the sky
While I'm as free as a criminal in jail.
I hope to join you one day
And soar in the sky with you,
Leaving the ground forever
And also leaving my troubles all behind.

Kevin Seon, Grade 7
Plainview-Old Bethpage Middle School, NY

Paradise Is Very Nice
Yesterday you were here,
today you are gone.
I gave a little tear,
until I thought of fun.
Even though I miss you so,
you're always here with me.
One day when I'm feeling low,
and I know you can't be seen,
I can see you in my mind.
I can feel you in my presence.
And even though I cannot find you,
it will make me less tense
to know you are safe,
to feel you are happy,
Because death is a beginning
of a new life!
After death is a paradise,
a place for a long holiday,
so relaxing and nice.
I know you love it, as much as I love you!

Domenic DiCenso, Grade 9
Unami Middle School, PA

Clouds
The sky is a serene, beautiful, bright blue,
But not always an authentic blue.
The clouds create
A bleached sky,
Clear in some spots
Gloomy storms in others.
The huge clouds are
Full-size obstacles in our lives.
The tiny clouds are
The little bumps in the road to overcome.
More times than not,
The fluffy white clouds,
The problems that can be solved,
Overpower
The dark storm clouds,
The dreadful, dreary moments
To once again create the sky and its beauty.

Jordan Zboray, Grade 7
Ocean City Intermediate School, NJ

A Bike in the Sky
I ride my bike through the sky.
I take a tour through the clouds.
I soar over the mountain tops.
I hear a zap a buzz a slap a fist against the alarm.
Just for now I come back to the world to see another
Yet another day of school

Ethan Goldberg, Grade 7
Oblock Jr High School, PA

Change
Oh…
Will it ever be the same?
Will this ever change…
Back?

You, never seem to see
What was right with me.
If there was a wrong
It wasn't ever long before you said —

Change! Change your ways,
Change for you, change for me, change the way
they want you to be.
I love you, I need you, please understand…

Now, maybe there was nothing right,
Maybe I was always wrong.
And to figure that out took me this long.

So I'll change. I won't change for you,
I won't change for them.
I'll change for me, because I want to be
Different.

Garrett Nickell, Grade 9
Lincoln Park Academy, FL

Kot

Kot. Felino. Gato.
It sits there
its tail twitching impatiently
just sitting there.
Minding its own business.
But of course,
I cannot mind mine.
How can I?
Especially
when it
meows at me.

Nikolas Oktaba, Grade 9
Bronx High School of Science, NY

The Meadow

The quiet, the peace and relaxation
that I cannot get anywhere else —
a spiritual release.
I love the connection I feel
to nature and to God.
I can only go with the best
of my friends and family.
The cold is like no other;
it is comfortable.
The meadow lets me hunt
just being with nature and God
making me feel wonderful.
The meadow gives me a sense
of pride knowing that
I am the fortunate one —
sitting for days and never
seeing another person.

Herbie Godfrey, Grade 7
Ocean City Intermediate School, NJ

Good Bye

You know what you did to me.
That was wrong.
Going around telling people lies.
What's going on?
Acting like everything
Is still tight and all right.
What has he turned you into?
You're not the person that I met,
The person that I cared about.
I tried to talk,
Show you the way
Open your eyes!
But every time
You just complained and denied.
You're being pulled out of my life,
But that doesn't really bother you.
So I guess I just have to say my
GOOD BYE.

Natalia Rosa, Grade 8
KIPP Academy Lynn Charter School, MA

Life

Life is like a rock climbing wall.
The bottom is where you start, and the top is your goal.
If you don't pick the right footholes and fingergrips, you don't get to the top.
If you don't make the right choices in life, you don't make your goal.
Make the right choices and you succeed.
Choose the right footholes and fingergrips, you make it to the top.
Do the right thing. Get to the top.

Allison Walton, Grade 9
Orono High School, ME

Dance

Gazing out onto the vivid stage
Awaiting my turn to shine
This is what I live to do.
The glistening lights, I glide across the floor.
Reviewing the moves in my head,
I have learned tricky but pleasing choreography.
Backstage, I am imprisoned in the darkness.
But onstage, I am free to dance my heart out
And dance like there is no tomorrow.
A little nervous, my heart is pounding like a beating drum.
I step into my position now at the center of the curtain.
The theater is dark, for a few seconds, like a winter's night,
As if to say, "It's your turn now, get ready."
I reminisce throughout the long year,
I have been reviewing each step and now, I am ready to perform.
The music begins to play and I slide across the dance floor.
Point my toes, extend my legs, sway my arms.
My nervousness wanes and excitement takes over.
I am doing what I love to do.
Dance.

Leslie Hirshberg, Grade 8
Eli and Bessie Cohen Hillel Academy, MA

The Unseen Scar You Leave

You look at me
But not inside me.
You judge me for who I was
Instead of who I am.
You look at me as if I have a deadly disease.
To the people that have hurt me I am an outcast.
You make fun of me because others have.
You hurt me and call me names.
You play tricks on me.
Through all this I am strong, I never shed a tear.
Instead, I give my love and compassion to the ones you hurt more than me.
So know this.
The ones who choose to love even though they have been hurt so many times
Are the ones who get the most love in the future.
So I will never hold a grudge.
I forgive YOU.
I forgive you because you don't know the pain you cause me.
You will never know
Until someone else hurts you like you have hurt me.

Laura Walker, Grade 7
Alton C Crews Middle School, GA

Mixed Emotions

There are many emotions inside me.
Although I hate letting my feelings out,
Sometimes, letting them out makes me feel free.
Everyone feels that way, without a doubt.
A teardrop shows the sadness that I feel.
I have a fear of the darkness at night.
My smile shows that happiness is real.
The joy I have shows my inner delight.
Anger comes when I scream at my brother.
Resentment shows in me if someone lies.
Love shows for my father and my mother,
But, no hate for someone that I despise.
The feelings that are inside me are true.
What do I feel now, do you have a clue?

Alyson Evans, Grade 9
Carbondale Area Jr/Sr High School, PA

Summer

Summer vacation
Is finally here!
I've been waiting for it;
The entire school year.
No more textbooks;
Not one more test!
Finally, I can
Get a well-deserved rest.

It's almost September,
And I want to go back!
I miss my friends, and
Soccer, and track.
Right now (during the summer) I'm so bored;
All I do is mope.
Well, school is not that bad,
So with school I can cope!

Heather Van Voorhis, Grade 8
New Jersey United Christian Academy, NJ

Free

She cries with sorrow
he wipes her tears
leads her to dance
she smiles, bright as the sun
floating on a cloud of dreams
head on his shoulder
he studies her, eyes the color of sapphires
his green with flecks of gold
leans toward her
kisses her tenderly
the cold disappears with the snow
God closes their eyes
hand in hand, heaven carries them up
finally happy, on a cloud
they are free

Jenny Pionzio, Grade 7
East Hampton Middle School, CT

My Homies

My homies are a lot of things,
They're like a pot of boiling grease,
Hot, heated and ready to pop!!!
They're like a wool sweater, so close
To make you safe and comfortable.
They are like writing a note,
Funny and sometimes random
And unpredictable.
But, they are good homies overall.

Valchas D., Grade 9
Audubon Youth Development Center, KY

Bugs

Oh, bugs, why must you annoy everyone?
I, along with others don't understand.
We go in the sun, trying to have fun.
But, because of you pests our day's not grand.
Some of you sting, pinch, and make us itchy.
But then there's others that don't do a thing.
I just hate the ones that make me twitchy.
Why can't I ever just enjoy the spring?
Why, oh why must you do this to us all?
It's not like we did anything to you.
You make us freak when you decide to crawl.
We run, swat, and jump and then we yell shoo.
Oh bugs, oh bugs the things I hate so much.
I wish I could crush you all in my clutch.

Kayley Liuzzo, Grade 9
Carbondale Area Jr/Sr High School, PA

The Red Sox

Just won the world series second in four years
The green monster in left
Pesky's Pole in right
Manny being Manny
Lowel the world series MVP
JD-Drew with a sweet lefty swing
Listen to the Red Sox's faithful sing
They are an offensive hitting machine
When Oritz is up to bat
You know you'll hear a "crack"
As the ball goes outta the park
Ellsbury diving to make the catch
Lugo and Pedrioa turning out the double play
Keeping the other team at bay
Varitek catching behind the plate
Wakefield pitching a nasty knuckle ball
Matsuzaka throwing lights out innings
Youkilis a golden glover
Can play 1st or 3rd with ease
The Red Sox are always ready to play
Against their rivals the Yankees

Zachary Zygmunt, Grade 7
Depew Middle School, NY

I Am a Man
I am a man, foolish and dreaming of new life, with significant meaning,
Using only wits, a strong trait of mine, I blunder about desperately seeking a sign.
With nothing left, I wait for adventures to unfold. Coveting them like a treasure of gold.

I am a man who takes life by the handle! No time to dawdle, no time to ramble.
I would rather find adventure, not let it find me! Soon I will set sail, least I be dragged out to sea.
Before I go now, please remember this: life flies by so fast, it's too easy to miss.

I am a man who is taking life slow. It's not on a schedule; it's got nowhere to go!
Why go out for adventure when you have it right here! I am truly honest and sincere
When I say that the Hare blew through life way too fast while the Tortoise lagged behind and had himself a blast.

I am a man who lives life to the fullest! But taking in doses is certainly surest,
The absolute way to ruin your fun for the rest of your days until they're undone.
If I've learned a lesson it's certainly this: live for the moment, but the moment don't miss.

Donald McWilliams, Grade 8
Westampton Middle School, NJ

When Parting
Love me New England,
Like I love your rocky coast,
The hidden rabbit-holes, and hence broken ankles, in
Your golden fields.
The crunchy, re-gifted snow,
And the emotion that's so easy to read in your blue-sky eye.
Love me forever,
Keep me out in the cold and guessing, drifting through the fogs
And then warm again, suddenly — just as always, I learn — stuck in your hearth;
The one you burn, and so —
For the firewood — thank you, cut like hair off your evergreen head.
Love me more than anyone,
But then there's your sister, the one crying at your feet, and burying said feet in the sand.
Throwing fits just to embarrass you, landing you on the news.
Running away to Europe's west coast.
And leaving behind her torn-up toy boats.
But you clean them up for her, responsibly, lovingly.
Or maybe just before you get a splinter.
Love me like that sister, your sister,
The one who moves away.

Kathleen Morrissey, Grade 9
Bridgewater-Raynham Regional High School, MA

Eternal Servitude
Slavery, slavery won't you let go of me?
In your bondage I'm still held, by those who want to weld me to eternal servitude!
By those who look down on me, because my ancestors were set free!
By those who do not wish me me well, because of the misfortune that befell
all those who were whipped, and who sowed the fields owned by those of old.

But why should I feel bad, because my ancestors survived something that blackens our nation's history?
Something that made my ancestors stronger, and then me,
something that yes, I'll have to wear for all eternity, but I'll wear it proudly as you'll see!

Slavery, Slavery I'll wear you proudly always!

Yanique Spigner, Grade 7
Westwood Jr-Sr High School, NJ

Courtyard Concert

A courtyard concert performed by Jews,
Nazis have guns that they will use.
Soldiers listen for entertainment,
Keeping all Jews in forced containment.
A courtyard concert where 'undesirables' play,
Waiting for freedom, day by day.

When that day finally comes…

A courtyard concert performed by Nazis,
No guns needed to celebrate peace.

Thomas Zamry, Grade 7
Glades Middle School, FL

Toni the Tiger

Everywhere I go, I don't want to know
That I share a name with a dumb cartoon
That song is playing everywhere I go
More of this torture, and I'll explode soon

On TV almost every night
That song mocks me again and again
The tiger is going to give me a fright
Why couldn't my mom think of a normal name?

People don't know how annoying that can be
I do love my name for what it really means
But not for the commercial on TV
My name is special, or that's what it seems

Hey Tony, I like the things you do
Kellogg's, why did he have to be Tony too?

Toni Walker, Grade 9
Unami Middle School, PA

When Your Heart Is a Balloon

When your heart is a balloon
All it does is pop
From things like a scissor,
To things like a thumbtack
To put it in words is yet
Too hard to describe
For all you do is tape it,
But never replace it,
Like stones in a bag
Making it heavier,
Never going away,
But pulling it down
How to describe when
Your heart's a balloon,
But just with never-ending
Holes.

Kristen Crasto, Grade 7
Florence M Gaudineer Middle School, NJ

Just Because

Just because you're my friend
I won't always tell you everything
I won't always open up
Just because you're my friend
We'll still get into fights
We won't always be happy with each other
Just because you're my friend
Doesn't mean we won't annoy each other
It doesn't mean I like you
Just because you're my friend — I won't always be there

Rebecca Nidle, Grade 7
Anthony Wayne Middle School, NJ

Life Is Like a War

Life is like a war,
Every day a battle with me trapped in the middle
If not one thing, then always another.

Actions don't just speak louder than words,
They scream in your face.
And words are like bullets
That pierce your heart.

Opposing forces trying to defeat each other,
But always miss greatly
And I am the one who is hit and wounded.

A never ending war,
But one day I hope they find peace
And let me go free.

Brianne Tartaglia, Grade 9
Unami Middle School, PA

Cats

Ten big cats went up a hill
One fell on a big windmill
Nine big cats were playing by the lake
One was jumping around and landed on a rake
Eight big cats were having fun
One got in trouble and was hit with a gun
Seven big cats were playing with Nick
One was rolling in the grass and got a tick
Six big cats ran in the door
One got shoved into a drawer
Five big cats went in a hot air balloon
One forgot a parachute and met its doom
Four big cats were in a plane
One disappeared because of David Blaine
Three big cats went to feast
One was mistaken and was eaten by a wildebeest
Two big cats went to school
One was naughty and was hit with a tool
One big cat had some fun
It got in trouble and was burned by the sun

Sam Gelber, Grade 7
Yellow Breeches Middle School, PA

Shade

Exhausted
I sit in the shade of the tent
Sheltered from the unblinking sun
Whose stare even now burns
My husband in the fields
As he scrapes the dusty earth
To raise a crop
That has not grown
Since the rain dried

I gaze down
Upon my dear child
Who sits in front of me
I see mirrored in her eyes
My own
A thousand tears
Of sweat
Are those eyes

I must be her shade
To shelter her
From the hot sun
Jeremy Gutekunst Perlman, Grade 9
Bronx High School of Science, NY

Silent Killer

Deep in the jungle coming,
Silent as a wisp,
Running through the rivers,
Cold and heartless, swift.

Coming in still night,
Coming in hot day,
It has not a preference,
It cannot be swayed.

Killing all it meets,
Keeping all their souls,
Trapping up their futile works,
And turning them to mold.

Medicines will come,
Treatments will then go,
Never will they rid the killer,
The virus will not go.
Cameron Cummings, Grade 9
Schenectady Christian School, NY

Freedom

steam simmering my lips
little kids singing
daisies in the morning
butterflies fluttering
soft, baby skin
Jeffrey Croft, Grade 7
Madisonville Middle School, TN

Impostors

One window is all we need:
To let go of the mask we have tightly tied to our faces.
We are all fakes, not showing the people who we really are inside,
War boils within our conscience, constantly holding back our genuine personality.
With one slip of the truth, we stand ashamed.
She lies to us,
He lies to us,
They lie to us.
Frauds are what we are.
We fear to be judged for the veracity.
Fear has grabbed us by the hand, unable to let go.
Let it all fade.
Yena Lee, Grade 7
Anthony Wayne Middle School, NJ

I Know It Is Not Your Fault

The last leg of the journey is ruined
The final memory I will have, but now it is destroyed
I move on to almost a whole new world
Carrying with me only the recollection of this demolition
Tears
I cry for the good times that could have been had
As well as the ones I must now remember alone
Hopes slashed I surrender to the despair that is to come
Life was so great too great it had to descend into
Darkness
Alone I must continue
Blindly stumbling on the path ahead with no clear destination
Clumsy and awkward
Destinations eternally forgotten, leaders dropped one by one
Now there is no one left to guide through the voyage of life
Time to spread my wings
But nobody is there to give the necessary push that propels me to flight
Suddenly I have been abandoned to fend for myself in an unknown wilderness
I am heated and bitter but
I know it is not your fault
Izzy Kornman, Grade 7
Solomon Schechter Day School, CT

Original

I don't *blend in* with the crowd,
I *stand out* against all my peers.
Most girls will try to fit in.
But that is not an issue for me.
I am myself, and always will be.
Nothing you say can change that.
I'm the only star in a foggy, clouded night sky.
I'm the beauty and radiance of a single dewy rose.
And I'm the Flamingo in a flock of Pigeons.
I am myself, and always just me.
Briana Graham, Grade 7
Ocean City Intermediate School, NJ

Fall

Memories of summer fade,
Orange, red, yellow,
Falling from branches.
Cool breeze flying by trees,
Branches bare, mortified, without leaves.
Unknown noises lingering through forests,
A rustling in a pile of leaves,
Branches wave like flags flying high.
A wolf's call is heard.
The herald of winter has come.

Haven Anderson, Grade 7
Trinity Middle School, PA

A Tribute to Mom

Mom, your sense of humor is dry
like a sauna,
and you can get me to smile
at my most dreadful moment.
Mom, your golden brown hair glistens
in the sunlight and reflects your warmth.
You're fiercely independent
and too stubborn to change your opinion
on anything!
You smell like a wild honeysuckle and
your olive complexion melts within the moonlight
creating a soft glow
you're a peacock in the sun on a rainy day
Mom, your heart of pure gold
beats for the ones you love.

Taylor Goebel, Grade 8
Beacon Middle School, DE

God Knows

The sky is falling, God is calling.
My name, I am forever ashamed.
People say blessed be,
Never take the Lord's name in vain.
But we are all the same.
Sinful, trying to live by the Bible.
Too worried about style and fancy things,
People trying to live in fame.
Always trying to please us.
Sin is only for a season,
God knows your true feelings.
When you're stealing, living, or breathing,
It's all the same, if you just believe in Him.
He will show you the light,
Teach you wrong from right.
Still in spite of wrong or right,
He will still love you every day and night.
God is my life,
No matter how hard the fight or struggle.
I will always love Him.
God knows I'm right.

Shane C., Grade 9
Audubon Youth Development Center, KY

Change of Heart

Teardrops fall, the pain is here
The heart is broken, of you I fear
The things you do to me, the pain I face
You in my life, it will never go away.
To see you! Not to see you!
Either way I cry to know you're not by my side
I hate you but, maybe not anymore.
You changed my heart from hate to love.
You hurt me to know that I will never be the one by your side.

Joan Collins, Grade 9
Miami Beach Sr High School, FL

Getting Through It

I know I will get through it sometime soon.
At the time it does not feel as though I will.
Work approaches fast, unlike a full moon.
Over flowing like a river when it fills.
I wish all the work would come to an end.
I feel overloaded with things to do.
I wish school and work was all pretend.
It feels as though I might catch the flu.

All of my finished work needs improvement.
I get lots of help and support,
I just need to add a little movement,
Make a difference and get a good report!

I am strong, determined and fit,
In the end, I know I will get through it.

Natalie Injaian, Grade 9
Unami Middle School, PA

Young Love

Young love, young love; the path too hard to see.
Young love, young love; smitten I may be.
But why for me has love turned to gray?
The peaceful feeling has been robbed away.

It seems in young years
We like to advertise our need for tears.
And why do we fake sadness
When we really feel that love is madness?

For others, in school and love, they fly so high.
They are athletic and young, but also numb.
Their song has already been sung
Because when they age they will run out of sky.

So young love, young love,
Thank you for what you have taught me —
To take the time to live and grow,
And only love the ones you know.

Nicholas Pisciotta, Grade 9
Flint Hill School, VA

Forever Apart

In my heart
You will forever stay
Until the sunlight fades away
Standing there
Forever apart
Waiting there
Without my heart
For you have taken it
So far away
Keep it safe
Or let it stay
I will wish
For our love to remain
Just one more kiss
To clear the pain
Say goodbye
Just walk away
Forever apart
Because you chose not to stay
Bethany Pearson, Grade 8
Yellow Breeches Middle School, PA

The Cat

I pounce on mice
I get low to the ground
My chances are like dice
I'm quick as sound
I get closer and closer
Until...
Bam! Dinner is served.
Courtney Dzurnak, Grade 7
St Anthony School, CT

Anymore

Covered in blood...
Covered in tears...
Covered in dirt...
Just a phantom on this world

The darkness of night is my cover
The wind is my guide
The sun, my enemy

You can't break me
You can't fix me
You can't hurt me
Anymore...
Karina Barreto, Grade 7
Port Chester Middle School, NY

Grass

Grass between my toes
Freezing cold dew cleans my feet
Skip in the green grass
Emily Bissell, Grade 8
Covenant Life School, MD

The Epic Game

This was the game the game to decide it all
19-19
The ball sitting in my clammy hands
Sweat drip
                    drip
                        drip
                            dripping down my face
The crowd so silent you could hear the sweat hitting the table
I stare at my enemy at the other end of the table
I throw the tiny white ball into the air
Smack! The opponent sees the ball he dives but it's too late
20-19
The crowd let out a small roar
The enemy looks down in deep despair he knows it's his last chance he serves it
I see it like it's in slow motion but it's moving like a cheetah catching its prey
I thrust my paddle up to block the shot he hits it back even faster
Stay calm I think
Whack! I hit it back it barely goes over the net
Landing on the white line at the end of the table then hits the floor
The game's over the crowd roars
I win 21-19

Alex Naglich, Grade 8
William Penn Middle School, PA

The Redemption*

The days run by, since I've last seen you
My heart is somber with the pain
I am filled with the sorrow of not seeing you
Will our paths cross each other again?

Since the great holocaust that overtook me, I have altered
My penitence has been served
My lamentable self has been starving for your company
Can you accept my faults for what they are?

We were a blossoming flower, with roots deep as the richest soil
A strong oak tree with leaves of love expanding
Those days, have long retreated
Jane, return to me my love

The Rochester you long knew is over
You left me here to suffer
My body is crippled, my heart in pieces, my compassion, still intact
Oh, how I pray for the days that the Jane, I love, will return.
Scott Glassman, Grade 9
Council Rock High School South, PA
*Inspired by "Jane Eyre."

The Winter Horse

A coat as soft as freshly fallen snow
Eyes as bright as the first rays of the sun hitting the snow
Hooves that sound like ice crystals hitting the ground every time he walks
Breath as cold lingering as first winter's chill
Hair as wild as a blizzard

Nichole Savell, Grade 9
Seminole High School, FL

Passing Ways

I never saw your face again.
As we passed by each other for the last time.
I asked myself why.
And found no true answer.
I said goodbye.
I found the wonderful grace in your reply.
I wanted you to stay
But my sadness spreads like a fire.
I thought and wondered.
But found solace only in the thought of more.
More of the happiness and good times.
More of the sadness of departure.

Byron Lambrou, Grade 8
Sanford School, DE

End of the Year

Notes are passing
Feet are tapping
Brains are cramping
Hands are packing bags
Eyes are watching the clock
While ears hear tick-tock
Palms are sweaty
The hall seems to be calling
Teacher gives a reminder
While guys silently mock her
Bodies race to the door
Ready to rush the hall's floor
The teacher continues to bore
Suddenly it's silent
Everyone's energy is spent
Watching the clock
My heart has stopped
A sudden burst of cheer
The end of the school year is finally here

Brooks Bell, Grade 8
Briarwood Christian Jr/Sr High School, AL

One Speedy Roller Coaster

The rushing water, voices of little kids,
the smell of the sweet cotton candy.
My energetic body was bouncing
to the loud music in my ears.
I felt the smooth rail
on the side of the fast roller coaster.
Then all of a sudden, boom!
I felt dizzy, nothing seemed still.
Now I couldn't smell the clean air,
or the cotton candy
or even the dried out minty gum in my mouth.
My hands were as rough as sandpaper,
gripping that rail tightly.

Brittany Bunda, Grade 7
William Penn Middle School, PA

The Night Sun

As darkness creeps in,
it comes out from the shadows.
Little pebbles of sparkle reflect off its smooth surface,
casting an eerie glow over the earth.
Lights up the night sky,
it completes the look of the great balls of gas.
Nothing could ever stop it, even daylight.
The night sun,
the moon.

Cara Minnix, Grade 7
Carson Middle School, VA

My Friend

Now that you're out of my life,
it's just not the same.

I was stabbed in the back
by one of my truest friends;
I thought you would be better than that.
I was wrong!

Someone better came along
and I got replaced.

You really surprised me
because you weren't the type
to follow the crowd.

All I want is my friend back!

Lucy Castillo, Grade 9
Bishop Ford Central Catholic High School, NY

Why?

Why are children hurt,
Why do babies cry,
Why can people be so cruel,
Why are we ridiculed…Why are we scared,
Why do we cry…Why do we swear,
Can we answer this, No!
Why do we feel…Why do we see
Why do we eat…Why do we sleep
Can you answer this, No!
What is grass…What are trees,
What is life…What is sad
What is air…What is water
Can you answer this, No!
There are many things we cannot answer
But we live with them each day.
We can't tell the future or what is in it,
But tomorrow's a new day,
And we can help it along
And show it the way
So it won't get lost
By night or day.

Shaina Ledford, Grade 7
Columbia Falls Elementary School, ME

Ambulance Siren

The ominous messenger of bad news echoes across the suburban landscape as if saying: "you could be next."
The ambulance siren keeps us on our toes, warning us not to get comfortable in our lives.
It tells us that a distant problem could become your personal disaster in an instant.
The ambulance is one of the only vehicles respected and feared upon our chaotic highways.
People know they would want the same thing done for them if they were in that ambulance.
The ambulance siren is a sinister reminder that nothing in this world is constant.

Evan Manuella, Grade 8
New Providence Middle School, NJ

I Dreamed

When I go to sleep at night I see horses running across the land. They band together running free as ever. As I see, they gallop as fast as thunder falling across the sky. They find a pasture and they graze. A blaze came by. It was the black, leader of the herd. As he approached them, the horses treated him with honor and respect. He held his head high with loyalty and pride. They ran together like thunder bashing across the open field, running as fast as an eagle could fly. It was like a thousand soldiers running for victory.

Tiffany Miller, Grade 8
Trigg County Middle School, KY

Once a Friend...Never Again

Remember when we used to fight over the stupidest things,
when we would get over it and then laugh two minutes later?
Or how about all of the good times we had?
Hangin' over the weekends, hangin' out at school and in lunch.
Well...now everything's different.
A lot was said between you and I.
We were at each other's throats day in and day out.
And from there on it all went down hill.
Until one day I finally realized what was happening.
We weren't meant to be friends as long as we tried.
The way we were, the way we talked and hung out, would never exist again.
We do try to get along.
We do try pushing our differences and all of our thoughts aside, and it was all working well.
But now I'm seeing the harder we try, the farther apart we become.
So I have one last thing to say.
You WERE once a good friend
NEVER AGAIN.

Lexi Kendziora, Grade 7
Depew Middle School, NY

Ms. Blue

A woman of the black race, that never really hides her face,
and represents herself in different ways, the first language arts teacher that I really had in middle school,
she is very cool for being old school, her mind is amazing and full of different things.

The independent woman with some soul and sass, a friend of Ms. Crowell that also teaches her GT class,
like a sister she is to Ms. Blue, for they teach in the same school,
they are like fraternal twins in almost every way, they burn candles almost every day,
except Ms. Blue is sharp around her edges but beautiful inside and out, like a rose in the garden of my mind.

Believing in her students that are trying to achieve, by being herself and not becoming deceived,
a lover of the theatre and Shakespeare's work, and you can't forget Langston Hughes poetry,
the same with her precious iPod, but last of all a love of my violin that I play the sweet melody of my life on,
she is the one the only and the all so true Ms. Tonya Blue.
The one and only believing, loving, understanding, educator.

Shafiqah Deaouvlt, Grade 9
Western School of Technical & Environmental Science, MD

Wished Away

Oh look, there goes a shooting star
The first time I've seen one, too
So glowing golden bright, so miraculously true
But wait! Oh foolish, silly me
Lost in my shooting star reverie
A wish! Oh that is what I need!
Upon that shooting star
They say that you're supposed to
They say you really are
But what shall I wish for? What do I need?
A gallant horse? A noble steed?
A castle home? An emerald, green?
A jack-in-the-box? A sapphire stream?
Oh, I'm not prepared for this
This wishing-on-the-spot
How I wish for time to consider
Some time, star please allot
Oh wait! I wish to take it back!
Oh, alas, I've wished again
Well, there goes my special wish
I should've wished for ten!

Meghan Walsh, Grade 8
Our Mother of Perpetual Help School, PA

His Love

God brought you in this world, and He'll bring you out.
But with His 24 hours a day, you must not make Him doubt.
He gave you everything for you to lead.
He gave you everything to supply your needs.
There's only one thing that keeps you up.
It's His grace and mercy, plus His tender love.

His love is so mighty, His love is so strong,
His love is so great that He gave us His Son.
His love keeps on giving to those who believe.
His love keeps on giving to those that want to succeed.
It's so everlasting to all the Earth,
So come to Jesus and it will all work!

Vladimir Bien-Aime, Grade 8
St Clare School, NY

Stranger

One man walks,
Another man stalks,
Waiting for the right time,
To go through with the perfect crime,
To take the life of a man,
Who only has a couple of bucks, his family and his van
He pulls a knife but whack!
The poor man fights back,
The fight lasted for like what seemed like hours,
Eventually the poor man overpowers,
The knife swinging bandit decides to take flight,
Once again the win goes to the guys that do right.

Patrick Mahony, Grade 7
Depew Middle School, NY

The Wind Song

A tree, blowing in the wind
  Bending this way and that
    Swaying to the rhythm, to the beat
      Shaking its leaves to express itself
        Letting out all its anger or joy
          While it dances to the Wind Song

Jessica Addesa, Grade 7
Depew Middle School, NY

Key Serve

Last set, match point.
H-e-a-v-y intimidation suffocates the player
As she takes confident S
                    T
                     E
                      P
                       S toward the base line.
Wiping off the fierce sweat which threatens vision,
She winds up her Wilson for the key serve.
Whack! The ball rockets between the players
Like a swinging pendulum on a grandfather clock.
Her shoes screech in pain as she scurries to a spot
To keep the ball in play.
Shuffling into position to take a volley,
Almost as if in s-l-o-w motion,
The ball flies safely into the doubles alley
Ending the match victoriously.

Emma Greco, Grade 8
William Penn Middle School, PA

I've Got Something to Say

I've got something to say.
I want to shout "Hey!"
I've got something to say.
Just listen to me
For once; maybe you'll see.
I've got something to say.
We all know you're bright,
But what you're doing isn't right.
We need you to hear
So you'll share in our fear.
I've got something to say.
I have to share,
I need to get this thought out of my hair.
You're hurting us all,
Soon we're all going to fall
I've got something to say.
We need you to think,
We're all just standing on the brink.
Just take a kneel,
And think about how she would feel.
I've got something to say. And you ought to listen.

Taylor Young, Grade 9
Unami Middle School, PA

Flight

Life is like a cocoon
that keeps making
more and more life;
new life of desires
and hopes and dreams,
all connected in life
with others as cocoons.

Life is like a cocoon,
all spun into a tangled ball
trapped within surroundings,
until at any moment,
a perfect blossom opens
and reveals a beautiful
butterfly taking flight.

Kodi Segich, Grade 7
Ocean City Intermediate School, NJ

Out of Sight

Out of mind
nothing is left behind
it strikes terror
it strikes fear
over head and underneath
all that was is now all gone
just left to sit in the sun
it spins here it spins back
staying out of range
not an arrow or a bullet can stop it
only those of natural force
can come about such an evil force
no one wins
some may die
but in the faint you will hear a cry
a cry for love
a cry of pain
most will die
we're all in vain

Dylan Johnson, Grade 7
Litchfield High School, CT

The Bird in Me

There is a bird in me,
With colors like a rainbow,
And feet like branches.
Its high-pitched sound
Rings like a bell,
Letting someone know it's there.
It flows like a river.
It lives in my heart, and
Makes me stay calm.
It makes me want to fly away.

Kaila DiOrrio, Grade 7
Christ the Teacher Catholic School, DE

A Window, a World

One window is all I need
To see the world
To plant a seed
That grows and grows
Outside my window
The highs and lows of this world
Sketched in my window
The seed grows to a sapling
And gets older
Less dynamic, more static
And the world grows colder
So I pull the shades
And block out the light
The innocent light
That flows through my windows
And the sapling is now a tree
Its bark slowly fades
And I realize
My window didn't change
But what I let myself see
Did

Katie Saulenas, Grade 7
Anthony Wayne Middle School, NJ

Intertwined

We collide
Our lives are intertwined
Your dream becomes my dream
My fear becomes your fear
The promises you make
Become mine to keep
The memories you hold
Are now mine to live
And when we collide
Our dreams are intertwined
We become one

Kathryn Rubin, Grade 8
Whitinsville Christian School, MA

Lost

I am looking at myself in the mirror
what's going on?
My heart beats no more,
my tears don't flow,
my cries are whispers.
Where is my voice?
Where is my strength?
Where is my hope?
…my faith?
…myself?

I am lost.

Roseberline Porcenat, Grade 9
Gateway High School, FL

The Worm

Once upon a time there was a worm,
It would squiggle and squirm.

Then came along a bird,
Which the worm had not heard.

Then the worm had a horrible fate,
It then became bait!

Olivia Rosato, Grade 7
Tarpon Springs Middle School, FL

One Body, One Mind

Big and vibrant,
small and meaningful,
each leaf affects the tree,
each mind affects the body;
its limbs spread far and wide.

As the tree grows,
the leaves will fall and die,
but then grow back again.
A cycle of life
that will never stop turning.

The mind will keep growing
through the good
and through the bad,
but the life of one
will always live on in another.

Anthony Wilent, Grade 7
Ocean City Intermediate School, NJ

Baby Blue Skies

The sky
Blue and white
Filling the air.
With the sun peering through
Warm and cool winds
But then…
The sky turns gray.
Thunder, Lightning
Rain, Hail
The sound of clicking and clacking
On the roof.
Then a big BANG!
When Mother Nature
Unleashes her power
The sky is glittering
Kids running scared
When it concludes
Friends and pets running
All this like nothing happened.

Sean Hawkins, Grade 7
Palmyra-Macedon Middle School, NY

Mother's Day

My mom is awesome
She helps me with my homework
She is good to me
And is nice as can be to me

Whatever she can't do
She always try tries again
She is always easy and cool
And just jumps in the pool

Sometimes I get mad
When I get bad grades
She helps me get them up
Like the backpacking through Europe

Dylan Kiser, Grade 7
Lashmeet/Matoaka Elementary School, WV

Relaxation

Water washing up on the shore, sunny and warm
Seagulls flying over, making noises
Waves crashing and washing away sand
Up above the shore, sun shining bright
No clouds in sight
My body full of warmth and it is peaceful
A gentle breeze through the trees
How long will I be there?
When will I be back?
I feel happy, calm, relaxed, warm, and peaceful
This place brings back fond memories
Relaxation, relaxation, relaxation.

Briana Sinclair, Grade 7
William Penn Middle School, PA

The Quiet Storm

Staring up at the midnight sky
Rain pouring down on me
Each individual drop is felt
As they fall from the unknown above
With closed eyes
I see your familiar face
And long to feel your touch once more
I'm hit with a hurricane of disbelief
You're gone…Forever
Coming to the reality that is
And the shock of what has been
I lay here grieving the loss of you
Hours of the night sneak past
I awaken from this deep slumber of thought and oblivion
Just as the sun is rising
Light envelops me in a blanket of warmth
And hugs me like an old friend
It is a new day

Kaylee Pofahl, Grade 8
Helen A Fort Middle School, NJ

My Favorite Place

The sun immediately warms my heart
the second it touches my face.

I'm in my place now.

Over the freeway sits the amazing city skyline
While driving along the streets, beautiful houses
Sit atop lush, beautiful gardens.

Outside my bedroom window,
Ripe fruits hang from their trees.

I'm surrounded by my family,
And every second, we're having a good time.

The beach has warm water
and a mountainous horizon.
The crashing waves take away my problems,
and the warm breeze takes away my words.

Now, this place is my paradise for two weeks.
One day, it will be my paradise
always.

Mary Mazur, Grade 9
Bishop Ford Central Catholic High School, NY

The Ugly Bud

She sits there, waiting, 'tis the season to bloom
But she hasn't yet sprung, so she suspects her doom.
As the other young stems, start to spread their petals,
She still must wait, for her bud is still settled.
She looks right beside her to see a beautiful flower
She feels so small, brittle, and without any power.
As days pass on, the lonely bud now awaits,
To become a hideous flower, a dreadful fate.
When that day came, when the other flowers were at high.
She had opened up her wings that were ready to fly.
Petals so lush and soft, just like a pillow,
So fluffy and white, just like a marshmallow.
Thy heart made of gold, her stem very green,
The once ugly bud, now an enchanting scene.

Nick Silva, Grade 8
Milford Middle East School, MA

Friends Forever?

I always thought we'd be friends forever…
So, why does it feel like we are slipping away?
You don't trust me anymore,
When it should be me not trusting you
You told my biggest secret
I've never opened my mouth on yours.
It feels like you're replacing me…
With something new and shiny
What happened to me thinking we'd be friends 'till the end?

Kristin Langford, Grade 7
Rock Mills Jr High School, AL

Boy, It's Cold Today

Boy, it's cold today,
The winter breeze is on its way!
What's there to do today?
I want to play, but I can't play.
It is really snowy outside,
But I'm grounded cause I lied.

Boy, it's cold today,
The winter breeze is on its way!
Outside it is dead silent,
All is calm and all is quiet.
Gather up with family and friends,
And have fun that never ends.

Boy, it's cold today,
The winter breeze is on its way!
Santa's sleigh is coming soon,
We open presents next day at noon.
Gifts there are for all to share,
Everyone will love and care.

Boy it's cold today,
The winter breeze is on its way!
Tushar Gupta, Grade 7
Westwood Jr-Sr High School, NJ

Waiting

Anxious to see what will happen
Time passing like the breeze
Patience wearing thin
Tick tock goes the clock as we
Wait
Miaya Torres, Grade 9
Highland Park Middle/High School, NJ

4 Seconds

4 seconds to live,
4 seconds to breathe.
Not enough time to do what I need.

A trip to the zoo,
And finding true love!
With only 4 seconds,
How can it be done!

4 seconds to run,
Right into the sun!
Trying to have fun,
With 4 seconds to spare!

Now my time has come,
4 seconds are gone,
4 seconds will come.
Then all will disappear!
Kyle Hosbach, Grade 7
Tohickon Middle School, PA

Three Stages

Tiny, squirmy, wondrous, unknown life forms.
Helpless from predators such as birds as well as humans.
Most are unable to live a full life.
But I know one caterpillar out of many who has made it this far.
She protects my tomatoes and is always around when I want her to be.
She is strong and intellectual although small and delicate.

But what is happening now?
She seems to be enclosed in some sort of tiny life sack.
How can one live with no food or air.
Wait! Something is happening again.
She seems to be getting released from her imprisonment.
Now she has wings.
She is fluttering about all orange and black.

Now I look back and realize how far she has come.
She came from being a gross looking bug
To a beautiful butterfly.
And here she comes.
When she lands, she is as light as a feather. Lighter.
I'm glad she remembers me.
It tickles as she lifts off and flies away.
Out of sight.
Ben Krenz, Grade 7
Palmyra-Macedon Middle School, NY

The Baby Girl

The baby girl was born. She was small and delicate.
Lightly colored with red on her cheeks. The baby girl was born.

She was brought home to lie in her bassinet.
She looked lovely. The baby girl was brought home.

They coddled the baby girl. Wrapped in pink blankets.
A sweet headband around her small head. The baby girl was coddled.

It was the baby girl's first birthday. She ate cake for her first time.
The birthday hat slid into her eyes. It was the baby girls first birthday.

A year later, the baby girl's second birthday. She tries to sing happy birthday.
She is greeted with gifts. It was the baby girl's second birthday.

It was the baby girl's third birthday. She has grown so big.
She is beautiful. It was the baby girl's third birthday.

It is now the baby girl's fourth birthday. She has grown to be sweet and innocent.
She enjoys her life, it's the baby girls fourth birthday.

I sit and admire the baby girl on her fourth birthday.
That baby girl is my little sister. I love that baby girl.
Jessica Martin, Grade 8
Westampton Middle School, NJ

Our Garden

The place where my grandma and I have a special bond,
Where sentimental value,
Grows deep within the roots,
Each and every petal becomes a special memory

The place where all my worries tumble away
With the rustling leaves,
Where being five years old felt like a big girl

My dirty knees become a custom,
While the spade becomes my best friend
The place where my grandma and I share a special bond,
Our Garden!

Tori Scott, Grade 8
Carthage Middle School, NY

How Do You Know When You Love Someone?

A love is the most beautiful creation
It's hard to believe sometimes it exists
Confused with liking or infatuation
Loving someone is more than just a kiss

Wasting time is just a confusing emotion
Cannot be seen, touched, or heard every day
Guilt's lush is lost far beneath this ocean
Running from truth, left with nothing to say

Let's hope, honestly, and appreciate
It is not perfect in this day so young
Put her needs first, I will accommodate
Never mix thoughts with feelings, notes are sung

Can't show them all of my care and sorrow
I will love them like there's no tomorrow

Alex Ressler, Grade 9
Unami Middle School, PA

My Love

I love this guy so much I don't know what to do
My mind was undecided, but my heart was always true
I still love you even after all the things you put me through
You make me smile continuously even when I'm feeling blue
The time that we shared I'll never forget
The way I am feeling about you I'll never regret
I've never felt this way
Neither have you I bet
I'll never let you go
Not just yet
I gave you my heart, right from the start
I hope that we never drift apart
When I'm with you I have so much pride
Too scared to show emotion, but my feeling I can't hide
I'll never leave you my heart is here to stay
I cherish every moment we share every single day

Gredesha Jones, Grade 9
Seminole County Middle/High School, GA

Ocean Blue

Ocean blue is the sunset outside my bedroom window
Ocean blue is how I feel when I lose someone I love
Ocean blue is what I taste when I drink salt water
Ocean blue is what I feel when I lose a competition
Ocean blue makes me want to go on a whale watch
Ocean blue is the ocean breeze
Ocean blue is serious and vibrant
Cool, thoughtful, nice
Ocean blue

Haley Miller, Grade 8
Gowanda Middle School, NY

The Minstrel's Song

The minstrel-boy has gone away to war,
To do his duty for country and for God.
The only possessions he carries are
His father's sword and his harp.
On his harp he plays,
And his voice sings away,
To a sad melody.
    "I am tired and weary,
    But I must fight on,
    'Til the Lord comes to call me away.
    In the morning it's bright
    And I continue to fight
    Until the day comes when I am laid down."
The minstrel was slain,
And moving with pain,
He tore his harp apart.
No one shall play those tunes again,
For those were the minstrel's songs.
He sang that sorrowful melody,
Until the day came for him to lie down.

Julia Buschmann, Grade 7
The Holy Name of Jesus Academy, NY

Unforgettable

She thinks of those moments over and over
She can't let go, the truth is in front of her.
It's been there all along, but she is blind.
She thinks and remembers "those moments were once mine"
She made a wrong decision, a mistake that she regrets.
It will follow her wherever she goes
Because she cannot forget
Yet, it's time to go on with her life
Because the past is over.
A memory that burns like the sun
An unforgettable mistake, a regret
A memory she'll never forget
Because she doesn't want to let go
And forget the moment that they met.

Francesse Mehu, Grade 9
Bishop Ford Central Catholic High School, NY

Realization

From the moment I was born,
They stayed, eager for my first breath,
From the day I began to talk,
They coaxed me to achieve my goal,

For all the times I fell,
They were my support,
For all the times I lost hope,
They urged me forward,

Through all the tough times,
They gave me a hand to hold,
Through all the tragedies,
They gave me a shoulder to cry on,

Even when I slept,
I knew there was someone caring,
So why, when I see fellow humans,
Hurt, damaged, and flustered,
Do I react with not even a tear?

Annemarie Chen, Grade 7
Anthony Wayne Middle School, NJ

My Notebook

The pages are full of writing,
And drawings of people fighting.
With scribbles here and there,
Writing this much is so unfair.

The cover is bent and torn,
For a new one I have sworn.
Most of the pages are crinkled,
but all of the page are wrinkled.

The wire is messed up and twisted;
I would never of missed it.
I wish I had a new notebook,
And now I'll begin to look.

Anastasia Kahlstorf, Grade 8
Garnet Valley Middle School, PA

Just Because I'm Young

Just because I'm young
Doesn't mean I act like a child
Doesn't mean I can't keep a secret
Just because I'm young
I'm not naïve
I'm not short
Just because I'm young
I can still be responsible
I can be serious
Just because I'm young
I can still stand on my own
I'm me and that's all I can be.

Ashley Bachkhaz, Grade 7
Anthony Wayne Middle School, NJ

Pets

Pets are the bright side of every day,
Their warming eyes will make you feel special in your own way.
Their presence and happiness brings joy to you,
The adventures in their faces makes you want to try something new.

When you have a lovely bond with your pet, your love is strong,
This love will tell you that it will last very long.
A new pet in the house will bring happiness to your heart,
Another reason to get a pet is because they are very intelligent and smart.

Pets are angels waiting to take you to heaven up above,
The most important part of them is their great and tender love.
The eyes of a pet tell to give some love up,
That is how I felt when I first saw my little pup.

Neal Selechnik, Grade 7
Westwood Jr-Sr High School, NJ

Rookie

STRIKE 2
The count is full
The batter touches his helmet pine tar smeared over the blue logo
Taking his time the batter steps into the white outlined box
The box that immobilizes him like a deer in the headlights
He touches the edge of his plate with his bat
The pitcher stares him down
Beads of sweat roll down his nose
Taking a look at first then second the pitcher goes into his windup
Clenching his bat he hears the catcher say
STRIKE 3
But the batter sustains his gaze
Already halfway through his windup, the pitcher kicks his leg up and jerks his head
The ball comes screaming towards the leather target
CRACK
The silence of the crowd is deathly
As the ball sails in the air towards the big green wall in left field
It intimidates the hitter, deciding if the ball, is a home run or a double
Finally the ball hits the edge of the wall
Floating in the air and suddenly a wind pushed the ball over the green wall
And into the fan's leather glove

David Richards, Grade 8
William Penn Middle School, PA

The Three Sisters

Once upon a day beyond the worlds away three sisters came into play.
Though days went on to days the sisters grew apart.
Once a triangle of praise has now become a haze.
Time and time they move until they settle into a groove.

When the sisters move on, the world goes away.
The *they* affect the *we* seen only by the eyes of me.
The sisters have to band
If only they would stand.

The world stands alone at night needing the sisters to unite.

Dominique J. Bell, Grade 9
Lee High School, AL

Independence Day

Your dim, cavernous mind
is a vast globe unpainted,
a virile beast dormant;
with immaturity it's tainted.

Intrigue has found the better of you;
with inquiries your mind is saturated.
You are now, at last, nascent,
with sciences you are infatuated.

Here is your stroke of success:
though what you have created,
your spark of genius,
has already been stated.

After this discovery,
you are no longer shrouded by the veil of naïveté.
No longer stained by the brush of stupidity;
the pains of Faraday's successes can now be alloyed.

For you did as he,
at a younger age;
thus, you — are superior.

Andrew Niess, Grade 8
Wissahickon Middle School, PA

Phrahgrai the Immortal Dragon

Existence of Phrahgrai much too much
Up stood Grath flail at hand
On he put his armor, bright and red
For ancient metal constructed it.

Vengeance seeking was the man
For this dragon had killed a friend
He charged Phrahgrai, flail raised high
Let out a bloodcurdling battle cry.

At memory sat his friend's face
His own well being forgotten
When flail impaled Phrahgrai's tail
Pleasure fell upon him.

The pleasure lasted momentarily
For Phrahgrai turned and lifted a forearm
Out shot tornado flame
That engulfed the mighty hero.

Now two friends sit in heaven
Looking down upon Phrahgrai
They are both happy now…
And Phrahgrai? He's hungry.

Brandon Herrington, Grade 7
Franklin Regional Middle School, PA

Riding from a Rainbow

Waves undulating in the salty sea air
Squished seashells beneath the toes
perched upon a rainbow boogie board,
the one with the elbow indents.
Hearing the rush of the blue water from behind
preparing for the worst
Afraid to drop beneath the salty sea
Zoom, the board zips off in front
Last inches of rainbow board in hand
murky water,
ice cold water.
Struggling for air, trying to reach the sun
that is as bright as a stadium light.
Shining sun is reached, gasping for air.
Trudging up the beach;
the slopping sand.
Only to see that no one noticed the fear,
despair, struggles,
That the rainbow board and I just went through.

Emily Drabeck, Grade 7
Trinity Middle School, PA

Publications of Two Minds

As the sunset, the moon arises
I raise my spectacles, and so I watch
A half lit Luna, and just one question
The reflections do not move, and so I starve
I'd write on my hand, my limited answers
Let the ink be absorbed, engraved in my knowledge
But ink I don't have, a hand is not present
My skin won't absorb, the reflections not move
As the sunset ends, the moon arises
I rest my head, and so I succumb
A full moon waiting, engulfed by the absence
A vivid illusion, my pen rests in place
I watch it rotating, and I simply stare
I do not reach for it, as if I would care
A few lines fly by, the clock hands stop
A reflex, I fix them, my pen rests in place
I dream all night, I wake up, forget them
I dream in spare time, I'm conscious, they're written

Katherina Gindinova, Grade 7
Intermediate School 239 Mark Twain, NY

A Blossoming Poem

Poetry is a flower,
Beginning with a seed in one's mind,
Sprouting from the ground onto paper.
Adorned by the leaves of stanzas,
Exuding fragrance of rhymes and rhythm,
Blossoming into a bright mellifluent verse,
Spreading joy to all who see it,
Bearing the fruits of inspiration,
And pollinating ideas to bloom again.

Archit Verma, Grade 8
Seven Bridges Middle School, NY

Giraffe

I'm getting dizzy
Climbing these spots,
Brown and black on a carpet of yellow.

Climbing every vertebrae,
Like they
Were only stairs.

The staircase never ends.
And to reach the top floor
Would hold great wonders.

Wheezing at the top
The view is limited,
For I am behind a tree
Which the giraffe finds to be
Very tasty.

Katie Talley, Grade 7
Yellow Breeches Middle School, PA

Place of Broken Woes

Forsaken girl with troubles many
Flees to find with angered fury
To a place where woes are broken
And sandbars leave the watcher looking
Ripples disturb the glossy lake
With serenity for a mere girl's sake
Who weeps in doleful gaze
As winds past in perfumed haze
To grant silent words unspoken yet
In hopes to comfort dreadful fret
Of an adolescent's mournful cries
Where on sand does she lie.

Emily Baer, Grade 9
Woodbridge Sr High School, VA

August

August flies in
With un-expectancy
It burns the ground
And up in the sky
It shimmers and sways
Until it leaves us all
Just as fast as it came
With an un-expecting bang
Gena Aiello, Grade 7
Anthony Wayne Middle School, NJ

Talent

Talent is unique,
It is a tough tornado,
It rarely arrives,
But when it does come along
It does so vigorously.
Timothy Ware, Grade 9
Unami Middle School, PA

We Love the Sun

Flowers are blooming
Bees are sipping nectar
The sun awakens
When the sun goes to bedtime
Moon takes substitute for the sun
The flowers won't get the sunshine they deserve
The flowers want it to be morning
If there's no sun, there are no flowers
No flowers, no bees, and then no honey for us to share
Flowers are cheering when sun's back
Is that why there's sunset because he doesn't like the flowers?
Guessing the flowers did nothing for the sun
Then depression comes on
The flowers die
We need the flowers desperately for energy but we still have the sun
Bees die, honey disappeared
The sun and flowers should make up
Are they even friends but the sun is so nice
The sun does everything for us like energy we deserve
But we don't do much for the sun
Does that mean our lives will disappear?

Lauren Grossman, Grade 8
C C A Baldi Middle School, PA

Angels Paint My Dreams at Night

I lay in bed, in peace at rest
I hear the angels sing
for every night as I sleep
angels paint my dreams

the angels come down
in robes of white
as typical angels do

they paint my sleeping mind
with billowing soft colors
like orange and pink and blue

they wrap my dreams
in soft white clouds
and send me drifting into the night

because my dreams
are painted with the hands of angels
and a hope for morning light

so as I drift to morning's break
my mind is wiped perfectly clean
for the hope of the angels tomorrow to come paint another dream.

Madison Knapp, Grade 7
Westwood Jr-Sr High School, NJ

I Miss You

I still can't believe you are so far away
After all this time, I still can't get over it
I know you're only a phone call away, but it's not the same
You used to be so close, but you went away
I want you to come back so badly,
But I know nothing I do or say will change this situation.
I just want to let you know that I've been missing you,
And I can't wait until the next time I see you
I love you always.

Lynn Buckvicz, Grade 9
Bishop Ford Central Catholic High School, NY

Uncle Mike

Uncle Mike
Hunting with me early in the morning,
Both us us clad in camo, toting guns through the fields.
His scratchy voice whispering, "There's a deer."
Green Arctic Cat quads, as green as grass,
Old Camaros and Chevelles,
Camping in the whole tri-state area,
John Deere tractors mowing the lawn.

Devon Hoskins, Grade 7
Trinity Middle School, PA

Blue Jays!

A single blue jay is standing guard,
Waiting for peanuts to be tossed in the yard.
When he spies them, he yells to the others.
Then they fight, like sisters and brother.
When all the peanuts are cleared from the yard,
They all run away except one, standing guard.

Holly Sofka, Grade 7
Mahanoy Area Middle School, PA

Opening Night

Silent confusion reigned.
Nervous eyes scanned the shadows.
Uneasy hands quivered.
Hushed preparation was being composed.
Suddenly, as if by magic, a perfect line formed.

One by one solemn figures filed onto stage,
Until lastly the conductor came.
Applause thundered from all directions like sirens,
Quickly modified into absolute tranquility.
Lights faded,
And it seemed Darkness had wrapped itself around the stage.

The musicians prepared for the moment.
Arms were raised and backs were straightened.
All eyes focused on one point.
Tension hung thick in the air like storm clouds.
With one movement of the conductor, music began,
Until you heard it — perfect harmony.

Brian Chin, Grade 9
White Station High School, TN

Kenya

K is for kind and I'm always on time.
E is for excellence because I am intelligent.
N is for nice because I always think twice.
Y is for yes because at sharing I try my best.
A is for attitude but I am not rude.

K eep in mind.
E ntertain everyone and get to know them.
N ever give up.
Y ou always stay ahead.
A ccept everyone in life.

K eep moving with a good life.
E nter things you know that's right.
N ever let someone upset you.
Y ield at things you think is wrong.
A ge is what you do so don't grow up too fast.

Kenya Turner, Grade 9
Seminole County Middle/High School, GA

Change

People change for the praise of others
People change to delight their mothers
People change because they don't like who they are
People change to shine like a star
People change to make a friend
People seem to change but just pretend
People change to be with someone they like
People change because they've found a new like
People change and later forget who they were
People change and life just becomes a big blur
People change to have a better life
People change to become man and wife
People change.

Michelle Sanchez, Grade 9
Bishop Ford Central Catholic High School, NY

What Friends Are

Friends are the ones who you can trust
The ones you can talk to
They are the ones you have
When you need a shoulder to cry on

They tell you the truth about what you do wrong
They are there to help you when you are in trouble
They are the ones you laugh and joke with

You should hold your friends close
They are some of the dearest people you have
Respect, care, and laugh with one another
You never know when you will need them the most

Sheela Fisher, Grade 8
Fairview Elementary School, NC

The Pak

Mom and Dad squeezed my hands tight as we pushed through the turnstile and the train was in sight.
There were hundreds of people all dressed in red all going to the "Pak," at least that's what they said.

Their shirts and hats gave it away, they talked funny, but the "Pak" was definitely Fenway.
So all together we rode on the "T," to think I was just seven and on my way to see Papi.

Just out of the subway, up ahead there it was, old red bricks and dull green metal and yet such a buzz.
Getting close wasn't easy, but we made our way, and with each step it felt more and more like my special day.

Through another turnstile my hands still held tight, but this time I was amazed at the sight.
I was in Fenway Park, a dream for someone who had never been, and soon I would see the guys battle for hopefully a win.

The Green Monster was really a wall, I guess because it was thirty seven feet tall.
And the scoreboard wasn't electric, it wasn't lit up, there were actually guys taking down numbers and putting them up.

In the eighth inning, the whole stadium sang a song so fine, I know it now, it's "Sweet Caroline."
These things I remember even more than the game, because Fenway Park is much more than a name.

I've gone back many times since, it never gets old, because there is always something new for my memory to hold.
They better never tear it down, I'll stand in front of the wrecking ball, 'cause Fenway Park should live forever and never ever fall.

Dean Badach, Grade 7
Westwood Jr-Sr High School, NJ

Rich Become Poor

When the rich become poor, and the poor become lost,
No one has a clue how much their lives really cost.
When spending becomes a job, and there is no cash to seek,
The cash in their wallets soon become too weak.
When they are taught money grows on branches, and learn they are working for leaves,
All you seem to hear are their sorrowful grieves.
When they finally learn that money isn't just paper used all the time,
Nothing is left in their wallets but a small lonely dime.

Nicole Tufaro, Grade 7
Thompson Middle School, NJ

Sound of a Free Man

'Twas not so long ago, as I can remember that my feet marched the walk, last year's September
An American rebel whose skin was white but for freedom, I was willing to fight
The hoses attacked night and day but our determined minds never gave way
"Equality! Equality!" we yearned but the stubborn whites had never learned
That integration was the only way to bypass the dark and dreary gray
Haze the troubled '60s brought as the battle for peace was constantly fought
The hatred killed as people cried but the need for justice never died
We dreamed of heaven, and breathed in hell as the weakening nation crumbled and fell
The love…absent; violence hung in the air the pain of evil was too much to bear
Drinks and drugs were an easy escape for the weak of the nation to blindingly take
If we were strong, unity would exist if we were strong, we would daily persist
A thing possible to pursue while our country waits for something new
A kind of change that must be seen before our country surrenders to green
From envy, hate, blood, and war a lifeless nation full of gore
I wished my country would come together so for peace, I wouldn't crave forever
My children need to know the truth, be able to forgive those like Booth
Acceptance of others is the ultimate way to reach the mountaintop far away
As a nation, we must see that this world is bigger than you and me

Tatiana Bowe, Grade 9
James Weldon Johnson Middle School, FL

Victorious — An Ode to Vikings

Trudging through the underbrush
charging over each rotting stump
through branches a many, plow and push
we rush and scream and stride and jump

Forests cleared, we were nearly dry
salty brine stung eyes of us
we roared to all who passed us by:
"Oh, we are victorious!"

Burst through the nearest door
of the nearest bar we could see
we wanted a feast and nothing more
of lamb and stew, of turkey and beef

We guzzled mead by the keg
slammed our flagons on makeshift tables
gurgling, giddy, drunk and we beg
ordered more ale of every label

No one cared about the time
or what would become of us
we roared to all who pass us by:
"Oh, we are victorious!"

Natalie Tessicini, Grade 8
Milford Middle East School, MA

Ignorance

Looking out of the window
Of the house that I am trapped inside,
I see the clouds of puffy white.
When they fall onto the harsh grass,
They will vanish into the sky.

When will I see the sun,
That calls out through the clouds that confine it?
It says to help, but our ears will be shut.
We will keep alive with ignorance,
And the clouds will continue to fall.

The window glass is breaking in two.
Oh, we will see a collision occur.
The glass was always shining, obeying the sun.
It cried out, but everyone was deaf.
They will run away, to avoid the pain.

As the sun continues to glow,
We will continue to live our lives
Of apparent happiness.
But the sun will die, and we will learn
That ignorance is not a virtue.

Emily Indig, Grade 9
Manalapan High School, NJ

The Unbreakable Tree

So firm and deeply rooted,
So pretty and gentle,
So strong during storms and trunk made of metal.
The leaves and branches are tossing and turning in the wind.
As the wind blows, the clouds are passing.
The tree is just sitting there,
Giving off oxygen allowing us to live.
The bark is steel, but the pulp is so soft.

Anthony Payne, Grade 7
Ocean City Intermediate School, NJ

A Rainbow of Truth

Oh, what does it take? I ask this out loud.
Uniqueness and change, I can hear it call.
And the choices we make; will we be proud?
Yearning and churning, deep inside us all.

Life is fragile and one must care for it,
And if only everyone could see.
Then maybe the world would be different.
And innocence would remain, finally.

Conformity is an evil indeed,
A spark that leads to hatred in this place.
I think: is it something we really need?
In the end, difference shan't be erased.

I am my own person, this I do know.
And with this awareness, I will let it show.

Lauren Handley, Grade 9
Unami Middle School, PA

Recall School Blues

It's time to start a new chapter.
We were fools then,
but it's time to get past that.
We played our roles and kept it cool,
stayed our ground and left a bold memory
Reminisce about the good days
and the bad ones too
Make friends, make enemies.
Change is for the better,
though it makes you feel worse
The world got turned upside down
and left a mark of identity
Never forget who was here first,
leaving a path for the next generation
It was fun, it was horrible
But we made it through.

Remember, remember
the 5th of September
when we invaded the school,
and changed it forever.

Madison Johnson, Grade 8
St Joseph the Carpenter School, NJ

Night and Day

His room is a pig pen,
and he thinks he's the
coolest thing in the world.
He treats me like I am six
and doesn't know when
to leave me alone.
The night owl takes
as long as a girl
to get ready
to surf
all summer
or play
ice hockey
all winter.
He is night.
I am day.

Taylor Schreffler, Grade 8
Beacon Middle School, DE

Watch Your Back

Wind
It's quiet yet very loud
It sneaks up behind you
Whispers in your ear
It is always when you least expect it
Wraps you up inside of it
It hugs you tighter than ever
Wind is sneaky
It will always catch up with you
No matter what
You better watch your back
Because that wind is always there
Megan Macchione, Grade 7
Westwood Jr-Sr High School, NJ

Football/Golf

Football
Dashing, thrilling
Throwing, catching, running
Football, helmets, golf ball, clubs
Swinging, chipping, putting
Skillful, moderate
Golf
Shaun Kotoski, Grade 7
Most Blessed Sacrament School, MD

Boys/Girls

Boys
Cute, loud
Talking, moving, playing
Love to play sports, love the color pink
Bothering, annoying, loving
Spoiled, pretty
Girls
Jon Carlos Fermin, Grade 7
St Agatha School, NY

Accept Me

I look around…
Cascading below me, there are many colored fish, like the rainbow.
I slowly rotate my body to look up.
Bubbles escape from my mouth through my face mask,
Looking like jellyfish gliding through the clear-blue water.

Above me, I see the crisp colors of sky blue and cloud white,
Overtaking my mind with all the wonders of the world.
People dream about traveling to the mysterious depths of the ocean…
But that is all behind me,
For that I have already accomplished.

Some people wish to fly,
Some people crave for fame…
But all I want is simple,
Please accept me…for me.

Alyssa Gogel, Grade 9
Unami Middle School, PA

Baseball's Most Nervous Moment

The wind up
The crowd went silent
We hoped that if the Yankees got a hit the Met fans wouldn't get violent
Here came the ball so fast it sounded like a Porsche speeding past
As you watched it into the catcher's glove it almost gave you whiplash
Everyone knew that it was ball four
The bases were loaded and now one run scored
The game was over
Officially done
Jeter had scored the winning run

Chris Cofrancesco, Grade 7
Westwood Jr-Sr High School, NJ

The Akzia*

Shoving, pushing
"OUCH!"
"Shhh."
The sound
of heavy boots,
heavy guns,
heavy, cold-blooded hearts.
Sweat pouring down.
Don't cry…
Screams, cries coming from outside.
Please don't cry…
SLAM! The door closed.
It's over…the akzia of the week is over.
How many more Jews? 10, 20, 50? Maybe more?
I have to survive. Survive the grief, the torment, the evil,
Survive the devil's work.
But I know, that when this is over, there won't be much of us left.
Like a tiger, on its way
to extinction.

Kayleigh Kirkpatrick, Grade 7
Carthage Middle School, NY
*Inspired by the book "Destined to Live"

An Ode to My Muse

I stare at this blank page wondering what to do
I wonder what my muse is up to
She has left me behind and has apparently forgotten
Something most important that had left me loose like cotton
I feel no inspiration that she was to bring
Nothing at all not even a ding
What to write on this empty page at hand
I don't even know what to plan
I wait and wait for my muse to return
I even start to feel concern
Where has she gone to, my lady of inspiration
I don't think muses can take a vacation
I glance at the page with a saddened feel
I feel shocked to what is revealed
An ode to her, my precious muse
Oh what wonderful, joyous news!
She has been here all along
Helping me to write this beautiful song
Thank you my muse as I dedicate this to you
Now I am ready to start fresh and brand new!

Kya Gibson, Grade 8
Intermediate School 383 Philippa Schuyler, NY

Raindrops

R aindrops fall so very far before reaching their destination.
A ll its elegance so intense, and such a mysterious finish.
I t takes so long for its creation.
N ot one, not half, but all of them.
D oes it know before its finish, its impending doom.
R ainbows result from this beautiful precipitation.
O n anything visible do they fall.
P laying outside ceases because of them.
S o miraculous yet causes so much discomfort.

Jeremy Reisman, Grade 9
White Station High School, TN

Chances

Everything you say or do
Whether you're laughing or screaming.
I am always there for you,
When I'm awake and when I'm dreaming.

No one else could take your place;
I can't stand to watch you go.
I will always see your face
Because in my head, I know.

I love the way we stay up late.
Why don't you say what's on your mind?
The way you laugh at your mistakes,
That just proves that love isn't blind.

These are more than just passing glances
Because I'm taking all the chances.

Brittany Purvis, Grade 9
Elmira Christian Academy, NY

I Too Have A Dream*

I too have a dream about American's future.
Healthy living, peaceful neighborhoods,
quiet corner stores,
more home schooled kids, and gun control.
Drug usage out and alcohol not around.
And music you can understand the words to.
I too have a dream about American's future.
We can all make it real if we just work together.
Let us lift up our voices and sing!
We know we can.
We know we can.
We know we can.
Thank God almighty, we know we can!

Lydia Johnson, Grade 8
Wise and Pure Jr High School, PA
*In honor of Martin Luther King, Jr.

Hometown

The sun comes up after every night,
To fill the day with joy and light.
The sun came up to shine on my hometown,
The sound of children laughing all around.
I visited my childhood house not wanting to say "Goodbye,"
I visited my old schools, middle and high.
The joy in my heart could never go down,
From the feeling I get when I visit my hometown.
My body is elsewhere, but my heart still fights,
To go back to my home where they treat me right.

Stephen Lundy, Grade 9
Lee High School, AL

Conflicts

As time passes
many hopeless things would change,
where everyone are friends,
no one is fighting.
You're not judged for how you are,
or what race you are from.
Everyone wouldn't be full of hate,
because others aren't like them,
People wouldn't be killed,
because of how they are
Many see no hope,
but as time passes.
You'll see different people helping each other
Not caring if the other person is the same race.
As they put their differences aside,
less fights would happen.
And stop to see through the eyes of each other.
See all the pain they go through
because of how they are.

Emily Martinez, Grade 9
Colonia High School, NJ

Free

Giving up the life
The things that I once knew
Letting go of my past
It's just so hard to do.

I try to forget
And try something new
I seem to regret
Everything that I do.

The boy that I love
Appreciates me
But when push leads to shove
There's things he can't see.

I hold back the feelings
I have in my heart
He still won't let me fall apart
He sets me free…

Veronica Cutler, Grade 9
Kittatinny Regional High School, NJ

everybody wears a mask

the people in the world
scared, sad, grumpy, mean,
gangster, beach boy
all lies i say
the world is halloween
all 365 days
every year
people need to grow up
be who you really are
don't be scared
so what if they judge
they're the scared ones
so be true

Robbie Hazel, Grade 8
Beacon Middle School, DE

Graduation

The day is really going fast
It's time to forget all of our past.
The teachers will be missing us
Our parents will be kissing us.

On the stage all ready to go
Our footprints left out in the snow.
Our world is starting as we know it
We're moving our stuff out bit-by-bit.

Entering the big world unknown
Ready to get our first bank loan.
Graduating isn't easy
Leaving all my friends behind me.

Krista O'Boyle, Grade 7
Mahanoy Area Middle School, PA

1960s*

1960 comes and goes with ax handles and mockingbirds,
With sit-ins in Greensboro, Mr. Ed and the Flintstones
Peace, freedom, and free love.
Let the people sing their song, let their voices drown the world!
Vietnam calls us in 1961 like a mother with open arms, we can't resist her pull
Hello Cuban Missile Crisis, Goodbye Norma Jean,
It's 1962 and Warhol pops on the scene
1963 brings tidings of silent grief
When John Fitzgerald Kennedy leaves gifts we must receive
An invasion of music our civil rights are ours
Baby boomers are legal '64 hardly sour
1965 there's rioting in Watts
Montgomery makes us cry our cause it seems lost
Enter 1966 we want our rights N.O.W.
Black Power raises its fist and Twiggy storms the world
Here comes 1967 with the summer of love
Ending war would be heaven, so we say to all
Hope seems lost in '68 with Bobby and MLK
But we don't lose faith we've seen the promised land
Woodstock is the place to be
That's one small step for man the moon is so sweet to see from 1969!

Juliette Holthaus, Grade 8
James Weldon Johnson Middle School, FL
*To the tune of "Across the Universe"

The Last Flight

It was a sunny day out,
and suddenly the courageous pilot
Alex Maximum found himself lost over
Enemy territory during World War II
He was low on fuel.

The bright sun disappeared from his face
Two Mig-15s on his tail.
They flew through his formation of B-24s that have weathered every impact.
The Migs with guns blazing separated him from the group.
His gunners fired back and blew one out of the sky.

But the second came from their 3 o'clock
the impact was so great the plane shook
and the tail broke free.
The plane spiraled earthward
with only a few hundred feet between him and the ground.

His gunners bailed.
He kept the plane up just long enough to save them, but couldn't save himself.
He was never heard from again.
His body found cold and dead.
With the victory he has won.

Gordon Sabol, Grade 8
Westwood Jr-Sr High School, NJ

Change

It's funny how things change
And how it worked out this way.
You still don't realize it was you
Who made it this way.
Most likely things will never go back —
Back to the way they were before
Like those memories that I still adore,
When everything was so simple
Like black and white, everything was so right!
So maybe I'm still that fool
If I keep reminiscing about you.
And maybe you weren't the one who changed
And maybe you're still the same
But something seems to have changed.
Maybe it's I who has changed
And no longer look at things in the same way.

Tiffany Marshall, Grade 9
Bishop Ford Central Catholic High School, NY

One Window

One window is all I need to see new things
To feel the warm sun
To see the blue sky
One window is all I need to see a new opportunity
To take it
And make it mine
One window is all I need to make something out of life
To build a new world
One window is all I need to be a better person
To change the world, to make a difference
One window is all I need to be me

Dana Avolanti, Grade 7
Anthony Wayne Middle School, NJ

Drums

Some kids are smart, they got the brain
Some kids are lame, they're all too plain
But not me, I got something more
Making music from the roof to the floor
Drums is the elixir that fills my soul
Makes me complete, makes me whole
To express myself, this is the way
Forget the world and just play
My heart's thumping makes the beat
Always moving, hands and feet
When I play, I just want to be heard
My drums speak for me, every word
Life's full of happiness, tears, joys
Pick up my sticks to make some noise
Drums and life aren't so different to me
We all got something that sets us free

Fabio Recine, Grade 9
Bishop Denis J O'Connell High School, VA

Midnight

In this dark room,
The only light, a candle,
Its flame licks the air.
I watch it leap and jump,
While the wax races down to the metal taper holder.
And the shadows dance on the wall.
A loud clang is heard. It echoes throughout the house.
My gaze is quickly taken to the source,
A grandfather clock.
Its hands, both rest together at the highest point.
Midnight.

Molly Yanchuck, Grade 7
Mahanoy Area Middle School, PA

Dreams

A dream is a wish,
Something that we must work for.
We may face obstacles,
We may encounter life changing decisions,
But in the end dreams are simply part of life.
They do not always work out how we want them to —
Good or bad,
Amazing or dull.
But it is not the dream that makes a difference in our life,
It is how we make the dream come true,
It is the strength we build,
The courage we strive for,
The love we earn,
And the determination in our hearts.

Mikaela O'Neil, Grade 8
Inter-Lakes Jr High School, NH

Daniel Paille

He passes the puck
Protects it well
Instigates others
And lays the lumber as well
His name is Daniel Paille
And he is the best
Every game he passes the test
He dangles the goalies
And gets assists
He comes down the ice
He gives a pass
For the goal that is the last
They celebrate a goal
That was very much needed
To give credit to a man who is not conceited
He never stops working
Never misses a chance
To live up to his potential
To be the very best
And remember the name Daniel Paille
Because Rick Jenneret will be saying it for a while

Anthony Yarussi, Grade 7
St Stephen's School, NY

Water

Inside this water,
There is a drink for the thirsty,
Hope for those stranded,
A source of life for all.
Without water we could never exist.

Shannon Boswick, Grade 7
Christ the Teacher Catholic School, DE

My Underground Trail

My underground trail,
It's my hide-out,
It's reality bail,
When there's a train,
In my underground trail,
I don't follow the light,
It leads me to a place,
Where I don't fit in,
With what I'm supposed to feel,
If I bring a red rose,
It would shatter to pieces,
Because it's real,
To be in my underground trail,
You have to be unrealistic,
And stand out or you will shatter,
Stand out or you will be nothing.

Karen Desir, Grade 7
John F Kennedy Middle School, FL

What I Left Behind

I look back slowly
Briefly glimpsing the confusion
Before turning away
I should not have looked back
I should have kept on walking
But my heart won't allow it
My friends and family all gone
Deep inside I can still hear them
Telling me to keep moving on
And not miss what I left behind

William Nuckols, Grade 7
Carson Middle School, VA

A Single Flower

I am one flower
in a huge garden.
My roots extend as they search
randomly for water
to help me grow.
My petals whistle a sweet melody
as the cool wind blows through.
My thorns are cool to look at
but yet, painful to the touch.
These are all parts that make
the plant of my life.

Max Rundgren, Grade 7
Ocean City Intermediate School, NJ

You and Me

I need you more than you need me
I want you with more passion than you will ever see
and the more I need and the more I want you the harder I will die
Cause I see you with her, I see that you think you need her
you think you want her, but can't you see
That you need me, that you want me
that we are meant to be
you and me
forever in peace, baby you inspire me
to be the way I wanna be
No fakes, all flaws
But you don't care, because you love me
as me
no one else but me…
But there is someone else
    You
I want you in my life for life
cause without you I am…incomplete

Ashley Green, Grade 8
Milford Middle East School, MA

My Future

They say it is in my hands.
But what if I don't want to hold anything just yet?
I haven't made up my mind.
So quit asking me questions.
I like lots of things.
Photography.
Environmentally friendly stuff.
Fashion.
Business and marketing.
Hey, maybe I'll be an eco-friendly designer who markets with photography.
But this is a big decision.
I mean, I have a general idea,
But my mind changes like the weather.
So get over it.
I'm not ready to decide,
What I want to do,
For the rest
    Of
        My
        Life.

Kellie Walsh, Grade 8
Beacon Middle School, DE

Video Games

I have a favorite hobby, they say I play too much.
The only problem is, sometimes my hand hurts from the controller being in my clutch.

I think I am an expert, I beat almost every game,
And if they had one, I know I'd make the gamers hall of fame.

Doesn't matter Wii, Xbox, or DS,
To me they are all the best!

Steve Walinski, Grade 7
Depew Middle School, NY

Inside a Cloud

Inside a cloud, such a heavenly sight,
are minuscule shimmers of vapor and light.
Forever they dance, water and air,
together they form a wondrous pair.
Today they shall move as never before,
cannot be explained, but cannot be ignored.
Forth they will go, away from this place,
leaving the sky with not but a trace.

Christine Leonard, Grade 7
Grace Lutheran School, FL

Lovely Days Living at Lake Erie

The sun shines bright on a relaxing beach
With infinite water all out ahead
The sand as hot as fire or as cold as ice cream
And the smell of a storm blowing in the wind

The taste of cool water slips into the mouth
The sound of splashes of water surrounds
From waves, from swimming, from walking about
In the water of Lake Erie this all can be found

The waves of Lake Erie attack with much zeal
Or calm little ripples crawling up the sand
Body surfing waves find great appeal
And tubing and kayaking are rather grand

The glistening diamond that is Lake Erie
I enjoy being there for the time that I get
The best part about it what I say finally
I spend it with family and I like that every bit

Ryan W. Matzke, Grade 9
Maple Point Middle School, PA

Why Did I

I was sitting on a tree, mentally
staring at the world below me,
thinking about the past and how
it went so fast. You don't know
what it's like to be left out,
you don't know what it's like to be
on the road with no friends on the
outside looking for happiness.
Why did I have to feel this way,
why did I have to feel so down and
lonely. Slowly I get up and pray,
hoping for a lovely day, looking
outside to see the sun, looking for
a day of fun. Why did I have to
be so sad when I could have been
so glad. Looking for friends I once
had until I met you. My day of
happiness finely came, because I met you
BEST FRIEND.

Danielle Boldt, Grade 7
Depew Middle School, NY

Thanksgiving

T asty desserts are made.
H appy faces fill the room.
A turkey is being carved into delicious layers.
N eighbors and family all get together,
K nives and forks for everyone.
S oft music is playing.
G ravy is passed around the table.
I ce-cold glasses clink together.
V arious pies are waiting to be eaten,
I n many different flavors.
N ew memories are made;
G ive thanks to everyone!

Taylor Stucchio, Grade 7
Unami Middle School, PA

Strength

Lord You are my soul
You are my air I breathe
You are my desire in life
You are my boldness
You are my holiness
You are my kindness
You are my calmness
You are my righteousness
You are my taste of food
You are my touch in feeling
You are my shield from hurt
You are my strong tower
You are my fighter
You are my lawyer
You are my desire
You are my soil
You are my former
You are my guider
You are my strength.

Lapoloean Washington, Grade 8
Seminole County Middle/High School, GA

Neighborhood Watch

Looking out the window on a warm summer day
All the kids are outside getting ready to play
I'm inside all alone, all by myself
All I can do is look at the pictures on my shelf
The kids outside having so much fun
I should do my homework because I have a ton
They hit the ball and WHACK!
The ball came flying up and CRACK!
My window shattered and glass broke
And they all laughed like it was a joke
So I got my paintball gun and pegged them all
Then one by one they began to fall

Alyssa Eckhardt, Grade 9
Colonia High School, NJ

Glittering Like a Thousand Mirrors
The beach is the place where I want to be,
Waves booming constantly throughout the day,
Swooping seagulls steal snacks,
People in the shade of umbrellas,
The hot sand oozing out from in between my toes,
Swimmers bobbing up and over the towering waves,
The sun blazing down upon us,
Random patches of clouds every now and then passing by providing relief from the sun,
Beach planes humming along flying their colorful advertisements,
Water lapping up onto the sand,
Glittering like a thousand mirrors,
The waves swooshing, swaying, splashing,
All that I know is that I will be back tomorrow,
There is nothing like a perfect beach day.

Daniel Kraus, Grade 7
William Penn Middle School, PA

Slipped
I wish I never dropped the ball
I could've had it all
I almost got the opportunity
to taste the sweetness of victory;
My team was down and I was up;
I ran forward and made a cut
Went past the safety and I was on my way
but then I slipped and felt dismay
My team was yelling and I grew angry then
asked the coach to put me back in
I heard hike then I made a dash,
I didn't slip and made it pass
I saw the ball in the air
I leaped up and everyone was scared
But then I felt something in my hands and then I looked down and the happiest moment of all,
I was in the end zone with the ball
I was so happy I almost did a flip;
then I realized I had to go to Dick's and buy new cleats so I didn't slip.

Marc Bethge, Grade 7
Depew Middle School, NY

Afraid of Love
Why yes, the word itself sends shivers through our spines
Isn't that being afraid of love?
Parents don't allow their kids to go out until they're old and mature enough
Isn't that being afraid of love?
What about shaking when you hear that someone has a crush on you?
Isn't that being afraid of love?
Being too scared to tell the person that you like about your innermost feelings for them
Isn't that being afraid of love?
Having butterflies in your stomach and your face gets red as an apple when you see that one special person
Isn't that being afraid of love?
A lot of people think of love as a beautiful, divine emotion, and I can agree with that
But most of the time, it's not like that in reality
It takes all your strength and courage to be able to face love
Love is that powerful and frightening, huh?

Clarissa Suparman, Grade 7
Pine-Richland Middle School, PA

Shy

Just because I can be shy
Doesn't mean I think I'm better
Doesn't mean I don't like you
Doesn't mean I don't care

Just because I can be shy
Doesn't mean I don't think about raising my hand
Doesn't mean I don't know the answer
Doesn't mean I'm stupid

Just because I can be shy
Doesn't mean the personality is dry
Doesn't mean I'm boring
Doesn't mean I'm not fun

Just because I can be shy
Doesn't mean I'm always shy
Doesn't mean I never talk
Doesn't mean I'm never loud

Just because I can be shy — try to get to know me better

Erika Pianin, Grade 7
Anthony Wayne Middle School, NJ

The World

The world would be a better place
If there were no killers and we were safe.
I would guide and guard people through the night
And protect them until the sky is bright.
The world would be a better place
If people in the world could see each other's beautiful face.
Everyone is beautiful it's true you see.
Take a look at a person like you and me.

India Pickren, Grade 8
Seminole County Middle/High School, GA

unloved

who will love the little girl who is feeling unloved
they say she bad all she need is a hug
who will find the little girl who's lost and all alone
she's looking for a mom she can call her own
who will accept the little girl who is feeling left out
no true friends no nothing all she has is doubts
who will tell the little girl that she is worth it
who will heal da pain cause she is hurting
who will cry for the little girl and catch her tears
she been crying alone all these years
what you blind need some glasses to see
that the little girl is exactly me
so love me please tell me you will
only love can heal what needs to be healed

Tashmere Fisher, Grade 8
Pineland Learning Center, NJ

Anger

I own the stars in the sky
I fueled the serpent in the Garden of Eden
My name is anger, pain
Bad seeds I plant in
I burn the feeling hope yet I fuel the emotion hate
I am the key dish on the platter of the Devil's plate
To disease, torture, pain I'm no stranger
I'm a monster hatred anguish and pain it's me anger

Titus Jones, Grade 7
Perquimans County Middle School, NC

Warm Summer Magic

The air is thick.
The breeze is warm.
The blanket that wraps itself around the sky
is studded with the brightest diamonds the gods can offer.
Her heavy hair dances gaily around her bright face, beckoning.
Her feet soar and leap over the soft grass,
leading her body further and further from
the cold that calls itself home.
With one last leap, she doesn't come back down.
Or look back.
Over the trees.
Over the cold.
Into the warmth.
Into the black abyss of the night.
With an echoed giggle,
and a twinkle into the black,
it's silent,
and all is still
on this warm summer's night.

Sydni Schiavone, Grade 9
Holley Sr High School, NY

When There Is No Going Back

What do you do when there is no going back
to being girls and boys?
What do you do to make time last
before packing away all your toys?
The clock keeps ticking your time away
until you will be young no more.
And you are trying to keep all this time
because you don't want to grow up anymore.
The transition between being a child and a young adult
is already a hard one to make without having to say goodbye
to friends moving far, far away.
So what do you do when there is no going back,
and when your time is running out?
How do you make the time you have left last,
when there is no time left to count?
You wanted to grow up when you were young
now you just want to be a kid.
Did your time seem to go by super fast?
I know mine sure did.

Victoria Fulfer, Grade 8
Yellow Breeches Middle School, PA

Picture

You put me in a frame
Where I don't always stay
I can be wild and crazy
I travel in your wallet
So you can show me off
To your family and friends
These memories that you keep with you
Will never end
You may love me or hate me
And I may or may not always be with you
But you will always remember
The good time you had!

Valerie Gottlieb, Grade 8
Covenant Life School, MD

My Fishing Pole

My fishing pole is my companion
through thick and thin
bending and flexing
under weight of a fish.
When we accomplish
the fish of the day
we go back to rest
for that day.

Griffin McDermott, Grade 7
Brielle Elementary School, NJ

Sizes

It may be just me,
maybe it's them.
They tell me, "No more!"
'cuz I'm too big, too little,
or even too thin!

To me it doesn't matter,
size that is.
To me it's a number,
why judge by this?

Being too thin can cause problems
or even extreme sickness.
Instead of being thin,
I'd rather have some thickness.

Ashlee Spencer, Grade 8
KIPP Academy Lynn Charter School, MA

Freedom

Thanksgiving
church bells ringing
pizza
blue sky on a sunny day
video games

Bradley Gill, Grade 7
Madisonville Middle School, TN

The Void

From long before the clock struck ten,
We knew the words to say.
But the clock kept ticking melodically
With every passing day.

The words grew thin and dreary,
Like the trunk of a withering tree.
They began to blow right past the ear,
Like the wind that carries its leaves.

So the hands on the clock passed eleven,
And our time grew stressed and tense.
And all the love that once was there
Has never been there since.

And you grew old and left me here
To sit and wonder why,
Why things became so miserable
And why you said goodbye.

But the clock still hasn't hit the twelve,
And the hands are moving slow,
So maybe we can fill this void
And allow our love to grow.

Nathaniel Lamkin, Grade 8
Masconomet Middle School, MA

Freedom

Tastes like a fresh salad
Sounds like birds chirping
Smells like cold milk
In the bright sunshine
With a nice warm blanket

Michelle Umphrey, Grade 7
Madisonville Middle School, TN

The Story of My Life

There is a part of me that's black.
I don't get along easy
Like two peas in a pod.
Get angry easily
People don't know how to stop
Me.

There is a part of me that's white.
Everyone thinks I am nice,
But people think too much.
They try to give me ice
People pay to do too much.
I am too nice to all my friends.
I am too kind to people around
Me.

Jacob Teates, Grade 8
Hopatcong Middle School, NJ

Black Angel

I live for the darkness,
My soul has been sold,
I no longer find joy,
My happiness old,
My body is weak,
I don't know myself,
My life is bleak,
I'm all alone,
In this big world,
I have meaning no more.

I live for the darkness,
My purpose is gone,
My only life is learning the tricks,
Of the Black Angel,
The angel of abyss,
The angel of sorrow,
Of death and hate,
The angel of darkness,
Is what I have become,
I am myself no more.

Anna Lier, Grade 8
Lumpkin County Middle School, GA

Heaven

I may not have wings
I may not have a halo
The world may not be the best
My days may not be the brightest
But even in my worst days
Having you by my side
Is like being in heaven

Melisa Matus, Grade 9
Miami Beach Sr High School, FL

Truth

The truth can hurt you,
But it can also make your day,
I thought so hard,
But never thought it would,
End this way.
The truth can,
Burn a hole
In your heart,
Or it can sew it back together,
It depends who told you,
Or how you take it,
It can,
Make you
Or
Break you,
But don't let it get to you...

Alexa Farner, Grade 7
Gowanda Middle School, NY

Mom
Moms are here
Moms are there
Some moms are looking down at us from the sky
Other moms don't get a chance to say goodbye
Days fly by
Before you know
It's time to let your daughter go
Don't be sad, you still have Dad
Be glad for all the times we've had together
Whether they were happy or sad
Some were even bad
I love you so much
Words can never describe
Lets keep the mother-daughter vibe!

Happy Mother's Day Mom!

Tayler Myers, Grade 9
Melbourne Central Catholic High School, FL

The Young
For some young people life is like a song,
waiting to be sung.
others it's a game,
waiting to be lost or won.
In both cases there are different outcomes,
but there are ways that you should live your life,
some fun, some serious.
But overall make sure you use every minute of your life,
because you only get one!

Bridget Fay, Grade 7
Nativity of Our Lord School, PA

Release into the Wind
Release it all out, into the wind,
All your colors, with their charm and grace,
Give your humid drops away,
And don't hide your true face.
Walk alone down that slippery path,
Run away from all the hate,
Don't tell them where you're going,
Tell them just that you'll be late.
Seep into that silence,
And blend in with those gray-colored walls,
Shut your eyes and ignore,
All their tales, so dull and tall.
Seek that truth, beyond their words,
Do not accept what is not right,
And make a shell of memories,
To help you survive the night.
Be what you have always been,
Do not bring out the hatred,
Sing your song, your melody,
And let your mind flow kindred.
Release into the wind.

Muna Al-Safarjalani, Grade 8
Alabama School of Fine Arts, AL

The Crash
Used to boost U.S. security
Billion dollar aircraft
Bat-like, stealthy, aerodynamic multi-role bomber
B-2 plunged to the ground
Bang!
From simple mechanical failure
Smoke billowing from the wreckage
People in tears
First to crash of 21
No injuries on the ground
Or damage to buildings
Both pilots in good health
Flying again next week

Steven Clark, Grade 9
Unami Middle School, PA

The Journey
Seeds!
I will wander no more —
as a budding child of the world,
putting down my roots in the nourishing earth,
planning for my growth in the future,
creating a solid foundation.

Leaves!
Stretching and grabbing at the gleaming sun,
learning as I sprout,
going out of my way —
to survive drought and storm,
transforming my face as seasons collide.

Flowers!
Living in bloom,
I stand radiant and tall,
expressing my love in colors,
knowing…hoping…wishing
my children will be wise —
as wise as I.

Alexis Gros, Grade 7
Ocean City Intermediate School, NJ

Friendship
Friendship towards another person is a feeling of
Warmth…
Truth…
And happiness.
A friend is someone who is always there for you.
They are there to catch you when you fall.
To keep your secrets,
And wipe your tears.
Do you know who your real friends are??

Amanda Borner, Grade 7
Gowanda Middle School, NY

My Diary

My diary,
A place for sorrow
A place for happiness
A place to hide
A place to seek for answers
A place to cry
A place to laugh
A place to curse your enemies
A place to unite
A place for fantasies
A place for the real world
A place for weakness
A place for strength
A place for knowledge
A place for imagination
What else can I say, for which the diary,
Is a place to write a life story.

Onyinyechi Obelle, Grade 8
Hackensack Middle School, NJ

Baseball

As I get hit in the face with a stick,
I fly in the air and glide.
I see a glove in my way — Smack!
I get thrown back,
as I hear you're out!

Frank Orellana, Grade 7
St Agatha School, NY

Storm Upon the Heart

Awakened at midnight,
by the crashing of thunder.
Laying by my window,
I started to wonder.

The streak of light,
clashing through the rooted trees.
They say it's a storm,
But beyond is the feeling of ease.

Earth is the heart.
Raindrops are tears.
Lightning is the break,
causing love to disappear.

The heartbreak,
leading to much despair.
The gloom,
causing young hearts to tear.

But at the end of the storm,
there's always a rainbow.
The sun shines brightly.
The heart lets itself go.

Agatha Ventura, Grade 9
Western High School, FL

Nonconformity

I do not change for them
For they are pure fools, all trying to be analogous
Each person is unique, and should not be the same, I am what I am

For this they only laugh and squirm
And do not see, how foolish they really are, similar to one, huge cloud of gas
I do not change for them

Everyone wearing the same jeans and playing the same game
Everyone almost looking like one, single, moving mass
Each person is unique, and should not be the same, I am what I am

They all circle around me, the only rational man, in an effort to condemn
They try to denounce me, and to no avail, I surpass
I do not change for them

I refuse to change, and they make me scram
They acted as though they were the outclass
Each person is unique, and should not be the same, I am what I am

The next day they come back, their fad now quondam
Everything was over, including their sass
I do not change for them
Each person is unique, and should not be the same, I am what I am

Saiganesh Ravikumar, Grade 7
Anderson Middle School (P.S. 334), NY

It Seemed Every Day Was Sunny

I'm realizing how much I've grown up, I went from a kid's 13 shoe to a woman's 7
I don't listen to lullabies, I choose my own music
I wear matching clothes, no more combos of stripes and polka dots
It seemed every day was always sunny
I don't chew Bubbalicious anymore, I chew Orbit and Stride
I wear real jewelry, not plastic
I miss the outdoor girl I was
When kick ball and hide and seek were a daily routine
It seemed every day was always sunny
When I pretended to be an Indian, my name was always Tiger Lilly
When I pretended to camp out at 12 noon
When I pretended to run away from home and really just hide in the closet
It seemed every day was always sunny
My nails are still painted, my hair is still golden
My eyes are still hazel, my smile is not gone
It seemed every day was always sunny
I'm accepted for who I am, not who I was
But I wish I could go back and relive the girl I was, everything was so simple
It seemed every day was always sunny, and now I think to myself
In another few years, will I think my days as a teenager never rained?
But, I know, it has.

Caroline Duerr, Grade 7
Brielle Elementary School, NJ

School Shootings

Gunshots heard from the deeply disturbed.
Once pure-hearted children, those who were lured
Into the path of violence and hate
Peers didn't know until it was too late,
Kids who were bullied took their revenge,
Wouldn't let anything get through their heads.

They ended up doing what they intended to do,
Only to end up hurting many others too,
Wanting to be a legend in the wrong ways,
They were falling into the horrible craze.
Rifles in hands as they targeted many,
They didn't stop until they killed plenty

How could this happen? We are partly to blame.
We were blinded from the signs until the tragedies came,
Many were injured, the innocent are dead,
Tears of their families and friends were shed.

So many times it has happened, so many times we've cried;
We shouldn't be satisfied until we've tried
To prevent this from happening ever again,
So get a head start, pick up a pen,
Send a message of peace like the one you've just read.

Grace You, Grade 7
Plainview-Old Bethpage Middle School, NY

Crimes of an Essay

Raise your pen and poise your sword!
We're fighting to the final word!

The wits, they crackle and clang and clash!
And nothing persuades us from doing the rash!

A bell will signal — the weapons begin
And show us why wrath is considered a sin.

They heed us no warning, they give us no time.
Our words laced with toxin committed the crime.

Syllables race across paper with speed:
We shall give no mercy for both have no need.

All plead stronger tactics, the mission confirmed.
The battlefield displayed why the authors did squirm.

In the vicinity lay corpses by twos
The occasional thinking cap, battered and bruised

The pen ceased movement (and swords) and then
We strike up a battle, quite gruesome again.

Alexandra Wolf, Grade 8
Milford Middle East School, MA

A Spark in the Dark

The day was gray and bleak
 Dragging on
  For seemingly eternity
But wait —
     One single ray
       So Bright and Golden
          Penetrating through the clouds

The room was dim and dreary
 No windows
  To let light tumble in
But wait —
     One candle lit
       Erect and Shining
          Illuminating the dark

The tunnel was long and twisted
 Wandering aimlessly
  Through all its turns
But wait —
     An opening is in sight
       Dazzling and Glowing
          The end of an arduous journey

Rivka Friedler, Grade 9
Torah Academy for Girls High School, NY

Just Alone

I hate because I want what they have
I admire because they have what I want
It is the tired magic that keeps me going,
Keeps me strong
It is the connection, that is what's important.
If I am not connected, than I am just alone.

Emily Fiumara, Grade 9
Garnet Valley High School, PA

Seeing Life Change Without Knowing What's Going On

Think of what you had
Even though you couldn't understand what was happening
You can read his face
But you just don't get what he's telling you
Can he be deceiving
Or is he telling the truth
Sometimes you just don't know
And you never will
With this situation
You might just have to return it
But after you do you find another that catches your eye
It twinkles like a star in the night sky
So you take a chance
And check it out
You then realize
He is the perfect one
And the one that you call Dad

Stephen Edwards, Grade 8
William Penn Middle School, PA

The Tree

The tree stands tall and proud,
like the stars in the sky up high,
it dances up high
as the wind whistled in the sky
like a bird singing, never stopping
the tree sings a lullaby
to the animals inside.
But what will it become?

Payton McLay, Grade 7
Grace Lutheran School, FL

A Single Flame

I swiftly writhe and gently swerve
but can fall still instantly
lunging and darting swaying to and fro,
A single element
pure
and strong,
Some think me a monster
a destroyer?
Death?
If only they knew
what life, warmth and light
I am,
I do not sing
nor do I
speak at all,
But I dance regally
when the breeze
plays her majestic tune,
I am eternal, infinite
and unceasing,
since before the beginning of time.

Sara Kowalski, Grade 7
Merrimack Valley Middle School, NH

Prayer of a Slave Child

We work all night,
we work all day.
We barely eat.
Oh, this I pray.
Look at these scars,
how big and deep.
They beat us 'til we fall,
they yell at us,
hit us,
abuse us.
Some of us faint,
most of us die.
Some run away
and never come back.
Our skin is dry,
oh, God, please save us.
This I pray.

Kaitlyn Bell, Grade 7
Swift Middle School, PA

Till I Met You

My life was empty, till I met you.
My life was full of sadness, till I met you.
I was hurt and weak, till I met you.
Failed and disappointed I felt, until the day I met you.
I thought I couldn't keep on, but I met you.
I thought my life was useless, until the day that I met you.
Now you're the joy and happiness in my life.
The silly little reason that makes me laugh.
You're my main reason I wake up in my everyday life
In the middle of the night
I look up in the sky staring at the bright shining stars
Hoping that like him, you won't let me fall.
Meeting you was just like love at first sight,
Like an angel descending from heaven in a bright light.
You dedicated your time in making it feel just right.
With you on my side; nothing can go wrong, you make it feel right
Even when something goes wrong.
Having you in this book of my life
You're the best chapter so far.

Alejandra Bilbao, Grade 9
Miami Beach Sr High School, FL

Strength

Strength is pushing, pulling, lifting, holding, standing, and defending
It's the measure of who we are
We use it to judge and to explore
Strength is pushing, pulling, lifting, and holding
Pushing, through everything the world throws at you
Pulling, others onto the right road,
Lifting, others up to more than they can be
Holding, everything together when it matters the most
Standing, up for what you believe in
Defending, those that you hold dear
Strength is emotions, intelligence, and morals.
Somewhere some of us sold it for "true" strength.
We already have it.

Brooks Jordan, Grade 8
Leesville Road Middle School, NC

Outsider

These days in schools could be better.
I get looks, whispers, and fake smiles, also people talking behind my back.
I keep all my opinions to myself.
Moreover, I am very soft-spoken. I do not talk to anybody.
They treat me as if I am a hideous creature.
They cannot see that I am just the same as everybody else.
I am a regular person.
They do not seem to see that.
My face is a symbol to be recognized.
I use my mouth to say what I feel and to state my opinions.
I use my ears to hear what they think of me and to hear the truth.
I use my eyes to see who they truly are.
In my mind, I am a mark in their minds.
They think I am an outsider.

Cassie Bavaro, Grade 7
Hoboken Charter School, NJ

One Window

One window is all I need…
to escape from myself,
from my fears,
from my mind.
One window is all I need…
to cause change.
to make a difference.
to save the world.

Andrea Bucci, Grade 7
Anthony Wayne Middle School, NJ

Different

Who am I different?????
What make me different
How am I different
When I am different
Why am I different
Who else is different
Do I like being different
How does it feel to be different
Why are we different
Shouldn't we be the same
Could we be the same
Who would make us different
We make ourselves different
Why…cause we want to

Michael Comerford, Grade 8
Hommocks Middle School, NY

Orange

Orange looks like a summer sunset
Orange sounds like a motor revving
Orange smells like a ripe orange.
Orange tastes like a fresh cut mango.
Orange feels like a fresh coat of paint.
Orange is the color of a flower
Orange messes around
Orange is orange.

Tyler Campbell, Grade 7
Gowanda Middle School, NY

Lily from Fire

It's hard to follow the right path
But this lily will rise to the challenge
This lily will rise from the fire
Breathe in life and
Breathe out problems
This lily won't give in
It will rise from the fire
It will follow its dream
And never give up
Because this lily is me

Wyneka Curry, Grade 9
Thomson High School, GA

Lost

I'm here on this Earth
Lost in the jungle
Where cats prowl at dark
But dogs cannot bark

I'm in Outer Space
Lost on the moon
Where Martians roam
Please take me home

I'm in a desert
Lost with the cacti
Where armadillos sing
And cars don't pass by

I'm up in the sky
Lost in a cloud
Where angels usually lay
Not making any sounds

I'm here in my home
Lost in my room
Daydreaming about where
I'll go soon

Carla Abrachinsky, Grade 7
Mahanoy Area Middle School, PA

Meadows of Freedom

All of these meadows are so graceful
All you see is the grass and sky
You always see the birds fly
Which makes it even more beautiful

Life should go to and fro
You should really know
That it's going to take you far away
Far away to maybe stay

The animals running to and fro
Horses, cows, and that Border Collie
Oh how it makes my heart so jolly
It gives me a feeling to want to go

And now you know
The world is free free to see
Act like you really know
Where it is you want to go

Where do you want life to take you
Someplace where the sky is blue
God will guide you the whole way
To that place you shall stay

Jana Farmer, Grade 7
L E Gable Middle School, SC

Missing

Help, I'm lost!
Can anyone save me?
I've gone away!
Can anyone hear me?

Can anyone save me?
I wish you were here!
Can anyone hear me?
Can you find me?

I wish you were here!
I want to be seen!
Can you find me?
What if I wasn't here?

I want to be seen!
Will anyone miss me?
What if I wasn't here?
Missing is what I am.

Will anyone miss me?
I've gone away!
Missing is what I am.
Help, I'm lost!

Bryanna Hoffman, Grade 8
Noble Middle School, ME

My Day at the Beach

Crashing waves,
The warm sandy beaches,
Hot summer days.
The seaweed a mountain high,
Crystal, clear water,
How I wanted to splash.
Excited, I ran towards the water.
I tripped,
The seaweed swallowed me whole.
I wrestled around to get up.
I would never splash again.

Natalie Nedley, Grade 7
Trinity Middle School, PA

Animal Inside — Greyhound

There is a greyhound in me.
With fur like a smooth blanket
And eyes like a penetrating glare
It howls like a wolf.
It runs like a cheetah.
It lives in my legs and makes me fast.
I wish that I could be as fast.
It makes me feel unmatchable.
It makes me want to sprint.

Zack Chen, Grade 9
Highland Park Middle/High School, NJ

Colors

C olossal amounts of yellow sunshine awaken the golden tints concealed in the ground.
O range, spherical blobs speckle the muddy brown fields in the distance.
L ovely red and rust leaves detach from their branches and progressively drift downward.
O h, what breathtaking, brightening sights are heading our way!
R eal oranges, reds, yellows, and countless others make their ways to the towering trees.
S unsets, bright and bold, end a colorful autumn day.

Sonali Shah, Grade 7
Unami Middle School, PA

The Moon

Its dusky shadows portraying a feeling of death and chilling sorrow.
The drumbeat of a million hearts, the sun is approaching.
Rushing to meet the moon, the sun wraps its muscular hellish hot arms around the body of the cold moon.
Telling no more people their life is up, the sun is out you will be born again.
The joyous return of the sun, a time for a fresh start.
Ducks drying their water soaked wings under the constant crispy warmth of the sun.
But there's not always a happy ending for everyone.
The moon hibernating like a butterfly in a cocoon waiting patiently for the sun to set.

Lauren Verhoef, Grade 8
Greencastle-Antrim Middle School, PA

Deer

In the woods beyond the trees the deer are crouched down on their knees.
Very graceful very sweet but so shy you will rarely meet.
How dare those hunters how dare those men shoot down these creatures but that's the end....

Raquel Wenk, Grade 7
Lancaster Mennonite School, PA

Charming Deception

A fire so great once burned within my circle of affection, only for you
Yet the doubts that lay behind my smile proceeded as I uncovered the truth
The fire blazing so red soon morphed into a black hole, for the love you claimed for me was untrue

Weeks later, as I saw you crossing my path, desire filled my heart to start anew
And when your eyes twinkled in the bright sun, it revealed the real you; a heartless fool, but I'm the fool
A fire so great once burned within my circle of affection, only for you

The laughs we shared remain unforgotten, yet the heartaches you caused opened my eyes, thank you
I yearn for my heart to be at ease; what I did only made matters worse, but I did what was honorable
The fire blazing so red soon morphed into a black hole, for the love you claimed for me was untrue

My feelings for you have turned into mere thoughts; you're a library book that is long overdue
Still, I wonder, was it your almost perfect smile that made me fall for you?
A fire so great once burned within my circle of affection, only for you

How could I have mistaken my handsome prince for you?
I now know that all those talks and sparkles in your eyes were lies waiting to be unveiled
The fire blazing so red soon morphed into a black hole, for the love you claimed for me was untrue

When you grabbed my hand and asked for a second chance, appalled, I withdrew
Again, I stayed true to myself, but a feeling of emptiness filled my heart, but that feeling always passes
A fire so great once burned within my circle of affection, only for you
The fire blazing so red soon morphed into a black hole, for the love you claimed for me was untrue

Stella Iskandarian, Grade 8
Public School 334 Anderson, NY

Butterfly Tempo

Ephemeral thoughts cascade through my mind
like a jungle's waterfall that roars but ends with
the trickle of a tiny brook or stream across the countryside.
The clouds, silver-white, flit intermittently across the sun:
sluggish yet gentle movements juxtaposed with
the hefty sigh of the wind that rushes through the gold-tipped,
impossibly green leaves basking in the late afternoon light.
If I could
capture this
fleeting moment
within my hands
would it flutter, fragile
like a butterfly
until I set it free
forever?
The days pass in front of my eyes so quickly
that the images blur and time seems to paradoxically
stand so still.
But I don't want to crush the butterflies in my hands
even if they would fly away and leave me with nothing, because
living forever in a moment means being trapped in it.

Lindsey Lam, Grade 9
Jericho High School, NY

My Dog Lady

L is for the love she showered me with.
A is for how she'll always be with me.
D is for the distress and sadness I felt when they took her.
Y is for you and the memories I'll never forget.

Kelsey McKeown, Grade 8
Spartanburg Jr Writing Project, SC

Survival

Racing for survival
Finding food in the trees
Running for your shelter
Defacing the leaves
Living in the treetops
Trying to fly with the birds
Most victims were black
In a time of survival it seems as if you're grouped in herds
No one cares if you're red, white or blue
In a time of survival all you have is you
In a time of survival all you have is your spirituality
Most people will regret tragedy because they didn't want
To face reality
You might not know how to survive in the open and out
But you know how to live when all is in doubt
Don't take little chances but
Don't waste time
They will really regret it when the Earth is past its prime
Everyone will regret everything
When it hurts to stay alive
Because all you have is your courage when you want to survive

Rachel Fletcher, Grade 9
Columbia High School, GA

Still I Cry

Tears fall into puddles of water drip, plop, drip
Still I cry
My eyes dry and soak into my skin like a sponge
Still I cry
The wind blows my tears in another direction
Like leaves being tossed in the wind
Still I cry
Then the sun lays to rest, birds fly freely
Still I cry
The winds are as strong as a tornado storm
While the waves are rapidly rumbling
And birds are cheerfully chirping
Yet I still cry

Cinnamon Wilcox, Grade 7
Herbert A Ammons Middle School, FL

Photograph

Indescribable words,
Something held in memories staying as sharp as birds.
Sitting in our past,
While months and years are going by fast.
Helplessly taking over our minds,
As days and fashions rewinds.
And time is being replayed,
While the world around us is delayed.
For all emotions suddenly run wild,
When you see your face as a child.
Loving how it used to be,
Playing with dolls and having tea.
If only words could describe this place,
Going through what's just time and space.
Where a photograph is the border line,
Through our past and present, flying time.

Kathleen Westervelt, Grade 9
St Anthony's High School, NY

The Tale of a Thousand Yawns

When there's a day when I finally sleep
That is the day I won't strike out and yell
Work gets in the way of counting my sheep
When I wake, I dread that wretched bell
I worry and work as my stress levels soar
I close my eyes tight and begin to dream
Need to stay awake a few minutes more!
I'll be back soon, to my gift so supreme
I'm finally done all I have to do
I crawl into bed, little time to spare
I drift off to sleep and dream sweet dreams, too
I hope to relax, really want to care
So that when the bell sounds I am prepared
I'll get up easy; as if I were dared

Samantha Kee, Grade 9
Unami Middle School, PA

Secrets

S ome people know them others don't
E veryone would like to know them
C ute, funny, fun, weird
R ude if you don't tell your friend
E veryone has a secret
T ell the right person
S ecrets

Shirley Rea, Grade 7
Perquimans County Middle School, NC

One Window

ONE WINDOW IS ALL I NEED
To see the beauty of me and
The things around me.
To smell the sweet flowers,
Or see the innocent birds.

ONE WINDOW IS ALL I NEED
To see what's inside of me.
To see that people care about me.
To see that people see me for me.

ONE WINDOW IS ALL I NEED
To see the hurt.
To see the tears.
To feel the pain.
Of the people below
Mourning,
For someone that they loved,
And that someone loved me.

ONE WINDOW IS ALL I NEED
To see everything.
Mallory Cohen, Grade 7
Anthony Wayne Middle School, NJ

Is It My Turn

Is it my turn yet?
Why am I still here?
What makes me better than others?

I am just she,
Standing here waiting,
Till death comes for me.

I who am helpless,
Cannot do anything,
I am so weak.

Waiting for my fate,
Lucky to be alive,
But wait…

Is it my turn yet?
Jessica Escorcia, Grade 8
Glades Middle School, FL

Into the World

Past the old gnarled oak tree, a hundred or more years old,
Under the wide wooden bridge
Beyond the gurgling stream,
Among the mottled bark and feathery leaves of the willow trees,
Towards the world I go.

Onto the wide moors,
Around the glassy lakes,
Amid the spirits in caves from long past,
With their memories in me,
I regard the world through your eyes.

Near a wood of bronze, black and green trees,
I look back, and
In my mind's eye, I see my home, a tent under a foliage of green,
The dappled light blowing softly in the breeze,
As I continue to travel on.

The wind rushes past,
Flying by on puffy white sails,
The mane of my steed, rushes past,
Like a glossy, rippling, brown water fall,
I look towards the future and the travels yet to come.
Pooja Krishnan, Grade 7
Carson Middle School, VA

Unanswered Prayers

I asked God for lenient parents, so that I could have all I asked for.
I was given strict ones, so that I would not be spoiled.
I asked for easy answers, so that I would be successful.
I was given mediocre grades, so that I work harder.
I asked for heaps of money, so that I could buy the world.
I was given pocket change, so that I learn to cherish my possessions.

I asked for love and care, so that I would be helped.
I was shown anger and hatred, so that I would be independent.
I asked for praise and recognition, so that I could be proud.
I was ignored and criticized, so that I learn to be humble.
I asked for a good life, so that I could be happy.
I was given sorrow and grief, so that I would not take things for granted.

I asked for a fair and just world, so that all would be well.
I was given a voice, so that I would speak out.
I asked for a look into the future, so that I would not be afraid.
I was given eyes and actions, so that I would find the future myself.
I got nothing that I hoped for, but everything I should have asked for.
Although in twisted ways, my prayers were answered.

I am most truly blessed.

Patricia Jančová, Grade 9
Unami Middle School, PA

Sunset

The sunset at the beach red, orange, pink
Bright sunlight, shimmering waters

Boats go by
While waves break up on shore

Where does the sun go?
Why does the sky change from blue to black?
How do boats float in the water?

I feel lucky today,
To be with my cousins watching the sunset

Sunset at the beach.

Khadijah Khan, Grade 8
Tarpon Springs Middle School, FL

Janiece

My name not like many others
Uncommon
Some pronounce it wrong
Janiece
Ja like the begging of an American name Jake
And niece the opposite of nephew
Picked by a confident woman
Married to another confident man
Left many years ago
To form a unique name of Latin beauty

Janiece Montas, Grade 7
Hoboken Charter School, NJ

Vacant Lot

The world is changing for the worst
Developing into a dark vacant lot
The lot is filled with murder, pollution and depression
I cry for this ground
I cry for its people
I cry for its disease
This acreage is abandoned, this piece of land is cold
We are tangled and engulfed in our own agendas
We hide from the world and pretend we are immortal
This vacant forgotten land is suffering
Our chance is now
We are the solution, as well as the problem
If we awaken and stand up,
Remove that battered blanket concealing our eyes we can help
We can make this vacant space delectable
But for now this area is in shambles
A wasteland of potential
Sorrowful, shameful
A vacant lot

Elizabeth Nylander, Grade 8
Milford Middle East School, MA

In Retrospect

Singing out the opening notes of the beloved song
A murmur rippling through the audience
Piccolos playing
Cymbals crashing
Violins soaring
Playing a long, plaintive melody
Full-throated
Deeply resonant
In its musical triumph
A visiting emotional experience
Incredible joy, sadness
A connection
Opening their hearts
Bringing tears to the eyes of all
A cultural experience
Suffused with importance
Coming to light is an opening
To a whole new dimension
In retrospect,
It's just music
Play an encore

Katherine Fein, Grade 9
Unami Middle School, PA

New Day

The sky is blue as so is the sea,
The earth is green as so is the grass.
As the sun begins to lower towards the deep blue sea,
The blades of grass begin to lie down towards the earth.
As the shadow of the sun glazes on the shimmering waters,
Then the almighty blades of grass retire of its beauty.
But as the time passes and the sun begins to rise again,
The dew of the grass begins to shimmer.
And as the sun rises so do the blades of grass.

Dalton Ruch, Grade 7
Chickahominy Middle School, VA

Life

Life is a wonderful thing that we take lightly
Wars and violence is a vision so unsightly
Why kill to get what you want?
Guns and bombs are what we use to taunt
Our enemies when we don't agree
Stop the violence, together we should run free
Of all the conflict we have in this world
To do this job it does not take one girl
But one nation to unify us all
No matter if you are short, skinny, fat or tall
It is better to use words instead of guns
Even with words we may come to problems
But these same words may lead to a resolution as well
No body bags, funerals, or prisoners in jail
Life is an important thing, don't take it lightly
Help unify us all, learn to embrace tightly.

Iseinie Mendez, Grade 8
Kappa V School, NY

The Fox

Through the woods he quietly sneaks
His coat all shiny, nice, and sleek
He pads silently to the top of the hill
Then raises his head to the midnight air
And lets the breeze run through his hair
He gazes at the moon
And hopes it will leave soon
He walks over the moonlit path
And leaps into the water
To take his midnight bath

Jenny Free, Grade 8
Durham Middle School, GA

Pitching

The best part of baseball is pitching
To hold the ball and all of its stitching
To throw a strike
With all your might
It is really not something worth ditching.

To be on the mound is the best
You stand with great pride on your chest
To pitch the ball
And hear the call…STRIKE THREE!
Take a seat with the rest.

Baseball is a whole lot of fun
But pitching is second to none
Stare down the batter
Like a mad hatter
And see that his at bat is done.

Larry Kelley, Grade 9
Unami Middle School, PA

Dedication to Soldiers in Iraq

You who are brave,
You who care,
You who support this country,
You protect us and cease our fears.

You who wish to be noble,
You who wish to be strong,
You who wish for your family,
You wish to go home.

You who are dedicated,
You who want to make a difference,
You who chose a daring path,
You never turned back.

You who endure long days,
You who work hard,
You who are powerful,
You protect our lives!

Hannah Garrison, Grade 8
Hyattsville Middle School, MD

What I've Learned

I've learned as a student in my nine naïve years
That to be a good friend you must simply be sincere
I've learned that an action may speak louder than a word
But it still horribly hurts when gossip is overheard
I've learned that grades are not everything as you will shortly see
In this lovely luscious land of America, the home of the free
I've learned that the easy way is not always the best path
For after you're all through there will always be aftermath
I've learned I have a passion for the stage to act
It was fabulous fun even when I had to "Quack"
I've learned that your marks are for you and only you
It may be hard to believe but it is tremendously true
I've learned that procrastination is the ensnaring enemy
It peeks into your worries, but then will furtively flee
I've learned that you don't have to be like the rest
If you tenaciously try hard and always do your best
I've learned not to worry about what other people think or say
Cause I have a brain of my own and there's not just one way
I've learned much as a student so let me give you some advice
Try to make good choices and before you talk, always think twice

Madelyn Crimmins, Grade 8
Most Blessed Sacrament School, MD

Silent Woods

The cool, quiet shadows of the woods invite me in,
Giving me instant relief from the hot summer sun,
Everything is hushed and still, in silent harmony,
Soft, fragrant breezes move through the trees, rustling the leaves,
Caressing my face, singing a song with grace,
Majestic trees, standing tall and proud, surround me quietly,
While dainty, simple wildflowers decorate their feet,
A world of ageless beauty, a peaceful and serene sanctuary.

Rebecca Angert, Grade 8
Whisconier Middle School, CT

Music You Are My Reason to Live

Music
You grab my soul and speak to me
heal my soul and tell me it's going to be okay
When I am alone and upset, I forget everything
you accompany me
You are my reason to live

If I am on the road or just at school you wait for me
With the time of the world, you soothe me
Indescribable feelings about you
You are my reason to live

You're like a loved one that no matter what happens you're there for me
To comfort me and you are like an energy drink that gives me that extra boost.
You're my Tylenol, Advil, Motrin, and maybe even a bandage
you heal my soul when I have a heart break
or just down in the dumps
without you life would be a world of black and white.

Lissa Urena, Grade 7
Westwood Jr-Sr High School, NJ

Tell Me Here Tell Me Now

Tell me can you take a child seriously
Tell me here
Tell me now
Why these children can't speak aloud
Why these voices of the future must die down
Why this world must undermine
The voices that are yours and mine
Could this be a sign?
Tell me here
Tell why
Our future has to die
Can a child change the world
Tell me does it matter?
How big you are?
How old you are?
Tell me now
Tell me why
Can you change the world at this time
Can you change this world
Can you be taken seriously?
To change the world is to make the difference

Edward Byrd, Grade 8
Mattei Middle School, PA

Separate

I awake to the voices
The angry, deafening voices that torment me,
That burn my ears like flames
I put my ear to the wall but they're gone like wind
The car pulls away and pungent pain punctures my heart
I asked myself, how, why
Too long, too fast, too late
I stuttered and I stumbled as I got back in bed
My eyes are closed like nothing's wrong but I know
While life goes on things remain
Separate

Will Hoehne, Grade 8
William Penn Middle School, PA

Animals

Animals are big and small
Animals are short and tall
Some of them are smelly and ugly
And some of them are beautiful and pretty

When animals don't like you they start a fight
They scratch, pinch, and bite
People are scared of lions and tigers
Because they are scary and they are biters

Many animals live in the zoo
But do not hurt them no matter what they do
Different animals live in each nation
But do not hurt them because they are God's creation

Nooreldeen Rostoum, Grade 8
Noor-Ul-Iman School, NJ

Jane Eyre

Jane Eyre is a very unfortunate child
From Mrs. Reed's house she was exiled
For Jane, her aunt had no compassion
To improve her life, Jane went into action

Jane was a great student at Lowood School
She moved up to a teacher by following each rule
For Mr. Rochester, Jane then did work
She and Adéle came together like clockwork

With her aunt, Jane tried to redress
But all they did was retrogress
Jane came back and fell in love with her boss
And the only thing she got from that was complete chaos

Jane became a beggar, wandering the streets
She finally found nice people to meet
They turned out to be related to her
This brought to Jane great pleasure

Her uncle bequeathed his fortune to her
It was big enough to be equal with her lover
In the end they lived happily ever after
The rest of Jane's life was filled with laughter

Jonathan Gordon, Grade 9
Council Rock High School South, PA

The Pencil

The lady's fingers move nimbly with expertise
Coating the formerly white sheet
With blossoming scenes.

The gentleman's hand flies across the page
Leaving in its messy tracks
The words of a tale.

The girl's weary arm reaches for a tool
And reluctantly begins to write
The paper for tomorrow.

The boy's hand stops as he wracks his brain
Then quickly resumes the scribbling
Of a card for a sick friend.

The child laughs as her arm zigzags back and forth
And on the wall she creates
A grand masterpiece.

The baby giggles and looks at the colored stick
Then happily chews on it
And continues to play.

Danielle Feffer, Grade 9
Home School, PA

Every Day

With each and every day,
The colors begin to fade,
Leaving nothing but a blackened slate.
With each and every day,
With every step I take,
Another step closer to hate.
With each and every day,
The dark will enclose me.
I long for the light.
But is it worth the strength?
With each and every day,
The joy will slip away.
Is this the path I want to take?
With each and every day,
The fear begins to rise,
Stretching the limits of my sanity.
With each and every day,
The dark will strangle me,
I turn and run for the light.

Vicki Williams, Grade 7
Depew Middle School, NY

This Is Who I Am

Freedom; be what you want to be
Freedom; equal rights for he or she

Freedom; all colors in unity
Freedom; no racism in communities

Freedom; don't tell me I can't
Freedom; this is who I am!

Krishanthi Devendran, Grade 8
Sewanhaka High School, NY

In the Room

In the room,
the jostling crowd
moves toward the cold.
To some it's just a normal feeling.
To me it's the cold indifference
of a new world to explore.
We have our special shoes,
like the staples for this new world —
without them, you can't survive.
I balance my way through the door
to that land of smooth, slick ice
like a baby dropped into a world
where it knows not its place in life.
I find it in me to take a chance —
leave familiarities behind
and glide around inside this space.
I'll find my way through this world
where the earth-bound learn to fly.

Rachel Fralick, Grade 8
Spartanburg Jr Writing Project, SC

Trees

I am like a tree because I'm beautiful in God's eyes,
Even though my leaves are crumpled and my roots are dry,
He says that I am precious and I was worth His time.

I may be cut down again and again but yet I will still rise,
I will lift my humbled hands and stretch them to the sky.
I praise the Lord Almighty for picking me up again,
I may have been cut deep and scarred but strong will I stand.

In life I go through many trials and storms,
And with each one there will be times where I will cry and mourn.
I will look toward the sky and wait for the break of dawn,
When it comes I will lift my voice and sing a grateful song.

Each storm makes me tough though my strength may be worn,
With each one that comes my roots become more strong,
Thank God that I wasn't made to endure this alone.

When the rain comes I thankfully drink it up,
For it comes to satisfy my thirst and fill me up.
But when my final days on this Earth have come,
God and I will finally join and again become one.

Desiray Simmons, Grade 8
First Assembly Christian School, NC

The Guy Who Saved Me

I tripped and fell.
I broke my beautiful white wings.
I can't stop falling.
Oh, is there anyone who can help me?!
From far mountains,
Across cold blue seas,
In a castle far away,
You came to save me.

You killed every cold, scary, ugly, demon,
With a white, shiny sword.
It was almost as if he was cunning in thin air.
For it was too easy for my prince.
As soon as he came towards me my broken wings were fixed.
As he got closer to me I stopped falling.
As he was an inch away from me I tripped into his arms.

I whispered, "Thank you for saving me."
He whispered,
"It is my duty to protect the woman I shall give my hand in marriage too."
I whispered, "Really?"
He said no more and leaned toward my face.
A kiss from his lips to mine sealed our love for each other.

Jennifer Winser, Grade 8
Westampton Middle School, NJ

Sew, Sew, Sew!

Sewing is such a dream;
It all starts with a 5/8 seam.
Why buy clothes at the mall?
Get a pattern, either Simplicity or McCall's.
Now buy your fabric at the store;
Pick something colorful, don't be a bore!

Cut out your fabric, be sure to pin;
With this new outfit you're guaranteed to win!
Now finally set the scene;
Begin by threading your machine.
Put in the bobbin and begin to sew;
Focus on the fabric and go, go, go!

To make sure your outfit will surely fit;
Use a double-stitch when sewing a knit!
Before you gather and take the lead,
A basting stitch is all you need!
Now the process is finally through;
Put on your outfit and be a whole new you!

Molly Spanfelner, Grade 9
Unami Middle School, PA

Change

I've been trying to figure out what I've left behind
Everything is changing
And everyone around me thinks that I'm going crazy
I'm in a different place now
And I don't know what to do
But when I took the first chance
I had the first glance to look at everything that's been going on
And everything that's tragic in my life
Has been changed by the magic of love
Now I am happy
I am in a better place
I know that things happen for a reason
But it all gets better soon
Each step I take gets harder and harder every day
And every time I see the ray of sunshine
It's always the way things happen

Muruvvet Cevik, Grade 9
Miami Beach Sr High School, FL

The Struggle

Every day you wake up knowing it's a new start,
Optimistic is what you should be,
Knowing day by day that you have to get up and go,
Not being able to take a rest just even for a second,
One day you will be at your greatest,
To be successful and rich like all the rest,
All those years of struggle came up to one successful day.

Mary Mubiru, Grade 9
Bishop Denis J O'Connell High School, VA

Lightning

It crashes down
Like a tiger pouncing on its prey
It lights up the sky like a giant veil of light
It comes when you are least expecting it
And then it's gone in a flash
It can appear anywhere in the sky
And then it leaves without a trace

Jeffrey Mariconda, Grade 7
Anthony Wayne Middle School, NJ

My Favorite Colors!

My Favorite Colors Are:

Orange, like the color of my cat,
   The color of a fire
   The color of the leaves in the fall.
   It's my favorite color of all,

Purple, is the color of my room,
   Like the color of my cousin's hair.
   The color of my favorite shirt.
   It's the color of my bike.

Green, like the color of the summer grass.
   The color of the forest trees.
   The color of my bathroom,
   It's the color of my aunt's pool in the winter.

Blue, like the color of the morning sky.
   The color of my baby sister's eyes.
   The color of my blue jean pants.
   It's the color of my favorite candy.

Chelcee Kelley, Grade 8
West Point Middle School, AL

Caring

Big cities, small cities
They're all the same
In this tough world
Money is what it's all about
You know that while you're walking
You see a run down house
You laugh out loud
But cry inside
Caring about it is not going to hurt
Even though you think it will
When you think about greatness, what goes through your mind
Do you think of billionaires
Or do you think of volunteers and donators
When you think about tragedy, what goes through your mind
Do you think about a stock market crash
Or do you think of Hurricane Katrina
If you care about other people you are not soft
You're just doing what this world needs more of

Sam McMillon, Grade 8
Beacon Middle School, DE

Great Sichuan Earthquake

It was a devastating earthquake, says the world, embracing chaos and pain and sorrow throughout itself. Cities are in ruins, says the destroyed car, flattened from the great force of the concrete of the building it was parked next to. Vehicles roamed upon the shattered roads, says the fallen rubble, and somewhere nearby, sirens go off. Screech says the ambulance, as they stop where help is needed. And then speed off towards to the infirmary. One by one they depart say broken wooden boards littered across the land, from one of the 5 million homes destroyed.

Many people were cluttered in there, say the hospital walls, all covered in white and with people running about. It was a period of panic, say the hospital tools, cluttered among the operation table with other devices as they were taken to be used. Time was essential, says the analog clock, as it rested on the wall peacefully while doctors kept glancing at it, wanting more time. They were too late says the amount of blood spilled, for there was over 500,000 deaths in Sichuan.

Why us, says the cold ground, since China has never experienced anything like it. Some ignored this event, or so they say, because they really didn't give a damn about it. And the other people? They all helped out with the tragedy, says the amount of money that was donated to aid this painful event. Millions of people are helping out to support this. "Will you help us too?" say the scarred hearts that have experienced this.

Russell Leung, Grade 8
Heritage Middle School, NJ

I Know Nothing in This World

I don't know where I am, can you tell me? Because no one else can
I'm lost in this world and I can't find my way out, can you show me?
Because no one else can

I just wonder, how is life supposed to be? Have you ever realized it's not the way you would hope?
So how do you know there's not someplace else out there,
Because anywhere's got to be better than here

To be able you find my way out, I have to find myself first, but how can I do that if no one else can,
Life would be a lot better if it wasn't like the Jerry Springer show
But it is, and now there's no going back, no going back

I just wonder, how is life supposed to be? Have you ever realized it's not the way you would hope?
So how do you know there's not someplace else out there,
Because anywhere's got to be better than here

Why haven't I found my true love? I'm not supposed to be invisible, maybe he's out there and feels the same way I do,
But what do I know? What will I ever know? Because as of now in this world, I know nothing

I just wonder, how is life supposed to be? Have you ever realized it's not the way you would hope?
So how do you know there's not someplace else out there,
Because anywhere's got to be better than here

I know nothing in this world.

Jamie House, Grade 9
Surry Central High School, NC

In Downtown Spartanburg

In downtown Spartanburg, cars speed through the busy streets,
and Papa's Breakfast Nook begins to fill up with hungry customers.
In downtown Spartanburg, the people of the Chapman Cultural Center get ready for their 10:00 opening,
and the public library waits for someone to come and take a bite of its knowledge.
In downtown Spartanburg, those men and women kind enough to keep our Barnet Park clean
are doing their job so I can sit here enjoying the beauty of my hometown.

Kennedy Byrd, Grade 7
Spartanburg Jr Writing Project, SC

The Forgotten Ball

I sit upon your front porch.
I am as red as a fiery torch.
You used to play with me,
But now you just don't care.
All the while, you sit and stare.
I was your best friend,
But now I don't know
If my heart can mend.
We had some good old times,
But now I sit here and listen
To the wind chimes.
I've sat through winter, spring, summer, and fall.
What am I but your old red ball?

Zachery Muscatello, Grade 7
Carson Middle School, PA

Summer Senses

Swish, swish, swish, waves lap against the beach
Seashells crackle under the clear blues of the water
Seagulls call, scrounging for food
Kids play in the sifting sand

A warm breeze wraps around me, comforting
Wet sand leaves squishy footprints
Dry sand, sifts softly
Cool water sneaks up on the beach as if it were watching

The rays of the sun are diamonds on the shining sea
Seagulls waddle across the hot sand in search of food

The light smell of saltwater dances through the air
Ice cream melts in my mouth as my senses draw in the beach

Calm.
Peaceful.
Relaxing.

Emily Clark, Grade 7
William Penn Middle School, PA

Discover Yourself

Dare to be yourself, just love what's real.
Make an entrance.
Be different, original, stronger, unstoppable.
Outshine the others.
Dream into the world of color.
Be happy, radiant, confident and irresistible.
Who says you can't go the distance and
Put your best foot forward?
Today's the day to mix it up and be crazy.
Unleash your inner voice, the real you!
It's important to believe that you can do anything you want,
You were born to rule.
Remember when you're strong, you sparkle,
And what makes you different is what makes you beautiful!

Victoria DeCesare, Grade 9
Unami Middle School, PA

Happiest Place on Earth

Mickey, Goofy, Donald too,
I'm excited to see all of you!
When I pass through those magical Disney gates,
Inside of me a joyful feeling creates.

Minnie, Pluto, and Daisy
The four theme parks are absolutely crazy.
There's nothing better than this happy place,
Where a child can eat waffles in the shape of Mickey's face.

Allie Zoccolo, Grade 8
William R Satz Middle School, NJ

My Dad

My dad saves lives.
He isn't an engineer or salesman.
He is a doctor and
Saving lives is his job.
It is an instinct for him:
Does everything he can to help
Comforts those in need
From cuts to car accidents
He does it all.
He may stay up through the night sometimes
But he does it to save lives
And my dad loves his job.

Dylan McDermott, Grade 7
Brielle Elementary School, NJ

Snow

Tiny snowflakes fall to the ground,
Crystal raindrops swirl.
Early morning sun shines around
To reveal it to the silent world.

It covers the Earth in purest white,
A secret for the dawn to keep.
No one else has seen the sight
Until the rest awake from sleep.

A clean blanket spreads over grass, hills, and trees,
Over icy lakes and sparkling streams.
None of the Earth's flaws can now be seen
When they are masked by beauty.

But when the early sun has risen higher
And beams its rays down from the sky,
Snow melts under the ball of fire
And it all is gone in the blink of an eye.

Tiny flakes, no one alike
Maybe will come on another night.

Rachel Herrington, Grade 8
Briarwood Christian Jr/Sr High School, AL

School

I cannot wait
To dive in a pool
To go to the beach
And not go to school
To get a huge tan
And go to the park
Hang out with my friends
Stay out after dark
But right now I'm in school
Watching the clock
Hearing its annoying
"Tick, tock, tick, tock"
And so, in a few months
It will be summer
But for now I'm in school
Boy, what a bummer

Arman Maqsudlu, Grade 7
Westwood Jr-Sr High School, NJ

Mom

You're sweet like candy.
You're as soft as the fur of a rabbit.
You make the best cookies ever,
And you don't have to try.
I wish you could be immortal
So you wouldn't have to die,
And I wouldn't have to miss you.
You make me feel loved by an angel.
You're worth staying on Earth for.
Aside from all of my friends at school,
And in my neighborhood,
You're my best friend.

Danielle Pitter, Grade 9
Colonia High School, NJ

Waves

Rocking a lullaby
I watch
The wave goes up
And crashes back down
Then the water retreats
To reveal a new set of sea shells
Hypnotized by the rhythm
I stand there

The sun beats down
Seagulls cry overhead
I watch a little longer
Before I decide
As beautiful
Yet scary
As they are it's time for me
To get over the fear
Of them taking me away

Kylie Piper, Grade 7
Carthage Middle School, NY

Heart Broken

Today's the day where I ask, is this a really big task?
I was yelling out loud, in front of a large crowd.
I went to her house, she was wearing a blouse.
She told me no, I made a new foe.
I was walking home, in me was a dome.
She told me, I have no chance. While my enemies put me in a trance.
I gave up, when she said no, when I realize it started to snow.
When we went to school, she made me look like a fool.
I sent her a note, that I wrote.
She wrote back, saying that I lack.
On the outside I was mad, but on the inside I was sad.
The only thing I infer, is that I loved her.

Alfredo Andrade, Grade 9
Colonia High School, NJ

How Long Is Forever

We were best friends forever from the start
We said it was about what was deep down within the heart
All those things you say you are not, now that's who you have become
How long is forever?
You change more than the weather outside
Some days you ignore me like I am invisible
Other days it seems you want the world to know that I am your friend
I don't know what to believe about my "best friend forever" anymore
How long is forever?
You hurt me right before my eyes, using me for when you need a friend
But when a better offer comes along I am dropped like last weeks garbage
I deserve more than what you give me
How long is forever?
I am finally letting go of the pain because I have thought about this way too long
My tears fall like rain
For me to keep on hurting because of you would be wrong
How long is forever?
I cannot take this friendship any longer
You have shown me in many ways that you are done too
We always said we would be best friends forever
Now I see clearly how it is...*forever is no more.*

Kristina Rossetti, Grade 7
Depew Middle School, NY

Life

Did it ever cross your mind
That you only had a short amount of time
To breathe and just live to see another day
You complain about everything and everybody
But who will you complain to when every living thing just went away
People don't know the absent so they don't have a clue
Knowing that God has heaven plans for them,
but few want to do what they want to do and
when death comes when least expected you panic
and say I don't want to leave life
Even when it was bad or good it won't feel right to not have life.
Now God is saying you would have unending life
Now it is time to go

Brian Scott, Grade 9
Seminole County Middle/High School, GA

Pull Me Down

The sun shines bright
As the rain pours
The sea lay calm
While the wind blows violently
Trees stay cemented to the ground
As the violent winds of tornados rip at them
She pulls me up
When they all push me down
He loves me
When everyone around despises me
They both keep me alive
When all else is hell

Andrea Beard, Grade 9
Fairhope High School, AL

The Nightmare!

When I was sleeping safe and sound,
The sounds of war drums were all around.
The enemy mortars hit us first,
The gas around us doubled our thirst.
The enemy troops were all around,
Was this the fate we were bound?
Seven of our unit fell and died,
The rest of us were forced to hide.
A thunderous booming voice thundered overhead,
"Get up for school, out of bed!"
I finally got up, "Thanks for saving our troops lives." I said.

Igor Polosukhin, Grade 7
Freedom Middle School, TN

Portrait of Ruin

I lay faceless in bane,
thunderstruck yet addicted.
Around me debris,
of what used to be
an El Dorado.
I fall in the ashen,
dismal and bleak
lustful for her touch
and finally…
Hell knows no bounds
as it breaks my embodiment.
I lay limp
in my self-constructed portrait of ruin.
Bloodlessly, I had initiated my own eradication.
until…
Her translucent aurora banishes holocaust
and harmony blankets life
as the future
taunts him
so.

Zaman Gilani, Grade 8
Intermediate School 98 Bay Academy, NY

The Soldier

Looking into his gleaming eye,
She sees fear.
Watching him as he goes off to war,
She stays strong for her two children.

Her husband comes home,
Six months too early.
Another one to feed by spoon,
She still stays strong.

She looks into his eyes,
Like looking into a child's.
He then realizes for the first time,
She is the real soldier.

Eily Walsh, Grade 9
Bishop Denis J O'Connell High School, VA

Off the Backboard

The round, blurry exterior of the ball
pounded the tough, polished floor.
Every repetition of the up-and-down motion
let out an echo of deep passion for the game.

Pass, "Bomp." The player caught the ball.
Without hesitation, he felt the need to share the object.
So with a light amount of communication
and some ridiculous arm strength,
he tossed the rock to another teammate.

"Bomp." Once again a player had received the ball
And with little time left on the clock
he discussed his next move with himself.
He pondered it and was going straight for the
fake drive to the bucket and just bank it in.

"3…2…1." The player shoots the ball.
"Swish." It goes in! Players congratulate him.
They hoist him to the highest point on their shoulders
then head to the locker room to celebrate the win.
After that, they dashed toward the bus to go
unwind and revel in their great accomplishment.

Alex Weinberg, Grade 8
William Penn Middle School, PA

Error

I had an error, I did not make the play to first
I really felt like I was the worst
I felt like everyone was down on me
I had no idea how much pressure I had on me
My coach had his head down like the world was over
This had felt like the worst day of my life
But I did not give up without a fight
The next batter hit the ball, I ran up without withdrawal
I made the play to first and now the worst day is over.

Brian Wilson, Grade 7
Depew Middle School, NY

The Night of an Owl

Posing on an oak tree's arm
Eloquently silent
Appearing to mean no harm
Frozen, hungry, patient

Two yellow moons stand on her face
Stationary, empty, spying
She eyes her prey at a steady pace
Before she springs, flying

A mouse or two, caught instantly
Constricted in her claws
Gliding, defying gravity
Soaring without flaws

Nestling to sleep as night drifts away
She remains to be unseen
Hidden by leaves that dance and sway

Concludes the owl's routine
Blair Bosshardt, Grade 7
Pine Crest School, FL

Crystal Beads

A grey and downing cloud
Floating up above
No one in this world
Meant for me to love.

A shiny silver rainbow
Hovering way up high
My will to live
Will never truly die.

No one I can trust
Where do I go now.
Mitch Halloran, Grade 7
St Anthony School, CT

Dancing in the Meadow

I dance in an empty meadow,
Yellow grass buried in snow,
Flowing black dress twirls,
As I go around in swirls.
Bright moon reflects in my eyes,
Distantly a black raven cries,
Dark hair fans out,
I dance away my doubt.
Serene smile as I sway,
All my fears I do slay,
Wind carries me along,
This is where I belong.
Elizabeth Barnett, Grade 8
Grant County Middle School, KY

Blue and Cyan

There is a part in me that is sky blue
polite, loyal
friendly
patient, kind
forgiving, pleasing.

There is a part in me that is curious cyan
thinking what will happen next.
Is it going to happen?
It is unknown.
And will it remain a mystery?
William Flyte, Grade 8
Hopatcong Middle School, NJ

Entish War Chant

To Celbain our feet will fall,
Like the horses,
Charging on the plain,
Our trunks and our branches,
Are the weapons of war,
Our bark our armor be,
Our voices sing,
Like a horn of men,
Flood the tower,
Destroy the gate,
And lay our enemies to waste,
For we roll on the beat of the drum!
Adrian Majerle, Grade 9
Lee High School, AL

The Runner

He never knows
running running
after nothing at all
The clock is ticking
pavement is hot
sun beating down
His feet hit the ground
a pattern in the steps
running running
The crowd cheers
the finish in sight
tick tock the clock goes
Faster faster
he steps on the ground
no sound comes now
nothing sounds anymore
the clock moves with no noise
his feet hit the ground
The finish comes
the noise comes back
the beat is loud
Dan Santalla, Grade 8
St Anthony School, CT

Homework

Homework is what I hate,
it is like a heavy weight.
We work all day in our schools,
then we come home and work like fools.
The doctors all say,
that we should play.
But we work all day,
so we have no time to play.
Adam Steiner, Grade 7
Depew Middle School, NY

Season to Season

A forest filled with dead trees
The ground covered in snow
Piles and piles of raked leaves
Plants no longer grow

The air is warming
The earth is thawing
April is coming
Winter is dawning

Birds begin to sing
Flowers once again bloom
As we welcome spring
We rid ourselves of gloom

The sun will shine
The grass will grow
The dirt will churn
The wind will blow

These things will never change
As the seasons come and go
From winter to spring
Why? The world may never know
Meredith Veit, Grade 9
Unami Middle School, PA

The Appreciation of Life

I have a lot of hate
But the love is there too
Always good things happening
Always a tragedy too hard to handle
Some need help to get through it all
The lucky ones
Get the help, no matter who that's from
And are the ones to give the help
The appreciation of life
Isn't from just what you do,
But also who helped you
See life through.
Kathryn Angers, Grade 9
Norton High School, MA

Taste

All in one bite, fluffy and sweet
How could something so good sweep me off my feet?
I love the taste it's so great every time,
One bite plus two equals all mines.
Filled with sweetness, just makes my jaw lock.
It may look like a little but it tastes like a lot.
So dark, and creamy, crumbly too,
I love chocolate cake. How about you?

L'Don Frierson, Grade 7
Perquimans County Middle School, NC

Yesterday

Dear Paul McCartney

Who had to go?
Why didn't she say?
Is that why you long for yesterday?

Did you know "Yesterday"
would make me think
of how much easier yesterday was,
when there were no tests,
or homework, or presentations
and how we both wish to go back
to that one special day
instead of being stuck in this shadow?

Dear Mr. McCartney
I hope tomorrow will be as it was yesterday.

Taylor White, Grade 7
Trinity Middle School, PA

What Is Life

What is life do you know
Is it just one big show
Can it be only a game
A race to get money and fame
Even though everyone's here
Can you feel love far or near
Is life supposed to bring pride and joy
Or hate between the girl and boy
Can life be stopped, paused, and replayed
Or does it sit there like a tree in shade
I think life is a blessing not a curse
A curse would be your body laying in a hearse
If life is so bad, if life is so sad
Why don't you walk around angry and mad
You're always cheerful and happy
Never mean and snappy
Before you say what life is really about
Hold your temper and don't shout
Life is more than dominance and fear
This whole poem should have made that very clear
Now I ask you once again, what is life tell me that my friend.

Johntavia Walker, Grade 8
Public School 3 D'Youville Porter Campus, NY

Yellow and Green

Yellow brings out spirit and joy in me.
When the sun is bright and shining
I'll be shining bright, too.
So when it is shining with yellow joy
Know that I'll be jumping for joy, too.
The sun is what makes me
Wake with lightning speed,
The way the bright yellow sun shines on my face.
Through the window in the morning,
The brightness of the yellow sun just makes
Me wake, with a bright smile on my face.

Green trees, leaves, and grass.
Green is the color of peace and life.
I go out to play.
I step out of the door.
I feel the rush of wind
And I know the swaying sound is beautiful.
Green trees.
When you feel the wind blow against your skin
It brings peacefulness.
Green is the color of my life.

Alnel Logan, Grade 8
Hopatcong Middle School, NJ

My Brother, Joe

He's not just my brother,
He's also my friend.
When I need someone to talk to,
I talk to my brother, Joe.

He is a very likable man.
And like all others, he has his faults.
But the good outweighs the bad
In my brother, Joe.

As an electrician, he's always on the job,
And several times he comes home with injuries.
And when an electrical job needs doing,
We go to my brother, Joe.

We talk about all kinds of things.
We'll talk about Mom's new recipes,
And when I want to laugh about our sister's crazy antics,
I laugh with my brother, Joe.

My bro and I have an age gap;
I'm fourteen years old, and he's twenty-five.
But he and I never look at our differences,
Because he's my brother, Joe.

Joshua Lewis, Grade 8
Whitinsville Christian School, MA

On the Inside

Inside this eraser are millions of words
That are hidden from anyone else
There are secrets too deep
To even be written down
And truths never told
There are mistakes fixed
And promises made
Knowledge is inside this eraser

Samantha Robeson, Grade 7
Christ the Teacher Catholic School, DE

Free

Soaring —
Set off by the first note
Flying with wide leaps
And a dazzling smile
Listening to every slight
Piece of music!
Jumping, spinning, gliding
Across the stage
Exploding with enthusiasm
Just setting myself free
Free to be me!

Phoebe Schumacher, Grade 7
Ocean City Intermediate School, NJ

Moon

The face of a man.
Edible.
    And made of cheese.
Glows.
    The light that lights the midnight sky.
Pulls.
    The waves of the ocean.
Floats.
    Through the galaxy's air.
But,
    It doesn't float away.
    Because where it lies is its home.

Meagan Mayers, Grade 7
Gowanda Middle School, NY

Happy as Me

Me as myself, is fine —
whether they think so or not,
I'm happy as me.

And like a tree,
standing tall — strong and thick,
with branches and beautiful leaves —

I am myself, and that is fine,
and am as happy as I please.

Cooper Kernan, Grade 7
Ocean City Intermediate School, NJ

Horseback Riding Camp

On my way to camp:
Butterflies in my stomach, of nerves and excitement
Carry me away
Arriving:
Overwhelmed, ecstatic, in heaven from the first moment
Tours of the picturesque barn and fields
Befriending the sweet-tempered horses
Meeting the campers
Swimming in the local lake
Going for the first fateful ride
New friends:
Friendships that will last a lifetime
Stories of tragedy, love, loss, life and laughter shared
Unbreakable bonds are formed during work, play, and the attempted hours of sleep
My first show:
Nerves bubbling and excitement flowing, pushing me to win two 1st place ribbons
Persevering through events, rain or shine, with adrenaline, sportsmanship, and fun
Leaving:
Oh how I hate to go
From this place that I have learned to love so
I can't wait for next summer to bring more adventures at camp...

Chelsea Colby, Grade 8
Inter-Lakes Jr High School, NH

Trust Is Not Just a Word

Trust is a just a word, but it has a powerful meaning.
People take trust for granted.
They think they can stab you in your back
And say a simple sorry
And they will have your trust back as fast as the wind blows.
But they are so wrong.

People don't know the hurt they cause because of their two-faced ways.
One minute they're all in your face, telling you stuff you want to hear.
The next minute you made the biggest mistake you ever did in your life.
You told that one fake person about the strife
You deal with in your life.

The next day you show up at school.
Everybody knowing your business.
People feeling bad for what you go through
Or people laughing at you and making fun of you.
Your heart cries out for help.
Then that one true friend will be there
And you will have them to cry on.
And you will have that very special bond.

One day you will find a true friend
And they will be there to the end.

Ayana Calhoun, Grade 8
Westampton Middle School, NJ

I Am Here for You Poppa*

What is strength? But nothing other than an emotion,
All I want is to make you have some hope.
Keeping you strong and going like a locomotion.
Your determination to go on helps me cope.
Inspiration and love is what you give me here,
Believe me when I say I'll help you fight.
You are someone I want to always keep near,
You are considerate, and fly like a strong kite.
I'm respectful to you, wanting you to stay.
You can always count on me to love you.
Wanting to see you get past the month May.
Believe me when I say my love is true.
You are a person I want to be,
I know every day you'll be what I see.

Brittany Julien, Grade 9
Worcester Vocational High School, MA
*Dedicated to my grandfather

Camping

Something about camping is magical.
The birds soaring in the air
The wind blowing through your hair.
The sound of leaves and twigs snapping as you walk.
The noise of a woodpecker, ratty-tat-tat.
The crackling of the evening fire.
The taste of that perfect s'more.
Ghost stories over a smoldering fire.
Going to bed in a snug sleeping bag.
Going to sleep thinking, "what a great day."
Camping is peace.

Joshua Grile-Nielsen, Grade 7
Chickahominy Middle School, VA

Goblin

Schizophrenia and depression have become a problem,
What used to be a smart man, has morphed into a goblin.
It is harder for me to give, and easier for me to take.
What used to be so real, has suddenly turned so fake.

He said things would change, but didn't warn me how much,
We have the same communication, how did we lose touch?
If I knew it could change overnight, I would never sleep.
If I knew how far to dig, I wouldn't have dug so deep.

Some choose to follow, but I choose to lead,
It brought me before a judge, forced to tell him how I plead.
On top of everything, I haven't any protection
Not worried about a thing, but to show her my affection
Left with no other choice, forced to grow up so quick
Growing up is not much of a treat, but maybe one big trick.

Brandon Gargiulo, Grade 9
Gulf Coast Marine Institute, FL

The Coward in Me

Run away and hide your face,
Run away with shame,
Run away from this evil place,
And wish away the pain.

Tammie Trinh, Grade 9
Bishop Denis J O'Connell High School, VA

Basketball

Shoes squeaking like little mice,
Ball bouncing up and down,
People yelling and cheering loud,
This is basketball.

Coaches yelling loud and clear,
Setting up plays to the left and to the right,
Teaching younger players how to play,
This is basketball.

Players dripping sweat by the gallon,
Playing hard with all their might,
Cheering their teammates on,
This is basketball.

People playing precisely and powerful,
Sounds all around like *swish, squeak,* and *yeah,*
People running up and down the court,
This is basketball.

Troy Becker, Grade 7
William Penn Middle School, PA

Beach

On a hot summer day with nothing to do
The possibilities are endless but it's up to you
Out of my personal favorites and you must agree
Pack a towel and sub and head for the sea

And while you are there what will you do?
The possibilities are endless, it's up to you.
Put out a towel and a get a nice tan
Or swim in the sea or build a castle of sand.
Play volleyball or watch two crabs fighting
Or perhaps do something a little more exciting,

Become close friends with a sea monster,
Discover a palace of mermaids
Make a sandwich of jellyfish jelly
Watch a school of fish parade
Be carried away by two seagulls
Or play tag with a shark

But before you know it, it's getting late, it's almost after dark.
What fun at the beach lets go again,
You look at yourself, you are bright red.
"Oops I forgot to put on sunscreen."

Alissa Musto, Grade 8
St Mary Academy-Bay View High School, RI

To Eyre is to be Human

As long as Jane could remember she was always alone
Her cousins were not amicable and at the sight of her Aunt Reed turned to stone
She was neglected for being "demonic" for being accused of committing sins
But when Brocklehurst tried to alienate her the condolences began to pour in

8 years she spent at her school before she applied for some work
She'd earn the title of governess and the one of teacher she'd shirk
She arrives at the estate of Thornfield stately in picture and frame
Likewise is its master he donned Rochester as his name

A man of harsh features with a dark secret concealed
Would one day become Jane's husband but for his actions God must level the playing field
He would lose his hand and the sight in his eyes
And still his Jane returns to him is that much of a surprise

Eddie Feller, Grade 9
Council Rock High School South, PA

The Story of Man

Purpose, that's what we are trying to find.
A reason for our existence to make our time here more bearable.
It's only natural, no one likes to feel they've been cheated out of something.
The promise of life and for what to die empty handed; No!
So we try to find that purpose, we search high and low, far and wide, almost everywhere our heart drags us to.
And while some do find what they are looking for, others still can't.
So life goes on for them, always thinking if they searched in the right places, if they searched hard enough, if they did all they could.
It's not until they are in their deathbed thinking back that they realize it was there all along...
"All that searching wasn't in vain," they might sigh.
The people they met, the stories they heard, the experiences they now have. I'm sure they wouldn't trade that for a second chance.
And maybe it's not exactly what they were looking for, but it's just as good, perhaps even...better.

Abimael Rubio, Grade 9
Southern High School, NC

Advice for Those Who Are Far Away from the People They Love

When they leave, tell them you love them, hug them,
hold them in your arms as hard as you can, finally let them go.
You can't do anything else.
Never forget them. Think about them a lot.
Call them, write to them, visit them, but don't stop to live.
Don't avoid other people. Make new friends. Go out. Cry and laugh.
Know that even if you can't see them, they are still there for you.
Be there for them too.
Have picture of them them in your room, look at them. Think.
Remember the moments spent with them. Smile with a tear in your eyes.
Talk about them with your new friends, never say bad things behind their back.
Let peace be between all your friends, your new ones and the others.
At night, cry thinking of them, but smile remembering their laugh, their voice, and their beautiful smile.
Look at the stars, they might be looking at them too, thinking of you. You all live under the same sky.
Go visit them whenever you can, but don't be scared if you can't go, they won't forget you.
Be nice to them and do everything you can to show them how you feel. Wish them luck.
The new friends will leave too, like everybody, but don't think they are leaving you,
they are just moving on with their life, like you do sometimes.
Start over, make new friends, but don't forget the others.
Wherever they are, miss them, love them and let them know that.

Zelda Wanstok, Grade 8
International School of Boston, MA

Dawn

The colors of dawn, soft and inviting
Beautiful, like the song of a bird
Graceful, like the movements of dance
Warm, like a fire on a winter's eve
Dawn, marking a new day, a new beginning

Sydney Collins, Grade 7
North Bethesda Middle School, MD

Beach Weeks

Waves rocking, sunscreen, big rides,
sun's high in the sky, very hot,
sandy hair, feet and hands.

Puffy white cloud, not covering the sun,
sun is warm on my face and back,

Squeaky sand, waves crashing upon the beach,
seagulls squawking, dogs barking,
frisbee throwing kids.

I am wondering, while laying out tanning,
in the heat of the afternoon sun,
will I always go here, why do I have to leave,
will this always be here?

I feel so happy when I am here,
and joyous, yet calm, relaxed, chill,
and peaceful, but out in the water,
I feel hyper and excited.

Fun in the sun!
Fun in the sun!
Fun in the sun!

Kayleigh Wilkes, Grade 7
William Penn Middle School, PA

The World

The world is such a great place
With so many different features,
God created each and every face
And He created all the different creatures.

The world is full of different kinds of people,
Many from a different race.
Some attend a church with a steeple
And some live ungodly upon this place.

God created everyone, young and old
And He has a great plan.
In the Bible He has told
His plan for each and every man.

In this world there are so many great wonders
From the deep seas, to the mountains that thunder.

Matthew McKinney, Grade 9
Elmira Christian Academy, NY

The Love of My Life

The love of my life is my boyfriend.
He's sharing, loving, and caring.
I love this boy with all my heart,
but the things he does make us tear apart.
We fuss and fight
then we are all right.
I love being around him so much.
He brightens up my day and makes me smile.
Whenever I'm mad and sad he knows how to make me glad.
If I didn't have him I don't know what I'd do.
The love he brings makes my whole life change.
He's not like all other guys
he accepts me for who I am.
That's why I'm glad that I have him.
I never pictured it being like this,
but I guess we where meant to be.
Truly I love him and hope he is the future husband for me.

Martequa Clark, Grade 9
Seminole County Middle/High School, GA

Day and Night

Day
Bright, safe
Enjoying, laughing, playing,
Sun, light, clouds, sight
But all too soon,
The twilight reigns,
The illuminating radiance of day gradually fades to dusk,
The sun disappears in brilliant flashes of orange and pink,
And then,
Stars, moon, shadows,
Sleeping, shivering, creeping, quivering,
Dark, dangerous,
Night.

Ryan Pindulic, Grade 7
Anthony Wayne Middle School, NJ

Hope in the Holocaust

As the days pass before me,
I feel death coming closer.
I envy the birds outside,
Free to roam where they choose.
Flying away into the red glowing sun,
Hope is all I have left.

They can take away my food, family, freedom,
But they can never take away my hope.
The only thing they have not taken from me,
The one thing that keeps me going every day,
Hope is all I have left.

Maricarmen Soto, Grade 8
Glades Middle School, FL

Music

Music is life.
It fills people with sorrow,
And also with joy.

It warms people's hearts,
Lifting all their worries.
It is their hope.

It connects people,
With its words and thoughts.
Music mends souls.

Music is cherished.
Music is everywhere.
Music is life.

Audrey Burnim, Grade 7
Hampstead Academy, NH

Freedom

a crisp apple
the birds of spring
a meadow of flowers
a flying bird in the sky
the warmth of a toasty fire

Denver Hedrick, Grade 7
Madisonville Middle School, TN

Looking Ahead

The clock is ticking on my life
This one life I have led
But now the time has come for me
To start to look ahead
I've thought of all the fun I've had
Thought of the things I've done
But now that I have thought about it
My life has just begun
I'm moving on to high school
A place where I'll learn some more
And for me to do my best
I know it will be a chore
Then onto college I will go
And onto bigger things
But I know if I try hard enough
I can do anything

Sam Mailand, Grade 8
Inter-Lakes Jr High School, NH

Fusion

It's in the past.
Let the world wait.
Make things right
And never let go.
Death is the end
But the end is only the beginning.

Tyler Gough, Grade 9
Hamburg Area High School, PA

Finally Six!

The fresh scent of blossoming flowers surrounds the newly cut grass,
and the sun gleaming down, singing with light.
Smoke floating in the air off the grill,
sending the scent of juicy meat throughout the people-filled yard.
My family and friends talking among themselves,
happy to be their for my big day.
Colorfully wrapped presents catching my curious eyes.
My grandma's famous birthday cake waiting to be eaten,
with seven candle propped on top (one being good luck, of course.)
Singing balloons tied in a bow at my seat as if I was a queen on my throne.
All of my friends having a great time playing made up games,
running around like someone's about to capture them.
Never did I want that day to end.
                    Bam!
The day went by and I was six.

Hannah Bullard, Grade 8
William Penn Middle School, PA

Horses

Riding together my horse and I, feeling free and as fast as could be
Nothing standing in my way, just my horse and me

Saddlin' up, takes no time
Jumpin' on high as the sky
Riding together my horse and me

Once again, riding together, my horse and me
Tomorrow awaits for another day of
My horse and me

Amanda Hurdle, Grade 7
Perquimans County Middle School, NC

You Are My King

A crown filled with jewels, isn't enough,
To show the world Your amazing love.
A rising mountain, touching the sky,
Isn't enough, to show the world why…
You are my Savior, You'll love me forever.
In some unknown way, You're there every day,
I really wanna find, how You could've died, for me.
But of course You are my King.
A marvelous, golden throne, isn't enough. To make Your name known.
A beautiful, white horse, isn't enough.
To show the world it will be rough.
But you'll be there 'cause…You are my Savior, You'll love me forever.
In some unknown way, You're there every day.
I really wanna find, how You could've died. For me.
But of course, You are my king.
Better than everyone else, with bigger power,
isn't enough, to show you're their strong tower.
You are my Savior, You'll love me forever.
In some unknown way, You're there every day.
I really wanna find, how You could've died for me.
But of course…You are my king.

Alyssa Martin, Grade 7
Burgin Independent School, KY

True Love

I found my true love,
he's kind of like a white dove.
He has a heart of gold,
but who knows it could be cold.
Not many people like him,
but I know he's smart and bold.
To me he'll always be there for me,
because I know his heart is pure gold.
No matter what the people think,
I care for him like he cares for me.
But that's what other people don't believe,
that he really, truly loves me.

Angela Cherry, Grade 8
Seminole County Middle/High School, GA

A Great Friend

A great friend is someone you can trust,
Someone who keeps you away from bad things like lust.

A great friend is someone who doesn't show sorrow,
Not today or even tomorrow.

A great friend is someone whose heart shines with a gleam,
Like a diamond in the water flowing down a stream.

A great friend is someone whose mind is fresh and clear,
But not like someone who is angry or has a sneer.

A great friend is someone who will never say never,
Someone whom you can trust forever and ever.

Claudel D. Noisette, Grade 9
Bishop Ford Central Catholic High School, NY

My Big Brother

It was a chilly summer night,
The lightning bugs were out and the fire was burning
It was just me and my brother
Roasting marshmallows while sitting by the toasty fire
Swatting at the mosquitoes as they bit our bare feet
It was just me and my brother
Zap! A bug flew into the bug zapper
While he was telling me my favorite stories
It was just me and my brother
He was teaching me how to cook a hot dog just right
When the firewood started to pop
It was just me and my brother
I'll never forget the fire as hot as an oven
And the wind that danced around us
It was just me and my brother
It was perfect

Ashley Beard, Grade 8
William Penn Middle School, PA

What Lies Behind?

You may look at someone
And judge them
Without even knowing,
What lies behind that face?
That unexpected personality?
That for some reason can't be explained
You may say it's one way
But when you actually get to really
Understand what lies behind
You will be forever wrong
You see people are not what
They appear to be no matter how much
You say or think you know them
We constantly change
At times without realizing
So next time you find yourself
Doing just this
Take a moment to think
What really lies behind that person
You are judging without reason?

Karina Sanchez, Grade 9
William Turner Technical Arts High School, FL

Beauty of a Thorn

Living
is like walking through a rose maze
Pleasant and beautiful
yet painful and hard to continue with
not knowing what a turn of the corner will bring
a bloom of rose petals
or a tangle of thorns
more than once wanting
wanting more than anything
to turn around
go a different way
redo something
but facing a thorn wall instead
Somehow
weaving your way through
all the way to the end
Turning around and finally appreciating the beauty
the beauty
of life

Joanna Ro, Grade 7
Carson Middle School, VA

Family

My family is something you can't explain.
Whenever we get together
we always have something to talk about.
We are the typical Italian family.
I have heard too many interesting stories to count
from the ones I love.
Now it's my time to make the stories.

Mary Ciampi, Grade 7
Brielle Elementary School, NJ

Him

I think about him every day.
No matter how hard I try,
I still find him dwelling in
The pit of my thoughts.
It never fails.
This individual is no longer
A holder of life, but
His spirit lives in me.
My mom says that at least he
Was able to be a part of
My life for ten years,
But that's the thing.
I miss my dad and I wish
He were here now.
I guess the doctors thought
I was too young to handle
The condition my father was in.
Although, they let me see him once.
The last thing he said to me was,
"I Love You…".
Now all I can do is daydream.

Najwa Watson, Grade 9
White Station High School, TN

Reality

Can you reach for the stars?
Can you touch the sky?
Is it a figure of you imagination?
Is it just a lie?

It's nothing more than a thought
some people may say
but I say if you can do it
do it anyway.

I think I can, I think I can
said the train
so the train ignored
all of the pain.

Zac Luther, Grade 8
Yellow Breeches Middle School, PA

Art, a Masterpiece on Its Own

Picasso and Monet
The supermen of art
Gorgeous drawings and colors
All over the paint splattered canvas
It may look like a mess
Though, you must look closely
You shall see a hidden splendor
With a diverse story in it
Every normal drawing
Has a unique secret within it

Sneha Iyer, Grade 7
Pine-Richland Middle School, PA

The Flower

Simply a flower
Growing on its stem low to the ground
Growing, flourishing, expanding
Slowly and steadily, hardly noticed
Until it breaks free in the wind.
Simply a flower, flying in the wind
Floating, twirling, spinning uncontrollably
Yet still dainty and fragile, as though it will fall apart any moment
As it passes through town.
Children look up as it passes by
Yelling, laughing, smiling
Trying to catch it, but that tricky flower
Continues to float by.
Adults look up as it passes by
The wise ones smile, enjoying its beauty
The busy ones continue to pass, despite their children's tugs and prods
And still some are not looking for any pleasant surprise or joy
They are the ones that will miss out on the smile it can bring.
Without a sound, the flower lands
And with a smile a young girl picks it up to give away
Simply a flower.

Jessica Reid, Grade 7
Williams Middle School, MA

The Race

Everyone ready? On the blow of my whistle, go!
The runners are lined up when we hear a loud blow,
We are off, running on the track,
Hoping we can keep up, so we don't get left back.

Now we are sprinting, like little kids chasing the ice cream man,
Just keep running, win the race! I know I can!
With the dirt flying up, with the sun in my eyes,
Still nothing can stop me, my eyes on the prize.

My feet hit the ground hard, my breathing is deep,
I pass the runner in second and this place I keep,
In the distance I hear people cheering, screaming my name,
"Don't give up!" and "You can win this game!"

One more lap, I'm wheezing like a machine,
I would not be surprised if my face was green,
When the runner in first starts to go slow,
I run like the wind, and to first place I go.

I can see the shadow of the runner behind,
But they won't catch up, the race is mine,
I run through the ribbon, I realize I had won!
My heart is pounding as loud as thunder, when the race is finally done.

Allison Recchia, Grade 7
Westwood Jr-Sr High School, NJ

Summer

In the morning, in the summer,
I wake up and see the sky,
I know this day won't be a bummer,
For the temperature is high.

Afternoon is great in summer,
I go and play outside,
My friend drives up; an in-comer,
I run so fast I almost glide.

Evening is so fun in summer,
I can't wait to see,
I tremble and feel number,
From excitement on TV.

When I go to bed in summer,
I shut my lights off,
And listen to the hummer,
Not a noise, or single cough,
Of the peaceful quietness, of sweet, warm summer.

Genevieve Cullen, Grade 7
Warren Middle School, NJ

Don't Call Me a Nerd

Just because I am smart,
    I don't get 100's on every quiz.
    I am not a nerd.
    I don't spend hours studying before a test.
Just because I am smart,
    I am not a bad athlete.
    I am not weird.
    I am not a bookworm.
Just because I am smart,
    I don't suck up to teachers.
    I don't watch the History channel.
    I don't enjoy homework.
Just because I am smart — don't call me a nerd.

Andrew Keane, Grade 7
Anthony Wayne Middle School, NJ

Family

Always there by my side
Always supporting me through the hard times
All the memories that we share
I know that I will always have someone who is there
The things you do to show me you care
Your love is so true that nothing can compare
Sure we have our differences, all families do
That will not affect our love for each other
I can always be myself around you
I can ask you for just about anything
We have our good times and our bad times
We may disagree and fight
But by the end of the day, I know everything will be all right

Taneeshia Gore, Grade 9
Unami Middle School, PA

Baby Jack

Do you understand as the pretty girls stop and stare
You observe your dad as you play
Declare your words in squawks and squeaks
Swim in the pool with one hand underneath
Half smile at your mom with your sea-blue eyes
Toss your brown hair from side to side
You watch the sea taunt you as it slowly creeps close
To your neatly laid out blanket threatening to destroy your toys
I watch and wonder what you'll be in coming years and days
But I will always love your pretty baby-blue eyes

Leigh Schaumburg, Grade 9
Riverside High School, SC

Poor, Lonely Bertha*

Once, beautiful and wealthy,
Now, crazy and insane.
Her family possesses a strong line of madness.
Rochester did not know,
Until after he had married her.
Her illness appeared after a few years.
No longer beautiful,
Now disheveled.
Betrayed by Rochester,
Alienated and forgotten,
Locked in the obsolete attic.
Madness drives her to escape.
Never wanting to see Jane happy.
Poor, lonely Bertha,
Never seen, only heard,
Considered negligible by all.

Kimberly Amato, Grade 9
Council Rock High School South, PA
*Inspired by "Jane Eyre."

Hello Summer

Hot sun, warm sand, cool water,
And just a few trees, rubbery green beach chairs.
Turtle statues sit stiffly on the edge of the beach
Soft clouds, blue sky, with a warm sun resting overhead,
Turquoise water glistening in the sun.
The unbearable hot sun kissing my shoulders.
The deep warm sand, covered with kids playing.
The wind as still as stone.
Water gently hitting the shore.

I'm so happy…excited…ecstatic

Hello summer
Hello summer
Hello summer

Sasha Skorodinsky, Grade 7
William Penn Middle School, PA

Jealousy

Jealousy is green.
It smells like burnt rubber.
It tastes like lemons and limes.
It sounds like dogs growling.
It feels like being boiled.
It looks like a monster.
Jealousy is being alone.

Claudia Mena, Grade 7
Westwood Jr-Sr High School, NJ

I Am Air

I'm swirling around
without a sound.
I'm in tight spaces,
wide open places.
over here, over there,
flowing through your hair
on a breezy day,
on a Saturday,
any occasion, anytime,
morning, or evening. I'm
invisible, unstoppable, imperceptible
coming in waves, flows, and spirals.
I get polluted,
by mankind
I am wounded.
I am vital,
in order for survival.
I am inhaled,
I am exhaled,
I am air.

Victoria Cocozza, Grade 8
Cinnaminson Middle School, NJ

Best Friends

Best friends
Until the end
That's who we are
Best friends

We make promises
We tell each other secrets
We have so much trust
In each other

We break promises
We tell lies
But we keep going
We don't let our friendship die

We are best friends
Until the end
Of all the promises I'll ever make
This is the one I will never break

Jaclyn Carlisle, Grade 9
Jemison High School, AL

What Am I Supposed to Do?

What am I supposed to do when I want us to meet somewhere,
And you don't answer your phone?
What am I supposed to do when we fight or have a big disagreement?
I want to straighten this out between us, but you don't want to talk to me.
What am I supposed to do when I say, "I love you."
But it's really wrong.
And you are kind of feeling strange because you might think we are going too fast.
So what am I supposed to do? Because I'm lost, "Help Me!"

Michele Parrish, Grade 7
John A Carusi Middle School, NJ

Thirteen

It's here! That special day is here.
Every kid hears how great it is.
Everything changes, everything becomes exciting.
Today's the day, I'm finally thirteen.

BUT according to my parents —
It just means more chores, more responsibilities, more, more, more…
They always ruin all of my fun
When all I want is to have more freedom,
more time with my friends.
Impossible — I can't fulfill their wishes now!

My life has become a ticking time bomb.
Oh No! Five, Four, Three, Two, One.
5:08 PM came all too soon.
There's no going back,
only pressing forward to fourteen, fifteen, sixteen,
and the rest of my life.

Brianna Hess, Grade 7
Ocean City Intermediate School, NJ

Tears of Love

The day that she told me,
I was speechless.
Not an amazed speechless
Not a pondering speechless
But a nothing-to-say speechless.
I was shocked at how such a thing could happen to me,
Why God would take her away from me in such a short time
Why nobody seemed to feel the way I felt.
She told me that everything was going to be okay and I reassured her.
But we both didn't believe it.
As time passed though,
We realized — realized the truth,
That a vast ocean couldn't keep us apart
That true friendship like ours could never be separated
That we were surrounded by angels, our friends.
And the day that she left,
I cried.
Not tears of joy
Not tears of sadness
But tears of love.

Grace Chuang, Grade 7
Kilmer Middle School, VA

Amazing Luna in the Sky

When you're lost and it seem like the end,
Look up to find a friend,

Amazing Luna in the sky,
I come out when owls fly,

I'm farther than you thought,
But closer than you think,
When the sun comes out,
I'm gone in a wink,

Once a month I won't be there,
You won't find me anywhere,
The next night look hard,
You'll see I'm just a shard,

But that's just what you see of me,
I'm a great entity,

Awesome Luna in the sky,
Coming out when owls fly,

And if you don't know me now,
Let me tell you how,
If the sun and I do mix,
You have a lunar eclipse.

Hannah Anderson, Grade 7
Pathfinder Academy, NH

We Will Remember You

The notes came from his lips
Like the love from our hearts.
His music came from deep within
Just like his laughter and his smarts.
He loved to be funny
And put a smile on your face
And he loved to play his music
No matter what the pace.
His jokes made us laugh
And his music touched our soul.
But what happened that day
Would definitely not leave us whole.
My heart is filled with sorrow
To hear what happened that day.
Tears will be shed by many of us now
But he wouldn't want to be remembered that way.
He will never be forgotten
For his life changed many.
And his soul will be remembered
In the hearts of plenty.

Stephanie Sheehan, Grade 9
Tottenville High School, NY

Thank You

Thank you is all I can say to a wonderful teacher
Thank you for being the one to show me right from wrong.
Thank you for believing in me and being the one to help me
Thank you is all I can say to a special person
Thank you for always telling me that I can do it.
Thank you for everything you've done for me
Now it's time to give you back a little more
For all you've given me
You really showed me how to work for success
Thank you!!!!!

Alicia Rodriguez, Grade 9
Miami Beach Sr High School, FL

5 Seconds

What could happen in just 5 seconds…?

Your life could be over, flashing before your eyes
People everywhere could, now going up to the skies
Your life as you know it, could completely change
Everything that was, is now rearranged

Or perhaps someone could hit that game-winning
Game changing, life changing buzzer beater
For just that moment he or she becomes the hero
5 seconds ago he could have been a nobody, a zero

What could happen in just 5 seconds…?

Matt Clark, Grade 7
Pine-Richland Middle School, PA

Crushed

You look pretty your eyes so beautiful your smile so great
your hair so perfect
you're smart you're athletic

you like soccer like I do
you're good at sports like me

we were good friends
I asked you out

you said no "we should just stay friends"
you told all your friends

I felt embarrassed
I felt ashamed

you misled me to think you liked me
you said no

you crushed me
I don't know how long it will take me to be me again

all I know is I wish it were different

Jeremy Kaufmann, Grade 8
Carthage Middle School, NY

The Summer I Was Twelve

The warm yet cool summer breeze
Weaving through our hair and cooling our necks
While we run on the dusty streets of that Lebanese village
With summery clothes and high spirits.

A trickling river nearby is where we refill our water bottles
And at the nearest restaurant white plastic chairs welcome us
As do huge platters of fresh watermelon and peaches
Each three times the size of a normal fruit.

Music from an old radio comes from the kitchen
As we wait for the Lebanese food to be cooked
We dance and sing along with a smile on our faces
Speaking of where and what we will go see next, as a family reunited for the first time at last.

Back into the van that fits seven people
Even though we are around fifteen in all, we manage to squeeze in; who's watching anyway?
Back on the road for more sightseeing while the radio is on maximum
Looking at the gorgeous view of Lebanon as we roll by.

Then a sudden blast and the sound of shattering glass and screaming,
Our smiles disappeared as if they had never been there
Covering our ears as an Israeli warplane flies right over our heads;
That was the end of the summer I was twelve.

Seraina Eldada, Grade 8
International School of Boston, MA

Just Me

My hair is curly like a wave whipping through the ocean of life.
My skin is silky brown like the pajamas that you see in the expensive stores in New York.
My eyes are delicate and small like little crystals.
My legs are long like the roots that plant a tree.
My arms are short like tree branches you find way at the bottom of a tall tree.
My teeth are as white as a pearl that was formed in the deep sea.
My nails are short and brittle like a cookie that has been left out too long.
My life is like a ball of yarn that keeps unrolling, every day unfolding something different.
My world is frequently turned upside down like an hour glass running out of time.
My family is like a bunch of unarranged clothes on my bedroom floor.
My friends are like candy; they may not always taste right but they come in handy.
My smile is radiant like the bright sun shining over the Earth.
My life is great but sometimes it gets a little shaky.
But in the end something beautiful is created like when an oyster makes a pearl.

Kimesha Keitt, Grade 7
Hoboken Charter School, NJ

The Seven Deadly Sins of Christmas

We all know that Christmas is the holiest day of the year, but even that cannot stop the sins. The seven deadly sins are vanity, greed, wrath, sloth, lust, envy, and gluttony. Wrath: two people fight over the last ham in the store with fists. Greed: as the Salvation Army bell rings people pass by putting in nothing, a penny, or a bottle cap. Vanity: a family is taking a professional portrait to commemorate themselves. Lust: a spoiled child stares into a window for the latest toy. Envy: a sibling despises the other for getting the toy he wanted. Gluttony: a family devours an entire Christmas dinner as a family outside watches, starving in the cold. Sloth: after Christmas entire families do nothing but watch holiday specials. These sins are dangerous enough on their own, but combined on the holiest day you'll be lucky not to burn in the deepest circle in the pit.

Sean Breslin, Grade 8
Beacon Middle School, DE

The Wind

You don't see it
You always hear it,
You can't smell it,
but you can feel it.
The wind is as sharp as a blade,
It's sometimes cool as lemonade,
Wind cannot be weighed,
but, wind can make people afraid
The wind can knock down trees
It can sometimes make a pleasant breeze
It carries pollen that makes people sneeze
it also carries those colorful leaves.
You don't see the wind,
you can sometimes hear it,
You don't smell it
but you constantly feel it
The wind

Nicole Schanzenbach, Grade 7
Westwood Jr-Sr High School, NJ

Scars

A tree once stood in a meadow,
so majestic and so proud,
then one terrible, vile day,
lightning came down from a cloud.
This tree, if it had a voice,
would have roared in pain,
then, once again, the skies open up,
and the tree is blessed by rain.
To this day, the tree still stands,
but its soul is in heaven's hands.
It shall never grow again,
as its spirit looks down on what it could have been.

Amanda Laidler, Grade 7
Vincent J Gallagher Middle School, RI

Midnight Sky

Laying on the grass, staring at the sky,
Shooting stars coloring the dark night
Hear the whisper of crickets as they cry.
The brightened moon casts a shadowing light.

As calm as children woken from nightmares
In their fathers' arms shunned from unseen fear,
As I lay there 'neath the sky, free from care,
On that summer night I think of ones so dear.

Burst of color as fireworks light the sky,
This beautiful night, making life so worthwhile,
And as I gaze at the art of the sky,
Darkness fills the sky with so much vile.

This dwindling light is becoming less,
Yet light overcomes the ceasing darkness.

Britney Marshall, Grade 9
Elmira Christian Academy, NY

Anger

A venomous cobra — anger slithers through me.
I am ready to strike; emotions coiled. Ready!

Don't tell me to calm down; I don't want to hear that.
I am filled with rage, fury. Geared for combat.

My mind will not be still; I want to scream and shout.
I despise the evil that's within and without.

Tensions could make me snap at any moment now.
I need you to help me. Oh, Lord, please show me how.

I want to harm and hurt, but you would have me love.
So, remove my desire; replace it with your love.

I'll give you this problem. I'll leave you this hate.
Oh, Lord, please take care of me before it's too late.

I'll give you these people; I'll leave them all to you.
For you alone are just, and you know what to do.

Dontae Barrett, Grade 7
Randolph County High School, AL

A Family

A family is full of people that care for you,
A family is full of people that love you,
A family is full of people that support you.
Family members will be there for you anytime,
They will also do almost anything for you.
A family consists of a mother, father, and kids,
There will also be aunts, uncles, and grandparents,
Some families also consist of great grandparents.
For a family to be moving smoothly everyone has to agree,
Also they will have to listen to other family members.
All families should love and care for each other,
A family should also support one another in any way possible.

Logan Reiselt, Grade 9
Corinth High School, MS

Evan Farmer

Evan

Short forgetful silly amazing
Lil bro of an artist and big bro of an alien
Lover of Ihop
The fears are death and spiders
Needs a microwave to cook on
I give my friendship to others
Would like to see the world
Resident of Highland Park
Farmer

Evan Farmer, Grade 9
Highland Park Middle/High School, NJ

God's Gift of Fall

The leaves are falling all around.
The chill is in the air.
The frost lies still upon the ground.
There's pumpkins everywhere.
The summer days seem long gone.
Flowers start to fade.
Autumn colors come in strong.
The good Lord's plans have been laid.

Julia Wojtko, Grade 7
Redeemer Lutheran School, PA

The Dark Days

I go back every once in awhile.
I can't go that Often.
I cry every time I see them,
Because it reminds me
Of those dark days.
The days I grew up without him,
When he just walked out,
Didn't even say bye.
Where I saw him get arrested,
Taken away in a cop car, drunk, pitiful
He watched as I cried my eyes out

Roses are red
Violets are blue
And so are the days
Thinking of you
Where you are
My memory of you fading

Mariah Minnerly, Grade 8
Louis M Klein Middle School, NY

Innocence of a Child

Oh to be small again
There was never anything wrong
And when the radio played,
I "knew" all the songs.

I would sing and dance
In front of everyone
And not care
If I were judged.

I made up stories and lives
For all the shapes in math.
Heart and Square were married.
Back then, everyone was friends in class.

I miss those days
When I loved to eat a PB&J sandwich
And trade my chips for cheese crackers
Oh to be small again.

Marie Leibfreid, Grade 9
Unami Middle School, PA

Where Is Life Taking Us?

We are brought into this world as mere helpless babies
We grow from infant to toddler
We begin to wonder and discover
Our body begins to grow along with our minds too
We're now a child, starting to learn
Now entering kindergarten, learning the ABC's
Getting older again, hitting age ten
Different obstacles now, like who's a good friend
Now entering middle school where all the drama begins
Graduating middle school, now becoming a sophomore
High school is a much bigger task than middle school was
This is a very long journey to when we receive our diploma
We start to select our college now,
Seeing what we want to do with the rest of our lives
Going through college we manage to come out on top
Starting a career and finding true love and getting married
Starting a family, now is where life begins to blossom
As we get older a new generation forms through our children
We're grandparents now, realizing our parents' lives came to a halt
Soon enough that will be our day too
Could you tell me: where is life taking us?

Nicole Navarra, Grade 9
Unami Middle School, PA

The Summer I Was Three

I peered from behind my mother's leg,
To which I clung for dear life.
A terrifying metal beast rose in front of me,
A deafening buzz escaping from its entrails.

I clung to my mother in a vain attempt
To save her from my newfound enemy.
But the beast seemed to have acquired total control over her
As she continued steadily, prying my hands from her thigh.

I closed my eyes as we walked in,
And the stench of old vomit and dust overwhelmed me.
I felt as if I was falling, and the world was spinning.
I shouted and my mother's hand clapped my mouth shut.

As I squinted through my eyelashes, I barely heard my mother's scolding.
I was too amazed by the recently developed knowledge
That the silver dragon was a means of transportation.
My foe had become my aid in gliding overseas.

I was in the plane on my way to Neverland, just like Wendy...
But I was flying atop a mystical creature, just like Hercules.
My little girl imagination was racing,
And I peered at the world through enchanted glasses.

Yasmine Harrison, Grade 8
International School of Boston, MA

Wind and Sun*
A quarrel arose between Wind and Sun.
"I have more power" claimed each one;
They spotted a traveler down below,
And agreed in turn their strength to show.
The winner'd be he who could make
The man his cloak from his back take.

Sure of success the wind went first,
Hoping the traveler's cloak to burst
By the violent force with which it blew.
Yet tighter his cloak the man held, for 'twas new.
Wind blew, but all in vain,
And gave up muttering, "What a pain."

The sweltering sun took its turn.
Its heat, the man it seemed to burn,
He quickly cast off his colored cloak
And ran to the nearest creek to soak.

So Sun beat Wind fair and square
And the moral is, have a care
For a moral there is of course,
"Persuasion is better than force."

Lilly Carlisle, Grade 7
The Holy Name of Jesus Academy, NY
*Based on "The North Wind and the Sun" by Aesop

Win This Battle
This cancer battle is long and hard;
Please don't send another get well card.
My hair is gone and my body is shaking
Having trouble just awakening.
I hope I can win this battle.

Throwing up not much to say,
Maybe some friends will come by to play.
Or someone just to say hey, but not today.
I hope I can win this battle.

The slow silent beats of the heart monitor echo in my ear.
Not giving my parents much to hear.
Finally the beats stop.
Then my eye lids suddenly drop.
Too late to win this battle.

Now I'm in heaven, cancer free.
Could there be a more wonderful place for me?
Look at me; God has finally set me free.
I have won this battle.

Chase Clark, Grade 8
Briarwood Christian Jr/Sr High School, AL

School
Wouldn't it be nice if kids ruled the school.
We would have a kid's lounge, maybe even a pool.
We would have gourmet lunches every day.
Then we would go outside and play.
We would have no teachers or homework.
Sometimes the kids might go a little berserk.
Whenever we felt like it, we would have nap time
Sometimes after our naps, we could go see a mime.
There would be nobody to tell us what to do.
We could rule the school just me and you!

Donald Kilian, Grade 7
St Stephen's School, NY

How to Park a Car
There is always a time when you must park,
But make sure you never do it in the dark.
Put the car into drive, and slowly move forward,
Being careful not to crash,
Otherwise both cars will have a huge gash.
Park between the lines,
To avoid getting the fines,
And to save yourself from being called a swine.
Put the station wagon into parking gear,
Alas, never fear, your car will still be here.
Get out of the car,
But before you get far,
See if you left a scar!

Chris Madden, Grade 8
New Providence Middle School, NJ

Seasons
The frost is gathering on my windows.
I blow warm air on the window.
My breath starts to freeze,
as I see sparkles on my window as it snows.
It is winter.

The flowers start to bloom in my front yard.
The grass gets greener in my backyard.
I hear bees buzzing,
as I step on my bike to ride far.
I feel it — it is spring.

The pool, you know how it is — only fun.
A swoosh of happiness makes me feel like number one!
Colorful beach balls, swimsuits —
It's melting, but just because of the sun.
It's good to be home — it's great that it's summer.

It's time for backpacks, homework, more.
No more relaxing, such a bore.
I bet all my teachers will be nice, though.
I can't help wondering what's in store,
for me when I arrive at school — oh my, it's fall.

Priyanka Srinivasan, Grade 7
Carson Middle School, VA

Sunrise/Sunset

Sunset
Gentle, colorful
Slipping, melting, glowing
Embers, nightfall, horizon, daybreak
Rising, popping, brightening
Brilliant, hopeful
Sunrise

Mignon Winterling, Grade 7
Most Blessed Sacrament School, MD

Tears

Drip, drop, spilling tears,
Weeping, under waning moonlight,
Tears hitting solemn tile.
The moon shares shimmering tears.
Love gone, though life must go on.

Matt Eisner, Grade 7
Pine Crest School, FL

More Years of War

Heading into more years of war
Vague campaign online
We should have avoided Iraq before.
My buddies are benign
The military shoots terrorists
We shoot our friends
They lurk in the mists
Our games lend
Distinguishably injured
A humble resistance
The enemies lack intelligence
Snipe them from distances
Freshly operated turrets.

Xavier Peter, Grade 9
Unami Middle School, PA

War to Peace

Shimmering swords clashing
Careworn eyes glaring
Sore fists bashing
Disgruntled people staring

Exhausted minds' fault
Soldiers' spirits losing
The fighting ceases and halts
People stop the bruising

Hope is in stock
The war is won
Enemies are shocked
Now they are shunned

Excited people cheer
Peace now no more fear

Matt Waldron, Grade 8
St Anthony School, CT

From the First Day*

Open view of life flows through my mind.
No longer trapped in a dormant stage.
Soon my body becomes entwined.
Not only with life but also its surroundings.
Because now everything is sounding so new to me.
But I'm not afraid because it's only she.
She reaches out her arms and picks me up oh so gently.
In the background I hear, "It's a newborn baby."
I giggle, I smile, I also cry.
A couple of my visitors just said good-bye.
So now I look around with my newly opened eyes.
Everything comes to me as a surprise.
But I already know there are more to come.
My dad couldn't be there because he's on the run.
But my perfect mom is there hovering above.
And no matter what happens in life we always exchange our love.

Terelle Belle, Grade 8
Beacon Middle School, DE
*Dedicated to my mom.

One with Water

Feet in the sand,
Rays of light touching skin.
Overwhelming warmth, inside and out.
Waves come crashing down as the tears begin to spill.
Can't the waves just take me in, swallow me whole and make me disappear?
Leaving this world behind, becoming one with water.
No more worries. No more fears.
Just calming sounds, and a beauty beyond belief.

Tracy Sanchez, Grade 9
Barbara Goleman Sr High School, FL

The Wind

The wind twirls and
dances to the music
of nature while the
trees do the same
in the wondrous blowing
of the wind. The

grass joins the trees
and the wind in
their dance blowing in
the breeze. The grass
stops its dancing as
well as the wind.
And the grasses and
the wind go to

rest with the fallen
flower petals and the
leaves as the grass's
blanket. And the clouds
act as the wind's
white puffy pillow. The
wind and the grass go to rest.

Charlie Patrick, Grade 7
Ocean City Intermediate School, NJ

The Real Easter Egg

The real Easter Egg is not what you think.
It is actually a symbol of life.
It's not milk chocolate, plastic, or colored in pink.
The real Easter Egg is not what you think.
That miraculous chick pops out of its shell in a blink
Showing a sign of spring, birth, and the Lord's sacrifice.
The real Easter Egg is not what you think.
It is actually a symbol of life.

Brittani Roussel, Grade 8
Princeton Elementary School, ME

Summer

Summer is the best
Season of the year.
Even though sometimes
The heat can be too much to bear.
School's out in the summer and
That means vacation and fun.
Before you look around, summer's done!
This summer, I hope to go on a cruise
To visit different islands
to see how people live.
Or maybe, I'll just go to the many sites
New York has to offer.
Like adventure parks, museums, beaches, and
Out-of-door concerts
These places have rides, candy, food, and more.
I can't imagine life without summer;
It would really be a bummer!

Quamari Haynes, Grade 9
Bishop Ford Central Catholic High School, NY

Developments

When I look at a development
All I see is death
I lose my breath
Because off all the death
Know why there is death,
Because,
Of all the trees that died
And all the animals that had to move,
But many did not make it
They died because of our selfishness
We wanted all the land
But I,
I reach out to the land and it takes my hand
I sit under the trees where I can see the bees
Buzzing around working so hard
And again we bombard them,
For their honey just to make money
We can be so selfish at times
So just listen to my rhymes
Let's change these times!
Leave your selfishness behind.

Brandon Kook-Whitley, Grade 8
Pennbrook Middle School, PA

All Locked Up

I never really noticed
the abandoned brick house
with boarded up windows,
locked doors,
and an overgrown yard.

Once, I saw the reason
the last stained glass window,
with a cross and angel
pictured in the beautiful multicolored glass
was boarded up,
a horrible kid,
threw a stone,
through the glass.

I wonder,
what happened to the owners,
maybe they died
in the spire that reaches up past
the third floor,
and maybe it is haunted.

Maybe, in time,
it will be torn down.

Addison Anderson, Grade 7
Trinity Middle School, PA

Lonely

Sitting here, I don't feel a thing.
Lonely inside, but I don't know why.
I feel numb, weak, lonely, and scared.
I try to talk, but nothing comes out.
I feel so alone; all I want to do is to shout.
I'm by myself, with my thoughts racing.
They go so fast, so I keep chasing.
I wish they were here, sitting with me,
holding me tight, saying they'd never leave,
talking to me while I'd cry on their sleeves.
I never got to know them;
I never got a chance!
Only one year old, what could I do?
With parents gone, I had no one to talk to
I feel so alone, but I don't want to cry.
Maybe this is the reason, I'm so shy.
Alone in the world with my words to myself,
They build so high like they're going to burst,
But I need to talk to someone first.
I need a person to be there for me.
I realize I just want to feel free!

Dominique Panton, Grade 9
Bishop Ford Central Catholic High School, NY

Not Worthy

He's gorgeous
I'm not gorgeous
At least…
I don't feel that way
He's gorgeous
I'm not
I like him
I don't think I'm his type
But I really don't know
I'm not gorgeous
Don't change for anybody…right?
He's supposed to like me for me
He's gorgeous
I'm not
What if I did change?
He's gorgeous
I'm not
I think I've already begun to change

Monique Walker, Grade 8
Mount Airy Middle School, MD

Today's Tomorrow

Today, was the day —
the day he took my breath away
when I stood
staring…into those
eyes that were deep ocean blue.
My heart exploded,
and I saw the fireworks.
I saw the blues,
reds, yellows, and oranges.
His silk black hair blew in the wind.
Somehow today was my tomorrow.
I still stare into those big
beautiful-deep-ocean blue eyes.

Jaclyn Chapman, Grade 7
Ocean City Intermediate School, NJ

The Heartbreaker

You put me through so much pain,
This relationship is not a game.
I'm done,
And I want you gone.
You fooled me,
You're out of my mind,
A new love I will find.
I'm in a jam,
My thoughts are in a cram.
I want to be done with you,
So get a clue.
You are never welcome back,
And that is a fact.

Stephanie Reczek, Grade 7
Depew Middle School, NY

Like a Father

I have an uncle
Like a father
Always there
Never runs
From my problems
Understanding,
Loving,
Perfect,
Like a father
At my dance recitals,
My games
Like a father
Cheering me on
To make the point,
The goal
Like a father
Clapping and cheering
Like a father
Proud of me
An uncle
Like a father.

Gabrielle Wimmer, Grade 7
Carthage Middle School, NY

Fire

I am fire.
I am as hot as the sun.
Orange is my color.
I warm humans in winter.
I am very dangerous to play with.
I damage animals' habitats.
Don't Touch Me!

Michelle Lam, Grade 7
St Agatha School, NY

I Miss You

You went to heaven
But you did not die
Your soul is still here
I shall not cry
You are not in pain
Nor temptation
You do not have sorrow
Nor frustration
I know you're okay
I know you're all right
I know you're beautiful
I shall have no fright
So I'm ending at this
What shall I do
Let us rest in peace
With the memories of you

Mandy Myers, Grade 8
Yellow Breeches Middle School, PA

Awards

You did the right thing
You did something great
For an award
That sits on your shelf
That symbolizes your achievements

But what would you do
If wrong was happening
You're the only one to help
And there is no reward?

Even though you think
There is no reward
There really is

Sitting on your shelf
That symbolizes your greatness
And now shimmers even brighter
Because
You chose
To do
The right thing.

Jonathan Busch, Grade 8
Carthage Middle School, NY

Inside This Book

Inside this book
There are hundreds of ideas
Wanting to express themselves
to the world
Waiting for just the right person
to find them, love them,
want to understand them,
Wondering how long
they will have to hold themselves in,
Dreaming of the day
someone will realize,
Dreaming of showing
what is inside them.

Ryan Franzoni, Grade 7
Christ the Teacher Catholic School, DE

Mighty Machine

The tank is a tough machine!
The cannons look like tusks.

Roaring up and down the forest!
Leaving footprints behind.

The armor can't be pierced.
Tough as nails like a beast!
The tank.

Giles Clemons, Grade 7
Oakvale Elementary School, WV

The Drug

Never was there a more powerful narcotic
That netted the souls of the next generation
Went by the benign name, video games
A more addictive drug we have never seen
That captures the mind and soul in a wink
And yet available it is for every child
Is it a joyful form of entertainment?
Or is it just another euphemism for poison
So now we must ask ourselves
What does it kill?
Our time or our brain.

Jonathan Lin, Grade 9
White Station High School, TN

Hey Is Anyone Listening

Hey is anyone listening,
We fly to Mars,
But now can't afford our cars,
We look for new land for a future home,
But signs of foreclosure are now in vogue,
NASA is trying to study all they can,
But is anyone listening to the average man,
We need better energy,
A new way to conserve,
But they keep poking holes in the stratosphere,
What's it going to take to help the poor down here,
I don't understand the point of going up there,
Hey is anyone listening?

Venessa Trofa, Grade 9
Danbury High School, CT

I Will Be

I will be: there for you always.
I'll never leave your side;
Be there for you all the time.
Though things will change,
This love will remain.
Forever and ever;
I will be.

It's time to truly realize,
What we need and have.
There's no doubt we need this love to last.
If I ever lose you, I don't know what I'd do.

Please don't let me go;
I need you. I love you.
Just remember me.
'Cause I will be...

Hayley Stettner, Grade 9
North Hills Jr High School, PA

Free to Be Me

Feel the rush,
            make sure it lasts.
Never be afraid to let it free.
I will never be the staple to hold
anyone back from being herself —
Rush of self
and no one else!
Put on the Earth to be
different and stand out
not to blend in with the public.
There is a difference from creating and finding —
finding the freedom to help
me on my journey.

Devon Tanski, Grade 7
Ocean City Intermediate School, NJ

Writing Is Like Friendship

Personality comes first,
Just like you need to know the person to be friends.
The characters can be happy or sad,
And so can your friends.
You should know what they're like
And know where they're going.
Your friends will tell you their hopes and dreams,
Just don't crush them.
Then comes the plot,
Give the characters something to solve on their own.
You and your friends will go through the good and the bad,
Let things take their course.
Get rid of the people who don't need to be there.
You will leave some friends behind,
But you won't forget them.
Help your characters deal with pain,
Your friends will deal with it too.
Next comes the end,
Everything will be solved, or not.
Your friendship may end,
But you'll deal with it, eventually.

Dara Driscoll, Grade 9
Unami Middle School, PA

Is That Me

Who is she
is she me
she's always depressed
never gets any rest
never sleeps at night
always scared of fright
she feels like she was stabbed in the back
she feels as ugly as a caveman
she feels like she's nobody
as if she doesn't exist
who is she
is she me?

Safa Ahmad, Grade 7
Depew Middle School, NY

The Lake

An old friend greets me as my bare feet slowly step on the cold, rocky shore.
Frigid, black water sloshes and churns as the late summer's cool wind whistles an old, unforgettable tune through my hair.
The aroma of crushed birch leaves and spruce needles bring back old memories,
pleasant ones and painful ones, all as vivid as the cloudy sky hovering so majestically above the swirly waters.

A sole loon cries out, its tremolo sounding like the fragile, broken melody of a forgotten dream.
I hear many miniature splashes as thousands of olive green, algae covered frogs plunge into their murky home.
Tremendous wing beats sound overhead as an osprey with ruffled feathers and a twisted, squeaky cry
soars high above the water's surface, scouring the lake for succulent trout.

The sun peeks above the horizon, turning the immense, wispy clouds
an extremely wide range of violet, crimson, and auburn hues.
I can taste the icy spray as the waves crash against the slippery rocks around my feet.
The clouds peek open, and the golden morning sun gently touches my face, as if to say, "welcome home."

Matthew Barrett, Grade 7
Westwood Jr-Sr High School, NJ

Girl Power

In bustiers and hot pants they come for a taste of girl power,
Geri Halliwell, Melanie Chisholm, Victoria Beckham, Melanie Brown, and Emma Bunton
Are the Spice Girls, but anyone can play,
Fashion books and reality shows,
Undying sisterhood.

Glitter splatters Wachovia Center with stands filled with ersatz Spices,
Fans scream with anticipation, smiles and lights,
And the eardrum shattering version of the wave only makes the Spice Girl magic.

Ginger, Scary, Posh, Baby, and Sporty each strutting solo stuff,
Girl-powering up their copper-hued outfits,
Whispering and giggling like school girls,
Their imperfection is, after all, part of their charm,
Spice Girls find it nice to be spice one more time.

Emanuela Spatola, Grade 9
Unami Middle School, PA

Realizing

When you're all alone and there's no one for you to talk to,
you doze off into another world escaping yourself from the reality and everyone around you.
That's when it all starts to hit you.
What are we all doing?
What is right, and what is wrong?
Is there such a thing as a perfect person?
No one knows the kind of pain that rushes through another's brain.
The mistakes that hold them back from their futures,
and the lies that remain unsolved; still till this day.
You ask yourself, "What is the cause of it?"
Why does it have to turn out this way?
There's no explanation, only change.
All you have is hope that keeps you standing here breathing today.
Fighting for what's right and what's wrong.
Realizing that we are all the same and nothing will change.

Jessica Lynn Bujdos, Grade 9
Brick Township High School, NJ

An Ode to My Puppy

I love you, puppy
You know I do
You make me feel happy when I'm feeling blue
Your sweet puppy kisses
They fill me with joy
You see me in my worst
But that doesn't matter to you
You love me for who I am
And I don't need to be anyone else
No matter what I wear
Or whether I have straightened my hair
Your loyalty never ends
You will always care
You will be there to protect me when I need it the most
You will always love me
And I will always love you

Emily Young, Grade 7
Christ the Teacher Catholic School, DE

You

When I lie down at night and close my eyes,
Your face is what comes to mind.
I start dreaming of you and sunset skies,
Never wanting to leave that place behind.
When I'm with you and your arms wrapped around me,
I feel so secure.
Etched in my thoughts, it's your face I see,
Our young love so pure.
Future plans drift through my dreams;
Life's greatest joys.
Picket fences and anniversaries all meet at the seams.
Thinking of pink — for girls and blue — for boys.
Being with you, I am now complete,
Our destiny, I am ready to meet!

Chelsea Wallis, Grade 9
Carbondale Area Jr/Sr High School, PA

Pass the Buck

The world is war torn and poverty stricken
Being taken over by disease and fear
So what does the average American worry about?
Celebrity, obesity
The legalization of marijuana
Then they blame the government
For issues they were apathetic about

But don't tell the Americans this
They'd just talk your ear off with excuses
Then move on, still dumb as doornails,
To debate whether or not Britney Spears is a good mother

Everyone in this country plays the victim
Eventually there won't be anyone left to pass the buck to
Then what will we all do?

Jackie Drayer, Grade 9
Countryside High School, FL

Sisters

My sisters are my best friends…
My forever friends
They are there constantly when I am weak or strong
When I call for them, I never wait for long
Someone to talk to, to cry with, to help
Someone to laugh with, to smile with, to love

My sisters are my best friends…
My forever friends
They are there when I need them
When I am healthy or sick
If I had to choose them I couldn't make a better pick
Someone to play with, to cheer up, to help
Someone to look up to, to hangout with, to love

My sisters are my best friends…
My forever friends
My life wouldn't be the same without them
When I am happy or sad
At them I can never stay mad
Someone to hug, to listen, to help
Someone to live with, to learn with, to love

My sisters are my best friends…my forever friends

Jackie Chiaravallotti, Grade 9
Unami Middle School, PA

Time to Make a Change

So little time
So many dreams
On to make a better world it seems
I have so many goals to set for myself and others
Why can't we all see each other as brothers?
Let's make an end to hatred and crime
And put children's futures in our prime
Put down the weapons of destruction
And help each other learn how to function
To our surrounding and to our environment
And let's stop being so rude and flagrant
All it takes is one person to make a change
God knows who it can be
Maybe him, her or even me
Get to know as many people as you can
Whether it's a child, woman or a man
Make a better world for you and your people
Be a good influence for younger kids and adults
Because you're a legend in the making
You will run into quite a few things that are strange
But thank you, for making a change

Richard Buhl, Grade 8
Mahanoy Area Middle School, PA

Snow

Soft, immortal, snow
slowly covering the ground
shining everywhere
Joseph Clarke, Grade 7
St Anthony School, CT

Winter

It's white and snow everywhere
No green in sight,
It's almost time for Christmas
Parents are buying presents,
Stores are running out of toys
There is no wrapping paper anywhere
People are decorating their houses
And hanging mistletoe,
Children are making snowmen
And hoping for a snow day,
Here comes Christmas
Kids tucked in their beds,
It is Christmas morning
Everyone is happy,
Gifts galore wrapping paper everywhere
Party time and people say…
Happy holidays to everyone,
And joy to all.
Zaida Smith, Grade 7
St Stephen's School, NY

Lying Awake in Bed

My face is to the ceiling
and my eyes are open wide.
I can hear winter wind
Whirling wildly outside.

The heater's kicking in;
it's pounding on the wall.
Pulling up my sheets,
I wait for dawn to call.
Katherine Videira, Grade 8
Harry B Flood Middle School, CT

Whispering Wind

A whisper travels through my ear
Something that I can barely hear
So close, yet so far
I catch it in a jar,
But nothing is there

I hear it swaying in the grass
I turn around and hear it pass
As I gaze my eyes and hear its call
Nothing is there nothing at all
It soon will travel back once again.
Jessica Overman, Grade 8
Covenant Life School, MD

The Day

The day my heart stops beating is the day I will die,
The day you stop loving me is the day my heart stops beating,
This is a mire example of cause and effect,
But I would like you to know,
I still love you even though you were the cause of my death.
Odane Lawrence, Grade 9
Belleville High School, NJ

Star

She told me I was a star that fell down from the sky
and that came for only one reason: to be her blessing 'till she die.

That fell down from the sky just to make her joyful.
To be her blessing 'till she die and make her so very hopeful.

Just to make her joyful, I was glad to do just that,
to make her so very hopeful, to give her a comforting pat.

And I was glad to do just that all throughout her years.
To give her a comforting pat and be there to wipe her tears.

All throughout her years, I was there right by her side.
Being there to wipe her tears and being her helpful guide.

I was there right by her side 'till there was no side to stand next to.
Being her helpful guide 'till there was no one to give guidance to

When there was no side to stand next to I didn't know what to do.
When there was no one to give guidance to.
I looked up at the stars and saw her face shining anew.
Garrett Eucker, Grade 8
Westwood Jr-Sr High School, NJ

Grandma

Oh how long it's been since I have seen your face
It feels that in order to see you I need to finish the race
You used to tell me I could be anything that I wanted
And to follow my dreams as far as they would lead
You told me that you would be there as long as you were in need
But why are you gone when I need you the most?
I would boast that you were the world's greatest grandma
When we would play for a while you told me you needed a rest
Every time I walked in the door you would give me the test
You told me that I was better than the rest
When we would cook we would sing our favorite song
Sometimes I read the recipe wrong
I would never tell you
You said to me that you would never leave
But you made me grieve
When the cancer finally got you
They told me you had gone to a better place
I felt as though you were as far away as space
Sometimes I wonder where you are
Then I hope and pray you are a star
Malina Bazink, Grade 9
Carbondale Area Jr/Sr High School, PA

Cool Summer Breeze

As I sway back and forth on a swing
The breeze rustles my hair like leaves on a tree
I look up in the sky
And a bare tree catches my eye

I wonder what's coming tomorrow
Will this bare tree still be here?
Will I still be swinging?
I close my eyes before the breeze hits my face
When I open them I see blank
The breeze has stopped
The world is dark
But I am still swinging

Alex Conoway, Grade 8
Davis Hills Middle School, AL

Step

Step into the circle, try to take me down
High legs, low legs, try to throw me around
Step onto the battle field, attempt to score a point
Use every muscle and every single joint
Step into the ring, try to stop my moves
I'll fight, kick, and scream just so I don't lose
Step onto the mat, I'll show you the way
Good luck my friend but, I'm not losing today
Step into my wrestling sanctuary, try your best
Try your moves, but I'll put you to the test
Step on the line once again, win or lose, I won't reject
I'll show all my opponents, all deserved respect

Jordan Schmick, Grade 8
Yellow Breeches Middle School, PA

The Unlimited Striver

As unlimited as the universe,
As hard as a rock,
Helen Keller rode on the rainbow,
As she went through all of her obstacles,
Like a short, sharp knife.

She was blind, and yet she saw.
She was deaf, and yet she heard.
Heard the cry of the world for help,
Saw the pain of everything around her,
And suffered with it.

She strived on, became unlimited, unbeatable, unbeaten.
Like a storm in the middle of the Atlantic.
She reached up, up, up,
And she touched the sky.

Ellen Sukharevsky, Grade 8
Milton Academy, MA

A Hot Summer Day

The flowers are blooming
The leaves are colorful
Birds are chirping
The sky looks light blue
People are everywhere
Everyone is having fun
The water in the lake is glistening
The sun is a pretty reddish orange color.

Quanita Tucker, Grade 8
Seminole County Middle/High School, GA

I Will Miss This

Dare I compare you and the morning sun?
You caress my heart in your secure hands.
Your smile brightens my heart's deep horizon.
The sun floods the set on the drowning sands.

Sun's warmth gives replenishing sensation,
But your touch curses with invalid taunt.
Though down inside the curse is worse than death,
Near temptation leaves my soul dry of breath

Today, you are key to my survival.
Tomorrow, the sun shortly sets again,
But of all I see in charm's arrival,
Its glow will always be just as brilliant.

Yes, how true it seems I shall long for this,
All your sweet sunsets will dearly be missed.

Katelyn Hand, Grade 9
Brookwood High School, AL

Punta Cana<3

Of all the places to see,
Punta Cana was the place to be.
The golden sun lit up the sky,
Making the crystal waters sparkle like a diamond.
On top of the water,
dolphins danced in the air,
but under the water,
it was like a dream.
The colorful fish swam with great ease,
they hid in the coral,
so they were not to be seen.
The coral reefs poked their heads
and broke the surface,
making it a sight to see.
As the fish took me on a journey,
I ended up in the heart of the reefs,
where all the fish came around me.
As the sun was going down,
the palm trees swayed in the wind,
A cool breeze hit everywhere,
Making it feel like this was paradise.

Lindsay Knowlson, Grade 7
Trinity Middle School, PA

Summer Days

Summertime is fun,
You get to play with all your friends,
You get to play in the pool,
And also do flips and back bends.

Sometimes it gets boring,
And it lasts very long,
And words couldn't describe it,
Even in a song.

When school starts again,
You shout and say "YAY!"
But after a month or two,
You'll wish it were a summer's day.

Michelle Stanhope, Grade 7
West Cary Middle School, NC

The Truth Is in the Chatter

The truth is in the chatter
The proof is inside
Rarest flavor
Endorsed with pleasure.
Rally for the way
And the wrongly convicted
Indulge in the love story
My heartbreaking judgment.
The secret between us
The moment of truth
My music.
My moment.
Face God
Beautiful-beneficial-infallible-love
Heal me
Love me
Label me
Redemption.

Tiffany Weir, Grade 9
Unami Middle School, PA

Untitled

I hate how "we" turned out.
A nightmare to be.
I loved you, how couldn't you tell?
We were so picture perfect in my eyes.
Now I know it was a bunch of lies.
My tears and blood came out for you.
Friendships lost because of you.
You're ridiculous, a coward.
Now you get "I hate you" with power.
I don't want you in my life,
But you won't leave my mind.
It's funny how you don't even care.
I put my heart on my sleeve,
Now you can leave.

Julia Kress, Grade 7
Depew Middle School, NY

What He Means

Your lips were so soft just as mine,
To this day you make my world shine.
I will love you forever as you love me,
I hold memories so people will see,
You have my trust and I hold his,
I hope this works and it won't be a miss.
You say he loves me and I love you too,
You are so far away so I start to feel blue.
I always sit there waiting for him to write back,
Sometimes I wait so long that it seems you are only a smack!!
My friends want you to call me and say you love me first,
When I am missing you, waiting for you, I can only out burst.
There is a problem though…
I never know what happens with you on the other side,
I won't ever know if I am your girl that is on the side but only as a guide.
I never want to set you free from my arms or let you go,
You are my best friend, you are more than that and isn't that so??
You are the sunshine in my world even when it's raining,
My never ending love for you is never ever draining.
You smile at me and I smile too,
In my life you are more than just my boo!

Jillian Salerno, Grade 7
Merrick Avenue Middle School, NY

My Heart, My Home

Well my life is at a big turning point
I just wasn't happy inside that hate filled joint
Wasn't sure what it was that made me so sad and what made me so sore
But I think it was just that feeling of not knowing where my home was anymore
I knew that home was always a place which I could be totally safe and warm
I lost that feeling of comfort when my heart got too ripped and torn
Didn't have everything that I once had space for in my heart
But now I'm realizing as I look past the lost and such
Look at what I found at the end of it all
I have learned so much
I have grown into something so much bigger than all that little stuff
And if I hold on to the things I lost
Then that will only make me feel uneasy and pay more than what it really costs
So I let it all go
And I now know
That my home was never gone
I know that my heart is my home
Everywhere I go it brings me a new dawn
All I need is the love that I carry along
And I can be totally unconditionally happy
Finally capable of really meaning it when I sing this song

Olivia Scammell, Grade 9
Princeton Science Academy, NJ

Fall

F iery leaves flutter off branches,
A ccumulating into big piles on the sidewalk and swirled by the wind,
L ike a paintbrush dyeing the world with autumn's passion,
L ike wet fingers splashing the world with joy.

Russell Maclin, Grade 7
Unami Middle School, PA

Good Night

Under a cloudless and starry sky,
I gaze in the campfire, cooking a s'more.
A cold wind dances through the night,
Kills my fire, extinguishing the light.

I stand up and run.
Covered in shivers,
I get in my tent,
And pull on a sweater.

I grope for my flashlight, blinded by dark.
Time is short; a chill's coming down.
As a mighty wind beats the tent tenfold,
I find the flashlight hilt in a jumble of clothes.

I gratefully flick the icy switch on,
The shining light turning the frozen tent golden.
Slipping on a second sweater,
I settle in, feeling much better.
After the clouds flow in and the wind stops howling,
My ears make out a blissful humming.

Good night, good night.

Keven Zhang, Grade 7
Carson Middle School, VA

A Passion

Like a drum that starts to sing
Or a bell that never stops its ring
The color of your hair or the shining of a star
Like your attitude, your passion explains who you are.
No one knows who made it start going,
But like your blood, it keeps on flowing
From your grandma, mom or a whole nation
To you, your children, and another generation
Maybe in Africa or somewhere far
Look deep, deep inside and you'll find a shining star
So whatever it is that keeps you going
Remember that your passion, like your blood,
Keeps on flowing.

Mattison Bond, Grade 7
Bertie Middle School, NC

Colors of Nature

All together as a rainbow
Falling down from the sky
It's time to let it go
Make it all just pass by
The branches reach out like a hand
The trees stand skinny and tall
Watching the rainbows as they land
On this calm day of fall
The river is a mirror on this day
I would want this to last and never go away

Elexus Buckner, Grade 9
Potomac High School, VA

Power of Nature

I believe in the power of nature —
the sound of the wind
calling out to me in fear,
blazes of fire destroying mankind,
placid waters going upstream,
light of the sun gliding
me upon my way,
and trees growing high to reach
for the sun's light.
The power of nature has always been,
but now it is in danger of being destroyed
by the power of man!

Dominique Meola, Grade 7
Ocean City Intermediate School, NJ

Life

I am…
Added but excluded
Extinct but overpopulated
Different but alike
Calm but disrupted
Amended but kept the same
Adjacent but remote
I feel like I'm…
Happy but sad
Brave yet afraid
Inflated but deflated
Stupendous yet trivial
Excited but reticent
Trapped like a soul yet free as a bird
Grounded like a dog but soaring through the skies

Christina Kinard, Grade 7
Paxon Hollow Middle School, PA

Wind

Wind is beautiful, magical, and great.
It is full of majesty,
Even controls all things' fates.
Wind may even cause a travesty.

Wind dictates where storms go,
Makes trees crash,
Even controls how water flows,
Wind controls how things smash.

Wind shows feeling,
Represents wind, summer, and fall.
It can help with the problems you are dealing.
Wind power can be all.

Jake Buchanan, Grade 7
Chickahominy Middle School, VA

The Poem Problem

I can't write a poem.
I am not a poet.
With all of the rhythms,
and all of the rhyming,
I know I just can't do it.

Try and try and try as I might,
the words just won't fall in all right.
I just can't think
about poems anymore.
It is time to say GOOD NIGHT!

Abbey Hoteling, Grade 7
Gananda Middle School, NY

Teenage Life

I love
Living
I love
My family
I love
Music
I love
Money
I love
To ride my bike
I love
Having friends
I love
To party
I love
Girls
I love
Everyday changes in my life
I love
My life
As a teenager

Derrick Hayes, Grade 7
Battin Middle School, NJ

Florida

Rays beat against your skin
Sand between your toes
amusement parks roaring
putting sunscreen on your nose.
little kids jump
little kids play
little kids bump
and little kids sway
Florida is bright as the sun
the grass is green
and the waters are blue
so come to Florida
for the view

Courtney Schultz, Grade 9
Countryside High School, FL

Fire

Fire runs over the land
It destroys everything in its path,
It roars like thunder and grows bigger and bigger,
It burns trees like matches in a fire,
Then after it is all and done,
The ground is littered with coals as black as the sky at night.

Joe Kelczewski, Grade 7
Westwood Jr-Sr High School, NJ

Dreams, Promises, and Love

Dreams, promises, and love.
What are they to us?
Are they things that we need in order to live happily,
Or are they just there to torture us?

Dreams, promises, and love.
What is so great about them?
They cause us pain in so many ways.
Dreams are crushed, promises are broken, and love is unfaithful.

Dreams, promises, and love.
Don't they have a good side just like everything else?
They could bring us so much joy.
Dreams are achieved, promises are kept, and love is faithful.

Dreams, promises, and love.
How will we know when they cause us pain or bring us joy?
We will never know which is which
Because we will need the pain to get us back on track,
and we will need the joy so we know there is still hope.

Kayla White, Grade 9
Thomas County Central High School, GA

Nothing But the Worst

Lately, I've caught myself thinking of one nice thing to say about you,
But those words are hard to think of, and even harder to say out loud.
I gave you more chances than anybody could count,
I tried to think that maybe I was the one that wasn't being a good friend,
I even considered the fact that it was my fault; but I knew it wasn't.
And the one time where I said this is the last chance, I really meant it;
But you didn't care, and you took me for granted again.
You talk about me with other people, and pretend everything's fine when I'm around.
I don't know what I actually saw in you the day we started talking;
Maybe it was how you seemed nice and you didn't seem stuck up.
But all of that is a lie because you're the farthest thing from a real person.
You sneak behind everybody's back and don't care about the consequences;
But maybe you should start caring because you're losing everybody.
I realize now our friendship was like a dying star.
It shined so bright, but not it's dying out;
Because the trust turned into doubt;
The laughs turned into tears;
The best friends turned into memories;
And until you realize how ridiculous you are,
I wish nothing but the worst for you.

Abby Heltman, Grade 7
Depew Middle School, NY

My Prince

He is a yellow lab
with brass tags and a red collar
that runs to me in my dreams.
Mom told me so much about him.
He was her best friend.
The drawing of him hanging above the couch
is always on my mind.
I've thought about him
and loved him,
but I have never known him.
I know he is watching me,
my guardian angel.
What was he like?
Did he love?
Would he love me, too?
Would he stay by my side,
like he did my mom's?
He knows me.
He loves me.
He is
my Prince.

Alice Roney, Grade 7
Merritt Academy, VA

War

Newspapers cannot end this conflict with pen
There are many small battles every day
War, this monster of mutual slaughter among men

Many people die once again
It should be over this year, they say
Newspapers cannot end this conflict with pen

They send out soldiers ten thousand times ten
We try to eliminate war with a war that does not pay
War, this monster of mutual slaughter among men

Civil men say, "This will be over when?"
"Surely there must be another way"
Newspapers cannot end this conflict with pen

Mortar so loud, no eggs from the hen
Starving men on their knees to pray
War, this monster of mutual slaughter among men

Men huddle together like wolves in a den
Hope dies out when the sun shines its final ray
Newspapers cannot end this conflict with pen
War, this monster of mutual slaughter among men

Michael Mondzelewski, Grade 7
Fort Couch Middle School, PA

Same Old Me, Same New Tree

I used to depend on my family and friends.
I used to be timid and shy.
I would always wonder about the "what ifs?" and "whys?"
I was always worrying, anxious, and afraid.

Now I'm no longer dependent on others,
And prefer to be alone.
I stand up for myself and drive my points home.
I still ponder over the way of the world
And dwell on what I do and don't know.
My leaves may have changed,
But this tree is still the same.

Emily Travers, Grade 7
Palmyra-Macedon Middle School, NY

What Is Freedom?

Freedom is a right,
Freedom is a gift.
Freedom is being who you want to be
And saying what you want to say.
It's eating ice cream in winter
Wearing your shirt backwards,
And wearing two different socks.

Freedom is coloring outside the lines,
It's making your own choices and choosing your own life
It's choosing your own faith, religion and ideas

Freedom is what you feel within,
The decisions you make
And the right we've earned.
Freedom is America
The land of the free
And the home of the brave.

Daniella Amell, Grade 8
Sewanhaka High School, NY

An Ode to Writer's Block

Oh boy
  Oh boy
    Oh boy
Writer's block
Oh how joyless like counting bugs you are
Usually I have a great idea
But you came along
And now I'm
    Stuck in quicksand
      Stuck in mud
        Stuck in *sticky* peanut butter
Oh how joyless you are
Joyless like living in a shed
  Joyless like getting swung by a brick at your head
    Joyless you truly are
Oh, how joyless you are, Writer's Block

Shawn Butler, Grade 7
Christ the Teacher Catholic School, DE

Dark Little Window

Faded images scurry across the tinted glass.
Painful tears pinch my lifeless cheek as I gaze up at the blackened sky.
Horrid reflections of what use to be makes me shiver and quake as you walk past.
Twisted memories grip at my empty heart piercing my hate and pain that leaves me cold and dry.
Your breath on my neck sheds tears of fooled thoughts and unwanted cries that I shed.
I let you in and gave you the world you took what you wanted and turned your back to me.
You started out sweet, gentle, and unique but then you changed and became what I feared.
I saw you go with sorrow tears regretting what you did because deep down inside you still believe we were meant to be.
Days so cold and lonely and each night I taste the pain so true.
I wish I could tell you I'm feeling better every day. That it didn't hurt when you walked off.
I miss you even though you hurt me.
I can't stand seeing something I want in front of me knowing I can't have it.
My whisper speaks a thousand words "I love you please stay."
In my heart to tell you the truth I can't find my way without you.

Ashley Mauricio, Grade 9
Colonia High School, NJ

The Trip to Victory

Second half, one minute left, tied two-two, Diaz throws the ball in from the eighteen,
It floats in the air until, it's caught still on the head of Mario.
The white and gold ball hits the green grass.
Mario heads for the goal full spring dribbling, dribbling between his two Puma cleats.
A defender comes into sight, Mario thinks of his next move.
He flips the ball on his back heel it f-l-i-e-s into the air over the defender's head.

       i   n
     a   b
The r   ow, a tricky play, but as Mario goes after the ball. Trip!!
The ref's whistle screams, as he flings his arm in the air.
A red card appears, the defender got a red card, and is out of this intense game.

The ref signals a penalty shot. Mario sets the ball up on a patch of grass, sweat flows off his face like a river.
The goalie rocks back and forth, trying to distract the shooter,
But nothing is getting through his padlocked mind. Mario runs top left corner in his head.
He kicks it,   e
Perfect   v
           r
        u
      c
The goalie d-i-v-e-s the crowd gets quiet so quiet you can hear a pin drop.
SWISH!! The net ricochets back the crowd goes wild and the team piles on Mario.

Ryan Carroll, Grade 8
William Penn Middle School, PA

Life's Joys

I lay, on my back and listen to the wind in the trees, seeing what everyone sees.
Many do not drink it in, but to pass it by is such a sin!
The world holds wonders bigger than you and I, from the tallest mountain to the tiniest fly.
Some people pass through life thinking only of their hardships and strife.
Intent on the destination, they don't see that life's a vacation.
The world is full of beauty, one just has to look! There's wonder in even the smallest nook.
Life is filled with amazing things, from the grass on the ground to the red robin's wings.
So, the moral of the story that I'm here to tell is "Please for your own sake, love life well!"

Eve Elizabeth Taft, Grade 7
Home School, NY

One Man

How can one man have so many names,
and have done so many awesome feats?
He is all, this one man I speak of,
a creator, a master, a judge.
But what does he know of this life?
What does he know of struggle, of strife, or of love?
Where has he gone in this time of need?
Have our sins really driven away this almighty being?
Or perhaps has he run.
Cowardly run far from everything we have,
run from our greed and need for war.
Gone and left us groping for answers.
Left us praying, asking, needing help.
Let our prayers stand quietly unanswered,
cordially ignored pushed to the side.
But hope does not die easily.
Hope grows like grass,
pushing stubbornly through sidewalk cracks,
Only to be stomped dead by soldier's marching feet.
Crushed by ourselves when no supreme beings help,
we turn upon ourselves in need for answers.

Eleanor Richard, Grade 8
Melrose Veterans Memorial Middle School, MA

Leaf

It's not just a leaf; it's this leaf!
Every little leaf out there has
its own unique personality.
The sweet innocent veins in this leaf,
just suck up the love from the tree.
When I look at this leaf,
I see my family inside
nurturing — a gentle touch
providing everything imaginable.
This tree with open branches provides this leaf
all that nature has to offer.

Amanda Conner, Grade 7
Ocean City Intermediate School, NJ

Dragon

The wings keep a beat in time with the Earth's heart,
Pulsing in rhyme, flying through the sky,
Scattering clouds aside, soaring in loops,
And shaming the graces of the ocean.
Strong muscles writhe beneath the scales of blue,
Catching the light and blinding those who watch.
Falling to the ground, pulling up into a graceful arch,
Spiraling straight through clouds of powdered snow.
Eyes like gems, whose depth never ends,
And breath of fire burning all in its path.
This is the mighty Dragon of legend
Come to life by ancient magic
That is to guard the portal
Between the magical world and ours.

Victoria Leonard, Grade 9
South Aiken High School, SC

Winter Rain

Pit, Pat, Pit, Pat.
The raindrops beat quietly against the windowpane.
Pit, Pat, Pit, Pat.
I have a message they seem to say.
Pit, Pat, Pit, Pat.
Please listen I pray.
The heavens are crying,
The rivers are flowing.
Oh, how terrible it is to see us falling.
The clouds are ill,
And I beg you, please be still.
Oh polluters, hibernate for just a day,
And I promise you for when you wake.
You will see our beauty,
How lovely we just are,
And how you need us to do our part.
Pit, Pat, Pit, Pat.
The children sigh.
Oh, how awful it is,
To see the heavens cry,
Winter Rain.

Carey Feng, Grade 8
Henry C Beck Middle School, NJ

Poetry

Poetry isn't just words on paper.
It's a piece of yourself to save, and look back on later.
It's an artist's painting, a singer's song.
It's an astronomer stargazing all night long.

It's a dancer's steps, a guitarist's strings.
It's an author's story, an eagle's wings.
It's a runner's heartbeat, a lover's heart.
It's a coach's team, it's a work of art.

It's a teacher's classroom, it's a mother's child.
It's an animal's freedom in the wild.
It's a doctor's patient, a lawyer's case,
It's designer's style a model's face.

It's a policeman's duty, a musician's notes.
It's a soldier's honor, an elective's votes.
It's an accountant's calculator, a child's childhood itself.
It's an avid reader going from shelf to shelf.

But no matter who you are, and no matter what you do,
Look deep down and find the poetry that's just right for you.
'Cause poetry isn't just words on a paper.
It's a piece of yourself to save, and look back on later.

Samantha Forbes, Grade 7
Carthage Middle School, NY

Defense

Defense,
I see the player sprinting down the field.
I flash the antagonizing smile,
the smile of a defender,
spreads across my face.

I thrash my stick high,
position my feet slightly slanted.
The player nears me.
I begin to scream "ball."
I push her,
drive her to the sideline.

Eventually she is off the field, completely.
She glares at me.
Her face scrunched with annoyance.
Her eyes filled with defeat.
She slams the ball into my stick.

I glare back.
My face, perfectly normal,
except,
the antagonizing smile,
the smile of a defender.
Jennifer Cannan, Grade 8
Carthage Middle School, NY

Magic

Powerful spirit
In the imagination
Magic in the air

Used to grant a wish
So it makes a dream true
And then be happy

Magic is in myths
Anything is magical
Even in our dreams

You can believe it
When you evenly see it
In your own hearts too.
Shreya Patel, Grade 9
Methacton High School, PA

Rising Against

I hold my head high,
You disgust me the way you lie.
You're not so perfect, are you?
I hate you more and more each day.
Fallen to the ground,
You said you'd catch me if I fell but now,
It's your loss, because you've lost me.
Avery Czechowicz, Grade 7
Depew Middle School, NY

What Do I Do?

I don't know who I should listen to.
My heart beats for you but I don't know what to do.
What would you do if two people were telling you two different things?
You're telling me to be with you but my friends don't want me to.
What do I do?
Do I listen to you or turn from you?
Do I listen to them and ignore you?
Do I listen to you and forget them?
What do I do?

Dana Martinez, Grade 7
Thorne Middle School, NJ

Bella

The Labrador ran through the house
with her icy cold, soaking wet nose, like a Dasani water bottle.
Along with the thudding sound of her paws —
which sounded like fireworks bursting in the sky — came mud galore!
Those gray, scratchy, oversized paws of hers
were like big chunks of meat slapping off a rock.

As Bella came in the house,
she tracked in musty grass and dark mud.
There were tracks of mud and grass
on the clean and sparkly kitchen floor.
Mom stomped in and saw what Bell had done
and roared so loud at the innocent puppy
it seemed as if it could rumble the stars out of place.
and Bella gave mom the "Puppy Dog Face."

Angelina LaBella, Grade 7
Trinity Middle School, PA

Those That Hold the Beauty of Truth

You tell me not to mention sufferings in life
Because it's everywhere and everyone knows
When there isn't one that hasn't gone through strife
You say writing is meant for beauty…nothing ugly or low
But the weight of the untold future is what I carry
I've seen my mother form a coat of steel, made from melted lessons
And sharp epiphanies molded onto her skin
Only does time toughen her to know what has to be done
She's a keeper most would say, a protector of sorts
I've seen my father talk whimsy of better things to come
Only hoping…but knowing a dream is what it's called,
A rosy blur thrashed by the sudden reality of what he's become
He's a sweet singer yet his sealed voice isn't shown
It is sold for the family's monthly sum
Living off fated choices as he hums weakly and true to its tone
I've been told not to lie but make fantasies
To stir my imagination in turn to get through scarcity
You say to write the world as beautiful, "true beauty"
But "false beauty" was made through the ignorance of reality
So I burnt the ugliness away until the bitter essence of true beauty is left
The true beauty of life, of suffering is only kept.

Julie Chen, Grade 9
Bronx High School of Science, NY

My Unsent Letter

Dear Mom,
I've learned everything from you:
I'm strong, I can do it.
It's never going to be easy, but it will be worth it.
I can conquer anything.
I've learned everything from you:
I'm human, I'm going to make mistakes,
It's my job to fix them, and learn.
Every day is a lesson,
Each lesson is something to cherish.
I've learned everything from you:
You showed me to be a good —
Friend, sister, daughter, niece.
I've learned everything from you:
Most importantly you've taught me to love.
Unconditionally.
This is my unsent letter, my thank you.
My promise to you, that you will be my best friend,
My soul mate.
Forever.
Love always, Me.

Jessica Ryan, Grade 8
Carthage Middle School, NY

Spring

The Earth awakens;
    new life begins.
Spring has arrived.
    Life's slumber ends.

The wet, soft ground
    reveals what's below.
The vivid colors
    bursting to show.

Limbs break out
    with buds so bright.
Reflecting against
    the cool, blue light.

In the air around
    and up above,
Feathered friends sing
    their lyrics of love.

A season of hope,
    spring's rebirth anew.
Cleansing creation
    with its morning dew.

Caroline Brennan, Grade 8
Briarwood Christian Jr/Sr High School, AL

Music

Music calms people and soothes everyone
The talent of being a composer is very hard
The grace of music enlightens everyone
The notes are like a language and cheers up everyone
When you're mad or sad your mood changes
And a smile shines on your face
After the slow pace of Beethoven's eighth

Shlomo Zelefsky, Grade 7
Yeshiva Ketana of Manhattan, NY

Soccer Fields of Fun

Goals stand tall, fields lined, trees waving
Birds in the sky call
Soft grass waves back and forth
Spring warmth
It's the evening, close to sunset
The sun casts an orange glow
The sun is settling down for a nap tonight
Sun reflects on the ripples of the puddles
My cleats squish in the wet soft grass
Soft gentle breeze rustles the trees
People's voices near and far
Voices are excited
Birds call and some dogs bark
The ball is being dribbled
Heavy breathing from running
I wonder if in the future it will be here
Holds a lot of emotional memories
Excited, happy, hyper and anxious to start
Field of fun
Field of fun
Field of fun

Sarah McComas, Grade 7
William Penn Middle School, PA

Cooking

Chopping, stirring, heating, baking
My mom is the most phenomenal cook in town.
She knows how to cook up a storm.

Teaching to chop
Showing to heat
Loving to bake
Hating to stir

Amateur cooks look for advice
from her.

The pans are greasy.
The aprons are shiny clean.
The spatula is dirty but,
Our bellies are full.

My mom the best cook in town.

Nick Parkes, Grade 7
Brookline Regional Catholic School, PA

If and I

If you say it's ok
I know it's ok.
If you say don't go there
I will avoid there at all costs.
If you hold me tight
I do not move.
If you push me away
I panic.
If you tell me a secret
I tell no one.
If you tease me
I know it's all in good fun
If you hurt me…
But you don't.
If you say "Trust me"
I give you my everything.
If you say "Little Sister"
I say "Big Brother."

Jillian Altrichter, Grade 8
Gravelly Hill Middle School, NC

Snowboarding

The thrill of the speed
Makes my adrenaline flow.
And I crouch low
As I flash by the white, glistening snow.

When it drops to zero below
I feel it down to my little toe.
So I sit down by the fire to warm up
And get all comfy, with a hot cocoa cup.

Ben DeVries, Grade 8
Covenant Life School, MD

Less Than Zero

Feels like less than zero now,
But I'm not quite sure how.
But it's not really me
Who's lowest as can be.
Everyone knows it's you.
You aren't even a two.
How does less than zero feel?
I've got to tell you, this is real.
I'm not the best, and I'm glad,
But your situation is really bad.
Less than zero is lower than low,
Because you never know where to go.
You're all alone in this life,
But that's your fault not mine.
So while you stay
Less than zero today,
I'm happy as can be
Just being me.

Katherine L. Burks, Grade 8
Southaven Middle School, MS

Here I Stand

Here I stand needing something to eat
Here I stand needing somewhere to sleep
But also I need someone to keep, me warm at night
I am so tired of my life of family strife!
So tired of being alone at night!
So here I stand asking you to change my life.

Mecca Wright, Grade 7
Sewickley Academy, PA

Dark

I sit there alone a child that no one wants to meet
That no one gives a chance
I sit and listen…of birds as they fly by
The sounds of yelling children as they play
My lights are turned off, and all my shades are pulled down
I can smell my mother's stew as it boils on the stove
As she dumps in those last few ingredients
The taste that could make any mouth water
I listen to the sounds of my father as he walks in the front door
I wait…and hear him walk up the stairs the sounds of his footsteps are closer now
Like the sounds of drums at a musical festivity
I hear my bedroom door click…
The sounds of the door as it swings open, travels through my empty room
I look up and now all I can do is wish…
Is wish…wish to see…
To be able to see again
The faces of the people I love so very much
To get out of the terrible twisted world I'm in
The Dark

Alec Lapan, Grade 8
Milford Middle East School, MA

Trapped

Trapped in a corner.
Helpless and
Trapped.
I sit there and witness
How can someone know they're doing harm,
Not only to her child, her spouse, but also to
Herself and continue to input the Devil himself
Into their body and spirit?
I can never fully understand, but I do understand that
Addiction is a powerful being.
I plead, "Stop! Please, stop! Don't you care enough to just stop?"
For one to devour a power greater than themselves
Takes pain, agony, willingness, and defeat.
One thing, one dose, one minute, that's all it takes.
But to defeat the drug, whatever that may be for you,
It takes a million other things,
A million other doses, and a million more minutes.
Until then,
Trapped in a corner.
Helpless and
Trapped.

Sequoyah Rodgers, Grade 7
Summerbridge Pittsburgh School, PA

Orange

Orange is a sunset going to sleep
Orange is the color girls look like after a fake tan
Orange is the taste after you ate a nice juicy orange
Orange is the feeling I gct when I'm happy
Orange looks like flowers blooming in the spring
Orange is what I feel after a Cleveland Cavaliers game
Orange is a happy color

Markie John, Grade 7
Gowanda Middle School, NY

Breath of Fresh Air

I am who I am,
I don't care what you think,
to be alive
and to live,
are two separate things.
To be alive is to judge those who live.
To live is to do things,
and to dream big.
I'm different than most,
some may say weird.
I'll shout it from the rooftops,
I'll show no fear,
and there will be no tears,
and most important of all,
I'll never let those judgments become sears.

Emily Hawkins, Grade 9
Summertown High School, TN

The Morning Sun

The deep ebony clouds crawl away,
Showcasing the dazzling sun.
As the sun boldly shines,
Gold, crimson, and violet hues paint the sky.

The dark, sinister night dashes away,
When the angelic sun beams a brilliant grin.
The shining light brings an essence of hope,
And no matter what the adversity,
The effect of the glow is always the same,
A widespread sanctuary.

The sprouts are able to grow,
Are able to stand up and kiss the sun beams.
When the spring sprouts grow,
Land sparkles from the dew and golden youth.

The point pushes out of the oblong egg.
From the small opening a beak appears.
Along with a tiny head,
And two vivid eyes,
A soft chirp fills the air.
The mother's eyes are now,
As exuberant as the dazzling, morning sun.

Mallika Patkar, Grade 7
Carson Middle School, VA

Rosewater

Every June, when butterflies flap their wings in the sultry air
When ice cream runs sticky down wrists
I go with my grandmother, my mother, my uncle
And a bouquet of delicate roses
Down to the river.
The river where my grandfather used to watch
The nearly invisible strength of the tides.
We say how we loved him,
Then we toss these roses and watch them drift,
Marching slowly onwards by the moon's direction
On the back of the languid river.

Today, in October, this river smells like
Gasoline!
Plastic bottles dance clumsily on its brown surface
Candy wrappers are their royal robes,
These kings of the littered water.
The roses are ephemeral, their petals are gone
Out to sea on the morning's sunlit waves, or
Down to the depths of the murky river
Deep within its eternal soul.

Sasha Dudding, Grade 9
Dalton School, NY

My Life

Bam, my tomorrow and today have gone right before my eyes
Sometimes I know my life is like a roller coaster ride
And as I take a deep breath and slowly sigh,
My eyes fill with tears as I begin to cry.

As I look up to the sky and see my feet on the ground
I still have noticed that I wear the king's crown
Now I remember who this person is standing before me
It was me all along, I just could not see.

I am as tall as a tree, as strong as a gorilla,
I am huge in my world, just ask Godzilla.
Now I know who I am and what I will become,
My life is as bright as the stars and the sun.

I am the king in my world and now I can rule,
I know that drugs and alcohol are not cool.
Now that I realized how much power that I have,
I can pick up the entire world, and still hold my mass.

Roses are red,
Violets are blue,
My life is now shining,
And the world is too.

V.J. Cabbler, Grade 8
Westampton Middle School, NJ

Sunset Boating

Bouncing on a tube,
a tug boat passes and
a small boat speeds by.
The sun bounces brightly
off the river.

Shadows disappear into darkness,
big puffy clouds lightly dot the sky,
water gushes and
waves lap the banks.
My cousin
giggles beside me.

Where is the tug going,
and what about the little red boat
zipping by?

Serenity, peace and
a giggly feeling
run in and out of me.
Bounce, dip, giggle
Bounce, dip, giggle
Bounce, dip, giggle.

Jessica Zarenkiewicz, Grade 7
William Penn Middle School, PA

Spring

Springing in full bloom
April brings colorful sights
New life and beauty

Taylor Ward, Grade 8
Covenant Life School, MD

If I…Would You?

If I said something
something dumb
that made no sense
would you laugh at me or with me?
If I cried
for something that seems pointless
or even with a reason
would you be there to wipe my eyes?
If I was bored nothing to do
and the nail polish was right there
would you let me paint your nails?
If I was down not a sound
not a grin or giggle
would you know something's wrong?
If I was scared late in the night
when the thunder goes boom!
would you stay up with me until it's over?
The most important thing of all.
If I said I love you
would you say I love you too?

Katherine Dirks, Grade 8
Beacon Middle School, DE

My Compass

The moon
is my night light that shines around the world,
revealing
spiritual pathways to new truths,
acting
as a flashlight guiding my soul through life,
beaming
light through the delicate stars a sparkling awareness for my mind's eye,
unveiling
dreams of the future shining down on delicate minds,
sparkling
diamond-like light reflects down on the world to bring a new life in the
    dark sky.

Paige Rauner, Grade 7
Ocean City Intermediate School, NJ

Rejection Is Less than Friendship

It was a day like any other
When secrets spread like wild fire
Poisoning the ears of all our peers
Secrets that were meant to be kept hidden
When a fake valentine was sent
She said she was only kidding
Avoiding you doesn't benefit to the pain that is penetrating into one's soul.
It hurt to breathe; to even think about you
Now we've gone through everything, we could ever possibly go through
Rejection is less than friendship
So I fought through, harder than you ever knew
The questions and the comments
It hurt, but I denied them
Your friendly gaze I saw every day
It hurt, but I looked the other way
I muster up all the strength I can to keep myself from stuttering
My life would be dreary, a blank canvas without you
Waiting for you to splash vibrant colors for the entire planet to view
Being strong tends to be tough but I did it for only you
Our friendship means the world to me
And that's beyond way more than enough

Kelly Spoor, Grade 7
Depew Middle School, NY

I Used To

I used to be small and closer to the ground,
but now that I'm tall it has all turned around.

I used to play tee ball and flinch at every hit,
but now if my opponent has the football, I put him to the ground lickety-split.

I used to have training wheels and stick to the asphalt,
but now I have a mountain bike and all the other kids gawk.

I used to like going fast throwing caution to the wind,
but now I broke my jaw and am more disciplined.

Jay Crimmins, Grade 7
Most Blessed Sacrament School, MD

The Soldier's Lament

I am a soldier lost at war
My name is forgotten forevermore
So now a nameless soul I'll be
Until the end of eternity

I am a soldier lost at war
My body covered in dirt and gore
Buried with a gravestone and spade
I sleep while memories of me fade

I am a soldier lost at war
I'll be in no historic lore
I won't even be a memory
But I do know that God remembers me

So know I lie in peace at death
Having drawn my final breath
This poem you read is all that remains
Of the millions of soldiers who have no names

Alexander Finegan, Grade 7
St. John the Evangelist Catholic School, GA

My Wicked, Wicked Sister

My wicked, wicked sister, a despicable, horrible sprout!
When I swallowed awful, poison pills she wouldn't help me out.
My terrible, terrible sibling watches suffering with malice,
She chained me in the cellar with our hissing kitty, Alice.
My evil, evil sister I mightily abhor,
Even our imaginary friends wage endless war.
My vile, vile sibling garners only my contempt,
Perhaps our bond grows tighter with each murderous attempt.
My nasty, nasty sister causes catastrophic pain,
She never flushes toilets, she spills and kicks and stains.
I hear that witchy creature is moving far away,
So now I daily scream "Yippee!" and hope that there she'll stay.

Ricky Posner, Grade 7
Kilmer Middle School, VA

I Thought

I thought I loved u
but now there's nothing,
at one point I wanted u to once care for me and
u never did,
when I die I hope you care
and go to my dead grave and say
"I wish I was with her and
gave her a chance instead of not caring,
I always did I just didn't tell her"
please care and help me instead of making me sad

Raven Druin, Grade 9
West Frederick Middle School, MD

Clutch

As I dribble the ball up the hardwood,
I think about my goal;
Get the ball into the hoop.
I sidestep my defender, leaving him hanging
As I dash toward the rim.
I brace myself, ready for contact,
As I scoop the ball into the hoop.
The ref blows the whistle, foul's the call.
I've made the basket, saved our season,
All with one play.
The game is over, but my mind plays the scene
Over and over and over.

Ryan Paige, Grade 8
Carthage Middle School, NY

Winning the Incubus

I know the aroma isn't from this
It is not from the flowers before me
The fragrance is from when I reminisce
The flowers merely represent my plea
This supplication in my heart tonight
Near the shadows of the moon veering red
I start to feel relics of my past fight
Though brutality is something I tread
I desire the war within to start
So I can be free of the wistfulness
So finally this scent will soon depart
I will saunter unscathed and with finesse
Victory is claimed by me! The owner
What other nightmares will dare to occur?

Ashleigh Binger, Grade 9
St Petersburg Catholic High School, FL

Dream

What do you do when the oppressor is the oppressed?
Why do I feel so stressed?
I've got my back against the wall
My mother always told me don't go chasing waterfalls
She had to believe
That she could achieve
He had to run
Just because he could have won
How do you find the blessing?
When you teach without a lesson
Who would procrastinate the date
That they find their soul mate
I wanted to sink beneath the surface and disappear
But I had something to learn life isn't always fair
Sunshine comes after the rain
I sit and ponder on what comes after the pain
One day I want to have an expensive car
Some people tell me that I won't get far
No matter how things may seem
I will hold fast to my dream

Tiara Carter, Grade 8
John W Dodd Middle School, NY

My Home Is Temporary

My home is temporary
Ma says
it's just 'till
the drought passes
and the crops come back

The fields will be full
with cabbages
corn, carrots
anything that I want to eat
we will have
but not now

Now I'm always hungry
it didn't used to be this way
we had a home
with lots of room
and plenty o' food
behind the house

Now it's different
Food is worse when we get it
but things will be better
because my home is temporary.
Sarah Scaffidi, Grade 9
Bronx High School of Science, NY

Escape

I want to escape
Escape from this town
Away from this life
Out of this world

I want to believe
Believe what you said
And all of your stories
Even your lies

I want to see
See all the damage
All that you've brought me
But I already know

I want to open
Open my eyes
To look at the world
Without thinking of you

I want to escape
Escape from this town
Away from this life
Out of this world
Tori Amorosi, Grade 7
Depew Middle School, NY

Moon

I am big, bright, and white.
I give light to the night.
I am big and round,
And hard to miss.
Sometimes I'm shaped like a banana.
At some point in time, I had visitors.
Some times you might not see me,
But I'm there!
Stephanie Rivera, Grade 7
St Agatha School, NY

In the Band Room

Broken reeds
scatter the floor.
Instruments in my way
as I trip through the door.

Friendly faces
smiling at me.
Playing my song
to soar high and free.

I hear the drummer
give a loud boom.
My home is right here
in the band room.
Kelsey Parker, Grade 9
Riverside High School, SC

I Stand Alone

I stand alone
Facing the sky
Whispering away
My heart's content

I smile alone
Laughing at myself
Enjoying the moment
But at a distance

I cry alone
Sorry for the world
And all the damage
That's been caused

I fight alone
Embracing my future
To help the people around me
To save the world

I stand alone
But you don't have to
Stephanie Kulaszewski, Grade 7
Williamstown Middle School, NJ

Snow

Falling, falling, falling,
Snow, snow, snow,
Swoosh!

Snow was falling.
Covering the ground,
Like a soft, white, blanket,
Putting the ground to rest.
Covering the world with calmness,
Waiting for more.

Children dreaming of snowmen,
Snow angels,
Hot chocolate,
And more.
Thinking that the snow was a dream.

The minutes passed by like years.
Ready to awake,
And run through the cold,
White,
Falling,
Snow,
Swoosh!
Abigail Hancock, Grade 7
Hightower Trail Middle School, GA

Bonfires

Wood crackling,
Smoke intoxicating,
Conversations rising,
Deep emotions.

Words crisp
Trapped
Silencing flames.
Heat like a vine,
Swirling around me
In the cool autumn night.

Woods,
Grazing,
Praying,
Hoping,
Wishing,
For that one twig everyone wants.

"It's mine, it's mine"
Marshmallow roasting,
Engulfed in flames,
The sweet scent,
Intoxicating.
Matt Gallagher, Grade 8
Carthage Middle School, NY

Dream Vocals

We have dreams
Some of us are wannabe singers
They are crushed
When they don't steal the night
When they're not stunning
But at least they can imagine
That they were the best
That they were beyond brilliant
One of the top ten
But welcome to reality
Sometimes you have to be very risky
He was risky, and it worked
Everyone wanted to be like him
They all compete, so that they won't go home
But only one's dream comes true
And only one is destined for superstardom
Only one is American Idol

Shauna Kelly, Grade 9
Unami Middle School, PA

Misunderstood

She was a beautiful girl who walked with her head held high
She had an amazing smile that brightened up the night sky
No one cared; no one knew…
behind that smile was sadness too.
She was surrounded by many but felt so alone
But no one could hear the emptiness in her tone.
She had this emptiness in her heart…
that was tearing her apart
She had nowhere to turn to…
No one had a clue…
No one knew what it was about
But yet no one cared to find out.

Jessica Amaya, Grade 9
Bishop Ford Central Catholic High School, NY

Bubbles

Bubbles floating through the air
Everyone looking at their bright blue glare
Never coming to a stop
Just keep going until they pop.

Chelsie Girolamo, Grade 8
St Anthony School, CT

Best Friends

They're there to help you when you're down;
Then other times you just want to jump around;
We yell, scream, and make crazy sounds;
Me without her is like a cheeseburger without cheese;
With her, my life is at ease;
We can't wait for summer '08 babe, it' going to be great!
There's no reason to hate;
Live life with your best friend,
And it will seem like it's never going to end.

LaKiesha Mellott, Grade 8
Yellow Breeches Middle School, PA

Nervousness

There is an emotion unlike the rest.
It doesn't make you feel your very best.
It's called nervousness.
Here's when you get it.
Before a big game or a doctor's visit.
When you are nervous, you get butterflies,
And you tend to tell little lies.
So that's the emotion of nervousness.
It's surely an emotion you'll want to miss.

Taylor Stepps, Grade 8
St. Hilary of Poitiers School, PA

Little Miracles

Small gifts of light on a gloomy day
A special visit they soon will pay
They help all people; you and me
Achieve our dreams and able to be:
A teacher educating an innocent child
A hairdresser whose hair she has just styled
A policeman saving someone's life
A chef cutting vegetables with his sharp knife
A doctor helping a kid with a broken arm
A firefighter rescuing someone from the fire's harm
An environmentalist saving the Earth
A business owner determining an item's worth
A scientist creating a cure for AIDS
A person standing up for the underpaid
Small miracles can give us so much more
Whatever your dream, they will help you soar
Achieve your goals and don't be hesitant
Who knows, some day you could be the president

Emily P. Calvert, Grade 7
Duluth Middle School, GA

Seeking True Love

When what one seeks is never found
Their soul is devoured by the hounds.

They twist and turn throughout the night
Hoping for true love come morning's light.

By day they roam the winding halls
Ever slowly their spirit falls.

Defying despair, there is still hope
Climbing ever higher up the slope

When this desired love is found
At last one's life is turned around

Brian R. Houle, Grade 9
Dighton-Rehoboth Regional High School, MA

Sensational Bliss

Laying on my soft beach towel, I gaze at the smooth warm sand surrounding me.
I stare out at the gentle sea, filled with giggling, splashing children.
Small waves grow, break, and slowly crash down on the children, swallowing them for a few seconds.
The waves bring in seaweed, shells, and other things onto the sand.
I glance up at the vast sky above me, peaceful and blue.
Puffy, scattered clouds slowly drift across the sky in the very soft breeze.
The sun shines down on me, gently and slowly tanning my skin.
I hear the gentle crash and rumble of the waves breaking onto the shore
as they carry careless, crazy kids, screeching and laughing.
Seagulls whine, beg, and cry nonstop, determined to get food.
I hear people's feet thump across the nearby sand, and the lifeguards whistling off in the distance.
When I come back this fall, will the beach still be cheerful and warm, or cold and dreary?
Will the once overly crowded shore be abandoned?
Is the ocean going to be rough and cold, or gentle and warm like before?
When I arrive at the beach in the summer, I am filled with peace, happiness, and wonderful memories.
I feel so warm and comfortable, and can't stop smiling.
When I'm sad or worried, I want to be there, and when I'm there, I never want to leave.
Bliss.
Bliss.
Bliss.

Erin Shellenberger, Grade 7
William Penn Middle School, PA

Take a Stand

Mistakes are made, promises are broken,
Time is paid, because bad choices were chosen
Yeah, I made a bad choice but haven't we all
Yeah, I might be locked up right now, but
Freedom still calls my name and still I stand tall.
Sometimes I get sad and the tears do fall because I now realize that I blew it all,
I had a chance, that I didn't take, but it's okay.
I'll add that to my other mistakes and
The consequences that came with them. My mistakes that is,
But soon I'll be able to look back on this. And know that I have learned my lesson.
Soon I'll be older and wiser, looking at this as a blessing.
People say home is where my heart is, I surely agree,
Because that is where my heart is. And there I'll know I am free.
I will be faced with another decision and that will be to do right.
And whether I stay or not will be my choice.
So I'll take responsibility and show the real me, and I'll show you all.
Just how great I can be, but I won't rub it in. I'll help you to change.
The feeling is great yet, it's strange.
I'll show you all that life is what you make of it.
So join me in making better choices and you won't regret it, yet you will benefit from it.
And take a stand you'll stand taller then ever before. Now isn't that clever.

Jennifer D., Grade 9
Willow Lane School, SC

Panda Bears

Panda bears, so big, like giants. They eat bamboo which is a type of grass. They are black with white spots, or white with black spots? Sure beats me, I cannot tell which. I picture them as big fluffy marshmallows with burn spots. Friendly from afar, yet vicious up close. So protective of their young, just as mothers are with their children.

Garrett Secli, Grade 7
Westwood Jr-Sr High School, NJ

Nature Walk

A walk through the park is like a breath of fresh air.
You feel that soft breeze blowing through your hair.
There are so many sounds and sights to see,
Now just relax and set yourself free.

You see the people jog on by,
Mothers with strollers trying to hush the cry.
Young boys on bikes, girls on swings,
Butterflies starting to spread their wings.

Squirrels running up the trees,
Flowers being tasted by buzzing bees.
Chirp, chirp here and there,
Birds are flying through the air.

Benches are lined with lunchtime folks,
Sounds of laughter, telling jokes.
Picnic baskets on the ground,
Little children running around.

I'm afraid our day has come to an end,
Home is just around the bend.
I know that you're sad, but the park is here to stay,
We can come back another day.

Taylor Benzin, Grade 7
Depew Middle School, NY

No More Homework

Doing homework is a bore,
I'd rather do my chores,
Than work on this piece of paper.
Homework is a waste of my life,
I'd rather get in a strife,
With my teacher.

Homework is a waste of my time,
I sit there as time passes me by,
Time,
Don't pass me by,
I need it for other things.
Like watching TV,
Or playing the Wii,
Maybe I'll learn something then.

I heard that homework can help you in school,
In my head I believe it's cruel,
All I have to do is pay attention in class,
Because it's an easy way to pass.
(Don't even get me started on projects.)

Robbielee Delle Site, Grade 8
Westampton Middle School, NJ

Looking Back

Looking back I see how you were always there for me,
through thick and thin we will be best friends forever,
instead of being mad when I say something stupid
you stick by my side and that's how I know
you are the best friend I always dreamed of.

Meghan Marlin, Grade 7
Depew Middle School, NY

To Be Human

Here's a story.
It's an interesting tale.
It's got everything everyone wants to read about.
It's got love, it's got hate.
It's got happiness and depression.
Anger, loss, betrayal.
Contentedness, euphoria, and success.
Failure, malcontent,
Morality.
Humanity.
This story,
It's a tale of emotions,
And instinct,
And rationality,
And, most of all,
One very special person.
Trying to blaze their own little path
Through Life's forest.
To make a difference.
To be noticed.
To be all that is human.

Nicholas Norberg, Grade 8
Haverford Middle School, PA

Learning

Now what do you know!
It's school time!!!
You are all new.
Kids make fun of you.
You feel very bad.
Your heart tells you to run away.
But you just can't.
Your parents force you to be good.
You try really hard to concentrate.
But it's no help because you don't understand.
You're tired of carrying heavy books
But no ENGLISH!!
When the school is over you are glad.
But are sent to SUMMER SCHOOL!
You work very hard and now know how to speak
Not perfectly — but ok!!
You make one friend and start paying attention.
Your teachers start talking to you and they even call on you.
You don't feel sad but sure miss your country.
LONG LIVE PAKISTAN!!

Arsalnna Sarwar, Grade 7
Intermediate School 141 Steinway, NY

Out for a Cold Ride

Black and white horses
Covered with snow
Uneasy to see the white
But the black was all around.
Birds in the air?
No blue jays or woodpeckers
For it was too cold
My frozen body now felt numb.
The aroma of pine trees soothed the nose
But there was nothing for my legs
Except the clothes I had on.
I could tell my legs were as red as the sun
For I could not move them at all.
Once I was home
I drank the snow off my gloves
For I was thirsty and tired
And the water pipes were solid rock.
I ran to the fireplace
And felt the snow melt away
Soon there will be more
A blizzard is on its way.

Alberto Mestre, Grade 7
Pine Crest School, FL

The Paper Airplane

I made a paper airplane,
And then, it I threw.
It hit on the dresser my model train,
Right into my train, it flew!

This was quite to my astonishment,
But then, quite to my fright,
Something happened that I had not meant —
The plane continued its flight!

I was very astonished and very surprised,
When out the window the plane flew!
I could barely believe my eyes —
The plane had busted right through!

Now I never again saw that paper airplane,
But I can tell you that it flew and flew,
Its flight path it continued to maintain,
And there is nothing more I can now do.

But from this story there is a lesson that's great.
Your words are like this paper airplane —
When hurtful words leave your lips it's too late.
So do not use them, for they cause pain.

Joshua Quinn, Grade 7
Home School, NY

My Best Friends

My friends are always there for me
They help me when I need a hand
I am there for them, and they are there for me
We are always happy and want to be together ALL the time
We make each other laugh out loud until our faces turn blue
We always have fun together no matter what we do
We guide each other to do the right thing
We care about one another
My friends are always there for me

Callie Andro, Grade 7
Pine-Richland Middle School, PA

Justin

I watch the fountain as I drive by.
Its rhythm is smooth and relaxing.
The rippling water is pouring, raining.
How wonderful it must be for a bird to fly past.

In the morning or night, what a beautiful sight.
Blue waves falling, passion, sadness, memories of you.
You were there for me through noise and softness.
Never leaving my side for the world until the accident;
Your life flashed before your eyes.
Here I am today, alive but without you.

One day we'll meet again under the fountain where we met, our first kiss.
The first day promising each other to be together always.
But then it happened, if only you were watching the road.
Why is that truck coming at me…
Justin! A regrace of hugs, joy, sorrow.
We're now forever in Heaven together.

Jessica Elia, Grade 7
North Myrtle Beach Middle School, SC

Triumph

Everyone feels it at one point in time
Butterflies in your stomach, before the big game.
You walk onto the field all you see are thousands of fans starting back at you.
You take your position on the field, your heart starts beating rapidly.
The whistle blows and you're off.
Your feet moving swiftly through the green grass,
Cold air smacking against your face as you run full speed to get the ball.
Now you have the ball, you're in control.
You're heading for the goal, dogging players left and right,
All the pressure is on you to make that goal.
You look left, look right
Then smack you're foot pounds against the ball as it rockets toward the goal.
The goalie dives to save and misses it.
The announcers scream "Goal!"
The fans explode in the stands whistling and screaming.
You feel as free as a bird.
A huge smile stretches across your face
You run down the sidelines giving high fives to all your teammates.
Now you're in control and the game is on!

Savanna Weight, Grade 8
William Penn Middle School, PA

Music

Rock, Country, Hip-Hop, and Metal…
Each type of music is like a rose petal.
Punk, Alternative, Jazz, and Blues…
Sit down, relax, and take off your shoes.
Every kind is important, but they aren't the same.
Who cares, music is the name of the game.
Music…
You hear it everywhere, but you do not realize,
It appears in every TV show although it seems disguised.
Whether it's a theme song or a dramatic game show tone,
You don't stop to think about it, but you're not alone.
Even in commercials you hear it.
Quiet in the background, or upfront just a bit.
Music…
It will completely alter the world.
As styles are forgotten, and new ones are eventually unfurled.
Everything will change.
New fans and new brands with a whole different range.
Music…
Is a never-ending voice,
For which you have a choice.

Brady Orcutt, Grade 7
Depew Middle School, NY

Cat Eyes

Cats' eyes are like a deep ocean, full of mysteries and wonder,
Their eyes are like maps, unending, waiting to be discovered.
When they are curious they grow large, filling with the world.
Cat eyes are going to be mysterious forever.

Taylor Kickbush, Grade 7
Gowanda Middle School, NY

The Race

Boom, we're off
Curve in, the starter yells
15 runners, 1 mile, 1 winner
Speed takes its place,
A line forms around the bend.
Loud breathing behind me, feet tapping, crowds cheering,
A rhythm begins, 3 laps left.
Quickly, they're catching up, I shout to my friend
Speed, once again takes its place,
Hurry, he's right behind you, the crowd hollers.
1 lap left, my breathing low,
My energy fading and others passing,
200 meters left
I begin to pick up speed,
100 meters, 1st place finishes,
50 meters, 2nd and 3rd.
Finally, I race across the finish line,
5 seconds behind my friend,
5:53:07, 5th place
A loss, yet a victory,
A victory for me, personally.

Zachary Israel, Grade 8
William Penn Middle School, PA

Mother

Your heart,
Softer than a feather against the ocean
Your smile,
Brighter than an illumination against my darkest days
You warm my soul
You are the long awaited breath of relief when lost in an ocean
A single star in the sky of a universe of the lonely
You are the colour in my dreams,
When life is a black and white film
An unexpected smile, after years of sorrow
You are the blood running through my veins,
The air I breathe,
My life and my soul;
My mother
I'll never leave your side,
You'll never leave my mind
I will not let you leave my heart
I won't let anything take you away from me
In my protection you'll always be
Until my last breath is drawn away and I am lifeless,
In my heart you'll be.

Almila Kakinc, Grade 9
McLean High School, VA

Letter from a Child

Dear Mother and Father

Wish the days when I was little would come back.
When I couldn't upset you.
No perfect child, but I wish I could be,
And although you anger me,
You're the perfect parents for me.

I know you can't take care of me all the time now,
But I want your attention.
I know I can pour my own drink.
But it feels nice to know that you care.
I'm always going to need you.

You're the adults; I'm the child
But I'm right, sometimes.
Though it seems I don't care about you
You're the only people that matter.
You're important to me.

I just want you to know
That I love you.

Your Child
Nyjah Ferryman, Grade 9
Bishop Ford Central Catholic High School, NY

Seems Senseless to Me

Why?
Why must soldiers die?
What about compromise?
Why must war be filled with lies?
Is the other country to blame?
Must we really go through all this pain?
War is gray,
And it won't listen to what you say.
Turmoil treads tyrannically.
We watch helplessly.
Seems senseless to me.
It's true irrationality.

Jeffrey Holmes, Grade 8
Redeemer Lutheran School, PA

Untitled

Here I am, as always
making my way through
these same old double doors
to get to the homeroom
that never lets out.

As I have often wondered,
is this all really necessary?
To continue on my way as
I have for the past 5 years?
Why not change?

But as always, I walk into
the sour faces of students
and instantly know I belong.
Another day of the recorded
"morning" from teachers alike.

Here I am, as always
making my way through
these same old double doors
as an untitled "morning"
as though the past 5 years
have accumulated into nothing.

Farrah Wong, Grade 7
Peabody Elementary School, MA

Summer Fun

Summer sure is fun
in the bright gleaming sun:
staying up all night,
sleeping in all morning,
swimming all afternoon.

But there's one day of summer
that is the worst day of all
and that is the last day of vacation,
and the beginning of fall.

John Radford, Grade 7
Elizabeth Seton Elementary School, PA

To Be Somewhere Else

They all say the same thing.
Be better, work harder, strive higher,
More effort, make the grade, get the win,
Don't lose, don't fail, don't mess up.
Practice, study, win, pass.
No.
Don't pass, ace. Don't win, demolish.
Wishing for the beat of crashing blue sweeping over the toasty tan sand.
Just laying in the cover of the palm, sipping, eyes closed, mind closed.
They all say the same thing.
Relax.
Don't worry, don't care, don't think.
Don't try to be something you're not.
Strive to be,
Because to be is enough,
When you are being somewhere else.

Sophie Giaquinto, Grade 9
Bishop Denis J O'Connell High School, VA

Gone

I lay down in the grass.
S P R E A D my body out and close my eyes.
The sun beats down on my face and body.
Its fingertips gently run all over me.
Warming me with their touch.
Birds' songs find their way to me; filling me with the joyous tune.
Grass is growing around me, growing T A L L E R.
Trying to reach, the sun; the sky, the clouds
Trees are dancing and swaying to the winds' harmonic song.
Whispering in my ear, twirling my hair.
The breeze is telling me to move forward.
My time here is almost over.
Finally, peace has reached me; and I must r e a c h out to it.
Grab it; embrace it, hold it tight and never let it go.
    I open my eyes.
The birds have flown away; trees cut down; grass is almost gone.
The beautiful sanctuary I once knew,
Now a cold, barren land.
The colors are gray and lonely.
The peace has left; e.s.c.a.p.e.d. from me; slipped away.
g o n e.

Kathryn Marshall, Grade 7
Ocean City Intermediate School, NJ

Under the Shining Sun

Sounds of excited and cheery laughter fill the still air
A glowing sun wraps around my body in a blanket of warmth
Kids dance and play along the sides of the park
They're talking in exuberant, happy voices
As a glinting light beams down into every corner
A light and buttery air flows through my lungs
Sweet scents of daisies and other flowers drift to my nose
A stream of energy rushes through my veins like a bolt of lightning

Anna Darnowsky, Grade 7
William Penn Middle School, PA

Snowstorm

I look outside the window
At the endless train of snow.
I look outside the window,
And see the great storm grow.
I step outside the door now
Into this icy flow.
I pick up the frozen water
Into my gloved hands
I shape it and it falls
Falls in snowy strands.
Soon I begin to shovel it
And the snow disappears bit by bit
I go inside, eat, drink, and sit
And I think of the snowstorm that just hit.

Martyn Mendyuk, Grade 7
Woodrow Wilson Middle School, NJ

My Brother

My brother is a brook
Making music from his bass guitar
And pounding on his drums
Like water smashing into rocks

My brother is a brook
Sticking up for me
Like a brook separates a piece of land
Helping me when I need him
Active, playing soccer and snowboarding
Like a brook active all day and night

Jason Garceau, Grade 8
Swift Jr High School, CT

Midnight

The moonlit path
It draws me in,
With silvery light
And cool, dark wind.

I go,
Down the path
Farther farther,
In the distance,
I see a sparkle.

The stream shines,
Lit by the ghostly light,
Like the stars are trapped,
In its endless cascade.

I cross the stream
Leave the world behind,
And continue down,
This path
Of cold night.

Hannah Thompson, Grade 7
Huntingdon Area Middle School, PA

Oh Florida

Oh Florida,
Your beaches are like no other
The sand between my toes
The sun gleaming on my forehead
The water dripping from my hair
Your beaches are like no other

Oh Florida,
Your parks are like no other
The squeaky swings swaying in the wind
The steep little slide on the other side
The metal monkey bars shining bright
Your parks are like no other

Oh Florida,
Your people are like no other
The smiles you pass walking down the sidewalk
The laughing you hear when little kids play
The affection friends and lovers are giving
Your people are like no other

Oh Florida!

Amanda Zizzo, Grade 9
Countryside High School, FL

My Garden

There is a garden,
That blooms at night,
When the wind blows, they look so bright,
The wind keeps blowing and they start to sing,
In a harmony way,
That when everybody passes by it sounds like symphony,
But when morning comes they go away,
Like nothing was there a single day.

Janey Canales, Grade 9
Parkdale High School, MD

Trick or Treat

Dark and creepy, fog and smoke
I really hope this is some kind of joke
Walking blindly in the night
Following the shadows from the moonlight
The path seems longer than before
I've walked so many times to the door.
Everything is so unreal more like a dream.
I thought by now I would have met up with my team.
It is getting scary and really no fun.
I wish I could find everyone.
We started out all together.
I hope this doesn't get worse before it gets better.
The door is opening
The candy is coming
This is great, no work at all
Trick or treating alone is great look at my haul!

Alan Wopperer, Grade 7
St Stephen's School, NY

Endless Rain
Drip, drip, drip
Off the rooftop raindrops slip.
For days and days it has rained,
Not a minute, has it skipped.
All the happiness it has drained,
The landscape is forever stained.
Will this madness ever stop?
Will this rain ever wane?
Stephany Rosa, Grade 8
St Stephen School, NJ

Crush
I gaze at you

The sun illuminates
Your hair

Stars glisten in
Your eyes

Fire flares in
My heart

I ask you
For a dance

You reply "of course"

We dance past
Twilight

You are lovely

You are my crush
Paul Zehr, Grade 8
Carthage Middle School, NY

Pappy
It was a hot summer day
at the flea market
and we were melting away
from the blazing sun
beating down on us,
but we couldn't leave yet,
not until we found
the perfect veggies for dinner.
From vendor to vendor
his brown wrinkled hands
inspecting every veggie
until he finds the perfect ones.
After we got the perfect ones
we walked through the crowd
back to his light blue car.
Tanner Lyon, Grade 9
Riverside High School, SC

I Am
(A Letter to My Aunt)
I am sophisticated in a way no one understands but you and me.
I am smart so everyone can see, that one day I'll make history.
I am hurt with the pain that you know I have dreaded with for so long,
Even though for most of it, I have done no wrong.
I am sad for the times I got you mad,
But most of the time, we were always glad.
I am mad that I never got to say goodbye,
But when I die, I will be greeted by you with a warm, meaningful "Hi."
I am cherishing the very moments we had before you closed your eyes.
Crying and getting mad at myself for not knowing when to say my goodbyes.
I am frustrated for being mad at you your last two weeks here,
Even though I wish I wasn't for something so mere.
I am taking care of the things you left behind:
Your kids, your siblings, nieces and nephews and myself as far as calming my mind.
I am trying not to cry, for you said not to,
But I can't help the fact that I miss you.
I loved you dearly and we had a love so strong,
That when you left, I hated listening to that Mariah Carey song.
Even though you passed, you're someone I'll always miss.

Signed,
Your Little Pocahontas
Chelsea Gray, Grade 9
Capital Preparatory Charter High School, NJ

Beauty
Beauty is the fiery golden sun rising above the sea,
Illuminating the backs of waves and heaps of sand.
Watching the ongoing waves slowly roll up with a hushed roar,
Quickly unfolding, smoothing out all bumps in its path with a low hiss…
It's as if it holds its breath and then exhales.
The only remnant of it is a white line of foam that once rode on the brink of the wave.

Beauty is the burning sun warming your body and kissing your cheeks.
It is relaxing in a sand chair and burying your toes in the sand.
It is the gentle warm breeze that makes your hair sway from side to side.
It is getting your toes wet while looking for shells.

Beauty is my footprints in the sand next to yours.
Andrea Solimando, Grade 7
Westwood Jr-Sr High School, NJ

Worth
1 penny is 1
2 pennies are 2
Wouldn't it make sense that I mean more to you?
I am not an item to be shown to your friends.
I am not an item that can be returned if you don't like it.
I am not going to be another trophy on your shelf,
next to all the other girls you told that you loved, and then pushed aside and told goodbye.
You told me goodbye once you saw that I was not good enough for your friends.
So we tried to be friends it didn't work, so now you're just part of my past.
Kirah Lenners, Grade 8
KIPP Academy Lynn Charter School, MA

Perfection and You

Some people have perfect bodies.
Some people have perfect minds.
Some people have perfect grades.
Some people have perfect lives.

Some people have perfect balance,
As they're running through the woods.
Some people make perfect paintings,
Because they know they should.

Some people have perfect attitudes,
And can put on perfect shows.
Some people have perfect manners
When they see someone they know.

Some people are just plain perfect.
I know this to be true,
But it's those slight mistakes and quirks
That made me fall for you.

Joseph Gillis, Grade 9
Homewood High School, AL

One Window

One window is all I need…
To look past this blurry mess
To see myself as I am
To see the true me
To see my life in fast forward
To let me be me

Christina Martinez, Grade 7
Anthony Wayne Middle School, NJ

Treasure

Family —
a hidden treasure
whose glittering glare
brings a plentiful light
that fills my soul.
But, many times
I take too much
for granted — not truly
seeing its worth.

Care —
is what is needed
because
in a blink of an eye,
a beat of a heart,
snap of a finger;
it can vanish —
leaving me alone
in complete darkness.

Delaney Heenan, Grade 7
Ocean City Intermediate School, NJ

My Mom

My mom is the best
She is the one I admire
No matter what happens
She is my role model
If something bad was to happen
She will find a way to resolve it
If I were to be sick
She will take care of me
No matter what happens
She is someone I trust because
She will always be there for me
She is someone I love with all my heart.

Brian Flores, Grade 9
Miami Beach Sr High School, FL

A Sad Cold World

Come with me to my world
With the flat black night
Where you can't see
Three feet in front of you
And the blood red sunsets
That fill your heart
With sadness and hate
Lie on lime green grass
That stains your clothes so easily
Above the stars that look
Like diamonds glowing
Just a few feet in front of you
The brown suede mountains
Look like a huge fountain
Of flowing chocolate
And the deep blue denim oceans
That are as cold
As a white pearl winter night.

Andrew Rogers, Grade 8
South Pittsburg High School, TN

Once?

O Man, where is thy kingdom?
Where is that which the Lord
gav'st thee to rule?
Did He not tell ye to be a king
over all the land?
Art thou not the one who
governs every beast?
Behold, Man, this is thy kingdom.
Thine subjects are dying
and thine land is being destroyed
by thy brethren.
Wilt thou suffer this to be?
O Man, the choice is thine.
Wilt thou act the king?

Laura Speake, Grade 9
Inter-Lakes High School, NH

Skating

the wind rustled my hair
down the hill, do I dare
scared to death I might fall
but if I live I will have a ball
the griptape stickin' to my shoes
come here, check out my moves
a drip of sweat drops down my face
another one follows at a steady pace
I speed down the hill, fast as lightning
I was scared, it was frightening!!
I open my eyes to see if I'm alive
I cross the finish line to dance and jive!
watch me do an ollie or a pop shove it
my passion is skating and I just love it!

Jackson Estes, Grade 7
Houston Middle School, TN

Young Love

She acts
like a cat
who wants to annoy me
and
like a dog
who wants to play a lot
and doesn't know when to stop.
She cries like the rain
and wants people to help her.

Randy Membreno, Grade 8
Beacon Middle School, DE

An Irregular Symmetry

This time is bright.
We don't dwell in black.
What are we if there is to be no light?
On the other side,
The darkness shines,
Where blaze turns to ice,
And day turns to night.
But, shouldn't the light need dark,
Just as a fire needs breeze?
As yin needs yang,
And as yang needs yin?
Where is the hope,
If there is no doom?
The light consumes the dark,
And the dark consumes the light.
Opposites come in pairs,
And pairs come in 2's.
Where light meets darkness,
And fire meets water,
Is an irregular symmetry,
Where harmony has power.

Jay Woo, Grade 8
Cresskill High School, NJ

Football

I play football for B.F. Raiders.
We beat Connellsville West, the Uniontown haters.

Our goal is to win the section crown.
We took all our opponents down.

We wanted to win and be the best.
We succeeded to do that after we beat the rest.

Warare Wilkerson, Grade 8
Ben Franklin School, PA

Trees

For me it's hard to think
A seed,
Water,
Sun,
Tree
How do they grow?
There is nothing to hold them up
Or keep them going
No mom,
No dad,
No family.
People say they are living,
But I would not be able to live,
Without a family.
They can't talk
Like *The Giving Tree*
But *The Giving Tree*
Had someone a li'l boy
Most trees are alone.

Bridget Podgorski, Grade 7
Christ the Divine Teacher Catholic Academy, PA

Life Somewhere Else

California mornings filled with warm sunny air,
Bright and beautiful.
Days perfect for bike riding,
I was young and full of curiosity,
Always wanting to push a littler further,
Always wanting to peek around the next corner.
So, I set out on my tiny bike, my parents and I,
Going wherever the wind took us,
Pedaling past the apple orchard,
Down the hill to the park.
The colorful trees called to me,
Wanting me to play joyfully in their crunchy leaves.
Simple images caught my attention.
A buzzing bee in a flower,
A butterfly fluttering throughout the rows of bushes,
Birds soaring way above the towering oaks.
I was three.
The world seemed so much larger than me.
Days went by so quick, like my life somewhere else.
And all I can remember, are those bike rides
Through the hills of California.

Michael DiFiore, Grade 8
William Penn Middle School, PA

In Love

Love is supposed to be the most wonderful thing in your life.
It is supposed to be when everything in your life is full of happiness.
And nothing can go wrong, when you have someone to help make you strong.
It makes you feel like nothing in the world can bring you down and everyone knows it in town.
When your life is turned upside down, and you feel the love all around.
You know you are in love when you change your life for them.
When you stop talking to all your childhood friends
When you stop dressing a certain way
When you wish he would always stay
You know you are in love when your best friend tells you are changing
And you say oh please you are going crazy.
When you stay home on the weekends just wishing he would call.
But when it comes down to the true feelings all he does is stall.
You know you are in love when you know it is about to end
But you still try to pretend
You know you are in love when you cry and cry but still you try.
Then you realize how you are losing yourself.
How everything that once mattered doesn't anymore.
And slowly you realized there's a lot more in store.
You wish that what is happening really isn't true
That love actually hurt you.

Jasmine Rodriguez, Grade 9
Miami Beach Sr High School, FL

Index